Adam Smith

Adam Smith

Systematic Philosopher and Public Thinker

ERIC SCHLIESSER

OXFORD
UNIVERSITY PRESS

OXFORD
UNIVERSITY PRESS

Oxford University Press is a department of the University of Oxford. It furthers
the University's objective of excellence in research, scholarship, and education
by publishing worldwide. Oxford is a registered trade mark of Oxford University
Press in the UK and certain other countries.

Published in the United States of America by Oxford University Press
198 Madison Avenue, New York, NY 10016, United States of America.

© Oxford University Press 2017

CIP data is on file at the Library of Congress
ISBN 978-0-19-069012-0

Each hand hath put on Nature's power

—Shakespeare, Sonnet 127

This book is dedicated to the economic theorists M. A. Khan, David M. Levy, and Sandra J. Peart, who have taught me true philosophy, especially philosophical friendship.

CONTENTS

PART 3   PHILOSOPHERS

PART 4   CONCLUSION

ACKNOWLEDGMENTS

Scholarship operates in a credit economy, but it is ultimately a collaborative enterprise. Thus, it is only fitting that, first, I thank Oxford University Press's generous and constructive referees. Their careful and elaborate reviews exposed my manuscript's weaknesses and aided my efforts to improve it. I hope the final product meets their exacting standards; even if it does not, I trust that they recognize that their labor improved the final product immeasurably. I hope they receive approbation from the impartial spectator within for their efforts. In addition, I want to thank my editor at OUP, Peter Ohlin, for his confidence and ongoing support.

I encountered Adam Smith in a scholarly context sometime around 1997 while a Ph.D. student at the University of Chicago. Since then I have defended a Ph.D. dissertation and published nearly twenty papers on his works. It is impossible for me to list all the scholarly debts to teachers, peers, referees, and students that I have incurred in nearly two decades of research and teaching on Smith and his many interlocutors. I have long lists of acknowledgments in all these works and have not duplicated these, so I apologize for any large and small omissions in what follows.

In the following pages, Adam Smith is primarily (albeit not exclusively) a philosopher with an interest in "instructing and entertaining" the public, which he, in part, helped fashion. Yet from the start, my research on Adam Smith has been encouraged by some truly eminent economists who have passed away, including Warren Samuels, Mark Blaug, Milton Friedman, James Buchanan, Nathan Rosenberg, Gordon Tullock, and Andrew Skinner. I have benefitted from their critical feedback, their time, and their criticisms. When I was an early career scholar, I had no idea how fortunate I was that they would find the time to engage with and facilitate my work. In particular, while instructing me in the fine points of the history of economics, they also instructed me non-trivially in philosophy and its history. I would have surely dedicated this book to Blaug if he were still with us today. (I already dedicated an edited volume to Samuels.) In addition, the late I. B. Cohen stimulated my interest in exploring the myriad connections between Smith and Newton, and an earlier version of Chapter 12 had been dedicated to his memory.

Among the living economists, I want to single out the members of the ill-fated History and Methodology of Economics group at the University of Amsterdam: John Davis, Marcel Boumans, and Harro Maas provided me with a near-ideal environment to study the history and philosophy of economics. I often think of these halcyon days now that I am, in turn, employed by the University of Amsterdam In addition, Vernon Smith, Bart Wilson, Ross Emmett, Jerry Evensky, Leon Montes, Maria Paganelli, Pete Boettke, Mario Rizzo, and my regular—albeit too infrequent—co-author, Spencer Pack, who will recognize some of our joint work, especially in Chapter 4 (but throughout the book), have always made me feel welcome among professional economists.

My interest in Smith was a late, acquired taste during my Ph.D. I first listened in on a spirited conversation about him between Lauren Brubaker and Fonna Forman in Classics Café. I am unsure if Ryan Hanley was already at Chicago, but all three of these scholars wrote dissertations focused on Smith important to my own intellectual development. Fonna and Ryan, in particular, have remained intellectual friends and occasional sparring partners since. I am very grateful to Fonna and the folks at Liberty Fund, whose generosity facilitated a memorable visit to Kirkaldy, in the company of Vernon Smith and Nick Phillipson no less, while researching this book. I owe a special debt of gratitude to Ryan, who read and commented on multiple drafts of this monograph during the last half-decade. At Chicago, I learned a lot about Smith (and Hume, Newton, Spinoza, etc.) from other Ph.D. students, especially Jen Boobar, Chad Flanders, Patrick Frierson (technically a Notre Dame graduate), Alessandro Pajewski, Erik Curiel, Kate Abramson, Michelle Mason, Jessica Spector, and Julio Tuma. While I overlapped with Deborah Boucoyannis at Chicago, her decisive influence on me occurred during the years 2012–4.

In addition to Hanley, Michael Gill and Sam Fleischacker, who hosted a memorable Ph.D. Seminar at "Circle," which many of us attended, and whose writings on Smith have set the standard I have tried to emulate since his first book appeared in 1999, commented on and read advance drafts of this monograph. Ryan, Michael, Sam, David Gordon, and several anonymous referees caught many mistakes, and their insightful comments improved the final product. I owe a huge debt of gratitude to Anna de Bruyckere for preparing the index with care.

However, it was a fortuitous encounter with Sonja Amadae, a pioneer in the contextual, philosophical study of twentieth-century economics, on a connecting flight between Indianapolis and Boston that is responsible for my interest in Smith as a philosopher of science and for turning the writings of economists and their effects into a subject of study. At the time Sonja was near completion of her dissertation, the backbone of her *Rationalizing Capitalist Democracy: The Cold War Origins of Rational Choice Liberalism* (2003). The appearance of this book also slowed down my research on Adam Smith, as it is one of the main reasons

I became increasingly preoccupied in mapping, in a series of expanding papers, what I call "The Rise and Fall of Chicago Economics: 1921–1976."

At Chicago, my main mentors in philosophy included Charles Larmore, Martha Nussbaum, Bill Wimsatt, Howard Stein, Daniel Garber, Abe Stone, Andrea Woody, Laura Snyder, Ian Mueller, John Haugeland, and Leonard Linsky. The last three of these have passed away. I am especially sad that I cannot offer a copy of this book to Ian, who, I am sure, would have noticed with some (perhaps bemused) regret that Marx's engagement with and penetrating criticisms of Smith are still not sufficiently acknowledged by me. Larmore and Garber were model supervisors. Larmore has remained a model of professional integrity, and Dan, especially, has been a wise teacher and friend throughout the years.

It is undeniable that exposure to the life and works of Nussbaum and one of my undergraduate teachers, Dan Dennett, has stimulated my ongoing reflections on the varied roles of professional philosophers in society. They taught me that rigor, originality, and social significance can be mutually reinforcing. I have been especially fortunate that Dennett, has included me in some of his recent European travels.

At Chicago, I was also lucky to discuss Smith's "History of Astronomy" with Noel Swerdlow in a reading group and to explore *The Theory of Moral Sentiments* alongside Mandeville's *Fable* with Mr. Ralph Lerner in a seminar. In addition, the late, generous Joseph Cropsey allowed me to pick his brain walking along the lakeshore while he was distracted by my bullmastiff.

Some bits of this book have been promised to grant agencies at The Netherlands Organisation for Scientific Research (NWO), Research Fund, Flanders (FWO), and Ghent University's BOF (Special Research Council) at one point or another. In addition, throughout my career I have been the beneficiary of largesse from Liberty Fund (and I am grateful to Doug Den Uyl, Christine Henderson, and Mark Yellin for their support and conversation). The support of these organizations has made me attractive to a number of employers and has allowed me to explore my scholarly interests under near ideal circumstances. In sum, I have been the lucky and grateful beneficiary of a rigged lottery.

Since I left Chicago, I have been employed by philosophy departments at Wesleyan University in Middletown, Washington University in St. Louis (in conjunction with social thought), Leiden University, and Ghent University. Throughout, my colleagues have very been supportive of my development as a teacher and philosopher, and they indulged my ongoing interest in Adam Smith. I want to single out Pauline Kleingeld, who was a model colleague in St. Louis and Leiden, and an exemplary department chair; and I want to mention the late José A. Benardete, who carefully read the footnotes of one of my writing samples (the origin of the present Chapter 15) and, after Syracuse hired me, berated me for being insufficiently ambitious—he then proceeded to take me out for lunch at every opportunity. Little did I know then he would become the main cause of my slow path in completing this project. To cut a long story short, he roped me, together with our wonderful and joy-generating student, Andrew Corsa, into his projects on magnanimity. One can discern a glimpse of José's vision in his *Greatness of Soul: In Hume, Aristotle and Hobbes, as Shadowed by Milton's Satan* (2013); the book is as fantastic it sounds! Along the way, and in addition to dramatic changes in political circumstances, I was stimulated to rethink my project—if identity is stable enough to allow the indexical—almost from the ground up.

Longer ago than I wish to remember, this book was solicited by Brian Leiter when I needed an entry on a grant proposal. I thank him for confidence. Much to my own amazement, I completed this book while employed as a political scientist at the University of Amsterdam in the research group, Challenges to Democratic Representation. I am exhilarated to be surrounded by so many dedicated scholars aiming to develop scholarly tools in order to understand and develop (sometimes prescriptive policy) answers to the major political questions of our times. I have been especially pleased to be permitted to co-teach with Niña Weijers and Michel Heijdra, a true public servant.

As it happens, when I walked into George Smith's year-long course on Isaac Newton at Tufts, I did so as an undergraduate student of political science, who, in the aftermath of the fall of the Berlin Wall, had grown dubious about the nature and content of "science" in political science. That same year, I took seminars with the late Michael Fixler on Milton and Rob Devigne on Thomas Hobbes. It was a decisive year in my scholarly life because for the first time I tasted the fruits of discerning the connecting principles among other people's projects. George first taught me the craft of research and the significance of rewriting. George's impact on this book is not insignificant: Chapters 11 through 13 all develop aspects of his teaching and our joint research on the reception of and debates over Newton's method(s). At Tufts I met Jody Azzouni, who taught me that systematic philosophy can be practiced even within the confines of analytical philosophy, and who has remained a generous philosophical interlocutor since.

At the start of these acknowledgments, I mentioned that scholarship is ultimately a collaborative enterprise. In my experience this is especially true of "early modern philosophy." During the last decade my philosophical development in it has been nourished by critical and helpful responses to my work, and many other many small acts of kindness, especially by Katherine Brading, Dana Jalobeanu, Michael Della Rocca, Lex Newman, Ursula Goldenbaum, Alison Simmons, Karolina Hübner, Don Ainslie, Wim Lemmens, Alan Nelson, Noa Shein, Dennis Des Chene, Karann Durland, Tom Stoneham, Omri Boehm, Yitzhak Melamed, Stephen Gaukroger, Charles Wolfe, Steve Darwall, Remy Debes, Maarten Van Dyck, Lisa Herzog, Craig Smith, James Harris, Warren Herrold, Alison Peterman, Aaron Garrett, Bill Harper, Sue James, Sandy Stewart, David Raynor, Michaela Massimi, Ursula Renz, Jacqueline Broad, Karen Detlefsen, and Catherine Wilson. In addition, I have been fortunate to work and publish with Chris Smeenk, Zvi Biener, Paul Russell, Sandrine Berges, Petra Van Brabandt, Mary Domski, Yoram Hazony, Karen Valihora, Tamas Demeter, Marcy Lascano, Christia Mercer,

Marietje van der Schaar, Martin Lenz, Anik Waldow, and Andrew Janiak, among others. I am grateful to Sandrine, in particular, for letting me use (drafts of) her translation of de Grouchy in this book. Those familiar with Andrew's book on Isaac Newton will recognize that the title of this book is a homage to it.

During the last decade, I have been reflecting on the institutions of science and professional philosophy. This book is, in part, the product of that reflection. It was inspired by the pioneering work of Heather Douglas. Much of that reflection took place publically at *NewAPPS*, where I was joined in daily conversation by a very gifted group of philosophers, and at *Digressions&Impressions*. I am lucky that Liam Kofi Bright often finds ways to turn what I say into a topic of more interesting conversation. Also, I am grateful to my two Ghent co-authors, Merel Levefere and Rogier de Langhe, for their willingness to assimilate me into their research program on science policy.

This book would never have been finished if it were not for the love and encouragement I received from my better half, Sarit. Because Smith teaches that "serious and strong expressions of" love "appear ridiculous" to others, I say no more on ours here. In fatherhood I have learned the truth of Smith's claim that "the agreeable passions of love and joy can satisfy and support the heart without any auxiliary pleasure." Avi, "you're my inspiration!" Moreover, thanks to the support and love of my parents and sister I can attest to the truth of one more Smithian claim, that there is a genuine "satisfaction in the consciousness of being beloved."

I close these acknowledgments with a note on my dedication. "True philosophy" and its conceptual sister "true liberty" are important concepts for Hume (see Schliesser 2014), and they guide my understanding of Smith's writings, but I did not fully understand their meaning in the sense provided by lived experience until I was first invited to the Summer Institute for the Preservation of the Study of the History of Economics hosted by David and Sandy in the late stages of my Ph.D. Through them I met Ali. I had no idea at the time that I was about to receive intense, graduate-level training in philosophy first at Carow Hall and then at Jepson year after year; even less could I have imagined the daily instructions not just in the fine points of mathematical economics, statistics, and economic theory, but also in modal logic, ordinary language philosophy, and deconstruction. But as much as I treasure these tutorials, I value (in the multiplicity of ways this word can convey) even more the daily missives in the arts and complexities of living a joyful, scholarly life. Thank you.

ABBREVIATIONS

Writings of Adam Smith

Ancient Logics = *"The History of Ancient Logics and Metaphysics" (reprinted in Smith 1982a)*

Ancient Physics = *"The History of Ancient Physics" (reprinted in Smith 1982a)*

Astronomy = *"The History of Astronomy" (reprinted in Smith 1982a)*

Corr. = *The Correspondence of Adam Smith (Smith 1987)*

Edinburgh Review = *"Letters to the Edinburgh Review" (reprinted in Smith 1982a)*

EPS = *Essays on Philosophical Subjects (Smith 1982a).*

External Senses = *"Of the External Senses" (reprinted in Smith 1982a)*

Imitative Arts = *"Of the Nature of that Imitation which takes place in what are called the Imitative Arts" (reprinted in Smith 1982a)*

Languages = *Considerations Concerning the first Formation of Languages (initially attached to TMS, now reprinted in Smith 1985)*

LJ = *Lectures on Jurisprudence (Smith 1982b)*

LJ(A) = *"Lectures on Jurisprudence, Report 1762–3" (reprinted in Smith 1982b)*

LJ(B) = *"Lectures on Jurisprudence, Report dated 1766" (reprinted in Smith 1982b)*

LRBL = *Lectures on Rhetoric and Belles Lettres (Smith 1985)*

TMS = *The Theory of Moral Sentiments (Smith)*

WN = *An Inquiry into the Nature and Causes of the Wealth of Nations (Smith 1981)*

All references to the writings of Adam Smith are, unless otherwise noted, to the Glasgow edition of his works by page number and, where possible, paragraph number. References to Smith's letters and lectures also include, where possible, a date.

Writings of David Hume

Ancient Nations = *"Of the Populousness of Ancient Nations" (in Hume 1987)*

Dialogues = *Dialogues concerning Natural Religion*

EHU = *An Enquiry Concerning Human Understanding*

EMPL = *Essays, Moral, Political, and Literary (Hume 1987)*

EPM = *An Enquiry Concerning the Principles of Morals*

First *Enquiry* = *An Enquiry Concerning Human Understanding*

History = *The History of England from the Invasion of Julius Caesar to the Revolution in 1688 (Hume 1983)*

N = *Natural History of Religion*

Second *Enquiry* = *An Enquiry Concerning the Principles of Morals*

Treatise = *A Treatise of Human Nature*

All references to the writings by David Hume follow, unless otherwise noted, the citation conventions of http://www.davidhume.org/. The exceptions are the references to EMPL and the essays therein (where the essay name and page numbers in Hume 1987 are used) and to History (where volume and page numbers of Hume 1983 are used).

Writings of John Locke

Essay = *An Essay Concerning Human Understanding (Locke 1975)*

Education = *Some Thoughts Concerning Education (Locke 1989)*

All references to Locke 1975 are to book, chapter, and paragraph. The references to Locke 1989 are by paragraph number.

Writings of Jean-Jacques Rousseau

Second Discourse = *Discourse on the Origin and Basis of Inequality Among Men (Rousseau 1997)*

Writings of Sophie de Grouchy

Letters = *Letters on Sympathy*

All references to Letters are to letter number in Sandrine Berges's translation.

Writings of Thomas Hobbes

All references to *Leviathan* are to chapter and paragraph in Hobbes 1994.

Writings of Spinoza

TTP = *Theological Political Treatise (in Spinoza 2016)*

All references to TTP are by chapter and paragraph number in Spinoza 2016. In addition, citation to the *Ethics* (in Spinoza 1994) are in customary fashion to the part, proposition, and definition or scholium.

BIBLIOGRAPHIC NOTE

Substantial elements of the following papers have been reused and rethought in writing this book:

Pack, Spencer J., and Eric Schliesser. "Smith's Humean Criticism of Hume's Account of the Origin of Justice." *Journal of the History of Philosophy* 44.1 (2006): 47–63 (in Chapter 4).

Pack, Spencer J., and Eric Schliesser. "Adam Smith, Natural Movement, and Physics" (2017,*Cambridge Journal of Economics*, in press; in Chapter 2).

Schliesser, Eric. "The Obituary of a Vain Philosopher." *Hume Studies* 29.2 (2003): 327–62 (in Chapter 15).

Schliesser, Eric. "Some Principles of Adam Smith's Newtonian Methods in *The Wealth of Nations*." *Research in the History of Economic Thought and Methodology* 23.A (2005): 33–74 (in Chapter 12).

Schliesser, Eric. "Wonder in the Face of Scientific Revolutions: Adam Smith on Newton's 'Proof' of Copernicanism." *British Journal for the History of Philosophy* 13.4 (2005): 697–732 (in Chapter 11).

Schliesser, Eric. "Adam Smith's Benevolent and Self-Interested Conception of Philosophy." In *New Voices on Adam Smith*, edited by L. Montes and E. Schliesser. London: Routledge, 2006.

Schliesser, Eric. "The Measure of Real Price: Adam Smith's Science of Equity." In *The Street Porter and the Philosopher: Conversations on Analytical Egalitarianism*, edited by David M. Levy and Sandra Peart. Ann Arbor: University of Michigan Press, 2008: 228–38 (in Chapter 8, Section c).

Schliesser, Eric. "Articulating Practices as Reasons." *Adam Smith Review* 2 (2006): 69–97 (in Chapters 2 and 4).

Schliesser, Eric. "Copernican Revolutions Revisited in Adam Smith by Way of David Hume." *Revista Empressa y Humanismo* 13.1 (2010): 213–48 (in Chapter 11).

Schliesser, Eric. "Reading Adam Smith After Darwin: On the Evolution of Propensities, Institutions, and Sentiments." *Journal of Economic Behavior & Organization* 77.1 (2011): 14–22 (in Chapter 2).

Schliesser, Eric. "The Piacular, or On Seeing Oneself as a Moral Cause in Adam Smith." In *Contemporary Perspectives on Early Modern Philosophy*. Edited by Martin Lenz and Anik Waldow Dordrecht: Springer Netherlands, 2013, 159–77 (in Chapter 5).

Schliesser, Eric. "Jonathan Israel, Democratic Enlightenment: Philosophy, Revolution, and Human Rights, 1750–1790." *Œconomia. History, Methodology, Philosophy* 4.4 (2014): 651–57 (in Chapter 16).

Schliesser, Eric. "Counterfactual Reasoning in Smithian Sympathy." *Revue Internationale de Philosophie* 270.4 (2015; in Chapter 5).

Schliesser, Eric. "Introduction." In *Sympathy: A History*, edited by E. Schliesser. Oxford: Oxford University Press, 2015 (in Chapter 5).

Schliesser, Eric. "The Theory of Moral Sentiments." In *Adam Smith: His Life, Thought, and Legacy*, Edited by Ryan Hanley. Princeton, NJ: Princeton University Press, 2016 (in Chapters 1 and 9).

Schliesser, Eric. "Sophie de Grouchy, Adam Smith, and the Politics of Sympathy." In *Feminism and the History of Philosophy*, edited by M. Lascano and E. O'Neill. Dordrecht: Springer (in press).

1

Introduction

Systematic Philosopher and Public Thinker

a. Systems in Adam Smith

This is the Hinge of your system.

—David Hume on *The Theory of Moral Sentiments*
to Adam Smith, July 28, 1759

In his 2015 intellectual biography of David Hume, James Harris notes that after the youthful *Treatise*, Hume does not describe his own writings as "systematic" or as belonging to a "system." This is surprising given how important systematicity is to the early Hume (Boehm 2016; Hazony 2014; Hazony and Schliesser 2016). For example, Hume writes in the Introduction to the *Treatise*: "to explain the principles of human nature, we in effect propose a compleat [*sic*] system of the sciences."

As the remark quoted above from the 1759 letter to Smith implies, Hume did not lose interest in other people's "systems." In fact, Hume's memorable deathbed scene (to be discussed in Chapter 15) reveals that Hume, as reported by Adam Smith, understands himself as battling other people's "systems of superstition" to the end of his life; so, even if Hume presents himself no longer as a systematic philosopher after the *Treatise* (but see Sabl 2012), he remains concerned with the effects of systematic thought on human affairs.

This book is about Smith's system and the effects he hoped to promote with it. Recent scholarly literature on Adam Smith, inspired in part by Hayek's concerns over social planning, has paid considerable attention to Smith's criticisms of the "man of system" who is "apt to be very wise in his own conceit" (TMS 6.2.2.17, 233; see, e.g., Craig Smith 2013: 550; Levy and Peart 2013: 387). Indeed, if one starts reading *The Theory of Moral Sentiments* (TMS) one quickly encounters Smith's concern with how "the judgments of mankind [can be] perverted by wrong systems" (1.1.3.3, 17). Shortly thereafter, he implies, in a deflationary manner, that a "system of philosophy" as such (so not its consequences) is not a matter of much interest (1.1.4.5, 21). Thus, one may easily be tempted into thinking that Smith agrees with the mature Hume's rejection, if it is one, of systematicity, in part because of systems' bad impact on human judgment. Even if one were to grant (as I do not) that these passages show that Smith rejects systematicity, Smith clearly does not think philosophy is inert in human affairs (cf. Arendt 2006: 243); systems can undermine what we ought to think or affirm.

It is possible that Smith intended to use "wrong systems" in the sense of "false" or "not true" systems, but Smith, who is an incredibly precise and meticulous author, could have stated *that*; so I assume that the category of "wrong systems" includes systems with bad moral and/or political consequences, including ones that may be true (in some sense).[1] Of course, if wrong intellectual systems pervert the judgments of ordinary citizens, one can, if one is responsible about one's intellectual efforts, adopt different kinds of intellectual strategies, including, albeit not limited to, aiming at abolishing all systems; hiding one's system from the masses (in the manner of a "Government House" utilitarian or a Platonic noble liar); or articulating intellectual systems that are thought to have less bad consequences either (a) by rhetorically blocking, somehow, such consequences or (b) by not being *wrong* in the relevant sense.

Either way, Smith, a teacher of rhetoric, clearly thinks it is legitimate to evaluate at least some scientific theories on their social consequences. In recent philosophy, this is studied as a species of so-called inductive risk (see, e.g., Douglas 2000), and sometimes I'll use that modern term to capture Smith's interest in the moral and political consequences of philosophizing to the public by the philosopher. I follow Smith in taking the nature of responsible public speech by philosophers or (more anachronistically) experts seriously.

By a "public philosopher," I refer to a philosopher who engages in his writings with a (sometimes imagined) public composed of literate citizens and/or who advises rulers and would-be rulers of the polity. For example, Hume starts his *Treatise* by explaining his wish "to try the taste of the public." (Treatise Ad.1) This is a bold stance of philosophical independence. While Hume hastens to add that "the approbation of the public I consider as the greatest reward of my labours" and that he is willing to be instructed by its judgment, he is coy about how exactly he will interpret its judgment, and there is no hint that he grants the public's taste authority over his work.

For most of his career Smith was less bold than Hume. This is revealed by a telling remark in the context of an opportunity to appoint Hume to a position at Glasgow University; as he wrote to his university colleague, William Cullen, in November 1751, "I should prefer David Hume to any man for a colleague; but I am afraid the public would not be of my opinion; and the interest of the society will oblige us to have some regard to the opinion of the public" (Corr. 5; see also TMS 6.2.3.3, 235, to be discussed in Section b of Chapter 9). It is notable that Smith

---

[1] For example, a system that states truths about society may also reinforce (a deplorable) status-quo bias. This danger is not merely a theoretical possibility but is always a real possibility in imperfect societies.

treats the university as a "society" (the topic of Part 2 of this book) with an identifiable interest (instead of "society" we would call a university "a corporation" or "institution"); and that he uses "public" and not "Kirk" here. Smith's position is clear: while university educators shape the minds of the young (especially of future members of the clergy and the medical and legal professions), they do so within constraints. One of these constraints is a kind of background, favorable opinion by the public of the university and its professors. In Smith's judgment the opposition to Hume's well-known lack of religious orthodoxy generates too much friction with the opinion of the public; it's not in the university's interest to generate such hostility. Thus, he sacrifices his own interest (and the demands of friendship and truth) for the sake of the larger university "society" he is part of.[2] This is because, on Smith's view, public authority in society is based on opinion and so must be attentive to it in various ways.

We see Smith call attention to this interest in the social consequences of scientific theories in the Introduction of WN: "Those theories [of political economy] have a considerable influence, not only upon the opinions of men of learning, but upon the public conduct of princes and sovereign states" ("Introduction and Plan of the Work," 8, 11; I explore this more fully in Chapter 12, Section a). A public philosopher need not be only a public philosopher; she can also teach, as Smith did, students in the lecture hall or be a private tutor or engage with other philosophers in letters or conversation on more esoteric matters that are insignificant to the public's flourishing.

While the term "inductive risk" is anachronistic, the consequentialist evaluation of theory is not; for example, Hume justifies his interest in offering a "science of man" in terms of its "utility"—that is, in its ability to produce good consequences in moral and political affairs (Treatise Intro.10). During the eighteenth century. theoretically aiming, in a philanthropic manner, at such good consequences, or aiming at human advancement, falls under the category of "beneficence" (Montes 2004; Schliesser 2006).

Smith is not alone in his interest in the relationship between systems of thought and inductive risk. One author he studied closely (see, e.g., External Senses), Berkeley, argues that systems of philosophy can have indirect effects on common life. In the 1713 "preface" of the *Three Dialogues*, Berkeley offers a kind of "intellectual trickle-down" theory:

> [I]f by their Speculations rightly placed, the Study of Morality and the Law of Nature were brought more into Fashion among Men of Parts and Genius, the Discouragements that draw to Scepticism removed, the Measures of Right and Wrong accurately defined, and the Principles of Natural Religion reduced into regular Systems, as artfully disposed and

---

[2] The first edition of TMS was published while Smith was still a (leading) member of Glasgow University's "society."

clearly connected as those of some other Sciences: There are grounds to think, these Effects wou'd not only have a gradual Influence in repairing the too much defaced Sense of Vertue in the World; but also, by shewing, that such Parts of Revelation, as lie within the reach of Humane Inquiry, are most agreeable to Right Reason, wou'd dispose all prudent, unprejudiced Persons, to a modest and wary Treatment of those Sacred Mysteries, which are above the Comprehension of our Faculties.

Thus, while Berkeley addresses his arguments to "those, who are most addicted to speculative Studies," the consequences of their combined judgments would radiate out to other (less speculation-addicted) learned persons, the professions, the wealthy, and, eventually, the lower orders of society. Here I do not mean to suggest that Smith accepts Berkeley's version of intellectual trickle-down or subscribes to Berkeley's theory of diffusion of ideas or even his hierarchical conception of society. If anything, in what follows I show that a position like Berkeley's, which can be traced back to Plato, is Smith's target throughout his works. I only note that Smith is not alone in recognizing the significance of some such intellectual trickle-down theory.[3]

In the quoted passage from Berkeley's *Dialogues* the word "system" is used to describe a mode of organization of the explanatory principles of a particular science (i.e., natural religion; in the Introduction to *Treatise*, Hume, too, treats "natural religion" as one of the sciences [Intro.4]; to the best of my knowledge Smith does not do so).[4] To be *systematic*, then, here means that such explanatory principles of a science, or intellectual discipline, *cohere* with each other and are properly *connected*. This is the central sense in which Smith also uses the term "system." Berkeley's plural ("systems") suggests that for him a single science or theory can contain multiple, coherent and properly connected explanatory principles and so can be a collection of systems. Presumably, once the systems are fully integrated into a single set of connected and coherent explanatory principles, a science can be thought of as a single system or a unified theory. It is not a huge leap from this intra-scientific (or intradisciplinary) notion of "system" to an inter-scientific notion of "system" in which the explanatory principles of different sciences cohere and are connected with each other (for more background, see Catana 2008).

This latter, inter-scientific notion of "system" is part of the self-described aim of Hume in *Treatise*: "we in effect propose a compleat [*sic*] system of the sciences"

---

[3] Kant, too, appeals (in *"Was Heist, sich im Denken orientieren"*) [see Kant 2012] to the analysis of a doctrine's effects in terms of the worthiness of freedom (of thought). That worthiness is understood by Kant in terms of both a doctrine's likely consequences, by way of intellectual trickle-down on a larger public, and its impact on other intellectual currents of thought (for discussion, see O. Boehm 2014: 221–2).

[4] In eighteenth-century philosophical jargon, a "principle" is an explanatory ground, often causal. In the context of a science or a discipline, "principle" is a foundation (e.g., an axiom, or common notion). See E. Chambers (1728) *Cyclopædia, or, An universal dictionary of arts and sciences* (872–3).

(Intro.7). In context, Hume suggests that such a complete system of all the sciences is possible only if one science, the science of human nature, or "the science of man," is epistemically foundational to the other sciences. In *Treatise* this science is composed of multiple systems (e.g., his system of generating "general idea" [1.1.7.16], "system concerning space and time" [1.2.4.1], etc.). Within this foundational "science of man," Hume recognizes some "elements" as the principles of his science (T 1.1.4.7; Hazony and Schliesser 2016). An epistemically foundational science is not logically required to complete a system of the sciences.

If a "system" has coherent and connected explanatory principles, and, according to Smith, "philosophy is the science of the connecting principles of nature" (Astronomy 2.12, EPS 45), then philosophy is the activity that generates the explanatory foundations of systems of thought. In Section e of Chapter 3, I'll explain the psychological mechanisms—the role of the intellectual sentiments, in particular—that according to Smith account for this activity. In Chapter 11, I'll recount both how, according to Smith, there is a regular pattern of development and Kuhnian revolutions, a dynamics of reason (Friedman 2001), within and among these systems, and his vision of philosophy's role within the division of labor.

Therefore, when in this book I treat Smith as a "systematic philosopher," I mean to describe Smith's interest in contributing to (i) the development of particular intra-scientific systems (note the plural), (ii) the creation of systematic science(s), (iii) the development of a system of the sciences, and (iv) the abstract reflection on the nature and development of systems as such—this is called "meta-philosophy" in recent terminology. In addition, (v) I treat Smith from the perspective of "systematic philosophy"—a term still used in contemporary philosophy, especially in Europe (where it is often used to convey an interest in theoretical as opposed to "practical" and "historical" philosophy).

Smith's interest in all five of these, especially the first three, will be developed at length in this book. Often I treat these as distinct topics, although occasionally I call attention to the ways in which Smith saw their connections. Sometimes this requires considerable exegetical detail because, while Smith is explicit about his interests in systematicity (a fact well known to scholars), he often submerges these connections. One of the central conceits of this book is that because he is primarily writing for the public, and not just "men of learning," he does not always spell out his moves and his originality because of his understanding of what it is to be a public philosopher (for more on this, see my methodologic remarks in Section d of this chapter). This helps explain that sometimes in WN Smith is even apologetic for being "extremely abstracted" (e.g., WN 1.4.43, 46; see also Section a of Chapter 12).

Thus, on the interpretation developed in this book, we should understand TMS and WN as works that instantiate responsible speech aimed at educating and guiding the public as well as being two of the main parts of Smith's system. In this section I discuss briefly an important feature of Smith's meta-philosophy;

in the next section I focus on Smith's insistence that he had developed a system of the sciences; and then in the final section of this chapter, I explain the method I adopt in my treatment of Smith.

Fleischacker (2004) has called Smith's interest in meta-philosophy (iv) itself a "system of scientific systems." For convenience, I adopt Fleischacker's terminology, but note that to accept Smith's interest in meta-philosophy does not entail seeing Smith as offering a system—in the sense of having coherent and connected explanatory principles—of scientific systems. For example, Brubaker (2006a) treats Smith as a systematic philosopher who avoids offering a positive system. Even Fleischacker tends to present Smith as embracing a proto-Wittgensteinian sensibility and suspicion about theoretical enterprises (Fleischacker 1999 and 2004: 23–7). Of course, if Smith *does* manage to offer such a "system of scientific systems," he would, in effect, have attained Hume's ideal of a (near) complete system of the sciences.

I disagree with Brubaker and Fleischacker. Despite the fact that, as we have seen, Smith makes deflationary comments about systems of philosophy at the start of TMS, Smith also notes that, as a matter of fact, the "love of system" can activate the most "noble and magnificent" political and philanthropic projects and the right sort of "public spirit." More surprising, perhaps, such love of abstract system(s) and system-inspired public spirit can even compensate for an absence of the love of humanity or "pure sympathy" in a political agent (see, especially, TMS 4.1.11, 185). In context, Smith emphasizes that "public welfare" can be an indirect, even unintended consequence of the desire to make actual a (proper) "system of government." Presumably, a system that can or does generate such "public welfare" is a *right* system. I treat Smith as aiming at such nobility and magnificence.

The intellectual trickle-down envisioned by Smith does not always follow Berkeley's path,[5] which predicts widespread adoption of philosophically discovered and widely diffused justified beliefs; rather, for Smith, public "happiness" and "welfare" can be an unintended side consequence of an aesthetic desire for "order" and "harmony" as perceived by an elite, political actor who pursues a kind of private, contemplative pleasure. This entails that for Smith, we need not always get lost in "the contemplation" of "noble" and "beautiful" theoretical objects (although, as we shall see, he recognizes the risk of intellectual escapism, too), but rather we are motivated to actualize them (e.g., improving roads, advocating export subsidies, etc.; TMS 4.1.11).

In fact, the "love of system" that Smith is alluding to in the quoted passage from TMS 4.1.11 is the fondness for mercantilism in Great Britain and physiocracy in France in his own age. These are the "two different systems of political œconomy" characterized and then polemically discussed in Book 4 of the *Wealth*

---

[5] At Ancient Physics, 10, EPS 116, Smith describes an instance of "intellectual trickle-down" of dangerous beliefs.

of Nations: "the one may be called the system of commerce, the other that of agriculture" (WN 4 Intro.2, 428).

As is well known, Smith was a critic of the mercantile system and physiocracy. He is aware that a love of system is not without danger; it can become excessive and then turn into a (problematic) "spirit of system," which can either produce actual wrongs or—Smith anticipates Kant here—treat people as inappropriate "means" (TMS 4.1.11, 185). In fact, later in TMS, in a passage added to the sixth edition (1790), Smith emphasizes that horrible things can occur when this love of system is transformed, in a revolutionary context, into a "spirit of system" and, subsequently, is turned into the ideologically driven "madness of fanaticism" (TMS 6.2.2.15, 232). Some scholars tend to discern in this later passage allusions to the unfolding French Revolution (influenced by Ross 1995: 393). And it might be thought that what is being targeted is the influence of Rousseau, who as many commentators have noted is, in fact, clearly alluded to in the pages just before the passage quoted above (i.e., TMS 4.1.8–9, 182–3).

Smith was, indeed, very well acquainted with Rousseau's "system" (as he describes it in his early review [Edinburgh Review 11, EPS 250]). But it is unclear why from Smith's vantage point, writing in 1790 before the Reign of Terror, the French Revolution would have involved "love of system," a special kind of factionalism, or the "madness of fanaticism." In fact, a glance at the student notes on Smith's *Lectures on Jurisprudence* reveals that Smith lectured on faction already in 1762-3 (see LJ 273, 321)—a topic that is also significant in the second edition of TMS (see, especially, the chapter on the "sense of duty" with its treatment of the "laws of faction" at TMS 3.3.44, 155). In WN (1776) Smith associates the twin evils of fanaticism and factionalism primarily with the dangers of clerical religion (WN 5.1.g.8, 793; 5.1.g.15, 796; 5.1.g.29, 801 and 5.1.g.34–6, 808–9). Therefore, while it is not impossible that Smith is alluding to the unfolding events in France, it is just as likely that Smith is referring more generically to the dangers when party loyalty in religion and politics as well as the desire for systematicity mix.

Smith was, of course, not the first to diagnose that "love of system" could be problematic in some contexts. The provocative philosopher John Toland argues in *Letters to Serena* (1704) that Spinoza is a sectarian philosopher who wishes to have disciples over whom he has a magisterial authority. (Toland allows that one can end up with disciples even if one did not wish so—Socrates is his main example.) According to Toland, one of Spinoza's main intellectual vices is, in fact, that he's "too much in love with his new world (for such is a system of philosophy)" (*Letters to Serena*, IV, p. 137).[6] Smith, too, allows that a system of philosophy

---

[6] In what follows, I'll return to Toland a few more times. In a later chapter (Section a of Chapter 11), I'll offer some speculative evidence that Smith read Toland. But here I just note that Toland's *Letters to Serena* were the target of a high-profile attack by Samuel Clarke in the 1705 Boyle lectures, *A Demonstration on the Being and Attributes of the Divinity*, a work that Smith is very likely to have read.

can be something like a new world (see also Hume EHU 10.20). In the context of describing the evolution of ancient systems of astronomy and natural philosophy, he also describes a form of intellectual escapism:

> When those philosophers transported themselves, in fancy, to the centres of these imaginary Circles, and took pleasure in surveying from thence, all those fantastical motions, arranged, according to that harmony and order, which it had been the end of all their researches to bestow upon them. Here, at last, they enjoyed that tranquility and repose which they had pursued through all the mazes of this intricate hypothesis; and here they beheld this, the most beautiful and magnificent part of the great theatre of nature, so disposed and constructed, that they could attend, with ease and delight, to all the revolutions and changes that occurred in it. (Astronomy 4.14, EPS 62; I return to Smith's account of such intellectual escapism in Chapter 11)

In Toland "love" of system seems to mean having too much *partiality* for one's intellectual commitments or productions such that one becomes unresponsive to objections and overlooks alternatives. This kind of partiality is also an intellectual vice according to Smith; for example, he criticizes "those who are fond of deducing all our sentiments from certain refinements of self-love [e.g., Hobbes and Mandeville], think themselves at no loss to account, according to their own principles, both for this pleasure and this pain" (TMS 1.1.2.1, 13). He is also critical of Hume for such partiality: "the same ingenious and agreeable author who first explained why utility pleases, has been so struck with this view of things, as to resolve our whole approbation of virtue into a perception of this species of beauty which results from the appearance of utility" (TMS 4.2.3, 188). Here Hume is charged of trying to turn the wrong principle into a system in his explanation of the origin of justice (see Chapter 4 for details). Smith insists that Hume's mistake is one common to "men of reflection and speculation" (TMS 4.2.11, 192). In fact, elsewhere, Smith accuses Hume of adopting a stance of "refined and enlightened reason" in explaining the origin of justice; he claims that Hume's mistake is a natural one ("we are very apt to impute") for a thinker to make. That is, Smith treats Hume here as a negative exemplar to diagnose the existence of a kind of common intellectual illusion that privileges mono-causal explanations, in which the good consequences of a particular feature of an institution can explain its origin (TMS 2.2.3.4–5, 86–7). Thus, regardless of whether Smith was familiar with Toland's writings, he also agrees with Toland's version of the misguided, too-partial love of system.

But when Smith talks of "love of system," he means to describe something subtly different from Toland's version: he wishes to convey that one is too inclined to think that one's explanatory principles are more coherent with each other than they really are, or that they are inappropriate for the situation at hand. Thus, with (excessive) "love of system" Smith diagnoses a kind of expert blind spot or overconfidence in one's theory in virtue of the connectedness of (and lack of gappiness between) its principles. Such "love of system" generates straightforward inductive risk. Obviously, the two versions of bad "love of system" (Toland's and Smith's) are often compatible with each other and, undoubtedly, accompany each other frequently.

It follows from Smith's position that he recognizes that being systematic— that is, aiming at internal coherence (recall the escapist astronomers who bestow "harmony and order" on the objects[7]—is not itself particularly truth-conducive. As he puts it in WN, there are many "systems of natural and moral philosophy" whose "arguments" rest on "very slender probabilities, and sometimes [are] mere sophisms" (V.i.f.26, 769). In fact, Smith argues that concern over how the appearance of systematicity in other people's theories and arguments can mislead explains the origin of logic as a device to detect fallacious inferences (WN V.i.f.26, 770).

As a terminological aside, and to avoid a common confusion, in eighteenth-century terminology "moral science" (or "moral philosophy") does not quite mean what we might think it means. Condorcet, for example, understood by "moral science … all those sciences that have as their object either the human mind itself, or the relations of men to another."[8] Moral sciences were opposed to physical sciences and distinguished by the kinds of causes to be discussed (Berry 2006). Moral sciences dealt with moral causes, wherein "moral" meant something like "social." For example, institutions, norms, education, language, emotions, and property relations were all thought of as moral causes; by contrast, geography, climate, mechanics, and matter theory were physical causes.[9]

Therefore, Smith's standard use of "moral" (as in "moral sentiments" and "moral causes") conforms closely to our notion of the "social." For example, when

---

[7] Smith echoes here Spinoza's criticism of the mathematical astronomers in the famous Appendix to *Ethics* 1. (For example, Spinoza writes, "those things we can easily imagine are especially pleasing to us, men prefer order to confusion, as if order were anything in things [*ordinem in rebus*] more than a relation to our imagination," and "there are men lunatic enough to believe, that even God himself takes pleasure in harmony; indeed there are philosophers who have persuaded themselves that the motions of the heavens produce a harmony.") But there is no firm evidence that Smith read Spinoza, although I will note a few more such allusions in what follows.

[8] Quoted from Hacking's translation in Hacking 1990: 38; Hacking (ibid., 220n3) gives as his source "Eloge de M. Burquet," in A. Condorcet-O'Connor and F. Arago (eds.), *Oeuvres de Condorcet* (Paris: Firmin Didiot Frères, 1847), 2: 410. Condorcet is also among the first thinkers to use "social science" in something like the modern sense. See Baker (1964) and Wokler (1987). (I thank Michael Kremer and Jeroen Van Bouwel for help on this note.)

[9] Therefore, eighteenth-century "moral" science and twentieth-century "social" science are closer in outlook than is commonly thought. Even so, the two practices have different presuppositions: social science often presupposes a version of the fact/value distinction, whereas in moral science "the natural course" or "nature" is often itself normative. If acting according to nature, or properly cultivated nature, is a key criterion or means toward the practice of virtue—as it is in many traditions—then moral science might be a guide to the practice of virtue.

Smith speaks of "irresistible moral causes" (WN 5.1.e.26, 752 and WN 5.3.5, 910), he is describing the effects of social circumstances. Thus, the distinction between, say, moral causation and physical causation is not the contrast between the ethical and the natural. As I explain in Chapters 2 through 4, a "moral sentiment" is a "social passion." However, I also argue there that a social passion is intrinsically normative because it is a cultivated feeling whose content always includes reliable expectations about responses by others. In what follows, I use "natural philosophy," "natural science," "science," and "philosophy" synonymously for Smith unless I note otherwise in context.

In sum, Smith's position entails that one constraint on the public presentation of scientific systems is that they must generate the right sorts of love and spirit among those who might use them, and avoid the excessive kind. Smith makes clear that the right sort facilitates feelings of humanity (TMS 4.1.11, 185–6). In fact, in the final edition of TMS, Smith specifies that one further feature that the right kinds of systems have in common is that they promote caution about implementation: "to insist upon establishing, and upon establishing all at once, and in spite of all opposition, every thing which that [systemic] idea may seem to require, must often be the highest degree of arrogance" (TMS 6.2.2.18, 234). The problem diagnosed here by Smith is not just intellectual arrogance or overconfidence, but, especially, the violence required to impose one's views on unwilling others. In WN, Smith himself promotes gradualism in the implementation of policies even those in accord with his own system, on grounds of "humanity" and fear of "disorder" (WN 4.2.40, 469). One way, then, to understand Smith's preference for his own "obvious and simple system of natural liberty" (WN 4.ix.51, 687) is that it does not involve such violent imposition. While Smith prefers the rule of law over what he calls "savagery," Smith does not ignore the fact that many laws explicitly or tacitly need to be backed up by force and violence to be authoritative. While the violence of law may be necessary sometimes, it is still violence. In light of this fact he urges caution in advocating the imposition of force on others (Pack and Schliesser 2017, who also argue that, following Aristotle, "natural" is often contrasted to "violent" in Smith).

To be sure, it does not follow that there is no constructive role for systems in public life according to Smith. The very passage in which Smith warns against the arrogant and dangerous imposition of ideologies starts with the claim, "some general, and even systematical, idea of the perfection of policy and law, may no doubt be necessary for directing the views of the statesman." (TMS 6.2.2.18, 234) Smith claims that the good political leader requires a unified and broad intellectual perspective to provide a normative and coherent ideal that orders and provides stability to political decision-making. In fact, the way Smith has worded it, it does not really matter if the system is true (so he is not claiming here that a statesman should adopt *his* system); any coherent ideology will do as long as it guides behavior in a gradual and humane fashion.

One reason, then, to be interested in Smith, in addition to the continued influence of some of the ideas that animate his writings, is not so much his noble intentions, but that, as a public philosopher, he takes the inductive risk that may follow from his systematic theorizing very seriously. Judged by the often humorless quality of his otherwise beautiful and eminently quotable (and sometimes sarcastic) writings, some readers may feel he took it too seriously.[10] In fact, he does not appeal to a doctrine of unintended or unknowable consequences to block concern over, and the evaluative relevance of, the utility of one's theories. One sub-theme of this book is that despite the justified interpretation of Smith as a preeminent thinker of unintended consequences, he argues that there are many circumstances in which plenty of consequences are foreseeable either by the agent involved and/or by informed spectators (these can come apart). In fact, in Chapter 12 I argue that Smith's account of the famous invisible hand in TMS and WN involves agents who *could* have known the short-term effects of their actions and would have known so if they were not in the grip of selfishness (TMS) and a false economic theory (WN).

I treat, then, Smith as an exemplar of a public thinker, who finds a way to convey the right sort of system to the public. I focus on his writings in order to uncover both how he understands the nature of such public thought as well as how he practices it. My study is incomplete because I do not explore his practice as a tutor and counselor to leading politicians of his day nor his classroom lectures (see Phillipson 2010). Reflection on such an exemplar also serves as useful preparation to the attempted renewal of the "old truths" of liberalism (Hayek 2011: 47). Such a renewal is urgently needed today.

---

[10] One discerning reader, Hume, had great fun informing Smith of the commercial success of TMS by alluding to the issues discussed pertaining to his self-styled practice as public philosopher:

My Dear Mr. Smith, have patience: compose yourself to tranquillity: show yourself a philosopher in practice as well as profession: think on the emptiness and rashness and futility of the common judgments of men: how little they are regulated by reason in any subject, much more in philosophical subjects, which so far exceed the comprehension of the vulgar.

Non si quid improba Roma, elevet, accedas examenque improbum in illa, perpendas trutina, nec te quaesiveris extra. A wise man's kingdom is his own breast: or, if he ever looks farther, it will only be to the judgment of a select few, who are free from prejudices, and capable of examining his work. Nothing indeed can be a stronger presumption of falsehood than the approbation of the multitude; and Phocion, you know, always suspected himself of some blunder when he was attended with the applauses of the populace.

Supposing, therefore, that you have duly prepared yourself for the worst by all these reflections; I proceed to tell you the melancholy news, that your book has been very unfortunate: for the public seem disposed to applaud it extremely.

It was looked for by the foolish people with some impatience; and the mob of literati are beginning already to be very loud in its praises. Three bishops called yesterday at Millar's shop in order to buy copies, and to ask questions about the author. (Hume to Smith, April 12, 1759)

b. Smith's Corpus as Two Systems of Philosophy

That Smith intended to be read as having developed an incomplete system of the sciences, he reiterates strongly at the start of the final (1790) edition of TMS published in his lifetime. Smith remarks,

> In the last paragraph of the first Edition of the present work, I said, that I should in another discourse endeavour to give an account of the general principles of law and government, and of the different revolutions which they had undergone in the different ages and periods of society; not only in what concerns justice, but in what concerns police, revenue, and arms, and whatever else is the object of law. In the Enquiry concerning the Nature and Causes of the Wealth of Nations, I have partly executed this promise; at least so far as concerns police, revenue, and arms. What remains, the theory of jurisprudence, which I have long projected, I have hitherto been hindered from executing, by the same occupations which had till now prevented me from revising the present work. Though my very advanced age leaves me, I acknowledge, very little expectation of ever being able to execute this great work to my own satisfaction; yet, as I have not altogether abandoned the design, and as I wish still to continue under the obligation of doing what I can, I have allowed the paragraph to remain as it was published more than thirty years ago, when I entertained no doubt of being able to execute every thing which it announced. (TMS Advertisement.2, 3)

Smith clearly implies that TMS and WN form part of a larger enterprise, which I call "a system of anthropic philosophy." I call it "anthropic philosophy" because Smith's theorizing is resolutely focused, despite occasional nods otherwise, on the human (see Chapter 2). This system would have included an unfinished work in legal theory and its development over time; part of the legal work is contained in WN (especially in Books 3 and 5; see Hont 2015). Smith does not use the word "system" in the quoted "Advertisement" to TMS, but given that these works are supposed to offer "general principles," he is describing his own enterprise as offering a foundation for systems. This interpretation is confirmed by that very "last paragraph" (of TMS), where Smith praises Grotius as offering the first attempt

> to give the world any thing like a system of those principles which ought to run through, and be the foundation of the laws of all nations: and his treatise of the laws of war and peace, with all its imperfections, is perhaps at this day the most complete work that has yet been given upon this subject. (TMS 7.4.37, 342)

Smith then comments that he

> shall in another discourse endeavour to give an account of the general
> principles of law and government, and of the different revolutions they
> have undergone in the different ages and periods of society, not only in
> what concerns justice, but in what concerns police, revenue, and arms,
> and whatever else is the object of law.

Therefore, Smith clearly wished to emulate the scope of Grotius's system in his own work. Near the end of his life, he claims that TMS and WN were part of such a larger, not entirely completed, system of anthropic philosophy.

TMS and his other writings belong to another project, too. Despite the immediate and ongoing success of TMS, Smith claims in the "Advertisement" of the (1790) sixth edition that he "always intended" to revise it "with care and attention" (TMS Advert.1, 3). One such change is, in fact, announced on the revised title page of TMS: he included "A Dissertation upon the Origin of Languages" (Languages), which Smith had already added to the third edition of TMS (1767; see also Smith's letter to Strahan, Winter 1766–1767, Letter 100; Corr. 122, which instructs his publisher that Languages "is to be printed at the end of" TMS). During the eighteenth century, TMS and Languages could, thus, be seen as mutually enlightening. For example, when Sophie de Grouchy produced her very fine, authoritative translation of TMS into French (1798), she appended her *Letters on Sympathy* to her combined translation of TMS and Languages. Inexplicably, the editors of the modern, Glasgow edition of Smith's works, which has become the standard one for most recent scholarly purposes, moved Languages into a volume (LRBL) with student notes—without even mentioning Languages in the title volume![11]

That is, TMS was meant to be read not only alongside WN and the never-completed legal work as part of a system of anthropic philosophy, but also alongside Smith's (to use Fleischacker's phrase) "system of the scientific systems." In Languages, Smith presents his Dissertation as a response to Rousseau's treatment in the *Discourse on the Origin and Basis of Inequality Among Men* on the origin of language—a topic heavily debated during the eighteenth century. Human equality is important in its own right, of course, as Smith argues we are "one of the multitude in no respect better than any other in it" (TMS 2.2.2.1, 83). Existing inequalities are a central part of wider Enlightenment debates about human nature and the nature of political and intellectual life in commercializing societies. But these debates also impinge on a second-order set of reflections about the *kind* of agents that can engage in and contribute to the development of "principles" of systems at all. For Languages is not just about the origin of language, but also an inquiry into the origins of the very cognitive *possibility* of "metaphysical analysis" (LRBL 216).

---

[11] Ryan Hanley's Penguin edition of TMS does better.

While Smith was a somewhat unfair critic of Scholastic metaphysics (WN 4.i.f.29, 771; see also the criticism of Stoic metaphysics at TMS 3.3.13, 143), it does not follow that he is against metaphysics as such. Like his friend Hume, whose interest in metaphysics has been rediscovered (Baxter 2008; Rocknak 2012) and who described his own work as a "true metaphysics" (EHU 1.12), Smith, too, is interested in the possibility and significance of metaphysics, as illustrated by his short history of ancient metaphysics.[12] In eighteenth-century context, this inquiry into which humans could or could not engage metaphysics is also, albeit not solely, a debate about human intellectual hierarchy (Garrett 2000, 2006; Levy and Peart 2008b; Sebastiani 2013; Smith 2015); the content and effects of Smith's predominately egalitarian stance on such hierarchy are discussed throughout this book.

In addition to Languages, some other parts of Smith's "system of the scientific systems" were deliberately saved from the flames and published posthumously by Smith's friends Black and Hutton in EPS (1795), including the history of ancient metaphysics just mentioned. This volume includes two essays, External Senses and Astronomy, which will play a significant role in my argument throughout this book. While the latter has been read and admired since Whewell's days and receives respectful attention from historians of economics (from Menger to Schumpeter), it remains oddly unappreciated by professional philosophers and historians of science despite anticipating many of Thomas Kuhn's best insights (Schliesser 2005). The former is Smith's most narrowly philosophical essay. It is an extensive engagement with the ideas of Berkeley and animal behavior in order to tackle Molyneux's question and external world skepticism (for details see Glenney 2011, 2014). Both essays are extremely useful to the student interested in Smith's philosophy of mind and metaphysics that are presupposed in WN and TMS.

In their advertisement to EPS, they write:

> The much lamented Author of these Essays left them in the hands of his friends to be disposed of as they thought proper, having immediately before his death destroyed many other manuscripts which he thought unfit for being made public. When these were inspected, the greater number of them appeared to be parts of a plan he once had formed, for giving a connected history of the liberal sciences and elegant arts. (Advertisement, EPS 32)

The saved fragments of the connected history of the liberal sciences and elegant arts focus—as the title page of EPS indicates—on "the principles which lead and direct philosophical enquiries; illustrated by the history of astronomy." Here we see further evidence of Smith's interest in describing other people's "systems of science." In fact, Smith will argue that once fruitful principles have been

---

[12] Smith did think, however, that "scholastic or technical system of artificial definitions, divisions, and subdivisions" are "one of the most effectual expedients...for extinguishing whatever degree of good sense there may be in any moral or metaphysical doctrine." (TMS 7.1.2.10.41, 291) I do not mean to suggest that Smith develops a metaphysics with the subtlety and quality of, say, Hume or Condillac. In fact, Smith is a critic of metaphysics when it becomes too subtle and with too many distinctions

discovered, such systems have a common pattern of development and series of revolutions among successive systems (see, especially, Chapter 11).

Black and Hutton describe Smith's project as the "Principles in the Human Mind which Mr. Smith has pointed out to be the universal motives of Philosophical Researches" (EPS 105). By insisting that for Smith these are "universal motives," in the "Human Mind," Black and Hutton put Smith on the side of an anti-hierarchical conception of human nature. With the right background conditions (law, order, education) *anyone* can become a philosopher—in Smith's memorable phrase, "the difference between the most dissimilar characters, between a philosopher and a common street porter, for example, seems to arise not so much from nature, as from habit, custom, and education" (WN 1.ii.4, 29).[13] Even so, Smith's phrasing is comparative ("not so much") and about what is commonly perceived ("seems to arise"). While Smith is definitely on the egalitarian side—we do not find in Smith a fondness for racial eugenics (as can be found in Berkeley's *Querist*) or dismissiveness of the intellectual capacities of "blacks" (as can be found in Hume's "Of National Characters" [see, especially, the notorious note 10 in EMPL, p. 634; Garrett 2000] and Kant's "On the Use of Teleological Principles in Philosophy" [Kleingeld 2007])—I also call attention to some of Smith's more elitist tendencies.

Thus, Smith's writings are embedded in two, larger Smithian projects, one a system of anthropic philosophy that focuses on the political, economic, legal, moral, and psychological (etc.) requirements "sufficient for the harmony of society" (TMS 1.1.4.7, 22) in the context of a broad account of the origin and causes of flourishing of law and government. This project is informed, even circumscribed, by a more theoretical account, the "system of scientific systems," that explains how from "savage" origins "remote from the societies of men" (Languages 1, LRBL 203) crucial intellectual features of human nature as found in civilization(s) themselves could have developed over long expanses of time (see also Steuart's obituary of Smith in EPS; Schabas 2006: 93). In addition to Languages and the essays collected in EPS, I treat Smith's biographical reflections on Hume's life, "Letter to Strahan" (which he published alongside Hume's autobiography in 1776), as a means into Smith's meta-philosophical reflections that inform his system of scientific systems.

c. A Bibliographic Interlude

As noted above, I treat Smith as a public thinker who was simultaneously a "systematic philosopher." In this section I describe key methodologic features of my approach to Smith and also call attention to some works that anticipate my general outlook.

((TMS 3.3.14, 143; 7.2.1.41, 291, and WN 5.1.f.29, 770). Such subtle metaphysics distances us from and undermines our disposition dispositions and is, thereby, likely to move us away from how we ought to behave. For example, he blames Scholasticism for the corruption of moral philosophy, which he calls "by far the most important of all the different branches of philosophy." (WN 5.1.f.30, 771)

[13] Habits are individual, while customs are social.

While Smith has been long studied by economists, especially historians of economics, and sociologists, Smith's status as a philosopher is frequently rediscovered (for an illustrative example, see Broad's [1950] review of Prior [1949]).[14] There has been a renaissance of engagement with Smith's moral philosophy (much of it influenced by the agenda set by Fleischacker [1999] and Griswold [1999]).[15] Smith's work in moral psychology, his views on moral luck (e.g., Nagel 1976; Russell 1999; Flanders 2006; Garrett 2005; Hankins 2016), his analysis of sympathy, and his moral phenomenology (Brown and Fleischacker 2010) have all become important subjects of study. These topics are regularly discussed in light of Smith's known engagement with the works of, say, Hume, Rousseau, Mandeville, and Hutcheson. There have been serious studies of Smith's moral philosophy that interpret him as a neo-Stoic (Raphael 2007), or as a kind of virtue-theorist (Hanley 2009), or, looking ahead to Kant, a kind of deontic theorist (Fleischacker 1999; Carrasco 2004; Montes 2004; Darwall 2006).

WN is now, for better and for worse, routinely read in light of TMS.[16] That is, thanks to the attention of notable contemporary philosophers and historians of philosophy (including, but not limited to, Martha Nussbaum, Axel Honneth, Amartya Sen, Ryan Hanley, Steve Darwall, Sam Fleischacker, Fonna Forman, Remy Debes, Charles Griswold, James Otteson, Maria Carrasco, Michael Frazer, Craig Smith, and Lisa Herzog), Smith is taken seriously as a *moral* philosopher, especially relevant for agents in liberal societies. My work is much indebted to their efforts. Even so, the working assumption behind this study has been that these efforts have given us a very partial understanding of Smith's project and its possible ongoing relevance, especially now that the survival of a liberal society cannot be presupposed even in its historical heartland.

By claiming that Smith is now commonly presented as a moral philosopher, I do not mean to suggest that other philosophical aspects of Smith's writings are entirely overlooked; Smith's philosophy of science (Montes 2003; Kim 2012), as known by Astronomy, is often invoked, in passing, and respectfully, and there is growing interest in his philosophy and sociology of religion. Even so, Smith's moral philosophy is rarely connected to his interests in say, metaphysics, his philosophy of language, his philosophy of mind, his response to skepticism, his philosophy of logic, or his aesthetics. To understand his views on these topics one need not explore the student notes to his lectures; the substance of his views on

---

[14] I am indebted to David M. Levy for insisting on the significance of Prior, who became simultaneously one of the leading historians of philosophy and logicians of the middle of the twentieth century, on Smith.

[15] The editor of a recent collection of essays even bemoans the lack of attention to Smith's political economy (Young 2009).

[16] One may wonder "why for worse?" The quick answer is that the moral and political philosophy of WN is thereby often neglected (but see Fleischacker 2004 and Rothschild and Sen 2006), even though these frame, in turn, TMS.

these matters can be read in the works he published during his lifetime or that were part of his intended *nachlass* (EPS).

This is not the first book that focuses on Smith and systems. Andrew Skinner's collection of essays (1979, republished in 1996), *A System of Social Science*, anticipates many of my methodologic claims (especially the significance of EPS to WN and TMS). My debt to Skinner is also personal; he commented on some draft chapters of my dissertation (in the late 1990s). Even so, Skinner is primarily focused on putting Smith's political economy in proper intellectual context and thereby making him accessible to the "modern economist" (see, e.g., 252). He thereby misses lots of conceptual distinctions and philosophical themes that were manifestly of interest to Smith but not to twentieth-century economists (as understood by Skinner).

Moreover, Skinner's essays were "by-products of editorial work done on the Glasgow edition of Smith's Works and Correspondence (Oxford, 1976–83)" (Skinner 1996: v). These essays, thus, often presuppose now-dated commitments inherited from other, earlier scholarly literatures. While I admire the labor Skinner and his editorial colleagues put into the Glasgow edition, I also have—as revealed in the previous section by my polemical remarks on the removal of Languages from TMS—come to disagree with their underlying vision of Smith's oeuvre that they have projected onto it (including his relationship to Stoicism).

Nicholas Phillipson's (2010) intellectual biography, *Adam Smith: An Enlightened Life*, also emphasizes Smith as a systematic thinker. I loved reading Phillipson's elegant book and I warmly recommend it as a contextualized introduction to Smith's thought and times. It has relieved me of the responsibility of adding a biographical essay to this study. But Phillipson's monograph is short on conceptual detail and, thereby, understates some of Smith's intellectual achievements.

Athol Fitzgibbons' (1995) *Adam Smith's System of Liberty, Wealth, and Virtue* anticipates my interest in connecting Smith's systematic ideas to his political theory. Moreover, he deserves praise for drawing attention to many serious differences between Hume and Smith. Unfortunately, the handling of their differences lacks conceptual care. For example, Fitzgibbons treats Hume's moral philosophy as a "selfish" philosophy and so conflates Smith's criticism of Hobbes and Mandeville with the criticism of Hume. In addition, Fitzgibbons treats Hume as a "positivist" (18), a "materialist" (16, 21), and a nihilist (15) without recognizing the tension among these categorizations. Finally, Fitzgibbons treats Smith's metaphysics and philosophy of nature as basically Stoic (18ff); while this is not implausible, in what follows I'll offer lots of reasons for challenging this ascription (see also Montes 2004; Brubaker 2006a; Hanley 2009; Andrews 2014a; Pack and Schliesser 2017).

Finally, I mention Mike Hill and Warren Montag's (2014) *The Other Adam Smith*. This is an exhilarating attempt to capture Smith's system and place its concerns within a range of eighteenth-century debates (over copyright, insurrection, and the emergence of bureaucratic state order). I read their book in manuscript and it jolted me—together with Ryan Hanley's careful and masterful (2009) study of Part 6 of TMS, *Adam Smith and the Character of Virtue*—out of a complacent sense that I understood Smith. Spurred on by their work, I returned to Smith's texts, which seemed stranger and more vivid than I had discerned before. Ultimately, we have written very different books, but mine would not have been possible without theirs and Hanley's.

d. Methodologic Remarks

I offer some remarks on the methodology I have followed in this book for two reasons. First, I blend practices, which are often used by competing schools in the history of philosophy, in idiosyncratic fashion. Here I do not offer justification for this approach (see Della Rocca 2015 for a defense of the compatibility between contextual and systematic approaches to the history of philosophy). Second, I deviate from some of my own, more polemical methodologic writings (e.g., Schliesser 2013).

In this book, I focus on writings available to a learned audience in, say, 1800 (Smith died in 1790). This entails drawing on and interpreting the writings published in Smith's lifetime and those published shortly after his death (so the corpus treated here is primarily WN, TMS, EPS, "Letter to Strahan," and Languages). While there is understandable scholarly interest in the discoveries of student notes taken from his lectures (e.g., Haakonssen 1989; Young 1997), we still lack an adequate treatment of many fine-grained details and even many doctrinal commitments of the *public* Smith. Thus, while I do not pretend that the student lecture notes do not exist—I draw on them for supporting evidence and to rule out some possibilities—they do not motivate my interpretations. The lectures were tailored to their audience (students, most of them under the age of twenty) in part as a species of moral education (see Heydt 2008 also for more nuance about this claim). While a "public" philosopher can engage in moral education of his students and be concerned with "inductive risk" in so doing, I assume that Smith distinguishes between the lecture hall and public instruction. In fact, Smith's lecture notes were not designed to be studied by posterity, and Smith tried to remove them from circulation by having them destroyed (see Phillipson 2010 for details on this and many of Smith's other acts of self-concealment).[17] One additional advantage of treating Smith in the way that I propose is that it sets the stage for a more thorough, historical work on Smith's reception.

---

[17] There are at least two other related issues. First, Smith seems interested in controlling his posthumous reputation (see Chapter 15 for more extensive elaboration). Second, Smith seems to reduce the corpus of material available to future readers in order to reduce any discordant notes between published and manuscript material; that is, he wishes to present himself as coherent as possible. When one's philosophy and public comportment match, one exhibits a certain kind of philosophical integrity (see Chapter 15).

When possible, I'll present and analyze Smith in his own conceptual vocabulary. Smith is a very careful, often talmudically precise and terse writer, whose prose is, in addition, eminently quotable. Even so, I deploy distinctions and terms from recent philosophy when these can help illuminate Smith's system; sometimes I also impose taxonomies on his text. Unlike most other historians of philosophy who draw on historical context, I maintain that the exclusive use of so-called actors' categories often distorts and confuses rather than produces historical understanding. This is because if one adopts, uncritically, the concepts and categories of the past one also takes sides, often unwittingly, in debates of the period; concepts are contested terrain, after all.[18] While no perspective on the past is fully neutral, sometimes an anachronistic vocabulary can do more justice to the various positions in a surveyed philosophical landscape. Proponents of the use of actors' categories worry that anachronism may remove the strangeness of the past; without denying such concerns, the Smith presented in these pages is in many ways a philosopher with unfamiliar commitments that are difficult to pigeonhole or classify.

In addition to relying on systematicity—that is, I interpret Smith's writings in light of each other—I use two other means of making available Smith's positions. First, I rely on a wide range of other, earlier readers of Smith to highlight and examine his works. Second, I put Smith in conversation with other philosophers, including not only the ones we know who shaped his philosophy, but also a few who may not have been known to him firsthand. I neither offer a history of Smith's reception nor do I trace intellectual lineages or sources to him. Smith was incredibly well read in an age of polymaths, and it will take more dedicated scholarship than I am capable of to master all the works he is responding to.

I largely aim to offer a generous exposition of Smith's views. Sometimes I reveal thereby some of his limitations (or my own). I have not shied away from occasional, explicit criticism, especially in Section b in Chapter 7 ("Even the Humane Smith").

By discerning the systematic connections in Smith's thought, this study also offers new ways of understanding Smith's philosophy, including aspects that are often taken to be familiar hitherto. Here, I offer four concrete examples that I develop in subsequent chapters.

1. I argue that while Smith certainly took experience and empirical science seriously, he should not be understood as an empiricist in epistemology and his moral epistemology; he relies crucially on innate ideas and innate mental structure.
2. This book gives the first extensive (albeit not exhaustive) study and taxonomy of Smith's theory of the passions, which I treat as the *elements* of his system (cf. Hume Treatise 1.1.4.7). In fact, I argue that the content of a social passion is inherently normative in Smith's approach.

---

[18] I owe this insight to Dan Schneider.

3. I argue that Smith is decidedly reserved about deploying mathematics within his political economy.
4. I argue that Smith's account of liberty should not be identified with the so-called liberty of the moderns, or freedom of contract. While Smith certainly was a defender of freedom of contract, his account of liberty is more expansive (and more attractive).

In sum, in the pages of this book one can find a sympathetic exposition of Smith's views. I often do so by extensive exegesis and by making explicit the distinctions and assumptions that Smith leaves implicit. As others have noted (Fleischacker 2004: 53), Smith often relies on immanent criticism. Not unlike J. S. Mill a century later, Smith also tends not to signal when he is original;[19] this should be distinguished from the charge that he was not sufficiently generous to others (as explored by Rashid 1998). It is not always entirely clear if his restraint on explicit theorizing (i) is a rhetorical choice, say due to concern about being thought an "abstruse" thinker (see, e.g., TMS 4.2.7, 189 and recall TMS 7.1.2.10.41, 291), or (ii) it follows from his concern with inductive risk, or (iii) it is a consequence of his aversion to a kind of scholasticism (WN 4.i.f.29, 771; these three reasons are compatible with each other). When he does engage in, say, metaphysics, he is more concerned with the psychological and social preconditions for its practice than contributing to metaphysical doctrine.[20]

e. Summary

I have organized this book thematically, moving, roughly, in Part 1, from an analysis of abstract human nature and its passionate constitution to Smith's analysis of important social institutions (science, markets, government, finance, etc.), in Part 2, in order to finish with Smith's treatment of higher things (religion and philosophy). While the latter chapters often presuppose distinctions and claims articulated in earlier chapters, I have tried to make the book as modular as possible—students and scholars interested in particular topics can skip ahead as needs must to sections of interest. However, a few important topics (Smith's aesthetics, his relationship to Hume, his account of social explanation, his treatment of uncertainty, etc.) are discussed throughout the work rather than as stand alone

---

[19] I owe the point to David Levy and I am here echoing the judgment of Levy's teacher, G. J. Stigler (1955), on Mill. Stigler insists that Mill's modesty is due to unselfish dedication of "his abilities to the advancement of the science." Leaving aside the peculiarity of a Chicago economist attributing such unselfish behavior to anybody, I suggest that Mill was following Smith in the way he writes for a public even in his more technical works.

[20] Having said that: as David Levy emphasizes, Smith tends to be very careful with modality and uncertainty. I have noted this throughout this book, but both topics merit further study.

chapters; I have used explicit cross-referencing to ensure that the full argument can, where necessary, be recovered with little effort.[21]

This book is divided in three unequal parts. The first part, Chapters 2 through 5, is devoted to treating the main *principles* and *elements* (in the Humean sense discussed above) of Smith's system of thought: his account of human nature and his account of social explanation, which I argue is a form of historical explanation. The two are related because for Smith human nature is itself a consequence of a long historical development. In particular, throughout these chapters, I offer an extensive analysis and taxonomy of his account of the passions (especially Chapter 3). While relying on Smith's relatively neglected distinction between natural and moral sentiments (see Carrasco 2004), I argue that instances of the latter are inherently normative, because in Smith's hands a moral sentiment, or a social passion, is a cultivated feeling that includes reliable expectations about responses by others. In addition, I show that in his account of ordinary human functioning a considerable role is played by instinctual responses and anticipations as well as innate mental content; I use this to undermine the idea that Smith is a (Humean) empiricist.

In the first part, I also offer new accounts of (i) the nature of good judgment according to Smith, (ii) Smith's treatment of the sympathetic mechanism, and (iii) Smith's account of judgments of propriety. All three topics have in common the role of causal analysis and causal judgment in Smith's system—something that tends to be obscured in and neglected by treatments of Smith as a sentimentalist (or moral sense theorist). I argue that the sympathetic mechanism relies crucially on counterfactual reasoning in the imagination; I show that judgments of propriety are, in fact, judgments of the proportionality of causal relata. In this part, building on my discussions of these issues, I also discuss Smith's treatment of conscience, the faculty of reason, the impartial spectator, and his treatment of moral rules.

I illustrate my analysis of Smith's account of human nature and social explanation by applying it to two topics: (i) Smith's account of the origin and nature of justice and (ii) Smith's treatment of a species of moral luck, the piacular, when one is the unwilling cause of somebody else's misfortune. Smith's account of property is central to his political (and legal) philosophy; it simultaneously extends Hume's analysis and is critical of it. Along the way, I show that Smith's moral theory distinguishes between a thin, albeit stable, universalist account centered on common humanity, and a thicker, society-specific account of revisable context-specific morality. Through this distinction I address the persistent concern that Smith's system tends toward a species of cultural relativism (Forman-Barzilai 2010). The treatment of the piacular usefully reveals some of the intricacies of

---

[21] Smith's views on taste, art, and aesthetics certainly deserve a more thorough treatment than I provide. I did not discuss Smith's treatment on the so-called naturalistic fallacy because I could not improve on Prior's contribution; see Prior 1949: 18.

Smith's approach to moral evaluation of individuals and also brings out his complex relationship to the nature of Enlightenment.

The second part (Chapters 6 through 12) is more heterogeneous but deals with Smith as social philosopher, including his philosophy of science, his political philosophy, and his political economy. I argue that while Smith is a kind of pluralist about human value (Gill 2014a, 2014b), and his ethics tends toward context-sensitive situationism, he is a consequentialist (but not a utilitarian) in his evaluation of social institutions (including, as we have already seen, the institution of philosophy). The consequentialism is embedded in a kind of group-selectionist argument on the development and evolution of norms and institutions. This coheres nicely (but does not necessitate) with another claim I argue for: that "society" is a key analytical category of Smith's political philosophy and political economy.

Building on research by others (Pack 1991; Rothschild 2001; Fleischacker 2004; Boucoyannis 2013), I show how his proposed tax regime and the fundamental measure of his political economy are geared toward benefiting the working poor. I show how these theoretical commitments follow from and are in accord with Smith's moral theory, especially a surprisingly robust conception of human flourishing and liberty. In addition, Smith advocated peaceful coexistence among different nations (note the plural in the title of WN) and peoples, and he was a critic of slavery and, despite favoring commercial states and the rule of law, was an enemy of the forceful extension of civilization. Even so, I argue that his constitution of an Atlantic empire is systematically biased against non-white subjects.

In Part 2 I also discuss Smith's practice as a political economist: I look at his methodology in action, describe the ends served by his key measures, and discuss how his method coheres with his social epistemology. I argue that Smith puts inquiry within the division of labor, but that he also tacitly relies on the impartial spectator within his analysis of communities of enquirers. I devote considerable attention to Smith's critical attitude toward the application of mathematics in political economy.

Chapter 10 presents a new interpretation of the "invisible hand" passages in EPS, TMS, and WN. I do so in order to characterize more precisely the ways in which the TMS and WN versions of the phrase help clarify Smith's account of social explanation. In particular, I call attention to the ways in which the invisible hand passages allow Smith to model the role and evaluation of knowledge among distinct agents, in particular the differences of perception between economic agents and (theoretical) spectators. In many ways this chapter provides some of the most surprising payoffs of my systematic approach to Smith.[22]

Finally, in Part 3 I discuss Smith's account of theology and philosophy. I argue that Smith treats theology as subservient to morality and offers a substantial defense of the public role of philosophy within commercializing societies, but this defense reveals a modest strain of (moral) elitism.

---

[22] I say "surprising" because the invisible hand has been the subject of huge amount of scholarly comment.

PART 1

PROPENSITIES AND PASSIONS

2

Passionate Human Nature

Despite Smith's reminder that we can sympathize to some degree with "all other animals" (External Senses, 6, EPS 136; Frierson 2006a, 2006b), nearly all of his philosophy is about the human, especially the social human (Macfie 1967). This is why I call his system an "anthropic philosophy." Even Smith's relatively neglected observations on animal development are written up with an eye toward explaining human cognition (External Senses, 49, EPS 150ff; in this he is following Hobbes, Locke, and Hume [see Fry 2016]). Although Smith writes about astronomy and the sciences of matter, and their histories, or (say) botany, he is ultimately more interested in developing arguments about how communities of inquirers function and, perhaps, articulating the nature and limits of knowledge, than in offering a comprehensive system of everything. Even the main point of Smith's careful and limited remarks on theology is to assert its subservience to what's moral for human beings. Therefore, throughout this book, as I offer details of Smith's philosophy, I also explain his precise views on what it is to be human and his vision of human potentiality.

The overall aim of this chapter is to offer a detailed survey of the main elements of Smith's understanding of human nature so that we are well prepared to understand his views on human flourishing as it is fleshed out in his moral psychology, his moral theory, his philosophy of science, and his political economy. I introduce this survey by offering a careful exegesis of one of the set-piece, opening passages in WN (1.2.1, 25). There Smith offers a template for what I call "Smithian social explanation." In this chapter, I use it to show how Smith's account of human nature enters into Smithian social explanation. In later chapters I distinguish Smithian social explanation from invisible hand explanations.

In this chapter I also start presenting Smith's account of the passions, which I flesh out in taxonomic detail over the course of the next two chapters. For while Smith does not name the elements of his system, he repeatedly calls attention to the "principles of human nature." (Recall from Chapter 1 that a "principle" is an explanatory ground, often causal, of a system.) For example, at the start of TMS, Smith writes, in one of the more Hobbesian (Cropsey 1957) passages of his oeuvre, "and from thence arises one of the most important principles in human nature, the dread of death, the great poison to the happiness, but the great restraint upon the injustice of mankind, which, while it afflicts and mortifies the individual, guards and protects the society" (TMS 1.1.1.13, 13; below I also explore Smith's many criticisms of Hobbes). Later Smith notes that it is universally accepted that "compassion," or fellow feeling with another's passion, is a "principle of human nature" (TMS 1.3.1.2, 43). Thus, and this is no surprise to the student of Smith, the "principles of human nature" include the passions.

My way of presenting Smith's account of the passions differs dramatically from Smith's initial presentation of the passions in TMS 1.2. In doing so I depart from other commentators. In TMS 1.2, Smith evaluates the passions from the point of view of propriety. He does so after having first introduced his readers to the outlines of his account of sympathy (TMS 1.2.intro.2, 27) and after having defined what he means by propriety (TMS 1.1.3.6, 18). In TMS Smith treats primarily of *moral* sentiments— that is, only a subset of all the passions. I argue that in addition to the moral sentiments, Smith recognizes other sentiments: the so-called natural sentiments and the intellectual sentiments. By evaluating the passions from the start of TMS from the vantage point of propriety, Smith is treating the passions from *within* moral life much the same way as Aristotle treats politics from within the political order in the *Politics* (for more on Smith's debts to Aristotle, see Berns 1994; Hanley 2006, 2009; Vivenza 2009; Pack 2010; Andrews 2014a; Pack and Schliesser 2017). In this chapter I embed Smith's theory of the passions in his understanding of the historical development of human propensities, including language, cognition, and reason.

a. Human Propensities and Smithian Social Explanation

This section explains what human propensities are according to Smith and how these fit into his larger explanatory and historical framework. I do so by offering a close reading of a key passage at the start of WN. Just after Smith introduces one of his important explanatory concepts, the division of labor, he adds this remark:

> THIS division of labour, from which so many advantages are derived, is not originally the effect of any human wisdom, which foresees and intends that general opulence to which it gives occasion. It is the necessary, though very slow and gradual consequence of a certain propensity in human nature which has in view no such extensive utility; the propensity to truck, barter, and exchange one thing for another. Whether this propensity be one of those original principles in human nature of which no further account can be given; or whether, as seems more probable, it be the necessary consequence of the faculties of reason and speech, it belongs not to our present subject to inquire. (WN 1.2.1, 25)

In later chapters I return to the significance of the division of labor in Smith's thought. My main point here is that Smith views human nature as a collection of propensities. A "propensity" is a stable inclination. Propensities do not always manifest themselves; they may require what I call "triggering conditions." That is, a propensity is a tendency in an agent that gets activated in certain specific circumstances of the environment or in the bodily and mental state(s) of the agent concerned. And even when such triggering conditions are present the inclination need not be always expressed in any individual over time or all individuals at a given time. A propensity is, then, a disposition. This means that whenever Smith speaks of "human nature" he is not describing an exceptionless type. I use the phrase "normological"—as opposed to "nomological"—to capture the kind of regularity Smith discerns in human nature. While nomological regularities are exceptionless laws, normological regularities are robust generalizations that allow exceptions. While to a modern eye a normological regularity can be treated like a statistical generalization, traditionally normological regularities tend to accompany functional, or teleological, explanations and, thereby, also allow misfirings or failures of functions. Most of the time, Smith's normological regularities are not based on statistical data, but sometimes (when discussing long-run prices of silver and corn) they are.

When Smith writes that something is "natural," he often means "for the most part" (e.g., WN 1.2.1, 160; Levy and Peart 2013: 380; see also WN 2.2.62, 305). Thus, Smith understands human nature as a collection of fairly stable dispositions.

These propensities can either be bedrock parts of human nature or the consequence of human nature as we find it today. (I am ignoring propensities that have disappeared.) I call the former "original propensities" and the latter "derived propensities." The terminology of "original" and "derived" propensities tracks Smith's treatment elsewhere:

> [Nature] has constantly . . . not only endowed mankind with an appetite for the end which she proposes, but likewise with an appetite for the means by which alone this end can be brought about, for their own sakes, and independent of their tendency to produce it. Thus self-preservation, and the propagation of the species, are the great ends which nature seems to have proposed in the formation of all animals. Mankind are endowed with a desire of those ends, and an aversion to the contrary. . . . But though we are . . . endowed with a very strong desire of those ends, it has not been entrusted to the slow and uncertain determinations of our reason, to find out the proper means of bringing them about. Nature has directed us to the greater part of these by original and immediate instincts. Hunger, thirst, the passion which unites the two sexes, the love of pleasure, and the dread of pain, prompt us to apply those means for their own sakes, and without any consideration of their tendency to those beneficent ends which the great Director of nature intended to produce by them. (TMS 2.1.5.10, 77–8)

Thus, on Smith's view, there are at least five "original and immediate" instincts— "Hunger, thirst, the passion which unites the two sexes, the love of pleasure, and the dread of pain"—that guide our behavior. Facilitated by at least two faculties (reason and speech), these original and immediate instincts can combine in various ways to produce stable original propensities (Wight 2009). In the conceptual apparatus of Smith's time, a "faculty" is itself a stable power or disposition of the human mind (e.g., TMS 3.5.6, 165, and Locke's *Essay*, Book II, Chapter XI; Smith also uses "faculty" to refer to a branch of learning or a university department as they are still called in Europe, but those senses of "faculty" do not concern us now).

However, Smith's use of "faculty" is often broader and vaguer than a disposition of the mind. For example, in "Of the External Senses," Smith writes that "The young of several sorts of quadrupeds seem, like those of the greater part of birds which make their nests upon the ground, to enjoy as soon as they come into the world the faculty of seeing as completely as they ever do afterwards" (71, EPS 162). Thus, for Smith, humans and animals alike possess faculties. Smith tends to use "faculties," "senses," and "instincts" as rough synonyms. For example, "Nature, it may be said, never bestows upon any animal any faculty which is not either necessary or useful, and an instinct of this kind would be altogether useless to an animal which must necessarily acquire the knowledge which the instinct is given to supply" (External Senses, 75, EPS 163; in context, Smith is describing the "instinctive perception" of distance). In addition to reason, speech, and the so-called external senses (sight, touch, smell, hearing, and taste), Smith also recognizes memory, reflection, and imagination as faculties of the human mind. More surprising, perhaps, is that Smith also talks of some of the natural passions, especially resentment, as a "faculty" (LJ(B), 344, 547). For example, early in TMS he writes, "Every faculty in one man is the measure by which he judges of the like faculty in another. I judge of your sight by my sight, of your ear by my ear, of your reason by my reason, of your resentment by my resentment, of your love by my love" (1.1.3.10, 19; see Griswold 1999 for significance of this passage and Prior 1949: 66ff).

The passage I quoted from TMS 2.1.5.10 (77–8) offers evidence of Smith's teleological conception of human nature. If one reads Smith's quoted phrase "Director of Nature" as sincere, one has evidence that God is responsible for the original constitution of human nature (this is the view defended by Evensky 2005). Even if one is disinclined to read Smith metaphorically at TMS 2.1.5.10, human nature is assimilated to animal nature and the two great ends (self-preservation and propagation of the species) of human nature are no different than those of all other animals. Our fundamental natural ends are reduced to mere material, animalistic survival and propagation. If Smith is read literally here, God's aim for us is, in addition to our individual self-preservation, our demographic expansion (echoing Genesis 1:28). Either way, this serves as evidence that for Smith, human dispositions are functional.

If providence is an essential part of Smith's system, as many readers are inclined to think, then TMS 2.1.5.10, 77–8, offers the best direct support for it.

But the providence on offer here is a very thin Deism; it's of the sort that could be embraced even by Hume's Philo in *Dialogues Concerning Natural Religion*:

> You ascribe, Cleanthes, (and I believe justly) a purpose and intention to Nature. But what, I beseech you, is the object of that curious artifice and machinery, which she has displayed in all animals? The preservation alone of individuals and propagation of the species. It seems enough for her purpose, if such a rank be barely upheld in the universe, without any care or concern for the happiness of the members, that compose it. (D 10.26)

Let us return to WN 1.2.1, 25; Smith thinks it is highly probable that the disposition to barter and truck is a derived propensity of human nature. He uses this point to offer a surprising, counterfactual explanation for why he believes that "the difference between ... a philosopher and a common street porter ... seems to arise not so much from nature, as from habit, custom, and education" and why "when they came into the world, and for the first six or eight years of their existence, they were a, perhaps, a very much alike, and neither their parents nor play-fellows could perceive any remarkable difference." Smith then goes on to argue that "without the disposition to truck, barter, and exchange, every man must have procured to himself every necessary and conveniency of life which he wanted. All must have had the same duties to perform, and the same work to do, and there could have been no such difference of employment as could alone give occasion to any great difference of talents" (WN 1.2.4–5, 28–29). That is, absent the disposition to truck and barter, all humans *must* have had to do pretty much the same work (as Smith considers the case in savage circumstances, WN Intro.4, 10). Smith comes close to suggesting that in a counterfactual situation in which humans lack the disposition to truck (etc.) a great difference of talents would have been pointless and so absent. Given that there are societies in which a great difference of talents is pointless, natural difference of talents ought to be limited.[1]

This propensity to truck, barter, and exchange presupposes the faculty of speech. In fact, Smith adds a complex, sixth instinct, "The desire of being believed, the desire of persuading, of leading and directing other people, seems to be one of the strongest of all our natural desires," to help explain the origin of the faculty of speech:

> The desire of being believed, the desire of persuading, of leading and directing other people, seems to be one of the strongest of all our natural desires. It is, perhaps, the instinct upon which is founded the faculty

---

[1] Smith here is clearly presupposing some kind of optimality principle not unlike Aristotle's and Newton's "nature does nothing in vain." He also seems to be presupposing that humans form a single kind (cf. Hume's "Of National Characters" n. 10 in EMPL, 634).

of speech, the characteristical faculty of human nature. No other animal possesses this faculty, and we cannot discover in any other animal
any desire to lead and direct the judgment and conduct of its fellows.
Great ambition, the desire of real superiority, of leading and directing,
seems to be altogether peculiar to man, and speech is the great instrument of ambition, of real superiority, of leading and directing the judgments and conduct of other people. (TMS 7.4.25, 336)

In contrast to Aristotle (*De Anima*), who presented man as the rational animal,
Smith insists that talking is what distinguishes humans from other animals.[2]
In fact, Smith clearly thinks some animals possessed the faculty of reason (this
echoes Hume's first *Enquiry*, essay 9, and the skeptical tradition since Montaigne
more generally [see Fry 2016 for useful nuance]). For Smith has been recorded as
saying,

dogs . . . by having the same object in their view sometimes unite their
labours, but never from contract. The same is seen still more strongly
in the manner in which the monkeys rob an orchard at the Cape of
Good Hope.—But after they have very ingeniously conveyd away the
apples, as they have no contract they fight (even unto death) and leave
after many dead upon the spot. ((LJ(A), 4.57, Wednesday, March 30,
1763, 352)

Thus, on Smith's view, some animals have intelligence, and are capable of society, but lack speech to negotiate the spoils of their joint endeavors, and other
contracts. Without language, the Hobbesian state of nature remains a permanent
possibility.
     On Smith's picture, we talk to others originally not so much to share truths as
such, but rather in order to guide other people's judgments so that they will be
favorable of us. As he writes in the continuation of the passage that I quoted at
the start of this section:

[Speech] is common to all men, and to be found in no other race of
animals, which seem to know neither this nor any other species of contracts. Two greyhounds, in running down the same hare, have sometimes the appearance of acting in some sort of concert. Each turns
her towards his companion, or endeavours to intercept her when his
companion turns her towards himself. This, however, is not the effect
of any contract, but of the accidental concurrence of their passions in
the same object at that particular time. Nobody ever saw a dog make

---

[2] Of course, given that *logos* can also be translated as "speech," it's not impossible that Smith was
echoing Aristotle.

a fair and deliberate exchange of one bone for another with another dog. Nobody ever saw one animal by its gestures and natural cries signify to another, this is mine, that yours; I am willing to give this for that. When an animal wants to obtain something either of a man or of another animal, it has no other means of persuasion but to gain the favour of those whose service it requires. A puppy fawns upon its dam, and a spaniel endeavours by a thousand attractions to engage the attention of its master who is at dinner, when it wants to be fed by him. Man sometimes uses the same arts with his brethren, and when he has no other means of engaging them to act according to his inclinations, endeavours by every servile and fawning attention to obtain their good will. He has not time, however, to do this upon every occasion. (WN 1.2.1, 25)

Smith distinguishes between two kinds of persuasion: a fawning or servile kind, which we share with animals, and a guiding kind, which humans alone engage in. The guiding kind of persuasion is, as he claims, governed by notions of fairness. Notably, neither relies on truth or force (of course, what is fair can be compatible with truth and force). The guiding kind of persuasion is clearly an important component of Smith's treatment of the role of discussion within commercial and moral exchange (Fleischacker 2004: 92–4; Otten 2016). I assume, and will exhibit in what follows, that when Smith aims at instructing the public, he engages in such guiding persuasion not so much aimed at teaching truth, but rather that he aims at and often relies on considerations of fairness by appealing to "our natural sense of equity" (TMS 2.3.2.8, 103). To be sure, Smith is not an enemy of the Enlightenment project of bringing truth to the masses (WN 5.1.9.14, 796; 5.1.f.50–56, 781–6), but as we'll see (Section c in Chapter 7) his defense of forms of public Enlightenment is primarily instrumental.

Even so, in the first instance, talk is a political instinct in the service of social hierarchy. In doing so Smith revives, not unlike other early modern reactions to Hobbes, Aristotle's conception of man as a political animal (Montes 2004; Fleischacker 2004: 92–4). Smith is aware of reports of other talking animals (e.g., Locke's parrot) and he calls attention to the existence of other social animals. But he thinks only humans talk to persuade others from "great ambition" and "the desire of real superiority." That is, we naturally desire high social status *within* groups. Smith's account also suggests, echoing Hume's "Of the First Principles of Government" and anticipating Madison's *Federalist* 49, that for Smith political leadership relies, in part, on the good opinion and beliefs of others. At WN 4.7.c.77, 625, Smith intimates that public opinion on both sides of the Atlantic would be powerful enough to thwart his suggestions for a union between Great Britain and her colonies that he thought could bring the "present disturbances" (WN 4.7.c.64, 615) to a peaceful resolution—something he left in WN just as the American War of Independence was getting under way.

In fact, according to Smith, the good opinion of others is crucial for most of us ("in the inferior and middling stations of life") in ordinary life; we "can never be great enough to be above the law," and, therefore, are almost always dependent "upon the favour and good opinion of their neighbours and equals" (TMS 1.3.3.5, 63). Smith relies here tacitly on the distinction made famous by Mill in *Of Liberty* between regulated physical force (that is, the impartial rule of law) and the coercive power of opinion.

To understand what Smith is saying in TMS 1.3.3.5, 63, we need to note that during the eighteenth century the prerogatives (including tax exemptions, primogeniture, etc.) of the feudal elite have not been swept away fully yet; some of the feudal lords are still exempt from the regular rule of law. Within the equalizing context of the impartial rule of law, ordinary people rely on the good opinion of others (in commerce, family relations, and mutual moral evaluation [see Otteson 2002a]). Such "favour" is not to be understood as a form of nepotism, but rather a consequence that is part and parcel of Smith's defense of bourgeois virtues: "What is the reward most proper for encouraging industry, prudence, and circumspection? Success in every sort of business" (TMS 3.5.8, 166; for more on Smith's defense of bourgeois virtues and Smith's views on justice in the market, see Herzog 2013, Chapter 6).

Moreover, in the last sentence ("he has not time . . . to do this upon every occasion") quoted from WN 1.2.1, 25, Smith suggests that if time were not scarce (Levy and Peart 2013), we would engage more extensively in the fawning kind of persuasion. Scarcity of time is at the limit just a statement of the necessity of our mortality, which I take to be an axiomatic element in Smith's philosophy. Because we lack time to get to know others and the world around us, we need heuristic tools to get around: maxims, proverbs, rules of thumb, satisficing, and intellectual systems are among such heuristics (Levy 1992b). Throughout Smith's writings we find extreme sensitivity to both the roles of such heuristics (for the most celebrated use in the invisible hand passages, see Chapter 10) and the role of scarcity—in fact, WN starts with the reminder of the miserable circumstances of "the savage nations of hunters and fishers." "Such nations . . . are so miserably poor, that, from mere want, they are frequently reduced, or, at least, think themselves reduced, to the necessity sometimes of directly destroying, and sometimes of abandoning their infants, their old people, and those afflicted with lingering diseases, to perish with hunger, or to be devoured by wild beasts" (WN Intro.4, 10).

According to Smith it is primarily when we are vulnerable (because, say, we lack power or property) that we will act in such degrading fashion. Yet, such servility is apparently a permanent option in our shared natures. Smith's larger project can be understood as decoupling commercial exchange from the fawning kind of persuasions common in hierarchical societies, while being increasingly aware that commercial life can also produce its own kind moral corruption (on the latter see Hanley 2009; Tegos 2013b). Part of Smith's moral defense of "commerce and manufactures" is that they

> gradually introduced order and good government, and with them, the liberty and security of individuals, among the inhabitants of the country, who had before lived almost in a continual state of war with their neighbours, and of servile dependency upon their superiors.[3] This, though it has been the least observed, is by far the most important of all their effects. Mr. Hume is the only writer who, so far as I know, has hitherto taken notice of it." (WN 3.4.4, 412; this is one of the few places Smith explicitly acknowledges his intellectual debts to Hume in print)[4]

Therefore, *some* freedom is presupposed when we can engage in the guiding kind of persuasion even if the same instinct is also a means toward the nonviolent subjugation of others.

Now I am in the position to start offering an analysis of Smithian social explanation: social phenomena (e.g., the division of labor), which have social utility, can be explained by the effects of the unforeseen (and unintended) workings of human propensities over time. Smith thinks that given our original and immediate instincts, the propensity to barter and truck must arise eventually; it is "the necessary, though very slow and gradual consequence." Much ink has been spilled over Smith as a theorist of unintended consequences (and invisible hands). But here I emphasize three related aspects of Smith's explanatory account:

i. It is causal ("necessary consequence"). Thus, while propensities are themselves normological, the persistent triggering of these and their expression can lead to nomological outcomes such that the outcome could not be otherwise— presumably as necessary as the fact that all humans are mortal. But like human

---

[3] Here Smith does not equate liberty and commerce. Rather, liberty is a state of mind or disposition (i.e., the absence of servility) that is the indirect consequence (via "order and good government"—that is, the rule of law that reduces uncertainty and increases the possibility to plan ahead) of commerce. I develop the significance of this in Section g in Chapter 8.

[4] The whole passage is worth quoting because it illustrates one of the methods by which Smith reads the historical record and how he understands the degrading nature of feudalism: "After the fall of the Roman empire. . .the proprietors of land seem generally to have lived in fortified castles on their own estates, and in the midst of their own tenants and dependants. The towns were chiefly inhabited by tradesmen and mechanicks, who seem in those days to have been of servile, or very nearly of servile condition. The privileges which we find granted by antient charters to the inhabitants of some of the principal towns in Europe, sufficiently shew what they were before those grants. The people to whom it is granted as a privilege, that they might give away their own daughters in marriage without the consent of their lord, that upon their death their own children, and not their lord, should succeed to their goods, and that they might dispose of their own effects by will, must, before those grants, have been either altogether, or very nearly in the same state of villanage with the occupiers of land in the country" (WN 3.3.1, 397).

mortality, the exact timing of a particular outcome is ordinarily unknown in advance to mortals.

ii. Smith's account is a historical explanation. By "historical" I mean to capture two features: (a) that the stable consequence would not have been in "view" (or predictable) to human observers of human nature at an early time and, so, also not capable of being intended; (b) that to be a cause does not require temporal contiguity between the cause and the effect. The same cause(s) can do their work over enormous expanses of time. Of course, this does not require magical historical action at a distance (with temporal gaps between micro-causes); at any given time the relevant propensities of human nature remain the same and this allows particular kinds of effects to accumulate over time. (Smith makes fun of claims surrounding the "levity and inconstancy of human nature" [WN 1.8.31, 93].)

iii. Smith's account does require that after certain consequences become visible to observer-participants they become self-reinforcing and generate a form of lock-in. Presumably this self-reinforcement is due to the fact that those who benefit from the cumulative consequences will help prevent backsliding from new social arrangements. (It may also be aided by the fact, as Marxists have noted, that those who do not so benefit will be deprived of various resources to prevent further change.)

Therefore, in the long run and in the aggregate, normological propensities will produce initially unpredictable, albeit definite and determined outcomes; (i–iii) are jointly characteristic of what I call "Smithian social explanation." Smithian social explanation is not *sub specie aeternitatis*; it takes epistemic limitation of the historical agents and the theorists of human history for granted. By calling it "Smithian," I do not mean to suggest he pioneered this kind of explanation or that (i–iii) are unique to his approach. As others have noted, the explanatory template that I call "Smithian social explanation" has clear roots in the writings of Mandeville and Hume (Rosenberg 1963; Hayek 1967; C. Smith 2006).

In Chapter 10 I argue that Smithian social explanations ought not to be confused with so-called invisible hand explanations in Smith. Here I just note that Smithian social explanation is the dominant form of social explanation in WN. For example, after discussing the division of labor, Smith turns to the origin of metallic money in WN 1.4. This, too, conforms to the structure of Smithian social explanation: "men seem at last to have been determined by irresistible reasons to give the preference, for this employment, to metals above every other commodity" (1.4.4, 38). Smithian social explanation is compatible with the development of institutions that do not presuppose government (division of labor, metallic money, justice, etc.) and those that do ("mints" as well as "aulnagers and stampmasters of woollen and linen cloth" [WN 1.4.7, 40]). But the latter can only occur in what Smith calls "improved" countries—that is, ones that already have considerable commerce. Other important institutions treated by Smithian social

explanations include the division of stock (WN 2.1), the natural progress of opulence (WN 3.1), and the origin of justice (WN 5.1.b; to be discussed in Sections a
and b of Chapter 7). As Otteson (2002a, 2000b) has emphasized, Smith's account
of these institutions bears a close similarity to his treatment of the origin of languages and morality elsewhere.

While Smith allows sudden political revolutions and economic shocks, changes
in the nature of a society's broader "stage of development" take place over very
long periods of time. From the start of WN Smith, thus, embeds his treatment of
political economy within an elongated account of historical time (Schabas 2006).
Smith's main historical distinction is among the four stages of civilization—
hunting, shepherding, agriculture, and commerce (WN 5.1.a, 689–708; Meek
1971). Smith thought that "progress" from one stage to the next was the "natural course of things." On the whole, Smith thought it was better to advance to a
higher stage, but he was aware that important moral qualities (say, magnanimity, courage, and self-command) could be lost along the way toward commercial
society. Moreover, he vigorously combated the idea, promoted by Hume ("Of
Refinement in the Arts," Hume 1987: 271), that advanced societies always exhibit
more "humanity" (TMS 5.2.9, 205–10; Harkin 2002). Smith did not believe that
it was inevitable that one moved from one stage to the next, nor that all stages
needed to be passed through to reach one stage or another (WN 3.i.3, 377; for
more discussion see Schliesser 2005; Hont 2015).

Each stage is characterized by a dominant set of social-political institutional
arrangements and norms. While some of Smith's technical economics is stage
specific, Smith does offer large-scale generalizations across such stages. For example, "The first duty of the sovereign, therefore, that of defending the society from
the violence and injustice of other independent societies, grows gradually more
and more expensive, as the society advances in civilization." The reason for this is
"the military force of the society, which originally cost the sovereign no expence
either in time of peace or in time of war, must, in the progress of improvement,
first be maintained by him in time of war, and afterwards even in time of peace"
(WN 5.1.a.42, 707). In context it is clear that "originally" refers to the shepherding age (when the kingly, great shepherds simply had large numbers of subservient retainers); "first" refers to the agricultural stage (when farmers would have
to be induced to take up arms); and "afterwards" to commercial periods (when
soldiering has become an expensive, specialized part of the division of labor—the
expense is also due to the high cost of state-of-the-art weapons technology).

Sometimes, Smith uses other historical conceptual distinctions: for example,
a "poor and barbarous nation" is opposed to an "opulent and civilized" one (for
the contextual significance of these terms see Pocock's majestic *Barbarism and
Religion*). Two such nations can exist at the same date, even though the "opulent
and civilized" society has already advanced to the agricultural or commercial stage,
while the "barbarous" other remains a shepherding (or very poor agricultural)
society. He can use the same concept to refer to similar stages of development

of countries far apart. For example, at one point he compares England "at the invasion of Julius Caesar, when its inhabitants were nearly in the same state with the savages in North America" of Smith's time (WN 2.3.34, 344; Hont 2015). The England of Smith's day is a commercial society, while the Scottish Highlands are less so (WN 1.9.c.4, 109).

Yet, Smith's terms are by no means static. For Smith also distinguishes between "Ancient," by which he means roughly the classical Greeks and Romans, and "Modern" times, by which he means roughly eighteenth-century Europe. It turns out that due to technological progress, in Modern times a "nation of hunters can never be formidable to the civilized nations in their neighbourhood," while in Ancient times a nation of shepherds would certainly be capable of beating a civilized nation on the battlefield (Hont 2015). Smith is confident enough of such normological invariances to offer counterfactuals (e.g., "If the hunting nations of America should ever become shepherds, their neighbourhood would be much more dangerous to the European colonies than it is at present" [WN 5.1.a.5, 692]). Despite Smith's critical stance toward the rapacity of European mercantile empires (WN 4.3.c.9, 493), he did not foresee the genocide of American natives, although he was aware that advances in the technology of firepower favor more recent opulent countries on the battlefield and even make the "permanency and extension" of civilization foreseeable (WN 5.1.a.44, 708).[5]

As Smith's conceptual opposition between the "barbarous" and the "civilized" reveals, Smith's treatment is not devoid of normative content; moving through the four stages is an "advance;" and stages can be "advanced" relative to each other (WN 5.1.a.3–8, 690–4). This does not mean that Smith does not recognize some losses as byproducts of such advances (see also Section b of Chapter 8). Moreover, he is very clear that so-called advanced civilizations can behave savagely. He is, for example, very indignant about the behavior of European colonists abroad: "The savage injustice of the Europeans rendered an event, which ought to have been beneficial to all, ruinous and destructive to several of those unfortunate countries" (WN 4.1.32, 448). Thus, while Smith applauds the permanency of civilization, by which he means societies that are governed by law, he is, unlike Hume (Sabl 2012: 65) and many nineteenth-century liberals (Pitts 2009), distinctly reserved about its *violent* extension.[6]

However, peaceable extensions of "civilization" can count on his support, which is one reason why he praises the union between England and Scotland and advocates a political "union" between Ireland and Great Britain in order to tackle existing (mutual) "hatred and indignation" (WN 5.3.89, 944; see Section a

---

[5] It follows that if Smithian "civilization" is good for self-preservation and population growth then civilization is, in fact, a way to secure the great ends of human nature as intended by the Director of nature (recall TMS 2.1.5.10, 78). Thus, Smith comes close to offering a religious sanction to the project of colonial civilization.

[6] Recent evidence shows that very late in life, Hume expressed misgivings about empire. See Baumstark 2012: 232-3. I thank Tomáš Kunca for calling my attention to it.

of Chapter 7). As these latter two examples make clear, Smith is unwilling to undo existing political settlements even if their origin is unjust (as in Ireland). Hence, politically, Smith is clearly a reformist, not a revolutionary.

In sum, Smith makes clear that from the point of view of WN, certain original propensities are epistemic bedrock. In Section a of Chapter 8, I argue that in WN and TMS when it comes to accounting for institutions with social utility, Smith hints at a group selection process. It is tempting to see in the passage quoted from WN 1.2.1 an analogy between the (slow, gradual, and unforeseen) development of social institutions and derived propensities. But in WN Smith leaves unclear both how original propensities play a role in producing derived propensities and the relationship among social institutions and development of human nature.

I close this section with a final, speculative observation on WN 1.2.1: it pertains to the thorny issue of the relationship between WN and Revelation. Recall above that I introduced Smith's four-stage stadial account of civilization (hunting, shepherding, farming, commerce). Of course, this echoes Biblical Revelation but also sits a bit uncomfortably with it. Early in Genesis we encounter the story of Cain (a farmer), who kills his brother, Abel (a shepherd), because he is jealous over God's (mysterious) unwillingness to accept his sacrifice (while accepting Abel's). In addition to being a farmer, Cain also founds a city. That is, in addition to cosmogony, the start of the Hebrew Bible is a kind of genealogy of civilization: first, in the Garden of Eden we are gatherers; then, second, humanity splits into mutually antagonistic shepherds and farmers; from the latter spring city governments with an impulse toward territorial (and other) ambitions. Jean-Jacques Rousseau certainly read the Bible this way (see his posthumous *Essay on the Origins of the Languages*, written about the time of the second *Discourse*) and sides with the more anarchic impulse of the "author of Genesis" (Hazony 2012: 308 n. 26).

Now consider this passage from David Hume:

> The bulk of every state may be divided into husbandmen and manufacturers. The former are employed in the culture of the land; the latter work up the materials furnished by the former, into all the commodities which are necessary or ornamental to human life. As soon as men quit their savage state, where they live chiefly by hunting and fishing, they must fall into these two classes; though the arts of agriculture employ at first the most numerous part of the society. ("Of Commerce," 1752)

"Of Commerce" introduced readers to Hume's political economy, and the quoted lines occur right after Hume's methodologic introduction to the subject in which he defends the worth of "abstruse" theorizing about economic affairs. Economically, people live by hunting and fishing without (much) division of labor. However, there is a division of labor between farmers and manufacturers in the state subsequent to savagery. Hume intimates that in the course of time this second stage is transformed from being primarily agricultural to a society focused on making things, including (eventually) so-called luxury items. Hume also notes a third kind of activity, (foreign) commerce, which promotes this transformation, but does not assign it a separate stage in history. (In fact, he thinks that trade can disappear from a large country without much loss; perhaps he had the historical example of China in mind or the narrative of Bacon's fable, *New Atlantis*.) Hume's genealogy is uninterested in shepherds and is hard to square with the Biblical narrative.

Unlike Hume, Smith does not ignore the shepherding stage. Smith recognizes that shepherding facilitates a life of leisure (WN 5.1.a.15, 697). Moreover, in Smith's account of the origin of government, the shepherding state, the "second period of society," is crucial because "some degree of that civil government" is introduced in it (WN 5.1.b.12, 715; as Boyd 2013: 446 notes, here Smith tends to treat "civil" as a synonym for "political," even though civil society should not be reduced to politics).

But unlike the Biblical narrative, Smith's account treats the shepherding stage as one to be overcome. Smith is hostile toward shepherding, and when in his first publication Smith reviews Rousseau's second *Discourse*, he criticizes its positive treatment of shepherding as sublime fantasy ("Edinburgh Review," 12, EPS 251). In WN Smith emphasizes that in shepherding societies conditions of great inequality and, thus, a servile relationship between "sovereign or chief" and subordinate "vassals or subjects" are generated (WN 5.1.a.15, 697; it is a key moment to help explain the origin of states that protect property). In this stage government is really no better than a protection racket; with a nod to Homer, Smith explains how in this stage, the sovereign is to be bribed for security. Thus, for Smith the inner logic of the shepherding stage leads to a great deal of morally deplorable political dependence: "during the continuance of this state of things, therefore, the corruption of justice, naturally resulting from the arbitrary and uncertain nature of those presents, scarce admitted of any effectual remedy" (WN 5.1.b.16, 718). For Smith, then, the advance from shepherding to a more regular administration of justice in agricultural and commercial society involves a reduction of uncertainty and an increase in morally laudable forms of independence.

In WN the Tartars and Arabs are the paradigmatic existing shepherding nations (WN 5.2.a.3, 817). In his published works, Smith is conspicuously silent on the ancient Hebrews. Even so, we know that in a lecture on Monday, February 28, 1763, Smith treats the "Children of Israel" as a "nation of shepherds" and equivalent to Tartars and Arabs of his time (LJ 4.77, 229). A few days before (Wednesday, February 23, 1763) Smith deviates significantly from the Biblical account by calling "the Jews . . . originally a tribe of Arabs" (LJ 4.44, 217). This may have been a transcription error, of course.

Either way, while one need not believe that shepherding is only glorified in the Old and New Testament, the image of the shepherd has a positive valence in both the Hebrew Bible (Psalms 23, where God is depicted as a good shepherd by King David, himself originally a shepherd) and among Christians with Christ's depiction as a good shepherd (John 10, especially). By contrast, Smith rejects the ideal of the shepherding life as unsuitable to man's nature and, thus, the idea that the "Good Shepherd" ought to be emulated: "to cultivate the ground was the original destination of man, so in every stage of his existence he seems to retain a predilection for this primitive employment" (WN 3.1.3, 378). Thus, there is little reason to think that Smith is a Biblical literalist.

None of this is meant to suggest that no Christian foundation for Smith's project is possible; since Max Weber we all know that capitalism and protestantism can go hand in hand. One of the most inspired readings of WN treats it as theodicy (Waterman 2002). I discuss this argument more fully in Chapter 6, but the just-quoted passage from WN (5.1.b.16, 718) already reveals there is good evidence to deny that Smith is committed to theodicy. Smith certainly draws on Christian imagery frequently, and like many social reformers before and since he draws on and redirects existing Christian virtues (Hanley 2009). But Smith's anthropology, one that focuses on "the propensity to truck, barter, and exchange," will, in fact, be deployed by Smith to criticize Christian duty, which orients us toward an afterlife without making much of a contribution to the "happiness and perfection of human life" here on Earth (WN 5.1.f.30, 771). The utility of Smith's science is—I quote Hume!—"to teach us, how to control and regulate future events by their causes" (EHU 7.29). Even if Smith is a pious Christian, his doctrinal focus is not on faith, but primarily on works that advance humanity's estate in this world. From a Christian perspective, Smith's writings tend toward the Pelagian heresy, or its modern cousin, Spinozism.

b. Mind, Language, and Society

This section argues that according to Smith linguistic development in humanoids presupposes mental development and, in turn, facilitates it. It shows how in Smith there is a careful analysis of the (possible) mechanisms by which our instinctive needs get transformed into stable derived propensities. In order to demonstrate this, I pay close attention to Smith's essay "The Origin of Languages." As I noted, Smith thought it important enough to include it with TMS. I then flesh out my argument with evidence from Smith's other writings.

Smith starts Languages as follows:

> The assignation of particular names, to denote particular objects, that is, the institution of nouns substantive, would probably, be one of the first steps towards the formation of language. Two savages, who had never been taught to speak, but had been bred up remote from the societies of men, would naturally begin to form that language by which they would endeavour to make their mutual wants intelligible to each other, by uttering certain sounds, whenever they meant to denote

certain objects. Those objects only which were most familiar to them, and which they had most frequent occasion to mention, would have particular names assigned to them. (Languages 1, 203–4)

According to Smith, it is possible that humans once existed without speech. Unlike Rousseau, who pretends to be offering an entirely hypothetical origin story of human nature and clearly signals that he does so in order to avoid religious controversy, Smith makes no explicit point in reminding his readers that his probable account does not fit the literal details of the Biblical creation story (Levy 1992b). Smith seems to assume ("naturally . . . form language") that there is in mankind an original propensity for speech, and that it will be triggered under specific circumstances. But the developed "faculties of reason and speech," which at the start of WN are presented as possible bedrock original propensity (recall Section a in this chapter), may well have an earlier natural origin and develop over time. In Languages Smith explores some of the mechanisms of such a development. The first steps toward a language can occur in the relatively vulnerable situation of two isolated individuals; language may originate outside the herd. Therefore, Smith's account is compatible with the idea that language originated (and even disappeared) more than once.

Against Rousseau's (and later Darwin's) speculation that language has its origin in a poetic and emotive language, Smith sees the origin of language in its concrete capacity to "denote certain objects." Even so, Rousseau and Smith agree that language has its origin in human need. In the wild, we start naming objects in order to have our companions help supply our "mutual" desires; this is how we "lead" and "direct" other people (recall TMS 7.4.25, 336). Thus, language facilitates exchange from the start. (See Berry 1974; Levy 1997; on this point, especially, Otteson 2002b.)

Smith's emphasis on the importance of the familiarity of the objects probably reflects (despite important differences between Hume and Smith to be developed below) a very Humean focus on the habituation that drives mental association. In Languages Smith goes on to develop an account in which language and mind co-develop. The argument unfolds slowly in Smith's hands. Smith informs the reader,

The man who first distinguished a particular object by the epithet of green, must have observed other objects that were not green, from which he meant to separate it by this appellation. The institution of this name, therefore, supposes comparison. It likewise supposes some degree of abstraction. The person who first invented this appellation must have distinguished the quality from the object to which it belonged, and must have conceived the object as capable of subsisting without the quality. The invention, therefore, even of the simplest nouns adjective, must have required more metaphysics than we are apt to be aware of. The different mental operations, of arrangement or classing, of comparison, and of abstraction, must all have been employed, before even the names of the different colours, the least metaphysical of all nouns adjective, could be instituted. (Languages 7, 207)

Before language is developed in the human species, humans are capable of mental operations: "arrangement or classing, comparison, and of abstraction." In Smith's scheme these belong to the most basic, most "original" dispositions of humanity. According to Smith these operations of the mind are originally nonlinguistic, although obviously once language is developed these operations can also involve linguistic items. These prelinguistic, mental operations are the functional cranes (Dennett 1995) that will help language, mind, and culture develop toward handling and expressing greater complexity (as we will see, Smith thinks there are path-dependent, local limits to this complexity).

Nouns get applied to familiar objects. The very possibility of applying what Smith calls a "noun adjective" presupposes having the capacity for contrastive reasoning and a mental capacity for classification and conceptualization of as well as abstraction from these experiences. On Smith's view objects must be conceived to be bearers of properties before adjectives can be applied to features of these objects. That is to say, from very early in human development we deploy a kind of natural metaphysics that prefigures Aristotle's. (Below I discuss Smith's attitude toward this natural metaphysics.) Moreover, in the quote Smith clearly conceives of nouns adjective with different degrees of metaphysical-ness—presumably here meant in terms of abstraction from the appearances. Abstraction turns out to be the key variable when Smith turns to prepositions: "The invention of such a word, therefore, must have required a considerable degree of abstraction ... Whatever were the difficulties, therefore, which embarrassed the first invention of nouns adjective, the same, and many more, must have embarrassed that of prepositions" (Languages 12, 210).

Smith treats abstraction as a mental power, but his way of doing so is unusual. For example, traditionally, geometric properties of phenomena were understood as abstracted from sensible qualities. This conception of abstraction involves a kind of subtraction or stripping away from sensory input (where we focus on only some elements and throw away the rest). For example, when the French natural historian Buffon describes the application of geometry to nature, he writes, "it is necessary that the phenomena we are concerned with explaining be susceptible to being considered in an abstract manner and that their nature be stripped of almost all physical qualities. For mathematics is inapplicable to the extent that subjects are not simple abstractions" ("Initial Discourse" *Histoire naturelle* [see Lyon 1976: 176]; Smith refers to Buffon's [1749] text in what is probably his first [anonymous] publication, the 1756 Letter to Edinburgh Review, 8, EPS 248 [Lomonaco 2002]). Sometimes Smith also uses "abstraction" in this sense.

But that's not Smith's standard way of understanding abstraction. For Smith, a thought is more abstract than another thought when it requires more discrete

mental "operations," or steps, to introduce during the history of human development. Thus, in addition to being a mental power or operation, abstraction functions as a kind of *measure* for metaphysical-ness. A thought is very abstract if
starting with sensations, as a baseline, it requires many further mental operations
to be thought. That can include the traditional kind of abstraction, of course (if the
stripping of qualities is done in careful order), but also many other kinds. Therefore,
Smith's general picture of mind is that it is akin to a kind of invisible machine that
is capable of different, countable, and sequential operations. Smith borrows the
idea of mental operations from Hume (see, especially, Treatise 1.3.8.15, where
Hume also notes "'tis very difficult to talk of the operations of the mind with perfect propriety and exactness") but not his treatment of metaphysical-ness.

Unfortunately, Smith does not explain some of the tacit commitments he
relies on here. For example, he seems to assume a kind of natural minimal unit for
each mental operation. He also seems to presuppose a kind of mental-least-action
principle such that in the course of human development we naturally find—or we
can rationally reconstruct *post facto*—the least required mental operations in each
step of abstraction. It is also unclear if for Smith the degree of abstraction is ultimately dependent on empirical facts about human cognitive architecture or the
logical complexity of the represented content.[7]

Smith conceives the historical development of more abstract components of a
language and mind as a necessary consequence (of human dispositions). That is,
we are in the realm of a Smithian social explanation of a useful human capacity
(it's historical, it's causal, and it gets locked in due to the advantages it confers).
Smith thinks that given our original and immediate instincts, the propensity to
reason and speech must arise eventually; it is "the necessary, though very slow
and gradual consequence," but one that encounters many obstacles along the way.
Here are two examples from Languages:

i. "[t]hough the different formation of nouns substantive, therefore, might, for
   some time, forestall the necessity of inventing nouns adjective, it was impossible that this necessity could be forestalled altogether" (Languages 10, 208)
ii. "[n]umber considered in general, without relation to any particular set of
   objects numbered, is one of the most abstract and metaphysical ideas, which
   the mind of man is capable of forming; and, consequently, is not an idea,
   which would readily occur to rude mortals, who were just beginning to form a
   language . . . In the rude beginnings of society, one, two, and more, might possibly be all the numeral distinctions which mankind would have any occasion
   to take notice of" (Languages 22–3, 214).

---

[7] The whole paragraph is indebted to Steven Horst. As he asked me in correspondence: is it possible that two token "thoughts" have the same content yet differ from one another in abstractness
depending on the actual chain of operations through which each was obtained? Smith lacks resources
to develop an answer here.

As the second quote, especially, makes clear, there is no doubt that Smith's account is meant to capture the reality that the full metaphysical nature of language develops only slowly. It also entails that mathematics can only be a late-stage development in the grand history of humankind (see also Astronomy 3.1, EPS 48).

Unfortunately, Smith leaves unexplained how a primitive ("savage") linguistic duo either re-enters society or founds its own society. But he clearly allows that language originates outside of society and that once existing, language and society can develop alongside each other. That is, even within the "savage" stage, Smith distinguishes between a pre-societal unity, or proto-society, and what he calls the "lowest and rudest state of society;" the latter is instantiated in his time by the fully linguistic hunter-warriors "among the native tribes of North America" (WN 5.1.1.2, 689–90).

Languages was published before the first edition of WN and available to its more attentive readers. There, recall, he wrote that he remains silent on the origin of the propensity to truck, barter, and exchange one thing for another. He allowed two options: (i) it might be one of those original principles in human nature of which no further account can be given; or (ii) whether it be the necessary consequence of the faculties of "reason and speech;" while treating the second as more probable (WN 1.2.1, 25). In Languages we discover that the faculties of reason and speech are themselves developed out of various preexisting instincts and are really composed of various propensities; different aspects of speech develop long before humanity first developed the full capacity of reason. Reason is here, thus, understood as a capacity to engage in systematic abstractions—that is, multiple, sequential mental operations. Thus, Smith's considered view seems to have been that while language develops to facilitate mutual exchange in order to satisfy our needs, the propensity to truck, barter, and exchange, which presupposes reason and speech and is governed by fairness, is probably a propensity that is itself a (much) later development in the natural history of the human species.

Smith's main point in all of this is that different parts of language presuppose different mental developments. So for Smith mental capacities must be developed slowly before classes of more abstract words can be invented.

Languages sheds some light on and is in turn illuminated by a passage from the better-known (among Smith scholars), posthumously published Astronomy:

> It is evident that the mind takes pleasure in observing the resemblances that are discoverable betwixt different objects. It is by means of such observations that it endeavours to arrange and methodise all its ideas, and to reduce them into proper classes and assortments. Where it can observe but one single quality, that is common to a great variety of otherwise widely different objects, that single circumstance will be sufficient for it to connect them all together, to reduce them to one common class, and to call them by one general name. It is thus that

all things endowed with a power of self-motion, beasts, birds, fishes, insects, are classed under the general name of Animal; and that these again, along with those which want that power, are arranged under the still more general word Substance: and this is the origin of those assortments of objects and ideas which in the schools are called Genera and Species, and of those abstract and general names, which in all languages are made use of to express them. (Astronomy 2.1, 37–8)

This treatment of ever-increasing abstraction in Astronomy compresses a process that gets decomposed analytically and "historically" in Languages. Yet, Astronomy also suggests that it is not merely *need* that drives the process; Smith also describes the vivid mental *pleasure* that comes from classification. As we have seen in the TMS passage on self-preservation and the propagation of the species (2.1.5.10, 77–8), nature's ends are brought about by (sometimes) pleasing instincts. Thus, Smith offers a careful analysis of the (possible) mechanisms by which our instinctive needs get transformed into stable derived propensities.

In *The Descent of Man* (published over a century after TMS in 1871), Charles Darwin, who engages with TMS, describes much the same process, but he adds one crucial element that is consistent with but, perhaps, not fully appreciated by Smith:

The mental powers in some early progenitor of man must have been more highly developed than in any existing ape, before even the most imperfect form of speech could have come into use; but we may confidently believe that the continued use and advancement of this power would have reacted on the mind itself, by enabling and encouraging it to carry on long trains of thought. (Darwin 2004: 110)

Darwin states clearly that the possession of rudimentary language itself also facilitates mental development.

Smith may have also discerned the possibility that mind and language can influence each other's development. As evidence for this claim, I focus on a passage that was probably written as a critical response to Hume's infamous insistence that there was no simple impression of the self to be found in him (Treatise 1.4.6.2). Smith argues:

But in this early period of the language, which we are now endeavouring to describe, it is extremely improbable that any such words would be known. Though custom has now rendered them familiar to us, they, both of them, express ideas extremely metaphysical and abstract. The word I, for example, is a word of a very particular species. Whatever speaks may denote itself by this personal pronoun. The word I, therefore, is a general word, capable of being predicated, as the logicians say, of an infinite variety of objects. It differs, however, from all other general words in this respect; that the objects of which it may be predicated, do not form any particular species of objects distinguished from all others. The word I, does not, like the word man, denote a particular class of objects, separated from all others by peculiar qualities of their own. It is far from being the name of a species, but, on the contrary, whenever it is made use of, it always denotes a precise individual, the particular person who then speaks. It may be said to be, at once, both what the logicians call, a singular, and what they call, a common term; and to join in its signification the seemingly opposite qualities of the most precise individuality, and the most extensive generalization. This word, therefore, expressing so very abstract and metaphysical an idea, would not easily or readily occur to the first formers of language. What are called the personal pronouns, it may be observed, are among the last words of a which children learn to make use. A child, speaking of itself, says, Billy walks, Billy sits, instead of I walk, I sit. As in the beginnings of language, therefore, mankind seem to have evaded the invention of at least the more abstract prepositions. (Languages 32, 219)

By Smith's lights the very idea of an "I" is "very abstract and metaphysical;" it is, thus, not the kind of idea that could be copied from a simple impression even in Hume's understanding of abstraction.[8] Smith is, thus, committed to the claim that *humans with selves* are a late arrival on the scene; they presuppose considerable mental, linguistic, and social development (recall that once off the ground, language and mind develop in society).

I call attention to three features about the last few lines of the passage quoted from Languages 32, 219:

i. Smith uses evidence from child development to capture the nature of minds of early humanoids. It is unclear if Smith knew personally this "Billy" or read about him, but here and elsewhere (Of the External Senses), Smith shows an interest in the details of human and animal development (Glenney 2011).

ii. Regardless of his sources, Smith's approach is very much in line with Lockean anthropology, where the savage mind is compared to the child mind (Berry 2006). Unlike many of his contemporaries (e.g., Adam Ferguson) that liken then-contemporary savages to children (the source of imperial ideology in which conquered nations require Western political/military guidance [Pitts

---

[8] "All abstract ideas are really nothing but particular ones, consider'd in a certain light; but being annexed to general terms, they are able to represent a vast variety, and to comprehend objects, which, as they are alike in some particulars, are in others vastly wide of each other" (Treatise 1.2.3.5).

2009: 37, 269]), Smith clearly has "early" and not existing savages in mind in the passage from Languages 32, 219.[9]

iii. Smith also expresses what has become known as Haeckel's Biogenetic Law: (a child's) individual development recaptures species development (now discredited). Something like this also seems to have tempted Rousseau in *Emile* and Vico (Danesi 1993), but while there are tantalizing similarities between Vico and Smith there is as of yet no evidence that Smith read *Scienza Nuova* (1725).

Now let's place Languages alongside an important paragraph from TMS in order to articulate the central point of this section. Smith writes,

Were it possible that a human creature could grow up to manhood in some solitary place, without any communication with his own species, he could no more think of his own character, of the propriety or demerit of his own sentiments and conduct, of the beauty or deformity of his own mind, than of the beauty or deformity of his own face. All these are objects which he cannot easily see, which naturally he does not look at, and with regard to which he is provided with no mirror which can present them to his view. Bring him into society, and he is immediately provided with the mirror which he wanted before. It is placed in the countenance and behaviour of those he lives with, which always mark when they enter into, and when they disapprove of his sentiments; and it is here that he first views the propriety and impropriety of his own passions, the beauty and deformity of his own mind. To a man who from his birth was a stranger to society, the objects of his passions, the external bodies which either pleased or hurt him, would occupy his whole attention. The passions themselves, the desires or aversions, the joys or sorrows, which those objects excited, though of all things the most immediately present to him, could scarce ever be the objects of his thoughts. The idea of them could never interest him so much as to call upon his attentive consideration. The consideration of his joy could in him excite no new joy, nor that of his sorrow any new sorrow, though the consideration of the causes of those passions might often excite both. Bring him into society, and all his own passions will immediately become the causes of new passions. He will observe that mankind approve of some of them, and are disgusted by others. He will be elevated in the one case, and cast down in the other; his desires and aversions, his joys and sorrows, will now often become the causes of new desires and new aversions, new joys and new sorrows: they will

---

[9] "A child caresses the fruit that is agreeable to it, as it beats the stone that hurts it. The notions of a savage are not very different." Smith then goes on to offer an example derived from "The ancient Athenians" (Astronomy 3.2, 49; TMS 2.3.1.1).

now, therefore, interest him deeply, and often call upon his most attentive consideration. (TMS 3.1.3, 110–1)

In order to explain his account of causation, David Hume uses a similar thought
experiment for different ends. (Recall: "Were a man, such as Adam, created in the
full vigour of understanding, without experience, he would never be able to infer
motion in the second ball from the motion and impulse of the first" [Abstract.11].)
Even if we leave aside some of Smith's hyperbole ("all his own passions will immediately become the causes of new passions" seems to require a rather unlikely,
instantaneous impact from society), the claim here about the need for society's
"mirror" is quite far-reaching: without society a solitary, Robinson Crusoe–like
individual is entirely outer-directed. (See also Hume's Treatise 2.2.5.21.) While
self-examination may be possible in principle, it will not be triggered outside
society. (In Section a of Chapter 11, I show that Smith rejects apolitical philosophy.) If taken literally, the passage also suggests that presocial (original) passions
are finite in number. Thus, according to Smith some passions are only possible
in society; other people's responses to our passion-driven behavior generate new
passions in us. I call the presocial passions "original passions" or "natural passions" because from the vantage point of Smith's causal analysis, they are part
of humanity's most original dispositions. I call the socially triggered passions
"derived passions."[10]

According to Smith, even the mental phenomena that are most "present" (i.e.,
the passions) would not be the focus of attention in the imagined counterfactual
situation. Smith's counterfactual relies on a distinction between having a mental
object in one's mind and being attentive to such an idea. Here he denies, thus,
the natural transparency of the mental—an influential thesis associated with
Descartes (with whose writings Smith was familiar).[11] Smith's position seems to
be that only being attentive to a mental object counts as genuine thinking. For
Smith (echoing Locke), consciousness is an attentiveness to one's experience.

To be clear, Smith is not claiming that our derived passions are entirely constituted by society; all he claims is that the "objects" to which passions are attached
become more varied. Not unlike Mandeville and Rousseau, Smith is very aware
that once in society, our derived passions easily start to multiply.

Smith never explicitly works out the relationship between what I have been
calling "original" and "derived" propensities, on the one hand, and, on the other
hand, the original and derived passions. It is tempting to see original passions as

---

[10] Note two things. First, in the body of the text, "original" is treated pragmatically depending on
use/context. For example, reason and speech may be treated by Smith as an original propensity in
some contexts, but when explaining the causes of their development not so. In addition, so far everything I have argued is compatible with the idea that for Smith there never was a presocial state in
human development, and that his supposing one is merely a device to exhibit some causal mechanisms. This is why I speak here of the vantage point of Smith's causal analysis.

[11] The thesis was already denied by Spinoza and Leibniz (whom Smith never mentions).

an instance of the original propensities of human nature and derived passions as an instance of the derived propensities, but conceptually this need not be necessary. The distinction between original and derived propensities is not about being in or out of society—it is fundamentally a temporal-causal distinction about what, for the sake of analysis, comes earlier in human development. By contrast, the distinction between original and derived passions is introduced in order to distinguish between passions that do not involve other people and passions that involve other people (in society); when it is fully fleshed out we will see that the distinction between original and derived passions will mark an important difference about the structure and nature of the passions. To simplify: social (that is, derived) passions will be inherently normative (and original passions not), and original passions will have fairly stable triggering conditions (while derived passions will have more flexibility).

From Languages we learn that these social achievements of selfhood presuppose considerable mental and linguistic development before they can be put into words (for another argument to this conclusion, see Nuzzo 2010). TMS (3.1.3, 110–1) adds that without society we will not even really think of some of the most salient parts of ourselves. From here it is a small, conceptual step to see that Smith rejects so-called Robinson Crusoe economics (Levy 1999).

This completes my introduction to Smith's account of human nature. We have covered a lot of material. In particular, I have introduced the nature of Smithian social explanation, I have analyzed his account of abstraction, and I have indicated the centrality of the passions to Smith's analysis of human nature. In the next two chapters I flesh out Smith's treatment of the passions and how these relate to other significant features of human nature and our moral lives, including, especially, reason, rationality, and judgment.

3

The Passions, Rationality, and Reason

In this chapter I describe the main components of Smith's theory of the passions. I offer a detailed taxonomy and conceptual analysis of the content and structure of the passions.[1] There can be no doubt that the passions are crucial to Smith's theory of human nature. Even so, I have not found a definition of the passions in Smith. But we can infer his views from his descriptions, and put them into some systematic order.

In this chapter, I discuss four kinds of passions: the natural passions, the proto-passions, the intellectual sentiments, and I conclude this chapter with a treatment of Smith's views on the derived passions. To be clear, these four categories should not be seen as being on par (as species that belong to a genus); the proto-passions make the natural passions possible, while the intellectual passions are themselves a species of the natural passions. My taxonomy is also not intended to be exhaustive. Along the way I also explain the way in which Smith thinks about rationality and the role of reason as an active principle. I do so in order to illuminate the way Smith integrates both feeling and reason into both his account of the passions and moral philosophy. In particular I show how in Smith's hands, sound judgment links the epistemic and moral features of his system. Finally, by drawing on Smith's account of the proto-passions and his treatment of reason as an active principle, I argue it is a mistake to understand Smith as a moral empiricist, as is commonly done.

[1] I do not follow Smith's order of presentation because I explain Smith's views on propriety and sympathy in later chapters. My departure from Smith's order of presentation is not just a difference in starting points and taxonomic organization. In what follows I explain the way the elements or building blocks of Smith's account hang together, and how according to Smith moral life is generated out of the raw materials of human nature. Smith does not entirely neglect those latter topics in TMS (as my citations below reveal), but he does not start from them nor does he discuss them fully. Even so, Smith added his essay on Languages to the third edition of TMS, and the vantage point of my approach is very much informed by reading the contents of that essay back into TMS as Smith could have expected some of his readers to do. In particular, in this chapter I avoid articulating Smith's views in terms of *his* distinction among the unsocial, social, and selfish passions, nor do I develop my approach in terms of his other distinction between the passions that originate in bodily states as opposed to habits of the imagination. Rather, I follow Smith's other division between the original (or natural) and derived (or social) passions (or sentiments).

a. Natural Passions

In this section I analyze the natural passions. In particular, I describe the generic content of any natural passion and the ordinary "life cycle" within a human being of a natural passion. The main aim here is to give Smith's account of the etiology of the natural passions.

Recall that among the "original and immediate instincts," Smith included "the passion which unites the two sexes" (TMS 2.1.5.10, 77–8). I take that to be one of the presocial original passions. But as we have seen, according to Smith the derived passions are only possible in society; they are triggered by other people's responses and attach themselves to a great variety of social objects (recall the treatment of TMS 3.1.3, 110–1, in Section b in Chapter 2). So far the relationship between original and derived passions has been left obscure. Moreover, it is not entirely clear what a passion is according to Smith. In this subsection I distinguish four aspects of original or "natural" passions.

Consider the following passage:

> When an object of any kind, which has been for some time expected and foreseen, presents itself, whatever be the emotion which it is by nature fitted to excite, the mind must have been prepared for it, and must even in some measure have conceived it before-hand; because the idea of the object having been so long present to it, must have before-hand excited some degree of the same emotion which the object itself would excite: the change, therefore, which its presence produces comes thus to be less considerable, and the emotion or passion which it excites glides gradually and easily into the heart, without violence, pain, or difficulty.
>
> But the contrary of all this happens when the object is unexpected; the passion is then poured in all at once upon the heart, which is thrown, if it is a strong passion, into the most violent and convulsive emotions, such as sometimes cause immediate death; sometimes, by the suddenness of the extacy, so entirely disjoint the whole frame of the imagination, that it never after returns to its former tone and composure, but falls either into a frenzy or habitual lunacy; and such as almost always occasion a momentary loss of reason, or of that attention to other things which our situation or our duty requires. (Astronomy 1.1-2, 34-5)

We have no evidence if Smith ever witnessed a real death by sudden passion (although he may have encountered it on the opera stage—his writings exhibit great familiarity with opera). Rather than worrying about the accuracy of Smith's account, I focus on his conceptual framework here. In these two paragraphs Smith uses "passion" and "emotion" interchangeably; he also uses "sentiment" as a further synonym for these two (e.g., Astronomy Intro.1, 33). In what follows, I'll use "passion" and "sentiment" interchangeably. Here Smith's main distinction is between expected and unexpected passions, although he is also relying on a further distinction between calm (painless, etc.) and strong (violent, etc.) passions.

One of Smith's main examples of a calm passion, the desire of bettering our condition, is the main engine of economic activity in WN:

> But the principle which prompts to save is the desire of bettering our condition, a desire which, though generally calm and dispassionate, comes with us from the womb, and never leaves us till we go into the grave. In the whole interval which separates those two moments, there is scarce perhaps a single instant in which any man is so perfectly and completely satisfied with his situation as to be without any wish of alteration or improvement of any kind. An augmentation of fortune is the means by which the greater part of men propose and wish to better their condition. It is the means the most vulgar and the most obvious; and the most likely way of augmenting their fortune is to save and accumulate some part of what they acquire, either regularly and annually, or upon some extraordinary occasions. Though the principle of expense, therefore, prevails in almost all men upon some occasions, and in some men upon almost all occasions, yet in the greater part of men, taking the whole course of their life at an average, the principle of frugality seems not only to predominate, but to predominate very greatly. (WN 2.3.28, 341)

A note on Smith's terminology: by "vulgar," Smith need not mean anything negative; it means (something akin to) "appropriate to ordinary people." Having said that, in context Smith conjoins "vulgar" with "prejudice" (WN 2.3.25, 340), so it certainly can have a negative connotation here. It is as if Smith is speaking from the vantage point of the landed gentry and the associated values of honor, who might accept prejudicial stories about poor people living beyond their means while telling members of the upper classes that if left alone ordinary people will show a great deal of prudence. Smith's stance is compatible with his sharing in other prejudices against the working poor, or it may just be a rhetorical stance. Having said that, Fleischacker (2004) is correct to emphasize that in an eighteenth-century context, Smith's preferred economic strategy of high wages for the working poor puts him on the more progressive side of the political spectrum (and at odds with then mainstream mercantile thought).

This leaves plenty of questions about the nature(s) of unexpected calm passions or expected violent passions (etc.). More important, what is the nature of the natural relationship of "fit" between a triggering object and the excited passion? Smith's wording above (Astronomy 1.1– 2, 34– 5) is compatible with each and every object (cars, watches, bookshops, tigers, etc.) having an accompanying passion. This would mean that as commodities and technologies multiply, the number of passions do, too. Such an interpretation is not false, but we can make Smith's picture of the life cycle of the passions and the details of the structure and content of the passions more precise than that.

Recall the distinction between natural or original and derived sentiments. Original passions are described as follows: "the objects of his passions, the external bodies which either pleased or hurt him, would occupy his whole attention. The passions themselves, the desires or aversions, the joys or sorrows, which those objects excited" (TMS 3.1.3, 110). Therefore, to a first approximation the contents of original passions are (a) desires or aversions, or (b) joys or sorrows. The relationship of "fit" is then fairly simple: triggering objects that are pleasing (or useful, tasty, etc.) excite a desire for or joy in experiencing that object. Thus, Smithian passions are not just caused by triggering objects, but also directed toward them. I assume, then, that a representation of the aimed-at object is also part of the passion. Therefore, the full content of an original passion is then something like a twofold relation: <a desire (or aversion)/a joy (or sorrow), an intentional object [that is, an idea of the triggering object]>.[2] (In what follows, I use "< ... >" to describe the mental content and I separate the distinct relata of this content by a comma.) This content is experienced either calmly or violently.

To be clear: when Smith writes of the "strong" or "violent" passions, he generally means to convey intensity of feeling (e.g., TMS 5.2.10, 207; sometimes Smith adopts the Humean terminology of "vivacity" to capture this, e.g., Astronomy 1.8–10, EPS 37 and TMS 3.3.34, 152). Sometimes Smith also means to convey that they are particularly robust passions (and relatively immune to education); he writes that

> the principles of the imagination, upon which our sense of beauty depends, are of a very nice and delicate nature, and may easily be altered by habit and education: but the sentiments of moral approbation and disapprobation, are founded on the strongest and most vigorous passions of human nature; and though they may be somewhat warpt, cannot be entirely perverted. (TMS 5.2.1, 200)

Sometimes, too, he means to convey the thought that a strong passion motivationally trumps other desires: "The desire of becoming the proper objects of this respect, of deserving and obtaining this credit and rank among our equals, is, perhaps, the strongest of all our desires" (TMS 6.1.3, 213); recall also "the desire

---

[2] My use of "intentional" to capture the aboutness of the world-directedness of a mental object is anachronistic in a way that may mislead (which is why I flag it). In seventeenth-century philosophical terminology an "objective idea" is directed at the world (and derived from a "formal idea"), but Smith does not use that terminology, so I have opted to use the more anachronistic term to capture his position.

of being believed, the desire of persuading, of leading and directing other people, seems to be one of the strongest of all our natural desires" (TMS 7.4.25, 336). There is a fourth non-trivial sense of a "strong passion." This is the manner of physiologic expression: "Grief and joy, for example, strongly expressed in the look and gestures of any one, at once affect the spectator with some degree of a like painful or agreeable emotion" (TMS 1.1.1.6, 11).

In general one can disambiguate the intended meaning of "strong" from context. But Smith leaves unclear if there is an intrinsic connection among the intensely felt, the hard-to-pervert, the motivational trumping, and the physiologically expressed passions. It is logically possible, after all, that some passions are intensely felt, yet systematically fleeting, or cleverly concealed. One may feel pangs of jealousy, but in virtue of, say, being a generous and socially astute character, maintain a poker face when experiencing it. (I return to this example below in Section f.)

Yet, Smith also speaks of the "strong passions of jealousy, fear, and resentment" (TMS 7.3.3.9, 323). This seems to suggest that these passions are not just intensely felt (and strongly expressed) but *ceteris paribus* also trumping passions with the exception, perhaps, of a heterosexual drive, which Smith calls "naturally the most furious of all the passions" (TMS 1.2.1.2, 28).[3] Thus, for example, Smith writes,

> This passion to discover the real sentiments of others is naturally so strong, that it often degenerates into a troublesome and impertinent curiosity to pry into those secrets of our neighbours which they have very justifiable reasons for concealing;[4] and, upon many occasions, it requires prudence and a strong sense of propriety to govern this ...
> (TMS 7.4.28, 337–8)

Therefore, it seems that Smith thinks that jealousy, fear, resentment, curiosity (of a certain sort), and the desire for heterosexual coupling just are intrinsically strongly felt and, absent a great deal of mental exercise, motivationally forceful. They also are all passions that involve other humans—that is, social passions; I explore this feature more fully below.

Either way, we are now in a position to offer a first pass at a schematic description of the (so to speak) life cycle, or natural history, of original passions:

(i) A passion is excited by its natural triggering object;
(ii) (in the imagination) we feel desire (joy) or aversion (pleasure) toward the triggering object and

---

[3] Given Smith's lifetime of sublimation (Ross 1995: 214), this passage is a quite remarkable expression of self-command.

[4] Smith pays attention to the political significance of this desire for privacy in his treatment of taxation (WN 5.2.b.6, 827; 5.2.f.5, 848; 5.2.g.4, 853; 5.2.k.65, 898), to be discussed in Section f of Chapter 8.

(ii*) we express this by way of characteristic facial and bodily movements;

(iii) if the passion is expected and calm, it then dissipates without much further notice;

(iii*) if a passion is unexpected and strong it can have a lot of somatic consequences, including a temporary or extended loss of reason as well as damage to the functioning of the imagination.

Presumably, if a passion is not so calm as to dissipate without much notice and not so strong as to lead to paralysis or worse, that is, it is an expected and (moderately) strong passion, then,

(iv) the excited passion will motivate some behavior to (or away from) the triggering object by promising pleasure (or pain) upon gratification.

It is thus clear that our natural passions have—to adopt some recent technical terminology—a world-to-mind direction of fit; they involve some desire to change the world so that it fits the object of the desire. As we see in the following sections and chapters, *all* of Smith's passions have *some* such action-guiding desire for change built into them. But it does not follow that Smithian passions are fitted to motivate always the same actions.

To avoid confusion, when I talk of a "natural" triggering object, I mean to capture Smith's language of the fit between the external object and the original passion in ordinary circumstances such that reliable expectations and dispositive habits are possible. A sweet-tasting candy has a corresponding, say, desire in us. This (normological) use of "natural," thus, allows our passions to misfire in some circumstances or to motivate behavior that need not be good for us, all things considered.

Before I turn to the structurally more complicated derived passions, we need to draw out the manner in which Smith distinguishes between expected and unexpected passions. This reveals a crucial feature in which Smith turns out to deviate significantly from the empiricism associated with Hume (and often attributed to Smith).

b. Proto-Passions, Preconceptions, and Why Smith Is Not an Empiricist

In this section I articulate Smith's account of the proto-passions or preconceptions (I'll use the terms interchangeably). They are of interest because they play a crucial, largely ignored role in Smith's moral psychology and epistemology. I argue that on Smith's account these proto-passions guide behavior of the very young as well as provide us with part of the content that needs to be developed to cultivate moral virtue. Thus, I argue against the common assumption that Smith is an empiricist in moral matters and epistemology (for the best, still useful treatment of Smith's empiricism see Bittermann 1940). This is not to deny that Smith thinks empirical knowledge is significant and instructive, but at crucial junctures in his system he relies on the presence of reliable (what we would call) "mental content" that is not the product of experience or induction.

One of Smith's most important commitments about the brain is that in ordinary circumstances our mental anticipations run ahead of the world (the brain's "ideas move more rapidly than external objects, it is continually running before them, and therefore anticipates, before it happens, every event which falls out according to this ordinary course of things," Astronomy 2.7, 41, to be discussed more fully in Section c). While surprising consequences follow from this commitment, some are commonsensical. For example, according to Smith expected passions occur in ordinary circumstances when we are already mentally prepared to experience them. This is intuitive, and it, as we shall see in Section d, is the foundation for his views on sound judgment. But it also has a peculiar consequence; it is, perhaps, not an unattractive feature of Smith's analysis that ordinarily we experience the same mental content twice: first, a less intensely felt and expressed "proto-passion" triggered by the idea of the triggering object in anticipation of the triggering object and then, second, the real passion after the occurrence of the triggering natural object.

The whole circumstance surrounding a proto-passion (its ideational trigger, feeling, and expression) takes place in the imagination. But the way even a proto-passion is expressed can be through (mild) facial movements, hand gestures, and some other somatic consequences that would ordinarily accompany the genuine passion. That is to say, for Smith the imagination can have a very real physiologic impact. (This is a fairly common position among early modern philosophers, including even those who sharply distinguish between mind and extension. For example, Spinoza treats the imagination as part of extension.) Smith is quite adamant about the extent of the somatic impact of experienced passions: "joy comes rushing upon us all at once like a torrent. The change produced therefore by a Surprise of joy is more sudden, and upon that account more violent and apt to have more fatal effects, than that which is occasioned by a Surprise of grief" (Astronomy, EPS 1.6, 36). Lurking below this treatment is the thought that our passions, sentiments, and emotions are physically instantiated by or the expression of micro-movements in our body, be it "spirits" (fluids) or particles (e.g., Astronomy, EPS 2.3, 39).

Thus, we can describe the life cycle of an anticipated natural passion as follows:

(0) Based on habit the imagination experiences an anticipatory idea of a triggering natural object and a proto-passion suitable to it is excited;

(i) a passion is excited by its natural triggering object;

(ii) (in the imagination) we feel desire (joy) or aversion (pleasure) toward the triggering object; and

(ii*) we express this by way of characteristic facial and bodily movements;
(iii) if the passion is expected and calm it then dissipates without much further
       notice;

Presumably, if a passion is not so calm as to dissipate without much notice and
not so strong as to lead to paralysis or worse then,

(iv)   the excited passion will motivate some behavior to (or away from) the trig-
       gering object by promising pleasure (or pain) upon gratification.

One important feature of these proto-passions is that they dampen the intensity of the to-be-expected experience and expression of the passions themselves.
Therefore, if we expect, say, to encounter snakes when we enter a jungle and
this naturally occasions a proto-passion of fear, we will be less fearful when we
encounter real snakes in a real jungle. (This may help in controlling the impulse
to run.)

One might object that I have offered very little textual evidence for Smith's
commitment to such proto-passions. Perhaps Smith did not quite see the implication I attribute to him? As it turns out, Smith explicitly discusses proto-passions
in terms of "anticipation or preconception" in an important passage in an essay
that receives too little attention:

> But all the appetites which take their origin from a certain state of
> the body, seem to suggest the means of their own gratification; and
> even long before experience, some anticipation or preconception of
> the pleasure which attends that gratification. In the appetite for sex,
> which frequently, I am disposed to believe almost always, comes a long
> time before the age of puberty, this is perfectly and distinctly evident.
> The appetite for food suggests to the new-born infant the operation of
> sucking, the only means by which it can possibly gratify that appetite.
> It is continually sucking. It sucks whatever is presented to its mouth.
> It sucks even when there is nothing presented to its mouth, and some
> anticipation or preconception of the pleasure which it is to enjoy in
> sucking, seems to make it delight in putting its mouth in the shape and
> configuration by which it alone can enjoy that pleasure. There are other
> appetites in which the most unexperienced [sic] imagination produces
> a similar effect upon the organs which Nature has provided for their
> gratification. (External Senses 79, 165)

Thus, Smith clearly commits himself to the existence of some such proto-passions
(the point was stressed in Hamilton 1861: 182). In fact, the two examples he
offers (appetite for sex and appetite for food) are two of the original, or natural,
passions we have identified above.

Moreover, Smith is adamant that such proto-passions are innate ("long before experience ... the new-born infant ... the most unexperienced imagination"). Thus, while it is, of course, possible that various proto-passions are themselves a consequence of habitual experience (that is a natural reading of Astronomy 2.7, EPS 41), Smith appears to think that as a group ("there are other appetites") the proto-passions are innate (in his terminology they are "provided by Nature"). Of course, that proto-passions are innate is compatible with the further claim that they require environmental cues or triggering objects to be activated. While below I describe some preconceptions that according to Smith do require such triggering objects, Smith clearly also thinks some of those innate proto-passions are self-activating: the infant "sucks even when there is nothing presented to its mouth." Even though Smith was a lifelong, childless bachelor, he showed an active interest in child development.

Smith's position is not the minimal claim that prior to experience these proto-passions exist as kind of very vague drives or content neutral mechanisms (e.g., Humean principles of association); rather, the proto-passions already have *considerable content about the world built into them*. It is not just that the anticipation of the motivational, significant pleasure is built into the proto-passion, but also some of the means by which to gratify the passion. Thus, the infant may lack the idea or representation of a mother's breast, but it certainly is more than a blank slate about the structure of its life-world. As Smith puts it (in treating the self-motion of a "new-born animal"):

> the very desire of motion supposes some notion or preconception of externality; and the desire to move towards the side of the agreeable, or from that of the disagreeable sensation, supposes at least some vague notion of some external thing or place which is the cause of those respective sensations. (External Senses 85, EPS 167)

The passage is quoted from a larger argument directed against external-world skepticism as well as Molyneux's Question (Glenney 2011; I return to this in Section c in Chapter 11.)[5]

To be clear: the natural passions that do have associated proto-passions are *triggered* by states of one's body; they take "their origin from a certain state of the body" and not by the natural triggering object that they are about, say, the mother's breast (see also TMS 1.2.1). Even so, the content of the natural proto-passion is not the state of one's body, but much more akin to the content one *would* expect in the (normal) original passion. Smith's treatment of smell, which

---

[5] The essay is explicitly framed as a response to Berkeley, but its target seems to be the ways in which Hume extended Berkeley's system. Smith's position, in which the external world is a constitutive principle of extremely basic human functioning, is reminiscent of Locke's use of touch (R. M. Shockey 2007).

simultaneously draws on and illuminates his account of the proto-passion that leads to infants' suckling behavior, nicely illustrates these issues:

> The Smell not only excites the appetite, but directs to the object which can alone gratify that appetite. But by suggesting the direction towards that object, the Smell must necessarily suggest some notion of distance and externality, which are necessarily involved in the idea of direction; in the idea of the line of motion by which the distance can best be overcome, and the mouth brought into contact with the unknown substance which is the object of the appetite. That the Smell should alone suggest any preconception of the shape or magnitude of the external body to which it directs, seems not very probable. The sensation of Smell seems to have no sort of affinity or correspondence with shape or magnitude; and whatever preconception the infant may have of these, (and it may very probably have some such preconception,) is likely to be suggested, not so much directly by the Smell, and indirectly by the appetite excited by that Smell; as by the principle which teaches the child to mould its mouth into the conformation and action of sucking, even before it reaches the object to which alone that conformation and action can be usefully applied.
>
> The Smell, however, as it suggests the direction by which the external body must be approached, must suggest at least some vague idea or preconception of the existence of that body; of the thing to which it directs, though not perhaps of the precise shape and magnitude of that thing. The infant, too, feeling its mouth attracted and drawn as it were towards that external body, must conceive the Smell which thus draws and attracts it, as something belonging to or proceeding from that body, or what is afterwards denominated and obscurely understood to be as a sort of quality or attribute of that body. (External Senses 80–1, EPS 165–6)

According to Smith our senses have some structure of the external world built into their normal functioning from the start. When we smell we automatically presuppose not just "some distance and externality, which are necessarily involved in the idea of direction" but even "some vague idea or preconception of the existence of that body." Therefore, our proto-passions help deliver to us the idea of a *structured external* world. While this idea is commonly vague, the worldly structure presupposed can sometimes even be relatively precise as in the "shape or magnitude" of the aimed-for breast when the infant is sucking.

Of course, in the example above, smell is triggered by an object other than a state of one's own body, but that does not undercut Smith's claim here. We do not innately smell bodies that are not present. But how and what we smell when triggered to do so draw on innate (proto-passion) mechanisms that have significant features of the world's structure built into them.

This whole section, thus, goes against the standard reading of treating Smith as an "empiricist" (see, for example, Raphael 2007: 26, 49–50). Raphael treats Smith's purported empiricism as so uncontroversial that he never bothers to offer evidence for this claim. Presumably, Raphael would cite the broad similarity between Hume's and Smith's philosophy—a view very common in scholarship. Yet, Raphael fails to note that Smith is committed to the existence of the very un-Humean notion of "preconceptions."

A skeptical reader might concede that, perhaps, in Smith's youthful views on child development such preconceptions play some role, but that this is irrelevant to Smith's moral empiricism (this is, in fact, what Raphael's claim probably amounts to). Such a hypothetical critic may even concede that when it comes to the origin of our ideas, Smith is less of an empiricist than previously thought, but that experience is crucial in the justification of moral ideas. I cannot refute this critic decisively.

Yet, once one is alert to the possibility that Smith allows some non-trivial innate content one can discern some such commitment at the core of his moral theory lodged in passages that are in other respects taken as good evidence for Smith's moral empiricism. For example, Smith writes:

> The wise and virtuous man directs his principal attention to the first standard; [a] the idea of exact propriety and perfection. [b] There exists in the mind of every man, [c] an idea of this kind, [d] gradually formed from his observations upon the character and conduct both of himself and of other people. It is the slow, gradual, and progressive work of the great demigod within the breast, the great judge and arbiter of conduct. This idea is in every man more or less accurately drawn, its colouring is more or less just, its outlines are more or less exactly designed, according to the delicacy and acuteness of that sensibility, with which those observations were made, and according to the care and attention employed in making them. . . . He has studied this idea more than other people, he comprehends it more distinctly, he has formed a much more correct image of it, and is much more deeply enamoured of its exquisite and divine beauty. He endeavours as well as he can, to assimilate his own character to this archetype of perfection. (TMS 6.3.23, 247; I have added letters to facilitate discussion)

There is no doubt that experience plays an important role here, and I suspect that the repeated emphasis after [d] on "observations" tempts many readers to read moral empiricism into Smith's position. But [a–c] also sustain an alternative and—given Smith's precise wording—more plausible reading. This alternative reading takes its cue from the fact that [b] and [c] make both a very strong claim and a surprisingly weak claim. Note the universal ("every") scope in [b]. Smith claims that *some* idea of "exact propriety and perfection" is present in *everyone*.

It is offered without Smith's habitual caution (it seems, naturally, normally, etc.). This might be a rhetorical flourish, of course. But in [c] Smith is not claiming that everybody has a fully determinate "idea of exact propriety and perfection"; rather, he is claiming that everybody merely has *some such* (vague) idea. This thinner reading of [c] is, in fact, part of the main point of the passage: most of us do not have an idea of exact propriety and perfection; we have to work very hard to *cultivate* it. Part of the virtue of the "wise and virtuous" is, as Smith expressly says, her hard work at studying the idea. One only gains a *"much more* correct image" (emphasis added) of the idea by applying oneself to becoming, as it were, a better lover ("more deeply enamoured") of virtue. Given that we are in the realm of "exactitude," Smith is claiming that the intellectual sentiments play a role in attaining virtue (Hanley 2013; see Section e and Chapter 9).

If one is primed to think of Smith as an empiricist, then [d] is read as Smith offering the inductive means by which [a] is acquired. There is a sense in which this is true. It's through the exemplars available within our culture and education that we refine our standard or picture of propriety. But this empiricist reading cannot explain how according to Smith the process of cultivation gets off the ground, and it does not do justice to the fact that in [b] and [c] Smith is claiming that *everybody* has some less correct and inexact (as well as less loved, etc.) idea of perfection. It's this latter idea that we imitate as well we can (TMS 6.3.26, 248; on the significance of imitation, see the groundbreaking article by Chandler 2013). What is the source and justification of that to-be-imitated "ideal of perfection"?

The answer to this last question leads us to another way to read [a–c]: [a–c] claims that we all have an inexact (less beautiful, etc.) idea of propriety and perfection. Presumably this less exact (or vague) idea is innate in us. We give this idea ever more exact content by the practice of adopting the stance of the studious spectator who loves and emulates virtue and beauty as instantiated in the "archetype of perfection."

Despite Smith's deployment of Platonic language, I use a scholastic distinction in order to illuminate Smith's position: the form of the idea is always present, but we give the idea matter through our moral cultivation. Obviously, the distinction is not Smith's (although he is no stranger to using Scholastic terminology to clarify his position, e.g., TMS 6.2.1.1, 219), but putting it like this allows us to make sense of a broader understanding of Smith's position. As Sam Fleischacker pointed out to me in correspondence as I was developing this particular interpretation of Smith, the "idea of a fully virtuous person, formally, is just the idea of a person whose sentiments are fully admired by the impartial spectator . . . while the material content of this idea, in each specific society" varies with "historical circumstances." Without using such scholastic terminology, I argue in Section c in Chapter 7 that Smith indeed holds a view very close to this neo-Aristotelian position.

Ultimately only a few attain a genuinely precise idea of propriety/perfection. The reading offered here does not rely on the unconscious, as it were, subsistence

of the innate, inexact idea; all it requires is that we ordinarily have "little conception of this ideal perfection, about which [we have] little employed [our] thoughts"
(TMS 6.3.26, 248). Smith explicitly equates "a thought or conception of any kind"
with an idea in Ancient Logics 3, EPS 121—the whole extremely long, controversial footnote signals that Smith is very interested in the provenance of views of
the sort being discussed here.

In the canonical history of early modern philosophy we are not unfamiliar with
the position thus attributed to Smith. We find a version of it in Spinoza's *Ethics*,
where Spinoza also insists that *everybody* has some adequate ideas (E3p1), and
that some model of goodness is to be imitated (Appendix to *Ethics* 4). Even if
Smith never read Spinoza, he would have found very similar ideas in Shaftesbury's
(1711) *Characteristics*, which appeals to innate and instinctive "pre-conceptions
or pre-sensations" to explain our aesthetic standards (Shaftesbury 1999: 325–6).
Not unlike Smith, Shaftesbury draws analogies between animal and human preconceptions. There is no doubt that Smith was a very critical reader of Shaftesbury.
But there are also more orthodox sources for Smith's position as I have developed
it. For example, Luther inspired in his followers the idea that postlapsarian man
had innate ideas that through original sin were, as it were, covered up and required
a mental emendation to remove (Roelants 2013). Given that preconceptions
have roots in both Stoic and Epicurean thought, a more remote source of these
ideas may be Seneca's *Letters*. Here we need not settle on Smith's source of his
Platonizing ("archetype of perfection") variant of this approach. When Smith was
appointed Professor of Logic in 1751, his (now lost) inaugural lecture was titled
De Origine Idearum (Berry 2013: 3)—presumably it would have contained some
historical survey of opposing positions on the topic. One might think that God is
the archetype of perfection. But in the context of criticizing Hutcheson's philosophy, Smith makes clear that divine and moral circumstances are so different that
imitatio dei would be inappropriate. God is "independent and all-powerful," while
we require "so many things external." We need a model or conception of virtue *apt*
for human beings (TMS 7.2.3.18, 305; Levy and Peart 2013: 382).

None of this to deny, of course, that Smith treats the existence of proto-passions as an empirical fact. Smith's position is certainly not strict rationalism.
Moreover, the fact that the origin of relevant moral ideas is, in part, innate does
not mean that their justification need not be empirical. I do not aim to rule out
all ways in which Smith may well be an empiricist; rather, my main point is that
by assuming that Smith is an empiricist, we miss crucial details of his position.

Having said that, the *a priori* "idea of exact propriety" is, on the reading developed here, a legitimate and authoritative one, something we have every right to
employ in our practical reasoning even before we cultivate it by way of inductive
practices; I take this to be the main payoff of my analysis of TMS 6.3.23, 247.
Once we accept that Smith is often a (friendly) critic of Hume we can see more
clearly the ways his moral psychology deviates significantly from Humean principles (see also Fleischacker 2012). In addition, below I argue that preconceptions

and reason play some justificatory role in his epistemology. Hence, here I inter-
rupt my analysis of Smith's accounts of the passions to describe his views on rationality and reason in the next two sections. This is of intrinsic interest, but it will
also allow me to explain Smith's views of the intellectual passions more easily.

c. Causation, Sound Judgment, and Environmental Rationality

In this section I argue that according to Smith sound judgments consist in having the right kind of habits—that is, ones that match the causal order of one's
environment. The significance of this is that it explains how Smith's epistemic
commitments about the nature of causal judgments illuminate his ethical commitments. Along the way, I further develop Smith's views on abstraction.

Recall this passage:

> It is evident that the mind takes pleasure in observing the resem-
> blances that are discoverable betwixt different objects. It is by means
> of such observations that it endeavours to arrange and methodise all
> its ideas, and to reduce them into proper classes and assortments ...
> When two objects, however unlike, have often been observed to follow
> each other, and have constantly presented themselves to the senses in
> that order, they come to be so connected together in the fancy, that
> the idea of the one seems, of its own accord, to call up and introduce
> that of the other. If the objects are still observed to succeed each other
> as before, this connection, or, as it has been called, this association of
> their ideas, becomes stricter and stricter, and the habit of the imagina-
> tion to pass from the conception of the one to that of the other, grows
> more and more rivetted and confirmed. As its ideas move more rapidly
> than external objects, it is continually running before them, and there-
> fore anticipates, before it happens, every event which falls out accord-
> ing to this ordinary course of things. (Astronomy 2.1–7, EPS 37–41)

According to Smith there is a pleasing psychological disposition that activates
the mind to notice and, perhaps, even search out resemblances between objects.
In the most Humean part of Smith's treatment above, the habitual observation
of the ordered, constant conjunction of two objects causes the habitual con-
joining of the two ideas of the objects in order to form an association between
them (as Smith says) in the imagination. In Hume's terminology of the Treatise
this is called a "natural relation" (1.1.5). In Hume the associative mechanism is
not exception-less, but a normological "gentle force, which commonly prevails"
(Treatise 1.1.4.1). Thus, Smith here echoes Hume's account of causation without
mentioning Hume or using "cause."

According to Smith the pleasing activity of classifying ideas leads into what we may call a "natural taxonomy" including abstract categories ("proper classes and assortment"). To be clear: Smith's views on the origin of a natural taxonomy do not commit him to claiming that such a natural taxonomy is true. In Ancient Logics Smith explains that our tendency toward natural taxonomy is at the root of the Aristotelian metaphysical system. Even so, Smith insists that many of the "doctrines" of Aristotle seem "to have arisen, more from the nature of language, than from the nature of things" (Ancient Logics 5, EPS 125) Smith shares here in a mistrust of the epistemic capacity of language more general among early modern thinkers (e.g., Berkeley's *Principles of Human Knowledge*, Introduction, Section 25). Not unlike Spinoza, who attributes Aristotelian teleology to a projection of human desire (and fear) in the Appendix to *Ethics* 1, Smith offers a psychological account to explain the theoretical illusion that misled earlier philosophers into erroneous conclusions. While Smith is not harshly critical of Aristotle's system ("with all its imperfections it was excusable, in the beginnings of philosophy, and is not a great deal more remote from the truth, than many others which have since been substituted in its room by some of the greatest pretenders to accuracy and precision" [Ancient Logics 5, EPS 125]), he does not endorse it as a true metaphysics, either.

Smith claims we naturally group things together by way of common, sensible qualities. During the nineteenth century this generates two conflicting interpretations of Smith's metaphysics. Sir William Hamilton treats Smith as a nominalist successor to Berkeley and Hume (Hamilton 1861: 321ff). In his argument, Hamilton, who is now best known being the target of Mill's attack on the commonsense school of philosophy (Mill 1865), relies exclusively on the following passage from Languages:

> It is this application of the name of an individual to a great multitude of objects, whose resemblance naturally recalls the idea of that individual, and of the name which expresses it, that seems originally to have given occasion to the formation of those classes and assortments, which, in the schools, are called genera and species, and of which the ingenious and eloquent M. Rousseau of Geneva finds himself so much at a loss to account for the origin. (Languages 2, 204–5)

Smith draws here on a mental mechanism defended by Hume (and attributed by Hume to Berkeley): "all general ideas are nothing but particular ones, annexed to a certain term, which gives them a more extensive signification, and makes them recall upon occasion other individuals, which are similar to them" (Treatise 1.1.7.1). This mechanism has become known as the "revival set" in Hume scholarship (Garrett 1997: 24ff). Therefore, Hamilton's interpretation seems well founded.

The mechanism plays an important role in Smith's philosophy: "the very appearances of grief and joy inspire us with some degree of the like emotions, it is because they suggest to us the general idea of some good or bad fortune that has befallen the person in whom we observe them … the general idea of good or bad fortune, therefore, creates some concern for the person who has met with it" (TMS 1.1.1.8, 12). Here we have a rather abstract idea generating some concern for another person. The significance of this is not limited to the fact that Smith is clearly entailing that (abstract) ideas matter, and thereby suggesting that what we teach can influence our readers' and students' concern for others. (He does not suggest that this concern is especially strong, nor that all general ideas have this capacity, nor that this is the only way to generate some such concern.)

Even so, we can find a more thorough alternative to Hamilton's interpretation earlier in the nineteenth century by Hamilton's teacher, Dugald Stewart (and Smith's first biographer), who treats Smith's account approvingly. Besides drawing on much the same passages in Languages, Stewart calls attention to two features of Smith's treatment overlooked later by Hamilton (who was the editor of Stewart's collected works). First, Smith is describing a mental mechanism that allows us to see one aspect of an object "apart from the rest." Second, this mechanism is properly understood as the power of abstraction (Stewart 1792: 155). The first claim is uncontroversial and compatible with a nominalist interpretation. But the second feature is controversial and potentially at odds with the nominalist interpretation of Smith. Moreover, Stewart locates this power of abstraction not in the imagination, but in the understanding (without specifically attributing this further claim to Smith). Smith is familiar with such a philosophy of mind because in introducing Aristotle's treatment of so-called specific essences, Smith describes a similar mechanism as follows: "Mankind have had, at all times, a strong propensity to realize their own abstractions" (Ancient Logics 5, EPS 125).

I am inclined to agree partially with Stewart's interpretation, then, that according to Smith our natural taxonomy is itself founded on the original propensity toward abstraction that leaves traces in all languages.[6] After all, recall that in Languages Smith had insisted that "the institution of this name, therefore, supposes comparison. It likewise supposes some degree of abstraction." *Even in naming* we rely to some degree on abstraction. But hereby Smith has inverted the Berkeley-Hume position: rather than using the "revival set" mechanism as a way to explain away abstract ideas, Smith suggests that this mechanism crucially relies on abstraction!

---

[6] See Smith's Astronomy:

Where it can observe but one single quality, that is common to a great variety of otherwise widely different objects, that single circumstance will be sufficient for it to connect them all together, to reduce them to one common class, and to call them by one general name. It is thus that all things endowed with a power of self-motion, beasts, birds, fishes, insects, are classed under the general name of Animal; and that these again, along with those which want that power, are arranged under the still more general word Substance: and this is the origin of those assortments of objects

Of course, from this alone it does not follow that Smith is not a nominalist, but in Section b of Chapter 2 we have already encountered quite a bit of evidence that Smith is not afraid to "operationalize" different degrees of "metaphysical-ness" in terms of abstraction from the appearances. But my agreement with Stewart's interpretation of Smith is partial because Stewart misses that for Smith to see one aspect of an object "apart from the rest" is just the mind's capacity, by way of discrete mental "operations," or steps, to remove or add qualities to sensation.

There is an important moral to be learned here that applies to all of Smith's writings. Often Smith works with Humean concepts and mechanisms, but in his discussion he frequently subverts these in subtle ways (Fleischacker 2012); Smith does so sometimes to strengthen Hume's main point, sometimes to radicalize Hume's aims, and sometimes to offer a dramatically different account. Thus, even when one notices Humean commitments in Smith one has to be cautious about conflating their positions.

One important issue that Smith leaves open in Languages is the extent to which living adults are capable of abstracting in more or less the same way. Hume had infamously insisted that Negroes were naturally inferior to whites, insisting on "original distinction between these breeds of men" ("Of National Character").[7] In his great treatise on political economy *The Querist*, which anticipates many of Smith's most subtle insights (Rashid 1990), Berkeley had traced a certain amount of (indigenous) Irish laziness to the hereditary dispositions (Berkeley 1751: 69–70).[8] Smith's French follower, de Grouchy (who translated Languages into French), had no doubt that mankind varies in its "ability to grasp abstract and general ideas." For de Grouchy this is the basis of her account of why it is so hard "to enlighten men, even concerning their own true interest" (LS, V). But there is no hint of Hume's racialized hierarchy in de Grouchy. On the whole Smith's theory seems more egalitarian about human cognitive capacity not just than Hume's position but also de Grouchy's

and ideas which in the schools are called Genera and Species, and of those abstract and general names, which in all languages are made use of to express them. (Astronomy 2.1, 38)

Stewart is clearly familiar with Smith's doctrine because he goes on to discuss approvingly Cook's treatment of Cook's encounter of the inhabitants of Wateeoo, who had never encountered sheep and goats before and classified them as birds. In Smithian fashion, Stewart (and Cook) defend the natives' mistake of classification as a natural one, and not as evidence for their lack of taxonomic or intellectual capacity (a view promoted, alas, by Hume in "Of National Characters"). The episode reveals that Stewart was willing to call attention to the more radical possibilities in Smith's public philosophy (cf. Rothschild 2001: 66ff on Stewart's role in playing down Smith's "real sentiments").

[7] In Hume's hand natural inferiority entails a kind of inherent limit to the (to adopt an Aristotelian phrase) second nature produced by social (Hume calls them "moral") causes such as institutions, norms, trade(s), and other cultural practices that fix and stabilize individual habits and thereby the collections composed of these individuals. This limit is purportedly characterized by an absence of cognitive or intellectual excellence not just at the collective level but even among the individuals who are part of the naturally inferior race(s). (I am using "race" here in its nineteenth-century sense, but Hume is clearly one of the sources of the later use.)

[8] The three crucial queries are:

position (recall: the difference "between a philosopher and a common street porter, for example, seems to arise not so much from nature, as from habit, custom, and education" [WN 1.2.4, 29]), but Smith leaves some crucial details unstated.

Smith's final move in the passage above (Astronomy 2.7, 41) is also not to be found in Hume (although itself is not un-Humean). For Smith, once associated, our ideas, including our natural relations, move more rapidly than the (external) objects that originated them. In adults this process creates a never-ending stream of mental anticipations of the world.[9] These mental anticipations play an important role throughout my account of Smith's understanding of human nature. When the world deviates from these anticipations this generates a painful emotion of wonder and the desire to alleviate that feeling, which, in turn, leads (and this is crucial for the larger aim of Astronomy) in some circumstances to the desire to inquire into the hidden structure of the world.

Before the rise of civilization, the natural response to such occasionally wonder-inducing events was different:

> [T]he origin of Polytheism, and of that vulgar superstition which ascribes all the irregular events of nature to the favour or displeasure of intelligent, though invisible beings, to gods, daemons, witches, genii, fairies. For it may be observed, that in all Polytheistic religions, among savages, as well as in the early ages of Heathen antiquity, it is the irregular events of nature only that are ascribed to the agency and power of their gods. (Astronomy 3.2, 49)

Smith intimates here that the very idea of making gods (or god) responsible for lawlike nature is, in fact, a late arrival in human history. (I return to this in Section a of Chapter 10.)

Let me now turn to a Smithian thought-experiment, which radicalizes one by Hume (Treatise 2.1.6.9) and gets us to the nub of my treatment in this section:

> Could we conceive a person of the soundest judgment, who had grown up to maturity, and whose imagination had acquired those habits, and that mold, which the constitution of things in this world necessarily impress upon it,

512. Whether our natural Irish are not partly Spaniards and partly Tartars; and whether they do not bear signatures of their descent from both these nations, which is also confirmed by all their histories?

513. Whether the Tartar progeny is not numerous in this land? And whether there is an idler occupation under the sun than to attend flocks and herds of cattle?

514. Whether the wisdom of the state should not wrestle with this hereditary disposition of our Tartars, and with a high hand introduce agriculture?

With a reference to Plato's *Laws*, Berkeley proposes a program of assortative mating (Berkeley 1751: 29).

[9] Smith anticipates here features of the "predictive brains" approach to psychology; see Clark 2013.

to be all at once transported alive to some other planet, where nature was governed by laws quite different from those which take place here; as he would be continually obliged to attend to events, which must to him appear in the highest degree jarring, irregular, and discordant, he would soon feel the same confusion and giddiness begin to come upon him, which would at last end in the same manner, in lunacy and distraction. Neither, to produce this effect, is it necessary that the objects should be either great or interesting, or even uncommon, in themselves. It is sufficient that they follow one another in an uncommon order. (Astronomy 2.10, 43)

Of course, instant transportation to other planets is impossible. But this does not mean the whole thought experiment is mere whimsy. The idea that "some other planet, where nature was governed by laws quite different from those which take place here" may have lodged itself in Smith's mind while reading Newton's *Opticks*: "it may be also allowed that God is able to create particles of matter of several sizes and figures, and in several proportions to space, and perhaps of different densities and forces, and thereby to vary the laws of nature, and made worlds of several sorts in several parts of the universe" (Query 31; Newton 1730 [1952]: 379–80). In Newton it is, thus, possible for the laws of nature to vary among causally disconnected solar systems or (more likely) galaxies (see Biener and Schliesser 2017 for discussion).

Anyway, there are two aspects about Smith's thought experiment that are crucial to the argument of this section and Smith's philosophy more generally. First, sound judgment is nothing but having the right kind of habits; that is, one's mental expectations match the world's natural order. Here it is left unclear to what degree we have any control over these habits. At any rate, for Smith, in a properly functioning person there is a reciprocal relationship between the habituated mental anticipations and sound judgment. The system of mental anticipation of a culture's common sense is—to adopt recent philosophical terminology (Sellars 1963)—that culture's manifest image.

Second, on Smith's view, (one version, perhaps, of) lunacy is having mental anticipations that are systematically out of kilter with the order in which objects appear. That is, when our firmest, most habitual, natural relations of causation closely track our natural or common environment, this is constitutive of (mental) sanity and rationality. In fact, in Smith's treatment of the impact of custom and education among so-called civilized societies (that is, in law-governed places), he describes immoral behavior with the same language as the thought experiment we're discussing: one is "transported to do any thing contrary to justice or humanity" (TMS 5.2.10, 207). It is as if Smith thinks of immoral behavior in terms of one's being an alien in one's own environment. According to Smith one way in which our ordinary sanity can sometimes come undone and even cause permanent lunacy is through the workings of the so-called strong passions (Astronomy 1.2, 35). Smith, thus, opens the door to treating immorality as a kind of mental disease familiar from nineteenth-century discussions of psychiatry (Goldstein 2002).

It may seem that my use of "rationality" here is unwarranted, especially if one's emphasis is on Smith the purported value-free "social scientist" (e.g., Campbell 1971). Even so, in his treatment of mental anticipations, Smith brings together two kinds of expectations, the empirical and the normative, in a manner akin to recent meta-ethics (see Michael Smith 1994: 88–91). The normative develops out of the predictive. I take it as uncontroversial that when Smith speaks of the "person of soundest judgment" he just *is* describing the exemplary, rational person.

Therefore, I call this kind of sound judgment—to use an anachronistic term in honor of a very great Smith scholar, the economist Vernon Smith—"environmental rationality." To be clear: what Vernon Smith (2003) means by "ecological rationality" is different from what I mean to capture about Adam Smith here! Vernon Smith's use of the term is about capturing the nature of a particular "rational order, as an environmental system that emerges out of cultural and biological evolutionary processes" (Smith 2003: 469). I use "environmental rationality" to capture the idea that according to Adam Smith an individual's (or a group's, society's, etc.) judgment is developed and calibrated in a particular environment. Of course, it is likely that a sound judgment developed out of tracking regular features in one's environment is a prerequisite for developing the kind of order that is of interest to Vernon Smith and others inspired by Hayek.

I also adopt the terminology of "environmental rationality" in describing Smithian sound judgment in order to highlight an otherwise little-noticed feature of Smith's conceptual framework. As Lauren Brubaker first noted (Brubaker 2006b: 202), when Smith talks of an "irregularity," this tends to be a regular deviation from the expectations of our environmental rationality (see TMS 2.3, *passim*) and even theoretical reason (see, especially, Astronomy 4.45, EPS 83, 4.68, EPS 99, 4.70–1, EPS, 100–1). By "theoretical" reason, I mean here the expectations as trained up on a scientific "system." In Chapter 11 (and more briefly in Section e in the present chapter), I explore the complicated relationship between such environmental rationality and theoretical reason (and more briefly religious reason in Chapter 14). Thus, one way to understand what I mean here by ordinary "environmental rationality" is as reasonable judgment within the manifest image.

d. Reason as an Active Principle

In this section I describe Smith's understanding of reason. I claim it plays a significant role in Smith's moral psychology. I explain this role by way of contrast with Hume's understanding of reason.

Consider this long passage:

> Let us suppose that the great empire of China, with all its myriads
> of inhabitants, was suddenly swallowed up by an earthquake, and let
> us consider how a man of humanity in Europe, who had no sort of

connexion with that part of the world, would be affected upon receiving intelligence of this dreadful calamity. He would, I imagine, first of all, express very strongly his sorrow for the misfortune of that unhappy people, he would make many melancholy reflections upon the precariousness of human life, and the vanity of all the labours of man, which could thus be annihilated in a moment. He would too, perhaps, if he was a man of speculation, enter into many reasonings concerning the effects which this disaster might produce upon the commerce of Europe, and the trade and business of the world in general. And when all this fine philosophy was over, when all these humane sentiments had been once fairly expressed, he would pursue his business or his pleasure, take his repose or his diversion, with the same ease and tranquillity, as if no such accident had happened. The most frivolous disaster which could befal [*sic*] himself would occasion a more real disturbance. If he was to lose his little finger to-morrow, he would not sleep to-night; but, provided he never saw them, he will snore with the most profound security over the ruin of a hundred millions of his brethren, and the destruction of that immense multitude seems plainly an object less interesting to him, than this paltry misfortune of his own. To prevent, therefore, this paltry misfortune to himself, would a man of humanity be willing to sacrifice the lives of a hundred millions of his brethren, provided he had never seen them? Human nature startles with horror at the thought, and the world, in its greatest depravity and corruption, never produced such a villain as could be capable of entertaining it. But what makes this difference? When our passive feelings are almost always so sordid and so selfish, how comes it that our active principles should often be so generous and so noble? When we are always so much more deeply affected by whatever concerns ourselves, than by whatever concerns other men; what is it which prompts the generous, upon all occasions, and the mean upon many, to sacrifice their own interests to the greater interests of others? It is not the soft power of humanity, it is not that feeble spark of benevolence which Nature has lighted up in the human heart, that is thus capable of counteracting the strongest impulses of self-love. It is a stronger power, a more forcible motive, which exerts itself upon such occasions. It is reason, principle, conscience, the inhabitant of the breast, the man within, the great judge and arbiter of our conduct. It is he who, whenever we are about to act so as to affect the happiness of others, calls to us, with a voice capable of astonishing the most presumptuous of our passions, that we are but one of the multitude, in no respect better than any other in it; and that when we prefer ourselves so shamefully and so blindly to others, we become the proper objects of resentment, abhorrence, and execration. It is from him only that we learn the real littleness of ourselves, and of whatever relates to ourselves, and the natural misrepresentations of self-love can be corrected only by the eye of this impartial spectator. (TMS 3.3.4, 136–7)

Now this passage is not wholly anti-Humean. For example, Hume ("Of Commerce," EMPL, 253–5) and Smith agree that commerce is a proper subject of speculation. They also agree that the "man of humanity" can (but need not) be a moral exemplar (on Hume's treatment of humanity see Debes 2007; Hanley 2011; Taylor 2013). Finally, Hume and Smith agree that when it comes to distant strangers benevolence and humanity are motivationally fairly weak (Nieli 1986; Forman-Barzilai 2010) and involve moral posturing. These are non-trivial points of agreement.

Even so, among other things, Smith is criticizing five Humean doctrines here. First (and this has been explained by Fleischacker 2004), Smith is targeting an infamous passage in Hume:

> Where a passion is neither founded on false suppositions, nor chuses means insufficient for the end, the understanding can neither justify nor condemn it. 'Tis not contrary to reason to prefer the destruction of the whole world to the scratching of my finger. 'Tis not contrary to reason for me to chuse my total ruin, to prevent the least uneasiness of an Indian or person wholly unknown to me. (Treatise 2.3.3.6)

From context it is clear that Hume is not saying that it is reasonable (or rational) to prefer the destruction of the whole world to the scratching of one's finger; he is making a claim about the motivational power of reason here. But, as Fleischacker argues, for Smith it is not from affect, but from reason ("the stronger power"), that we resist the idea that we prefer the destruction of the whole world to the scratching of one's finger.

And this gets me to Smith's second criticism of Hume. Hume is notorious for claiming that "Reason is, and ought only to be the slave of the passions, and can never pretend to any other office than to serve and obey them" (2.3.3.4). Now behind Hume's claim is the view that according to Hume reason is not a so-called active principle (3.1.1.7). By contrast, "conscience" and a "sense of morals" are active principles according to Hume (3.1.1.10). An active principle is a "force or efficacy" (1.3.14.10). Interestingly enough, then, in Hume reason is by itself not a mental cause, while conscience *can* motivate actions. (See Cohon 2008 for a far more subtle reading of Hume's views on reason than I can provide here.)

Now in the long quote above, according to Smith reason *is* a so-called active principle. This is a second departure from Hume, and helps explain why for Smith reason can correct the sentiments even in the case of what our proper response to a very distant earthquake ought to be. A defender of Hume might object here that according to Hume "reason requires such an impartial conduct" (Treatise 3.3.1.18). Hume goes on to claim that

> our passions do not readily follow the determination of our judgment. This language will be easily understood, if we consider what we formerly said concerning that reason, which is able to oppose our passion; and which we have found to be nothing but a general calm determination of the passions, founded on some distant view or reflection.

Thus, Hume and Smith agree that reason can "oppose" or correct our passions. But in Hume reason is always itself a fairly feeble "calm determination," while in Smith "it is a stronger power, a more forcible motive." That is, the difference between Hume and Smith is best characterized as one of degree here, but it is non-trivial nevertheless, and this is emphasized by the two other differences.

Third, in Smith's system reason is often synonymous with "conscience" (and also "the inhabitant of the breast, the man within, the great judge and arbiter of our conduct," etc.), and this is a big departure from Hume. In Hume "reason" is largely restricted to being an inferential (non-formal) reckoning faculty (Owen 1999) that gives rise to representations (see also Cohon and Owen 1997). Yet, in Smith the operation of reason has clearly a more expanded, substantive moral domain. In the quote above Smith emphasizes that when it comes to our actions, which "affect the happiness of others," reason reminds us that "we are but one of the multitude, in no respect better than any other in it." Reason is a corrective here; it informs us that each of us ought to be counted equally.[10] This is why Maria Carrasco (2004) argues that in Smith "reason" is generally an instance of practical reason. Insofar as Smith is, as I argue in Chapter 8, a consequentialist in his evaluation of social institutions, this role of reason inclines him toward accepting equal consideration of everyone as a non-negotiable rational constraint.

In fact, Sarah Otten (2016) has called attention to the fact that when discussing Plato's moral psychology, Smith writes about reason as

> the judging faculty, the faculty which determines not only what are the proper means for attaining any end, but also what ends are fit to be pursued, and what degree of relative value we ought to put upon each. This faculty Plato called, as it is very properly called, reason, and considered it as what had a right to be the governing principle of the whole. (TMS 7.2.1.3, 267)

Here we need not assume that Smith agrees with Plato that reason is the governing principle of the soul, but he clearly does agree with Plato that reason is the "judging faculty."

---

[10] To be clear, it is not only reason that does so; it has been argued persuasively that Smith's analysis of civility also "presupposes an underlying moral equality between persons" (Boyd 2013: 453).

Fourth, as de Grouchy notes (LS, VI, 162), Smith insists that "reason is undoubtedly the source of the general rules of morality, and of all the moral judgments which we form by means of them" (TMS, 7.3.7.2, 320). That is to say, for Smith reason can be an *inventive* faculty, while for Hume it is primarily an inferential faculty. However, as de Grouchy reminds us, Smith goes on to deny that reason plays a role in the origin of all our moral judgments. (Smith relies on a distinction between direct moral judgments and judgments we make by applying moral rules.)

Neither Hume nor Smith explicitly discusses the nature and range of active principles very often in their moral psychology. But an important treatment occurs in material that Smith added to the final edition of TMS, where he explains that sympathy for one's children is "by nature" much more efficacious than sympathy for parents. The affections founded on the former (such as tenderness) are active principles (TMS 6.2.1.3, 219). Now for a proper understanding of Smith's larger philosophy this is very significant because it nicely illustrates the fact that for Smith sympathy is not just a judgment, but it can also be motivating. (See Montes 2004, who has refuted the claim promoted by the editors of the Glasgow edition of TMS that sympathy is entirely different from the motive to action!)

I conclude with a fifth difference. In the long quote above, Smith is targeting Hume's claim in the Second *Enquiry* that "humanity . . . alone is the foundation of morals, or any system of behavior" (EPM 9.6). According to Smith humanity is too "soft" a power! Thus, while Smith does not deny that Humean humanity has the right kind of formal features (that is, it is in principle equally available to everyone and provides identical judgments), it does not have the motivational pull for a morality worth having (Pack and Schliesser 2006).

Before I turn to Smith's explicit treatment of the natural and moral sentiments, and his moral theory more generally (sympathy, moral rules, social utility, impartial spectator, etc.), I first complete my introduction to his theory of the passions.

e. Natural Unexpected Passions: The Intellectual Sentiments

In this section I analyze Smith's treatment of the intellectual sentiments. I do so by distinguishing the generic content of original passions and intellectual sentiments. The aim of this section is to explain how Smith's account of the sentiments provides a framework for his epistemology and, more indirectly, his aesthetics and moral psychology.

Smith's Astronomy is devoted to the three so-called intellectual sentiments (Cropsey 1957: 43, n. 3 introduces this phrase): wonder, surprise, and admiration. Two of these (wonder and surprise) are paradigmatic, unexpected sentiments and, thus, lack proto-passions: "What is new and singular, excites that sentiment which, in strict propriety, is called Wonder; what is unexpected, Surprise;

and what is great or beautiful, Admiration" (Astronomy Intro.1, EPS 33; on the connection between grandeur and admiration, see Hume's EPM 7.16). Of course, this passage suggests that for Smith admiration is also ("beautiful") an aesthetic sentiment, not just an intellectual one (Valihora 2010: 141). Therefore, one of the intellectual sentiments is also properly aesthetic.

According to Smith, even full-blooded admiration requires an unexpected component: "an object with which we are quite familiar, and which we see every day, produces, though both great and beautiful, but a small effect upon us; because our admiration is not supported either by Wonder or by Surprise" (Astronomy Intro.6, EPS 34). In fact, wonder and surprise are not treated as emotions fitted to triggering objects. Smith is very explicit about this: "Surprise, therefore, is not to be regarded as an original emotion of a species distinct from all others. The violent and sudden change produced upon the mind, when an emotion of any kind is brought suddenly upon it, constitutes the whole nature of Surprise" (Astronomy 1.5, EPS 35). Thus, it turns out that in one sense surprise is parasitic on other emotions; it is, we might say, a "second-order passion. (This is not to be confused with Smith's "secondary passions," which "arise from the situation of love" [TMS 1.2.2.4, 33].) We would not feel surprised if we encountered something unexpected in placid manner. On Smith's view we need to be scared, elated, overjoyed (etc.) before we can feel surprised. Surprise is a "momentary emotion;" wonder, which is often quick on the heels of surprise, is generally the more enduring passion (Astronomy 2.8, EPS 41).

As commentators have noted, Smith identifies two kinds of wonder. Recall Smith's description of the pleasing activity of classifying ideas that lead into a natural taxonomy (cf. Astronomy 2.1–2, EPS 37–8). Wonder precedes the act of classification and is triggered by encountering "something quite new and singular" (Astronomy 2.3, EPS 39). The inability to group the new idea (itself produced by or copied from the triggering object) produces a whole characteristic symptomology:

> The imagination and memory exert themselves to no purpose, and in vain look around all their classes of ideas in order to find one under which it may be arranged. They fluctuate to no purpose from thought to thought, and we remain still uncertain and undetermined where to place it, or what to think of it. It is this fluctuation and vain recollection, together with the emotion or movement of the spirits that they excite, which constitute the sentiment properly called Wonder, and which occasion that staring, and sometimes that rolling of the eyes, that suspension of the breath, and that swelling of the heart, which we may all observe, both in ourselves and others, when wondering at some new object, and which are the natural symptoms of uncertain and undetermined thought. (Astronomy 2.3, EPS 39)

Recall that the structure of the content of a natural passion is something like this: <a desire, an idea of the triggering object>. By contrast, the content of the first species of wonder is more like this: <a painful uncertainty, lack of filling-location in the natural taxonomy (for the idea of the triggering object)>.[11] Moreover, such wonder produces a quite vehement physiologic and behavioral response. Unlike most of the natural sentiments, which are fitted toward highly specific triggering objects, the intellectual sentiments are observer-relative:

> The same orders of succession, which to one set of men seem quite
> according to the natural course of things, and such as require no inter-
> mediate events to join them, shall to another appear altogether inco-
> herent and disjointed, unless some such events be supposed: and this
> for no other reason, but because such orders of succession are familiar
> to the one, and strange to the other. (Astronomy 2.11, EPS 44)

The expert and untrained eye do not discern the same "things," and consequently have different occasions for wonder (see also Astronomy 2.2, EPS 38).

Smith's treatment of this first kind of wonder is reminiscent of Spinoza's account in the *Ethics* (especially E3P52 demonstration and scholium).[12] Both Smith and Spinoza treat wonder (*Admiratio*) as something that occurs by way of the imagination. In particular, when a mental object stands in isolation from other such objects it produces a painful feeling.[13]

Smith is aware that the Latin *Admiratio* can refer to both wonder and admira-tion, but English allows greater precision: "Wonder, Surprise, and Admiration, are

[11] Not all wonder is painful according to Smith. Sympathetically mediated wonder may be pleasing (TMS 1.1.2.2, 14) as is the wonder we feel at the representational exactitude in painting and sculpture (Imitative Arts 1.16, EPS 185). This seems to be the norm in Hume: "The passion of surprise and won-der, arising from miracles, being an agreeable emotion, gives a sensible tendency towards the belief of those events, from which it is derived" (EHU 10.16; see also Treatise 1.3.10.4).

[12] "PROP. LII. If we have previously seen an object together with others, or we imagine it has noth-ing what is common in many things, we shall not consider it so long as one which we imagine to have something singular.

Demonstration: As soon as we imagine an object we have seen with others, we shall immediately recollect the others (E2p18 and E2P18S), and so from considering one we immediately pass to consid-ering another. And the reasoning is the same concerning the object we imagine to have nothing what is common to many things. For imagining that is supposing that we consider nothing in it but what we have seen before with others.

But when we suppose that we imagine in an object something singular, which we have never seen before, we are only saying that when the mind considers that object, it has nothing in itself which it is led to consider from considering that. And so it is determined to consider only that. Therefore, if we have seen, and so on, Q.E.D.

Note.—This affection of the mind, or this imagination of a singular thing, insofar as it is alone in the mind, is called wonder [*admiratio*]; but if it is aroused by an object we fear, it is called consternation, because wonder at an evil keeps a man so suspended in considering it that he cannot think of other things by which he could avoid that evil." I am quoting Spinoza in the standard format by book and proposition.

[13] As Spinoza puts it in his treatment of the individual passions, *Admiratio est rei alicuius imaginatio, in qua mens defixa propterea manet, quia haec singularis imaginatio nullam cum reliquis habet connexionem* (E3p52S, Aff. Def. 4).

words which, though often confounded, denote, in our language, sentiments that are indeed allied, but that are in some respects different also, and distinct from one another" (Intro.1, EPS 33). Thus, Smith might be taken to innovate away from Spinoza (where *Admiratio* tends to be used in both senses).[14]

In ordinary circumstances, when we can exhibit what I have called environmental rationality, our mental anticipations run ahead of the world (cf. Astronomy 2.7, 41, quoted in Section c above). But sometimes we encounter an unusual order among the relations of objects (none of which needs to be itself unusual). This will also trigger a second species of wonder:

> [s]uch is the nature of this second species of Wonder, which arises from an unusual succession of things. The stop which is thereby given to the career of the imagination, the difficulty which it finds in passing along such disjointed objects, and the feeling of something like a gap or interval betwixt them, constitute the whole essence of this emotion." (Astronomy 2.9, EPS 42)

Presumably, the same kind of vehement (and painful) somatic response occurs on occasion of the second kind of wonder as it does in the first kind of wonder, but Smith is silent about this.

Structurally, Smithian wonder is very similar to fear, so much so that Smith takes Milton to task for confusing the two (Astronomy Intro.5, EPS 33)! According to Smith fear "is a passion derived altogether from the imagination, which represents, with an uncertainty and fluctuation that increases our anxiety, not what we really feel, but what we may hereafter possibly suffer" (TMS 1.2.1.9, 30). The uncertainty and fluctuation of the train of the imagination is common to wonder and fear.

There seem to be four main differences between wonder and fear. First, fear has an orientation toward the future built into the content of the passion; we anticipate unpleasant consequences, but because we recoil from these the imagination vacillates. Wonder itself (as opposed to the action it may guide) need not be so oriented toward the future. Second, the somatic consequences of fear are, in principle, less vehement than those accompanying strong wonder. This is so because, third, when we fear we tend to foresee a particular danger; we are not confronted

---

[14] Smithian admiration is closely connected to Spinozistic devotion (*Devotio est amor erga eum, quem admiramur.*) Smith never mentions Spinoza. Smith was familiar with four and arguably five authors/works that engage with Spinoza in serious fashion: Bayle (he owned his *Dictionary*; Berry 2013: 90); Maclaurin (Astronomy 4.58, 90); Clarke (TMS 7.1.3, 265ff); Diderot and the Encyclopedia project (Edinburgh Review 5–6, EPS 245–246). Below I present very suggestive evidence he was familiar with Toland's *Letters to Serena*. For recent work on Hume and Spinoza, see Della Rocca 2014. For Smith and Spinoza, see Hill and Montag 2014. All that we can say with confidence is that Smith departs from Hume in interesting ways that bring him surprisingly close to Spinoza.

with an unnamed/unclassified void (Astronomy 1.4, EPS 35). Fourth, on Smith's view fear becomes self-reinforcing when in the context of political uncertainty (or worse) it guides explanation of natural events. Thus, the uncertainty due to a lack of justice can generate direct political fears and indirect religious fears, which in turn generate more uncertainty (Astronomy 3.1, EPS 48). The foundation of the rule of law is the social remedy that reduces uncertainty; wonder, by contrast, is, in the right political and institutional circumstances, in principle a self-correcting passion.

The first kind of wonder leads to an expansion of the natural taxonomy correcting the manifest image. In addition, the second kind of wonder leads to an imaginative search for "intermediate, though invisible, events, which succeed each other in a train similar to that in which the imagination has been accustomed to move, and which link together those two disjointed appearances." The invisible mechanism (or "chain") is itself patterned on the disrupted visible pattern of objects. Therefore, when we feel wonder we invent invisible analogies to the visible world in order to remove the painful mental vacillation. This is "the only means by which the imagination can fill up this interval, is the only bridge which, if one may say so, can smooth its passage from the one object to the other" (Astronomy 2.8, EPS 42). Of course, in practice introducing an invisible mechanism may not entirely satisfy the imagination (which according to Smith is looking for a stable, enduring, and recurring object to fill in the gap): "even the vague hypotheses of Des Cartes, and the yet more indetermined notions of Aristotle, have, with their followers, contributed to give some coherence to the appearances of nature, and might diminish, though they could not destroy, their Wonder" (Astronomy 2.9, EPS 43). Thus, systematic explanations that provide the chains that fill the gaps in the imagination reduce wonder, and in their remainder (anticipating Herschell 1830[15] and Mill's [1843] method of difference) also encourage (among other incentives) the ongoing effort at improving explanations.

Thus, in accord with tradition going back to Aristotle and Plato, Smith argues that natural inquiry and accordingly expanded taxonomies develop in order to get rid of the painful feeling of wonder. This, in turn, allows him to define "philosophy," which just "is the science of the connecting principles of nature" (Astronomy 2.12, EPS 45). Recall from Section a of Chapter 1 that a "system" has coherent and connected explanatory principles. Therefore, we can say that for Smith, starting from the manifest image, philosophy is the impulse toward systematicity that results in systems of thought that, in turn, may be made to cohere in (a) scientific image(s).[16] As we will see in Chapter 11, according to Smith, there is a regular pattern of development and revolution within and among these systems.

---

[15] Herschell (1830: 12) explicitly refers to Smith's definition of a philosopher from WN.

[16] It does not follow that this is all there is to philosophy as Smith understands it.

Here Smith leaves ambiguous, first, when the "experience that common obser-vation can acquire" (Astronomy 2.12, EPS 45), which grounds our natural tax-onomy, shades into a philosophical (or scientific) taxonomy, and, second, when the "amazement," "terror, and consternation" that is at the root of the polytheis-tic account of "intelligent, though invisible causes" (Astronomy 3.1–2, EPS 48–9) that fill in the gaps of nature shades into "Philosophy," which

> by representing the invisible chains which bind together all these dis-jointed objects, endeavours to introduce order into this chaos of jarring and discordant appearances, to allay this tumult of the imagination, and to restore it, when it surveys the great revolutions of the universe, to that tone of tranquility [*sic*] and composure, which is both most agreea-ble in itself, and most suitable to its nature. (Astronomy 2.12, EPS 45–6.

Thus, we can describe the natural life cycle of unexpected, natural passions (wonder and surprise) as follows:

(i)   A passion is excited by either an unexpected object or by a disruption to our regular train of thought;
(ii) Depending on our expectations we may feel, say, joy (sadness) and then surprise;
(iii) As our surprise subsides, the imagination vacillates because it cannot find a filling-location in the natural taxonomy for the idea of the triggering object; and (iii*) we express this by way of "staring, and sometimes . . . rolling of the eyes . . . suspension of the breath, and . . . swelling of the heart";
(iv) The excited wonder will motivate either an expansion of our taxonomy or a search for the invisible chains that bind together all the disjointed objects.

What this natural history reveals is that while the fundamental aim of inquiry may be mental repose or tranquility, Smith conceives of the intellectual sentiments as being action-oriented; they stimulate more inquiry or taxonomic revision. (In Chapter 11, I'll argue that for Smith further revision to theory or taxonomy is always a possibility.)

More important, it follows from Smith's position that all inquiry can, in prin-ciple, be a means toward changing how we conceive of environmental rationality; it is, after all, a response to noticeable deviations from the previous standard of judgments. In doing so, by way of scientific inquiry, experts train up and develop a new standard of judgment about what is reasonable in a context expanded from ordinary, or "common," life. The intellectual sentiments occur within the manifest image (and may have helped constitute it) but create the conditions of revision to the manifest image or the development of a more narrow scientific image as understood only by the experts. This entails that, in principle, sound judgment may track a moving target. It helps explain the common phenomenon that one's generation's firm, sound judgment comes to be experienced as mere artifice or prejudice in later generations.

f. Derived Passions

In this section I analyze the derived passions. I argue that an important difference between original and derived passions is that the structures of the life cycle and generic content of derived passions are potentially far more complicated than those characteristically found in original passions. To articulate these differences, I distinguish between "natural" and "social" objects. Original passions are triggered by and directed toward natural objects; derived passions are triggered by and, in part, directed at social objects, including other people. The natural versus social objects distinction is a *conceptual* distinction only introduced to clarify Smith's position because (a) it is quite likely, of course, that one and the same entity can be a natural and social object at the same time; (b) such feelings can be instantiated in the same human being because we can have "original passions" when we are the "person principally concerned" and we can have social passions when we are a "spectator" (TMS 1.1.3.1, 16).

Either way, Smith calls attention to the fact that derived passions can induce us to feel "elevated" or feel "cast down" (recall TMS 3.1.3, 110–1). Presumably this is accompanied by a certain valence (e.g., joy or increased power accompanying elevation, hurt or impotence accompanying being cast down.) The derived passions triggered by social objects make us view ourselves in terms of *relative position* toward others. The "position" is established by how *we* take *others* to judge *us* (recall "He will observe that mankind approve of some of them, and are disgusted by others" [TMS 3.1.3]). Obviously, depending on our character we may interpret what we "observe" in distinct ways. (Smith regularly calls attention to our self-deception; see TMS 3.4.5.) Hence, the content of a derived passion will include a threefold relation: <(i) some desire (aversion, joy), (ii) an idea of the triggering social object, (iii) our (empowering/impotent) sense of ourselves moving up or down in the estimation of an (internally) selected group of observers>.

Moreover, derived passions can cause new passions ("his desires and aversions . . . will now often become the causes of new desires and new aversions" [TMS 3.1.3, 111]). Therefore, social passions often induce second-order passions, which can themselves cause a whole chain of passions parasitic on each other (it is not at all clear that Smith thinks the iteration needs to end).

In Section a above of this chapter, I mentioned a hypothetical case in which the intensity of a felt passion and the intensity of its expression come apart. Such a possibility turns out to mark an important distinction in Smith's system:

> There are some passions which it is indecent to express very strongly, even upon those occasions, in which it is acknowledged that we cannot

avoid feeling them in the highest degree. And there are others of which the strongest expressions are upon many occasions extremely graceful, even though the passions themselves do not, perhaps, arise so necessarily. The first are those passions with which, for certain reasons, there is little or no sympathy: the second are those with which, for other reasons, there is the greatest. (TMS 1.2.Intro.2, 27)

This example is about derived passions because the expected sympathetic response(s) of others feature significantly in their content. Thus, not only are there strongly felt but barely expressed passions, which do not tend to generate sympathy (these are in Smith's terms "indecent" passions[17]), but there are also other, barely felt and strongly expressed passions that *do* tend to generate sympathy (Smith's "decent" passions).

We can now redescribe the etiologic life cycle of expected, social passions:

(0) Based on, say, habit, the imagination experiences an anticipatory idea of a triggering social object and a proto-passion suitable to it is excited;

(i) a passion is excited by its triggering social object;

(ii) (in the imagination) we feel some desire (aversion, joy), an idea of the triggering social object, and an (empowering/impotent) sense of ourselves moving up or down in the estimation of an (internally) selected group of observers; and (ii+) we express this by way of characteristic facial and bodily movements; but (ii*) the relationship between (ii+) and (ii*) can be modified in light of the norms that govern expected social responses.

(iii) if the passion is expected and calm, it then dissipates without much further notice. Presumably, if a passion is not so calm as to dissipate without much notice and not so strong as to lead to paralysis or worse, it will be followed by either

(iv) an open-ended number of second-order passions (all of which can instantiate the (0–ii*) cycle), which eventually will result either in an expected and calm passion, or

(v) the excited social passion will motivate some behavior to or away from the triggering object.

From the vantage point of Smith's larger social theory, the crucial items in this life cycle are (ii) and (ii*). These two both make references to *reliable expectations* about responses by others.

Some might object that I am making much of relatively few passages in TMS. I plead guilty to the charge, but, first, the distinction between original and social

---

[17] Here's an instance where Smith's culturally loaded normative judgment is evident, yet even if not shared anymore this does not undermine the underlying logic of the analysis of Smith's account of the passions.

passion is presupposed in a passage on the Imitative Arts: "Whatever we feel from instrumental Music is an original, and not a sympathetic feeling: it is our own gaiety, sedateness, or melancholy; not the reflected disposition of another person" (Imitative Arts 2.22; EPS 198; cf. Chandler 2013: 135). A sympathetic feeling presupposes an internalized expectation about how we expect others to behave under normal conditions (that is, it is environmentally rational). Thus, second, expected social passions are governed by norms; they are *cultivated* sentiments. Smith's favored way of calling such cultivated, social passions is "moral sentiments." In the next chapter, I offer a detailed analysis of the relationship between the natural and moral sentiments. Here I just note that I have shown that for Smith the natural sentiments are not normative, while the moral sentiments are (anticipating Mill in Chapter 3 of *Of Liberty*; see Mill 1864: 108). In the next chapter I say more about the role of the natural sentiments in Smith's system, and I explain how Smith accounts for the transition between natural and moral sentiments.

But I end this chapter on Smithian passions by calling attention to Smith's discussion of a non-trivial derived, (a fifth kind) strong passion:

> The great source of both the misery and disorders of human life, seems to arise from over-rating the difference between one permanent situation and another. Avarice over-rates the difference between poverty and riches: ambition, that between a private and a public station: vainglory, that between obscurity and extensive reputation. The person under the influence of any of those extravagant passions, is not only miserable in his actual situation, but is often disposed to disturb the peace of society, in order to arrive at that which he so foolishly admires. (TMS 3.3.31, 149)

Here it looks as if some strong passions are a consequence of a mismatch between the feeling and its triggering object; perhaps because there are no "natural" triggering objects for these derived passions or, more likely, we imagine the existence of triggering objections. Crucially, this mismatch generates political disturbances. For Smith man is a social animal and this animal is governed by emotions that are rarely fitted to, or in harmony with, the present social order. It is, thus, misleading to treat Smith as the theorist who assumes or naturally expects social harmony (cf. Force 2003: 80; Fitzgibbons 1995: 140).

From Natural Sentiments to General Rules and Moral Sentiments

> But though man is thus employed to alter that distribution of things which natural events would make, if left to themselves; though, like the gods of the poets, he is perpetually interposing, by extraordinary means, in favour of virtue, and in opposition to vice, and, like them, endeavours to turn away the arrow that is aimed at the head of the righteous, but to accelerate the sword of destruction that is lifted up against the wicked; yet he is by no means able to render the fortune of either quite suitable to his own sentiments and wishes. The natural course of things cannot be entirely controlled by the impotent endeavours of man: the current is too rapid and too strong for him to stop it; and though the rules which direct it appear to have been established for the wisest and best purposes, they sometimes produce effects which shock all his natural sentiments.
>
> —TMS 3.5.10, *168*

This chapter is devoted to explaining the moral significance of what Smith calls the "natural sentiments." I illustrate the significance of the natural sentiments by their role in extended case studies: they help us understand Smith's criticism of Hume's account of the origin and morality of justice. In doing so I also explain the difference between natural sentiments and moral sentiments, and why despite the undeniable significance of feelings in his moral theory, Smith should not be considered a moral sense theorist.

a. Natural Sentiments

> Smith observed "man in nature and in society without prejudices."
> —Sophie de Grouchy (LS, IV)

In TMS Smith deploys a systematic distinction between natural and moral sentiments. In a landmark (2004) article by Maria Carrasco the importance of the distinction was first noted. It has greatly influenced my understanding, but in what follows I tend to emphasize different aspects of the distinction than she does.

Smith does not alert the reader to the distinction between natural and moral sentiments. In fact, the first explicit mention of the phrase "natural sentiments" is only in Part 2 of TMS (in a heavily reworked passage throughout the editions):

> All our natural sentiments [of untaught nature but of an artificial refine- ment of reason and philosophy our untaught, natural sentiments, all] prompt us to believe, that as perfect virtue is supposed necessarily to appear to the Deity, as it does to us, for its own sake, and without any further view, the natural and proper object of love and reward, so must vice, of hatred and punishment. (TMS 2.2.3, 91)

The bracketed text refers to the third, fourth, and fifth editions of TMS, where Smith helpfully explains that natural sentiments are the untaught (that is, uncul- tivated) original passions. These natural sentiments are directed toward the idea of the triggering object (virtue or vice) and have a fitting accompanying feeling (love/desire to see rewarded and hatred/desire for punishment).

Even though such natural sentiments are in some attenuated sense social passions (they pertain to situations involving more than one person), the con- tent of these sentiments makes no reference to the estimation of an (internally) selected group of observers. Even our "belief" in the response of the Deity is "for its own sake." Thus, in Smith there is a distinction between the uncultivated feel- ings humans "naturally" possess (that is, natural sentiments) and the cultivated feelings humans acquire from local social institutions or practices that accultur- ate them (that is, moral sentiments). Only the moral sentiments involve an esti- mation of the expected responses of an internally represented, select group of observers. In the bracketed passage Smith appears to have toyed with the idea that these natural sentiments are the psychological causes of our belief in a God that rewards and punishes. In this chapter I ignore the theological and political significance of Smith's naturalistic explanation of our belief in such a God.

Smith's distinction between natural and moral sentiments does important work in his moral philosophy. I offer an extended example to illuminate this. I show how an appeal to the natural sentiments informs Smith's response to Hume's account of the approval of justice.

i. Smith's Criticisms of Hume's Account of Property

To understand Smith's response to Hume, I offer an extended, albeit incomplete, summary of Hume's account of the origin and approval of justice.[1] For Hume the rule of law is based upon "convention." He presupposes "a sense of common

---

[1] This section draws on work that I first presented with Spencer Pack in Pack and Schliesser (2006).

interest; which sense each man feels in his own breast, which he remarks in his fellows, and which carries him, in concurrence with others, into a general plan or system of actions, which tends to public utility . . . in this sense, justice arises from human convention" (EPM Appendix 3.7). Moreover, "When men have found by experience, that 'tis impossible to subsist without society, and that 'tis impossible to maintain society, while they give free course to their appetites: so urgent an interest quickly restrains their actions, and imposes an obligation to observe those rules, which we call the *laws of justice*" (Treatise 3.2.11.4, emphasis in original). The laws of justice should be respected because they serve the needs of society and, thereby, the agents that constitute it.

Hume lists three "inconveniences, which proceed from the concurrence of certain qualities of the human mind with the situation of external objects," that are ultimately addressed by the human institution of the rule of law: (i) our "limited generosity" or "selfish" nature; (ii) the mobility of external goods; and (iii) these goods' relative "scarcity in comparison of" our "wants and desires" (Treatise 3.2.2.16; 3.2.2.18). As he puts it in the Second *Enquiry*: "[W]herever any benefit is bestowed by nature in an unlimited abundance, we leave it always in common among the whole human race, and make no subdivisions of right and property" (EPM 3.1.4). These three conditions work together to be inconvenient because, according to Hume, "avidity" is an "insatiable, perpetual, universal" part of human nature, so that we go unsatisfied; "there scarce is any one, who is not actuated by it." This is the main passion that is "directly destructive of society" (Treatise 3.2.2.12; for a different view of avarice, see "Of Avarice" in EMPL). It appears that Hume accepts, following Locke (Education, §110), that this passion is innate. For example, at Treatise 3.2.5.9, Hume talks about the "natural and inherent principles and passions of human nature; and as these passions and principles are inalterable." Hume's position contrasts, in advance, with Rousseau's claim in the *Second Discourse* that such avidity is only acquired as one of the negative effects of civilization.

Somewhat surprisingly, at first sight, it seems as if Hume's "inconveniences" and his insistence that "the opposite passions of men impel them in contrary directions" (3.2.2.11) have considerable affinity with Hobbes's account, especially the insistence on self-interested human nature.

Furthermore, Hume seems to echo one of the more striking moments in Hobbes when he asserts that justice is the sense that "all the members of the society express to one another, and which induces them to regulate their conduct by certain rules" (3.2.2.10). This is because, in *Leviathan*, the commonwealth is, when not founded through conquest, instituted by a covenant "of every man with every man . . . as if every man should say to every man, I Authorise and give up my Right of Governing my selfe, to this Man, or to this Assembly of men" (II.17; see also II.18).[2] Both thinkers seem to be claiming that the rules of justice should

---

[2] I refer to *Leviathan* by chapter and paragraph numbers in Curley's edition.

be understood, or conceptualized, as originating at a particular moment in time when all the potential members of a society say something to all the other members about their wish to be ruled by law (cf. History 2.106).

However, Hume's descriptions of the events leading to the origins of justice sit uneasily with some of his other more "evolutionary" claims in the same paragraph and elsewhere in the Treatise (for more on this tension in Hume see Haakonssen 1981: 17–8). For example, "the rule concerning the stability of possession," Hume writes, "arises gradually, and acquires force by a slow progression" (3.2.2.10, 315). In the same paragraph, Hume also goes on to describe, in a manner reminiscent of Mandeville (Rosenberg 1963; Hayek 1967; C. Smith 2006, 2009), the development of languages, and (later in human and societal evolution) money as a universal equivalent in the exchange of commodities as arising gradually.

Moreover, the evolutionary picture is supported by Hume's understanding of the psychology of "rude and savage men"; they are not capable of dreaming up the "idea of justice" (Treatise 3.2.2.7). Justice is, then, for Hume a distinct intellectual achievement of mankind that, in turn, is the pre-condition for civilization. Hume's story makes clear what the conditions for this achievement are.

I focus only on two connected, Humean arguments in his criticism of the very idea that justice has its origin in a simple promise or contract. While Hume admits that even "savage and uncultivated" people can be made sensible of the interest in keeping promises (Treatise 3.2.5.11), he claims, anticipating Nietzsche in the second essay of Zur Genealogie der Moral, that a "promise . . . is naturally [Hume means here in the state of nature] something altogether unintelligible" (3.2.5.4). Note, again, Hume's insistence that the "savage" will not understand something that the contract tradition ascribes to it. Moreover, for Hume, "promises have no force, antecedent to human conventions" (Treatise 3.2.5.7). The condition of justice, which creates some stable property relations, and thus an interest in keeping promises, is—to introduce a Kantian-sounding phrase—a *social condition of the possibility* for the giving of promises (Treatise 3.2.5.8–10). That is, for Hume promises first arise only when there is an interest in keeping them.[3] As he explains in the Second *Enquiry*, "the rules of equity and justice . . . owe their origin and existence to that utility, which results to the public from their strict and regular observance" (EPM 3.12). Humean conventions are necessary in the same way as the historical-causal mechanism that Smith relies on in deriving nomological outcomes from—persistently triggered and expressed—propensities that are themselves normological in Smithian social explanations (described in Section a of Chapter 2).

For Hume it is our self-interest that is the prime cause of the origin of the convention of law in conditions of limited benevolence and scarcity. It is only by "establishing the rule for the stability of the possession, that this passion restrains

---

[3] Hume's claim is a conceptual one; Hume's treatment echoes Spinoza's argument directed against Hobbes's position in Chapter 16 of the *Theologico-Political Treatise*.

itself" (Treatise 3.2.2.14). Thus, justice comes into being to defend property rights (especially external goods); as Hume writes, "the origin of justice explains that of property" (3.2.2.11). Hume's summary in the Second *Enquiry* is quite clear:

> Few enjoyments are given us from the open and liberal hand of nature; by art, labour, and industry we can extract them in great abundance. Hence the ideas of property become necessary in all civil society: Hence justice derives its usefulness to the public: And hence alone arises its merit and moral obligation. (EPM 3.13; SBN 188; in Chapter 10, I'll discuss how Smith's invisible hand of TMS develops Hume's observation of the open and liberal hand here.)

Thus, Hume insists that the moral obligation that justice can command is also derived from its utility to society. He explains in the Treatise that after the interest in the law is "establish'd and acknowledge'd, the sense of morality in the observance of these rules follows naturally, and of itself; tho' 'tis certain, that it is also augmented by a new artifice, and that the public instructions of politicians, and the private education of parents, contribute" to a sense of duty involved in observing property rights (Treatise 3.2.6.11).[4] Moreover, it is a good thing that there is education in the morality of justice because, as Hume notes in a different context, many individual instances of justice (say, returning some stolen food from a poor man to a miser) may appear quite "cruel" (Treatise 3.2.1.13–4). This sense of morality is supported by the "pleasure" we receive "from the view of such actions as tend to the peace of society, and an uneasiness from such as are contrary to it" (Treatise 3.2.6.11; see also EPM Chapter 5). While Hume admits that the establishment of a right to property involves the use of some reason—after all, it involves a gradually evolving recognition among individuals through "ballancing the account" (Treatise 3.2.2.22) of a "general sense of common interest" (3.2.2.10, see also 3.2.2.22)—it is also founded on a pleasurable sentiment.

To sum up Hume's views: he distinguishes among (1) nature, which creates us wanting more than is provided naturally, (2) reason, which, however weakly and slowly, allows us to discover over time with others, and (3) conventions that enable us, by harnessing our interest, to overcome some of the limitations of nature. For Hume, the origin of and continuing adherence to justice, as "a whole plan or scheme" (Treatise 3.2.2.22), are founded on its perceived utility to society as well as the pleasure this brings us. The utility consists mainly in the "peace and order" it establishes in society (3.2.2.22, 319; recall also 3.2.2.14, 316). To put this in Smith's terms, the "love of system" is in Hume (cf. "a whole plan or scheme") part of the feeling that ensures our adherence to justice.

---

[4] Hume is here critical of Mandeville's position in the *Fable*, which ascribes to "dexterous management of a skilful politician" some role in setting up the institution of justice (not just a role in the maintenance of the institution).

By contrast, Smith explicitly and repeatedly argues the claim that for a proper explanation of the origin of justice, we cannot point to its utility (Raphael 1972). As Smith writes, "it is seldom this consideration which first animates us" against "licentious practices." All men, "even the most stupid and unthinking, abhor fraud, perfidy, and injustice, and delight to see them punished. But few men have reflected upon the necessity of justice to the existence of society, how obvious soever that necessity may appear to be" (TMS 2.2.3.9, 89). In fact, Smith devotes the whole of Part Four of TMS to a respectful criticism of Hume's views, which he thinks more suitable to "men of reflection and speculation" (TMS 4.2.12, 192) rather than people in a purportedly, pre–law-governed, savage situation.

On Smith's view, although we often employ both efficient and final causes in our description of the phenomena of nature, and it is often quite natural to do so, we (moderns) know we can account for them with efficient causes. When we contemplate human affairs, however, we find it much more difficult to distinguish between efficient and final causation. Hume's picture, while the product of "a refined and enlightened reason," is erroneous because it imputes to reason "the sentiments and actions by which we advance those ends" that are really the product of "natural principles" (TMS 2.2.3.5, 87). By pointing to "utility" as the explanation of the origin of justice, Hume has conflated final and efficient causes! Of course, from Hume's early (July 1739) letter to Hutcheson, Smith's teacher, onward, Hume was a fierce critic of final causes: "I cannot agree to your sense of *Natural*. Tis founded on final causes, which is a Consideration, that appears to me pretty uncertain & unphilosophical" (*Letters* 1, p. 33). Smith turns the tables on his friend by deploying the same kind of argument that Hume had used against Smith's teacher, Hutcheson. Note that Smith does so without vindicating final causes as such.[5]

Smith's main complaint against Hume is that the perception of utility is a secondary consideration that may enhance and enliven the feeling that gives rise to the moral sentiment; the perception of utility is not the "first or principal source" of the emotion that produces the moral sentiment. It is a contingent fact of nature that the useful and the virtuous can coincide (TMS 4.2.3, 188). Nevertheless, Smith maintains that the "sentiment of approbation always involves in it a sense of propriety quite distinct from the perception of utility" (TMS 4.2.5, 188). According to Smith we approve of an action not because we find it useful to society, but because we judge it right. In contradistinction to Hume, Smith writes: "It seems impossible that the approbation of virtue should be a sentiment of the same kind with that by which we approve of a convenient and well-contrived building; or that we

---

[5] At TMS 2.2.3.5, 87, Smith allows that human aims and mental intentions can be understood as final causes that help explain individual human actions. But it does not follow from this that Smith allows either general final causes (that govern providence as such) or particular final causes (i.e., miracles). As we have seen, Smith's account of the ends of general providence is extremely thin: self-preservation and propagation of the species (TMS 2.1.5.10, 77-8; for an alternative to Smith on final causes, cf. Kleer 1995).

should have no other reason for praising a man than that for which we commend a chest of drawers" (TMS 4.2.4, 188). Thus, for Smith social norms arise for considerations that have little to do with utility. ('Utility' here clearly does not mean what later Bentham and Mill meant by it.) Of course, once such utility is widely felt and perceived, the institution of justice may become further entrenched in the manner accounted for by Smithian social explanation.

Smith criticizes Hume's claim that our approval of justice is originally derived from our appreciation of the social institution's utility. This is the wrong kind of sensation. The crucial argument in favor of Smith's alternative source is this:

> [S]o when a single man is injured, or destroyed, we demand the punishment of the wrong that has been done to him, not so much from a concern for the general interest of society, as from a concern for that very individual who has been injured. It is to be observed, however, that this concern does not necessarily include in it any degree of those exquisite sentiments which are commonly called love, esteem, and affection, and by which we distinguish our particular friends and acquaintance. The concern which is requisite for this, is no more than the general fellow–feeling which we have with every man merely because he is our fellow-creature. We enter into the resentment even of an odious person, when he is injured by those to whom he has given no provocation. Our disapprobation of his ordinary character and conduct does not in this case altogether prevent our fellow-feeling with his natural indignation; though with those who are not either extremely candid, or who have not been accustomed to correct and regulate their natural sentiments by general rules, it is very apt to damp it. (TMS 2.2.3.10, 89–90)

Smith claims that we naturally sympathize (from common humanity) even with the "natural" indignation of (an unfairly) injured odious character. It is the "immediate and instinctive approbation of the very application [of punishment] which is most proper to attain [the welfare and preservation of society]" (TMS 2.1.5.10, 77; on the role of resentment in Smith's moral philosophy, see also Campbell 1971: 186–204). This sympathetic resentment is the right kind of sentiment to do the explanatory job Smith has set himself—this is discerned by de Grouchy's observation that "our moral sentiments originated in natural and unthinking sympathy for others' suffering" (LS, VI).

Smith, thus, avoids offering (i) too abstract a sentiment (e.g., Humean "utility;" "general interest of society"); (ii) too moralized a sentiment (e.g., love of virtue); or (iii) too "exquisite" a sentiment (love, esteem, and affection). The first cannot ground an institution whose fruits can only be discerned after its establishment; the second (and sometimes the first, too) presupposes (viz. justice) what it is trying to explain; the third sentiment ties us to particular people but does not provide us the right sort of social glue for enlarged societies. (See also Hanley 2014.) Smith's position does not require that we always enter into the proper resentment of an odious to us person. He is calling attention to a disposition that can originate a norm and maintain it once the norm is off the ground. It is, thus, quite possible that before the norm had been established the expression of the disposition, while instinctive, was less regular and frequent (or firm) than after its establishment.

We have seen that Smith lists resentment among the original passions (recall its inclusion among "jealousy, fear, and resentment" [TMS 7.3.3.9, 323]). According to Smith there is nothing especially human about resentment; "all animals" are also capable of "resentment and gratitude" (TMS 2.3.1.1, 94). Even if we recognize some exaggeration in Smith's rhetoric, we should recognize that for Smith, what we may label "natural resentment" seems "to have been given us by nature for defence, and for defence only" (TMS 2.2.1.4, 79). Our natural resentment makes possible, even prior to the establishment of the rule of law, our sympathetic desire for retaliation, which "seems to be the great law which is dictated to us by Nature" (2.2.1.10, 82), and this sentiment undergirds later systems of justice. Thus, according to Smith,

> In order to enforce the observation of justice, therefore, Nature has implanted in the human breast that consciousness of ill-desert, those terrors of merited punishment which attend upon its violation, as the great safe-guards of the association of mankind, to protect the weak, to curb the violent, and to chastise the guilty. (TMS 2.2.3.4, 86)

In these passages Smith asserts that "consciousness of ill-desert" has been put by nature not in our brain or in our reason, but in our breast. While Smith hedges his bets a bit (he uses repeated "seems"), this suggests that he considers resentment and our occasional desire for retaliation an innate or natural passion (see, also, Pack 1997: 128–30). This is compatible with the view expressed in WN, where resentment is already present in a hunting society, the earliest stage of development (WN V.i.b.2, 709). Of course, in practice resentment can in some circumstances be "generous and noble" (TMS 1.2.3.8, 38), but it can also be bad; the effects of resentment need to be *restrained* by justice or otherwise society will perish (TMS 2.2.3.3, 86; for a development of the political significance of this fact see also Schwarze & Scott 2015). So there is no doubt that for Smith the natural passion can be corrupted in society such that the institution that is built on it may be required to check it (this is clearly indebted to Hume's account of justice).

But for Smith's account to work we must also have an original propensity for the "general fellow-feeling which we have with every human being merely because he is our fellow-creature." In TMS Smith is silent about the origin of this propensity, and it may seem that Smith's account awaits something like Darwin's position:

> These sensations were first developed, in order that those animals would profit by living in society . . . With respect to the origin . . . of the

social instincts, we know not the steps by which they have gained; but we may infer that it has been to a large extent through natural selection. (*Descent*, Darwin 2004: 128–9)

However, Smith insists that we have the capacity to feel "with every man merely because he is our fellow-creature." Strikingly enough, Smith does not rest the capacity on the recognition of our fellow humanity or species; presumably that idea of humanity or species would be too "metaphysical" a thought only possible *after* the development of society (recall Languages in Section b of Chapter 2). Smith agrees with Hume that resentment arises from an original instinct (see also Laing 1926 on Hume on instinct).[6] But Hume limits its presence to those who have a "warm concern for the interests of our species" (EPM 5.2.39). Given that some fellow-feeling is required to ground the institution of justice, Smith needs a more diffuse and less "metaphysical" and less "species-ist" feeling for his account not to be circular. In fact, there is good textual evidence that Smith's account can be saved from such circularity. For Smith writes,

fellow-feeling which Nature has, for the wisest purposes, implanted in man, not only towards all other men, but (though no doubt in a much weaker degree) towards all other animals. Having destined him to be the governing animal in this little world, it seems to have been her benevolent intention to inspire him with some degree of respect, even for the meanest and weakest of his subjects. (External Senses 6, EPS 136)

Here Smith offers a natural mechanism by which mankind can implement the command to "have dominion over the fish of the sea, and over the fowl of the air, and over every living thing that moveth upon the earth" (Genesis 1:28).

Therefore, our natural sympathetic resentment is itself the combination of two original passions, (i) a very broad capacity for fellow feeling with other creatures and (ii) natural resentment at harms done to them. Steve Darwall (2006: 84) has rightly emphasized that for Smith resentment is a call for respect, even for other living things. As Smith writes, the object of resentment is

chiefly intent upon, is not so much to make our enemy feel pain in his turn, as . . . to make him sensible that the person whom he injured did not deserve to be treated in that manner. What chiefly enrages us

---

[6] I thank James Hill for calling my attention to Laing. I found Hill's unpublished work on Hume on instinct very useful.

against the man who injures or insults us, is the little account which he
seems to make of us. (TMS 2.3.1.5, 95–6)

It is, thus, intimately linked with Smith's moral egalitarianism among humans.
Smith does not challenge the idea that mankind has dominion over animals. Even
so, it follows from Smith's position that if we are capable of recognizing injuries
done to animals, we can also feel appropriate sympathetic resentment on their
behalf and, thus, the institution of justice can, at least partially, be extended to
them. After all,

> animals are not only the causes of pleasure and pain, but are also capa-
> ble of feeling those sensations, they are still far from being complete
> and perfect objects, either of gratitude or resentment; and those pas-
> sions still feel, that there is something wanting to their entire gratifica-
> tion." (TMS 2.3.1.4, 95)

This is why it is legitimate in Smith's view to punish and reward animals sometimes, and presumably to prevent "brutality" to animals (TMS 2.3.1.4, 95; for
more work on Smith's environmental ethics along similar lines, see Frierson
2006a, 2006b).

One significant feature of this is that on Smith's view an individual need not
even be capable of reason in order to be the proper recipient of respect. A person
might sometimes influence another person's (or animal's) actions in a way that
treats the second person with respect, without ever presenting her with imper-
sonal considerations that she might evaluate for himself and choose to treat as
reasons to act. So being paternalistic toward somebody or some animal may,
thus, cohere with treating them with respect. How this is supposed to work is not
spelled out in detail by Smith.

These features of Smith's treatment of sympathetic resentment are missed by
Jesse Prinz in his influential account (2011). Prinz explicitly draws on Smith's
definition of sympathy in order to show that (a) selective or partial application
of sympathy is pervasive in our lives and (b) sympathy is not very efficacious.
Purporting to disagree with Smith, Prinz rejects relying on sympathy as necessary
for moral life and insists that what is needed is recognition of "common humanity . . . combined with a keen sense that human suffering is outrageous" (Prinz
2011: 229). But, of course, this just *is* Smith's analysis of sympathetic resentment,
which presupposes such common humanity. (I elaborate on the significance of
common humanity in Section c in Chapter 7.) Prinz's mistake is to think that
Smith's account cannot differentiate between the different uses for different
kinds of sympathy and antipathy in his moral psychology.

Thus, in Smith's system "natural" sentiments must do important work to
ground the social institutions that allow for enlarged societies. (Smith does not
use the language of "natural sentiments" very often, but for a striking passage see

TMS 3.5.10, 168–9, which is the epigraph to this chapter.) Smith denies Hume's suggestion (see Second *Enquiry* 3.2.40) that justice is either the result of reflection (cf. TMS 4.2.12, 192) or itself an original instinct. For Smith this is a false choice. (Perhaps, in response, Hume would insist that in his treatment Smith has broadened the very idea of justice beyond property to include all kinds of other harms.) Paradoxically, for Smith, the same passion, resentment, that can destroy society (TMS 2.2.3.3, 86) is required to get the social institution of justice going, thus enabling increasingly complex society: we find "original" propensities in human nature (e.g., the natural sentiments or original passion) that help ground derived propensities (e.g., moral sentiments), which are regulated and corrected, in part, by general rules.[7]

This is not to deny that there is a question-begging aspect to Smith's account. The point of departure of de Grouchy's criticism of Smith is her claim that "Smith contented himself with asserting its existence, and expounding its principle effects: I regretted that he held back from investigating further that he did not discover its first cause and show, at last why sympathy is the property of every sensible being susceptible to reflexion" (LS, I).

De Grouchy's point is that Smith takes the existence of sympathy for granted in his analysis. She is correct that nowhere in his published writing does Smith explain sympathy's origin analogous to, say, the manner of explaining the development of language and mind in Languages (which she had also translated into French); nor does Smith ever acknowledge the potentially question-begging claim that sympathy is a universal disposition.

De Grouchy did take on the challenge: "to account for the sympathy we feel for the moral suffering that is common to all members of our species, we need to go back to the cause of our particular sympathies, because they are the causes of our general sympathy" (LS, II). If one were to grant that sympathy exists universally (or at least widely enough in "savage" society), Smith's arguments against Hume and his positive account of the origin of justice can follow, so de Grouchy offers to correct Smith from within (for more on de Grouchy's positive views, see Forget 2001, 2003; Tegos 2013a; Berges 2015a, 2015b; also Schliesser 2017a, 2017b).

Without doing justice here to her full analysis, let me simply note that de Grouchy concludes as follows:

> I have shown how moral pains and pleasures are born out of physical sympathy that has become personal, strengthened by diverse circumstances, rendered more active and energetic by enthusiasm. But the origins of this sympathy for another person do not depend on the

---

[7] Smith's treatment may well have been inspired by Butler (MacLachlan 2010). Price was also inspired by Butler's *Dissertation* when Price criticized "Hutcheson's benevolence-monism" for attributing "to agents exceedingly complicated calculations about what will produce the greatest good for all of humanity" (Gill 2014a).

nature of that person's pains or pleasures. We suffer when we see him suffer, and the thought of his torments makes us suffer because we feel that the same torment would hurt us too. It is clear, therefore, that what we have found to be true of physical pains will also be true of moral pains provided we are subject to them. The sight, the memory of the moral suffering of another affect us like the sight or the memory of his physical suffering.

Here are therefore, new ties of sympathy by which we are united to mankind, as well as a wider range of human relationships.

Not only is the sight or memory of other's pains and pleasures, moral or physical, followed in us by pain and pleasure of our own, but, as we have already explained, this sensibility, once awakened, can be renewed in us simply by the abstract idea of good and evil. This results in a personal motivation to do good and avoid doing evil, a motivation which follows from the fact that we are sensitive beings capable of reasoning, and which can, in subtle souls, serve at once as guide to the conscience and a prime mover of virtue. (LS, III)

This is indeed a level of detail that is entirely absent in Smith on why sympathy is shared by all the members of the species. It is a remarkably egocentric model (and echoes Mandeville as well as Rousseau's adjustments to Mandeville's approach in ways discerned by Smith in Edinburgh Review): our moral ideas are derived from *our* suffering at the sight at others' suffering and the mental abstractions from our impressions of it. For de Grouchy moral sentiments presuppose considerable social and psychological development. To avoid confusion, we need to distinguish between de Grouchy's explanation of the *origin* of our moral sentiments, which is social in character and presupposes considerable interaction between many contextual factors over time, and her account of the *nature* of our moral sentiment, which even in its focus on duties to others is strikingly self-regarding. Ultimately, this makes her treatment of sympathy, as Ryan Hanley first pointed out to me, closer to Rousseau's use of "pity" than Smithian sympathy. (In her *Letters*, de Grouchy does not hide her admiration for Rousseau.)

I turn to my second example of the significance of Smithian natural sentiments, which will illuminate Smith's moral theory by discussing some crucial aspects of the relationship among natural sentiments, moral sentiments, and the general rules. I do so to point to an issue that haunts Smith's moral psychology: what if a set of social norms and mores makes a whole society complicit in some evil? While Smith explicitly denies that all the norms could be immoral, Smith recognizes, as we have seen, that society can persist with some unjust practices, while even claiming "public utility" (and "remote interest" [TMS 5.2.15, 210]) on their behalf.

ii. The Natural Sentiments and General Rules

In the context of his treatment of negligence, Smith writes, "law is approved of by the natural sentiments of all mankind" (TMS 2.3.2.9, 103). In context, Smith is not claiming that all law is approved by the natural sentiments of mankind. (He is merely discussing the requirement to compensate a victim in cases of unintended negligence.) Rather, all he is claiming is that there are laws, generally laws that exist in "all" societies, that are approved by the natural sentiments. (Here Smith almost sounds like a natural law theorist; see Angner 2007.)

This is not to deny that Smith recognizes that in real life heated passions are in themselves unreliable guides to what we ought to feel. For even though "the passions, upon this account, as father Malebranche says, all justify themselves, and seem reasonable and proportioned to their objects, as long as we continue to feel them" (TMS 3.4.3, 157; see also Astronomy 3.1, EPS 48), in practice, "none but those of the happiest mould are capable of suiting, with exact justness, their sentiments and behavior to the smallest difference of situation, and of acting upon all occasions with the most delicate and accurate propriety" (TMS 3.5.1, 162). Smith explains that even when we have calmed down we tend to be self-deceptive and too partial to ourselves. He concludes: "This self-deceit, this fatal weakness of mankind, is the source of half the disorders of human life" (TMS 3.4.6, 158; our propensity toward self-deception is the great theme of TMS 3.3; see also Gerschlager 2002).

In fact, according to Smith, for most of us being taught to follow general rules is the means toward correction of such self-deception:

> The regard to those general rules of conduct, is what is properly called a sense of duty, a principle of the greatest consequence in human life, and the only principle by which the bulk of mankind are capable of directing their actions. Many men behave very decently, and through the whole of their lives avoid any considerable degree of blame, who yet, perhaps, never felt the sentiment upon the propriety of which we found our approbation of their conduct, but acted merely from a regard to what they saw were the established rules of behaviour. The man who has received great benefits from another person, may, by the natural coldness of his temper, feel but a very small degree of the sentiment of gratitude. If he has been virtuously educated, however, he will often have been made to observe how odious those actions appear which denote a want of this sentiment, and how amiable the contrary." (TMS 3.5.1, 161–2)

According to Smith *many of us* probably *never feel* the right kind of (moral) feelings as we go about our lives. Sometimes this is due to the fact that some of us are simply *incapable* of feeling the right kind of moral feelings, but even those of us with this kind of psychological deficit can still do our duty "without any hypocrisy or blamable dissimulation, without any selfish intention" by following the *taught*, general rules of morality. In fact, even though the majority ("the bulk") of people are capable of feeling the right kind of moral feelings, they, too, are, in practice, guided by general rules.

The previous paragraph raises troubling issues for Smith's position. First, it entails that much of Smith's detailed moral phenomenology as presented in TMS relies on a subtle compact with the reader, who will pretend, counterfactually, that she really feels the right feelings in the many imaginative examples offered by Smith (even though Smith's position entails she will not do so in practice). It entails that when Smith speaks of "common sense" (TMS 3.2.4, 115; 3.6.1, 171; 3.6.12, 176, etc.) and its role in directing our behavior, he cannot be relying on our real sentiments, but rather he relies on the guidance of general rules that help us act as if we had the right feelings. Readers of TMS often extoll Smith's moral phenomenology without fully recognizing that our purported recognition of Smith's descriptions of the intricacies of our moral experience is by his lights also a kind of subtle, albeit desirable, form of self-deception. As Smith says in Imitative Arts (1.4) of a "copy of a picture," that it "derives its merit, not so much from its resemblance to the original, as from its resemblance to the object which the original was meant to resemble" (EPS 178); we are kind of flattered by the experience we were meant to exhibit.

Second, given "the inequalities of humour to which all" of us "are subject" (TMS 3.5.2, 163), the institutions by which a society ensures the "discipline, education, and example" of general rules are, in fact, crucial for the ongoing functioning of society (for more on this, see Section b in Chapter 14). From a political point of view the conditions for moral education are, thus, vital. As we will see, in Book 5 of WN, Smith gives considerable attention to educational reform (see especially 5.1.f *passim*).

The educational reform side of Smith's project is more pronounced in his French translator and critic, de Grouchy, than in Smith. She accepts something akin to the Smithian distinction between natural and cultivated sentiments; she makes it central to her political reform program that is based on the claim that our vices "are less the result of nature than of a few social institutions; if the fact that there were too few reasons to abstain from unjust behaviour was nearly entirely the result of these institutions, then one would have to try and reform them and cease to calumniate human nature" (LS, VI, 164; see also LS VIII). For de Grouchy, "social institutions have, in most countries, more often degraded nature than perfected it." (LS, VII). De Grouchy and Smith agree on the crucial role of conscience, and they agree that it, too, is frequently corrupted by customs and social institutions. This is why it is so important for de Grouchy that in educating children we "cultivate" the proper "natural sensitivity to other people's pleasures, and especially the happiness they derive from contributing to it" (LS, III). Extending Smith's arguments, de Grouchy's *Letters* provide a far-reaching program of social and legal reform and moral education (see letters five through eight).[8]

I return to the main argument. We should not ignore the fact that in TMS 3.5.1, 161–2, Smith makes a striking contrast between the (few) with the "happiest mould," which can be perfected, and "the coarse clay of which the bulk of mankind are formed"; the coarser sort "cannot be wrought up to such perfection" (see also Frazer 2010: 152 on Herder). Smith does not explain if the differences between "happy moulds" and those with "coarse clay" are innate, or if these differences are themselves a consequence of interaction with the society and family one is born into.

There is a persistent strain in recent scholarship to read Smith—with an appeal to Smith's claim that "the difference between the most dissimilar characters, between a philosopher and a common street porter, for example, seems to arise not so much from nature, as from habit, custom, and education" (WN 1.ii.4, 29)— as embracing "methodologic analytical egalitarianism" (see, especially, Peart and Levy 2005; Levy and Peart 2008a, and the essays collected in Levy and Peart 2008b). A methodologic analytical egalitarian is a theorist who embraces, as a norm of inquiry (not an ontology), motivational homogeneity across agents.[9] This homogeneity is compatible with differences in observed behavior, but such differences are, in the context of inquiry, attributed to culture, education, incentives, norms, and institutions. In particular, methodologic analytical egalitarianism entails a reflexive demand that the theorist understands herself as motivationally similar to the agents studied. There is evidence that Smith embraces such reflexivity (as I note in Chapters 11 and 12) and that his public philosophy is motivated by norms that are compatible with such methodologic analytical egalitarianism.

Even so, the natural reading of TMS 3.5.1, 161–2, seems to suggest that there are differences in our morally salient psychological makeup regardless of their source, and this should encourage some caution about attributing to Smith a firm commitment to methodologic analytical egalitarianism (even at WN 1.ii.4, 29, Smith's use of "seems" exhibits his own caution on the subject). If, however, the very possibility of the existence of somebody with a "happy mould" is entirely dependent on social and educational (etc.) institutions, then a society without

---

[8] In the body of the text I emphasize the commonalities between de Grouchy and Smith. But by focusing on the compassionate elements of sympathy she pushes Smith's thought back toward Rousseau's philosophy and, as Tegos and Berges have argued, turns Adam Smith into a moderate sentimentalist-Republican, harbinger of the French Idéologues (Tegos 2013a; Berges 2015a, 2015b). In my work on de Grouchy (Schliesser 2017a, 2017b), I tend to treat de Grouchy as a sentimentalist-consequentialist who, inspired by Cesare Beccaria, anticipates features of Bentham's and Mill's program.

[9] This position is naturally opposed to two alternatives. The first is a theory that embraces differentiated human nature; the differences also reflect axiological hierarchy. This seems to be Aristotle's position (say, on natural slavery) in Book 1 of *Politics*, and is revived regularly by modern eugenicists. Second, a theory with differentiated human nature but without (axiological) hierarchy among the differences. This seems to be Socrates' position in the true city (or "city of pigs") of Book 2 of *Republic*, and some contemporary standpoint theorists (e.g., E. Anderson 1995).

somebody *ever* feeling the right kind of moral feelings about a salient moral horror is possible.

But what, then, is the *source* of general rules according to Smith? Here our natural sentiments and the reactions of others play a crucial role:

> Our continual observations upon the conduct of others, insensibly lead us to form to ourselves certain general rules concerning what is fit and proper either to be done or to be avoided. Some of their actions shock all our natural sentiments. We hear every body about us express the like detestation against them. This still further confirms, and even exasperates our natural sense of their deformity . . . We thus naturally lay down to ourselves a general rule, that all such actions are to be avoided, as tending to render us odious, contemptible, or punishable, the objects of all those sentiments for which we have the greatest dread and aversion. Other actions, on the contrary, call forth our approbation, and we hear every body around us express the same favourable opinion concerning them. Every body is eager to honour and reward them. They excite all those sentiments for which we have by nature the strongest desire; the love, the gratitude, the admiration of mankind. We become ambitious of performing the like; and thus naturally lay down to ourselves a rule of another kind, that every opportunity of acting in this manner is carefully to be sought after.
>
> It is thus that the general rules of morality are formed. They are ultimately founded upon experience of what, in particular instances, our moral faculties, our natural sense of merit and propriety, approve, or disapprove of. We do not originally approve or condemn particular actions; because, upon examination, they appear to be agreeable or inconsistent with a certain general rule. The general rule, on the contrary, is formed, by finding from experience, that all actions of a certain kind, or circumstanced in a certain manner, are approved or disapproved of. (TMS 3.4.7–8, 159)

Smith's language here is a bit deceptive; none of us living in civilized society are in the position he describes. We have *inherited* (culturally) nearly all the general rules. In fact, the principles behind Smith's argument are clear from reflection on the fact that Smith neatly repeats and summarizes the core of this passage later (at TMS 7.3.2.7, 320)[10] in explicit response to Hobbes's "odious" arguments built on the fiction of a "state of nature" (TMS 7.3.2.1, 318). It is useful to

---

[10] "These first perceptions, as well as all other experiments upon which any general rules are founded, cannot be the object of reason, but of immediate sense and feeling. It is by finding in a vast variety of instances that one tenor of conduct constantly pleases in a certain manner, and that another as constantly displeases the mind, that we form the general rules of morality" (TMS 7.3.2.7, 320).

assess how Smith understands the aim of Hobbes's approach before I analyze Smith's account of how the natural sentiments give rise to general rules. This will help us better understand the goals and significance of Smith's treatment.

After summarizing the core Hobbesian doctrine, "that antecedent to the institution of civil government there could be no safe or peaceable society among men" (TMS 7.3.2.1, 318), and explaining briefly what follows from it, Smith writes,

> It was the avowed intention of Mr. Hobbes, by propagating these notions, to subject the consciences of men immediately to the civil, and not to the ecclesiastical powers, whose turbulence and ambition, he had been taught, by the example of his own times, to regard as the principal source of the disorders of society. His doctrine, upon this account, was peculiarly offensive to theologians, who accordingly did not fail to vent their indignation against him with great asperity and bitterness. It was likewise offensive to all sound moralists, as it supposed that there was no natural distinction between right and wrong, that these were mutable and changeable, and depended upon the mere arbitrary will of the civil magistrate. (TMS 7.3.2.2, 318)

Smith reads Hobbes as intending to solve primarily a theological-political problem: how to handle (competing) clerical ambition(s) without generating preconditions for breakdown of legal order and precipitating civil war. This is not the place to explore how apt this reading of Hobbes is.[11] But if the aim is to refute Hobbes (in TMS 3.4.7–8, 159 and 7.3.2.7, 320), then what "a sound moralist" needs to show is how from natural, human propensities the existence of moralized general rules worth having can (necessarily) be generated without requiring the assistance of either religious revelation or state intervention. Smith echoes a famous controversy in the wake of Spinoza, associated with Bayle's name, about to what degree a society of atheists is possible. Smith's teacher Hutcheson allowed, without emphasizing it, that an atheist could be virtuous (Gill 2006: 173); this is, in fact, the reason why he was accused of heresy in 1737 (Wright 2009: 36, n. 102). In the *Philosophical Dictionary* (1756) Voltaire also answered in the affirmative and treated the Senate of Rome on the precipice of the Republic's collapse as an exemplar but, with a sneer to Spinoza's denial of final causes ("some geometers who are not philosophers have rejected final causes"), thought it pernicious (Atheism II).

As is well known, the concern with refuting Hobbes (and Mandeville) is arguably signaled in the first sentence of TMS—"How selfish soever man may be supposed, there are evidently some principles in his nature, which interest him in the fortune of others, and render their happiness necessary to him, though he derives nothing from it except the pleasure of seeing it" (TMS 1.1.1.1, 9)—as well as in

---

[11] Even if Smith is right about Hobbes's intentions, his reading of Hobbes seems unduly narrow, as if mistaking it for the stated purpose of Spinoza's *Theological-Political Treatise*.

the critical nod to "those who are fond of deducing all our sentiments from certain refinements of self-love" (TMS 1.1.2.1, 13). If Smith succeeds at this, then he undercuts the need for both clerical control over law and the Hobbesian absolute sovereign. Of course, Smith is not alone in trying to offer such an account; a similar project is to be discerned in Book 3 of Hume's *Treatise* and other eighteenth-century moralists (Gill 2006).

However Smith can seem to beg the question by also mentioning "our natural sense of merit and propriety" (TMS 3.4.8, 159) if the natural sense of merit and propriety are thought of as already properly moral. The whole anti-Hobbesian exercise is to generate general moral rules in the context where morality has not been established properly yet. Smith need not have referred to "our natural sense of merit and propriety" in this context, so he need not have begged any questions. Having said that, Smith need not think that the *natural* sense of merit and propriety is itself "moral" in the sense under debate. In Chapter 5, on the mechanics of the sympathetic process, I show that for Smith our natural sense of merit and propriety can be articulated entirely in a strictly causal fashion.

Anyway, let me now turn to articulating how according to Smith our natural sentiments and the reactions of others generate moral rules (in TMS 3.4.7–8, 159). This has five steps. First, as we have seen (TMS 2.1.5.10, 77–8), Smith grants Hobbes's claim that we have a natural desire for "self-preservation" (TMS 7.3.2.1, 318); however, Smith would insist that we also have natural desires for "the love, the gratitude," and "admiration of mankind" and an equally strong desire for avoiding being thought "odious, contemptible, or punishable." Thus, by nature we are sociable animals (here Smith is echoing a standard seventeenth-century response to Hobbes found in Grotius, Puffendorf, and others). Smith puts this in terms of us having *both* "selfish and original passions" (TMS 3.3.3, 135; see also 3.3.35, 152), as if he wants to keep our natural passions distinct from the selfish. (See also his treatment of the Stoics at TMS 3.3.11, 140; Smith does not disapprove of the selfish passions as such. There are plenty of circumstances where we can, in fact, approve of the [moderate] expression of these, too [TMS 1.2.5].) Therefore, Smith certainly thinks even "the rudest vulgar of mankind" are naturally endowed with some of the so-called social passions ("generosity, humanity, kindness, compassion, mutual friendship and esteem," TMS 1.2.4.1, 38–9; by "rudest vulgar" Smith means those uneducated and living in the most uncivilized, savage state). Recall also the first sentence of TMS (quoted just above). Smith takes it for granted that we would agree with him that "a parent without parental tenderness, a child devoid of all filial reverence, appear monsters, the objects, not of hatred only, but of horror" (TMS 6.2.1.7, 220). Of course, there can be occasions in which self-preservation and our desire for the affection of others come into conflict, especially when the institution of justice is near collapse (or has collapsed), but what Smith's argument requires is that they need not necessarily conflict always. In fact, Smith is explicit that our "state or sovereignty" is "by nature, therefore, endeared to us, not only by all our selfish, but by all our private benevolent affections" (TMS 6.2.2.2, 227) such that for Smith ordinary patriotism even nationalism is not an expression of (immoral) partiality (from the perspective of, say, Stoic cosmopolitanism), but an expression of our more generic desire for virtue.

Of course, Smith thinks that in actual circumstances that approach the state of nature, humans are very fearful, frail, and even morally unworthy creatures:

> that cowardice and pusillanimity, so natural to man in his uncivilized state, still more disposes him [toward fearing invisible gods]; unprotected by the laws of society, exposed, defenceless, he feels his weakness upon all occasions; his strength and security upon none. (Astronomy 3.1, EPS 48)

Second, we observe how others interact, and, third, we are naturally led to find some of their behavior shocking. This component relies on the fact that naturally fear and resentment are intrinsically strongly felt and ordinarily motivationally forceful. (Recall my treatment of the natural passions in Section a of Chapter 3.) Fourth, our natural shock is sanctioned by the responses of (uninvolved) others.

We can grant Smith's point if we allow him that shock gets activated in response to abject cruelty and unfairness, or anything that severely violates "our natural sense of equity" (TMS 2.3.2.8, 103). According to Smith "shock" is generated by our noticing the absence of prosocial feelings in others (TMS 6.2.1.7, 220; see also 1.1.2.1, 13; 1.1.2.3, 15; 2.1.5.3, 75, and especially, when we had thought otherwise before 5.2.2, 200), even toward animals (TMS 2.3.1.3, 95), even more so when such actions provide evidence for "the little account which he seems to make of us" (TMS 2.3.1.5, 96; for more on the significance of this, see Darwall 2006). Of course, "shock" can also be generated if we notice that we ourselves have become incapable of feeling for others (TMS 1.1.2.6, 16) or awareness of the extent of someone's hatred (TMS 2.1.1.6, 69). An interesting case of "shock" occurs if others unfairly take us to lack prosocial feelings, even though we are innocent of the charge (TMS 3.2.11, 119).[12]

Of course, cruelty, unfairness, and lack of concern with equity are immoral, too, but for Smith our reliable and systematic feelings about acts of wanton cruelty and unfairness ground our capacity to be moral, including our judgment of such acts as immoral. Moreover, Smith thinks that we also disapprove of the absence of such resentment when it would be appropriate. As he writes approvingly, "even the mob are enraged to see any man submit patiently to affronts and ill usage" (TMS 1.3.3.3, 35). In context, it is clear that Smith thinks that in general "the mob's views" are not a very good measure of morally appropriate feelings.

---

[12] Smith thinks that significant deviations from our habitual aesthetic norms and standards also generate shock (TMS 5.1.8, 219).

Fifth, over time such reactions "are universally acknowledged and established, by the concurring sentiments of mankind" (TMS 3.4.11, 160). If we allow Smith some rhetorical excess, this is all Smith needs for his purposes. (For a nice treatment, see also Otteson 2002a.) The natural sentiments can thus be taken to ground the general rules that can be appealed to when proper feelings are absent. The general rules are also very useful in correcting our partiality (TMS 3.4.12, 160). But Smith stresses that they are not themselves "the ultimate foundations of what is just and unjust in human conduct;" nor is it the case (as Smith suggests eminent authors had claimed) that "the original judgments of mankind with regard to right and wrong, were formed like the decisions of a court of judicatory, by considering first the general rule, and then, secondly, whether the particular action under consideration fell properly within its comprehension" (TMS 3.4.11, 160).

It is worth explaining why this is so, despite the fact that the same mechanism that is the foundation of the establishment of general rules is also almost all that's needed for the mechanism by which the contents of our sentiments are properly moral. Recall that the content of a moral sentiment involves <(i) some desire/aversion, (ii) an idea of the triggering social object, (iii) our (empowering/impotent) sense of ourselves moving up or down in the estimation of an (internally) selected group of observers>. What's missing from the mechanism that establishes general rules is the creation of the habit that we apply (or, to use one of Smith's favored phrases in the first third of TMS, "bring home") the anticipated reactions of others to our sense of self. As Smith puts it in another context:

> Our whole sense, in short, of the merit and good desert of such actions, of the propriety and fitness of recompensing them, and making the person who performed them rejoice in his turn, arises from the sympathetic emotions of gratitude and love, with which we bring home to our own breast the situation of those principally concerned. (TMS 2.1.5.3, 75)

Even if we adopt the general rules as our own, we have not thereby internalized the way we might move in the estimation of the right kind of observers. That is, to a first approximation in Smith "conscience" and "the impartial spectator within" are synonymous (TMS 3.3.4, 137).

Rather than articulating Smith's account of the impartial spectator here, I can now explain why widely recognized law is, according to Smith, fundamentally rooted in our natural sentiments. In Smith this is the case because he allows that "all general rules are commonly denominated laws" (TMS 3.5.5, 165). Hence, in Smith we find the claim that all *authentic* positive law is responsive to our natural sentiments. Clearly my use of "authentic" is rather charitable to his position. The claim relies on the idea that the natural sentiments (and the general rules that they support) underwrite a relatively *thin* universal common morality based on an aversion to cruelty (Forman-Barzilai 2010: 232–8; see Shklar 1989 for a modern expression).

In the following section I explore the nature of Smithian conscience and how it relates to his larger views on what he calls the "moral faculties" and what has sometimes been called the "moral sense."

b. Moral Faculties: The Moral Sense and Conscience

In treating reason as an active principle (Section d in Chapter 3), I noted that both Hume and Smith also treat conscience as an active principle, and that Smith treats "reason" and "conscience" as synonymous. But I did not explain the nature of "conscience" there. In this section I characterize Smith's account of conscience and his treatment of moral sense.

One might think, perhaps, that in Smith's system, conscience just is the moral sense. There is, in fact, a long tradition of reading Smith as a so-called moral sense theorist not unlike other eighteenth-century British moral philosophers. Smith is categorized as belonging to the "sentimental school" in Selby-Bigge's influential (1897) anthology of the *British Moralists*.[13] We have already seen in the previous section that Smith denies that most of us feel what we ought to feel most of the time (TMS 3.5.1, 161–2). In addition, when it comes to conscience, Smith explicitly rejects the idea that it is a moral sense: "The word conscience does not immediately denote any moral faculty by which we approve or disapprove. Conscience supposes, indeed, the existence of some such faculty, and properly signifies our consciousness of having acted agreeably or contrary to its directions" (TMS 7.3.3.15, 326).

Thus, Smithian conscience is not a moral faculty but a form of self-awareness about our having acted properly according to and under the guidance of "some such faculty." This is why in the previous section I wrote that in Smith "conscience" and "the impartial spectator within" are approximately synonymous (TMS 3.3.4, 137).

The phrase "some such faculty" might lead one to believe that there is a moral sense that directs conscience. In fact, one might be tempted to infer that Smith also accepts the existence of a moral sense from the following long, complex passage:

> These researches, however, when they came to take place, confirmed those original anticipations of nature. Upon whatever we suppose

---

[13] It seems this was Rawls's original source for his understanding of Adam Smith (Levy and Peart 2013: 378).

that our moral faculties are founded, whether upon a certain modification of reason, upon an original instinct, called a moral sense,
or upon some other principle of our nature, it cannot be doubted,
that they were given us for the direction of our conduct in this life.
They carry along with them the most evident badges of this authority, which denote that they were set up within us to be the supreme
arbiters of all our actions, to superintend all our senses, passions,
and appetites, and to judge how far each of them was either to be
indulged or restrained. Our moral faculties are by no means, as some
have pretended, upon a level in this respect with the other faculties
and appetites of our nature, endowed with no more right to restrain
these last, than these last are to restrain them. No other faculty or
principle of action judges of any other. Love does not judge of resentment, nor resentment of love. Those two passions may be opposite
to one another, but cannot, with any propriety, be said to approve
or disapprove of one another. But it is the peculiar office of those
faculties now under our consideration to judge, to bestow censure or
applause upon all the other principles of our nature. They may be considered as a sort of senses of which those principles are the objects.
Every sense is supreme over its own objects. There is no appeal from
the eye with regard to the beauty of colours, nor from the ear with
regard to the harmony of sounds, nor from the taste with regard to
the agreeableness of flavours. Each of those senses judges in the last
resort of its own objects. Whatever gratifies the taste is sweet, whatever pleases the eye is beautiful, whatever soothes the ear is harmonious. The very essence of each of those qualities consists in its
being fitted to please the sense to which it is addressed. It belongs to
our moral faculties, in the same manner to determine when the ear
ought to be soothed, when the eye ought to be indulged, when the
taste ought to be gratified, when and how far every other principle of
our nature ought either to be indulged or restrained. What is agreeable to our moral faculties, is fit, and right, and proper to be done;
the contrary wrong, unfit, and improper. The sentiments which they
approve of, are graceful and becoming: the contrary, ungraceful and
unbecoming. The very words, right, wrong, fit, improper, graceful,
unbecoming, mean only what pleases or displeases those faculties.
(TMS 3.5.6, 164–5)

The context of this passage is Smith's insistence that "reasoning and philosophy"
(viz. "these researches") confirm what human nature already believes—that is,
that "those important rules of morality are the commands and laws of the Deity,
who will finally reward the obedient, and punish the transgressors of their duty"

(TMS 3.5.2, 163).[14] Regardless of Smith's own philosophy (or beliefs), this is an odd claim to make for two reasons. First, Smith is at least indirectly familiar with philosophical criticism, which insists that such a Deity is an anthropomorphic fiction or projection. In the Newtonian works written by Samuel Clarke and Colin McLaurin (Smith refers to Clarke at TMS 7.1.3, 265ff, and to McLaurin in Astronomy 4.58, 90), Smith could read elaborate descriptions and attempted refutations of Spinoza and Spinozism. Moreover, even if one were to grant that Hume would concede that, perhaps, "God" was the first cause of the universe, the whole tenor of Hume's philosophy is directed against accepting that there is anything that really corresponds to our idea of an anthropomorphic, agential God.

Second, in context Smith explicitly allows that it is not a forgone conclusion that we naturally end up with a monotheistic framework; by nature in a "rude" society, it is originally far more likely that we end up with "pagan superstition" (recall TMS 3.5.4, 164; see also Astronomy 3.1, EPS 48). This is, in fact, Hume's position in the *Natural History of Religion*. Thus, very subtly, in a passage that, as the editors of TMS suggest, otherwise has strong echoes of Butler, Smith raises the question under what social conditions we would have a propensity toward monotheism.

Perhaps Smith's use of "confirmed" signals that he agrees with the Newtonian arguments. But to "confirm" need not mean "to prove;" during the eighteenth century, it could just as well mean "to sanction," "to authorize," or "to approve." For example, in a passage important to Smith's political philosophy, he writes that the public-spirited statesman "will accommodate, as well as he can, his public arrangements to the confirmed habits and prejudices of the people" (TMS 6.2.2.16, 233). In this latter instance, Smith's "confirmed" means something like "well established," but certainly not true (cf. "prejudices").

This is not the place to decide Smith's considered views on the relationship between naturally established beliefs and philosophically established beliefs. The context is an extremely delicate religious and political matter. Certainly an eighteenth-century Scottish university professor would choose his words carefully to avoid conflict with the Kirk. He witnessed the opposition to attempts to get David Hume appointed in Edinburgh and Glasgow. He was familiar with the troubles that even the very popular Hutcheson, who frequently invoked providence and freely appealed to final causes, experienced with ecclesiastical authorities (recall Wright 2009: 36, n. 102).

Either way, in TMS 3.5.6 it seems that Smith commits himself not just to the existence of "moral faculties," but also to the claim that [A] they can be "considered as a sort of senses." In particular, Smith seems to commit himself to the normative claim that [B] "What is agreeable to our moral faculties, is fit, and right,

---

[14] This is one of the tenets of Spinoza's "universal religion" to be promoted among the vulgar (see *Theological-Political Treatise*, Chapter 14 [III.178]).

and proper to be done" and to the semantic claim that [C] "The very words, right, wrong, fit, improper, graceful, unbecoming, mean only what pleases or displeases those faculties." I do not wish to deny that Smith is committed to both [B] and [C], although I argue below that on closer inspection of Smith's moral theory, the details of especially [B] turn out to be something quite unexpected. In this section I just wish to deny that this passage commits Smith to being a moral-sense theorist.

But what about [A]? Does Smith commit himself to the claim that our moral faculties are a kind of moral sense? Smith himself recognized that the line between moral sentiments and a moral sense is a fine one. Here is how Smith introduces the topic:

> According to some the principle of approbation is founded upon a sentiment of a peculiar nature, upon a particular power of perception exerted by the mind at the view of certain actions or affections; some of which affecting this faculty in an agreeable and others in a disagreeable manner, the former are stamped with the characters of right, laudable, and virtuous; the latter with those of wrong, blamable, and vicious. This sentiment being of a peculiar nature distinct from every other, and the effect of a particular power of perception, they give it a particular name, and call it a moral sense. (TMS 7.3.3.2, 321)

Therefore, according to Smith a moral-sense theorist is committed to the idea that there is in us a separate moral sense—that is, a distinct capacity to perceive, and fitted to, distinct pleasing and displeasing moral feelings. Smith attributes such a doctrine of such a direct internal sense to his teacher, Francis Hutcheson (TMS 7.3.3.6, 322). With delicious irony Smith objects "that it is strange that this sentiment, which Providence undoubtedly intended to be the governing principle of human nature, should hitherto have been so little taken notice of, as not to have got a name in any language" (TMS 7.3.3.15, 326; recall that Hutcheson often invoked providence). Smith marshals numerous what he takes to be "unanswerable" objections against the doctrine of a specific internal sense (TMS 7.3.3.12, 324; see Prior 1949: 72–4).

Faced with Smith's criticism of the existence of a moral sense in 7.3.3, the editors of the Glasgow edition, who are committed to defending the reading of Smith as a moral-sense theorist, added a footnote to TMS 3.5.6, 164–5: "The paragraph probably formed part of an early version of Smith's lectures" (TMS 164, n. 1). It is possible that the editors are right about the provenance of the paragraph in Smith's lectures, but it does not follow there is a tension between TMS 3.5.6 and TMS 7.3.3. To see that there is no tension I introduce a distinction between a "full-blooded moral-sense theorist" and a "weak moral-sense theorist." A full-blooded moral-sense theorist is somebody like Smith's description of Hutcheson—that is, a philosopher committed to the position that there is in us an authoritative, internal sense with a distinct capacity to perceive, and is fitted to, distinct pleasing and displeasing moral feelings. A weak moral-sense theorist is somebody who thinks that some collection of our natural sentiments or original passions exclusively grounds the moral character of our felt judgments.

As the quoted passages from TMS 7.3.3 reveal, Smith is not a full-blooded moral-sense theorist (see also Gill 2014a). In fact, he thinks the fact that we are far more likely to be self-deceived than mistaken in our judgments about others is a separate argument against the existence of an internal moral-sense faculty (TMS 3.4.5, 158). As I have demonstrated (in Section a of Chapter 2), even Smith's "some such faculty" (at TMS 7.3.3.15, 326) need not refer to a single, stable disposition of the mind; Smith tends to use "faculties," "senses," and "instincts" as rough synonyms. Thus, to say that there is "some such faculty" commits Smith to less than meets the eye. At its most deflationary, it could just mean that conscience is guided by some passion(s). Of course, to be guided or directed by some such passion does not mean it is itself an effect of it as it necessarily would be if conscience were a passive principle. Given that conscience is an active principle, the "guidance" of these passions does not itself necessitate conscience.

Now in 3.5.6 Smith first says that "our moral faculties are founded, whether upon a certain modification of reason, upon an original instinct, called a moral sense, or upon some other principle of our nature." Here he allows two named options—(i) a modification of reason or (ii) an original instinct—but he explicitly does not exclude the possibility of (iii) "some other principle of our nature." Now this unnamed alternative (iii) could be what I have been calling a "derived" passion or a cultivated sentiment.

It is not entirely clear what Smith means by "founded" in this context. It looks like the "principle" sought just means another psychological propensity, but one with the highest "authority" to settle one's *ought(s)*. We can reject (i) as a description of Smith's position; he certainly allows reason to play some role in his moral philosophy, but if reason is synonymous with conscience (as it sometimes seem to be for Smith), then reason should be included among the moral faculties for him and (to avoid circularity) it cannot be their foundation. That leaves (ii) and (iii).

Second, Smith claims that "it is the peculiar office of those faculties now under our consideration to judge [etc.] ... They may be considered as a sort of senses of which those principles are the objects." Smith's claim is very weak here; all he is suggesting is that for the sake of argument and explication one can treat the moral faculties as *akin to* the senses. But nothing in the whole long paragraph of 3.5.6 forces a choice between (ii) and (iii). Insofar as Smith allows (iii) or a combination of (ii) and (iii), then in TMS 3.5.6 he is not even a moral-sense theorist in the weak sense.

It is, however, undeniable that Smith thinks that the natural sentiments play some role in grounding morality (recall the arguments of Section a above). Thus, in this very weak sense Smith is a moral-sense theorist. But only if we think that Smith is a kind of meta-ethical moral monist does this imply that the sentiments ground the whole of moral theory. But as I have argued in this chapter, the natural sentiments ground at most justice and the moralized general rules, which should not be confused with either the whole content of morality or virtue, nor whatever grounds moral judgment in ordinary situations. It is by no means obvious that the sentiments ground these other features of morality. We should resist the temptation to read meta- ethical monism into Smith. (For extended arguments to this effect, see Gill 2014a, although he may not agree with my rejection of Smith as a moral-sense theorist.)

Moreover, I have already suggested that the natural sentiments ground at most a relatively thin common universal morality. This needs to be argued more fully, and I do so in Chapter 7. In addition. I have not yet articulated how Smith proposes to evaluate the moral character of social institutions. Finally, in the next chapter, I argue that moral judgments of propriety and merit do not themselves only rely on the natural sentiment according to Smith. Hence, let us turn to two of Smith's crucial moral concepts: sympathy and propriety.

5

The Sympathetic Process and Judgments of Propriety

In this chapter I describe Smith's views on the workings of the sympathetic process that feed into sympathetic judgment(s). I show that in anything but the most simple forms of sympathy, the sympathetic process presupposes and crucially depends on counterfactual, causal reasoning. In particular I argue for four related claims:

(i)   that according to Smith the sympathetic process depends on a type of causal reasoning that goes well beyond the kind of simulationist theory standardly attributed to him;

(ii) that the Smithian imagination in the sympathetic process works by way of counterfactual reasoning and that even the feelings we ought to feel as a consequence of the sympathetic process need not be actual, but counterfactual (see also Valihora 2010: 143);

(iii) that Smithian agents are non-trivially understood as belonging to the causal order of nature (in this chapter, I illustrate (iii) through an extended digression on Smith's views on a certain form of moral luck); and

(iv) that Smithian judgments of propriety are intrinsically judgments about the proportionality of causal relations.

The idea that sympathy depends on the workings of the imagination is not new. But in such accounts, the imagination tends to be treated as a device that gets us to "change places with others" by way of projection (Griswold 2006: 85–90). This approach has support in Smith's text, but it systematically ignores the significance of causal and counterfactual causal reasoning in Smith. To put the point that I shall argue for in Humean terms: in the sympathetic process the Smithian imagination primarily deploys natural relations of causation and resemblance (Treatise 1.1.4).[1]

---

[1] It does not deploy only natural relations; sometimes it deploys what Hume calls "philosophical relations" (Treatise 1.1.5ff), and this helps explain why sympathy need not be truth-apt.

This chapter proceeds as follows. In Section a, I present what I take to be the standard, feeling-focused reading of Smithian sympathetic process and outcome—one that emphasizes the mutual modulation of feelings between spectator and moral agents. In Section b, I provide evidence for the claim that the sympathetic process crucially involves counterfactual causal reasoning. One important feature of my argument is that this is so in what I take to be the paradigmatic or exemplary form of sympathy—what we may call "perfect sympathy" or in Smith's terminology "natural sympathy"—the attachment "among men of virtue" (6.2.1.18, 225; on the "men of virtue" see also Chapter 9 and Section d in Chapter 15). A crucial claim is that judgments of propriety and merit are in a non-trivial sense causal judgments; when we make a moral judgment we do so after mentally inspecting, as it were, the proportionality of the relata that enter a cause-and-effect relation. This section is followed by two digressions that are meant to illuminate and support it. In Section c I analyze what Smith means by proportionality. In the long Section d, I discuss a peculiar feature of Smith's approach to moral luck, "the piacular." Smith's views on what it is to be an unwilling cause of other people's harms are very unusual, but I explain them by building on my treatment of Smithian environmental rationality (recall Section c in Chapter 3). In Section e, I discuss the nature and the extent of the role of counterfactual reasoning within the sympathetic process.

a. Sympathetic Process (Feelings)

In this section, I offer a first approximation of the sympathetic process. It is deliberately simplified in order to articulate the sequential nature of the sympathetic process. In subsequent sections, I analyze and offer an improved and partially different account of how we should understand the steps and character of the sympathetic process.

For the sake of clarity I adopt a distinction from Montes (2004) between "sympathy as a process" and "sympathy as an outcome." When one starts reading TMS one quickly encounters what appears to be a definition of sympathy: "Pity and compassion are words appropriated to signify our fellow-feeling with the sorrow of others. Sympathy, though its meaning was, perhaps, originally the same, may now, however, without much impropriety, be made use of to denote our fellow-feeling with any passion whatever" (TMS 1.1.1.6, 10). This makes it sound as if "sympathy" means something like the following: feeling another's emotion regardless of the nature of the emotion. It makes it seem that sympathy is primarily something felt. In fact, this is indeed so, when we regard "sympathy" as an outcome. In this sense we can, in principle, sympathize with "all other animals . . . even for the meanest and weakest of his subjects" (recall External Senses 6, EPS 136). But only in rare cases will an animal sympathize with our feelings. Thus, even when we understand sympathy as an outcome we will want to distinguish between instances of mutual sympathy (e.g., TMS 1.1.2, 13ff) and what one can label "one-way sympathy."

A few pages later Smith articulates the process by which mutual fellow-feeling is attained:

> In order to produce this concord, as nature teaches the spectators to assume the circumstances of the person principally concerned, so she teaches this last in some measure to assume those of the spectators. As they are continually placing themselves in his situation, and thence conceiving emotions similar to what he feels; so he is as constantly placing himself in theirs, and thence conceiving some degree of that coolness about his own fortune, with which he is sensible that they will view it . . . As their sympathy makes them look at it, in some measure, with his eyes, so his sympathy makes him look at it, in some measure, with theirs, especially when in their presence and acting under their observation: and as the reflected passion, which he thus conceives, is much weaker than the original one, it necessarily abates the violence of what he felt before he came into their presence, before he began to recollect in what manner they would be affected by it, and to view his situation in this candid and impartial light. (TMS 1.1.4.8, 22)

Here is a way to capture the sequential nature of this process to a first approximation:

(i)   a felt circumstance by the person principally concerned due to a moral situation that is observed empirically by

(ii) spectators and moral agents, who place themselves in the situations of the person principally concerned by way of the imagination, and this involves

(iii) a sympathetic mutual modulation (informed, perhaps, by observations about how the person principally concerned is reacting), which, in turn, produces

(iv) a conceived reflected passion within each participant (both the person principally concerned and the spectator[s]) in the sympathetic process, and this

(v)   alters the intensity of the feelings of all the participants in the process; after several rounds of (i–v), perhaps, this produces

(vi) fellow-feeling (sympathy) between the spectator(s) and the person principally concerned. This produces

(vii) a second-order, pleasing feeling (TMS 1.1.2.1, 13).

Therefore, the outcome of a well-functioning sympathetic process is in the first instance two feelings: (a) the shared experience of a passion (whose intensity has been transformed) and (b) the pleasurable knowledge of this sharing—that is, a sympathetic pleasure. As Smith puts it, mutual "Sympathy . . . enlivens joy and alleviates grief. It enlivens joy by presenting another source of satisfaction; and it alleviates grief by insinuating into the heart almost the only agreeable sensation which it is at that time capable of receiving" (TMS 1.1.2.2, 14).

If we just focus on the role of feelings in Smithian sympathy, then the process and outcome of sympathy may seem to form a seamless whole, which is really about the transformation of feelings by way of the passions (for excellent treatment see Otteson 2002a). This is nicely illustrated by the following passage in Smith: "our propensity to sympathize with joy is much stronger than our propensity to sympathize with sorrow; and that our fellow-feeling for the agreeable emotion approaches much more nearly to the vivacity of what is naturally felt by the persons principally concerned, than that which we conceive for the painful one" (TMS 1.3.5, 44).

Smith's language of "vivacity" resonates with what we may call a "Humean reading" of Smithian sympathy. By this I do not mean just the focus on feelings, but also the significance of what has come to be known as the "contagion" model of the transmission of sympathy in Hume's Treatise (e.g., 3.3.2.2; see Morrow 1923: 67–8, who emphasizes the connection between it and Hume's "social philosophy"). In Hume and Smith, by way of the imagination the sympathetic process transforms a person's conceived feeling into a related kind of feeling (in Hume the sympathetic process is "the conversion of an idea into an impression by the force of imagination"; Treatise 2.3.6.8). Even so, there are non-trivial differences between Hume and Smith on sympathy. (Fleischacker 2012 has explored many significant ways in which Humean and Smithian sympathy differ.) For example, in Hume's approach relatively dull ideas are turned, as it were, back into vivacious impressions, that is, for Hume the sympathetic process is always vivifying; in Smith emotions are turned into reflected passions and this is only sometimes vivifying. (Smith also treats sympathy as a reflected passion at Imitative Arts 2.22, EPS 198, and TMS 6.2.1.1, 219.)

Awareness of the very possibility of mutual sympathy creates an incentive to enter into the sympathetic process: "As the person who is principally interested in any event is pleased with our sympathy, and hurt by the want of it, so we, too, seem to be pleased when we are able to sympathize with him, and to be hurt when we are unable to do so" (TMS 1.1.2.6, 15). It's almost as if there is also a further, parasitic pleasure on the anticipation of the pleasure that mutual sympathy will produce. Rather than seeing this parasitic pleasure as a damaging infinite regress, Smith regards it as the possible seeds of a virtuous cycle, where we draw each other into sympathy and delight in anticipating it. As Smith puts it in an anti-Hobbesian passage crucial to his political philosophy: "Man, it has been said, has a natural love for society, and desires that the union of mankind should be preserved for its own sake, and though he himself was to derive no benefit from it. The orderly and flourishing state of society is agreeable to him, and he takes delight in contemplating it" (TMS 2.2.3.6, 88; see Hanley 2013).

Before I analyze the sevenfold sequence (i–vii) inferred from TMS (1.1.4.8, 22), note that according to Smith "nature teaches the spectators to assume the circumstances of the person principally concerned, so she teaches this last in some measure to assume those of the spectators." I read this as another articulation of Smith's claim that we are naturally (and, if the right triggering conditions are present, frequently) sociable (recall Section a(ii) in Chapter 4; Montes 2004) and eager to enter into the sympathetic process when we observe a moral situation; we are pleased to imagine what the person principally concerned must have felt. According to Smith it takes much more effort and, perhaps, even some proper acculturation, education, or cultivation to do so when we are the person principally concerned. To put this plainly: when we are in the midst of a moral agency we find it hard to imagine how we are being seen and evaluated. In fact, it is a consequence of our awareness of the existence of spectators who, in fact, enter into our situation and our imagination of their doing so that helps create the circumstances by which we calm down and can start to adopt a more dispassionate perspective on ourselves. Smith tends to associate this awareness as a consequence of being in school (e.g., TMS 3.3.22, 145), but for some of us it is a life-long process.

b. Sympathy and Knowledge of Causal Relations

"Sympathy" is derived from the Greek συμπάθεια, the state of feeling together (derived from the composite of fellow [συν] and feeling [πάθος]). A solid Latinate translation would be compassion, but this has too narrow a connotation for us. Correctly or not, Smith suggests that sympathy originally had the more narrow meaning:

> Pity and compassion are words appropriated to signify our fellow-feeling with the sorrow of others. Sympathy, though its meaning was, perhaps, originally the same, may now, however, without much impropriety, be made use of to denote our fellow-feeling with any passion whatever. (TMS 1.1.1.5, 10)

Despite the fact that throughout the philosophical tradition "sympathy" is used to denote many different kind of and most uses tend to have five features in common (see Holmes 2012; Brouwer 2015; Emilsson 2015; Schliesser 2015: 6–9):

1. Sympathy is used to explain apparent or joint action at a distance.
2. The likeness principle—that is, the very possibility of sympathy presupposes that it takes place among things/events/features that are in one sense or another alike, often within a single being/unity/organism (which can be the

whole universe); these are to be contrasted with the antipathy (ἀντιπάθεια) of unalikes.

3. The cause(s) of sympathy is invisible to the naked eye.
4. The effect(s) of sympathy can be (nearly) instantaneous.
5. Sympathy is, in principle, bidirectional even if the elements or agents that enter into a sympathetic relationship vary in their power to do so.

A standard case that involves all five features is mentioned by Smith: "Men of the most robust make, observe that in looking upon sore eyes [of another person] they often feel a very sensible soreness in their own" (TMS 1.1.1.3, 10). In fact, Smith is also explicit in treating sympathy as an "active principle" (6.2.1.3, 219).

All five features, taken individually or combined, occur in cosmological, physical, and psychological accounts of sympathy. All five features are compatible with non-miraculous mechanisms. Sometimes sympathy is a useful, innocent placeholder while one is searching for underlying explanations for many different kinds of causal processes.

The likeness principle is important because it is meant to capture the fact that sympathy is not just introduced to refer to apparent distant action but mutual action or at least the capacity for co-affectability (which is also implicit in features 1 and 5). In a sympathetic relation, all the relata participate or engage; this is why, in fact, sympathy is thought to be an active principle. This is not to deny that there are cases of sympathy where one of the relata is not really active: Smith has a famous example of sympathizing "with the dead" (TMS 1.1.10.13, 12). But in such cases, the inactive relatum is conceived of or imagined as active somehow.[2] To sum up: in its traditional usage, "sympathy" is a concept that picks out a structurally distinct step in a causal process. Its presence may, but need not, invite further inquiry.

With that in mind, I focus more closely on the causal nature of the sequence (i–vii) of the sympathetic process articulated in previous section. I distinguish among the following three different ways in which causation plays a role in this sequence:

[a] the sequence (i–vii) is not merely temporal but also causal (i.e., Smith's "to produce," "makes," "necessarily abates," etc.). From one phase to another in the sympathetic process we are part of a causal sequence.
[b] We deploy (counterfactual) reasoning about causes within different steps in this sequence. That is, in the absence of such reasoning about causes, the sequence (i–vii) will only produce what Smith calls merely "extremely imperfect" sympathy (TMS 1.1.1.9, 11).
[c] I also argue that the reasoning described in [b] is itself a form of mental causation (akin to natural relations in Humean association in the imagination; see Treatise 1.1.4 and 1.3.14.31).

---

[2] I thank Kathryn Pogin for discussion.

Recall the following passage in TMS:

> There are some passions of which the expressions excite no sort of sym-
> pathy, but before we are acquainted with what gave occasion to them,
> serve rather to disgust and provoke us against them. . . . The general
> idea of good or bad fortune, therefore, creates some concern for the
> person who has met with it, but the general idea of provocation excites
> no sympathy with the anger of the man who has received it. Nature,
> it seems, teaches us to be more averse to enter into this passion, and,
> till informed of its cause, to be disposed rather to take part against
> it. Even our sympathy with the grief or joy of another, before we are
> informed of the cause of either, is always extremely imperfect. (TMS
> 1.1.1.7–9, 11)

Smith claims that what we might label "instinctual sympathy" only goes so far. In
some contexts, without knowledge of the causal circumstances that produce the
passions in the agent concerned, the sympathetic process will always lead to what
Smith calls "imperfect sympathy." It seems to follow from Smith's adopted terminology that there exists some (non-instinctual) sequence that leads to perfect, or at
least much less imperfect, sympathy. It can be described as follows: following (T0)

   (i)   a felt moral situation that is experienced or observed empirically by
   (ii) spectators and moral agents, who place themselves in each other's situa-
         tions by way of the imagination including
  (ii*) knowledge of (moral) causes that gave rise to the moral situation, and (ii–
         ii*) involves
  (iii) a sympathetic mutual modulation (informed, perhaps, by observations
         about how the other is reacting), which, in turn, produces
   (iv) a conceived reflected passion within each participant in the sympathetic
         process, and this
   (v)   alters the intensity of the feelings of the participants in the process; after
         several rounds of (ii–v), perhaps, this produces
   (vi) fellow-feeling (sympathy) among spectators and persons principally con-
         cerned, and this produces
  (vii) a second-order pleasure about (vi).

The addition of (ii*) is not *ad hoc*; it reflects significant currents in Smith's thinking about moral evaluation and moral agency. Consider a standard summary that
Smith provides about the natures of propriety and impropriety, on the one hand,
and merit or demerit, on the other hand:

> It has already been observed [TMS 1.1.3.5, 18], that the sentiment or
> affection of the heart, from which any action proceeds, and upon which

its whole virtue or vice depends, may be considered under two different aspects, or in two different relations: first, in relation to the cause
or object which excites it; and, secondly, in relation to the end which
it proposes, or to the effect which it tends to produce:[3] that upon the
suitableness or unsuitableness, upon the proportion or disproportion,
which the affection seems to bear to the cause or object which excites
it, depends the propriety or impropriety, the decency or ungraceful-
ness of the consequent action; and that upon the beneficial or hurtful
effects which the affection proposes or tends to produce, depends the
merit or demerit, the good or ill desert of the action to which it gives
occasion. (TMS 2.1.Intro.2, 67)

There is a lot going on here, and I am not going to provide even the semblance
of a full treatment of the Smithian concept of propriety or merit. All I claim is
that causal relations are constitutive of the nature of both Smithian propriety
and merit. That is, the two central Smithian moral judgments can be characterized schematically in the following temporal sequence: (u) an exciting cause,
which produces (v) a sentiment of heart, which leads to (w) an action and (x) its
foreseeable effects, and, of course, (y) the actual effects produced by (w). First,
judgments of propriety and impropriety, which are principally concerned with
judgments of situations, are judgments of the *proportionality* among (u)–(v)–(w)–
(x). Meanwhile, second, merit and demerit, which are fundamentally judgments
of character, focus on the *proportionality* among (v)–(w)–(y). These two sequences
are fundamentally causal in nature (i.e., "excites," the effect it produces, etc.).

Brown (2009) has offered a wonderful analysis of this passage (that is, TMS
2.1.Intro.2, 67) and calls attention to (u) in order to deny that the step between
(v) and (w) is causal. She does this because she wants to distinguish Smith's
account of agency in TMS from Humean compatibilism. (It is important to
Brown's larger context that Smith's views on agency are distinct in TMS and WN.)
In particular, she thinks that in Smith there is a "non-causal" account of action
(Brown 2009: 61). Her view echoes Griswold (1999), who had argued (against
Cropsey 1957) that Smith embraces an incompatibilist account of the freedom of
the will. But even in TMS Smith never refers to free will, and when he discusses
"the will" at all it only refers to "the will" of the "Deity" or "the great Director of
the universe" (TMS 3.5.12, 170; 3.6.12, 176; 6.2.3.4, 236; 7.2.3.20, 305)—often
in summary of other theorists' positions.

In fact, if we were to take some of the evidence that Brown marshals for her
position literally, then Smith would be a member of a philosophical tradition that

---

[3] One may have thought to distinguish the two relations Smith describes in terms of the kind of
causes they involve. The first involves (to adopt Scholastic terminology) efficient causes and the second final or teleological causes (ends). But Smith goes on to assimilate teleological causes to efficient
causes by treating them as ordinary effects. This is one reason for my deflationary interpretation of
Smith's treatment of final causes.

denies any causal power to finite beings other than God. This is because, as she argues, sometimes (e.g., TMS 1.1.3.5, 18; 1.1.3.9, 18; 2.3.Intro.1, 92; 2.3.Intro.6, 93) Smith embraces the locution "gives occasion to," when describing the transition from (v) to (w) (Brown 2009: 60). Smith certainly is familiar with the writings of Malebranche and other so-called Occasionalists (e.g., TMS 3.4.3, 157; Astronomy 3.1, EPS 48; Edinburgh Review 10, EPS 250, where Régis and Malebranche are presented as "refinements upon the Meditations of Descartes;" see also Smith's long footnote in the Ancient Logics, EPS 123). But such an Occasionalist reading of Smith simply cannot be sustained because in some of the very same passages from TMS that one would have to cite, Smith happily embraces causal languages to describe the affairs of finite beings. Moreover, in WN Smith also uses "occasions" (e.g., WN 1.1.4, 15; 1.1.10, 22, etc.), where even by Brown's lights Smith is constructing a "system of causal relations" (Brown 2009: 66).

Of course, the sequence (u)–(v)–(w)–(x) is a gross simplification and ignores considerable complexity in Smith's treatment of propriety and agency (etc.). But it is crucial that in describing the content of our moral judgments, Smith introduces the language of causal relations. In particular, when we make a moral judgment (of propriety, merit) we do so after mentally inspecting, as it were, the *proportionality* of the relata (say, (u) and (x)) that enter a cause-and-effect relation. As Smith notes, he is here adopting a feature of Clarke's system for his own ends (TMS 7.2.1.48–9, 293–4; this may be thought an additional argument for my claim that Smith is no empiricist).

c. Judgments of Proportionality

In this section I analyze what a judgment of proportionality amounts to in Smith's system. In particular, I explore the degree to which this judgment involves something more akin to a mathematical or an aesthetic judgment.

One might think that Smith's terminology (in TMS 2.1.Intro.2, 67) provides further evidence for his Humean debts. And indeed, Smith's terminology echoes the manner in which Hume treats the natural relation of cause and effect at Treatise 1.1.4. (Recall also Smith's treatment at Astronomy 2.2-7 in Section c in Chapter 3.) At first sight Smith is deploying a Humean framework about the nature of causation here, in which causes are regular successions of a certain sort. But Smith also subtly diverges from Hume, for Hume accepts the following position: "An effect always holds proportion with its cause" ("Of Interest," EMPL 297). I have dubbed this "Hume's ninth rule" because it follows from the conjunction of Hume's fourth and seventh (out of eight) "rules by which to judge of causes and effects" (Treatise 1.3.15; Schliesser 2008). Smith also tacitly appeals to an instance of Hume's ninth rule in his political economy: "The constancy and steadiness of the effect, supposes a proportionable constancy and steadiness in the cause" (WN 1.5.40, 63; see also WN 1.9.h.9, 232).

Thus, Smith's position is that when something like Hume's ninth rule obtains, we are inclined to make judgments of propriety and merit. But he is absolutely clear that in our moral life the ninth rule regularly does not hold—it is not as if judgments of impropriety need to be rare. Or to put the point somewhat differently: Smith thinks that moral causes and effects can be (even monstrously) out of proportion (e.g., TMS 1.1.3.1, 17; 7.2.22, 246; 7.2.28, 250), and this is something that is much harder to incorporate into Hume's framework. (I return to the role of Hume's "ninth rule" and judgments of proportionality in Smith's and Hume's political economy in Section c of Chapter 13.)

Of course, as Smith makes clear, sometimes judgments of proportionality require distance: "I can form a just comparison . . . in no other way, than by transporting myself, at least in fancy, to a different station, from whence I can survey both at nearly equal distances, and thereby form some judgment of their real proportions" (TMS 3.3.2, 135). We cannot be too close to the relata that are being compared.

As Griswold (2006) has emphasized, Smith is adamant on the existence and source of the "precise and distinct measure," which "can be found nowhere but in the sympathetic feelings of the impartial and well informed spectator" (TMS 7.2.1.49, 294; Smith is distinguishing his theory from Clarke's here). By contrast Smith is frustratingly silent about the *nature* of proportionality that goes into the judgment about the relata that enter a cause-and-effect relation.[4] It is unclear if Smith wishes to privilege a mathematical or aesthetic interpretation of proportionality. As happens throughout his writings, he often bring the two together (e.g., Astronomy 4.5, EPS 57; Astronomy 4.28, EPS 71; Astronomy 4.50, EPS 80–1; Imitative Arts, 2.32, EPS 206; Imitative Arts, Annexe 5–6, EPS 211–3). In TMS Smith regularly appeals to the musical language of "concord" and "harmony" to describe mutual sympathy and the pleasures it generates (e.g., TMS 1.1.3.1, 16 and 2.3.1.4, 94). Griswold (1999) has pushed the aesthetic interpretation of Smith's account of moral judgment, and it has been recently reiterated by Valihora (2010) and Chandler (2013).

One might strengthen Griswold's case with an appeal to Hume's important essay, "Of the Standard of Taste." Hume writes, "the principle of the natural equality of tastes is then totally forgot, and while we admit it on some occasions, where the objects seem near an equality, it appears an extravagant paradox, or rather a palpable absurdity, where objects so disproportioned are compared together." For Hume good taste simply involves, in part, just recognizing proportionality and disproportionality.

Even so, I am inclined to emphasize the mathematical over the aesthetic side in understanding Smith's account of proportionality. The reason for my inclination

---

[4] This is especially surprising given that traditionally geometric and arithmetical proportion are associated with different kinds of justice (e.g., Aristotle's *Ethics*, Book V), including different conceptions of just prices.

is twofold. First, Smith has a lack of confidence in the stability of our sense of beauty:

> The principles of the imagination, upon which our sense of beauty depends, are of a very nice and delicate nature, and may easily be altered by habit and education: but the sentiments of moral approbation and disapprobation, are founded on the strongest and most vigorous passions of human nature; and though they may be somewhat warpt, cannot be entirely perverted. (TMS 5.2.1, 200)

Contra Hume, Smith claims that aesthetic taste is just not very stable among different contexts.

Second, in particular, Smith explicitly identifies judgments of proportionality with mathematical skill right at the start of TMS and clearly distinguishes these from judgments of taste/beauty:

> It is the acute and delicate discernment of the man of taste, who distinguishes the minute, and scarce perceptible differences of beauty and deformity; it is the comprehensive accuracy of the experienced mathematician, who unravels, with ease, the most intricate and perplexed proportions. (TMS 1.1.4.3, 20)

This is not to deny that according to Smith taste and mathematical skill can be combined (and I will return to this passage in treating Smith's philosophy of science). Either way, it seems, then, that according to Smith at bottom *our judgments of propriety and merit are constructed out of judgments of (mathematical-like) proportionality about how the motives and expected consequences fit in certain situations as measured by the cultivated feelings of a proper judge (the impartial spectator) rooted in our natural passions.*[5]

The major problem with attributing this view to Smith is that it would seem to put moral judgment out of reach for ordinary people, even if we recognize that this may also help explain why Smith advocates the teaching of geometry to "children of common people" (WN 5.1.f.55, 785). One way to respond to this challenge is to bite the bullet and accept that Smith is an cultural-intellectual elitist about moral judgment (e.g., Brown 2009). But there is a lot of evidence that this is not Smith's preferred position (e.g., Fleischacker 2013). I think the truth about Smith is a bit messier.

Recall that according to Smith we *all* have an *inexact* idea of perfection (TMS 6.3.23, 247, discussed in Section b of Chapter 3), so in principle all of us can

---

[5] My analysis has shown that—*pace* Prior 1949: 74 and 91—Smith does have some resources to step "toward the notion of the truth of a 'judgment of propriety,'" although I do not claim his position gets there all the way.

become discerning judges. Moreover, modeling our behavior on a less than fully exact idea may be sufficient to help us navigate through much of ordinary life. But Smith also thinks that in practice few of us approach the position of a genuine impartial spectator—this would require a rare combination of fully developed moral virtues, and, given the significance of the conception of proportionality defended here, also intellectual virtues (Hanley 2013; see also Chapter 9 below). Therefore, for Smith anybody can, in principle, develop properly cultivated ability for moral judgment, but, in practice, few do. This is compatible both with attributing an analytical egalitarian position to Smith as well as the more elitist interpretation that I favor (recall my discussion in Section a of Chapter 4 about TMS 3.5.1, 161–2, and Smith's contrast between "happiest mould" and "the coarse clay of which the bulk of mankind are formed, cannot be wrought up to such perfection").

I have not explained Smith's concept of an impartial spectator yet, so this story still needs to be fleshed out further. Moreover, as Hanley notes (quoting TMS 7.2.1.50, 294): "while propriety is an 'essential ingredient' in every virtuous action, it is not the sole ingredient" (Hanley 2013: 223). But first we need to complete our analysis of the role of counterfactual reasoning within the sympathetic process itself.

d. Counterfactual Reasoning in the Sympathetic Process

In this section I call attention to the significance of counterfactual reasoning within the sympathetic process. I argue that the process does not only rely on counterfactuals, but is also meant to support them.

Earlier I offered a partial quote from TMS 1.1.4.8, 22. I now reproduce the full passage:

> In order to produce this concord, as nature teaches the spectators to assume the circumstances of the person principally concerned, so she teaches this last in some measure to assume those of the spectators. As they are continually placing themselves in his situation, and thence conceiving emotions similar to what he feels; so he is as constantly placing himself in theirs, and thence conceiving some degree of that coolness about his own fortune, with which he is sensible that they will view it. *As they are constantly considering what they themselves would feel, if they actually were the sufferers, so he is as constantly led to imagine in what manner he would be affected if he was only one of the spectators of his own situation.* As their sympathy makes them look at it, in some measure, with his eyes, so his sympathy makes him look at it, in some measure, with theirs, especially when in their presence and acting under their observation: and as the reflected passion, which he thus conceives, is much weaker than the original one, it necessarily abates the violence of what he felt before he came into their presence,

before he began to recollect in what manner they would be affected by it, and to view his situation in this candid and impartial light. (TMS 1.1.4.8, 22; emphasis added to highlight the text originally omitted)

I offer two claims on the emphasized part of the passage. First, my speculative gloss on Smith's "constantly" here is that Smith means to convey that our imaginative projection into the situation of others (both as spectators and as the person principally concerned) occurs very rapidly. If that is right, I am inclined to interpret the sympathetic process as relying on some kind of unconscious habits similar to, but not identical to, the associative habits in Humean natural relations. Recall from Section b in Chapter 2 that Smith is not committed to the transparency of the mental, so he can allow unconscious thought. As Smith puts it, we "do this so easily and so readily, that I am scarce sensible that I do it" (TMS 3.3.2, 135—in context, Smith is explaining our practice of spectator-taking by way of our practice of visual depth perception). Second, Smith explains that when we imaginatively place ourselves in each other's situations, we do so by counterfactual analysis.

Once one pays attention to it, Smith's moral philosophy is suffused with counterfactual reasoning. I quote two prominent passages (much discussed in Smith scholarship):

1. "As we have no immediate experience of what other men feel, we can form no idea of the manner in which they are affected, but by conceiving what we ourselves should feel in the like situation" (TMS 1.1.1.2, 9; this is known as the "the brother is upon the rack" passage).
2. "We sometimes feel for another, a passion of which he himself seems to be altogether incapable; because, when we put ourselves in his case, that passion arises in our breast from the imagination, though it does not in his from the reality" (TMS 1.1.1.10–11, 12; this is the so-called "calamity of the poor wretch" passage).

We need, therefore, to rewrite the sequence of steps in the sympathetic process: following (T0)

   (i) an intensely/passionately felt moral situation that is experienced or observed empirically by spectators and moral agents
  (ii+) by way of (potentially very rapid and unconscious) counterfactual reasoning within the imagination about causal processes involving persons and situations of spectators and moral agents, who place themselves in each other situations, by way of the imagination including
  (ii*) knowledge of (moral) causes that gave rise to the moral situation, and (ii+–ii*) involves
 (iii*) a frequently counterfactual sympathetic mutual modulation (informed, perhaps, by observations about how the other is reacting), which, in turn, produces

(iv) a conceived reflected passion within each participant in the sympathetic process, and this

(v) alters the intensity of the feelings of the participants in the process; after several rounds of (ii+–v), perhaps, this produces

(vi) fellow-feeling (sympathy) among spectators and persons principally concerned, and this produces

(vii) a second-order pleasure about (vi).

In fact, Smith explicitly allows that the sympathetic process can be counterfactual all the way down:

> No actual correspondence of sentiments, therefore, is here required. It is sufficient that if he was grateful, they would correspond; and our sense of merit is often founded upon one of those illusive sympathies, by which, when we bring home to ourselves the case of another, we are often affected in a manner in which the person principally concerned is incapable of being affected. (TMS 2.1.5.11, 78; see Sidgwick 1892: 214)

Notice that (ii+) and (ii*) both presuppose considerable prior projectable knowledge about how agents act and react to a wide variety of circumstances. We need to have considerable psychological and social knowledge before we can be genuine moral judges at all in addition to possessing a sense of the moral norms that might govern these circumstances. Moreover, (iii*) presupposes considerable skill at emotional attunement, while (ii*) presupposes considerable demands on our abilities to discern social causes. No doubt other moral skills are also presupposed. Even so, the significance of counterfactual reasoning in the sympathetic process is this: the fact that when we make a moral judgment, we do so after mentally inspecting, as it were, the proportionality of the relata that enter a cause-and-effect relation. This capacity to discern such proportionality turns out to require that we are also capable of including or supplying nonfactual relata to this judgment.

As Warren Herold first pointed out to me when he commented on an earlier draft of this chapter, I have, in fact, understated the role of counterfactuals in the sympathetic process; it "also makes use of what might be called counterfactual identities or personal profiles." Herold's claim makes sense if we remember that we often make judgments about characters;[6] we develop reliable expectations about the behavior of characters.[7] These expectations support counterfactual identities. Moreover, Herold rightly claims that according to Smith "we identify

---

[6] At one point, in Smith's lifetime, TMS acquired a telling subtitle: "An essay towards an analysis of the principles by which men naturally judge concerning the conduct and character, first of their neighbours, and afterward of themselves."

[7] This may be even more so in societies not unlike Smith's with fairly fixed "stations" and "offices," where personal and social identity match in the formation of character.

the relevant counterfactuals not before engaging in the process, but during it by exploring the extent and limitations of our capacity for imaginative engagement with feelings that are not our own." I have no doubt that more analysis will reveal further complexities.

Before I turn to Smith's treatment of the impartial spectator, I draw out the significance of Smith's idea that moral judgment involves judgment of (moral) causes and that in doing so we properly see ourselves as (moral) causes.

e. The Piacular, or On Seeing Oneself as a Moral Cause in Adam Smith

In this section I explore, in depth, Smith's account of a version of moral luck (for an excellent recent treatment see Hankins 2016). I do so, primarily, to respond to the possible objection that my reconstruction of Smith's moral theory in the previous sections cannot possibly be right because (so the objection would go) it would counterintuitively imply that for Smith it is appropriate to see oneself as a cause, and this would involve Smith in a kind of category error. As it happens, Smith endorses the counterintuitive consequence; he does so for reasons that reveal quite a bit about the intellectual moral universe that he inhabits. To get Smith's views in focus we must understand his views on a peculiar concept, the "piacular." The three main paragraphs of TMS in which he discusses this unusual concept (2.3.3.4–5, 107 and 7.4.30, 338–9) were all added to Smith's final, sixth edition: TMS 2.3.3.4–5 are inserted in Smith's treatment of moral luck, while TMS 7.4.30 is inserted in a complex discussion of Smith's views on sincerity, inquisitiveness, and casuistry. It is, thus, possible that when he wrote the first edition of TMS, he did not entirely foresee the implications of his own views, but once he noticed it he did not shy away from making these explicit.

What follows presupposes that in Smith's thought there is a surprisingly tight link among nature's regularity, our rationality as well as sanity, and moral judgment in the manifest image. It also assumes on the presented evidence that even the sympathetic process itself is not only a causal process but also relies on our ability to discern causal relations. Thus, in Smith's thinking about morality, the very fact that we are fundamentally part of the chain of causes plays a non-trivial role. If we now connect these aspects to the earlier observation that when we make a moral judgment we do so only after mentally inspecting, as it were, the proportionality of the relata that enter into the cause-and-effect relation, we can infer that on Smith's view, when we are functioning properly we have been attuned in a stable, well-ordered environment to make such proper judgments. This is what I have been calling "environmental rationality."

i. We (Ought to) See Ourselves as Causes!

In this section I argue that according to Smith we ought to see ourselves as causes. Consider the following passage:

> A man of humanity, who accidentally, and without the smallest degree of blamable negligence, has been the cause of the death of another man, feels himself piacular, though not guilty. During his whole life he considers this accident as one of the greatest misfortunes that could have befallen him. If the family of the slain is poor, and he himself in tolerable circumstances, he immediately takes them under his protection, and, without any other merit, thinks them entitled to every degree of favour and kindness. If they are in better circumstances, he endeavours by every submission, by every expression of sorrow, by rendering them every good office which he can devise or they accept of, to atone for what has happened, and to propitiate, as much as possible, their, perhaps natural, though no doubt most unjust resentment, for the great, though involuntary, offence which he has given them. (TMS 2.3.3.4, 107)

In brief, the piacular is the feeling that arises when we have been an involuntary cause of another's harm. It is a feeling of shame that is akin—but not identical— to what is commonly called "agent-regret." In its discomfort the piacular motivates compensatory behavior of atonement that is governed by highly specific norms. In Bernard Williams' influential (1976) treatment, agent-regret also motivates atonement. In what follows, while unpacking Smith's understanding of the piacular, I occasionally remark on the ways in which it is similar to agent-regret. I do so to highlight the crucial normative differences between the Smithian piacular and agent-regret (cf. Hankins 2016).[8]

As has been argued thus far, if we are part of a voluntary cause-and-effect sequence, then the categories of propriety/guilt and merit/demerit are appropriate. If, however, we find ourselves part of an involuntary cause-and-effect sequence, then the category of the piacular can be appropriate—after all, it is predicated on "the man of humanity" (TMS 2.3.3.4, 107). In some other contexts "the man of humanity" is treated as akin to the right kind of impartial spectator (see especially TMS 2.2.3.11, 90; 3.3.4, 137; and 3.3.26, 147, including non-trivial criticism of Hume's notorious treatment of scratching of one's finger at Treatise 2.3.3). Of course, this is not to deny that not all men of humanity are always

---

[8] According to Hankins, "shame typically leads individuals to withdraw from social situations in order to insulate themselves from criticism, whereas piacular guilt, like agent's regret, typically leads individuals to approach others in order to atone or make amends" (Hankins 2016: 737, n. 54). This may be true typically, but I note below that piacular shame is according to Smith a form of pollution in which we try to remove the stain by approaching others.

praiseworthy; according to Smith, "we so frequently find in the world men of great humanity who have little self-command, but who are indolent and irresolute, and easily disheartened, either by difficulty or danger, from the most honourable pursuits" (TMS 3.3.37, 153). However, in the case in which the man of humanity is an involuntary cause, his response is not faulted by Smith in any fashion. In the example above, this can be seen in the way Smith explicitly treats the resentful response of the victim's family as "most unjust," even though their feelings are quite "natural." By contrast, if the man of humanity had been a voluntary cause of the victim's death, their feeling of resentment would have been just. One of the useful aspects of the piacular feeling, then, is to "learn to dread that animal resentment" (TMS 2.3.3.4, 106).

This example also teaches that the natural sentiments, on which the institution of justice is founded, can—once the institution of justice is in place—themselves be "most unjust." This is not because the feelings themselves have been somehow perverted in society and, therefore, "misfire"; Smith is no Rousseau. Moreover, the victim's family's feelings of resentment remain "natural" responses to their loss; they do "fit," as it were, the occasion, except that it turns out our passionate nature has not been constituted to discriminate properly between voluntary and involuntary causes of harm of close kin. In fact, Smith comes thereby close to suggesting that in a hypothetical state of nature it would not pay to discriminate between voluntary and involuntary causes of harm.

Also, we are led to think that the feelings of the "man of humanity" are perhaps not so natural—at least in the sense that most of us (who are probably not regularly men or women of humanity) will mistakenly try to use our lack of culpability or blameworthiness as a way to avoid the feeling of the piacular (I return to this below). Even so, as earlier commentators have emphasized, echoing Williams (1976), if we lacked any feeling whatsoever about even the involuntary harm caused to others by us, something would also be amiss—a robotic "not my fault" somehow makes the situation worse. That is to say, we are causes, and it is part of our humanity that we ought to understand ourselves as such. In its acknowledgment of the significance of outside causes to our well-being, this is a most unStoic move in Smith's thought. We become inhuman when we fail to acknowledge the moral significance of fortune.

Here I introduce a polemical aside in order to undermine the idea that Smith is some kind of Stoic. I do so by way of responding to Raphael and Macfie's introduction to the Glasgow edition of TMS, where they argue for three influential theses. (i) "Adam Smith's ethics and natural theology are predominantly Stoic," which, they claim, "is the primary influence on Smith's ethical thought. It also fundamentally affects his economic theory" (11). (ii) "Essentially . . . WN and TMS and are at one" because Smith's moral defense of self-interest as a form of prudence ties them together. Raphael and Macfie conclude, "there is a difference of tone, but both books treat the desire to better our condition as natural and proper" (11). Their analysis of the second thesis follows from the first because "the moral quality

of prudence depends on its association with the Stoic virtue of self-command"
(9). The second thesis allows them to dismiss the *"Das Adam Smith Problem"*—that
is, the perceived conflict between an egoistic theory of self-interest in the view
of human nature presupposed in WN, and a sympathy-based concept of human
nature that appears to dominate TMS. This is why they conclude, "the so-called
'Adam Smith Problem' was a pseudo-problem based on ignorance and misunderstanding" (20). A crucial step in Raphael and Macfie's argument in dismissing
Das Adam Smith Problem is the third thesis: (iii) "sympathy is the core of Smith's
explanation of moral judgment. The motive to action is an entirely different matter. Smith recognizes a variety of motives, not only for action in general but also
for virtuous action. These motives include . . . self-love. It is this . . . that comes
to the fore in WN" (22). Raphael and Macfie recognize that Smithian sympathy
is to be distinguished from the Stoic and Humean kind, but insist that sympathy
cannot be motivating. As we have already seen, their reading of sympathy cannot
be sustained (see also Montes 2004). Here I raise some further problems for their
first thesis.

In their introduction, Raphael and Macfie note that "Stoicism is given far more
space [in TMS] than any other 'system', ancient or modern, and is illustrated
by lengthy passages from Epictetus and Marcus Aurelius" (5). But this is by no
means conclusive for settling Smith's attitude toward the Stoics, as reflection on
the implication of one of his remarks suggests: "Seneca, though a Stoic, the sect
most opposite to that of Epicurus, yet quotes this philosopher more frequently
than any other" (TMS 7.2.4.5, 307–8)! They insist, however, that Smith's mention of the invisible hand shows that he embraces a Stoic, cosmic harmony view
of nature; I shall challenge this reading in Chapter 10. Nevertheless, even Raphael
and Macfie note three minor differences between the Stoics and Smith in moral
matters: (i) Smith's rejection of Stoic views on suicide, (ii) Smith's rejection of
"the Stoic 'paradoxes' that all virtuous actions are equally good and all failings
equally bad" (9), and (iii) Smith's rejection of the Stoic view that world citizenship
should "obliterate stronger ties of feeling for smaller groups" (10). Yet, Raphael
and Macfie ignore Smith's repeated criticism of Stoic "apathy" and the auster-
ity of Stoic morality (e.g., TMS 3.3.14–16, 143, and 7.2.2.46–47, 292–3); they
ignore evidence that Smith is very critical of Stoic cosmology (Astronomy 4.15,
EPS 63), which undermines their claim that Smith endorses a Stoic picture of
cosmic harmony (e.g., "the plan and system which Nature has sketched out for
our conduct, seems to be altogether different from that of the Stoical philosophy" [TMS 7.2.1.43, 292]). Most astoundingly, they ignore Smith's claim that "the
Stoics, whose opinions were, in all the different parts of philosophy, either the
same with, or very nearly allied to those of Aristotle and Plato, though often disguised in very different language" (Ancient Logics 9, EPS 127; see also Ancient
Physics 11, EPS 116). We can debate the accuracy of Smith's assessment, but it
follows that we have to be cautious in attributing to Smith a Stoic viewpoint if a
Platonic or Aristotelian source is just as likely. Nevertheless, Raphael and Macfie's

Stoicizing reading of Smith has dominated the reception of Smith until very recently (for criticism see Montes 2004; Brubaker 2006a, 2006b; Hanley 2009; Pack 2010, Andrews 2014a, 2014b; Pack and Schliesser 2017).

I return to the main argument. Smith appropriates an old concept, the "piacular." The term is derived from the Latin *piāculum*, which means propitiatory sacrifice, and from *piāre*, which means to appease. In Smith, this presumably unpleasant feeling we ought to have when we are the involuntary cause of harm to others leads, as its etymology suggests, to compensatory behavior (as it also does in Williams' case of agent-regret).

ii. Norms of Appeasement, or On Experts and Smith's Embrace of Fortune . . .

In this section I first describe the norms of piacular appeasement. Then I turn to consider why they help explain, in part, Smith's need for the use of this concept and not, say, guilt or regret. Along the way, I explain the role of fortune in Smith's thought.

When Smith introduces the piacular, he does so with a dramatic case—one is the involuntary cause of the death of another. But as becomes clear in the very next paragraph, many other cases of causing involuntary harm to others can induce the piacular feeling. As Smith writes:

> The distress which an innocent person feels, who, by some accident, has been led to do something which, if it had been done with knowledge and design, would have justly exposed him to the deepest reproach, has given occasion to some of the finest and most interesting scenes both of the ancient and of the modern drama. It is this fallacious sense of guilt, if I may call it so, which constitutes the whole distress of Oedipus and Jocasta upon the Greek, of Monimia and Isabella upon the English, theatre. They are all of them in the highest degree piacular, though not one of them is in the smallest degree guilty. (TMS 2.3.3.5, 107)

Here Smith describes three different "piacular plays." All four named protagonists in these plays violate pre-established marriage rules, and all repay their debt by suicidal death or, in Oedipus' case, with blindness and the giving up of political power. However, the involuntary harm caused is not always death. For example, Jocasta's crime is unknowing incest, while Isabella's is unknowing adultery. Even so, all four are "in the highest degree piacular." This suggests, first, that the piacular comes in degrees, but, second, that perhaps above a certain threshold of harm (for instance, the violation of a major social institution), the piacular just becomes maximal.

Furthermore, TMS 2.3.3.4 makes clear that it is not just the harm caused that matters but also the relative social status between the cause of harm and the victim of harm, at least insofar as compensating the victim is concerned. This suggests that the discharge or the atonement of the piacular feeling is sensitive to social context and status. However, in the dramatic cases described in 2.3.3.5, the discharge involves death or (sacrificial) suicide by the female characters. From this I infer that, on the one hand, when the harm caused is primarily (or solely) to others, the "price" of atonement is governed, in part, by the relative social status of the victim and the involuntary cause. On the other hand, when the harm caused is a violation against a fundamental institution of civil society (marriage and family laws, etc.), then the "price" required is the ultimate sacrifice (at least on the theatrical stage).

As noted, Smith returns to the piacular in Part VII of TMS, and his treatment here sheds some further light on the norms governing atonement:

> It is not always so with the man, who, from false information, from inadvertency, from precipitancy and rashness, has involuntarily deceived. Though it should be in a matter of little consequence, in telling a piece of common news, for example, if he is a real lover of truth, he is ashamed of his own carelessness, and never fails to embrace the first opportunity of making the fullest acknowledgments. If it is in a matter of some consequence, his contribution is still greater; and if any unlucky or fatal consequence has followed from his misinformation, he can scarce ever forgive himself. Though not guilty, he feels himself to be in the highest degree, what the ancients called, piacular, and is anxious and eager to make every sort of atonement in his power. Such a person might frequently be disposed to lay his case before the casuists, who have in general been very favourable to him, and though they have sometimes justly condemned him for rashness, they have universally acquitted him of the ignominy of falsehood. (TMS 7.4.30, 338–9)

This paragraph is offered in the midst of Smith's critical treatment of casuistry (see also WN 5.1.f.30, 771, to be discussed below). This paragraph confirms that the piacular comes on a continuum that is governed by the harm caused. Smith implies that we can make relatively clear judgments about differences in the harm caused. If the harm is fatal to others, one is piacular in the highest degree. This suggests that the norms governing the price of the atonement are determined by the kind of harm (to norms of society, others, self, etc.) and the extent of that harm (how fatal, etc.), both of which take precedence over the relative social status of the victim and involuntary cause.

Also, Smith does not treat the feeling of the piacular as a mistake in some way; rather, here the "real lover of truth" embraces the feeling. It is hard to imagine that Smith would use this description for somebody fundamentally in error in her reactive attitudes. As such, it seems that both the virtuous ("man of humanity") and the wise ("lover of truth") can have this feeling. In fact, as I remarked above,

Smith thinks it is in some sense not a natural propensity to feel piacular. When we are neither virtuous nor wise, we are more likely to seek out the clerical experts (casuists), who—on payment—might sometimes be able to provide us with plausible reasons to evade feeling what we ought to feel. That is to say, ordinarily we sense that we ought to feel something—that there is an apt response—to situations producing harm to others in which we have been an unwilling cause. And yet, unless virtuous and wise, we also tend to go out of our way to avoid feeling it. Given this, part of the indictment against casuistry concerns the way in which it commercially facilitates moral-psychological escapism. In contrast to many of his modern admirers, Smith does not think that all free markets are always just. Moreover, as the analytical egalitarian reading of Smith has emphasized (Peart and Levy 2005; Levy and Peart 2008a, 2008b), Smith is especially suspicious of the manner in which the market for (moral) experts operates.

While here Smith does not further elaborate on the significance of relative social status in governing the norms of atonement, he does reemphasize that in the worst cases atonement will never fully succeed in discharging the piacular feeling. In such cases one "can scarce ever forgive" oneself and, recall, during one's "whole life" one considers "the accident as one of the greatest misfortunes that could have befallen" oneself. This thought extends beyond the pagan origins of the piacular, where "proper atonement" can end the "vengeance of that powerful and invisible being" (TMS 2.3.3.4, 107).

In addition, we learn from this passage (TMS 7.4.30, 338–9) why Smith is eager to distinguish the piacular feeling from guilt, and why earlier he had called it a "fallacious sense of guilt." The reason for this is that the piacular is a species of shame. This sets Smith clearly apart from a Williams-inspired reading in terms of agent-regret, which does not invoke shame (cf. Hankins 2016). While Smith never defines shame, for him it is primarily a consequence of the inward judgment of the imagined impartial spectator, even in an otherwise innocent person; see, for example, his treatment of the case of the "unfortunate" and "innocent" Calas, who is condemned by religious bigots for murdering his son, for whom the very idea of a posthumous (and unjust) infamy causes shame (TMS 3.2.11, 120). In particular, in Smith, shame is connected to ideas of being permanently stained or polluted (TMS 7.4.13, 333).[9] Given that the virtuous ("man of humanity") and the wise ("lover of truth") can have this feeling, I see no reason to doubt that the impartial spectator can endorse piacular judgments.[10]

Moreover, Smith's reflections on the piacular can be connected to the material covered in earlier sections of this chapter (and the treatment of environmental rationality in Section c of Chapter 3). If it is constitutive of human beings to be, in

[9] As noted above, Hankins (2016) misses that shame may motivate attempts to efface the "stain."

[10] Hume is also no stranger to taking the pollution metaphor seriously; see Hume's treatment of Queen Elizabeth's response to Bishop "Bonner, from whom she turned aside, as from a man polluted with blood, who was a just object of horror to every heart susceptible of humanity" (History 4:4).

part, a cause and, furthermore, if all causes are experienced as the Humean feeling of necessity, then it may well be the case that some lucky "causes" will simply get to glide through life. Meanwhile, other "causes," who may be largely indistinguishable from their fellow "causes," will be marked just in virtue of the harms that follow from their existence.

While much of TMS and the account of the "irregularity of sentiments" in particular is quite compatible with and, at first blush, even seems explicitly designed to elicit the approval of providential arguments (for example, even in context, Smith frequently talks of "Nature's intentions," "the Author of nature's plan," the "wisdom and goodness of God," etc.), *in this context* Smith is explicit that it is "Fortune, which governs the world" (TMS 2.3.1, 104). This is no slip of the pen: Smith's embrace of the piacular points toward an acknowledgment of the Epicurean system, which was then commonly associated with either the rule of chance or Spinozist necessitarianism—both of which are compatible with the rule of Fortune as presented by Smith. While I have a lot more to say about Smith's relationship to religion, Smith's treatment of the piacular does not only call attention to his anticlericalism but also raises serious problems for treating Smith as fundamentally Christian.

Smith's interest in the significance of fortune tends to be overlooked, but is, in fact, explicitly signaled, in the famous first sentence of TMS: "How selfish soever man may be supposed, there are evidently some principles in his nature, which interest him in the fortune of others, and render their happiness necessary to him, though he derives nothing from it except the pleasure of seeing it" (TMS 1.1.1.1, 9; a few paragraphs later he notes [recall] that "the general idea of good or bad fortune, therefore, creates some concern for the person who has met with it" [1.1.1.8, 11]). Nearly all informed readers recognize that this is a response to the Hobbes–Mandeville thesis (the "selfish hypothesis"). Smith is making a rather strong claim about the intrinsic properties of human nature; our nature is, in part, disinterested enough in wanting others to be happy. Smith treats this as evident.[11]

Smith uses "fortune" in different ways; sometimes it just means "wealth." Thus, for example, a famous sentence in WN (quoted above) reads, "An augmentation of fortune is the means by which the greater part of men propose and wish to better their condition" (2.3.28, 341). Smith also often uses "fortune" and "misfortune" in the sense of "flourishing" and "misery." But sometimes he is very explicit that he is using "fortune" as a way to convey something chancy: "The man who, by some sudden revolution of fortune, is lifted up all at once into a condition of life, greatly above what he had formerly lived in, may be assured that the congratulations of his best friends are not all of them perfectly sincere" (TMS 1.2.5.1, 41).

---

[11] Smith allows that seeing other people's happiness is pleasurable, and that may be thought to concede too much to the selfish hypothesis.

Our interest in the fortunes of others may not always be a cause of pleasure, after all. (Our sympathy with other people's [sudden] joy is weak according to Smith.) Fortune coincides with what the "vulgar" call "chance."

This use of "fortune" is not an isolated occurrence. One of the most important passages in TMS (and it fits the general argument of WN) condemns Mercantilistic, colonial empires and slavery:

> There is not a negro from the coast of Africa who does not, in this respect, possess a degree of magnanimity which the soul of his sordid master is too often scarce capable of conceiving. Fortune never exerted more cruelly her empire over mankind, than when she subjected those nations of heroes to the refuse of the jails of Europe, to wretches who possess the virtues neither of the countries which they come from, nor of those which they go to, and whose levity, brutality, and baseness, so justly expose them to the contempt of the vanquished. (TMS 5.2.9, 206–7)

For present purposes, the significance of this passage is not Smith's moral and political condemnation of slavery and imperialism (nor his somewhat surprising appeal to Rousseau's noble savage–like imagery); I return to that below. Rather, Smith resists in seeing in this world-historical event the working of either providence or historical necessity. There is no unintended consequence here that justifies the suffering of the "vanquished;" there is no hint of a remedy that will fit in some kind theodicy of necessary commercial development. Bad (and good) things happen to innocent people for no cosmic reason at all.

It does not follow that Smith was in all things a modern or revived Epicurean (as Reid suggests in response to TMS [see Norton and Stewart-Robertson 1980; Stewart-Robertson and Norton 1984]). But we may also understand at least some of Smith's criticisms of Hobbes and Mandeville (and even Hume) as in-house debate.

As we have seen, cases of the piacular are marked by a *disproportion* (in Smith's sense) between cause and effect; the worse the case of the piacular, the more this is so. They thus represent a very real danger to the mental health of well-formed minds. In this sense, the most piacular events are very much like the cases Smith describes of sudden, unexpected events:

> The passion is then poured in all at once upon the heart, which is thrown, if it is a strong passion, into the most violent and convulsive emotions, such as sometimes cause immediate death; some-times, by the suddenness of the ecstasy, so entirely disjoint the whole frame of the imagination, that it never after returns to its former tone and composure, but falls either into a frenzy or habitual lunacy; and such as almost always occasion a momentary loss of reason, or of that attention

to other things which our situation or our duty requires. (Astronomy
1.2, 34–5)

Therefore, piacular atonement serves three, related purposes: (i) the appeasement of the resentment of the victim (and her family); (ii) the potentially futile
attempt at discharging the unpleasant inward feeling of shame; (iii) acknowledging that one is, in some sense, a marked or polluted cause not because of
original sin, but because of the rule of fortune. Only (i) is compatible with
agent-regret, whereas the other two indicate that Smith's piacular is a distinct
feeling much closer to shame than regret. As we will see in the next section,
Smithian shame also generates a compensatory desire (to remove the feeling
of distress).

It would be tempting to conclude the treatment of the piacular here. However,
we have not yet explained why in reflecting on this atonement Smith introduces
the language of sacrifice and why he claims an ancient pedigree for the piacular.
To answer these questions I turn to the general mechanism of which the piacular
is an instance.

iii. Superstition and Grandeur

In this section I analyze the psychological mechanism of which the piacular is an
instance. In particular, I emphasize the ineliminable role of superstition in the
piacular.

In the context of Smith's second treatment of the piacular in TMS 7, he
describes the general psychological mechanism of which it is an instance:

> The consciousness, or even the suspicion of having done wrong, is a
> load upon every mind, and is accompanied with anxiety and terror in
> all those who are not hardened by long habits of iniquity. Men, in this,
> as in all other distresses, are naturally eager to disburthen themselves
> of the oppression which they feel upon their thoughts, by unbosoming
> the agony of their mind to some person whose secrecy and discretion
> they can confide in. The shame, which they suffer from this acknowl-
> edgment, is fully compensated by that alleviation of their uneasiness
> which the sympathy of their confident seldom fails to occasion. It
> relieves them to find that they are not altogether unworthy of regard,
> and that however their past conduct may be censured, their present
> disposition is at least approved of, and is perhaps sufficient to com-
> pensate the other, at least to maintain them in some degree of esteem
> with their friend. A numerous and artful clergy had, in those times
> of superstition, insinuated themselves into the confidence of almost
> every private family ... and hence the origin of books of casuistry.
> (TMS 7.4.17, 333–4)

To oversimplify somewhat: in normal circumstances one must find some compensating mechanism to rid oneself from psychological distress.[12] *Any* discreet, sympathetic person would be able to do the job. On Smith's anticlerical interpretation, the clergy's development of casuistry exists to supply this need. Smith suggests that in more Enlightened "times," one can dispense with this role for the clergy.

It is tempting to think that according to Smith his (and our) times are no longer superstitious—that this is simply run-of-the-mill Enlightenment rhetoric of progress. But if that were the case, it would make no sense for Smith to introduce the language of the "piacular" into his treatment of that species of shame involved in being an involuntary cause of harm. After all, from the point of view of reason, propitiatory sacrifice and a focus on purification just seem highly superstitious. Moreover, while I suspect that many reasonable readers would be willing to agree with Smith that some response is appropriate to being an unwilling cause of harm (for instance, a response along the lines of, say, Williams' agent-regret), few would want to follow Smith into the language of pollution and shame.

Smith himself signals that he is at least aware that on this score he is hardly being a "modern." He describes the feeling as "what the ancients called, piacular." These ancients are pagans of the "heathen religion." The word "piacular" and its variants are extremely rarely used in extant Latin works (and seem entirely absent in the Christian Roman sources). However, Livy seems to be Smith's source on the piacular. We know from Smith's lectures on Rhetoric that he knew Livy well, although the piacular is also mentioned in Lucan's *Pharsalia*, a text he would have (re-)read in light of the epigraph of Book 3 of the Treatise (Russell 2008: 75–80; when Durkheim discusses piacular rites at length, without mention of Smith, he traces the concept back to Pliny's Natural History (Durkheim 1912: 557).

In fact, in LJ, "superstition" is basically treated as synonymous with attempts at bribing deities (with prayer or sacrifice) for some favor to alleviate one's fear. Smith treats Ancient slaves' inability to engage in sacrificial bribing of the gods as one of the main causes of the growth of Christianity:

> I observed before that superstitious fears and terrors increase always with the precariousness and uncertainty of the manner of life people are engaged in, and that without any regard to their religion. . . . Slaves were of all others the most dependent and uncertain of their subsistence. Their lives, their liberty, and property were intirely at the mercy of the caprice and whim of another.—It was therefore very hard that they who stood most in need of some consolation in this way should be intirely debarred from all religious societies, {which might at least sooth their superstitious dreads}. The gods then were alltogether locall or tutelary; they did not conceive any god that was equally favourable to the prayers of all. . . . Besides, the deities then could never be addressed empty handed; who ever had any request to ask of them must introduce

---

[12] Environments in which one practices "long habits of iniquity" are profoundly irregular.

it with a present. This also intirely debarred the slaves from religious offices as they had nothing of their own to offer; all they possessed was their masters. . . . This it was which made all religions which taught the being of one supreme and universall god, who presided over all, be so greedily receivd by this order of men. (LJ, Tuesday, February 15, 1763)

Smith's neo-Lucretian, even proto-Nietzschean, account of the original success of Christianity (prior to its clerical corruption) makes no reference to the truth of its doctrines and leaves out mention of miracles and saints. Rather, he treats paganism as creating a kind of market failure in the market of consolation in the context of extreme uncertainty that monotheism, which accepts payments in the currency of prayer, rectifies.

If Smith had just used the language of shame and avoided the language of sacrifice, it would not be clear that the third aspect of atonement I called attention to above (recall [iii]: acknowledging that one is, in some sense, marked or polluted) is all that significant. But Smith's treatment of the piacular emphasizes sacrifice. Thus, Smith's whole discussion of the piacular swerves uncomfortably toward the position that there are circumstances in which piacular shame is justified while being akin to superstition. Presumably, the only reason why the piacular is not ultimately classified as an instance of superstition is because the wise and virtuous are not motivated in their atonement by that fear that is held to be the essential core of superstition (see Hume's "Of Superstition and Enthusiasm," EMPL, 73–7).

The significance of the nature of superstition in the piacular becomes clear when we reflect on a closely related case in Smith:

> Gratitude and resentment . . . are excited by inanimated, as well as by animated objects. We are angry, for a moment, even at the stone that hurts us. A child beats it, a dog barks at it, a choleric man is apt to curse it. The least reflection, indeed, corrects this sentiment, and we soon become sensible, that what has no feeling is a very improper object of revenge. When the mischief, however, is very great, the object which caused it becomes disagreeable to us ever after, and we take pleasure to burn or destroy it. We should treat, in this manner, the instrument which had accidentally been the cause of the death of a friend, and we should often think ourselves guilty of a sort of inhumanity, if we neglected to vent this absurd sort of vengeance upon it. (TMS 2.3.1.1, 94)

A stone that hurts us is also an involuntary cause of harm. In this sense, it is structurally identical to cases of the piacular. Reactive attitudes toward a stone that harms us are *natural and even humane*, and yet they are "improper" and "absurd." While Smith clearly could have thought that piacular shame and the feeling of pollution would also be absurd—as many modern moral philosophers are wont to think, opting instead for the more sensible notion of agent-regret (Hankins 2016)—Smith suggests that the piacular feeling is perhaps not so absurd. According to him, the piacular feeling of shame teaches us "to reverence the happiness" of our "brethren" (TMS 2.3.3.4, 106). Thus, paradoxically, it is when we are most like a stone in the inevitable causal chain of nature that we are most in a position to be taught the proper attitude toward our common humanity (which is really quite different from a stone). A further important consequence, according to Smith, is that we are forced to adopt a kind of general do-no-harm principle: "to tremble lest [we] should, even un-knowingly, do any thing that can hurt" our fellow brethren (TMS 2.3.3.4, 106). This principle is central to Smith's political philosophy (see section c.i. in Chapter 7).

To avoid confusion, I am not claiming that Smith thinks that propitiatory sacrifice is always superstitious. As he wrote in the original ending of the first through fifth editions (though this was removed in the sixth edition):

> The doctrines of revelation coincide, in every respect, with those orig-
> inal anticipations of nature; and, as they teach us how little we can
> depend upon the imperfection of our own virtue, so they show us, at
> the same time, that the most powerful intercession has been made,
> and that the most dreadful atonement has been paid for our manifold
> transgressions and iniquities. (TMS 2.2.3, 92)

Here, Smith is self-consciously echoing the New Testament; for instance, "Look, the Lamb of God, who takes away the sin of the world!" (John 1:29) and "This cup is the new covenant in my blood, which is poured out for you" (Luke 22:20).

Much has been made about the removal of these lines, but if we assume for the sake of argument that Smith was entirely sincere in these lines (and ignore the Epicurean treatment of Fortune above), there are two things to note about the case of the ordinary piacular. First, Smith provides no hint that he is assimilating the piacular to an instance of the imitation of Christ; second, Christ's sacrifice does not eradicate the need to purify the person who does unwilling harm, even if granted that Christ's remission of sin need not alleviate the guilty feeling that accompanies sin.

Even if the foregoing is correct, it is still somewhat unclear why Smith harkened back to a heathen concept that, at the very least, flirts with superstition in the way it is associated with ideas that emphasize propitiatory sacrifice, purification, and pollution. Perhaps it must be conceded that there is something fundamentally unreasonable about it.

However, Smith claims that the payoff of these not-quite-reasonable ideas is that "the happiness of every innocent man is, in the same manner, rendered holy, consecrated, and hedged round against the approach of every other man." The insight here is a simple one, namely that we require some of these not-entirely-reasonable notions in order to activate feelings that will make us care in the right way for "the happiness of every innocent man." On this point, Smith's writings reveal a concern with the fact that even humane philosophers, who ought to know better, sometimes do not consider the happiness of all. As he writes regarding Plato's attitude toward infanticide: "The humane Plato ... with all that love of mankind which seems to animate all his writings, no where marks this practice with disapprobation" (TMS 5.2.15, 210). Given that Plato was untouched by doctrines of original sin, Plato ought to have seen infants as entirely innocent, but he fails to show sufficient regard for them.

In particular, Smith recognizes that our ordinary sentiments fail to ensure that we take the happiness of all innocent people into consideration. As Smith writes in a passage added to the second edition of TMS:

> It is not the love of our neighbour, it is not the love of mankind, which upon many occasions prompts us to the practice of those divine virtues. It is a stronger love, a more powerful affection, which generally takes place upon such occasions; the love of what is honourable and noble, of the grandeur, and dignity, and superiority of our own characters. (TMS 3.3.5.4, 137)

Smith rejects here both Hutcheson's benevolent "love of mankind" and Christian neighborly love as providing, in practice, the proper motivational pull. Rather, a willingness to care about the happiness of all requires what he calls divine virtues, including those that are in some sense a kind of superior or highly elevated self-love (Hanley 2009). We have to be motivated by both a love of what is honorable and noble as well as dare see ourselves as great souls in a certain fashion (see Chapter 15). The highest form of the piacular is exhibited only in those capable of such divine virtues. This leaves open, of course, why Smith thought such people, in particular, require that others are rendered holy to them.

iv. Natural Sentiments and Enlightenment, or Nature Versus Reason

In this section I argue that despite Smith's commitment to an Enlightenment project of spreading knowledge through the population, his moral philosophy reveals that he thought that superstitious beliefs play an integral and, ultimately, ineliminable positive role in our moral life. This does not mean he thought most superstitious beliefs ought to be encouraged—he clearly thinks that values like impartiality and equal worth are fundamental to moral judgment (Darwall 2004).

As we have seen, according to Smith, in cases of inanimate instruments that harm us, nature and reason need not be in harmony with each other. Another instance of this is his claim: "That kings are the servants of the people, to be obeyed, resisted, deposed, or punished, as the public conveniency may require, is the doctrine of reason and philosophy; but it is not the doctrine of Nature" (TMS 1.3.3, 53). In this context, Smith seems to side against the Lockean doctrine with nature (see also TMS 3.3.8, 139; see also Frazer 2010: 108 on LJ(A) v.126, 320).

Instances of the piacular, then, are significant because, from the point of view of environmental rationality, in them nature itself is revealed as—to use a Smithian word—irregular: the family and friends of those harmed feel a natural but nonetheless unjust resentment. And while Smith implies that the majority of us who find ourselves in the unlucky position of being unwilling causes will likely flee to casuists (clerical or secular) who can supply us with excuses to avoid carrying around our discomfort and offer us ways to atone, a few, more noble and sensitive souls—those with the soundest judgments—will remain marked forever. Smith seems to have believed that reflection on cases of the piacular can help us appreciate the moral significance of everybody.

Thus, I read Smith as embracing the idea that aspects of superstition play an essential and sometimes positive role in the workings of our moral life (Garrett 2005). One might think that my evidence for this claim is slender given that it hangs on the interpretation of three paragraphs added to the final edition of TMS. But consider also the following passage:

> If the injured should perish in the quarrel, we not only sympathize with the real resentment of his friends and relations, but with the imaginary resentment which in fancy we lend to the dead, who is no longer capable of feeling that or any other human sentiment. But as we put ourselves in his situation, as we enter, as it were, into his body, and in our imaginations, in some measure, animate anew the deformed and mangled carcass of the slain, when we bring home in this manner his case to our own bosoms, we feel upon this, as upon many other occasions, an emotion which the person principally concerned is incapable of feeling, and which yet we feel by an illusive sympathy with him. The sympathetic tears which we shed for that immense and irretrievable loss, which in our fancy he appears to have sustained, seem to be but a small part of the duty which we owe him. The injury which he has suffered demands, we think, a principal part of our attention. We feel that resentment which we imagine he ought to feel, and which he would feel, if in his cold and lifeless body there remained any consciousness of what passes upon earth. His blood, we think, calls aloud for vengeance. The very ashes of the dead seem to be disturbed at the thought that his injuries are to pass unrevenged. The horrors which are supposed to haunt the bed of the murderer, the ghosts which, superstition imagines, rise from their graves to demand vengeance upon those who brought them to an

untimely end, all take their origin from this natural sympathy with the imaginary resentment of the slain. (TMS 2.1.2.4, 71)

The part of the sympathetic process that enlivens an idea can naturally and justifiably draw on counterfactual imagery that by Smith's light is "superstition." This superstition is the product of "Nature," which has "stamped upon the human heart, in the strongest and indelible characters, an immediate and instinctive approbation of the sacred and necessary law of retaliation" (TMS 2.1.2.4, 71). Or, to put it simply, at the heart of those natural, sympathetic mechanisms and reactive attitudes that form the foundations of moral thinking and justice, we encounter superstition. Thus, while Smith has a very different account from Hume of the role of the natural sentiments in generating the institution of justice, not unlike Hume (see EPM 3) he ends up calling attention to the way in which these institutions cannot do without some manner of thought that seems absurd from the point of view of a rationalizing Enlightenment.[13]

An uncharitable reader might think Smith's project is part and parcel of Enlightenment elitism, which notes the "absurd," "improper," and even "superstitious" nature of mankind. But, as we have seen, Smith's approach includes the wise and virtuous among those who draw on superstitious elements. There is, thus, no reason for thinking that the "precise and distinct measure" that can be found "in the sympathetic feelings of the impartial and well-informed spectator" would be entirely exempt from such superstition (see also Section d in Chapter 11).

With that in place, I now turn to explaining Smith's conception of the impartial spectator.

f. The Impartial Spectator

In this section I explain the nature of Smith's treatment of the impartial spectator. Spectatorial moral theory can be found in works as diverse as Plato's *Laws* and Hume's *Treatise*, but Smith offers one of the most detailed account prior to the twentieth century. Here I focus primarily on explaining Smith's account of the moral development of an impartial spectator.

Because of a comment by John Rawls, Smith's treatment has been assimilated to Firth's Ideal Observer theory (Rawls 1971: 184–5; Firth 1952). But this is misleading. First, Firth's Ideal Observer theory posits an ideal figure who is omniscient, omnipercipient, disinterested, and dispassionate. Firth attributes to his spectator the kind of properties we find in the agents who populate (then contemporary) neoclassical models of economics. But these are far removed from Smithian imperfect and situated spectators. As D. D. Raphael usefully emphasizes,

---

[13] Of course, some of us may lack fear, and so we will not ourselves be superstitious even if we engage in superstition.

Smith's impartial spectator only shares with Firth's Ideal Observer the quality of disinterest—if "disinterest" is understood as impartial (Raphael 2007: 44; to be sure, Firth's theory was never offered as an interpretation of Smith). Second, Raphael is alert to the use of Firth in Rawls's treatment of the impartial spectator as a device of utilitarian theory; he correctly criticizes Rawls for treating Hume and Smith as classical utilitarians (Raphael 2007: 45–6; cf. Rosen 2005). It is certainly misleading to treat Smith as an act-utilitarian or straightforward consequentialist (Montes 2004: 105–13). Duty plays a very large role in Smith (Montes 2004: 112–29).

Yet, while the details of Rawls's argument cannot be supported, Raphael does not appreciate Rawls's core insight. Raphael ignores lots of evidence from TMS and WN that, befitting a student of Hutcheson, Smith is often willing to endorse (median-based) consequentialist conclusions when evaluating social institutions (see Chapter 8).

Therefore, in what follows I discuss Smith's account of the psychological and social mechanisms that facilitate the development and cultivation of impartial spectators. I explain how according to Smith the impartial spectator within (i) judges by way of the norms of society one has been socialized in, but (ii) is capable of doing so in defiance of actual social judgments. I look closely at the resources available to Smith to support judgments that go against existing social norms.

Recall from Section c of Chapter 3 that the content of all derived or social passions involves three features: <(i) some desire (aversion, joy), (ii) an idea of the triggering social object, (iii) our (empowering/impotent) sense of ourselves moving up or down in the estimation of an (internally) selected group of observers>. It's the third, other-regarding feature that makes all our social passions, in principle, always possible *moral* (in the modern sense) sentiments. This is because if our social passions incorporate the standards of the right sort of observer—Smith's impartial spectator, whose sympathetic feelings, are (recall) a "precise and distinct measure" (TMS 7.2.1.49, 294)—then they are properly moral.

Of course, just because our social passions *can* incorporate the estimation of the right sort of observers does not mean they do so *in fact*. What drives us to have properly cultivated feelings? It turns out that another group of natural passions do important work:

> MAN naturally desires, not only to be loved, but to be lovely; or to be that thing which is the natural and proper object of love. He naturally dreads, not only to be hated, but to be hateful; or to be that thing which is the natural and proper object of hatred. He desires, not only praise, but praise-worthiness; or to be that thing which, though it should be praised by nobody, is, however, the natural and proper object of praise. He dreads, not only blame, but blame-worthiness; or to be that thing which, though it should be blamed by nobody, is, however, the natural and proper object of blame.

> The love of praise-worthiness is by no means derived altogether
> from the love of praise. Those two principles, though they resemble
> one another, though they are connected, and often blended with one
> another, are yet, in many respects, distinct and independent of one
> another. (TMS 3.2.1–2, 113–4; added to the sixth edition of TMS)

Smith thinks we desire love, to be lovely, praise, and to be praiseworthy (etc.).
Strikingly, when describing our desire for being lovely, our desire for praiseworthiness, our dread of being hateful and blameworthy, Smith does not treat us
as persons, but as "things" that are in principle subject to the justified praise/
love bestowed by a counterfactual audience that judges one even when "nobody"
is around to actually do so. That is, the desire for praiseworthiness, the desire
to be lovely, the dread of being hateful, and the dread of blameworthiness rely
on the same cognitive mechanisms that operate during the sympathetic process: counterfactual reasoning about causes (now understood as "things") in the
imagination.

Smith insists that the love of praise and the love of praiseworthiness are "in
many respects, distinct and independent of one another." In particular, he denies
(against the selfish hypothesis of Hobbes and Mandeville) that the love of praiseworthiness is derived from or an extension of the love of praise. Rather, he claims
"the love of praise seems, at least in a great measure, to be derived from that
of praise-worthiness" (TMS 3.2.3, 114; also added in sixth edition). Smith's is a
conceptual-developmental point; in the right kind of circumstances, our experience of desiring to be praiseworthy triggers our natural desire for praise. The right
context is informed by Smith's view that "the love and admiration which we naturally conceive for those whose character and conduct we approve of, necessarily
dispose us to desire to become ourselves the objects of the like agreeable sentiments, and to be as amiable and as admirable as those whom we love and admire
the most" (TMS 3.2.3, 114).

Earlier in TMS Smith writes that "approbation heightened by wonder and
surprise, constitutes the sentiment which is properly called admiration" (TMS
1.1.4.3, 20). The editors of the Glasgow edition of TMS claim that this statement
contradicts the account offered in Astronomy because there Smith claims that
"Wonder, Surprise, and Admiration, are words which, though often confounded,
denote, in our language, sentiments . . . distinct from one another" (Astronomy
Intro.1, EPS 33). But in the very same sentence of Astronomy, Smith also calls
these sentiments "allied" and only "in some respects different." Thus, there is no
contradiction. According to Smith, when we admire something, we feel approval
with a mixture of surprise and wonder. What I have called "the triggering condition" is what's really distinct about these passions: "What is new and singular,
excites that sentiment which, in strict propriety, is called Wonder; what is unexpected, Surprise; and what is great or beautiful, Admiration" (Astronomy Intro.1,
EPS 33).

Given that the content of admiration includes both surprise and wonder, it is itself intrinsically an unsteady feeling. Recall from Section e of Chapter 3 that surprise and wonder cause a vacillation in the imagination. (Smith insists that even though admiration includes the unpleasantry of wonder, it is itself an "agreeable" sentiment [TMS 3.2.3, 114]). Therefore, when we encounter people whom we love and find great and beautiful, we have a drive to discharge the feeling (Valihora 2010). But unlike ordinary instances of wonder and surprise, where we are motivated to expand our taxonomy or search for invisible chains, Smith insists that in cases of loving admiration we want to imitate so we can become loveable and admirable ourselves. It's this imitative practice and the preexisting "ideal of perfection" (TMS 6.3.23, 247; recall Section b in Chapter 3) that triggers the natural propensity to love praiseworthiness (Chandler 2013).

Ordinarily love and admiration are first prompted by a child's parents. We can illustrate this by drawing on Smith's biography. Recall that Smith grew up without a father, but he had a considerable attachment to his mother. Upon her death he writes his publisher Strahan:

> tho' the death of a person in the ninetieth year of her age was no doubt an event most agreable to the course of nature; and, therefore, to be foreseen and prepared for; yet I must say to you, what I have said to other people, that the final separation from a person who certainly loved me more than any other person ever did or ever will love me; and whom I certainly loved and respected more than I ever shall either love or respect any other person. (June 19, 1784, Corr., 275)

Smith remained an admiring and respectful child nearly his whole life.

In one sense Smith's theory is extremely promising; all humans start out as children, so we all encounter conditions that will trigger the desire for praiseworthiness (even if we are orphans, there will be surrogate parents of various sorts). Unfortunately, there is no guarantee that we will have proper objects of imitation. There is a sense in which a young child cannot help loving her parents and finding them beautiful. This is all that's needed for Smith's theory because he does not require that the parents really are loveable and beautiful; they just need to be thought so to trigger eventually the conditions that will promote in us the desire of praiseworthiness. But this is not to deny that Smith did not recognize that our childlike tendency to admire the great and beautiful is not also deeply problematic:

> THIS disposition to admire, and almost to worship, the rich and the powerful, and to despise, or, at least, to neglect persons of poor and mean condition, though necessary both to establish and to maintain the distinction of ranks and the order of society, is, at the same time,

the great and most universal cause of the corruption of our moral sentiments. (TMS 1.3.3.1, 61; added in the sixth edition)

Our moral sentiments are "corrupted" when we habitually include in them the
estimation of the wrong kind of observers. Smith has no doubt that, in practice, "The great mob of mankind are the admirers and worshippers, and, what
may seem more extraordinary, most frequently the disinterested admirers and
worshippers, of wealth and greatness" (TMS 1.3.3.2, 62). Thus, in itself ordinary
development can generate proper cultivation, but it is not likely to do so. For
"we frequently see the respectful attentions of the world more strongly directed
towards the rich and the great, than towards the wise and the virtuous. We see
frequently the vices and follies of the powerful much less despised than the poverty and weakness of the innocent" (TMS 1.3.3.2, 62). Smith really condemns
the ways of the world and is really on the side of "the study of wisdom and the
practice of virtue" (TMS 1.3.3.2, 62). In particular, a reformist-minded reader of
Smith (e.g., de Grouchy, Wollstonecraft, Paine, Millar) might well conclude that if
we were exposed to institutions that were less likely to facilitate the disposition
to worship the rich and powerful, there might well be less corruption of the moral
sentiments. Institutions that facilitate egalitarian outcomes will help turn us into
more moral persons (Herzog 2013: 109; Herzog 2014).

But Smith does not approach the sordid facts merely from the vantage point
of a moralist; he recognizes that the same mechanism that is (a) needed to trigger the development of an impartial spectator, in fact, (b) generally corrupts our
moral sentiments and (c) also is "necessary both to establish and to maintain the
distinction of ranks and the order of society!" (TMS 1.3.3.1., 61). In (c) Smith
suggests that our admiration for superiors is part of the cognitive mechanisms
that ground and preserve social hierarchy and with it social order (see also TMS
6.2.21, 225–6; Khalil 2005; Tegos 2013b). Even if Smith were an anarchist, his
talk of "society" (not government) implies that no "social order" is without some
such moral corruption. Given that Smith is, thus, committed to the claim that
all "civil government supposes a certain subordination" (WN 5.1.b.3, 710), even
the "obvious and simple system of natural liberty," which Smith promotes (e.g.,
WN 5.9.51, 687), also presupposes cognitive mechanisms that will also facilitate
and almost certainly produce the corruption of the moral sentiments. (Smith tells
the same story about our "admiration of success" [TMS 6.3.30, 253, added to the
sixth edition.)

Therefore, while we should not turn a blind eye toward Smith's perfectionist
and reformist aspirations, he accepts part of Rousseau's verdict about some of the
negative consequences of living in society. Smith's commitment to (c) is also an
important difference between Smith and his more radical admires like Paine and
de Grouchy. The latter, for example, believes there is "the sentiment of natural
equality which causes us to feel jealousy, or at least a certain harshness towards
everything that is above us" (LS, IV, although in context she assumes it is less

common among the English). Paine is more willing than Smith to propose institutions that might be thought to facilitate directly reduced disparities in wealth and status (*Agrarian Justice*; Anderson 2016).

Anyway, nearly all of us encounter conditions that will trigger the desire for praiseworthiness. These desires will be proper if they can be approved by the impartial spectator within. Let us turn to Smith's account of the origin of the impartial spectator and the circumstances in which it give its proper verdict. Recall Smith's thought experiment about "a human creature" that grows to "manhood in some solitary place:"

> Bring him into society, and he is immediately provided with the mirror which he wanted before. It is placed in the countenance and behaviour of those he lives with, which always mark when they enter into, and when they disapprove of his sentiments; and it is here that he first views the propriety and impropriety of his own passions, the beauty and deformity of his own mind. (TMS 3.1.3, 110)

We learn to judge (ourselves and others) morally and aesthetically from the judgments of the people who surround us as we grow up. We then develop the habit of seeing ourselves from without:

> In the same manner our first moral criticisms are exercised upon the characters and conduct of other people; and we are all very forward to observe how each of these affects us. But we soon learn, that other people are equally frank with regard to our own. We become anxious to know how far we deserve their censure or applause, and whether to them we must necessarily appear those agreeable or disagreeable creatures which they represent us. We begin, upon this account, to examine our own passions and conduct, and to consider how these must appear to them, by considering how they would appear to us if in their situation. We suppose ourselves the spectators of our own behaviour, and endeavour to imagine what effect it would, in this light, produce upon us. This is the only looking-glass by which we can, in some measure, with the eyes of other people, scrutinize the propriety of our own conduct. If in this view it pleases us, we are tolerably satisfied. We can be more indifferent about the applause, and, in some measure, despise the censure of the world; secure that, however misunderstood or misrepresented, we are the natural and proper objects of approbation. On the contrary, if we are doubtful about it, we are often, upon that very account, more anxious to gain their approbation, and, provided we have not already, as they say, shaken hands with infamy, we are altogether distracted at the thoughts of their censure, which then strikes us with double severity. (TMS 3.1.5, 112)

Thus, in practice, as we grow up, we internalize the values and expectations of our community, and we learn to see ourselves in light of their opinions. In effect, both our social feelings (or derived passions) and evaluations of these feelings refer to the estimations of others. If these are in accord with each other, we feel empowered; if they are really at odds, we're ashamed. Smith emphasizes the point with similar language ("elevated with secret triumph of mind") in the conclusion of his chapter criticizing Hume's theory of justice at TMS 4.2.12, 193. But, crucially, as we develop the habit of referring our feelings and actions to the judgments of *imagined* others, we already can, in principle, become independent of their actual praise or blame. At TMS 3.1.5, 112, Smith subtly implies that we are more likely to become independent of society's actual judgment if we are inclined to like how we see ourselves. Therefore, a kind of inborn or properly cultivated self-satisfaction not humility may, in fact, be necessary to become the right kind of judge who does not fall victim to fashion and social corruption either by correctly applying the general rules of morality latent in society or by actually attaining the right kind of distance oneself. Presumably such a self-satisfaction may lead to a form of socially useful pride. (Another careful reader of Smith, Malthus, also calls attention to "decent and useful pride" [Malthus 1992: 239].) So we should not be surprised that for Smith the "divine virtues" can only be practiced by people who feel what he calls (recall) the "dignity, and superiority of our own characters" (TMS 3.3.5.4, 137; see also Hume's Treatise 3.3.2.8; and for excellent discussion, see Taylor 2016).

Of course, there is a fine line here: in practice, we are likely to overvalue the way we see ourselves. Smith is especially adamant that in the heat of our "selfish passions" before and after we act, we are likely to see ourselves with a "very partial" view (TMS 3.4.1–3, 157). Thus, Smith has no doubt that "self-deceit, this fatal weakness of mankind, is the source of half the disorders of human life" (TMS 3.4.6, 158–9).

It should be clear now why earlier I emphasized the significance of the counterfactual reasoning within the sympathetic process. This is because before the impartial spectator can attain a judgment, we divide ourselves, "as it were, into two persons" (TMS 3.1.6, 113). In general, the impartial spectator just is the internalized judgment of a properly impartial, properly indifferent (but not unfeeling), properly distant, well-informed person whom we imagine within us and who then engages "us" in the sympathetic process by way of counterfactual reasoning.

So far I have emphasized that the impartial spectator within (i) judges by way of the norms of society one has been socialized in, but (ii) is capable of doing so in defiance of actual social judgments. Even so, this may be thought not sufficient for a morality worth having. After all, what if the norms of society are corrupt—as Smith certainly thinks is possible? Smith discusses an example of a whole society having an erroneous judgment on a *particular* moral issue. In the context of criticizing Aristotle's and Plato's views on infanticide he writes,

> When custom can give sanction to so dreadful a violation of humanity, we may well imagine that there is scarce any particular practice so gross which it cannot authorise. Such a thing, we hear men every day saying, is commonly done, and they seem to think this a sufficient apology for what, in itself, is the most unjust and unreasonable conduct. (TMS 5.2.15, 210)

Therefore, Smith clearly recognizes that (c) "environmental rationality" (recall Section c of Chapter 3) does not always track all of what humanity demands from us (see also his criticism of infanticide in China in WN 1.8.24, 90; China is a wealthy society that suffers from imperfect institutions; see Hanley 2014 for judicious analysis).[14]

But first, it is worth asking what resources are available to properly cultivated impartial spectators so that we can go against what is "commonly done" within Smith's moral theory. In a part that was added to the sixth edition of TMS, Smith writes:

> In estimating our own merit, in judging of our own character and conduct, there are two different standards to which we naturally compare them. The one is the idea of exact propriety and perfection, so far as we are each of us capable of comprehending that idea. The other is that degree of approximation to this idea which is commonly attained in the world, and which the greater part of our friends and companions, of our rivals and competitors, may have actually arrived at. We very seldom (I am disposed to think, we never) attempt to judge of ourselves without giving more or less attention to both these different standards ... So far as our attention is directed towards the first standard, the wisest and best of us all, can, in his own character and conduct, see nothing but weakness and imperfection; can discover no ground for arrogance and presumption, but a great deal for humility, regret and repentance ... The wise and virtuous man directs his principal attention to the first standard; the idea of exact propriety and perfection. There exists in the mind of every man, an idea of this kind, gradually formed from his observations upon the character and conduct both of himself and of other people. It is the slow, gradual, and progressive work of the great demigod within the breast, the great judge and arbiter of conduct ... He feels so well his own imperfection, he knows so well the difficulty with which he attained his own distant approximation to rectitude, that he cannot regard with contempt the still greater imperfection of other people. Far from insulting over their inferiority, he views it with

---

[14] I have a tendency to downplay Smith's debts to Stoicism, but it is undeniable that here Smith sides with Epictetus (see the *Discourses* 1.23.8–10). I thank David Levy for discussion.

the most indulgent commiseration, and, by his advice as well as example, is at all times willing to promote their further advancement. (TMS 6.3.23–5, 247–8)

According to Smith, the first standard can always inspire critical reflection, including humility. As he puts it at the start of TMS: "we very frequently make use of two different standards. The first is the idea of complete propriety and perfection, which, in those difficult situations, no human conduct ever did, or ever can come up to; and in comparison with which the actions of all men must for ever appear blameable and imperfect" (TMS 1.1.5.9, 26). So, as long as a society has notions of exactitude and perfection in it, some critical distance toward prevailing norms can be generated immanently (see also Frazer 2010: 105; for a different approach see Golemboski 2015).

According to Smith, it clearly helps if within society there exists an "archetype of a perfection" or a conception of the "divine artist" whose handiwork can be emulated (TMS 6.3.25, 247). In the preface to the *Principia*, Newton had encouraged his readers to emulate "the most perfect mechanic of all."[15] Regardless if Smith recalls his Newton, Smith is drawing on classic Christian-Platonic themes here. Setting aside Smith's religious views, Smith recognizes that "the very suspicion of a fatherless world" (TMS 6.2.3.2, 235) may undercut the social utility of certain religious ideas. Absent the idea of a "divine artist," it may (as Locke argued in defense of Protestant mutual toleration) be harder to properly activate or cultivate conscience.

Recall that (at TMS 7.3.2.2, 318) Smith reads Hobbes as intending to solve primarily a theological-political problem: how to handle (competing) clerical ambition(s) without generating preconditions for the breakdown of legal order and civil war. Then what "a sound moralist" also needs to show is how, from natural, human propensities, an impartial spectator worth having can (necessarily) be generated without requiring the assistance of either religious revelation or state intervention. That is to say, this passage also bears on the controversy over the degree to which a society of atheists is possible. Here Smith seems to be implying that some religious commitments involving perfection and infinity need to be in the culture in order to create norms that can offer immanent criticism. It would follow from this that one needs to be very cautious about removing or undermining certain kind of theistic ideas.

However, Smith could also have thought that the study of mathematics (the science of exact proportion) could furnish the appropriate critical distance from contemporary mores and public opinion. As he writes in a different context,

---

[15] "[T]he whole subject of *mechanics* is distinguished from *geometry* by the attribution of exactness to geometry and of anything less than exactness to *mechanics*. Yet the errors do not come from the art, but from those who practice the art. Anyone who works with less exactness is a more imperfect mechanic, and if anyone could work with the greatest exactness, he would be the most perfect mechanic of all" (Isaac Newton, *Principia* 1999: 381–2).

"mathematicians, on the contrary, who may have the most perfect assurance, both of the truth and of the importance of their discoveries, are frequently very indifferent about the reception which they may meet with from the public" (TMS 3.2.20, 124). It should not surprise us, then, that when Smith presents his educational reform in WN, he thinks it is crucial that the "common people" are

> instructed in the elementary parts of geometry and mechanicks, the literary education of this rank of people would perhaps be *as complete as it can be.* There is scarce a common trade which does not afford some opportunities of applying to it the principles of geometry and mechanicks, and which would not therefore gradually exercise and improve the common people in those principles, the necessary introduction to the *most sublime* as well as to the most useful sciences. (WN 5.1.f.55, 785, emphasis added)

Smith's rationale is, in part, clearly connected to his views on what became known as "human capital" theory (Blaug 1976; Teixeira 2007). Clearly he thinks that a generally educated workforce can be more productive, and in this sense geometry and mechanics are very useful. Moreover, in context it is clear that Smith also thinks his educational reforms would improve the quality of soldiering (WN 5.1.f.56–9, 786–7). One can recognize this point while emphasizing that Smith distinguishes between selling one's productive capacity as opposed to selling oneself (Herzog 2013: 70–1).

But we should not overlook the moral animus behind Smith's program. Smith emphasizes not just the direct social utility of these sciences, but also their sublimity and the way they complete the literary education of ordinary people—that is, a kind of indirect utility. While Smith may sometimes be using "sublime" in different senses, he also associates it with Burkean ideas of the infinite and eternal (and infinite and eternal being; I leave aside her the direction of influence between Burke and Smith). As he writes in a passage added to the sixth edition of TMS: "The idea of that divine Being, whose benevolence and wisdom have, from all eternity, contrived and conducted the immense machine of the universe, so as at all times to produce the greatest possible quantity of happiness, is certainly of all the objects of human contemplation by far the most sublime" (TMS 6.2.3.5, 236).[16] It follows from Smith's account that he ought not to undermine this sublime idea.

Just before, Smith had argued that an education that includes the "elementary parts of geometry and mechanicks" may be able to combat the "torpor" of "mind" that Smith thought subsequent to a "whole life . . . spent in performing a

---

[16] The passage clearly shows that Smith is familiar with the religious psychological and cultural roots of utilitarianism.

few simple operations, of which the effects too are, perhaps, always the same, or very nearly the same" (WN 5.1.f.50, 782). Smith's educational reform program stems from his concern for the mental well-being of the laboring class and is crucially focused on moral and political consequences: "The torpor of his mind renders him, not only incapable of relishing or bearing a part in any rational conversation, but of conceiving any generous, noble, or tender sentiment, and consequently of forming any just judgment concerning many even of the ordinary duties of private life." Of the great and extensive interests of his country, he is altogether incapable of judging; (WN 5.1.f.50, 782). De Grouchy follows Smith in thinking that "the main objects of education should be to provide some ease in acquiring general ideas and in experiencing ... abstract and general sentiments" (LS, V). Geometry and mechanics were understood as sciences that relied on abstraction and dealing in the most general ideas.

So, on Smith's view, the extensive division of labor associated with the mechanization of work is for all its economic benefits a very important source of corruption of the moral sentiments. And Smith clearly thinks that rather than preaching more (religious) morality, some mathematical and scientific literacy is a better source of keeping our passions appropriately moral. In particular, Smith believes that the "study of science and philosophy" can have social utility in suppressing "enthusiasm and superstition;" this is why he advocates mandatory exams in them for anybody who wants to practice a profession (WN 5.1.9.14, 796; 5.1.f.50–6, 781–6). For all his praise of the good moral-political consequences of the Scottish presbytery, Smith argues that religious education needs to be supplemented by a more worldly education; this is necessary to maintain freedom, public accountability, and order in a modern society (WN 5.1.f.61, 788).

Regardless what one thinks of the merits of Smith's diagnosis of the potential moral incompetence of the working classes and his proposed solutions, Smith's claim that we sometimes judge our own and other people's efforts by a standard of exact propriety and perfection is not sufficiently appreciated by those who worry how in Smith's moral psychology or moral epistemology a critical stance can be developed. It is a very important issue to Smith, as he explained his Letter No. 40 to Sir Gilbert Elliot, when preparing revisions to be included in the second edition of TMS: "that our judgments concerning our own conduct have always a reference to the sentiments of some other being, and to shew that, notwithstanding this, real magnanimity and conscious virtue can support itself under the disapprobation of all mankind" (Corr. 49; Brubaker 2002 and Corsa 2015 provide excellent discussion). Given that for Smith "real imperfection" is present in *all* of humanity's works, there will *always* be room for immanent criticism. (For more on the ways that Smith anticipates critical theory, see Otten 2016.) To be clear: on the whole, any possible, genuine impartial spectator will always deliver the most context-sensitive judgments of propriety.

However, for some readers Smith's position will be inadequate. For it is unclear how Smith can feel confident that the moral-psychological development of a genuine impartial spectator is, in principle, always possible. For it seems to follow from his principles that in some societies the sentiments are quite widely corrupt (see Sidgwick 1892: 218). Smith does not ignore this implication. For example, about his own society, he regularly criticizes "The savage injustice of the Europeans" in their colonial imperialism (e.g., WN 4.1.32, 448), and he suggests that under feudalism "The lords despised the burghers, whom they considered not only as of a different order, but as a parcel of emancipated slaves, almost of a different species from themselves" (WN 3.3.8, 402; see also TMS 6.2.1.13, 223). Smith recognizes that even to recognize other humans as fellow humans can be a moral achievement in some cultures.

Thus, Smith also discerns that in the context of militarism, when there is extreme inequality of power and fortune, we should not expect much moral sensitivity (WN 4.7.c.80, 626). As Smith puts it, "before we can feel much for others, we must in some measure be at ease ourselves" (TMS 5.2.9, 125). Some social orders undercut this systematically. So, the argument for commercial society is, in part, that it makes better moral functioning possible (Herzog 2013: 109; Herzog 2014. Even so, Smith denies that (nearly) all of a society's mores can be entirely corrupt (TMS 5.2.15, 211). In the context of Smith's consequentialist approach to evaluating social institutions, I critically discuss his argument in Chapter 8 by returning to his treatment of infanticide.

PART 2

SOCIETY

6

Society and Political Taxonomy

Individuals, Classes, Factions, Nations, and Governments

In this chapter I discuss some of Smith's more important economic and political categories. I argue that it is misleading to understand Smith as a methodologic individualist (cf. Arrow 1994: 2). In particular, I argue that "society" is a crucial category in Smith's political philosophy.

Smith is often taken to be a methodologic individualist. This makes good sense, of course: one of his characteristic claims—in the way it mixes empirical and normative commitments—is that the "private frugality and good conduct of individuals, by their universal, continual, and uninterrupted effort to better their own condition" and not "the profusion of government" is the source of English "wealth and improvement" (WN 2.3.6, 345). Smith treats it as an empirical fact that self-interested behavior ("bettering" on one's "condition") combined with individual decent behavior ("good conduct") leads to good outcomes ("wealth and improvement.")

Moreover, "consumption is the sole end and purpose of all production; and the interest of the producer ought to be attended to, only so far as it may be necessary for promoting that of the consumer" (WN 4.8.49, 660). Surely, Smith has in mind *individual* consumption here. One can quote a few more of such passages. From the vantage point of the great twentieth-century debates over, say, markets versus regulation, state versus individual (etc.), Smith must appear as a rather robust individualist. This, too, has informed my decision to focus extensively on Smith's account of the individual passions in the previous chapters of this book. But close analysis of Smith's account of the derived passions has already indicated that some of the most important of our private feelings always refer us to (the imagined estimation of) others. And, in fact, "the chief part of human happiness arises from the consciousness of being beloved" (TMS 1.2.5.1, 41; see also TMS 3.1.7, 113; 3.5.8, 166; 6.2.1.19, 225).

But neither the individual nor government is initially the main focus of Smith's political economy and his political philosophy. One might think this claim is a bit absurd because a critic might claim that the nation is clearly Smith's focus by pointing to the title of WN, which refers to "nations." And, indeed the first sentence of the book would seem to confirm this: "THE annual labour of every nation is the fund which originally supplies it with all the necessaries and conveniences of life which it annually consumes, and which consist always, either in the immediate produce of that labour, or in what is purchased with that produce from other nations" (WN Intro.1, 10). Here a nation is said to labor (or produce) and consume necessaries and conveniences or trade these with other nations. The very next sentence seems to suggest that nations are composed of a "number" of consumers (WN Intro.2, 10), and readers can be forgiven if they infer these must refer to individuals as ultimate elements of nations. In fact, still on the first page, Smith draws a stark contrast between the "miserably poor," savage nations of "hunters and fishers," which face "the necessity sometimes of directly destroying, and sometimes of abandoning their infants, their old people, and those afflicted with lingering diseases, to perish with hunger, or to be devoured by wild beasts," and the "civilized and thriving nations" (WN Intro.4, 10; going over the same point a few pages later, Smith contrasts a "rude" vs. an "improved" society [WN 1.1.4, 15]). In the very same discussion of savage nations, Smith introduces individuals, alongside families and tribes (WN Intro.4, 10). Without denying that individuals matter a lot to Smith, this chapter aims to correct a one-sided focus on the individual.

This is because, in his treatment of the thriving nations, Smith writes,

> the produce of the whole labour of the society is so great, that all are often abundantly supplied, and a workman, even of the lowest and poorest order, if he is frugal and industrious, may enjoy a greater share of the necessaries and conveniences of life than it is possible for any savage to acquire. (WN Intro.4, 10)

Workmen, order(s), and society are, in fact, more significant analytical categories in WN than, say, individual, family, and nation. For example, "society" is used ten times more frequently than "consumer."

To be precise, throughout WN Smith is concerned with describing the transition from circumstances of society in which individuals and their families matter to those circumstances in which properly divided workmen do. Here is a characteristic passage from the start of WN in which Smith illustrates one of his core economic axioms, that "That the division of Labour is limited by the Extent of the Market:"

> In the lone houses and very small villages which are scattered about in so desert a country as the Highlands of Scotland, every farmer must be butcher, baker and brewer for his own family. In such situations we can scarce expect to find even a smith, a carpenter, or a mason, within less than twenty miles of another of the same trade. The scattered families that live at eight or ten miles distance from the nearest of them, must learn to perform themselves a great number of little pieces of work, for which, in more populous countries, they would call in the assistance of those workmen. (WN 1.3.2, 31)

Densely populated societies with lots of consumers will have more division of labor and will be more productive and, thus, wealthier than dispersed societies (composed of "very small villages" and "families") without an extensive division of labor.

Thus, Smith calls attention to the fact that given the accidents of history, states and nations can be composed of different kinds of society. We tend to associate post-Treaty-of-Westphalia (1648) Europe with the nation-state. But during the eighteenth century, Great Britain alone included several, only loosely integrated nations (English, Scots, Irish, Welsh, etc.) some of whom—as the example above of Scotland indicates—involve themselves more than one society (Ireland is divided along the "most odious of all distinction, those of religious and political prejudices … [which] commonly render the inhabitants of the same country more hostile to one another than those of different countries ever are" [WN 5.3.89, 944]). As Smith repeatedly points out, in his day a huge number of "restrictions are imposed upon the inland trade," and "regulations take place through the whole kingdom" (WN 4.8.21 and 23, 650). Formal and informal trade barriers keep societies distinct. WN is, in fact, one long argument for the claim that by not preventing trading between societies, a nation and nations may become a more homogeneous (and wealthier) society, even as the occupations within and among them become ever more specialized and differentiated (anticipating Gellner 1983).

But Smith does not claim that the existence of trade alone will always create integrated societies; one reason why he advocates a political and economic "union" between Ireland and Great Britain (and praises the 1702 union between England and Scotland) is that sometimes the impartial administration of law is a precondition to break down internal practical barriers. With such a union "the people of all ranks in Ireland would gain an equally compleat deliverance from a much more oppressive aristocracy" (WN 5.3.89, 944).

Thus, societies are a distinct analytical category between individuals and governments.[1] In the extremely poor savage stage(s), there are sometimes no governments "above" society (that is, the savage state is anarchic). It is also compatible with Smith's view that with trade integration a transnational "society" can develop, but he recognizes that trade can just as easily cause friction:

> Commerce, which ought naturally to be, among nations, as among individuals, a bond of union and friendship, has become the most fertile source of discord and animosity. The violence and injustice of the rulers of mankind is an ancient evil, for which, I am afraid, the nature of human affairs can scarce admit of a remedy. But the mean rapacity, the monopolizing spirit of merchants and manufacturers, who neither are,

---

[1] David Levy has suggested in private correspondence that you can understand Smith's focus on society if you see it as combining Smith's commitment to scarcity of time (and human finitude more generally) with sympathetic agency, which limits attention. (See also Forman-Barzilai 2010: 150; Griswold 1999: 305.)

nor ought to be the rulers of mankind, though it cannot perhaps be corrected, may very easily be prevented from disturbing the tranquillity
[*sic*] of any body but themselves. (WN 4.3.c.9, 493)

He was almost certainly familiar with Addison's (proto-Kantian) argument that
trade was conducive to peace (see, e.g., *Spectator* No. 69, Saturday, May 19, 1711).
Yet, Smith clearly does not believe that universal peace is likely. In fact, while Smith
promotes trade, he is aware that trade also increases the likelihood of war (Paganelli
2013: 343 cites WN 4.8.53, 661 and 5.3.37, 920; see also Van de Haar 2013). The
lack of "remedy" for the "violence and injustice of the rulers of mankind" suggests
that he does not believe in genuine theodicy (cf. Waterman 2002; recall also WN
5.1.b.16, 718). But he does think that if the proper "rulers of mankind" can be
taught their true interests, then many trade-related wars can be averted.

Even so, once there is more than a modest amount of possessions, government
will be developed to secure property rights. (Remember, this is a normological
claim; it will not always happen, but over time it is likely that it will.) While Smith
recognizes the significance of and argues for the independence of society from
government (I ignore his priority dispute with Ferguson),[2] one of the first points
he makes in WN is that good government can make a non-trivial difference to the
flourishing of society and its least advantageous members: "It is the great multiplication of the productions of all the different arts, in consequence of the division of labour, which occasions, in a *well-governed society*, that universal opulence
which extends itself to the lowest ranks of the people" (WN 1.1.10, 22 [emphasis
added]). In fact, the following is a useful hermeneutic heuristic: throughout WN
when Smith focuses primarily on economic analysis, he writes about "society;"
when he focuses on moral or political matters, he will speak of "civilized society"
(e.g., WN 1.8.39, 97) or "political society" (1.8.36, 96).

There is a methodologic point lurking here. When in WN Smith deploys concepts like "family," "village," or the "individual" he tends to be describing societies
in early stages of development. Generalizations about these societies do not necessarily project to advanced agricultural or commercial societies. Unless Smith
specifies these, it is not always easy to tell which ones do or do not. But Smith
sometimes make the scope of the generalization explicit. For example:

every prudent man *in every period of society*, after the first establishment of the division of labour, must naturally have endeavoured to
manage his affairs in such a manner, as to have at all times by him,
besides the peculiar produce of his own industry, a certain quantity of

---

[2] One reason I ignore it is that the significance of (civil) society is clearly noted already by Locke and
Hume (and undoubtedly others). In the Introduction to the Treatise, Hume writes that "politics con-
sider men as united in society, and dependent on each other," and he repeatedly returns to the issue
(Treatise Intro.5); on Locke see Chapter 7 of the Second *Treatise* (Seligman 1995).

some one commodity or other, such as he imagined few people would be likely to refuse in exchange for the produce of their industry. (WN 1.4.2, 37–8; emphasis added)

I have been unable to find an explicit definition of "society" in Smith's writings. They are said to have "general circumstances," and one very significant measure of these is what Smith calls "an ordinary or average rate both of wages and profit in every different employment of labour and stock" (WN 1.7.1, 72; in the next paragraph Smith adds "average rate of rent," although that is also influenced by what he calls "natural or improved fertility"). Leaving aside momentarily the details, this suggests that for Smith once one has advanced beyond being an extremely "rude" society, a "society" just *is* some combination of laws, institutions, norms, and productive capacity shared by a particular "neighborhood," or as he puts it a few pages later, "different employments, and . . . different laws and policy" (WN 1.7.36, 80).

In practice, when speaking about "societies," Smith distinguishes between societies that have a very different, predominant social organization (that is, they are organized around the "stages" of fishing/hunting, shepherding, agriculture, or commerce) and "societies" within "stages," which tend to be distinguished by the extent of the shared market with (as we will see below) a predominant shared staple, which "regulates" other commodities. But predominant characteristics of a stage are not merely economic. For example, "in commercial countries," the "authority of law is always perfectly sufficient to protect the meanest man in the state." This is, in fact, what helps explain the dispersion of extended families and the lack of predominant significance of these in commercial stages: "Regard for remote relations becomes, in every country, less and less, according as this state of civilization has been longer and more completely established" (TMS 6.2.1.13, 223).

Moreover, "great" (i.e., very large or very powerful) reasonably advanced societies are also divided among different economic classes with often very different predominant sources of income (rent, wages, profit) and often different conflicting interests. To put it crudely, according to Smith rent and wages rise with the increasing prosperity of society (for explicit statements on wages see WN 1.8.21–2, 86–7; on rents see WN 1.11.p.1, 264). By contrast, Smith thinks that in rich societies the rate of profit is low (WN 1.9.20, 113), while in poor societies it would be high, and "it is always highest in countries which are going fastest to ruin" (WN 1.11.p.10, 266). Smith claims that in prosperous countries (that is, those in which capital had already been accumulated) "mutual competition" among merchants, who have abundant sources of capital, would drive down profit rates (WN 1.9.2, 105; cf. Turgot [1770] 1889, §XC, where competition is absent), while poor and declining countries would scare off merchants, thus increasing potential profit for the adventurous few. For Smith high wages and high profits do not tend to go together; he did recognize an exception to this general rule in "the peculiar circumstances of new colonies," where profits, due to relative lack of stock, and wages, due to high growth, could both be high (WN 1.9.11, 109). One may be tempted to claim that Smith thought that the rate of growth determines the rate of profit, but it is important to see that Smith thought that the unusual circumstance of the American colonies (abundant fertile land, unusually low prices for land, etc.) was an exception that proved the rule. Of course, the rate of growth can influence the rate of profit for Smith, but, ordinarily, profit is more closely (and inversely) linked to growth.

All this implies that in Smith's opinion there is, except in new colonies, an inherent conflict over resources between the wage-earning laborers and the profit-oriented merchants (WN 1.8.11, 83 and WN 1.11.p.8–10, 265–7). That is, a "society" is not by definition harmonious. In fact, Smith claims that the political backwardness of the lower classes and the landed classes vis-à-vis the merchant class is due to their inability to understand their own political interests in a commercial society even though theirs better coincides with it (WN 1.11.p.7– 10, 265–7; much of WN is one big lament on how the merchants and tradesmen have hijacked the economic instruments of the state to their own advantage). The causes for the failure of the workers and the landholders to properly understand their own interests and how they are affected by regulations are not identical. Smith thinks that the former often lack basic education and are too overworked to gather and properly analyze the necessary information (recall WN 5.1.f.50, 781). The latter are often spoiled by luxury, which makes their minds "incapable of that application ... which is necessary in order to foresee and understand the consequences of any publick regulation" (WN 1.11.p.8, 265; see also WN 1.11.a.1, 223 and 5.2.c.13, 831). Therefore, classes have distinct interests. Admittedly, unlike his intellectual rival, James Steuart (1966), Smith does not generally use "class" in the relatively modern sense I have been doing here (but see WN 1.8.26, 90).

Smith often uses the term "orders" to refer to these three classes. For example, in most countries "rent and profit eat up wages, and the two superior orders of people oppress the inferior one. But in new colonies, the interest of the two superior orders obliges them to treat the inferior one with more generosity and humanity" (WN 4.7.b.3, 565). I assume that Smith is being descriptive in deploying hierarchical language, but it is also possible that he is being sarcastic (because he is criticizing their immoral behavior).

But sometimes Smith uses "orders" in more fine-grained, constitutional fashion. Consider the following passage(s) from TMS:

> Every independent state is divided into many different orders and societies, each of which has its own particular powers, privileges, and immunities. Every individual is naturally more attached to his own particular order or society, than to any other. His own interest, his own vanity, the interest and vanity of many of his friends and companions, are commonly a good deal connected with it. He is ambitious to extend

its privileges and immunities. He is zealous to defend them against the encroachments of every other order or society.

Upon the manner in which any state is divided into the different orders and societies which compose it, and upon the particular distribution which has been made of their respective powers, privileges, and immunities, depends, what is called, the constitution of that particular state.

Upon the ability of each particular order or society to maintain its own powers, privileges, and immunities, against the encroachments of every other, depends the stability of that particular constitution. That particular constitution is necessarily more or less altered, whenever any of its subordinate parts is either raised above or depressed below whatever had been its former rank and condition.

All those different orders and societies are dependent upon the state to which they owe their security and protection. That they are all subordinate to that state, and established only in subserviency to its prosperity and preservation, is a truth acknowledged by the most partial member of every one of them. It may often, however, be hard to convince him that the prosperity and preservation of the state require any diminution of the powers, privileges, and immunities of his own particular order or society. This partiality, though it may sometimes be unjust, may not, upon that account, be useless. It checks the spirit of innovation. It tends to preserve whatever is the established balance among the different orders and societies into which the state is divided; and while it sometimes appears to obstruct some alterations of government which may be fashionable and popular at the time, it contributes in reality to the stability and permanency of the whole system ...

The man whose public spirit is prompted altogether by humanity and benevolence, will respect the established powers and privileges even of individuals, and still more those of the great orders and societies, into which the state is divided. Though he should consider some of them as in some measure abusive, he will content himself with moderating, what he often cannot annihilate without great violence ... When he cannot establish the right, he will not disdain to ameliorate the wrong; but like Solon, when he cannot establish the best system of laws, he will endeavour to establish the best that the people can bear. (TMS 6.2.2.7–10, 230–1 and 6.2.2.16, 233; see also WN 4.5.b.53, 543)

In this context an "order" is a subset of a political subentity with recognized legal rights and (economic) privileges and duties. (An "order" and a "society" can coincide.) In Books 3 and 4 of WN, Smith describes how these are a legacy from attempts by the kings to reduce the power(s) of the great lords. But Smith clearly signals that members of an order have more "attachment" to each other (than to members of other orders) from "interest and vanity;" this is a consequence of mutual sympathy by partial spectators (see also the treatment of "contagion" when discussing the dangers of faction at TMS 3.3.43, 155). While Smith does not defend the "zealous" defense of orders, he certainly expresses a preference for the political status quo; if changes, which are not forthcoming on their own, are desirable and in the interest of, say, preserving the state or ameliorating existing abuses, the relative powers of orders should be respected as much as possible.

Mereologically, "different orders and societies" *compose* a state (as parts of a whole). In addition, for many analytical and political purposes, orders and societies can be taken to be independent entities. But ultimately, when it comes to their existence and survival, "all those different orders and societies are dependent upon the state to which they owe their security and protection." Thus, as a theorist of advanced, civil society, Smith is no anarchist (although, as we have seen, he allows that a less advanced society can exist in partial anarchy). More subtly, he is also clear that the state is not an extra layer merely, as it were, bolted on to these orders and societies (in order, say, to solve coordination problems), but rather by granting legal privileges, the state helps *constitute* these orders.

This is not to deny that these passages help explain the many reasons why Burke so admired TMS (see Burke's Letter to Smith, September 10, 1759, Letter 38, Corr. 46–7). By contrast, de Grouchy distinguishes between rights rooted in natural equality and special group "prerogatives" (LS, VI) rooted in infringements against natural equality. By employing (and transforming) Smith's conceptual apparatus she argues for a more radical position than Smith: she would reject Smith's counsel for "respect" for "the established powers and privileges even of . . . the great orders and societies." (For more on de Grouchy's important argument at LS, VI, see Schliesser 2017a and 2017b.)

One kind of zealous "order" raises Smith's concern and ire: "faction" or a "cabal" (TMS 3.3.25, 146; TMS 3.3.33, 151), which Smith tends to associate with a propensity to "violence" (e.g., TMS 3.3.36–7, 152–3; TMS 6.3.26, 249), often descending into civil war (see also TMS 6.2.2.12–5, 231–3). As Smith puts it, "of all the corrupters of moral sentiments, therefore, faction and fanaticism have always been by far the greatest" (TMS 3.3.43, 156; see also Hume's Letter 140 to Smith, discussing Benjamin Franklin, on February 13, 1747: "Faction, next to Fanaticism, is, of all passions, the most destructive of Morality"; Corr. 171) Not unlike Hobbes (recall TMS 7.3.2.2, 318), Smith is especially concerned with ecclesiastical faction, but he also recognizes what we would call ideological factions, and what Smith calls the fanatical "spirit of system," leading to "madness of fanaticism" (TMS 6.2.2.15, 232; see also 6.3.12, 242). And Smith is at his most Hobbesian when he notes that "both rebels and heretics are those unlucky persons, who, when things have come to a certain degree of violence, have the misfortune to be of the weaker party" (TMS 3.3.43, 155; for excellent treatments of Smith on faction, see Brubaker 2006a and Peart and Levy 2009).

Finally, these are not the only significant distinctions with great societies recognized by Smith. We have already seen Smith discuss the different "ranks" within society. It is terminology that reminds us of the ongoing impact of feudalism in eighteenth-century society. In general Smith distinguishes between the well-born, high aristocratic ranks and what he often calls the "inferior" ranks. In between are the people of "middling" rank; these include what Smith call the "liberal professions," doctors, lawyers, educators, and so forth (e.g., WN 5.1.g.14, 796; recall "the middling and inferior ranks of people in Scotland;" WN 5.3.89, 944).

I close this taxonomic chapter with a final, more speculative thought. What I have called the "social" or derived passions (Smithian *moral* sentiments) always have a reference to expected responses of others as part of their content. This means that some of our most important feelings and experiences always have a non-trivial reference to the norms of society as such or relatively stable and significant sub-orders of society. While the content of derived passions may be cultivated through interaction with particular individuals, the content of these passions reaches beyond these to wider shared norms (recall Section f of Chapter 3). This may help explain Smith's emphasis on societies and orders rather than on individuals, even in WN.

7

Adam Smith's Foundations for Political Philosophy

Early in WN, Smith writes, "In the progress of society, philosophy or speculation becomes, like every other employment, the principal or sole trade and occupation of a particular class of citizens" (WN 1.1.9, 21). The main point, of course, is that after a certain level of development, philosophy is a part of the division of labor and, thus, governed by economic and psychological incentives—the philosophical analyst is put inside the analysis. This is a core, reflexive commitment of methodological analytical egalitarianism (Levy and Peart 2008a, 2008b). More important for present purposes, Smith puts his treatment of the effects of "progress" on employment in a political context: the philosopher belongs to a class of "citizens." Thus, Smith rejects the fantasy of apolitical philosophy. For Smith, in fact, all modern exchange has a social-political context.[1] This is best seen by reflecting on the framing of the beginning and end of WN.

In this chapter I sketch Smith's political philosophy. In particular, I explore the significance of Smith's understanding that his political philosophy is the activity of a citizen. That is, I treat his approach to his own theorizing as belonging to a particular community at a given time and place. Even so, Smith's project neither is exclusively descriptive of it nor only focused on what is commonly thought attainable. I argue that for Smith the historical baseline of one's time has normative significance. This does not mean he resists changes from the status quo, but it also means that whatever changes he proposes are constrained by existing institutional arrangements (for recent discussion, see Lawford-Smith 2013).

Part of the philosopher's task reveals itself as offering visions of society that, while not impossible, are more just and more reasonable. One way in which such a vision can be offered is by way of historical narrative, which not just reveals the nature of the historical baseline but also makes visible a second-order reflection on the ways the baseline might be altered. In doing so, one offers an image that

---

[1] As Seneca emphasizes in his *Letters*, not all philosophy engages in monetized trade with society, Smith can grant that, but Smith seems reluctant to allow pure speculation that is not in some sense part of society's commerce.

may speak simultaneously to one's own society and those in others, including future ones (Schliesser 2013).

a. "A New Utopia"

In this section I describe Smith's project of political reform for the completion of the British constitution that would put the relationship among Great Britain and her colonies on a new foundation. I call special attention to the significance of this project for Smith's vision for Ireland, Scotland, and America. What this reveals is that Smith hoped to help create a largely pacific, law-governed Atlantic empire in which all citizens are treated equally under the law.

Consider, first, one of the most oft-quoted passages at the start of WN: "It is not from the benevolence of the butcher, the brewer, or the baker, that we expect our dinner, but from their regard to their own interest. We address ourselves, not to their humanity but to their self-love, and never talk to them of our own necessities but of their advantages" (WN 1.2.2, 26–7). It is at the core of most Smith-as-individualist readings, and nobody would deny, of course, that in economic transactions self-love matters a lot. Sam Fleischacker has done nice work noting the significance of mutual persuasion that Smith presupposes here (2004: 91).[2] As Fleischacker notes, Smith adds in the very next line: "Nobody but a beggar chuses to depend chiefly upon the benevolence of his fellow-citizens. Even a beggar does not depend upon it entirely." Beggars, who were denied the franchise in Smith's time, are fellow citizens, too. For Smith, modern commerce takes places in political context. Even the existence of distinct trades of butchers, bakers, and brewers is context-dependent; recall that in "the Highlands of Scotland, every farmer must be butcher, baker and brewer for his own family" (WN 1.3.2, 31).

This social-political context of commerce reaches its crescendo in the final chapter, somewhat misleadingly titled "Of Public Debts," of Book V of WN. This is because submerged in WN is an ambitious program of political reform (not revolution); as Smith writes, a "new Utopia, less amusing certainly, but not more useless and chimerical than the old one" (WN 5.3.68, 933). Thus, while undoubtedly much of WN concerns itself with descriptive economics and practical matters, the book also contains a serious project of institutional reform (see the classic, Rosenberg 1960; Muller 1993)—one that even if it were unlikely to be implemented in practice, is self-consciously meant to be an attainable ideal in this world.

We know that WN was essentially complete by 1773, but that when Smith went to London to have it printed, it was held up by revisions related to Smith's

---

[2] Cf. Graeber 2014: 335, who treats Smith here as denying the reality of the role of credit in exchange and offering a "utopian" picture of a pure cash exchange. Smith goes on to say that it is "by treaty, by barter, and by purchase purchase, that we obtain from one another the greater part of those mutual good offices which we stand in need of" (WN 1.2.3., 27). It unclear why Graeber thinks this commits Smith to denial of credit.

preoccupation with—in Hume's phrase—the "Fate of America" (Hume to Smith, February 8, 1776, Letter 149, Corr. 185; see also the editor's introduction to Appendix B in Corr. 377–80). Certainly, WN engages with considerable focus on the relationship between mercantilism and the brewing discontent leading to the American Revolution (Skinner 2009: 263–70).

But while topical when WN was written, Smith's program encompasses a project for "extending the British system of taxation to all the different provinces of the empire" (WN 5.3.68, 933; I return to this sentence in the next section). Such an extension of the system of taxation would also require allowing

> into the British parliament, or if you will into the states-general of the British Empire,[3] a fair and equal representation of all those different provinces, that of each province bearing the same proportion to the produce of its taxes, as the representation of Great Britain might bear to the produce of the taxes levied upon Great Britain. (WN 5.3.68, 933)

So Smith proposed an institutional reform that would include a representative parliament proportional to the taxes levied in a particular region. In effect, in the run-up to what came to be known as the American Revolution, Smith agrees with the colonists there should be no taxation without representation (see Griswold 1999: 307).

Smith's program has three great main aims. First, it would address the legitimate grievances of the Irish:

> By an union with Great Britain the greater part of the people of all ranks in Ireland would gain an equally compleat deliverance from a much more oppressive aristocracy; an aristocracy not founded, like that of Scotland, in the natural and respectable distinctions of birth and fortune; but in the most odious of all distinctions, those of religious and political prejudices; distinctions which, more than any other, animate both the insolence of the oppressors and the hatred and indignation of the oppressed, and which commonly render the inhabitants of the same country more hostile to one another than those of different countries ever are. Without a union with Great Britain, the inhabitants of Ireland are not likely for many ages to consider themselves as one people. (WN 5.3.89, 944)[4]

---

[3] This suggests that Smith takes the Dutch republic's confederacy as his model or ideal type. He may have been inspired by Hume's "Idea of a Perfect Commonwealth," which is self-consciously and explicitly modeled on and a purported improvement over the Dutch republic.

[4] Smith treats a society based on birth and fortune as a useful second best; a society based on wisdom and virtue would be better, but he takes it to be unattainable:

> Nature has wisely judged that the distinction of ranks, the peace and order of society, would rest more securely upon the plain and palpable difference of birth and fortune, than upon the

By creating political union, Ireland would gain impartial administration of law and could not be treated as a religious and economic colony anymore. Here Smith has clear moral and political aims for his project; he wishes to eliminate a system that favors "religious and political prejudices" and that incites "hatred and indignation" so opposed to Smith's aim of promoting "happiness and perfection of human life" here on Earth (recall WN 5.1.f.30, 771). Moreover, Smith explicitly advocates that such a union would be accompanied by "an extension of the freedom of trade" (WN 5.3.72, 935) between Ireland and Britain—fulfilling the hopes of Bishop Berkeley and the Irish school of development (cf. Rashid 1988), for, at the time, there were tariffs on many Irish goods before they could enter the British markets. In addition, it would create *unity* among the *Irish* who, currently divided by religion and property, by being treated as equals within a larger political whole would also become "one people." Here Smith gives a glimpse of his sense of the kind of mechanisms that produce political cohesion. The point here is that Smith takes it as a normatively desirable task to produce such Irish unity.

Second, such an Imperial parliamentary union would address the legitimate grievances of the American colonists with whom Smith shared not just the political idea that there should be no taxation without representation, but also the significance of happiness to any political order. (See, e.g., the emphasis on the "liberty, reason, and happiness of mankind, which can flourish only where civil government is able to protect them" [WN 5.1.g.24, 803]; for more on the American Founding Fathers' debts to Adam Smith, see Fleischacker 2002 and McLean 2010; for more on Smith's sources, including Franklin and Kames, see Corr., Appendix 2, p. 379). In fact, Smith also echoes some of the American colonists' grievances against British mercantile restrictions imposed on the colonies—he refers to these also as "impertinent badges of slavery" (WN 4.7.b.44, 582; see also 4.7.c.64, 614–5). His proposed constitutional scheme would also "deliver" the colonists

> from those rancorous and virulent factions which are inseperable [*sic*] from small democracies, and which have so frequently divided the affections of their people, and disturbed the tranquillity [*sic*] of their governments, in their form so nearly democratical. In the case of a total separation from Great Britain, which, unless prevented by a union of this kind, seems very likely to take place, those factions would be ten times more virulent than ever. (WN 5.3.90, 945)

---

invisible and often uncertain difference of wisdom and virtue. The undistinguishing eyes of the great mob of mankind can well enough perceive the former: it is with difficulty that the nice discernment of the wise and the virtuous can sometimes distinguish the latter. (TMS 6.2.1.20, 226)

Clearly, Smith thinks that some social hierarchy is necessary for a society to subsist.

With his eye on ancient examples, Smith even predicts the likelihood of "open violence and bloodshed" among the democratic colonies in case of independence.[5] Without suggesting that he predicted the American civil war, it is notable that he left the material in the book long after the political moment had passed.

Third, connected to this second aim is this: Smith presents his program as a natural fulfillment of the promise inherent in the Whig settlement of 1688. He adopts the language of a living, imperfect constitution[6] that stands in need of completion: "there is not the least probability that the British constitution would be hurt by the union of Great Britain with her colonies. That constitution, on the contrary, would be completed by it, and seems to be imperfect without it" (WN 4.7.c.77, 624). Smith offers a non-revolutionary ideal, one that under the rule of law respects "the natural and respectable distinctions of birth and fortune" at least in the short run. Therefore, Smith is not proposing the direct abolishment of rank (which he takes to be necessary for social order). He does advocate policies (the abolishment of entails and primogeniture, the imposition of taxes on luxury, enrichment of entrepreneurs and merchants, etc.) that will make the system of rank that favors distinctions of birth less likely to endure in the long run (see Chapter 8).

Even though by 1776 the moment to implement Smith's proposal had passed, it is presented as non-utopian. By "utopian" Smith means "useless and chimerical," that is, a fanciful even impossible composite that has realistic elements. Smith's now-standard judgment on *Utopia* echoes Hume's "Of a Perfect Commonwealth," (EMPL, 514) and, especially the opening paragraph of Spinoza's *Political Treatise*, where Utopia is treated as a chimera.[7] I leave aside here to what degree this is a fair reading of *Utopia*. It follows, however, that Smith thinks of his own proposal as useful and feasible in a certain sense. I write, "in a certain sense," because by the last edition of WN it is pretty clear that Smith's project is not going to happen. The non-utopian character of the proposal becomes especially clear when we reflect on the fact that from the point of view of, say, humanity, impartiality, and morality, Smith has made some stark, even immoral concessions to political reality. In the next section, I explore these.

b. Even the Humane Smith

In this section I argue that Smith's projected law-governed polity systematically excludes non-Europeans from equal treatment. This is a puzzle because Smith is not attracted to the racist ideologies that were being developed in the eighteenth century (recall Hume's racialized hierarchy in "Of National Characters"); he is a

---

[5] It seems to follow that Smith is in favor of large (Madisonian) democracies and small monarchies.

[6] I am not suggesting that Smith is the first to suggest this, but his role in developing such a view seems to have been neglected in the history of jurisprudence.

[7] http://oll.libertyfund.org/titles/1710#Spinoza_1321.01_847,

critic of slavery. In addition, we can infer from a letter by Hume to Smith (January 20, 1755, Corr. 18), that Smith had been very critical of Hume's treatment of the Irish massacre—the whole tenor of Hume's treatment of the Irish massacre of 1641 in his *History* is to justify English rule over the Irish. Moreover, he recog-' nizes that "less advanced" societies may promote genuine virtues that are rarely cultivated in civilized societies, which often promote viciousness (Harkin 2002).

For close to a century, scholarship on Adam Smith was dominated by *Das Adam Smith Problem* (for a good history, see Montes 2004, Chapter 2). Das Adam Smith Problem evolved into many different kinds of varieties and prompted a lot of fantastic research (Otteson 2002a; Montes 2004; Paganelli 2008). At bottom, it discerns a tension between the purported self-interested agents of WN and the sympathizing agents of TMS as fundamentally at odds with each other. Moreover, and this is my present motive to bring up the topic, Das Adam Smith Problem tends to view WN as a value-free descriptive book, the predecessor to so-called positive economics, and TMS as a moralizing book. While the problem has, I think, no able defenders left, its afterlife persists in an ongoing general tendency to see WN as an amoral (not immoral) work (but see Evensky 2005 and Rothschild and Sen 2006).

On the very first pages in the Introduction of WN, Smith clearly signals his moral and humanitarian concerns to be addressed by the book. The first three paragraphs of the general Introduction treat of "every nation," but in the fourth Smith draws a contrast between "savage nations of hunters and fishers" and "civilized and thriving nations," prefiguring his stadial theory, in part (recall Chapter 2). In the Introduction, the point of the contrast between savage and civilized is to point to the practices of "sometimes of directly destroying, and sometimes of abandoning their infants, their old people, and those afflicted with lingering diseases, to perish with hunger, or to be devoured by wild beasts" in savage societies. By contrast, in civilized countries

> the produce of the whole labour of the society is so great, that all are often abundantly supplied, and a workman, even of the lowest and poorest order, if he is frugal and industrious, may enjoy a greater share of the necessaries and conveniences of life than it is possible for any savage to acquire. (WN Intro. 4, 10)

Smith offers a stark contrast here, one that anticipates the more famous (Lockean) trope articulated shortly hereafter: "the accommodation of an European prince does not always so much exceed that of an industrious and frugal peasant, as the accommodation of the latter exceeds that of many an African king, the absolute master of the lives and liberties of ten thousand naked savages" (WN 1.1.11, 24).

A large part of WN is, as indicated by its full title, about explaining the source of the differences between these two contrasting situations and also to explain how a nation can become thriving and flourishing. In both passages Smith picks out moralized features of the "savage" situation: in the African king passage, Smith calls attention to the lack of freedom, if not outright slavery, of most of the "savages." In the quote from the general Introduction, Smith points not just to natural evils, but also to practices that do not just lack compassion, but from the point of view of even "common humanity" (e.g., WN 1.8.16, 86) are extremely disconcerting, including infanticide, which Smith (recall) calls a "dreadful violation of humanity" (TMS 5.2.15, 210). Thus, the environmental rationality of a political, institutional context does not always promote what *we* would consider moral behavior (recall Section f of Chapter 5). Leaving aside here the very interesting issue of how the impartial spectator would evaluate tragic choices in the context of "necessity," there is no doubt that part of Smith's general argument in favor of commercial "civilization" is that in it many more people will be happier and will be in contexts that facilitate moral behavior. This is why he criticizes "The humane Plato ... [who] with all that love of mankind which seems to animate all his writings, no where marks this practice with disapprobation" (TMS 5.2.15, 210).

This is because Smith's view entails that in the progress of economic development, there will be many more opportunities not just for liberality, but for avoiding immoral behavior (less infanticide, less slavery, better treatment of the aged and infirm, etc.). This holds true even if Smith also thinks that *within* civilized contexts there can be circumstances of inequality that facilitate immoral behavior (recall Section f in Chapter 5). This is not to deny that Smith also recognizes genuine moral loss that can be the consequence of economic improvements (Harkin 2002, 2005). As he puts it in a celebrated passage,

> The same contempt of death and torture prevails among all other savage nations. There is not a negro from the coast of Africa who does not, in this respect, possess a degree of magnanimity which the soul of his sordid master is too often scarce capable of conceiving. Fortune never exerted more cruelly her empire over mankind, than when she subjected those nations of heroes to the refuse of the jails of Europe, to wretches who possess the virtues neither of the countries which they come from, nor of those which they go to, and whose levity, brutality, and baseness, so justly expose them to the contempt of the vanquished.
>
> This heroic and unconquerable firmness, which the custom and education of his country demand of every savage, is not required of those who are brought up to live in civilized societies. (TMS 5.2.9–10, 206–7)

Smith is an adamant and vocal opponent of European colonial and imperial enterprises (Muthu 2008). There are three important features to this passage, two of which are directly relevant for this section. First, Smith wants to deny that the colonial and imperial enterprises are *intrinsic* features of advanced civilization. Rather, they attract the least attractive of European characters; their "savage injustice" (WN 4.1.32, 448) and baseness are something even worse than "the mean rapacity, the monopolizing spirit of merchants and Manufacturers" (WN 4.3.c.9, 493). Thus, Smith clearly wants to distinguish between the virtues associated with commerce (e.g., prudence, more possibilities of exercising humanity, etc.) and those perversions that are (perhaps intentional) byproducts by the "mercantile spirit" of colonialism (WN 4.7.b.50, 584; see Hanley 2009). Smith regularly ties European colonies to mercantilism and the "monopoly of . . . commerce" (WN 4.7.b.63, 590). He does not think that international commerce is necessarily exploitive. As he puts it, "These misfortunes, however, seem to have arisen rather from *accident* than from any thing in the *nature* of those events themselves" (WN 4.7.c.80, 626; emphasis added). In context, Smith is referring to the very unequal military power between Europeans and colonized peoples.

Second, Smith thinks that different societies have locally appropriate moral outlooks reinforced and cultivated by local "custom and education;" earlier, I tried to capture this feature of Smith's thought with the language of "environmental rationality." Yet, despite these environmental differences, Smith is presupposing a common humanity here. Smith has and wishes to promote an attitude of respect toward the "savages" (despite the fact that to us "savage" has a jarring connotation). He is here assimilating the rhetoric (indebted to Rousseau, perhaps) of the noble savage to his own ends.

Third, Smith resists here a providentialist reading of history and theodicy. Rather than speaking of providence or the Author of nature (and such locutions), he introduces the more Epicurean language of "fortune's empire." There is no (hidden) divine plan that somehow vindicates the suffering of the colonized peoples (cf. Waterman 2002). They are also in no sense deserving of it.

Yet, earlier I quoted a sentence from WN 5.3.68, 933, only partially. The full sentence reads: "By extending the British system of taxation to all the different provinces of the empire inhabited by people of either British or European extraction, a much greater augmentation of revenue might be expected." The full sentence, thus, excludes many subjects without European roots in Smith's political non-utopian program. (Notice, too, that Smith is clearly trying to increase tax revenue.)

Smith does not explain why he would include only people from British or European extraction in his project in the political union with the Americas. But his proposal pointedly excludes the "blacks," who, Smith notes, "make the greater part of the inhabitants both of the southern colonies upon the continent and of the West India islands, as they are in a state of slavery, are, no doubt, in a worse condition than the poorest people either in Scotland or Ireland" (WN 5.3.77, 939). While this makes clear that Smith is no friend of slavery (WN, 4.7.b.53–62, 586–9 and WN 3.2.10, 388; see especially TMS 7.2.1.28, 282), his political program for the colonies does not directly address the reality of slavery and seems to reinforce a limited political franchise along racialized lines.

It is not impossible that Smith may have presupposed that a political union with Britain would have, if implemented, eventually abolished slavery in the

American colonies.[8] But Smith does not offer any hint that he foresees this possibility, so we cannot infer that he was thinking along those lines. Even so, it would be equally rash to assume that Smith believed that the slaves were somehow unfit for political participation. As I have noted, there is no evidence that Smith shared in the racial, hierarchical prejudices of his contemporaries (such as Hume or Kant), which was often connected to divine providence (see J. E. H. Smith 2015). The whole tenor of Smith's writings goes against natural hierarchy (Peart and Levy 2005; for a more balanced assessment see Fleischacker 2013). This was noted at once: Smith's earliest public critic, Governor Pownall, was very critical of Smith's rejection of natural hierarchy. In a letter to Smith, Pownall by contrast affirms innate natural differences: "Nature has so formed us, as that the labour of each must take one special direction, in preference to, and to the exclusion of some other equally necessary line of labour, by which direction of his labour, he will be but partially and imperfectly supplied." Pownall's (Platonic) position extends seamlessly into natural hierarchies, and Smith is rightly viewed as an opponent to these.

So why is Smith willing to promote a political program that, along the way, will maintain foreseeably great injustice, even if one can grant this is not its main aim? An obvious passage to bring to bear on Smith's exclusion of non-Europeans is one he added to the final edition of TMS (recall):

> He will accommodate, as well as he can, his public arrangements to the confirmed habits and prejudices of the people; and will remedy as well as he can, the inconveniences which may flow from the want of those regulations which the people are averse to submit to. When he cannot establish the right, he will not disdain to ameliorate the wrong; but like Solon, when he cannot establish the best system of laws, he will endeavour to establish the best that the people can bear. (TMS 6.2.2.16, 233; see also WN 4.5.b.53, 543, and WN 5.1.g.38, 810)

Smith's non-utopianism makes him aim for achievable ends. Crucially, that means taking into account not just "rooted prejudices of the people" but also a respect for "the established powers and privileges even of individuals, and still more those of the great orders and societies" in one's political program. From the point of view of humanity, this accommodative, ameliorative strategy is not very inspiring; it can also run the risk of too much appeasement of an unjust status quo. It is crucial, however, that one also continues to attempt "reason and persuasion" to undo injustices. Smith's public philosophy is not one that advocates turning a blind eye toward injustices in the name of reason of state or political expediency.

---

[8] It is unfortunate that we do not have his reaction to the decision in *Somerset v. Stewart* (1772) in London.

Finally, Smith's proposed parliamentary "union" also excludes the inhabitants of the territories acquired by the East India Company. Smith clearly prefers direct Crown rule over India, which would involve impartial law, to mercantile rule (WN 5.3.91, 945). But even though the closing lines of WN end on a call for Britain "to accommodate her future views and designs to the real mediocrity of her circumstances" and to recognize that the British have engaged in fantasy in thinking they possess "a great empire on the west side of the Atlantic," Smith does not explicitly advocate abandoning the rest of the "whole empire" (WN 5.3.92, 947). Thus, it would be a mistake to treat Smith as a full opponent of the colonial project.

All in all, we can admire that Smith was a fierce opponent of slavery and mercantile imperialism; in addition, there is no hint of scientific racism in his writings. But his political project, which presupposes a shared Atlantic community, is based on geographic extraction, and this geographic-cultural preference unintentionally ends up prefiguring, alas, some of the worst projects of subsequent centuries (Pitts 2009).

c. Belonging to Society

In this section, I argue that Smith's genealogy of how property arises offered in WN has normative significance. In particular, I claim that Smith distinguishes between original property rights, which are nearly absolute, and "derived property rights," which might be protected by different institutions or customs:

> [O]f the acquired and useful abilities of all the inhabitants or members of the society. The acquisition of such talents, by the maintenance of the acquirer during his education, study, or apprenticeship, always costs a real expence, which is a capital fixed and realized, as it were, in his person. Those talents, as they make a part of his fortune, so do they likewise of that of the society to which he belongs. The improved dexterity of a workman may be considered in the same light as a machine or instrument of trade which facilitates and abridges labour, and which, though it costs a certain expence, repays that expence with a profit. (WN 2.1.17, 282)

This vivid paragraph is often quoted when scholars discuss the history of the so-called human capital concept (e.g., Spengler 1977). After all, Smith does not shy away from likening the skilled laborer to a machine. And, indeed, there is a sense that on Smith's view, as commerce progresses with the mutual influence of specialization driven by the division of labor and technological innovation, the affective nature of all workers can, in principle, transmute into something more homogeneous, machine-like. At its most extreme this leads to, as we have already seen, the workers' "torpor of mind" (WN 5.1.f.50, 782), which requires its own ameliorative project.

What is less remarked upon is that Smith is adamant that the "capital fixed and realized" consequent education (apprenticeship, etc.) also is part of, even owned by, the "society" to which the laborer "belongs." This is not a slip of the pen in Smith; it's the point of his book to help explain what causes the "wealth of nations," after all. To be precise: on my reading, Smith's "as it were" modifies the claim about where capital is fixed and realized, not the claim that his talents belong in some measure to society.

Smith is not merely making an empirical claim about how our talents belong to society. Behind it stands a moral vision opposed to the very idea of "sovereign individuals" who "sell their human capital in the market" often attributed to him (e.g., Herzog 2013: 15; see also 66ff). By contrast, Smith talks about the way in which the employer "shares in the produce of their labour, or in their value which it adds to the material upon which it is bestowed" (WN 1.8.8, 83). This emphasis on profit as a "share" (Smith repeats the word in context) speaks of a very different vision (cf. Pack 2013: 529).

But in what moral sense can our embodied human capital said to "belong," in part, to society? To answer this question, I first explore Smith's genealogy of how property arises, and then I call attention to the normative significance of Smith's argument in WN.

i. The Genealogy of Property

In WN, Smith offers the following account of the origin of property; I quote in full before I comment on the passage:

> Among nations of hunters, as there is scarce any property, or at least none that exceeds the value of two or three days' labour, so there is seldom any established magistrate or any regular administration of justice. Men who have no property can injure one another only in their persons or reputations. But when one man kills, wounds, beats, or defames another, though he to whom the injury is done suffers, he who does it receives no benefit. It is otherwise with the injuries to property. The benefit of the person who does the injury is often equal to the loss of him who suffers it. Envy, malice, or resentment are the only passions which can prompt one man to injure another in his person or reputation. But the greater part of men are not very frequently under the influence of those passions, and the very worst of men are so only occasionally. As their gratification too, how agreeable soever it may be to certain characters, is not attended with any real or permanent advantage, it is in the greater part of men commonly restrained by prudential considerations. Men may live together in society with some tolerable degree of security, though there is no civil magistrate to protect them from the injustice of those passions. But avarice and ambition

in the rich, in the poor the hatred of labour and the love of present ease and enjoyment, are the passions which prompt to invade property, passions much more steady in their operation, and much more universal in their influence. Wherever there is great property there is great inequality. For one very rich man there must be at least five hundred poor, and the affluence of the few supposes the indigence of the many. The affluence of the rich excites the indignation of the poor, who are often both driven by want, and prompted by envy, to invade his possessions. It is only under the shelter of the civil magistrate that the owner of that valuable property, which is acquired by the labour of many years, or perhaps of many successive generations, can sleep a single night in security. He is at all times surrounded by unknown enemies, whom, though he never provoked, he can never appease, and from whose injustice he can be protected only by the powerful arm of the civil magistrate continually held up to chastise it. The acquisition of valuable and extensive property, therefore, necessarily requires the establishment of civil government. Where there is no property, or at least none that exceeds the value of two or three days' labour, civil government is not so necessary. (WN 5.1.b.2, 709–10)

Smith's approach presupposes both his account of the passionate propensities of human nature (at least ten passions are mentioned) and his four stages of civilization, those based on hunting, herding, agriculture, and manufacture (WN 5.1.a, 689–708; see Meek 1971 and Skinner 1996). Smith's framework is itself an elaboration and extension of Hume's sketch of a three-stage model in "Of Commerce" (EMPL, 256; cf. Meek 1976: 30–1 helpfully calls attention to Hume's Treatise 3.2.8). Each stage is, for Smith, distinguished by a predominant form of socioeconomic organization.

Note, first, that Smith agrees with Locke and against Hobbes and Hume that there can be some justice and property, as well as society, without government. Within a broadly Humean framework of moral psychology and the evolution of human institutions, Smith severs the intimate connection that Hobbes and Hume made between justice and property. Unlike Hobbes and Hume, for Smith justice is not a necessary condition of property. Nevertheless, he assumes that in a hunting society, property will always be fairly limited. Thus, there will be very limited incentive to set up an administration of justice. In Smith's terms, there can be society with possessions before there are law-governed rules of property.[9]

Second, Smith recognizes harms to one's frame of mind, body, and property (cf. Treatise 3.2.2.7). According to Smith, in a hunting society, men can harm each other's reputation and person. In affirming the former, Smith disagrees with

---

[9] In the body of the text I am accentuating the differences between Hume/Hobbes and Smith, but one might well argue that both Hume and Hobbes also allow some possessions in the state of nature.

Hume, for whom we "are perfectly secure in the enjoyment" in the internal satisfaction of the mind. But while "Envy, malice, or resentment" may prompt us to
injure others, according to Smith, there is little reason to expect this to happen
very often because in a hunting society we are not frequently ruled by these passions (in this Smith agrees with Hume; see Treatise 3.2.2.12). There is little "interest" to be derived from inflicting such harm. In a hunting society, then, there will
be no need for the rule of law or extensive property rights because there is little
or no harm that needs to be prevented by it. Therefore, "Men may live together in
society with some tolerable degree of security, though there is no civil magistrate
to protect them from the injustice of those passions." Before one assumes that
Smith ascribes entirely to what Hume calls the poetic "fiction of the golden age"
(Treatise 3.2.2.15), Smith only speaks of a "tolerable degree of security."

All of this accords well with Smith's criticism of Rousseau in his earliest publication, "The Letter to the Edinburgh Review;" Smith finds Rousseau's description
of life in the state of nature one-sided: "Mr. Rousseau, intending to paint savage
life as the happiest of any, presents only the indolent side to view." According
to Smith, Rousseau leaves out the "most dangerous and extravagant adventures"
(¶12, 251). This attack on one-sidedness recurs; Smith's main criticism of other
moral philosophers is precisely that their systems are also "derived from a partial
and imperfect view of nature" (TMS 6.1.1, 265).

For Smith, law develops when there is an interest in it. Smith thinks an "advantage" in harming others can only arise when there is more extensive and unequal
property distribution. This cannot occur in a hunting society and only comes about
after a major change; shepherding must become a predominant form of social
organization (WN 5.1.b.12, 715). Even in this stage, it may take considerable time
before formal rules of justice are developed; not only must inequality arise, but,
at first, this inequality will enable the rich to have a "natural authority over all the
inferior shepherds or herdsmen of his horde or clan" (WN 5.1.b.11, 714). Yet, eventually, "avarice and ambition in the rich" and "hatred of labor and the love of present
ease and enjoyment" as well as the sheer "indignation" and "envy" in the needy poor
make another person's property a tempting target. In Smith's view, once poor or
rich, people can be motivated by very different passions. While for Hume greed is
the prime cause of the origin of the convention of law (Treatise 3.2.2.12), Smith only
assigns it a partial cause in the smaller, albeit more powerful, part of society. Unlike
Hume, Smith does not offer an explanation drawn in terms of a single passion here.
In this, Smith is merely following Hume's methodologic advice in avoiding a "love of
simplicity" in explaining human affairs (EPM, Appendix 2, "Of Self-Love").

Moreover, Hume's account gives the impression that the rule of law is in the
interest, both initially and thereafter, of everybody. It is true that Smith thinks
the rich and the poor both eye each other's property, so both could benefit from
order following its establishment. Nevertheless, he has no doubt that "Civil
Government, so far as it is instituted for the security of property, is in reality
instituted for the defence of the rich against the poor, or of those who have some

property against those who have none at all" (WN 5.1.b.12, 715). After all, Smith only singles out the rich man's nighttime security (WN 5.1.b.2, 710)!

But this account raises a question: why, for Smith, is being law-abiding moral at all if it is so clearly partial to the needs of the rich? Smith is not blind to the widespread benefits of order that law entails (WN 5.3.7, 910 and WN 2.1.30, 284–5). Nevertheless, Smith's attack on Hume's account of the moral authority of utility undercuts Smith's ability to point to the benefits of the rule of law as a source of our moral obligations to the follow the law; at best it is of secondary importance: "it is seldom this consideration which first animates us" against "licentious practices" (TMS 2.2.3.9, 89). As we have already seen, Smith has recourse to a different story: "Actions of hurtful tendency ... seem alone to deserve punishment; because such alone are the approved objects of resentment, or excite the sympathetic resentment of the spectator" (TMS 2.2.1.2, 78). Our natural passion of resentment makes possible, even prior to the establishment of the rule of law, our desire for retaliation, which "seems to be the great law which is dictated to us by Nature" (TMS 2.2.1.10, 82). This sentiment undergirds later systems of justice. A main reason to have an institutionalized system of justice is the prevention of private vengeance rather than deterrence (Simon 2013: 406–8).

Now that we have a sense of Smith's accounts of natural resentment and natural origins of property, we are in a position to appreciate his account of what happens once system(s) of justice get developed away from these origins.

ii. Original and Derived Property

In the context of a critical discussion of attempts to prevent competition by guild and apprenticeship laws and so on, Smith echoes Locke:

> The property which every man has in his own labour, as it is the original
> foundation of all other property, so it is the most sacred and inviolable.
> The patrimony of a poor man lies in the strength and dexterity of his
> hands; and to hinder him from employing this strength and dexterity
> in what manner he thinks proper without injury to his neighbour is a
> plain violation of this most sacred property. It is a manifest encroach-
> ment upon the just liberty both of the workman and of those who
> might be disposed to employ him. (WN 1.10.c.12, 138)

Smith's conception, with its emphasis on the work performed by a poor person's hands (cf. WN 1.2.40, 469), is quite narrow. It is, for example, narrower than Rousseau's in his *Discourse on Political Economy*:

> [I]t is certain that the right of property is the most sacred of all the
> rights of citizens, and more important in some respects than freedom
> itself; either because it bears more directly on the preservation of life;

or because, goods, being easier to usurp and more difficult to defend
than persons, greater respect ought to be accorded to what can more
easily be seized; or finally, because property is the true foundation of
civil society, and the true guarantee of the citizens' commitments: for
if goods were not in accord with persons nothing would be so easy as to
elude one's duties and scoff at the laws. (DPE, 42)[10]

At WN 1.10.c.12, 138, Smith relies on neither God's will, nor on a metaphysics
of persons, nor on the Lockean claim about mixing in substances, nor even being
the first on the scene to ground the property right. Even so, it is not merely bald
assertion. To see why, focus on Smith's claim that "the property which every man
has in his own labour ... is the original foundation of all other property." There
are five crucial points in this passage.

First, the right is "original" because it is rooted in our *natural* sentiment (or
original passion) of sympathetic resentment when confronted with "injury."
This focus on injury is why protection of this is supported by the sympathetic
resentment of any impartial spectator, which can establish "plain" or "manifest"
violations.

Second, the stress on "original" is, thus, not ultimately temporal, but conceptual. This is because it appears that the normative force of the claim of any
form of ownership is (potentially) available to each of us: the claim is derivable
from everyone's labor. Of course, the use of "original" may bring to mind Locke's
founding story and others like it, but in context it need not do so; Smith's claim
is intelligible without it. Smith could be saying that, while we inherit a world full
of property arrangements, each one of us is—if we (can) labor—a moral source
of our property. Smith's claim differs from Locke's conception in an additional,
subtle fashion: Smith does not appeal to an *original* state of nature to found the
claim. The "foundation of all other property" is available to us to this day (note
Smith's use of "has" and "is"). Smith's picture is neutral between strategies that
insist that the state of nature is ongoing (e.g., Spinoza) or a fiction to be discarded
(e.g., Hume). There is no need to tell a justificatory story about ancient (or fictive)
origins of property rights.[11]

[10] I have consulted and slightly modified Victor Gourevitch's 1997 translation:

*Il est certain que le droit de propriété est le plus sacré de tous les droits des citoyens, et plus important
à certains égards que la liberté même; soit parce qu'il tient de plus près à la conservation de la vie; soit
parce que les biens étant plus faciles à usurper et plus pénibles à défendre que la personne, on doit
plus respecter ce qui se peut ravir plus aisément; soit enfin parce que la propriété est le vrai fondement
de la société civile, et le vrai garant des engagements des citoyens: car si les biens ne répondaient pas
des personnes, rien ne serait si facile que d'éluder ses devoirs et de se moquer des lois.* (OC, III, 264)

For a very good treatment see Hanley (2012).

[11] Some such strategy has been revived by Matthiasse Risse (2012), who, in Chapter 6, traces the
strategy to a "secularized version" of Grotius. Here I ignore the differences among Smith, Grotius, and
Risse. For an excellent treatment of Grotius and Risse see Olsthoorn (2017).

Third, the passage points to Smith's moral egalitarianism and universalism: the normative authority for appeal is available to us all ("poor man") and to this day (repeated "is"). If we leave aside for the sake of argument Smith's gendered language and the disabled, this is an egalitarian conception, especially in light of Smith's use of a "poor man."[12] It provides supporting evidence for Fleischacker's interpretation of Smith's moral egalitarianism (see Fleischacker 2004, Chapter 4, Section 16; cf. Frazer 2010: 220 n. 45; for a contrary approach, see Brown 1994: 83–94. Recently, Fleischacker 2013 offers a careful restatement).

Fourth, the basic form of (property) right is thus work and the right to contract it as long as one does not harm others. Smith here anticipates the famous articulation of the (more expansive) harm principle in the fourth article of the 1789 *Declaration of the Rights of Man*: "Liberty consists in the freedom to do everything which injures no one else."[13]

Fifth, our injuries can come in degrees. In the passage not all property is called "most sacred and inviolable," but only "the property which every man has in his own labour." And if there is "most sacred and inviolable" property, this implies that in societies with advanced division of labor there can be less sacred and less inviolable "other property" with fewer "plain violations." Smith implies that different kinds of property, however sacred, may have differing range of (weaker) protection accorded to them. Guild members, for example, would have thought of guild laws as protecting their sacred and inviolable rights, also perhaps as part of the fundamental order of society, so Smith's rhetoric is no doubt carefully chosen. Unlike Locke, however, and echoing Hume, Smith tends to avoid the language of rights and social compacts. But he does not avoid it entirely; Smith does call property rights "sacred" at WN 1.11.c.27, 188, and less clearly at WN 4.7.b.44, 582.

---

[12] Given Smith's gendered language it should come as no surprise that feminists have been critical (e.g., Bodkin 1999 and Kuiper 2006; for a more balanced assessment, see Harkin 2013). While I would argue that Smith's conception is not inimical to working women, what matters for present purposes is that contrary to what is often claimed, Smith *does* recognizes women's work (e.g., WN 1.8.15, 85; 1.8.51, 103; 2.5.21, 366), including a non-moralistic treatment of the "unfortunate" women who work as prostitutes (WN 1.11.b.41, 177). Therefore, there is no reason to assume he would deny that women's work cannot generate the normative authority. For a richer discussion of one pioneer feminist (Sophie de Grouchy)'s reception of Smith, see Schliesser (2017b). Having said that, while Smith was not blind to the "very severe" oppression of women (LJ(A) 3.13, 146), he is not a proto-feminist in the manner of Mandeville, Toland, or even his student James Millar.

[13] The English translation supplied by the Avalon Project: http://avalon.law.yale.edu/18th_century/rightsof.asp. In French, "*La liberté consiste à pouvoir faire tout ce qui ne nuit pas à autrui.*" I have consulted the version republished by the Constitutional Council of the French Republic: http://www.conseil-constitutionnel.fr/conseil-constitutionnel/francais/la-constitution/la-constitution-du-4-octobre-1958/declaration-des-droits-de-l-homme-et-du-citoyen-de-1789.5076.html

Thus, in different societies, what we may call acquired, "derived property rights" might be protected by different institutions or customs[14] (see Simon 2013 for an excellent discussion on the distinction between natural and acquired rights in Smith). As we have seen, our *moral* sentiments are cultivated by institutions that embody local norms of reasonableness, many of which may remain suboptimal from the point of disinterested, impartial utility. From the point of view of our natural sentiments, this is sometimes a good thing. In LS, de Grouchy makes this point very explicit; according to her, property rights and crimes against them come in degrees. It is half of the core principle behind her reform of the penal code. She attacks the failure of European criminal codes to match penalties to crimes (LS, VIII); this failure has had the unintended consequence of licensing "lesser crimes, and they can also be considered the cause of greater crimes, since it impunity of the former which inspires the confidence needed to commit the latter." Lesser crimes go unpunished because humanity "almost always keeps one from denouncing minor thefts" if the penalty is severe (e.g., death penalty for theft; LS, VIII).

Presumably Smith's unfinished work on jurisprudence would have developed some such story in greater detail. In WN Smith does not offer arguments for his assertions about plain and manifest violations, nor does he tell what limits there are to such claims. Can one prevent others from marrying and procreating? What violations are unambiguously discerned by our natural sentiments? Is there an order among them? Smith's account leaves too many unanswered theoretical questions to count as a fully satisfactory political philosophy.

In de Grouchy's hands property rights are derived from "labor," especially because work generates reasonable expectations. As de Grouchy explains: "by taking it away from him, making his work useless, depriving him of what he had long looked forward to, and of the possession he deserved, we hurt it more than we would, should we deprive him of a similar harvest that just happened to be within his reach" (LS,VI). De Grouchy offers here an account very much in accord with Smith's philosophy (we find it in the student notes to Smith's lectures on jurisprudence unavailable to de Grouchy—see LJ(A) i.13–5, 17; Fleischacker 2004, 159, 191), but one she develops by creatively extending Smithian themes. She may have been inspired by Smith's account of the impartial spectator's approval of the prudent man, who certainly develops "probable expectation" (TMS 6.1.11–3, 215–6). But in context Smith does not connect it to the grounding of property rights.

But grant me, for the sake of argument, that Smith deploys something like a systematic distinction between original and derived property rights. The former are shared by everybody and involve clear violations of things due to us anywhere and anytime. They are the common core in the universal principles or "dictates"

---

14 To be clear: the original/derived property distinction does not match up exactly on the original/derived passion distinction.

of "humanity"—Smith's term for the moral norms shared by all of us. In WN Smith uses "common humanity" to describe subsistence wages in places as far apart culturally and institutionally as China (WN 1.8.24, 89) and Great Britain. (WN 1.8.28, 91) Elsewhere, slaveholders are described as not just lacking crucially "humanity" toward their slaves (WN 4.8.b.3, 565). When Smith explains the paradox that free people (i.e., English colonists) tend to treat their slaves worse than in a country ruled by "arbitrary" power (i.e., French colonists), he argues that in "free" colonies, where slaves are viewed as mere property and where the ruling classes are secure from the magistrate's meddling in their property, magistrates are prevented from interceding out of "common humanity" (WN 4.7.b.54, 587). In Smith "humanity" is the opposite of cruelty (e.g., TMS 7.3.3.9, 323) and appeals to our pity (e.g., TMS 1.2.4.3, 40). It is the passion that can even make us wish to pardon the guilty (e.g., TMS 2.2.3.7, 88 and 2.3.2.5, 101).

Granting that Smith operates with a (sometimes tacit) original/derived property distinction helps explain otherwise puzzling remarks. For example, Smith is careful not to claim that we have an absolute right to the fruits of labor; we can legitimately be taxed, after all. As Smith writes, partially echoing the American colonists, "Every tax, however, is to the person who pays it a badge, not of slavery, but of liberty. It denotes that he is subject to government, indeed, but that, as he has some property, he cannot himself be the property of a master" (WN 5.2.g.11, 857). Here's a way to understand what Smith has in mind: as free people, we recognize that the size of and the right to our (derived) property is the product of our shared activities. Even when we enjoy "perfect liberty" (that is, we can switch occupations freely [e.g., WN 1.10.a.1, 116]), we are subject to government. (For more on Smith's account of liberty, see Section g in Chapter 8.) So none of us can claim an inviolable, absolute right to all of it. One can see in this, as Steve Darwall has urged on me, a reflective endorsement from the perspective of having an equal authority to make claims and demands on one another at all. It's this feature of Smith's account that explains why our embodied human capital is said to "belong," in part, to society. The very institutions that can prevent our slavery are the grounds for claiming some share of the value we generate.

Now we can see how the genealogical and conceptual points hang together. Smith's genealogy (recall WN 5.1.b.2, 709–10) reaffirms that we recognize mutual possessions prior to establishment of civil law, which, in turn, is the result of growth of inequality. Smith's genealogy teaches that derived property is, as Hume emphasizes for all property, conventional.

Smith's historical account of the four stages teaches that each stage is characterized by specific property and other institutional arrangements, which, in turn, are suited to fit local needs. This is because, in WN, the genealogical account of the origin of property is offered in the context of discussing the second duty of the sovereign, to establish an exact administration of justice. Smith defends the thesis "that an exact administration of justice, requires ... very different degrees of expense in the different periods of society" (WN 5.1.b.1, 709). This parallels the reason Smith provides in explaining why he offers a brief history in analyzing the first duty of the sovereign—that is, "protecting the society from the violence and invasion of other independent societies;" we learn that "the expense both of preparing this military force in time of peace, and of employing it in time of war, is very different in the different states of society, in the different periods of improvement" (WN 5.1.1.1, 689). History can teach that the appropriate or reasonable cost of government is stage-dependent.

Of course, as society changes, the needs of society will change, too. Nevertheless, as we have seen already in the case of Athenian legal infanticide, "[L]aws frequently continue in force long after the circumstances which first gave occasion to them, and which could alone render them reasonable, are no more" (WN 3.2.4, 383). There is, thus, considerable inertia, or, to use Bill Wimsatt's (1986) phrase, generative entrenchment, in the institutions of society. Thus, for Smith the "reasonable" content of derived property rights are a contingent matter determined by the needs and organization of historically specific societies.

According to Smith, in shepherd and agricultural societies, justice is quite arbitrary. For example, in feudal times, the countryside was ravaged, while the cities and burghs became the scene of order only after the king decided to ally himself with them against the barons (WN 3.3.11–2, 404–5). For Smith, part of the moral argument in favor of the commercial stage is that commerce creates conditions in which property rights become secure:

> [C]ommerce and manufactures gradually introduced order and good government, and with them, the liberty and security of individuals, among the inhabitants of the country, who had before lived almost in a continual state of war with their neighbours and of servile dependency upon their superiors. This, though it has been the least observed, is by far the most important of all their effects. Mr. Hume is the only writer who, so far as I know, has hitherto taken notice of it. (WN 3.4.4, 412)

Smith thinks that in countries without commerce, cattle or, in a shepherding society, surplus from land would be used by the rich to maintain idle retainers. Such retainers are a source of military power and, because of the feudal lords' ambition, disorder. Only when the rich have the option to spend their surplus on vanity-satisfying goods and the number of retainers decreases, while the power of the king, who is the source of more regular administration of justice, would grow, could this disorder start to decrease (WN 3.4, *passim*). Of course, there is a chicken-and-egg problem here:

> Commerce and manufactures can seldom flourish long in any state which does not enjoy a regular administration of justice, in which the people do not feel themselves secure in the possession of their property, in which the faith of contracts is not supported by law, and in which

the authority of the state is not supposed to be regularly employed in enforcing the payment of debts from all those who are able to pay. Commerce and manufactures, in short, can seldom flourish in any state in which there is not a certain degree of confidence in the justice of government. (WN 5.3.7, 910)

Thus, commerce leads to good order (politically and morally, see Paganelli 2013), yet some order is necessary for commerce to flourish. For Smith some trade can exist in the state of nature, but for extensive, flourishing trade to exist, people need to feel secure in their property. The form of government that creates secure administration of justice is, however, itself the result of commercial society. Smith's solution to this problem is to insist that the growth of commerce is a "gradual" and a "slow and uncertain" process during the course of centuries (WN 4.4.10–23, 418–26). He does not say so, but he implies that the growth of commerce and the rule of law can be a mutually reinforcing, concomitant process. (Smith is clearly following Hume here; see Hayek 1967: 113; Rothschild 2001: 10.) For Smith, commerce and law are created through the reasonable expectations of people about the security of contracts and the regulation of creditor/debtor relations.[15] Once there is some (by no means complete) "confidence" in the rule of law, commercial transactions can extend over time, and long-range planning and investment becomes profitable.

In Smith's Great Britain, property rights have come to be experienced as sacred and inviolable because they have been around for a long time and they have had a longstanding Parliament and competing law courts jealous to keep guard, however imperfectly, over their safety. They are, however, only a late development in the history of Western Europe; in the past, property rights were precarious and uncertain. Smith is aware, however, that a person, an institution, or a practice can be made to appear sacred in the eyes of the people even when it is not (WN 5.1.g.6, 791; 5.1.g.22–3, 802).

Moreover, Smith knows that in the case of corn (i.e., edible seeds), protecting property rights is less than "sacred" in practice:

The laws concerning corn may everywhere be compared to the laws concerning religion. The people feel themselves so much interested in what

---

[15] This undercuts significantly, but perhaps not wholly, Graeber's argument against Smith that Smith presupposes that "property, money, and markets" existed "before political institutions" (2014: 24ff). Graeber's argument relies on reading the stylized example of barter exchange at WN 1.2.3., 27, as offering Smith's historical anthropology. While it is clearly true that Smith appeals to the "trucking disposition" in order to explain, perhaps mistakenly, the origin of the division of labor (by way of a Smithian social explanation), it does not follow that Smith is appealing to the naturalness of barter either to limit the role of government to merely maintaining the soundness of the currency or to argue for the economy as a self-sufficient object of inquiry distinct from ethics or politics (cf. Graeber 2014: 25).

relates either to their subsistence in this life, or to their happiness in
a life to come, that government must yield to their prejudices, and, in
order to preserve the public tranquility, establish that system which
they approve of. It is upon this account, perhaps, that we so seldom
find a reasonable system established with regard to either of those two
capital objects. (WN 4.5.b.40, 539)

Whatever institutional arrangements are made, they must (in the sense of: cannot avoid) account for the "prejudices" of the people when dealing with important matters such as food and religion—if public order is to be maintained. As
Madison recognized,

all governments rest on opinion ... When the examples, which fortify
opinion, are antient as well as numerous, they are known to have a dou-
ble effect. In a nation of philosophers, this consideration ought to be
disregarded. A reverence for the laws, would be sufficiently inculcated
by the voice of an enlightened reason. But a nation of philosophers is
as little to be expected as the philosophical race of kings wished for by
Plato. And in every other nation, the most rational government will
not find it a superfluous advantage, to have the prejudices of the community on its side." (Madison, *Federalist* 49)

This illuminates why Smith gives a qualified endorsement of an act of Parliament
in the following terms: it was "though not the best in itself ... the best which, the
interest, prejudices and temper of the times would admit of" (WN 4.5.b.53, 543;
Hont and Ignatieff 1983, 20). Moreover, Smith thinks that the laws of England,
which at one point prevented middlemen from dealing in corn, encouraged the
people's prejudices in the wrong way (WN 5.5.b.21–6, 532–4). Hence, one reason
to instruct the political elite in true political economy is to encourage them to
design laws that, while still placating the prejudices of the members of the polity,
prevent an encouragement of these prejudices (see also Fleischacker 1999: 176–7).

Therefore, the content of original property is not established by history; at
most, Smith's moral psychology and historical account can reinforce it. History
teaches that the content of the derived property rights cannot be fixed. What will
count as reasonable is a contingent affair. Moreover, history teaches that political
prudence demands that legal institutions should accommodate local prejudices
without encouraging them. Insisting on absolute rights, even if reasonable, could
cause political disasters.

In this section, I have argued that Smith's turn to genealogy exhibits the contingent nature of the content of our derived property rights (and social institutions in general). Smith teaches that the "reasonable" content of such rights tend
to fit the past, local needs of a particular society, given the prejudices of the population. So property arrangements are a solution to a past problem, but future

needs may change. This is why the scope and nature of our right to derived property may change. It explains why derived (property) rights are never absolute and always context-sensitive and historically conditioned.

By contrast, all of us are the normative source for some fundamental rights rooted in our common humanity. The dictates of humanity, which is connected to a harm principle, suggest we should not be cruel to others and should treat each other with respect; we should not be owned by others, etc. (cf. Frazer 2010: Chapter 6, where he attributes to Herder the view that I discern in Smith).

iii. The Turn to History: The Enlightenment Imperative

I argue that a turn to history can correct one-sidedness and make the inquirer aware that future impartial spectators may improve on one's explanations and evaluative criteria. In particular, according to Smith, history teaches one to appreciate impartial, causal explanation while making one familiar with the idea of possible, future revision.

If the study of history yields no more than the contingent nature of the content of our derived property rights and social institutions in general, why spend so much time developing historical narratives about the origins of social institutions? There are four strands in Smith's philosophy that can account for this. As we have seen in the previous section, (1) the content of the right is articulated by way of a historical analysis. The historical account (2) provides a normative baseline with which to evaluate moral and social institutions. It (3) does justice to an Enlightenment imperative, one that demands non-miraculous, causal explanations for our practices. Finally, the historical account (4) enables a moral theory in which explanation and justification are mutually reinforcing. In this section I focus on strands 2 through 4.

One important reason to turn to history is that it can provide a useful baseline or measure in evaluating legal arrangements. The previous section already contains some evidence for this. What will count as "reasonable" is a contingent affair, determined by the provisional, social organization and needs of a society; this will never be fully rational. One can learn from the study of history that in our evaluation one must allow for suboptimal arrangements that meet the standards of local prudence and do not offend local prejudices (recall also the treatment of TMS 6.2.2.16, 233).

Moreover, the messy historical details are a kind of antidote against philosophers' tendency to offer "partial and imperfect" accounts of nature (TMS 6.1.1.1, 265). To this day philosophers tend to avoid messy details of the world of experience (Fleischacker 2004, 270–1; we will see in Chapter 10 that according to Smith philosophers are prone to mental escapism). For the Smithian philosopher, Hobbes's state of nature sets the baseline too low, while Rousseau's sets it too high. In Smith's hunting stage (as close as he gets to the state of nature), there is a "tolerable degree of security" (WN 5.1.b.2, 709). From this point of view, feudalism is definitely undesirable: ordinary people are "almost all slaves" (WN 3.2.8, 386). But some herding and agricultural and most commercial societies will be definite advances over the state of nature in many respects, especially in terms of, say, material comfort (even of the poorest members of society) and military might (recall the "African king" trope at WN 1.1.11, 24).

There is, thus, a final sense in which history offers a valuable baseline. In WN, Smith tends to compare the situation of a society across whole centuries (Schabas 2006). This historical sense allows one to ignore short-term fluctuations when one evaluates institutions of society. Moreover, it also offers the proper perspective when one advocates or evaluates policy/legal changes; one may ask, given one's historical experience and one's theoretical understanding provided by one's science of human nature, whether, say, proposed legal changes will "ameliorate" or worsen the conditions of the working poor in the long term. Of course, this historical perspective should not be abused to ignore genuine, short-term, or inhumane conditions. Smith, following Hume, is clear that in case of, for example, famine, otherwise "sacred" property rights may be revoked (see Fleischacker's 2004: 210 discussion of WN 4.5.b.39–40, 539).

Thus, using history as a baseline is an antidote against philosophers' tendency to examine and evaluate institutional arrangements from ideal points of view. History has a moderating effect. When we propose changes or innovations we should evaluate them in light of our historical experiences, but without appealing to tradition to justify ongoing injustices. That is, the existence of a tradition can be a (deplorable) excuse, but not itself a justification.

Of course, the treatment of property is not the only place in Smith's oeuvre where he offers a historical account, but he does not offer much explanation for his historical turn. Astronomy is supposed to instruct the reader in the unexpectedly large role of the sentiments wonder, admiration, and surprise in intellectual pursuits (Intro. 6, 34). In a narrow sense this is the point of Smith's essay, which is reflected in its full title: "The Principles which lead and direct Philosophical Enquiries: Illustrated by the History of Astronomy." Yet while Black and Hutton, Smith's original editors, promise the readers of Astronomy "satisfaction and pleasure" ("Advertisement by the Editors"), Smith claims that the history of philosophy offers "the most entertaining and instructive" account (Astronomy 2.12, EPS 45–6). This suggests the piece is not merely offered for satisfaction and pleasure. Black and Hutton call attention to Smith's intention to write "a connected history of the liberal sciences and elegant arts." Thus, one may ask why this would provide the most instructive material. In Chapter 10, I argue that Astronomy defends a subtle, naturalistic picture in which the potential, open-ended nature of physical inquiry, with changing norms of theory acceptance, is reconciled with a realist stance toward the claims made by the best available theory. Therefore, a turn to history can make the inquirer aware that future impartial spectators may improve on one's explanations and evaluative criteria.

So far, I have treated Smith's turn to history in relative contextual isolation. Smith did not pioneer the application of genealogical methods in the human sciences; we find so-called natural histories of human affairs in Bacon, Spinoza, and Mandeville, to name just a few. I find it useful to contrast Smith's treatment of genealogy with Toland's use. Toland's (1704) *Letters to Serena* focuses his genealogy on the idea of the immortality of the soul, the subject of the second letter. In paragraph 1 of Letter 2, the "immortality of the soul" is treated as a "truth" known to classical sources independent from and preceding Biblical revelation (p. 20; in fact, he insists that the doctrine is unknown to the Old Testament [Letter II, p. 56]). In the very next paragraph (2), Toland offers a concise statement of his methodology:

> To persons less knowing and unprejudiced than Serena, it would [be] found strange perhaps to hear me speak of the soul's immortality, as of an opinion, which, like some others in philosophy, had a beginning at a certain time, or from a certain author who was the inventor thereof, and which was favoured or opposed as peoples' persuasion, interest or inclination led them. Letters II.2 (p. 21; I have modernized his spelling)[16]

In this passage, Toland subtly shifts from treating the doctrine of the immortality of the soul as a truth to an invented opinion with a potentially definite natural history. Moreover, he treats the acceptance of the doctrine in terms of the rhetorical force, the agents' incentives, and the psychological needs of speakers and audience alike. While he explicitly allows that we have "reason," which—with practice—can be made immune from the falsehoods taught to us from earliest age, his account of his genealogical method omits treating reason's discovery of the doctrine. In fact, he suggests that (the mutually inconsistent) philosophers should just stop talking about the immortality of the soul now that the truth of the doctrine has been revealed. Toland grants that "it is impossible that God should lie; and what he has revealed, though not in every thing falling under our comprehension, must yet be true and certain" (Letter 2, p. 66). Even so, Toland's method treats doctrines as valuable and acceptable in a social discourse without

---

[16] Serena is the official addressee of the *Letters*; she is a high-status, educated interlocutor. The preface to the *Letters* offers a resounding defense of intellectual, gender equality. Toland suggests that it is either "inveterate custom" or the "design in the men" that causes female exclusion from the "world of learning." In general, Toland thinks nurture is responsible for much of our (very flawed) "second nature" in women and men. Thus, while Toland accepts a universal human nature, it is according to him extremely plastic (anticipating Mandeville and Smith). Echoing Plato and Malebranche, he suggests that belief and character formation starts in the womb and is developed (or degenerated by) our major social institutions (family, church, universities, etc.)—he treats our acculturation as inevitable, but as practiced as a form of social disease (cf. "infection").

regard to (revealed or discovered) truth, and this is indeed how Toland proceeds to investigate ancient sources on the topic.

There is a tendency to treat Toland and Smith as being in opposite camps of the Enlightenment (see, e.g., Jonathan Israel, who treats Smith as a so-called moderate and Toland as a radical). But when in the *Letters* Toland briefly turns to what can be learned from the Ancients, it turns out to be reducible to this: "the punishment of the wicked and the recompense of the good, not being contained in fables, but exhibited to our eyes, each party is every day put in mind of his duties; and by this custom there grows the best and most useful reformation of manners" (*Letters* II, p. 50—quoting Diodorus Siculus). Thus, regardless of whether unmasking is the main purpose of Toland's *Letters*, he has a political message, too. Rather than telling people tales of Hell and Purgatory, society would be much better, even best served by the strict enforcement of justice (this is the wisdom of the Ancients worth finding for those who know how to read, according to Toland). This is a reformist, not a radical, message and entirely compatible with Smith's position, except that Smith thinks one should be cautious in aiming to abolish religion.

Let's return to the main argument. Despite the well-founded reservations of Emma Rothschild (2001), much scholarship on Smith explicitly or implicitly takes its interpretations from his first biographer, Dugald Stewart, at face value. Rothschild convincingly shows that Stewart's biography is, in part, an attempt to distance Smith from any association with the French Revolution. Even so, Stewart can provide some useful insights. Interest in "theoretical or conjectural" history— that is, to show, in Stewart's words, how in the absence of reliable "information" (Stewart 2.45, EPS 292) an event "may have been produced by natural causes" (Stewart 2.47, EPS 29)—is widespread among Smith's Scottish and French contemporaries. According to Stewart, one important motivation for offering a conjectural history is to put a "check" to "that indolent philosophy, which refers to a miracle, whatever appearances, both in the natural and moral worlds, it is unable to explain" (Stewart 2.47, EPS 293). Thus, according to Stewart, conjectural history is part of a more fundamental Enlightenment project in which explanations are demystified and, to use an anachronistic term, secularized.

Now despite the fact that Smith also writes histories about well-documented cases, this is an important clue. In LRBL, in the context of praising Machiavelli, Smith remarks that the "chief purpose of History [is] to relate Events and connect them with their causes without becoming a party on either side" (2.70, Lecture 20, Wednesday, January 12, LRBL 115). This use of history fits quite naturally with Smith's (cautious) enlightenment project on behalf of the public (e.g., WN 1.10.c.40, 151). He believes that the "study of science and philosophy" can have a social utility in suppressing religious "enthusiasm and superstition;" this is why he advocates mandatory exams in them for anybody who wants to practice a profession (WN 5.1.9.14, 796; 5.1.f.50–6, 781–6). Smith thinks that an educated populace is necessary to maintain freedom, public accountability, and public order in a modern society. He worries about "gross ignorance and stupidity" in the modern world

(WN 5.1.f.61, 788). He worries that men become incapable of "bearing a part in any rational conversation" and of "forming any just judgment concerning many even of the ordinary duties of private life" (WN 5.1.f, 782). Thus, history teaches one to appreciate impartial, causal explanation while making one familiar with the idea of possible future revision. The fact that we find this idea in the lectures suggests that my reconstruction of Smith's published views is not implausible.

Now one may think that my account of Smith suggests that history shows that all previous understandings (property, moral theories, astronomy) that claimed to be objective were in fact limited or partial; that history teaches us that our convictions about what is sacred or established fact will seem less secure to future generations. It is tempting to think Smith agrees with Hume's barely disguised glee that much law has its origin "more on taste and imagination than on any solid argument." (Second *Enquiry*, Appendix 3.10). This account of Smith would put his genealogical project in the unmasking vein familiar from Toland. But we have already seen that Smith is more than willing to "accommodate, as well as he can," the "confirmed habits and prejudices of the people" rather than to undermine the public's beliefs. Therefore, even leaving aside his commitment to public Enlightenment, it is unlikely that Smith intends the main point of his turn to history to be deflationary in a general sense.

Dugald Stewart claims that conjectural history aims to show how, in the absence of reliable information, an event may have been produced by natural causes. While I agree with this, this formulation underestimates the project in Hume and Smith. They also articulate constraints on the development of social institutions. Recall (from Section a of Chapter 4) that according to Hume, "rude and savage men" are not capable of dreaming up the "idea of justice" in the state of nature (Treatise 3.2.2.7). The condition of justice, which creates some stable property relations and, thus, an interest in keeping promises, is—to use a Kantian-sounding phrase—a condition of the possibility for the giving of promises (Treatise 3.2.5.8–10). For Hume, promises first arise, and then necessarily (3.2.6.1), only when there is an interest in keeping them. Hume articulates here a kind of *conceptual social necessitation relation*. Such a relation does not hold in all social contexts, but only when the conditions that give rise to them obtain.

Smith's account of the origin of justice echoes the conceptual structure of Hume's argument. For Smith, law arises only when there is an "interest" in it. As we have seen, for Smith, against Hobbes and Hume, the unequal distribution of derived property is a social condition of possibility for the existence of regularly administered civil law (cf. Fleischacker 2004: 180–93). Smith's conjectural history aims, in part, at exhibiting such necessary conceptual and causal relationships. This goes some way toward explaining why, even if Smith recognizes the normative force of the original property right, he would offer a historical account alongside it. Smith is not merely after explaining how our conventions may have come into being without miracles but is also articulating what elements are constitutive in it. That is, while Smith shares with the modern followers of Nietzsche and Foucault the sense that genealogy reveals contingent features of our present arrangements, he is equally likely to emphasize the conceptual-necessitation relations, or forced moves, that occur through history. These forced moves can then figure in what I have called a Smithian social explanation.

Now throughout his writings Smith insists that philosophy is a social practice in which one uses reasons to appeal to each other's (imagined) approval (External Senses 18, EPS 140, and 12, EPS 137; see also Astronomy 4.15, EPS 63–4 and TMS 3.2.20–2, 124–5; I develop this point in Chapter 10). This is no accident. Smith treats the moral deliberation of our impartial spectator when, say, we attempt to act with self-command and propriety as discursive; it's the "voice" of "reason" (TMS 3.3.4, 137; Fleischacker 1999).

My suggestion about Smith's turn to history is, thus, as follows. It represents Smith's recognition that in an Age of Enlightenment, when Newtonian natural philosophy has become capable of offering real, albeit revisable, causal explanations (see Chapter 10), there has been a fundamental change in what is demanded of an explanation, including moral-historical ones. Once, following Hume, the experimental method has been introduced into moral and political affairs, one cannot turn the clock back to a more rationalistic or revelatory approach. When we adopt an inquisitive stance, we demand an impartial, causal account of why certain norms are possible for beings like us before we accept that they are binding on us. We do so even at the risk that the genealogy changes our self-conception.

My main proposal is this: for Smith, accounts of the naturalistic development of social institutions of property and their articulation in our practices and theorizing are partially constitutive of the normative force of these institutions. Of course, this account is not the sole authority of the normative force of these institutions. Smith himself emphasizes that for most of us, most of the time this force is derived from longstanding moral rules, whose authority, in turn, may be seen to be derived from other (divine) authorities (TMS 3.4–5). But in a world of Enlightenment, any appeal to authority, whether reason or revelation, is always open to further investigation. We may turn to history to learn how our social institutions fit our (past) needs, which provides a normative baseline with which to evaluate changes in our social institutions. In doing so, the historical account does justice to our Enlightenment Imperative, one that demands non-miraculous, causal explanations for our practices. These explanations teach us something about the social conditions of possibility of our institutions. The historical account enables a moral theory in which explanation and justification are mutually reinforcing for beings self-conscious of their status as intellectual animals. That is to say, while Hume thought that after the "true philosopher" had defeated various kinds of "superstition and enthusiasm," one could return to and defend a kind of "common sense," Smith saw that reflection can make the environmentally rational, common sense, including our moral self-understanding, itself a moving target. We must live with this uncertainty.

8

Social Institutions and Consequentialism

In the first few sections of this chapter I argue that when it comes to evaluating social institutions, Smith is a particular kind of consequentialist—one who favors the welfare of the working poor. I illustrate this by way of an analysis of (1) the so-called real price, Smith's central measure of welfare in WN, and (2) Smith's proposed progressive tax regime. I also argue that Smith's consequentialism should be distinguished from utilitarianism. I then turn to a consideration of what might explain Smith's theoretical bias toward the working poor. Finally, I discuss the principles that, according to Smith, govern the duties of the legislator and then analyze his account of liberty.

a. Society, Justice, and Group Selection

In this section, I argue that Smith offers a very thin group-selection argument, in which institutions that promote martial virtues and minimal intragroup justice are required for the enduring survival of any society.

Recall Smith's criticism of Aristotle and Plato for their failure to condemn Athenian infanticide. Smith adds the following claim:

> There is an obvious reason why custom should never pervert our senti-
> ments with regard to the general style and character of conduct and
> behaviour, in the same degree as with regard to the propriety or unlaw-
> fulness of particular usages. There never can be any such custom. No
> society could subsist a moment, in which the usual strain of men's con-
> duct and behaviour was of a piece with the horrible practice ["murder
> of newborn infants"] I have just now mentioned. (TMS 5.2.16, 211)

Let us assume, for the sake of argument, that there is a non–question-begging way of characterizing and connecting particular social institutions (customs, practices, laws, etc.) with the "general style and character of conduct and behavior"

such that environmental rationality is possible. Here Smith presupposes a more general social theory that he may have inherited from Hume (see the "indissoluble chain" in "Of Refinement in the Arts") or, especially, Montesquieu (e.g., *Spirit of the Laws*) and that Ferguson popularized in *An Essay on the History of Civil Society*.

A casual glance at the chapter heading in Book 5, "Of the Publick Works and Institutions for facilitating Commerce of the Society," suggests that Smith used the term "institution" rather widely. For Smith human institutions include roads, bridges, canals, harbors, companies, schools, universities, religious orders/ministries, the monarchy, the armed forces, slavery, taxation policies, and legal arrangements (especially on land and inheritance of property). Let's also assume that for Smith one of the dimensions along which one can characterize and evaluate both particular social institutions and the general style and character of conduct and behavior is moral. In the infanticide example (TMS 5.2.15, 210), Smith uses the language of "propriety," "murder," and "unlawfulness," even though in Athens exposure of children was legal. It's clear that Smith thinks that after Athens attained sufficient wealth, an Athenian-bred impartial spectator ought to have condemned infanticide. Before I turn to Smith's grounds for claiming this, I focus first on his more general claim here that "custom should never pervert our sentiments with regard to the general style and character of conduct and behavior." While Smith did not encounter Nazi villains or totalitarian dictatorships, he did criticize "the savage injustice of the Europeans" in their colonial imperialism (WN 4.1.32, 448), and he regularly holds up feudalism (e.g. WN 3.3.12, 405) as an instance "where men are continually afraid of the violence of their superiors" (WN 2.1.31, 285; Smith also lists "Turkey" and "most other governments of Asia" of his time as further examples).

Smith's argument seems to be that a society can persist with some unjust practices even while claiming "public utility" (and "remote interest" [TMS 5.2.15, 210]) on their behalf. However, a society cannot subsist if the general style and character of conduct is unjust. For Smith, "justice ... is the main pillar that upholds the whole edifice. If it is removed, the great, the immense fabric of human society ... must in a moment crumble into atoms" (TMS 2.2.3.4, 86). Even if we allow for some poetic license, it is tempting to see in all of this a proto-Darwinian point of view, especially because Darwin expressed nearly the same sentiment in *Descent*: "No tribe could hold together if murder, robbery, treachery, &c, were common; consequently such crimes within the limits of the same tribe 'are branded with everlasting infamy'" (Darwin 2004: 141).

The line of reasoning in TMS 5.2.15–6, 209–11, and the passage just quoted from *Descent* is a very thin group-selection argument. Smith and Darwin are not claiming here that there is differential selection among different groups based on their customs. Rather, they are claiming that the very *possibility* for a society to remain a distinct group presupposes a minimal amount of intragroup justice.[1] Of

---

[1] The survival of totalitarian regimes and certain kinds of dictatorships make such a judgment appear questionable.

course, both Smith and Darwin believe that a failure to keep some group/tribal identity over time will lead to a massive unlikelihood that members of the tribe or group will reproduce, which undercuts one of nature's "two great ends" (self-preservation and propagation of the species; recall TMS 2.1.5.10, 77–8). This is why one can discern in them a group-selection argument. In *Descent* Darwin's group-selection argument is more developed and explicit; as he writes shortly before the passage just quoted, "those communities, which included the greatest number of the most sympathetic members, would flourish the best, and rear the greatest number of offspring" (Darwin 2004: 130). Smith makes no mention of selection, so the evidence for even a thin group-selection argument in Smith is not overwhelming. Nevertheless, the claim is reinforced by Smith's obsession with the martial virtues in TMS (e.g., 1.3.2.5, 54–5; 6.3.17, 244) and WN (e.g., 5.i.f.59, 786–7), as documented by Montes (2004).

Above I quoted part of the well-known "torpor of mind" passage deploring the negative externalities of hyper-specialization on the conditions of the working poor; Smith remarks that a man "generally becomes as stupid and ignorant as it is possible for a human creature to become," rendering him "incapable of defending his own country in war." He goes even further, claiming that "[h]is dexterity at his own particular trade seems, in this manner, to be acquired at the expence of his intellectual, social, and martial virtues" (WN 5.i.f.50, 782). As he writes a few pages later, "the security of every society must always depend, more or less, upon the martial spirit of the great body of the people" (WN 5.i.f.59, 787). It is this concern with bare survival that explains why even "the man of humanity" will, despite misgivings, go along with the fate of

> A centinel [*sic*] . . . who falls asleep upon his watch, [who] suffers death by the laws of war, because such carelessness might endanger the whole army. This severity may, upon many occasions, appear necessary, and, for that reason, just and proper. When the preservation of an individual is inconsistent with the safety of a multitude, nothing can be more just than that the many should be preferred to the one. (TMS 2.2.3.11, 90–1)

So the requirements of martial virtue that ensure group survival are scattered throughout Smith's writings. For Smith, without institutions that promote martial virtues and minimal intragroup justice, *society and even the multitude* will not survive as either a society or a multitude.[2] Smith thought society ought to

---

[2] In the text I treat Smith's "multitude" and "society" as entities to be distinguished, on the one hand, from the state or government, which ensures the maintenance of justice or impartial law, and, on the other hand, from the mob, which in Smith uniformly has a negative valence (which has, for example, "undistinguishing eyes" [TMS 6.2.1.20, 226] and tends toward "foolish admiration" [TMS 6.3.30, 253]). For Smith's views on the multitude see Hill and Montag 2014.

promote practices that ensure its own survival. This is why one can claim that we can find a very thin group-selection argument in Smith.

Before I turn to clarifying the relationship between the evolution of social institutions and considerations of utility, we can now make precise Smith's denial that (nearly) all of a society's mores can be entirely corrupt. On his view, in any society there always must be some favored in-group that is treated with justice, and this practice ought to make possible the development of genuine impartial spectators. Absent such a minimal level of intragroup justice, it makes no sense to even talk of "society."

But, unfortunately, as we have seen, a militarist society with extreme inequality of power and fortune also facilitates much moral insensitivity toward nonprivileged insiders and outsiders generally. Moreover, Smith does not think this tendency has been overcome; he is insistent that commercial societies, when they allow monopolistic enterprises to rule (colonial) territories, are also capable of developing such insensitivity. He castigates the East India Company not just for "the embezzlement and misapplication" of tax revenue (WN 5.2.91, 946; see also 5.2.d.9, 840) but also for generating a "government," which is "necessarily military and despotical" (WN 4.7.c.104, 638).

In practice Smith offers little comfort to the victims of the militarily superior society. Smith's hope for mutual deterrence as a consequence of "extensive" mutual "commerce" because "nothing seems more likely to establish this equality of force than that mutual communication of knowledge and of all sorts of improvements" (WN 4.7.c.80, 626–7) is just a "likely" hope, not a guarantee. There is no evidence that Smith thinks that the suffering absent such equality of force is necessary for some greater good.

b. Utility and Social Institutions

In this section I argue that when it comes to the moral evaluation of social institutions, Smith is a consequentialist. In particular, I argue that he advocates institutions that have a propensity to promote the welfare of the working poor, who are the majority in his own day. To be clear, Smith is not a utilitarian in the sense of Hutcheson or, later, Bentham. Smith does not recognize a utilitarian calculus.

So far I have emphasized the deontic elements in Smith's moral theory (Montes 2004: 105–13). In Smith's theory of what we may label "individual morality," the impartial spectator's judgments of propriety focus primarily on intentions and their foreseeable, intended consequences. Even Smith's account of merit, which is the moral category that governs our considered judgments of the actual consequences of actions, ultimately "arises from the sympathetic emotions of gratitude and love, with which, when we bring home to our own breast the situation of those principally concerned" (TMS 2.1.5.3, 75) and, thus, involves a judgment of propriety. Even so, Smith does not want to deny any role for utility; as he concedes to Hume, perception of it can enliven the sentiment of justice (recall TMS 4.2.3, 188; see also Sidgwick 1892: 213).

By contrast, when it comes to Smith's moral evaluation of social institutions, he generally focuses on "consequences upon the general welfare of the society" (WN Intro.8, 11; see also WN 1.11.p.8, 265). As we have seen in the case of the sleeping sentinel, Smith thinks that regardless of individual judgments of propriety, the legislator can uphold institutions with an appeal to social utility when society's survival is at stake (see Levy 1995; Witztum and Young 2013).

An illuminating example of Smith's consequentialist reasoning occurs in Book 5 of WN:

> By a very exact account it appears, that, in 1755, the whole revenue of the clergy of the church of Scotland, including their glebe or church lands, and the rent of their manses or dwelling houses, estimated according to a reasonable valuation, amounted only to 68,514*l*. 1*s*. 5*d*.1/12. This very moderate revenue affords a decent subsistence to nine hundred and forty-four ministers. The whole expence of the church, including what is occasionally laid out for the building and reparation of churches, and of the manses of ministers, cannot well be supposed to exceed eighty or eighty-five thousand pounds a year. The most opulent church in Christendom does not maintain better the uniformity of faith, the fervour of devotion, the spirit of order, regularity, and austere morals in the great body of the people, than this very poorly endowed church of Scotland. All the good effects, both civil and religious, which an established church can be supposed to produce, are produced by it as compleatly as by any other. The greater part of the protestant churches of Switzerland, which in general are not better endowed than the church of Scotland, produce those effects in a still higher degree. (WN 5.1.g.41, 813)

The presbytery of Scotland is praised not just for its relatively successful religious effects ("uniformity of faith," "fervour of devotion") but also for its socially useful moral-political consequences (viz. "the spirit of order, regularity, and austere morals"). It does so very cost-effectively. The good social effects are *primarily* felt by "the common people" (WN 5.1.g.38, 810; this whole paragraph, on the sympathetic affection and mutual "kindness" between "presbyterian clergy" and "common people," is worth reading).

Smith's judgment on the good social consequences of the "presbyterian clergy" seems genuine (and not just a relative judgment among established churches). But (*pace* Waterman 2002: 914–5) in the list of positive consequences, Smith does not praise the doctrinal truths of the Scottish church; in fact, he goes out of his way to note that the Scottish clergy caters to "the prejudices of people" (WN 5.1.g.38, 810; recall the discussion of Section c in Chapter 7). And Smith does not hide the fact that the politicking surrounding "a certain concurrence" from the parish in the choice of clergy "keep up" the "fanatical spirit, either in the clergy or in the people of Scotland" (WN 5.1.g.36, 809).

Thus, Smith praises an institution for its positive impact on the common people even though it also has unpleasant secondary consequences upon, say, the intellectual elite of Scotland. His teacher, Hutcheson, and his friend, Hume, were once among the intended targets of the "fanatical" faction of the Kirk. In fact, Smith thinks that with established churches some such negative political influences cannot be avoided; this is why he advocates a "plan" of "no ecclesiastical government" (WN 5.1.g.8, 792–3; see Section b in Chapter 14 for more details). Smith's evaluation of religious institutions is exemplary in its careful cost/benefit analysis of its impact primarily on ordinary people. The costs are calculated financially while the benefits are measured by his judgment on morals and politics. Smith is not primarily treating their impact on economic growth, although Smith thinks that the "spirit of order, regularity, and austere morals" may have a positive externality on economic growth if it is conducive to prudential saving and law-abidingness generally.

So it should come as no surprise that, for example, Rawls tends to treat Smith casually as a utilitarian (1971: 22 n. 9). Rawls may have been influenced in doing so by Sidgwick, who treats Smith (and Hume taken together) as a (flawed) anticipation of the "explanations of the origin of the moral sentiments which have been more recently current in the utilitarian school" (Sidgwick 1892: 218; see also Edgeworth 1881: 97–8, who treats Smith, Bentham, J. S. Mill, and Sidgwick as developing the same utilitarian "system").

The connection of Smith's thought with utilitarianism is no surprise: Smith had a clear and deep influence on two of the most important utilitarians, J. S. Mill and Alfred Marshall. There are many continuities between Smith and the classical political economists who followed him throughout the nineteenth century. Even so, there are four important reasons to resist a taxonomy in which Smith appears as a utilitarian:

1. It does not fit the details of the deontic aspects of his moral theory, especially for individuals.
2. Nowhere does Smith show an interest in maximizing any quantity.
3. Smith rejects ethical monism (Gill 2014a), a philosophical vice he associates with Hobbes and Mandeville.
4. We do not find in Smith the kind of formulas that his teacher, Francis Hutcheson, promoted in evaluating the virtue of an action.[3]

---

[3] The second and fourth points may well be connected to what I call Smith's anti-mathematicism (see Chapter 13).

The second point is nicely illustrated by a passage from WN in which Smith defends what we would call "living wages" for the working poor:

> Servants, labourers and workmen of different kinds, make up the far greater part of every great political society. But what improves the circumstances of the greater part can never be regarded as an inconveniency to the whole. No society can surely be flourishing and happy, of which the far greater part of the members are poor and miserable. It is but equity, besides, that they who feed, cloath and lodge the whole body of the people, should have such a share of the produce of their own labour as to be themselves tolerably well fed, cloathed and lodged. (WN 1.8.36, 96)

In such passages Smith is responding to Mandeville and mercantilist others, who had argued that even in a wealthy country poor people should be kept poor in order (a) to keep the economy competitive with poorer countries, and (b) to create an incentive for the poor to keep working hard (for good discussion see Fleischacker 2004). It is no surprise that Samuel Whitbread appealed to Smith to argue for a minimum wage in Parliament in 1795 (Rothschild 1992: 85, 2001: 61–69). For Smith social consequences are linked to equity. Smith advocates institutions that have a propensity to promote the welfare of "the greater part." But he does so without trying to maximize their welfare or general welfare; his aims are more modest—that is, he is aiming for conditions in which they are "tolerably well fed" and so forth. This is not to deny that Smith recognizes that *within* these institutions some individuals can be understood to be maximizing whatever they deem valuable (security, profit, power, income, applause, etc.). Throughout his writings Smith discusses the prevalence of "avarice and ambition" (e.g., TMS 1.3.2.1, 50; WN 5.1.b.2, 709).

Moreover, Smith's focus on the "greater part" is informed by concern for those who do the actual (hard) work. He is concerned with institutions that improve the lot of the working poor—that is, "the interest of the many" (TMS 2.2.3.11, 91; see Herzog 2013: 28). David M. Levy has nicely tried to capture the spirit of Smith's project by treating Smith as a median-based utilitarian (Levy 1995), but it would be more precise to treat Smith as a median-based consequentialist when it comes to social institutions.

This is not to deny that with Smithian principles one could turn Smith into a utilitarian. In her *Letters on Sympathy*, de Grouchy does so in a very subtle fashion. She offers a streamlined account in which our pleasures and pains are linked to social utility. To put this starkly: by tacitly bypassing Smith's criticism of Hume's account of the origin of justice, she can transform the Smithian moral apparatus into a coherent, hedonistic consequentialism.

By contrast, Smith has (at least) a two-tiered analysis in which the principles that underwrite our judgments of institutions are distinct from our judgments of agents (and their characters). It is not so much the absence of the "objective" impartial spectator that distinguishes Smith's theory from de Grouchy's, but her willingness to forego judgments of propriety as an authoritative source of approval. Some will see in this a loss of appreciation for moral particularity, but others will welcome it as a move toward consistency that generates the very possibility of social reform, especially if respect for particularity is used to stifle the very possibility of progressive reform. This is because for Smith judgments of propriety are always judgments of local situations (TMS 1.1.1.1, 12). I do not wish to imply that de Grouchy could not consistently recover an analysis of propriety or find other ways to do justice to moral particularity, but it does not seem to be of major interest to her.

In the next two sections I illustrate Smith's consequentialism by focusing, first, briefly on the nature of one of Smith's most important theoretical concepts, the measure of real price, and, then, by looking at Smith's tax policy. In the final two sections of this chapter I explore the moral grounding of Smith's version of consequentialism when it comes to social institutions.

c. The Measure of Real Price: Adam Smith's Science of Equity

In this section I argue that Smith's main measure for welfare, "real price" (WN 1.5, especially 1.5.22, 56), is especially appropriate to capture the living standards of the working poor. Here I reveal this by analyzing Smith's measure of the measure. Along the way, some common confusion about "real price" is dismantled. In so doing, I elaborate on the line of argument that has been developed during the last three decades that has explained and emphasized Smith's attempts to further the interests of the working poor (for some of the best work, see Pack 1991; Fleischacker 1999; Rothschild 2001; Fleischacker 2004; Boucoyannis 2013).

In his discussion of exchange value (following WN 1.4.14, 46ff), Smith draws distinctions between "natural" and nominal/market prices as well between an absolute or "real" and nominal/market prices (this list is not exhaustive). In this section I just explore Smith's distinction between real and nominal prices (I focus on natural prices in Section b of Chapter 12).

Let me provide a simple, anachronistic example to illuminate what the distinction is driving at. When somebody's paycheck increases by 5%, we call that a nominal increase. But we need the inflation number, say, 3%, before we can judge the real increase of the salary (a little less than 2%). For Smith, the nominal price of the wage earner is the number on the check, or as he says, "the quantity of money," whereas the real price is constituted by the "necessaries and conveniencies of life" given in return for this quantity of money (WN 1.5.9, 51) or, to put it differently, by the labor "commanded" or "purchased" (WN 1.5.19, 55).

Two initial points need to be made here. First, the nominal price of things can only be measured at any given time: "at the same time and place, therefore, money is the exact measure of the real exchangeable value of all commodities. It is so, however, at the same time and place only" (WN 1.5.19, 55). There is, thus, no relevant distinction between real and nominal prices at a single location in time. That is, for most practical purposes—"the business of common life" (WN 1.5.4, 49)—and in the absence of hyperinflation, nominal prices are all that matter; the price mechanism provides merchants and laborers with the information they need (WN 1.5.20, 55).

Second, in my wage earner example, I assume some familiarity with the notion of purchasing power. As Smith writes, "The power which that possession immediately and directly conveys to him, is the power of purchasing; a certain command over all the labour, or over all the produce of labour which is then in the market" (WN 1.5.3, 48). The ability to command labor is not obviously the same as purchasing power; in contemporary thought this involves a weighted basket of goods. The ability to command "the produce of labor on the market" at a given time ("then in the market") is akin to purchasing power. As others have shown, Smith introduces real prices in order to measure something akin to what we would call welfare (Blaug 1959). According to Smith, work or labor can be irksome, and everybody wants to save "toil and trouble" (WN 1.5.2, 47) and command other people's labor (embodied in their products and services). He goes on to claim that labor "never varying in its own value, is alone the ultimate and real standard by which the value of all commodities can at all times and places be estimated and compared" (WN 1.5.7, 51).

For present purposes, the importance of this quote is to illustrate why Smith cares about an ultimate and "real" standard. Before I get to that, note two issues. First, there is a persistent confusion stemming from this quote (WN 1.5.7, 51): the word "labor" can be (and is) interpreted in two ways: (1) as a number of man-hours and (2) (to use modern terminology) as units of disutility—that is, the psychological and social cost of work to the individual, the "toil and trouble" mentioned before. If all work has the same character (that is, if man-hours and units of disutility are somehow related), then these two interpretations coincide. Smith thinks they do so, in fact, *only* in a hunting economy.

Second, since Ricardo's time the phrase "real price" has often served as encouragement to emphasize the ontological aspects of Smith's approach—labor as an ultimate and real standard of value. Many readers forget, however, that Smith only introduces a notion of a real price as a measure of "value in exchange" (WN 1.4.15, 15), which he distinguishes from "value in use" (WN 1.4.13–8, 44–6). Whatever else the distinction between "value in use" and "value in exchange" is supposed to do for Smith, there can be no doubt that he thinks any given commodity can have at least two kinds of values: use and exchange. Neither has ontological priority. Real prices measure only one kind of value: exchange. Moreover, Smith indicates that he not only knows quite well that some jobs are more enjoyable than others (even if they require the same amount of labor), but also that the value we put on the same job necessarily varies from one society to another or even within society depending on, say, one's social rank (e.g., WN 1.10.b.2–3, 117–8). Thus, for Smith, a real price can never measure some fundamental entity beyond exchange (cf. Maifreda 2012, Chapter 5).

Yet, even if one were to grant that Smith *did* want to call attention to some ontological element, a focus on ontology misses the purpose: Smith wants to be able to compare purchasing power in different times and places. As he writes, "In such a work as this, however, it may sometimes be of use to compare the different real values of a particular commodity at different times and places, or the different degrees of power over labour of other people which it may, upon different occasions, have given to those who possessed it" (WN 1.5.22, 55). The idea of a "real price" seems to be absent from LJ. It appears to be a conceptual innovation designed for the theoretical purposes of WN.

Here I have not done full justice to the intricacies of Smith's exposition. But, let us assume, for the sake of argument, that a criterion of welfare has been established. The question remains, whose welfare is to be measured? To answer that question we need to analyze the method of measurement that Smith advocates; this reveals his purpose.

If one wants to compare the wealth of different locales at the same time or people's welfare at different times, one cannot simply compare the nominal (money) prices of goods. The value of gold and silver is not invariant across time, and not even across place. In a complex commercial society it is impossible to calculate real prices directly without solid data: "the current prices of labour at distant times and places can scarce ever be known with any degrees of exactness" (WN 1.5.22, 55). The nominal wages of labor are uninformative if we do not know what they buy. Even if one thinks that one ought to measure the "toil and trouble" of work, how does one go about doing this across many centuries?

Smith chooses the price of "corn" (the eighteenth-century word for edible seeds) as a kind of second-best way of measuring the real price of things:

> Those [prices] of corn, though they have in few places been regularly recorded are in general better known and have been more frequently taken notice of by historians and other writers. We must generally, therefore, content ourselves with them, not as being always exactly in the same proportion as the current prices of labour, but as being the nearest approximation which can commonly be had to that proportion. (WN 1.5.22, 56)

Thus, Smith chooses corn for five reasons.

First, because rents were often paid in corn, relatively reliable and very long-running data were available to him (see the quote above). Smith discusses the quality and sources of these data at WN 1.11.e.16–38, 200–10. His long "Digression concerning the Variations in the Value of Silver during the Course of the Four last Centuries" at the end of WN Book 1 (pp. 195–267) exploits such data with a careful analysis covering more than 500 years. Smith's data start in 1205, although he also uses ancient sources going back to Roman times (see for a terrific, concise analysis see Rockoff 2013).

Second, although there are many short-term fluctuations in the price of corn (due to variations in harvests and political conditions), over the long term its price is relatively stable due to the near-constant cost of production (WN 1.11.e.28, 206, and 1.5.16–7, 53–4). However, there are many complications. For example, because the price of corn is tabulated in nominal prices, Smith needs to devise a way to compare the coinages of different periods. This is not an exact science, and Smith returns to it throughout WN (e.g., 1.4.9–10, 41–4; 1.11.e–i, 195–234). Also, when a society moves from one technological stage of development to another, the corn wage may change (1.5.15, 53). Thus, the measure works best *within* one of the stages of development (e.g., agricultural, commercial) rather than *among* them.

Third, Smith thinks that "[T]he desire of food is limited in every man by the narrow capacity of the human stomach" (WN 1.11.c.7, 181). He thinks that demand for bread would not increase very much with an increase in the standard of living (WN 1.11.d.1, 193 and TMS 4.1.10, 184; Hueckel 2009: 235). He specifically contrasts the limited demand for corn with demand for "the conveniences and ornaments of building, dress, equipage, and household furniture," which, as Rousseau had argued, "seems to have no limit or certain boundary" (WN 1.11.c.7, 181).

Fourth, because "men, like all other animals, naturally multiply in proportion to the means of their subsistence, food is always, more or less in demand" (WN 1.11.b.1, 162). This means there is a relatively constant demand for the main staple in proportion to the population. "In Europe corn is the principal produce of land which serves immediately for human food. Except in particular situations, therefore, the rent of corn land regulates in Europe that of all other cultivated land" (WN 1.11.b.35, 175). Glenn Hueckel has nicely captured Smith's point as follows: "corn rents determine the opportunity costs which must be met if the land is to be turned to an alternative use" (Hueckel 2009: 241; for minor exceptions see 256, n. 12).

Fifth, corn is the most useful yardstick, given his interest in advancing the interests of the working poor in Europe over time. This is because "Corn, besides, or whatever else is the common and favourite vegetable food of the people, constitutes in every civilized country, the principal part of the subsistence of the labourer" (WN 1.11.e.29, 206; cf. 1.5.15, 53). The price of corn is only a useful proxy-measure of the purchasing power of the poor because it makes up most of their subsistence (in advanced countries). By contrast, the price of corn is less significant as such a measure for the rich—for whom the part of the budget devoted to subsistence is insignificant—even though, as we have seen, Smith thinks that as a basic staple corn will "regulate" the price of all other things (WN 1.11.b.34–5, 175).

Of course, corn is not the staple everywhere. In China, for example, the workers' staple is rice, and in other places it is potatoes (1.11.b.36–40, 175–7). Comparing the absolute prices between economies (societies) with different staples can be a qualitative affair only. By contrast, in economies with the same staple, the price of that staple can be used to compare welfare across time, although it is harder to do so across major institutional changes such as those that occur in moving from one stage to the next. This is why Smith notes that "It regulates the money price of all the other parts of the rude produce of land, which, in every period of improvement, must bear a certain proportion to that of corn, though this proportion is different in different periods" (WN 4.5.1.13, 509).

In Smith's time, the working poor make up the vast majority of the people (recall "Servants, labourers, and workmen of different kinds, make up the far greater part of every great political society"). Thus, Smith's measure captures the welfare of most people. Smith does not seem to be bothered that his measure may not capture total welfare. To repeat,

> [w]hat improves the circumstances of the greater part can never be regarded as an inconveniency to the whole. No society can surely be flourishing and happy, of which the far greater part of the members are poor and miserable. It is but equity, besides, that they who feed, clothe, and lodge the whole body of the people, should have such a share of the produce of their own labour as to be themselves tolerably well fed, clothed, and lodged. (WN 1.8.36, 96)

Smith's "science" is not value-neutral; it is interested in the conditions of flourishing (Rasmussen 2006; Hanley 2009) and driven by equity. This is made further evident by his appeals to the readers' "humanity" and "reasonableness" (e.g., WN 5.2.e.6, 842; 2.e.19, 846; 1.8.36, 96; 1.8.44, 100; 4.8.19, 648). One can, of course, also understand the main point of WN 1.8.36, 96, as an appeal to the enlightened self-interest of the leaders of a great political society, and read the argument from "equity" as secondary.

Even so, Smith's choice of measure is at once practical and equitable. The measure reveals the purpose behind the concept. In search of expert consensus in economics, thinkers as diverse as Sidgwick, J. N. Keynes, Robbins, and Milton Friedman taught economists to distinguish sharply between so-called positive and normative economics (Schliesser 2016a). This suits the technocratic temperament of post–World War II economics. It is a core commitment of the present book that Smith's approach to political economy is, despite the considerable new insights developed in more recent economics, in many respects wiser and more humane. Smith's example shows that one can, in fact, generate robust analysis of empirical life by deploying moralized concepts.

The interpretation offered here is, in fact, a return to the original reception of Smith; Thomas Malthus anticipates the main point of this section very nicely:

> THE professed object of Dr Adam Smith's inquiry is the nature and causes of the wealth of nations. There is another inquiry, however, perhaps still more interesting, which he occasionally mixes with it, I mean an inquiry into the causes which affect the happiness of nations or the happiness and comfort of the lower orders of society, which is the most numerous class in every nation. (Chapter 13; Malthus 1992: 181. I thank David Levy for calling my attention to this passage.)

d. Progressive Taxation

In this section I argue that Smith's tax policies reveal a progressive bias (Peacock 1975: 562; Pack 1991: 64–9). Smith's tax policies are designed with the following maxim (the first of four) in mind:

> The Subjects of every state ought to contribute towards the support of the government, (1) as nearly as possible, in proportion to their respective abilities; that is, (2) in proportion to the revenue which they respectively enjoy under the protection of the state. The expense of government to the individuals of a great nation is like the expense of management to the joint tenants of a great estate, who are (3) all obliged to contribute in proportion to their respective interests in the estate. (WN 5.2.b.3, 825. The division into three points has been added to facilitate discussion.)

The main point of this maxim is to ensure fairness in taxation. Of course, what this means is quite ambiguous. 1, 2, and 3 *could* all be given a progressive slant. While it may seem that 2 advocates a flat tax rate (not exactly progressive), all it requires is that the richer one is, the more one is taxed; it does not say anything, one way or another, about exact rates of taxation. If, say, according to Smith (by 3), the rich have a disproportionate interest in the state—they benefit far more from the defense of property than the poor—then they should pay higher taxes, especially if one assumes that the poorest members have less ability to give up a part of their income. Moreover, note, too, that the passage (in 2) makes clear that according to Smith it is the judicial "protection" of the state that creates at least some of the conditions that allow for financial success.[4]

---

[4] Rothbard, who is very alert to the significance of society in Smith (recall Chapter 6), misses that Smith is talking of judicial protection here (cf. Rothbard [2006] 1995: 470–1).

Smith is not suggesting here that one's income ("revenue") and one's ability are somehow related; throughout WN Smith is explicit that in his time many who derive great income from inherited wealth lack abilities. Rather, here "ability" is almost certainly short for "ability to pay" (a phrase Smith uses at WN 5.2.g.7, 855, when discussing a French poll tax). Thus, (1) is a fairly progressive claim—the poor and working poor spend most of their income on so-called necessities, while the rich spend an increasing ratio of their income on so-called conveniences and "luxuries" (see the next block quote below).

The analysis proposed here is, of course, not the only reasonable reading of the passage, but several of Smith's tax proposals reveal a progressive bias, and these tend to support the present approach (Fleischacker 2004: 193–202). These provide the relevant context for interpreting the maxim. Let me provide several examples of Smith's progressive tax recommendations. First, when discussing the advantages of a tax on house rents, Smith writes:

> The luxuries and vanities of life occasion the principal expense of the rich; and a magnificent house embellishes and sets off to the best advantage all the other luxuries and vanities which they possess. A tax upon house-rents, therefore, would in general fall heaviest upon the rich; and in this sort of inequality there would not, perhaps, be anything very unreasonable. *It is not very unreasonable that the rich should contribute to the public expense, not only in proportion to their revenue, but something more than in that proportion.* (WN 5.2.e.6, 842; emphasis added)

Here, Smith is explicitly rejecting the flat tax reading of his own maxim in favor of a (mildly) progressive tax policy.

Second, while discussing ways to pay for public works (roads, canals, etc.) that facilitate commerce, Smith advocates that

> When the toll upon carriages of luxury upon coaches, post-chaises, etc., is made somewhat higher in proportion to their weight than upon carriages of necessary use, such as carts, waggons etc., the *indolence and vanity of the rich is made to contribute* in a very easy manner to the *relief of the poor*, by rendering cheaper the transportation of heavy goods to all the different parts of the country. (WN 5.1.d.5, 725, emphasis added)

Here Smith is not only arguing that the rich should pay more in proportion than the poor, but that in doing so the poor are explicitly benefited. This is not just an empirical claim; Smith's own estimation of his maxims asserts their "evident justice and utility" (WN 5.2.b.7, 827).

Once one pays attention, one can find similar comments elsewhere in WN. Note, for instance, Smith's criticism of the window tax: "the principal objection to all such taxes is their inequality, an inequality of the worst kind, as they frequently fall much heavier upon the poor than upon the rich" (WN 5.2.e.19, 846). He also invokes "equity" and "justice" to argue in favor of taxes on "brew or distill for private use" that will fall on the rich (WN 5.2.k.45, 888–9 and 5.2.k.55, 893).

Moreover, in his comment on his fourth maxim, Smith advocates being cautious about taxes on "branches of business which might give maintenance and employment to great multitudes" (WN 5.2.b.6, 826). In context, Smith's stated motive is prudential (it will also reduce ability to pay), but humane concern over the fate of the "great multitudes" may also be an obvious motive here (as it is explicitly when industries protected by duties on imports "employ a great multitude of hands. Humanity may in this case require that the freedom of trade should be restored only by slow gradations, and with a good deal of reserve and circumspection" [WN 4.2.40, 469]).

It is no argument against my claim that Smith did not propose an income tax that would have allowed for even greater progressivity. The arguments he gives against the income tax are practical: in Smith's time it is hard to know what people's incomes are (WN 5.2.k.1, 869) and it would be difficult to collect in a just way. Smith frequently worries about the tax inspectors' invasions of privacy, which may cause "unnecessary trouble, vexation, and oppression" (WN 5.2.b.6, 827; he calls this an "inquisition" at WN 5.2.f.5, 848; see also 5.2.g.4, 853 and 5.2.k.65, 898; on Smith's attention to the desire for privacy recall also the "very justifiable reasons for concealing" our secrets from "our neighbors" [TMS 7.4.28, 338]). Moreover, he is only against estate taxes on children who live with their father and rely on his income. The inheritance of financially independent children may "without more inconveniency than what attends all duties of this kind, be liable to some tax" (WN 5.2.h.4, 859; Fleischacker 2004: 303, fn. 27 notes that Tom Paine proposed estate tax schemes that are consistent with Smith's principles).

Finally, Smith does not, in principle, view taxes negatively. As he writes while discussing the poll tax (recall): "Every tax . . . is to the person who pays it a badge, not of slavery, but of liberty. It denotes that he is a subject to government, indeed, but that as he has some property, he cannot himself be the property of a master" (WN 5.2.g.11, 857). In fact, Smith knows he is exaggerating; not all taxes are a badge of liberty—ones that involve invasive home visits are viewed as "a badge of slavery" (WN 5.2.e.16, 846).

Smith develops and endorses a tax policy that has progressive consequences. Having said all of that, I do not want to convey the idea that progressivity is the most important feature of Smith's approach to taxation. His comment on his second maxim reveals his more fundamental concern: "The certainty of what each individual ought to pay is, in taxation, a matter of so great importance, that a very considerable degree of inequality, it appears, I believe, from the experience of all nations, is not near so great an evil as a very small degree of uncertainty." This clarity to the individual taxpayers also reduces opportunities for "corruption" (WN 5.2.b.4, 825–6).

There is an important point lurking in this paragraph. For Smith, the ultimate point of law is to reduce uncertainty and generate reasonable expectations (recall the treatment of environmental rationality in Section c of Chapter 3) that secure liberty and flourishing. Therefore, tax laws (and laws more generally) should be developed that minimize the evils for which they are ultimately intended to be a remedy. *Wrong* systems increase uncertainty and have foreseeable negative consequences even if they may maximize income to the state or provide opportunities for well-connected (rent-seeking) insiders; throughout Smith's works we find examples of responsible policy advice that pays attention to the downside risks of implementation and is especially careful about pushing those risks on less powerful others.

e. On Theoretical Partiality Toward the Working Poor

In this section I address the following questions: other than political preference, what could justify focusing on actual welfare consequences for the working poor? Why would this be identified, in practice, with what Smith calls "the general good" (WN 4.2.44, 472)? Could an impartial spectator approve of this? My approach to these questions will be somewhat speculative and surprisingly practical. I argue that according to Smith partiality toward the working poor might be justified by the need to offset, as it were, the known existence of political biases toward the rich within existing polities.

In Book 4 of WN, Smith critically discusses two rival economic systems: "the system of commerce," or mercantilism, and "the other that of agriculture," or physiocracy. Smith also suggests that both systems reflect "the different progress of opulence in different ages and nations" (WN 4.intro.2, 428; I leave aside here to what degree Smith's description of mercantilism itself *constructs* a unified, doctrinal system [in order to refute it] where previously there had been none [for critical remarks see Rashid 1988: 346]). Smith, thus, implies that these systems are partial representations of reality, reflecting the interest of the dominant class or rank of a particular society or stage of development. More subtly, he also offers many examples of how these partial systems influenced policy, and he worries how, indirectly, they may "corrupt morals" (WN 4.8.20, 649), recognizing the potentially destructive moral trickledown of ideology.[5] Mercantilism, especially, encourages the dishonorable project of violent colonialism and (local) exploitation; the laws promoted by it "may be said to be all written in blood" (WN 4.8.17, 648; Paganelli 2013: 342). Smith implies that his own project does not similarly favor a particular class/rank or sector/order.

In fact, Smith is also clearly committed to the idea that government should be impartial. As he puts it, "To hurt in any degree the interest of any one order

---

[5] Recall my treatment of Berkeley's Introduction to his *Three Dialogues* in Section a of Chapter 1.

of citizens, for no other purpose but to promote that of some other, is evidently contrary to that justice and equality of treatment which the sovereign owes to all the different orders of his subjects" (WN 4.8.30, 654). Absent further argument one would expect the impartial spectator to approve of *this* strict legal and administrative equality over the one that favors the working poor that I have attributed to Smith.

Of course, it is possible that Smith believed that favoring the working poor does not hurt anybody. After all, on Smith's account the working poor do best when the economy is growing fast—there is an expanding pie for everybody (Boucoyannis 2013). As Smith puts it, "The progressive [that is, growing] state is in reality the chearful and the hearty state to all the different orders of the society" (WN 1.8.43, 99; see Rasmussen 2006).

I suspect that Smith's reasons to favor focusing on furthering and measuring the welfare of the working poor are rooted in the non-ideal, permanent realities of the world; intentionally favoring the working poor may, in fact, produce more equal treatment of all. For there is plenty of evidence that Smith thought that in most circumstances the rich can take better advantage of any system of rules.

First, in "disputes with their workmen, masters must generally have the advantage" (WN 1.8.14, 56). This is bad enough, but employers have the factional ability to cloak the use of their power in secrecy. As Smith writes,

> We rarely hear, it has been said, of the combinations of masters; though frequently of those of workmen. But whoever imagines, upon this account, that masters rarely combine, is as ignorant of the world as of the subject. Masters are always and every where in a sort of tacit, but constant and uniform combination, not to raise the wages of labour above their actual rate. To violate this combination is every where a most unpopular action, and a sort of reproach to a master among his neighbours and equals. We seldom, indeed, hear of this combination, because it is the usual, and one may say, the natural state of things which nobody ever hears of. Masters too sometimes enter into particular combinations to sink the wages of labour even below this rate. These are always conducted with the utmost silence and secrecy, till the moment of execution, and when the workmen yield, as they sometimes do, without resistance, though severely felt by them, they are never heard of by other people. (WN 1.8.13, 55)

Here the natural state of affairs is by no means just (or efficient). It is a mistake to assume that Smith thinks ordinary workplace relations are harmonious. According to Smith employers understand their self-interests just fine: they have a monetary interest to keep wages low, and they have a reputational interest among their peers to be seen as tough on their workers. Note that Smith's argument does not primarily center on the economic incentives governing cartels of businessmen.

Rather, he points out that their perceived toughness on the workers will count as smart business sense, raising their status among their peer group (see also TMS 3.6.6, 173; Levy and Peart 2007 nicely compare this to Smith's treatment of faction in TMS).

The rich show self-command by not talking about their successful business practices. As Smith puts it, the "bustle and business of the world" is part of the "great school of self-command" (TMS 3.3.22, 145 and 3.3.25, 146). In TMS Smith praises self-command, "not only itself a great virtue, but from it all the other virtues seem to derive their principal lustre" (TMS 6.3.11, 241). But when self-command is in the service of one's narrow self-interest, as one of those "qualities most useful to ourselves" (TMS 4.2.6, 189), there is nothing especially virtuous about it (see Heath 2013 for an excellent analysis of the variety of self-interest in Smith).

Second, of course, to maintain their power, employers do not just rely on their combined power in the labor market; they also have easier access to politicians. As Smith argues:

> Whenever the legislature attempts to regulate the differences between masters and their workmen, its counsellors are always the masters. When the regulation, therefore, is in favour of the workmen, it is always just and equitable; but it is sometimes otherwise when in favour of the masters. Thus the law which obliges the masters in several different trades to pay their workmen in money and not in goods, is quite just and equitable. It imposes no real hardship upon the masters. It only obliges them to pay that value in money, which they pretended to pay, but did not always really pay, in goods. This law is in favour of the workmen. (WN 1.10.c.61, 157–8)

Throughout WN Smith calls attention to what contemporary economists call "rent-seeking behavior" by well-connected elites. On Smith's telling, the mercantile system is based on it (see also Ekelund and Tollison 1981). Thus, whenever the legislature manages to pass a pro-worker bill, however imperfect, it must have faced considerable opposition; it almost certainly is addressing a genuine problem. Of course, in Smith's time there was a limited franchise, so the legislature would rarely pass a bill that would cause genuine hardship on the franchised classes. The legislature's limited efforts on behalf of the workers would, thus, be balancing a weighted scale. There is some evidence that Smith thought a widened franchise would be beneficial (WN 4.7.b.51, 585), but he devotes little attention to it (Rasmussen 2013: 68).

Note that in both cases Smith offers universal generalizations: (i) "masters are always and every where in a sort of tacit, but constant and uniform combination" and (ii) "when the regulation, therefore, is in favour of the workmen, it is always just and equitable." He omits his more customary "perhaps" or "almost." They are not unlike a related claim, (iii) "Before the institution of coined money, however, unless they went through this tedious and difficult operation, people must always have been liable to the grossest frauds and impositions" (WN 1.4.7, 40).

At first blush claims (i) through (iii) appear logically on par with, say, the most significant axioms of his political economy, for instance (iv) "as it is the power of exchanging that gives occasion to the division of labour, so the extent of this division must always be limited by the extent of that power, or, in other words, by the extent of the market" (WN 1.3.1, 31) and (v) " the exchangeable value of every thing must always be precisely equal to the extent of this power which it conveys to its owner" (WN 1.5.3, 48).

Even so, claims (iv) and (v) are theoretical commitments of Smith—they belong to the analytical core of what we would call Smith's economics. They come close to being conceptual truths in Smith's analysis. By contrast, claims like (i) through (iii) turn on Smith's observations on and analysis of human nature. In all these three cases, Smith is clear that absent some countervailing institutions (the law, publicity, etc.) powerful people will exploit those who lack the power to do so (i.e., they presuppose the "love of domination" [see LJ(A) iii.114, p. 186 and iii.130, p. 192]). It is important to recognize this not just because it puts to rest any idea that Smith thought that left to (their commercial) selves, people would just be kind to each other because of some natural harmony. They reveal that, according to Smith, humanity and beneficence demand from us the promotion of some institutions (Rosenberg 1960) in light of existing human nature.

In addition to the two reasons I have offered, there is a third (more speculative) reason that may explain why Smith goes beyond the demands of strict impartiality and equality in favoring the working poor in his institutional design. As opposed to our context-sensitive, (ideally) impartial and exact judgments of propriety of characters and situations, we are in our judgments about social institutions always *partial* and imprecise spectators (Levy 1995). By this I do not mean that we can never abstract away from our rank/order/class interests. Rather, I mean that according to Smith it is nearly impossible to get a comprehensive view of what exactly is going on in the complex machinery of society in real time (see, especially, WN 1.1.11, 23—Smith is writing in an era prior to the massive data collection of national economic bureaucracies, but the problem is still with us, as recent experience of systemic risk in financial markets reveals). This is exemplified by the very first example of WN, in which the division of labor puts different branches of work in different, partially occluded workhouses (WN 1.1.2–3, 14; Levy 1995).

Moreover, according to Smith we cannot trust our ordinary judgments about these matters. In his comment on the famous pin factory example, Smith emphasizes the fact that "the rapidity with which some of the operations of those manufactures are performed, exceeds what the human hand could, by those who had never seen them, be supposed capable of acquiring" (WN 1.1.7, 16). Economic reality can go beyond what we take to be possible—empirical observation and theory (in Smith's terminology "reason and experience") supply us with the evidence for this (cf. Smith's description of Galileo: "It was then that Galileo, by explaining the nature of the composition of motion, by showing, both from reason and experience, that a ball dropt from the mast of a ship under sail would fall precisely at the foot of the mast, and by rendering this doctrine, from a great number of other instances, quite familiar to the imagination, took off, perhaps, the principal objection which had been made to this hypothesis" [Astronomy 4.44, EPS 83]).

Smith's stance has a familiar and a less familiar component to it. I focus on the relatively familiar features first, for the causes driving individual human actions are too diverse (and stubborn!) to be directed from above. As he writes in TMS: "[I]n the great chess-board of human society, every single piece has a principle of motion of its own, altogether different that which the legislature might chuse to impress upon it" (TMS 6.2.2.17–8, 234). Hence, not only is the problem of state direction of the economy computationally intractable (as suggested by WN 4.9.51, 687), but the legislator also has no reliable source of information about the diverse preferences of individuals (as implied by TMS 6.2.2.17–8, 234). Therefore, for Smith, "[T]he law ought always trust people with the care of their own interest, as in their local situations they must generally be able to judge better of it than the legislator can do" (WN 4.5.b.16, 531; for similar comments see 5.2.c.18, 833). This shows that one reason for Smith's argument in favor of relatively unregulated markets is epistemic: individuals will have better knowledge of their own circumstances than the ruler will.

In fact, an important source of information that individuals will rely on is markets. Markets can, given the right circumstances, provide, to use a modern phrase, a relatively effective signaling system (e.g., WN 4.5.b.24–5, 533–4). However, Smith does not attribute any magical powers to "the haggling and bargaining of the market," because he notes that it only works "according to that sort of rough equality which, though not exact, is sufficient for carrying on the business of common life" (WN 1.5.4, 49). Smith is relying on a distinction between common life and another more exact realm—presumably (mathematical) science. Smith is, in fact, pointing out that markets are good enough for the business of common life, but that the data they provide are insufficient for a more exact enterprise. As Smith puts it: "I have no great faith in political arithmetick, and I mean not to warrant the exactness of either of these computations" (WN 4.5.b.30, 534; see also Hume's Treatise 1.2.4.29 and 1.4.1.1–2).

The concern with exactitude shows up again shortly thereafter (recall): "[A]t the same time and place, therefore, money is the exact measure of the real exchangeable value of all commodities. It is so, however, at the same time and place only" (WN 1.5.19, 55). Smith is aware that the prices provided by market exchange only offer exactitude in a very limited sense. All of this suggests that the "men of learning" of his time, with an interest in constructing an exact science, should not focus exclusively on markets. What is unclear is if Smith thought that this was due to some principled reason about the intrinsic nature of markets or if this was exclusively due to the limited character of the data provided by the markets in his day. (I explore these issues more fully in Chapter 13.) Either way, markets are not the only source of information worth relying on; Smith also talks about the importance of knowing the characters of participants in the marketplace (e.g., WN 2.2.62, 305–6).

The epistemic weakness of the rulers shows up in other places as well, and it carries over into a morals argument for individual freedom. For example, the quote about the "great chess-board of human society" is lifted from a passage where Smith worries about "fanaticism" caused by the "spirit of system" or "faction" in turn influenced by the enthusiasm of the masses (TMS 5.2.2.15, 232–3; see Brubaker 2006a, 2006b). That is, Smith's argument against state direction of the economy is not exclusively epistemic; he also stresses the political dangers of state tyranny (e.g., WN 4.2.10, 456). We find similar considerations at work when Smith discusses efficient and just ways to collect taxes; he often notes that reliable information is not available and that it would require an "inquisition" on the part of the magistrate to obtain it (WN 5.2.f.5–9, 848–50; 5.2.g.4, 853; 5.2.j.2, 867). This is why

> the sovereign is completely discharged from a duty, in the attempting to perform which he must always be exposed to innumerable delusions, and for the proper performance of which no human wisdom or knowledge could ever be sufficient; the duty of superintending the industry of private people and of directing it towards the employments most suitable to the interest of society. (WN 4.9.51, 687)

In the previous three paragraphs, I have emphasized familiar features of Smith's position echoed most prominently by his free-market followers. But there is also a more unfamiliar aspect of Smith's stance. It has to do with Smith's remarkable self-awareness about the potential shortcomings of the theorist. In later chapters I offer a more complete account of Smith's epistemology and the circumstances of theorizing, but here we just need to recognize a crucial assumption of Smith, one that is very prominent in his account of the development of the impartial spectator—that is, the fundamental uncertainty that each of us has in our *own* judgments: "our uncertainty concerning our own merit, and our anxiety to think favourably of it, should together naturally enough make us desirous to know the opinion of other people concerning it" (TMS 3.2.24, 126; see also TMS 3.2.28, 127). As we have seen in my treatment of the intellectual passions in Section e of Chapter 3, this uncertainty about self is pervasive in the context of inquiry. This is because uncertainty drives inquiry: "wonder, that uncertainty and anxious curiosity" (Astronomy 2.4, EPS 40).

Thus, inner uncertainty is matched by the ongoing uncertainty of the theorist during inquiry. Smith diagnoses two potential, pernicious consequences of this uncertainty: when "love of system" is transformed into (i) "spirit" of system (TMS 4.1.11, 185 and 6.2.2.15, 232), or what we would call "expert over-confidence" (recall: "The over-weening conceit which the greater part of men have of their own abilities, is an antient evil remarked by the philosophers and moralists of all ages" [WN 1.10.b.26, 124–5]) and (ii) what we would call expert "groupthink." (Smith explores an instance of (ii) when he points out that at the start of the seventeenth century the Copernican system was accepted by "astronomers only," but that the "learned in all other sciences, continued to regard it with the same contempt as the vulgar" [Astronomy 4.36, EPS 77].) (i) and (ii) are what we may label intellectual vices, special instances of the all-too-common "self-deceit, this fatal weakness of mankind" (TMS 3.4.6, 158; see Gerschlager 2002). Thus, theorists are most in need of practices that correct for their often unacknowledged biases. In contemporary social science correcting for biases is generally understood as de-biasing or removing biases. But one can also correct bias by introducing a countervailing bias.

Given that Smith is self-conscious of the fact that intellectual systems tend to have a bias toward the interests of the more powerful economic and political classes (recall my treatment of WN 4.intro.2, 428, at the start of this section), which also have more ability to influence political and economic outcomes; given that he is so aware of theoretical vices; and given that also he takes for granted that no comprehensively complete understanding of the economy is possible, I speculate that Smith thought it made moral sense to introduce a theoretical bias *toward* the interests of the working poor into one's analysis. (For a striking example of this, see my treatment of Smith's approach to financial regulation in Section h below.)

With that in mind, we can turn to Smith's analysis of "general principles" of legislation. I introduce his views by way of the very informed reception of these by Mary Wollstonecraft.

f. The Role of the Legislator; Private Virtue, Public Happiness

> A truly benevolent legislator always endeavours to make it the interest of each individual to be virtuous; and thus private virtue becoming the cement of public happiness, an orderly whole is consolidated by the tendency of all the parts towards a common centre.
>
> —Mary Wollstonecraft, *A Vindication of the Rights of Woman*, Chapter 9 (Wollstonecraft 1995: 234)

By reflecting on Mary Wollstonecraft's reception of Smith, I argue that Smith promotes an institutional and economic framework in which human "flourishing" is possible throughout WN (see also Rasmussen 2006). In particular, I also suggest he prepares the philosophical groundwork for the more ambitious projects promoted by Paine and de Grouchy.

The main point of Wollstonecraft's *Vindication* is, of course, to argue that "to render [women's] private virtue a public benefit," women must be granted (equal) civil rights. But not unlike Smith, she does so with a vocabulary that is clearly meant to echo and rebuke Mandeville's "private vices, public benefits."[6] Wollstonecraft insists that a wise legislator can create the proper institutional framework in which all of humankind can sensibly and successfully pursue their interests in virtue and consequently serve the greater (and orderly, not to say happy) good.

From context, it is unclear if Wollstonecraft's "benevolent legislator" in the epigraph to this section must perform ongoing calibration—her "always" is ambiguous between (a) a legislator, who *is setting up* laws of society, is benevolent if and only if she "endeavours to make it the interest of each individual to be virtuous" and (b) once the laws are set up, the legislator must keep calibrating. Smith's unnamed, great rival, James Steuart, argued for ongoing "attention" by the "statesman" to a whole variety of ever-changing economic and political affairs (Steuart 1966, Chapter 27). Smith clearly targets Steuart in WN:

> To judge whether such retaliations are likely to produce such an effect, does not, perhaps, belong so much to the science of a legislator, whose deliberations ought to be governed by general principles which are always the same, as to the skill of that insidious and crafty animal, vulgarly called a statesman or politician, whose councils are directed by the momentary fluctuations of affairs. (WN 4.2.39, 468)

We know that Smith was deliberate about not naming his rival: "I have the same opinion of Sir James Stewarts Book that you have. Without once mentioning it, I flatter myself, that every false principle in it, will meet with a clear and distinct confutation in mine" (Letter 132, to William Pulteney, Sept. 3, 1777, Corr. 164). Anyway, Smith draws a sharp contrast between the "legislator" and the "statesman." His is the "science of a legislator" (Haakonssen 1981), who focuses on "general principles" and, presumably, the basic rules and laws of society (although Smith is not shy about going into a great deal of detail about particular rules). Given that Wollstonecraft's language here is more akin to Smith's "science of the legislator," interpretation (a) seems more plausible.[7]

Now in the context of the quoted epigraph, Wollstonecraft names as her target "Rousseau, and a numerous list of male writers" who "insist that she should all her life be subjected to a severe restraint, that of propriety. Why subject her to

---

[6] Mandeville's own proto-feminism has been unfairly ignored in recent times (but see J. Taylor, forthcoming).

[7] I thank Lena Halldenius for discussion. Halldenius has reminded me that Wollstonecraft primarily takes society as given.

propriety—blind propriety, if she be capable of acting from a nobler spring ... ?" One might think that among the "numerous" she also has in mind Smith, who is, after all, the theorist of propriety. But we are immediately alerted to how unlikely this inference is: not only would Smith reject blind propriety—his is a theory of *spectatorial* judgment—but Smith was also a known critic of slavery (recall WN 4.7.b.53–62, 586–9 and WN 3.2.10, 388; see especially TMS 7.2.1.28, 282), and in the same paragraph Wollstonecraft makes it very clear where she stands on that issue. Moreover, elsewhere in *Vindication*, Wollstonecraft tends to invoke Smith as a "respectable authority."

In fact, in the epigraph passage above Wollstonecraft follows Smith in two ways. First, she implicitly links Rousseau to Mandeville. In Smith's first publication, Edinburgh Review, Smith sums up his treatment of Rousseau's Second *Discourse* as follows: "It is by the help of this style, together with a little philosophic chemistry, that the principles and ideas of the profligate Mandeville seem to have the purity and sublimity of the morals of Plato, and to be only the true spirit of a republican carried a little too far" (Edinburgh Review 12, EPS 251).

Smith charges that Rousseau is somewhat of an extremist in his political convictions (notice that "little too far"!). Smith claims that despite contrary appearances ("seem"), Rousseau is at bottom in the same boat as the "profligate" and scandalous Mandeville—an *ad personam* attempt to convict Rousseau through guilt by association. Yet, in an ironic twist, Smith attacks Rousseau's false appearances. After all, for Rousseau "unmasking" was an important activity (Starobinski 1988; see also the second passage that Smith translates from the Second *Discourse* at Edinburgh Review 14, EPS 253). What is the false appearance? According to Smith it is Rousseau who may appear to us as a modern Plato. Smith contests this appearance. In the passage, Smith is not criticizing Plato or Platonism; the criticism of Rousseau is done by means of a *praise* of Plato's "morals," which are said to be pure and sublime. (Recall that the reason why Smith targets Plato's lack of criticism of infanticide is Plato's "humanity.")

In Smith's diagnosis, Rousseau and Mandeville share four important features. First, against the more popular reaction to Hobbes, both suppose "that there is in man no powerful instinct which necessarily determines him to seek society for its own sake." Second, they suppose the "same slow progress and gradual developments of all the talents, habits, and arts which fit men to live together in society, and they both describe [it] ... in the same manner." (On Mandeville and unintended order explanations see Heath 1999; C. Smith 2009.) Moreover, according to both, "those laws of justice, which maintain the present inequality amongst mankind, were originally the inventions of the cunning and the powerful, in order to maintain or to acquire an unnatural and unjust superiority over the rest of their fellow-creatures." Finally, they agree that pity "is possessed by savages and by the most profligate of the vulgar, in a greater degree of perfection than by those of the most polished and cultivated manners" (11, EPS 250–1).

However, Smith does not gloss over their differences; he recognizes that Rousseau is a fierce critic of Mandeville. Smith singles out the importance, for Rousseau, of pity in producing the virtues. This is perceptive, given how important pity will be in Rousseau's later works (Dent 1988, Chapter 4). This anonymously published piece first appeared under Smith's name in the 1797 French edition of Smith's posthumous EPS. Thus, it is unlikely that Wollstonecraft knew she was echoing Smith on the first point (although not impossible, given the circles she traveled in in Paris).

De Grouchy, who also echoes Smith's language on Rousseau, may well have consulted the French edition of EPS while she was preparing her translation of TMS. In an extraordinary passage near the end of Letter IV (thus halfway through LS), while comparing Rousseau favorably to Voltaire, she writes:

> Rousseau spoke more to conscience, and Voltaire to reason. Rousseau established his opinions through the force of his sensibility and of his logic . . . The first [Rousseau], having taken certain of his principles too far has given us a taste for exaggeration and peculiarity; the second, too often satisfied with using ridicule as a weapon against the worst abuses has not succeeded in rousing against them that healthy indignation which, if less efficacious than scorn in punishing vice is nonetheless more active in fighting it. Rousseau's morality is engaging if severe, and moves the heart even while disciplining it. Voltaire's more indulgent morality is perhaps less moving and because it requires fewer sacrifices and it gives us a lower opinion of our own strength and of the perfection we are capable of reaching. Rousseau talked of virtue with as much charm as Fenelon, and from the empire of virtue itself. . . . The first will renew age after age our enthusiasm for liberty and virtue. (LS, IV; on Fenelon, see Hanley 2016)

De Grouchy's assessment of Rousseau's rhetorical "charm" echoes Smith's rhetorically charged summary of Rousseau's achievement. But de Grouchy sides against Smith (and Voltaire) in defending Rousseau's rhetoric as helping the cause of virtue in the long run. Yet, despite her high praise for Rousseau, she agrees with Smith that Rousseau takes his principles "too far." No doubt the aftermath of the French Revolution and its Terror, in which her husband, Condorcet, lost his life, instilled in her an appreciation of Smithian moderation.

Second, in the epigraph passage quoted above, Wollstonecraft echoes an absolutely central paragraph in TMS:

> It is thus that man, who can subsist only in society, was fitted by nature to that situation for which he was made. All the members of human society stand in need of each others [sic] assistance, and are likewise exposed to mutual injuries. Where the necessary assistance is

reciprocally afforded from love, from gratitude, from friendship, and
esteem, the society flourishes and is happy. All the different members
of it are bound together by the agreeable bands of love and affection,
and are, as it were, drawn to one common centre of mutual good offices.
(TMS 2.2.3.1, 85)

Wollstonecraft and Smith agree that within the context of extensive division of
labor, we can create institutions that facilitate what we may call a "noble commerce of mutual friendship" such that a society is flourishing and happy. In WN
Smith echoes this passage in the most important egalitarian-consequentialist
sentence of the whole book (recall): "No society can surely be flourishing and
happy, of which the far greater part of the members are poor and miserable"
(WN 1.8.36, 96).

The very next paragraph after 2.2.3.1 in TMS is often taken as Smith's considered statement of rejecting a society of generosity. Smith writes, "Society may
subsist among different men, as among different merchants, from a sense of its
utility, without any mutual love or affection; and though no man in it should owe
any obligation, or be bound in gratitude to any other, it may still be upheld by
a mercenary exchange of good offices according to an agreed valuation" (TMS
2.2.3.2, 85–86). The articulation of a society of negative freedom can certainly be
found in WN: "That security which the laws in Great Britain give to every man that
he shall enjoy the fruits of his own labour, is alone sufficient to make any country
flourish" (WN 4.5.b.43, 540). Even so, there are at least three very good reasons
to resist this more minimal interpretation of Smith and accept Wollstonecraft's
nobler reading of Smith.

First, throughout WN (Pack 1991), Smith castigates "the mean rapacity, the
monopolizing spirit of merchants and manufacturers," singling out their "interested sophistry" (WN 4.3.c.9–10, 493–4; see also TMS 4.1.10, 184). For example,
he points out that "our merchants and master-manufacturers complain much of
the bad effects of high wages in raising the price, and thereby lessening the sale
of their goods both at home and abroad. They say nothing concerning the bad
effects of high profits. They are silent with regard to the pernicious effects of their
own gains. They complain only of those of other people" (WN 1.9.24, 115). Thus,
it would be very strange if Smith would endorse a society of merely "mercenary
exchange."

Second (and this is more interesting), just before these two paragraphs at TMS
2.2.3.1–2, Smith claims that

A superior may, indeed, sometimes, with universal approbation, oblige
those under his jurisdiction to behave, in this respect, with a certain
degree of propriety to one another. The laws of all civilized nations
oblige parents to maintain their children, and children to maintain
their parents, and impose upon men many other duties of beneficence.

> The civil magistrate is entrusted with the power not only of preserving the public peace by restraining injustice, but of promoting the prosperity of the commonwealth, by establishing good discipline, and by discouraging every sort of vice and impropriety; he may prescribe rules, therefore, which not only prohibit mutual injuries among fellow-citizens, but command mutual good offices to a certain degree. (TMS, 2.1.8, 81)

Thus, in TMS, Smith cautiously embraces the nobler road, pointedly calling attention to legal enforcement of responsibility of preventing infanticide and promoting care for the elderly. This is the crucial difference between a law-governed civilized nation and the savages (Boyd 2013: 448–50).

The executive should not only enforce the laws to prevent mutual harm (a classic liberal position [see C. Smith 2013 for twentieth-century refinements of this]), but he can also demand, by commanding "mutual good offices," that people help each other (Pack 1991; Fleischacker 2004). This is reinforced by his claim that the "laws of all civilized nations . . . impose upon men many other duties of beneficence." Smith does not go as far as Paine's *Agrarian Justice* (Anderson 2016) or Condorcet's mandatory, mathematically sophisticated welfare programs (see the tenth stage in his *Sketch for a Historical Picture of The Progress of the Human Mind*), but he clearly does not rule out state intervention to ensure that citizens support each other. Toward this end the civil magistrate need be motivated by neither humanity nor equity, nor moral repulsion over "vice;" a Bismarckian desire for public order (e.g., to prevent revolutions or riots) may encourage the magistrate to enforce duties of beneficence.

Unfortunately, Smith is exceedingly vague and cautious about how this ought to be brought about in practice: "it requires the greatest delicacy and reserve to execute with propriety and judgment. To neglect it altogether exposes the commonwealth to many gross disorders and shocking enormities, and to push it too far is destructive of all liberty, security, and justice" (TMS 2.2.1.8, 81). Smith is clearly worried about what we would call government abuse. In discussing a variety of tax regimes Smith also worries about abuses (recall, e.g., WN 5.2.h.16–7, 863).

One might be inclined to think that despite my claims, Smith *does* embrace the more minimal position in WN: "it is by treaty, by barter, and by purchase, that we obtain from one another the greater part of those mutual good offices which we stand in need of" (WN 1.2.3, 27). But, third, this is entirely compatible with (a) dealing with each other in the spirit of friendship and (b) the magistrate enforcing *some* mutual good offices despite the role of commerce in securing the greater part of these.

Even so, it might seem that (a) goes against the spirit of WN, where Smith writes that "In civilized society" we stand "at all times in need of the cooperation and assistance of great multitudes," while one's "whole life is scarce sufficient to gain the friendship of a few persons" (WN 1.2.2, 26). Thus, one might claim that according to Smith (a) is simply impractical. But in WN Smith also claims that "Commerce . . . ought naturally to be, among nations, as among individuals, a bond of union and friendship." Thus, in some normatively important contexts, commerce can itself become a source of friendship.

That is, throughout Smith's writings we are offered two competing interpretations of commercial society: (i) the sophistry-ridden, jealous one animated by "the mean rapacity" merchants, which Smith links to the immoral projects of mercantilism, and (ii) one that has space for "generous, noble, or tender sentiment" (WN 5.i.f.50, 782). In fact, (ii) is articulated in the context of fears about the damage done to the worker by extensive division of labor. Of course, Smith recognized that, in practice, (i) often predominates. His is a normative view that promotes (ii). One way to understand the critics of Smith is that they have generally tried to tar him with a ("greed is good") version of (i), which sometimes is promoted by friends of capitalism (for a useful overview see Wight 2005).

Thus, throughout WN Smith promotes an institutional and economic framework in which human "flourishing" is possible (Rasmussen 2006), not just of "commerce and manufactures" (WN 5.3.7, 910; of course, Smith does not ignore the duties of the sovereign that facilitate commerce [e.g., maintenance of public works]). In a discussion critical of the medieval Church he writes:

> The constitution of the church of Rome may be considered as the most formidable combination that ever was formed against the authority and security of civil government, as well as against the liberty, reason, and happiness of mankind, which can flourish only where civil government is able to protect them. (WN 5.1.g.24, 802–3)

In context, Smith's point is not just that a minimal civil government that offers "secure" law is necessary for human flourishing; according to Smith, people cannot be genuinely happy if they believe the "grossest delusions of superstition" (WN 5.1.g.24, 80). Smith does not fully explain this latter claim, but presumably he associates "superstition" with unnecessary (religious) fears, and he explicitly mentions "the delusions of enthusiasm and superstition, which, among ignorant nations, frequently occasion the most dreadful disorders" (WN 5.1.f.61, 788). That is to say, the government has duties to promote "reason" (or right thinking) among its citizens. In Smith, this duty is not a list of dogmas that need be taught; rather, citizens need to be offered various what we might call "medicines of the mind." (For more on Smith's views on education, see Weinstein 2013.)

Smith argues that a wise legislator must create and enforce various incentives to stimulate mandatory education of the young in philosophy (WN 5.1.9.14, 796 and 5.1.f.50–6, 781–6). Presumably, this would teach future citizens the rudiments of mathematics and orderly views of nature (Rasmussen 2013: 58). Given the epistemic demands of measuring propriety (TMS 1.1.3, 16–9; see Forman-Barzilai 2006), this may well be required for the proper functioning of morality.

While Smith hopes that such education would lend genuine stability to government (WN 5.f.61, 788), he also recommends public "diversions" (e.g., "painting, poetry, musick, dancing" and "all sorts of dramatic representations and exhibitions") to "amuse" people's minds and make political and religious fanatics the objects of "ridicule" (WN 5.1.g.15, 796–7). Thus, for Smith, philosophy can play some role in an Enlightenment project against religious enthusiasm and support public order. Smith is not an optimist about this because he is aware that "the private" and "publick morals of the Romans" were superior to those found in the philosophy-rich Greek city-states with their musical education (WN 5.i.f.39–40, 776–7; Smith is especially concerned with dangers of fanaticism and factionalism in context).

Among other duties, a Smithian legislator of a potentially flourishing society should promote voluntary exchange of the right sort. As Wollstonecraft and Smith understood, this should not be obsessed with absolute property rights. In particular, they both advocated the abolition of inherited property. This becomes very clear in Smith's attack on the practice of entails in WN (an "entail" is the restriction of property by limiting its inheritance to the owner's lineal descendants or to a particular class thereof, usually the first-born male). In his account of the development of property rights in Europe, Smith writes:

> They are founded upon the most absurd of all suppositions, the supposition that every successive generation of men have not an equal right to the earth, and to all that it possesses; but that the property of the present generation should be restrained and regulated according to the fancy of those who died perhaps five hundred years ago. Entails, however, are still respected through the greater part of Europe in those countries particularly in which noble birth is a necessary qualification for the enjoyment either of civil or military honours. (WN 3.2.6, 384)

The main point of this passage is that the dead have no hold over the living. (See Fleischacker 2004 on LJ.) One is reminded of Jefferson's famous quip about the need for a revolution in every generation. Nevertheless, this statement can suggest that not only was Smith only in favor of equality, calling the denial of equal right to property in every generation the most absurd supposition, but he also thought that market interference (in this case, preventing normal buying and selling of any division of property) is preventing equality from coming about, while providing an instance of the absurdity of absolute property rights. (Of course, somebody could object by claiming that a more natural reading of the passage is that "equal right" only modifies "every generation" and that he says nothing of an equal right to property of members of every generation. But if one accepts this reading, then the argument against entails loses much of its force.)

It is a corollary of my reading that, in order to be consistent, Smith has to be skeptical about the right to bequest. In his published works, Smith does not say much about this topic. He certainly does not oppose inheritance taxes (WN 5.2.h.4, 859). However, Fleischacker (2004) presents a reading of LJ, especially LJ(A), 63–9, that provides evidence for the idea that Smith was less than enthusiastic about the right to bequest.

Moreover, Wollstonecraft and Smith both oppose any system that consists "in multiplying dependents and contriving taxes which grind the poor to pamper the rich;" they agree that "Taxes on the very necessaries of life," which fall disproportionately on the poor, are not merely unjust but also have a worse moral-psychological-political cost in that they "enable an endless tribe of idle [rich] to pass with stupid pomp before a gaping crowd, who almost worship the very parade which costs them so dear" (Wollstonecraft 1995: 237, cf. TMS 1.3.2.2, 51). Now we are in a good position to turn to Smith's position on liberty.

g. Liberty

In this section I argue that for Smith, liberty involves a combination of self-ownership, the ability to exercise one's judgment, and the possibility to make meaningful choices; it presupposes a sense of security that is only possible under the rule of law. Understanding this helps us put Smith's defense of the "obvious and simple system of natural liberty" (WN 4.ix.51, 687) in moral context and illuminates the meaning of Smith's claim that "liberty, reason, and happiness of mankind ... can flourish only where civil government is able to protect them" (WN 5.1.g.24, 802–3).[8] Most of the evidence for the main argument in this section comes from WN because I do not want a critic to think I am reading TMS into WN on this very point.

Smith introduces liberty, seemingly *en passant*, right at the start of *Wealth of Nations*: "One of those boys, who loved to play with his companions, observed that, by tying a string from the handle of the valve, which opened this communication, to another part of the machine, the valve would open and shut without his assistance, and leave him at liberty to divert himself with his play-fellows" (WN 1.1.8, 20). In context, he is explaining how technological improvements are often made from the bottom up, as it were, on the work floor by relatively youthful "common workmen;" the contrast class is filled with "philosophers" (who within the division of labor also make contributions to technological improvement). While Smith is illustrating technology-driven productivity gains (C. Smith 2006), he is also making a point about intellectual egalitarianism (the working class and the young can be just as smart as the educated gentry). According to Smith,

---

[8] In what follows, for the sake of simplicity, I ignore all the passages where Smith discusses liberty in the context of the militia/standing army debate (Montes 2009) because there he sometimes uses "liberty" in the Republican sense when he is discussing Republican defenses of the militia.

boys—and it is possible that these are quite young—want to play.[9] In the quoted passage, "liberty" means something akin to control over one's time in a manner of one's choosing. It does not mean "freedom of contract" because in the passage, through labor-saving technical innovation, the boy, who is under contract, creates liberty for himself to do something else than work.

One may think that the use of "liberty" in the quoted passage is a kind of throwaway remark. This is because we all know that, for Smith, the "system of natural liberty" involves free trade (WN 4.7.c.44, 606; see the use of "liberty" at WN 5.1.e.10, 735), free movement (WN 4.7.c.54, 610), and, not the least, free settlement, based on the liberty to contract and self-employment (e.g., WN 5.1.g.14, 796).[10] Liberty is about the possibility to compete in free markets. We can point to this oft-quoted passage to illustrate the standard claim:

> All systems either of preference or of restraint, therefore, being thus completely taken away, the obvious and simple system of natural liberty establishes itself of its own accord. Every man, as long as he does not violate the laws of justice, is left perfectly free to pursue his own interest his own way, and to bring both his industry and capital into competition with those of any other man, or order of men. (WN 4.9.51, 687)

In this section, I do not re-enter the ongoing debate over to what degree Smith accepts limitations on natural liberty. Here I just want to note that in this passage liberty is the freedom to pursue one's own interest in one's own way in light of the harm principle (recall the discussion of WN 1.10.c.12, 138, in Section c of Chapter 7):

> The patrimony of a poor man lies in the strength and dexterity of his hands; and to hinder him from employing this strength and dexterity in what manner he thinks proper without injury to his neighbour is a plain violation of this most sacred property. It is a manifest encroachment upon the just liberty both of the workman and of those who might be disposed to employ him.

Based on such passages it is natural to think, of course, that Smith understands this pursuit of one's interest entirely in economic or commercial fashion. Here "liberty" really seems to mean liberty of contract (as long as one does not harm

---

[9] Child labor increased in Smith's era (Humphries 2013).

[10] "The state, by encouraging, that is by giving entire liberty to all those who for their own interest would attempt, without scandal or indecency, to amuse and divert the people by painting, poetry, musick, dancing."

others). But it is worth noting that here, too, the freedom of contract is founded in a kind of self-ownership (of body), or foundational property right that allows one to control oneself in a manner one thinks proper (recall Section c of Chapter 7). That is to say, we have found the following three ways of understanding liberty in Smith:

- It involves control of one's time in a manner of one's choosing (e.g., also WN 5.1.a.25, 700).[11]
- It is the pursuit of one's interest in one's own way (e.g., also WN 4.7.b.4, 567).[12]
- It involves self-control in a manner one thinks proper (e.g., also WN 5.1.g.19, 799).[13]

These three uses of "liberty" clearly have a family resemblance and seem to be species of the same general concept. The latter two occur in economic and legal contexts, but the first involves a kind of freedom from working (to pursue leisure activities/play). The general concept involves (some mixture of) actual self-ownership, the ability to exercise one's judgment (Fleischacker 1999 has emphasized this), and the possibility to make meaningful choices. In fact, the general concept presupposes also a further subjective fact, the "sense" of being secure: "But upon the impartial administration of justice depends the liberty of every individual, the sense which he has of his own security" (WN 5.1.b.25, 722–3). Here "liberty" is the sense of security that is made possible by the impartial rule of law. It's this merited sense of security that provides the moral underpinnings of Smith's defense of the rule of law.

As we have seen, the absence of such rule of law generates fear and uncertainty, while the partial application of the rule of law generates, in addition to fear and uncertainty, anger. In fact, it is significant that for Smith, the strict rule of law makes possible not only liberty and happiness, but also reason, which can only function properly in the absence of fear and uncertainty (recall "liberty, reason, and happiness of mankind . . . can flourish only where civil government is able to protect them" [WN 5.1.g.24, 802–3]). This hints at a social conception of reason (see Chapters 10 and 11).

---

[11] "The soldiers, who are bound to obey their officer only once a week or once a month, and who are at all other times at liberty to manage their own affairs their own way, without being in any respect accountable to him" (WN 5.1.a.25, 700). Because it involves the militia debate, I do not quote in the main body of the text.

[12] In addition: "Were the students upon such charitable foundations left free to chuse what college they liked best, such liberty might perhaps contribute to excite some emulation among different colleges" (WN 5.1.f.12, 763).

[13] "The rights, the privileges, the personal liberty of every individual ecclesiastic, who is upon good terms with his own order, are, even in the most despotic governments, more respected than those of any other person of nearly equal rank and fortune."

A skeptical reader may argue that the first instance of "liberty" quoted at the top of this section is just a slender example, and we should not read too much into it, and that all the other examples can be assimilated to economic functions. After all, Smith seems to define "perfect liberty" as the situation where one "may change his trade as often as he pleases" (WN 1.7.6, 73).

But, in fact, Smith uses "liberty" in the sense I have been articulating in one of the key passages of the analytical core of his system:

> Equal quantities of labour, at all times and places, may be said to be of equal value to the labourer. In his ordinary state of health, strength and spirits; in the ordinary degree of his skill and dexterity, he must always lay down the same portion of his ease, his liberty, and his happiness: The price which he pays must always be the same, whatever may be the quantity of goods which he receives in return for it. (WN 1.5.7, 50)

Enormous amount of ink has been spilled over these three sentences (which are often treated as Smith's account of the labor theory of value [recall Section c above). To be anachronistic, in the passage Smith is describing a kind of opportunity cost involved in labor. It's also natural to those influenced by modern economists to read the passage as describing a kind of standardized disutility in work.

Here I just focus on Smith's claim that equal quantities of labor involve giving up "the same portion of his ease, his liberty, and his happiness." What matters for present purposes is that rather than describing paid/contracted work as an *instance* of liberty, work is the *hardship* that involves a *giving up* of liberty and ease, even happiness.[14] The inability to make meaningful choices is why, for Smith, the very rich and powerful generally (and counterintuitively) *lack* liberty:

> It is this, which, notwithstanding the restraint it imposes, notwithstanding the loss of liberty with which it is attended, renders greatness the object of envy, and compensates, in the opinion of mankind, all that toil, all that anxiety, all those mortifications which must be undergone in the pursuit of it; and what is of yet more consequence, all that leisure, all that ease, all that careless security, which are forfeited for ever by the acquisition. (TMS 1.3.2.1, 51)

In addition, WN 1.5.7, 50 is also an expression of Smith's egalitarian commitment to what we may call "equal liberty."[15] Smith's example is built on describing the liberty of "the labourer." We may miss this because of the eternal character of

---

[14] Smith does not really allow cheerful work in the analytical core of his system, although he recognizes it elsewhere (see Chapter 15).

[15] I thank a generous reviewer for pressing this point.

the generalization ("at all times and places"), but Smith is claiming that the liberty of each, while alive (in "health, strength and spirits"), is at stake here.

To sum up: for Smith, the core concept of liberty presupposes the sense of security that is a consequence of living under the impartial rule of law, and this liberty involves a kind of self-ownership that allows one to exercise one's judgment in order to make meaningful choices.[16] One of these choices is the liberty to contract, but such liberty of contract is by no means the paradigmatic instance of this liberty, because one gives up liberty to exercise it; if anything, to play, while under contract, is to *be* at liberty. In fact, for Smith labor and liberty are contraries: "a life like what the poets describe in the Fortunate Islands, a life of friendship, liberty, and repose; free from labour, and from care, and from all the turbulent passions which attend them" (TMS 1.2.2.2, 32).

h. Regulating Markets

In this final section I describe the role of government in regulating markets according to Smith. I focus on his proposed regulations of financial markets; these reveal that that in addition to his general consequentialist streak, Smith evaluates particular financial instruments by exploring the foreseeable impact on the working poor. He focuses on the distribution of costs if and when things go wrong. This exemplifies his approach to responsible theorizing when it comes to inductive risk.

There is no doubt that Smith was against the government's micromanaging the economy:

> The statesman, who should attempt to direct private people in what manner they ought to employ their capitals, would not only load himself with a most unnecessary attention, but assume an authority which could safely be trusted, not only to no single person, but to no council or senate whatever, and which would nowhere be so dangerous as in the hands of a man who had folly and presumption enough to fancy himself fit to exercise it. (WN 4.2.10, 456; recall the distinction between statesman and crafty politician at WN 4.2.39, 468 discussed in Section f above)

Throughout WN Smith advocates the removal of barriers that prevent individuals, especially poor individuals, from making their own choices. This is why he attacks the poor laws of England, which prevent the poor from migrating between

---

[16] In the Advertisement to the fourth edition of WN, Smith announces that he finds himself "at liberty to acknowledge my very great obligations to Mr. Henry Hope of Amsterdam." To credit one's sources, to give another his public due, is a sign of such liberty among scholars.

parishes (WN 1.10.c.44ff, 152ff). In addition, he argues, "To remove a man who has committed no misdemeanour from the parish where he chuses to reside, is an evident violation of natural liberty and justice" (WN 1.10.c.59, 157; Smith's comment refers to the case of somebody who wishes to live in a parish where he was not born).[17] Thus, while Smith certainly offers economic arguments for increased freedoms, a part of his argument is clearly ("natural liberty and justice") moral. Guild and apprenticeship laws, which prevent people from moving between jobs, are both a violation of "just liberty" (e.g., WN 1.10.c.12, 138) and among the main causes why prices remain above the natural price—that is, they make life expensive for working poor. At WN 1.7.6, 73, Smith links the natural price, "perfect liberty," and the right to change one's trade as often as one pleases (see also WN 1.7.30 79; 1.10.a.1, 116). Of course, throughout WN Smith attacks both explicit barriers to internal and external trade and many more hidden barriers to trade and movement (e.g., the whole of WN 1.10.c, 135ff).

But it does not follow from Smith's epistemic, moral, and political rejection of government's micromanaging of economic affairs that (i) the science of the legislator will always propose the same institutional regime and, thus, (ii) the science of the legislator will always advocate free-market solutions in all respects. On (i), Smith's "general principles" can take into account stadial-historical differences, the path-dependency of existing institutions, and the circumstances one can find oneself in (e.g., geographic distribution of resources and population, relative competitive advantages, and military needs, among others).

On (ii), it has long been recognized that Smith allows that the legislator may need to set up government functions not handled by entirely free markets (e.g., Stigler 1971; Samuels and Medema 2005). Smith foresaw a government role in designing institutional regimes that maintain public works (e.g., canals, roads, postal services, education). All of Smith's proposals in these matters exhibit a careful assessment of how economic and other incentives might conspire to produce outcomes unintended by the legislation; he discusses what we now call "principal-agent" problems (e.g., WN 5.1.e.10, 735) and "regulatory capture" (e.g., WN 1.10.c.61, 157–8) as well as the rent-seeking, financial (and, thus, political) control by private firms of state functionaries, including ambassadors (e.g., WN 5.1.e.10, 736).

In addition to advocating a standing army (much against the chagrin of his Scottish friends [Montes 2009]) and ensuring a "martial spirit," Smith also advocated a role for government in public health:

> Even though the martial spirit of the people were of no use towards the defence of the society, yet to prevent that sort of mental mutilation, deformity, and wretchedness, which cowardice necessarily involves in it, from spreading themselves through the great body of the people,

---

[17] Parishes were responsible for poor relief among their parishioners.

would still deserve the most serious attention of government, in the same manner as it would deserve its most serious attention to prevent a leprosy or any other loathsome and offensive disease, though neither mortal nor dangerous, from spreading itself among them, though perhaps no other public good might result from such attention besides the prevention of so great a public evil. (WN 5.1.f.60, 787–8)

Moreover, in the movement from imperfect laws to the system of natural liberty, the legislator has to proceed gradually and carefully. I have already called attention to Smith's ameliorative attitude that is very pronounced in TMS (recall 6.2.2.16, 233). In WN he writes, "With all its imperfections, however, we may perhaps say of it what was said of the laws of Solon, that, though not the best in itself, it is the best which the interests, prejudices, and temper of the times would admit of. It may perhaps in due time prepare the way for a better" (WN 4.5.b.53, 543). Here Smith does not invoke providence or necessary progress. When proposed changes impact "great multitudes . . . Humanity may in this case require that the freedom of trade should be restored only by slow gradations, and with a good deal of reserve and circumspection" (WN 4.2.40, 469). Smith is no advocate of "shock therapy."

Smith is aware that sometimes one needs to balance different demands of justice. Thus, from the point of view of what we would call "antitrust" regulation, it would make sense to ban regular meetings among merchants. As Smith comments: "It is impossible indeed to prevent such meetings, by any law which either could be executed, or would be consistent with liberty and justice. But though the law cannot hinder people of the same trade from sometimes assembling together, it ought to do nothing to facilitate such assemblies; much less to render them necessary" (WN 1.10.c.27, 145).

Furthermore, Smith's general principles are compatible with the idea that if a free market produces what we would call "negative externalities," an ameliorative regime can be introduced that either prevents the worst features of the negative externalities or produces compensatory mechanisms. In light of our own ongoing financial crisis, it is quite striking that the financial services industry figures prominently in the more celebrated examples of Smith's deviations from purist free-market principles. I have already mentioned Smith's defense of (modest) usury laws (WN 2.4.15, 357ff—that is, legal restrictions on interest that prompted a famous response by Bentham [see Levy 1987 and Hollander 1999 for excellent treatments]).

When it comes to the complex financial services industry, economic agents may not, in fact, understand all the consequences of behavior (see, especially, one of the great set-pieces of WN, Smith's lengthy, scathing treatment of the financial manipulations of so-called bills of exchange, at WN 2.2.67–75, 309–15). His general counsel is to match temporally banking assets with liabilities—in effect, advising "no real estate" in bank portfolios (Rockoff 2013: 318). Here I focus on

Smith's justification of the regulation of financial industries. While Smith analyzes the banking sector, he argues that

> To restrain private people, it may be said, from receiving in payment the promissory notes of a banker, for any sum whether great or small, when they themselves are willing to receive them; or, to restrain a banker from issuing such notes, when all his neighbours are willing to accept of them, is a manifest violation of that natural liberty which it is the proper business of law, not to infringe, but to support. Such regulations may, no doubt, be considered as in some respect a violation of natural liberty. But those exertions of the natural liberty of a few individuals, which might endanger the security of the whole society, are, and ought to be, restrained by the laws of all governments; of the most free, as well as of the most despotical. The obligation of building party walls, in order to prevent the communication of fire, is a violation of natural liberty, exactly of the same kind with the regulations of the banking trade which are here proposed. (WN 2.2.94, 324)

In context, Smith is advocating the legal limitation of the use of banknotes to relatively high denominations. Banknotes were issued by private banks and can be understood as IOUs that give the holder of the note a right to demand its exchange into legal currency (i.e., gold or silver). In the case of a bank run or a bank bankruptcy, such notes would be worthless.

Now the "security of the whole society" is the "general principle" that Smith is appealing to justify legislation that infringes on "natural liberty." Let's grant Smith that (a) this is a good principle, (b) the harm that is to be prevented really occurs, and (c) the law would work as he foresees. Even so, Smith interprets "security of the whole society" in rather broad fashion. Financial collapse is extremely harmful, but unless a country is, say, deeply indebted to foreign nations, it need not endanger the survival of the whole society (leaving aside the fact, of course, that undoubtedly some folk may do quite well during a financial crisis). Thus, it turns out that "security" is really a weaker standard than survival.

Smith thus allows the legislator some leeway to develop regulations of financial industries in order to prevent quite general harms to active participants (i.e., the "private people" willing to accept "promissory notes") and innocent bystanders (those harmed in a financial crisis). This fits the consequentialist streak in Smith's attitude toward evaluating society's institutions that I have emphasized in this chapter.

But this is not the whole story; the case also reveals a paternalist aspect of Smith's stance. A few paragraphs above Smith explains his motive for restricting the use of banknotes to "dealers and richer folk": "But the frequent bankruptcies to which such beggarly bankers must be liable, may occasion a very considerable inconveniency, and sometimes even a very great calamity to many poor people who had received their notes in payment" (WN 2.2.90, 323).

This reveals that in addition to his general consequentialist streak, Smith evaluates particular financial instruments by exploring the foreseeable impact on the working poor. He focuses on the distribution of costs if and when things go wrong (that is, a situation of inductive risk). He does not engage in weighing the probability of those calamities happening, nor the long-term benefits that result from small-denomination banknotes (on Smith's reservations about exact reasoning in economic life, see Chapter 13). Smith seems to think it is obvious that banks either will occasionally go bankrupt (Smith witnessed several Scottish bank crises in his life) or will exploit their financial advantage at the expense of their customers.

This does not mean that such weighing is entirely irrelevant. Smith advocates a policy (limit paper currency to larger notes) so that "banks and bankers might still be able to give nearly the same assistance to the industry and commerce of the country, as they had done when paper money filled almost the whole circulation" (WN 2.2.93, 323). Thus, Smith promotes institutional regimes that, perhaps, do not promise the maximally possible economic growth (the "flourishing" state, which promotes the conditions of the working poor most; recall WN 1.8.36, 96) but in which the working poor are more (most) protected from the fallout when things go wrong. Thus, the evaluation of an institutional regime involves not just its justness, potential for growth, and impartiality (etc.), but also an analysis of the distribution of possible costs to the working poor when things go wrong. He analyzes the downside risk to those unrepresented in the corridors of power, and he assumes a risk aversion among them (no surprise if he thinks that famine or starvation is a real consequence of loss). What is left obscure, of course, is if in Smith's proposal the working poor are now also excluded from some of the non-trivial benefits of using small denominations.

9

Virtue

So the virtues of sensibility and self-command are not appre-
hended to consist in the ordinary, but in the uncommon degrees
of those qualities.... Virtue is excellence, something uncom-
monly great and beautiful, which rises far above what is vulgar
and ordinary.

—TMS 1.1.5.6, 25

In the middling and inferior stations of life, the road to virtue and
that to fortune, to such fortune, at least, as men in such stations
can reasonably expect to acquire, are, happily in most cases, very
nearly the same. In all the middling and inferior professions, real
and solid professional abilities, joined to prudent, just, firm, and
temperate conduct, can very seldom fail of success ... The success
of such people, too, almost always depends upon the favour and
good opinion of their neighbours and equals; and without a tolerably regular conduct these can very seldom be obtained. The good
old proverb, therefore, That honesty is the best policy, holds, in
such situations, almost always perfectly true. In such situations,
therefore, we may generally expect a considerable degree of virtue;
and, fortunately for the good morals of society, these are the situations of by far the greater part of mankind.

—TMS 1.3.3.5, 63

In this chapter I discuss two features of Smith's account of virtue. First, I argue
that there is a significant tension in Smith's treatment of virtue. The tension is
exemplified by the contrast between the TMS passages just quoted. Sometimes
Smith writes of virtue as something rare and sometimes he writes of it as something that one can expect to encounter reliably in others. Second, I analyze
Smith's treatment of the model of moral excellence, "the wise and virtuous" person. I argue that the content of his excellence reveals this is a practiced judge of
character entrusted with the wise enforcement of the law. That is to say, I claim
that the core of Smith's theory of virtue unexpectedly grounds the political order.
However, I also emphasize that Smith recognizes many forms of excellence.

a. Virtue as Excellence or Virtue in Common Life?

At the start of Part 7 of TMS, Smith writes:

> In treating of the principles of morals there are two questions to be
> considered. First, wherein does virtue consist? Or what is the tone
> of temper, and tenor of conduct, which constitutes the excellent and
> praise-worthy character, the character which is the natural object of
> esteem, honour, and approbation? And, secondly, by what power or
> faculty in the mind is it, that this character, whatever it be, is recom-
> mended to us? Or in other words, how and by what means does it come
> to pass, that the mind prefers one tenor of conduct to another, denomi-
> nates the one right and the other wrong; considers the one as the object
> of approbation, honour, and reward, and the other of blame, censure,
> and punishment. (TMS 7.1.2,265)

I offered my account of Smith's answers to the second question in Section b of
Chapter 4 and Section c of Chapter 5, so here I focus only on the first question.
However, note that the way Smith formulates both questions in terms of "tenor
of conduct" implies that to be virtuous means having the right sort of character,
that is, the collection of robust dispositions that make us who we are. In the following section I explore Smith's claims about what constitutes such an excellent-
in-virtue-of-character, but in this section I address an apparent, central tension
in Smith's philosophy.

We need to recognize that Smith's articulation of the excellent-in-virtue-
of-character does not exhaust the category of things that elsewhere in TMS
Smith also claims to be praiseworthy. As we have seen by Smith's lights we
make, for example, many judgments (of propriety, impropriety, merit, and
demerit) of people's behavior in particular situations that we are inclined to
call "moral," not just judgments of character as such. Such situational behavior
certainly may be praiseworthy (e.g., TMS 2.2.1.6, 80). In fact, without reference to character, actions can also be praiseworthy (TMS 3.2.26–9, 126–7 and
TMS 7.2.1.50, 294).

If one allows that the feeling of the piacular (recall, the one that arises when we
have been an involuntary cause of another's harm) is also in our sense a "moral"
attitude, then sometimes it is even praiseworthy to feel the right sort of feeling in
response to an *incident*. Of course, the fact that we do so might shed light on the
robustness of our character. Either way, from our vantage point, Smith's "principles of morals" are not restricted to judgments of character (Gill 2014a).

But even if we restrict our attention to excellent-in-virtue-of-character, we need
to recognize that Smith says things about "virtue" that would be, if not inconsistent,
at least in tension with each other if we assume that virtue is a single thing feature or
property and that "virtue" (and its cognates) refers to this one thing only. I offer two

examples of this tension. First, while the "ordinary degree of proper beneficence which experience teaches us to expect of every body" is not praiseworthy, that "which goes beyond it" is explicitly said to be praiseworthy (TMS 2.2.1.6, 80). But going beyond what we expect of everybody need not be "uncommon" (recall TMS 1.1.5.6, 25) if by "uncommon" we mean "extremely rare." This could be true whether what we "expect" is an empirical generalization or a normative expectation (recall Section c of Chapter 3, and my appeal to Michael Smith 1994: 88–91).

On Smith's account our expectations are a consequence of our habitual environment—recall my treatment of environmental rationality (Section c of Chapter 3). It is, thus, context-sensitive in such a way that we can develop fairly minimal expectations that are easily exceeded if we travel to other communities. I grew up in an environment where stopping in front of a red light at a pedestrian crossing was extremely unusual; in lots of communities it is a very robust norm.

Second, even if one allows that, as Smith implies, virtue comes in degrees, it looks as if the passage from TMS 1.1.5.6, 25, also implies that even a "considerable degree of virtue" ought also to be relatively rare. But TMS 1.3.3.5, 63, clearly suggests that a considerable degree of virtue is widely instantiable, if not instantiated. (I have quoted both passages at the top of this chapter.) I use the odd locution of "possibly widely instantiable" because TMS 1.3.3.5 describes "circumstances" in which the expectation of encountering a considerable degree of virtue is *reasonable* (even if it almost never occurs).

Given that TMS 1.3.3.5 offers what is ordinarily seen as Smith's defense of the so-called bourgeois virtues (McCloskey 2006; Herzog 2013), this tension is not trivial if we take, as I do, that Smith wishes to defend, on balance, the virtue of commercial society. Moreover, TMS 1.3.3.5 is also crucial for the claim that Smith embraces a conception of morality that, echoing his teacher Hutcheson, allows ordinary people to be virtuous (Fleischacker 2013), even if Smith may not go as far as Hutcheson.[1] This kind of moral egalitarianism would not be possible if the "greater part of mankind" would find itself in "situations" in which virtue cannot be safely exercised.

---

[1] Hutcheson allows that anybody can be a hero:

At present, we shall only draw this one, which seems the most joyful imaginable, even to the lowest rank of Mankind, viz. "That no external Circumstances of Fortune, no involuntary Disadvantages, can exclude any Mortal from the most heroick Virtue." For how small soever the Moment of publick Good be, which any one can accomplish, yet if his Abilitys are proportionably small, the Quotient, which expresses the Degree of Virtue, may be as great as any whatsoever. Thus, not only the Prince, the Statesman, the General, are capable of true Heroism, tho these are the chief Characters, whose Fame is diffus'd thro various Nations and Ages; but when we find in an honest Trader, the kind Friend, the faithful prudent Adviser, the charitable and hospitable Neighbour, the tender Husband and affectionate Parent, the sedate yet chearful Companion, the generous Assistant of Merit, the cautious Allayer of Contention and Debate, the Promoter of Love and good Understanding among Acquaintances. (F. Hutcheson *An Inquiry Into the Original of Our Ideas of Beauty and Virtue*, Treatise II, Section 3, XV)

To be sure, there is a compelling argument that, according to Smith, in *some* societies such "situations" are rare. Part of Smith's *moral* argument against feudalism turns on its undermining of the ordinary exercise of virtue (see also Section f of Chapter 5). But the point of TMS 1.3.3.5 is to claim that in a commercial and law-governed (that is, "civilized") society—as Smith understood to be his own—such circumstances would not be rare.

The wording of TMS 1.3.3.5 is no slip of the pen on Smith's part, because when he describes the "inferior prudence" of the man who lives within his income, he claims:

> In the steadiness of his industry and frugality, in his steadily sacrificing the ease and enjoyment of the present moment for the probable expectation of the still greater ease and enjoyment of a more distant but more lasting; period of time, the prudent man is always both supported and rewarded by the *entire* approbation of the impartial spectator, and of the representative; of the impartial spectator, the man within the breast. (TMS 6.1.11, 215; emphasis added)

As many commentators have noted when trying to reconcile the ways in which TMS and WN cohere (say, in context of resolving Das Adam Smith Problem—recall Section b of Chapter 7), it is a core claim of Smith's political economy that such prudence is widely dispersed in a society with rule of law: "the principles of common prudence do not always govern the conduct of every individual, they always influence that of the majority of every class or order" (WN 2.2.36, 295; see also WN 1.11.n.1, 256, where the contrast between fortune and prudence is tied to different forms of political organization).

So, in order to save Smith from contradiction, he needs to allow [A] that (i) to be truly virtuous and (ii) to be praiseworthy by the impartial spectator can come apart (with (ii) being the wider category) and [B] that virtue is not "far above" ordinary behavior, after all, so that we can ignore the stuff about unusual excellence. As we have seen, a good case can be made that (i) and (ii) come apart in the right way, so we can leave that aside.

However, I also accept Ryan Hanley's argument that, on balance, Smith is wedded to the idea of virtue as excellence (Hanley 2013: 224–5; crucially, whatever the content of this excellence, it cannot be one-sided at the expense of other virtues). Hanley's argument is rather persuasive in light of his detailed treatment of Smith's additions to TMS in the final edition, especially Part 6. In his last thoughts on the matter Smith embraced virtue as excellence. Thus, I conclude that there is a genuine tension in Smith that so far has not been eliminated (for more on this tension, see Shin 2014).[2]

---

[2] One anonymous referee suggested that such a tension is to be expected in an Aristotelian virtue account.

The significance of this tension is that Smith wants to defend ordinary moral experience in law-governed civilization (Fleischacker 2013). Yet, Smith requires his treatment of virtue as excellence in order to articulate some standards that go beyond ordinary moral life but are capable of criticizing it. As he puts it in a letter to Sir Gilbert Elliot (Corr., Letter No. 40, 49), Smith says that his moral philosophy is designed to show that "real magnanimity and conscious virtue can support itself under the disapprobation of man-kind." As I argue in Chapter 15, Smith treats Hume as the exemplar of a "wise and virtuous person" that instantiates the very existence of somebody who can offer to improve the norms of society, even under the disapprobation of his community.

b. Excellent-in-Virtue-of-Character

In this section I argue for two claims. First, one of the most significant exemplars of moral excellence, the wise and virtuous person, turns out to be a highly skilled judge of character capable of being entrusted with the proper enforcement of the law. This implies that TMS is not just a book in moral psychology but should be seen as contributing to political philosophy. This excellence involves a robust disposition to behave according to some "tone of temper." In particular, Smith treats this disposition as a "temper of mind" (Hanley 2013: 230–2). Second, Smith embraces multiple models of virtuous excellence (Hanley 2013: 222).

Sometimes Smith writes as if there is only one model of virtue. For example, he writes in a passage that I have already emphasized: "The wise and virtuous man directs his principal attention to the first standard; the idea of exact propriety and perfection" (TMS 6.3.25, 247; recall Section b in Chapter 3). This suggests that there is a single standard and that the wise and virtuous orient themselves toward it. And Smith states that the "precise and distinct measure . . . can be found nowhere but in the sympathetic feelings of the impartial and well informed spectator" (TMS 7.2.1.49, 294; recall Section c of Chapter 5). As I have argued, these cultivated feelings involve non-trivial epistemic judgments that rely on sophisticated (and sometimes subconscious) counterfactual reasoning; Smith, too, calls attention to both the non-trivial epistemic contributions ("precise," "exact," "well informed") to these judgments and the moral significance of treating everybody equally. To be an excellent moral judge is an exacting skill, which requires keeping in mind that even the most outstanding person is, as "reason" teaches, "but one of the multitude" (TMS 3.3.5, 137; recall Section d of Chapter 3).

"Admiration and respect" are "due only to wisdom and virtue" (TMS 1.3.3.1, 61–2). But in context, Smith famously claims that in practice most people offer more frequently admiration and respect to wealth and greatness. We do so, in part, because that's what we experience ("see") in the world. This is the "great and most universal cause" of the corruption of our moral sentiments (recall Section b of Chapter 5).

Not unlike the rich and great, the "wise and virtuous" also desire "to deserve, to acquire, and to enjoy the respect and admiration of mankind." As we have seen (recall Section e in Chapter 3), admiration is both an intellectual and aesthetic sentiment: we admire those things that are great and beautiful (Astronomy, Intro.1, EPS 33; Valihora 2010: 141; at TMS 1.2.3.6, 37, Smith emphasizes the musicality of admiration). The wise and virtuous person aims, in part by "emulation" of other wise and virtuous, to imitate the "more correct and more exquisitely beautiful in its outline" ideal standards. (For how this works in more detail see Griswold 1999: 331 and, especially, Chandler 2013; on emulation see TMS 3.2.3, 114.)

But that does not exhaust everything the wise and virtuous person aims for; she also aims at "respect." In context, Smith does not make clear what "respect" entails, and it is no help when later he calls the impartial spectator the "respectable judge" (TMS 3.3.25, 147). We seem trapped in some circle here (see also 6.2.1.18, 224), with respect being that which is due to a respectable judge (etc.); if one "associates chiefly with the wise and the virtuous, though" one need not "become either wise or virtuous," but one "cannot help conceiving a certain respect at least for wisdom and virtue" (6.2.1.17, 224). Respect ought also to be taught and learned at home (TMS 6.2.1.10, 222). Moreover, it does not inspire confidence in our respectful judgments of others if respect may also just be the product of daily familiarity (TMS 6.2.1. 16, 224).

Fortunately, Smith also connects the desire for respect to a sense of equality among one's recognized peers (TMS 6.1.3, 212–3; see also 6.3.39, 256, and 6.3.48, 260). As mentioned in Section a of Chapter 4, Darwall (2006) has offered a detailed account—centering on a second-person perspective that we adopt with each other in a moral community—of how recognition of such mutual equality is entailed by our justified resentment at injury: "What chiefly enrages us against the man who injures or insults us, is the little account which he seems to make of us" (TMS 2.3.1.5, 96). Thus, the wise and virtuous person desires to be thought beautiful for her excellence as well as, surprisingly enough, to receive *in practice* the recognition already *properly* due to being an equal member of a moral community. That is to say, she has a heightened sensitivity to her membership in a— to speak metaphorically—moral universe.

So far I have described what the wise and virtuous person aspires to, but I have not stated yet what her excellence consists in, although having such a heightened sensitivity obviously gives considerable clues to what Smith might have in mind. He says such excellence involves practicing "humble modesty and equitable justice" (TMS 1.3.3.2, 62). Unfortunately, he does not comment much on the nature of such modesty (a key virtue in Wollstonecraft's *Vindication*). But in his addition to the final edition of TMS, Smith explains that the "whole mind" of "the wise and virtuous" is "deeply impressed, his whole behaviour and deportment are distinctly stamped with the character of real modesty; with that of a very moderate estimation of his own merit, and, at the same time, of a full sense of the merit of other people" (TMS 6.3.25, 247–8). I propose (i) to treat the part after the semicolon (i.e., "with that … other people") as an explanation of the nature of "real modesty." Recall, too, from Section b of Chapter 5, (ii) that judgments of merit involve the proportionality among a sentiment of heart, which leads to an action and its foreseeable effects, and, of course, the actual effects produced by it. From (i) and (ii) it follows that modesty involves a proper estimation of the consequences of character in others and oneself.

Moreover, Smith tends to treat "justice" as a broader category than Hume, who tends to equate justice with the defense of property; justice is no more than the proper rule of law (recall Section a of Chapter 8). In brief, "equitable justice" just means treating people equally and giving them what is properly due to them in a legal context. On this conception, justice is the virtue that belongs to the "civil magistrate" (TMS 2.2.1.8, 81.)

So, surprisingly enough, when we connect the chain of implications, the wise and virtuous person is not just an ideal citizen, but somebody who is a skilled judge of character entrusted with the wise enforcement of the law. It need not be the case that such a person is always so entrusted; thus, we can express Smith's position on the wise and virtuous person that she is the type of person who is best entrusted with the maintenance of the legal order. It is, thus, sensible that such an excellent person deserves our respect and admiration because she guards our shared freedoms. If this is right, then, one of Smith's most important moral exemplars is fundamentally committed to a moral understanding of political life.

While this line of thought must remain somewhat speculative, it is also in evidence in Smith's claim that "The wise and virtuous man is at all times willing that his own private interest should be sacrificed to the public interest of his own particular order or society" (TMS 6.2.3.3, 235). In fact, we have already encountered this idea before: recall from Chapter 1, when Smith explained in his letter to Cullen that he would sacrifice his own interest in the university's corporate interest, "I should prefer David Hume to any man for a colleague; but I am afraid the public would not be of my opinion; and the interest of the society will oblige us to have some regard to the opinion of the public" (Corr. 5). Whatever one may think of Smith's stance, we may also recognize that Smith tried to achieve a kind of philosophical integrity—that is, a coherence between his stated moral theory and his own actions.

One might object to the proposed analysis of what the wise and virtuous person practices by claiming that the proper upholding of law ought to be recognized, in fact, by more than a few spectators. Yet, I do not see why this needs to be so. If properly understood, Smith is making the very important claim that the proper rule of law does not needlessly draw attention to itself; we do not "see" it very much even in the best of times. In fact, such an approach to law contrasts starkly with the manifest spectacles of torture and execution that Smith vividly describes from the first pages of TMS onward (e.g., TMS 1.1.1.2, 9; 1.2.1.12, 30; 1.3.1.11, 47). When alerted, anybody can recognize the significance of the most perfect wise and virtuous practices, but given what we experience (and things have not gotten better since Smith's day), few do.

So far my argument has focused on only one excellent-in-virtue-of-character. It's clear that the perfectly wise and virtuous person is among the most highly valued by Smith (cf. TMS 3.3.35, 152),[3] but it does not follow that there are no other excellent-in-virtue-of-characters worth emulating and imitation. For example, Smith writes that

> A sacred and religious regard not to hurt or disturb in any respect the happiness of our neighbour, even in those cases where no law can properly protect him, constitutes the character of the perfectly innocent and just man; a character which, when carried to a certain delicacy of attention, is always highly respectable and even venerable for its own sake, and can scarce ever fail to be accompanied with many other virtues, with great feeling for other people, with great humanity and great benevolence. (TMS 6.2.intro.2, 218)

Smith draws here a character of a "perfectly innocent and just man." This is also an excellent-in-virtue-of-character, but one who may lack wisdom. In fact, while the wise and virtuous character is all about a certain form of moral equality and the wise enforcement of the law, the perfectly innocent and just character *refrains* from harming vulnerable others (among other virtues). The wise and virtuous character concerns the public virtue of "beneficence" (TMS, 2.1.8, 81; see especially the treatment of the Roman exemplars of "noble beneficence" at TMS 2.1.5.3, 75). By contrast, the perfectly innocent and just person promotes the private duty of "great benevolence." (Montes 2004: 106 calls attention to the distinction between beneficence and benevolence in Smith.)

In fact, throughout TMS Smith draws vivid exemplary characters with excellent dispositions. For example, the "great Duke of Marlborough" is an exemplar of a "great warrior" but also (unusually for such a warrior) possesses "temperate coolness and self-command" (TMS 6.3.28, 251). There is also "the great leader in science and taste, the man who directs and conducts our own sentiments, the extent and superior justness of whose talents astonish us with wonder and surprise, who excites our admiration, and seems to deserve our applause" (TMS 1.1.4.3, 20). Finally,

> the leader of the successful party ... may re-establish and improve the constitution, and from the very doubtful and ambiguous character of the leader of a party, he may assume the greatest and noblest of all

---

[3] TMS 3.3.35, 152 talks of "the man of the most perfect virtue," while omitting mention of wisdom. He naturally generates love and reverence and is deserving of our admiration. Smith's conception of *his* proper role is explored at length in Hanley (2009).

characters, that of the reformer and legislator of a great state; and, by the wisdom of his institutions, secure the internal tranquillity [*sic*] and happiness of his fellow citizens for many succeeding generations. (TMS 6.2.2.14, 232; see Sabl 2012: 164-7 on Hume's History 6.247 on General George Monk).

All these characters have particular, cultivated virtues, practices, and, especially, mental dispositions associated with them. This just reinforces the fact that even Smith's conception of virtue is not monistic (Gill 2014a).

As Heydt (2008) has emphasized, Smith's vivid drawings of exemplars function not merely as descriptions but are also meant to be instructive. An older generation of scholars tends to cite a passage from an extended footnote by Smith against the very idea of a normative dimension to TMS: "Let it be considered too, that the present inquiry is not concerning a matter of right, if I may say so, but concerning a matter of fact" (TMS 2.15.10, 77). But in context (it's a quote from the chapter on judgments of merit), Smith is making a distinction between an inquiry into the "principles" upon which "a perfect being would approve of the punishment of bad actions; but upon what principles so weak and imperfect a creature as man actually and in fact approves of it." He is claiming that for his enterprise a realistic human anthropology is required rather than a divine one that is beyond our reach (that is, ought implies can). He does so to establish what creatures like us ought to do.

10

Three Invisible Hands

> [I]deas are not anyhow and at random produced, there being a certain order and connexion between them, like to that of cause and effect; there are also several combinations of them made in a very regular and artificial manner, which seem like so many instruments in the hand of nature that, being hid as it were behind the scenes, have a secret operation in producing those appearances which are seen on the theatre of the world, being themselves discernible only to the curious eye of the philosopher.
> —George Berkeley, *Principles of Human Knowledge*, Section 64

Since an article by Alec Macfie (1971), scholars have recognized that Smith uses the phrase "invisible hand" three times in EPS, TMS, and WN. Recently the never-to-be-forgotten Warren Samuels bequeathed us a lifetime of scholarship on the enormous variety of interpretations and usages that Smith's "invisible hand" has generated (Samuels 2011). Despite Emma Rothschild's valiant effort to convince scholars that Smith uses the phrase as an ironic joke (1994), little agreement on the meaning of the phrase has emerged. In fact, with a revival of interest in the religious and theological underpinnings of Smith's economics and the degree to which Smith anticipated the modern gospel of free markets, the invisible hands have taken on new urgency.

Even if one were to grant that the phrase "invisible hand" may have been an ironic joke, I have come to believe that the phrase conveys a set of concepts that are important to Smith (Fleischacker 2004: 138–42). I started Chapter 2 by quoting a passage on the origin of the division of labor in Chapter 1 of Book 1 of WN. I treated it as an exemplary argument pattern of Smith's approach to a considerable number of social phenomena (e.g., division of labor, but also origin of money, justice, language, even morality [Otteson 2002a]) that may have beneficial social consequences; these can be explained by the unforeseen and unintended necessary workings of human propensities over long stretches of time. While this is not the only kind of explanation Smith offers—he also describes quite a bit of intended and foreseeable rent-seeking (e.g., Buchanan, Tollison, and Tullock 1980) by the merchant class—the invisible hand passages do shed additional light on, and should be distinguished from, Smithian social explanations.

Therefore, in this chapter I discuss the three versions of the invisible hand in light of each other. I offer detailed textual analysis of them in order to argue that what I call "Smithian invisible hand processes" are not identical to what I have called "Smithian social explanations." I show that any given iteration of a Smithian invisible hand process is a relatively short-term process in which an agent produces unintended and, to him or her, unknown consequences. Crucially, I argue that in invisible hand processes the consequences are, in principle, knowable to the right kind of observer (either theoretically informed or by accumulated common sense) at the time. By contrast, Smithian social explanations involve cases where the consequences are visible or knowable only after the fact. Generally they take place over much longer amounts of time than any given invisible hand process. Smithian social explanations can include invisible hand processes as subcomponents (or mechanisms) but should not be conflated with these. I have left the temporal contrast vague, but the effects of Smithian invisible hand processes always become visible within a human life. By contrast, the processes described in Smithian social explanation accumulate over centuries.

a. The Invisible Hand of Jupiter, and Miracles

In this section I offer a detailed reading of the passage that contains the "invisible hand of Jupiter" in Astronomy. In addition to the significance for our larger understanding of invisible hand processes, I call attention to the importance of the passage to a proper understanding of Smith's religious epistemology; Smith's narrative also implies that belief in miracles is superstitious. Smith writes:

> Hence the origin of Polytheism, and of that vulgar superstition which ascribes all the irregular events of nature to the favour or displeasure of intelligent, though invisible beings, to gods, daemons, witches, genii, fairies. For it may be observed, that in all Polytheistic religions, among savages, as well as in the early ages of Heathen antiquity, it is the irregular events of nature only that are ascribed to the agency and power of their gods. Fire burns, and water refreshes; heavy bodies descend, and lighter substances fly upwards, by the necessity of their own nature; nor was the invisible hand of Jupiter s ever apprehended to be employed in those matters. But thunder and lightning, storms and sunshine, those more irregular events, were ascribed to his favour, or his anger. Man, the only designing power with which they were acquainted, never acts but either to stop, or to alter the course, which natural events would take, if left to themselves. Those other intelligent beings, whom they imagined, but knew not, were naturally supposed to act in the same manner; not to employ themselves in supporting the ordinary course of things, which went on of its own accord, but to stop, to thwart, and

to disturb it. And thus, in the first ages of the world, the lowest and most pusillanimous superstition supplied the place of philosophy.

But when law has established order and security, and subsistence ceases to be precarious, the curiosity of mankind is increased, and their fears are diminished. The leisure which they then enjoy renders them more attentive to the appearances of nature, more observant of her smallest irregularities, and more desirous to know what is the chain which links them all together. That some such chain subsists betwixt all her seemingly disjointed phaenomena, they are necessarily led to conceive; and that magnanimity, and cheerfulness, which all generous natures acquire who are bred in civilized societies, where they have so few occasions to feel their weakness, and so many to be conscious of their strength and security, renders them less disposed to employ, for this connecting chain, those invisible beings whom the fear and ignorance of their rude forefathers had engendered. Those of liberal fortunes, whose attention is not much occupied either with business or with pleasure, can fill up the void of their imagination, which is thus disengaged from the ordinary affairs of life, no other way than by attending to that train of events which passes around them. While the great objects of nature thus pass in review before them, many things occur in an order to which they have not been accustomed. (Astronomy, 3.2–3, EPS 49–50)

In Chapter 11 I return to Smith's description of the movement of historical character types that evolve from fearful to cheerful, from pusillanimous to magnanimous, from weakness to strength, and so forth. In Chapter 15 I return to Smith's characterization of the cheerfulness of the generous soul in my discussion of his obituary of Hume. In context, Smith is describing the origin of (natural) philosophy. On his account, (a) established law and (b) a leisure class with cultivated interests are jointly a necessary condition for the existence of philosophy; it is left unclear if they are sufficient. Law is crucial to reduce daily fear and uncertainty and to create the very possibility of leisure (presumably because it generates a class that can enjoy and have reasonable expectations about the fruits of surplus). Smith is silent about the role of slavery in generating the possibility of leisure.

Leisure supplies the very possibility of breaking through savage-state environmental rationality; that is, in properly functioning persons there is a reciprocal relationship between the habituated mental anticipations and sound judgment (recall my discussion in Section c of Chapter 3). Philosophy starts in wonder, and wonder is the passion that opens up the possibility for adjusting existing manifest image. It turns out that the "great objects" in the heavens supply the first philosophical systems according to Smith (see Astronomy 4.1, EPS 53). In the next chapter I return to this account to explore what happens to environmental rationality when links are introduced from ordinary experience to more specialized scientific "systems" of thought.

Here I focus on the fear-ridden prehistory before the origin of law and philosophy. In Smith's stadial theory, a pre-legal period refers either to the hunting stage or to the early shepherding stage. Both tend to be denoted as "savage." (They are akin but not identical to a Hobbesian state of nature.) In this stage the objects that constitute ordinary environmental rationality are all treated as necessary ("fire burns, and water refreshes; heavy bodies descend, and lighter substances fly upwards, by the necessity of their own nature"). In Ancient Physics (1–8; EPS 106–11), Smith describes the origin of a theory of four elements in more detail. From the vantage point of necessity humans appear as irregular.

Crucially, the way in which humans are irregular is that we can act for an end in order to interfere with nature's necessity. Humans introduce alternative possibilities into nature. Our pre-law-governed environmental rationality consists, in part, in judging which of these novel possibilities are themselves to be expected.

Smith claims that the gods are introduced by way of analogy to account for the most astonishing of the infrequent and—from the point of view of our environmental rationality—irregular events (that fall, thus, outside environmental rationality). Thus, the original gods are an anthropomorphic projection to account for the unexpected and fear-enhancing deviations in nature's ordinary necessity. These gods are imagined to have their own (and unknowable) fear-inducing ends and passions, and they act on these accordingly.

Thus, Astronomy's "invisible hand" is an anthropomorphic projection of the fearful and ignorant savage's imagination to account for events that deviate from his or her environmental rationality (that is, the realm of ordinary necessity). It ascribes to the deities *particular* providence (as distinct from general providence, which can govern nature's most general necessity). Heathen superstitions introduce godly intervention to explain unusual events. This projection of particular providence is said to be a form of the "lowest and most pusillanimous superstition."

I offer one final, more speculative comment on Smith's approach to Astronomy's "invisible hand." Smith offers what we would call "an error theory" about the savages' beliefs; they think that unusual events in the world are governed by passionate gods' actions, but in reality these are just anthropomorphic projections (see Kail 2007 on Hume for a useful taxonomy of such projections). The error theory diagnoses the savages' expectations, which are associated with necessity, and deviations from these are associated with godly interventions. By labeling all of this "vulgar superstition" (etc.), Smith indicates he does not believe any of it.

Smith's treatment of heathen belief as imaginative projections springing from fear and ignorance has an Epicurean flavor reminiscent of Hume's *The Natural History of Religion* and Spinoza's Appendix to *Ethics 1*. To some of Smith's posthumous readers (recall that these essays first appeared after his death in 1795), there may be a troubling consequence of this account: Smith explains how the heathen gods' actions appear as miraculous interventions in ordinary course of nature (associated with necessity) as projections from the savages' imagination. This is because a divine intervention in the course of necessity with the aim of some particular providence is ordinarily labeled a "miracle" by many of Smith's Christian readers.

Let's turn to examining the two other "invisible hands" in TMS and WN.

b. The "Vain and Insatiable Desires" of the Rich

In TMS the "invisible hand" appears in the course of a much-studied, lengthy, and rhetorically complex passage. I argue that, in fact, it reveals in Smith recognition of two kinds of social processes: one that he identifies with the natural deception of the imagination and the other with the invisible hand. I quote most of the passage before commenting on it:

> Our imagination, which in pain and sorrow seems to be confined and cooped up within our own persons, in times of ease and prosperity expands itself to every thing around us. We are then charmed with the beauty of that accommodation which reigns in the palaces and oeconomy of the great; and admire how every thing is adapted to promote their ease, to prevent their wants, to gratify their wishes, and to amuse and entertain their most frivolous desires. If we consider the real satisfaction which all these things are capable of affording, by itself and separated from the beauty of that arrangement which is fitted to promote it, it will always appear in the highest degree contemptible and trifling. But we rarely view it in this abstract and philosophical light. We naturally confound it in our imagination with the order, the regular and harmonious movement of the system, the machine or oeconomy by means of which it is produced. The pleasures of wealth and greatness, when considered in this complex view, strike the imagination as something grand and beautiful and noble, of which the attainment is well worth all the toil and anxiety which we are so apt to bestow upon it.
>
> And it is well that nature imposes upon us in this manner. It is this deception which rouses and keeps in continual motion the industry of mankind. It is this which first prompted them to cultivate the ground, to build houses, to found cities and commonwealths, and to invent and improve all the sciences and arts, which ennoble and embellish human life; which have entirely changed the whole face of the globe, have turned the rude forests of nature into agreeable and fertile plains, sand made the track less and barren ocean a new fund of subsistence, and the great high road of communication to the different nations of the earth. The earth by these labours of mankind has been obliged to redouble her natural fertility, and to maintain a greater multitude of

inhabitants. It is to no purpose, that the proud and unfeeling land-lord views his extensive fields, and without a thought for the wants of his brethren, in imagination consumes himself the whole harvest that grows upon them. The homely and vulgar proverb, that the eye is larger than the belly, never was more fully verified than with regard to him. The capacity of his stomach bears no proportion to the immensity of his desires, and will receive no more than that of the meanest peasant. The rest he is obliged to distribute among those, who prepare, in the nicest manner, that little which he himself makes use of, among those who fit up the palace in which this little is to be consumed, among those who provide and keep in order all the different baubles and trinkets, which are employed in the oeconomy of greatness; all of whom thus derive from his luxury and caprice, that share of the necessaries of life, which they would in vain have expected from his humanity or his justice. The produce of the soil maintains at all times nearly that number of inhab-itants which it is capable of maintaining. The rich only select from the heap what is most precious and agreeable. They consume little more than the poor, and in spite of their natural selfishness and rapacity, though they mean only their own conveniency, though the sole end which they propose from the labours of all the thousands whom they employ, be the gratification of their own vain and insatiable desires, they divide with the poor the produce of all their improvements. They are led by an invisible hand to make nearly the same distribution of the necessaries of life, which would have been made, had the earth been divided into equal portions among all its inhabitants, and thus without intending it, without knowing it, advance the interest of the society, and afford means to the multiplication of the species.

When Providence divided the earth among a few lordly masters, it neither forgot nor abandoned those who seemed to have been left out in the partition. These last too enjoy their share of all that it pro-duces. In what constitutes the real happiness of human life, they are in no respect inferior to those who would seem so much above them. In ease of body and peace of mind, all the different ranks of life are nearly upon a level, and the beggar, who suns himself by the side of the highway, possesses that security which kings are fighting for. (TMS 4.1.9–10, 183–5)

Recall from Section c of Chapter 3 that environmental rationality involves having the right kind of mental habits (that is, the train of ideas in one's imagination matches the world's natural order); for Smith, in a properly functioning person there is a reciprocal relationship between the habituated mental anticipations and sound judgment. In the passage above, Smith introduces an important, what I will call a "physiologic constraint" on the workings of the imagination: when we are sick or depressed ("pain and sorrow") we experience the world in gloomy fashion, while when we are really healthy we tend to wear rose-tinted glasses, especially when it comes to evaluating the worth of the external trappings of the rich and powerful. As Smith puts it earlier in TMS: "This disposition to admire, and almost to worship, the rich and the powerful, and to despise, or, at least, to neglect persons of poor and mean condition . . . is, at the same time, the great and most universal cause of the corruption of our moral sentiments" (TMS 1.3.3.1, 61).

That is to say, according to Smith we rarely have "sound judgment." According to him we tend to have systematic biases in our perceptions, including about ourselves when it comes to the conditions that create "real satisfaction." Therefore, unlike modern economists, Smith thinks there are objective facts of the matter when it comes to our well-being. Moreover, he assumes a theoretically privileged position—he purports to know what makes us happy even if most of us rarely exhibit this.

In fact, systematic biases toward the wealthy and against the poor as well as our own self-deceit (Gerschlager 2002) are recurring themes not just in his moral philosophy, but also in his political economy:

> The over-weening conceit which the greater part of men have of their own abilities, is an antient evil remarked by the philosophers and moralists of all ages. Their absurd presumption in their own good fortune, has been less taken notice of. It is, however, if possible, still more universal. There is no man living who, when in tolerable health and spirits, has not some share of it. The chance of gain is by every man more or less over-valued, and the chance of loss is by most men undervalued, and by scarce any man, who is in tolerable health and spirits, valued more than it is worth. (WN 1.10.b.26, 124–5; for discussion see Paganelli 2003)

Here Smith again invokes a physiologic constraint in diagnosing widespread epistemic ("abilities") and economic ("good fortune") overconfidence, with the latter even more prevalent. The correct estimation of "real satisfaction" is, in fact, the product of the "abstract and philosophical light." Thus, Smith is not just denying that sound judgment is common but is also claiming that it is a rare consequence of, in part, a second-order reflection on our ordinary situation. As I argued in Section b of Chapter 2, according to Smith abstraction is a different kind of mental activity than the natural train of ideas in the imagination. Smith does not tell us here how one acquires this second-order, expert reflection.

Ordinarily, the trappings of riches and power provide us with pleasing aesthetic spectacles that motivate us to try to acquire these for ourselves; we just lose sight of what gives us real satisfaction. Oddly enough, when we are physiologically most healthy "our imagination" is most likely to make us less sane than we ought to be. This creates a natural "deception" with predictable consequences: it "rouses and keeps in continual motion the industry of mankind." This "industry" has an especially important further, unintended consequence: it has caused mankind to "invent and improve all the sciences and arts, which ennoble and embellish human life." Thus, the desire to acquire the beautiful and noble-seeming trappings of wealth and power in the mistaken belief that this will make us satisfied led to the at least initially unintended growth of civilization, including the "arts and science," which do, in fact, ennoble our lives (for more on this, see Schliesser 2006). Another important side effect is that the circumstances that lead to famine and infanticide are reduced and the sustenance of "a greater multitude of inhabitants" than otherwise would have been possible.

Smith's account here conforms to a pattern characteristic of Smithian social explanation (recall Section a of Chapter 2). To summarize: (i) it is causal and (ii) it is a historical explanation. By "historical" I mean to capture two features: (a) that the stable consequence would not have been in "view" (or predictable) to observers of human nature at an early time (and thus not capable of being intended) and (b) that to be a cause does not require temporal contiguity between the cause and the effect. (iii) Smith's account *does* require that after certain consequences become visible to observer-participants, they become self-reinforcing. Thus, in the long run and in the aggregate, normological propensities will produce initially unpredictable, albeit definite and determined outcomes. In addition, an important feature of Smithian social explanation, which I had not emphasized before, is also visible here: (iv) it supports counterfactual judgments—the process characterized by the Smithian social explanation describes not just what happened, but also how it differs from what would have happened without the process characterized by the Smithian social explanation.

One might think that the invisible hand is just a vivid expression of Smithian social explanation, but it turns out that in context Smith applies the phrase *not* to capture the behavior of the people who are trying to emulate or become like the wealthy, but in order to discuss or capture the consequences of the behavior by the "rich." Therefore, now we need to figure out if Smith's analysis of the consequences of the behavior by the rich is also an instance of Smithian social explanation or, as I argue, something subtly different.

In TMS the invisible hand is, through the gratification of the "vain and insatiable desires" by the rich, said "to make nearly the same distribution of the necessaries of life" (TMS 4.1.10, 185). Smith is relying on a distinction between necessaries and conveniences in life. (Sometimes he also makes a further distinction by adding to these [a subset of the conveniences] "amusements" [e.g., WN 2.2.5, 287]) or "superfluities" (see below). In Smith and other eighteenth-century authors, the necessaries of life are contrasted with the conveniences of life. It turns out that there is no hard-and-fast distinction between the two, but we can recognize paradigmatic cases of each: "diamonds [are] the greatest of all superfluities ... [while] food, the first of all necessaries" (WN 1.11.g.28, 224). We might define conveniences operationally as the things we are willing to give up in times of financial (or worse) distress (WN 1.11.e.38, 210; WN 1.7.9, 74). Let's stipulate that necessaries are what's needed for bare subsistence (as seems to be implied by WN 3.3.12, 405). The reason why there is no hard-and-fast distinction between the two categories is that Smith recognizes that society's "custom" can alter one's perception of what is necessary, including for "respectability" or "decency" (e.g., his example of the gendered differences in wearing shoes at WN 5.2.k.3, 870). Thus, necessaries are context-relative, in the same manner as the environmental rationality of sound judgment.

Now often people see in this invisible hand passage Smith's commitment to a benign Stoic providentialism (Viner 1972 [2015]). Given that Smith uses the phrase "Providence" and ends it on the Stoic trope that "the beggar, who suns himself by the side of the highway, possesses that security which kings are fighting for," this reading makes a lot of sense (Fleischacker 2004). But regardless of what else Smith is saying, it is worth emphasizing that he is making a fairly weak claim here; the invisible hand equalizes the bare necessities of life only to some degree. Insofar as there is any material trickle-down effect, it is fairly minimal.

Smith's claim is even thinner than first impressions suggest. This is because we are also told something about how to interpret the quantity of the "necessaries of life" here. Smith qualifies the distribution of the necessaries of life with the further claim: "which would have been made, had the earth been divided into equal portions among all its inhabitants." This is a counterfactual. The question is what hypothetical time (and, thus, population size) Smith has in mind when he discusses equal portions of the Earth: (i) at creation, (ii) during the pre-legal savage period, (iii) at the establishment of property relations during the pastoral stage; (iv) at the present (c. 1776), or (v) say, at any given time. Regardless how one answers this question, by Smith's own lights simply dividing the Earth—he does not even say the fruits of the Earth—in the absence of exchange relations, the division of labor, or derived property rights is going to produce rather small quantities of anything. This is because we need the long-drawn-out process fueled by the deceptions of the imagination to make the Earth fertile!

Hence, when the baseline in the counterfactual is a Hobbesian state of nature or conditions of near starvation, the invisible hand is advancing the interest of society when the rich select the most agreeable parts. In miserable times, such as feudalism or the remnants of feudalism—and the context suggests this is what Smith has in mind (note the references to the "proud and unfeeling landlord" who "views his extensive fields," seems to live in a "palace," and employs "thousands")—even the poor get more than they would otherwise have. Of course, the political claim is important in the context of Hume's and Smith's attack on feudalism and their interpretation of how feudalism was undone by the feudal lords' (and the clergy's) insatiable interest in luxury goods.

But if the baseline in the counterfactual is a society with advanced division of labor, then the claim that Smith makes on behalf of the invisible hand as presented in TMS, however interpreted, is quite implausible by Smith's own lights.

This is because in such a society the poorest members have higher standards of living than the rich and powerful at earlier stages (recall Smith's deployment of the trope that an "industrious and frugal peasant" has a better accommodation than an "African King" in WN 1.1.11, 24). Thus, I conclude that granting that Smith is presupposing providentialism here, he is making this claim: even during the worst political times, the consumption of the rich will help the poor do better than in a pure Hobbesian state of nature.

Finally, "without intending it, without knowing it," the vain rich "advance the interest of the society, and afford means to the multiplication of the species." Does this conform to the four criteria that fit what I have called "Smithian social explanation"? Recall that these are as follows:

(i) It is causal.
(ii) It is a historical explanation—that is, (a) that the stable consequence would not have been in "view" (or predictable) to observers of human nature at an early time (and, so, not capable of being intended) and (b) that to be a cause does not require temporal contiguity between the cause and the effect.
(iii) Smith's account does require that after certain consequences become visible to observer-participants, they become self-reinforcing.
(iv) It supports counterfactuals.

It certainly fits (i), (ii[b]), and (iv), but I am not fully certain that it fits (ii[a]) and (iii).

First, let us consider (ii[a]). It is certainly the case that from *the point of view of the rich* (ii[a]) obtains; they neither know nor intend the consequences. But it does not mean that such knowledge would be, in principle, unavailable to humans at the time. At first sight there is little evidence to settle this either way. We do not find any hint that there are theoretical "men," who are fond "of appearing to understand what surpasses the comprehension of ordinary people" (WN 4.11.38, 678–9; see also Astronomy 4.33, 75) and who can settle this question on our behalf.

Yet, upon closer inspection of the invisible hand passage, Smith indicates that it does not require a sophisticated grasp of consequences to see what is going on in these circumstances; he explicitly appeals to "the homely and vulgar proverb, that the eye is larger than the belly, never was more fully verified than with regard to him." Like maxims, proverbs are accumulated folk wisdom (Levy 1992b: Levy and Peart 2004) Any human being can know (maybe from honest self-examination) that "the capacity of his stomach bears no proportion to the immensity of his desires."

Let us consider the other part of the claim, that

> The rest he is obliged to distribute among those, who prepare, in the nicest manner, that little which he himself makes use of, among those who fit up the palace in which this little is to be consumed, among

those who provide and keep in order all the different baubles and trinkets, which are employed in the oeconomy of greatness; all of whom
thus derive from his luxury and caprice, that share of the necessaries
of life, which they would in vain have expected from his humanity or
his justice.

This involves neither theoretical knowledge nor special observational skills. It
is true that (many of) the rich do not discern any of this; they are very partial
spectators of the consequences of their actions, but that's because they take
absolutely no interest in those who provide them with their goods. Elsewhere
Smith argues that under feudalism "The lords despised the [city] burghers,
whom they considered not only as of a different order, but as a parcel of emancipated slaves, almost of a different species from themselves" (WN 3.3.8, 402).
Thus, (ii[a]) does not obtain, and, therefore, this instance of the invisible hand
does not conform to the paradigmatic form of Smithian social explanation.

What about (iii)? Is this an instance of a self-reinforcing process? This is a bit
harder to evaluate from context alone. As it happens, the landlords' consumption of "different baubles and trinkets" is part of a *transformative* process that is,
in fact, self-reinforcing. In one of the great set-pieces of WN, Smith explains the
consequences of the landlords' consumption of "baubles and trinkets:"

> The tenants having in this manner become independent, and the
> retainers being dismissed, the great proprietors were no longer capa-
> ble of interrupting the regular execution of justice, or of disturbing the
> peace of the country. Having sold their birth-right, not like Esau for a
> mess of pottage in time of hunger and necessity, but in the wantonness
> of plenty, for trinkets and baubles, fitter to be the play-things of child-
> ren than the serious pursuits of men, they became as insignificant as
> any substantial burgher or tradesman in a city. A regular government
> was established in the country as well as in the city, nobody having suf-
> ficient power to disturb its operations in the one, any more than in the
> other. (WN 3.4.15, 421; see also WN 5.1.g.25, 803–4)

Thus, the invisible hand episode in TMS has an unexpected afterlife in WN with
quite unintended but also intrinsically unforeseeable consequences. In this
instance Smith's history reads like a Biblical morality play; the landlords lose their
authority by pursing unmanly ends.[1]

This opens the possibility that, in fact, there are two kinds of patterns of
unintended consequences in Smith's thought: (a) ones that are foreseeable by

---

[1] Smith treats the rise of royal power at the expense of aristocracy as a good thing because it
extends the reach of the rule of law ("a regular government was established in the country as well as
in the city.")

discerning spectators (and agents) in real time and (b) ones that are, in principle, only visible after the historical fact. Tentatively, I propose that when Smith uses the phrase "invisible hand," he has in mind (a) and not (b). Moreover, it seems that the paradigmatic form of Smithian social explanation (b) can include as a sub-component an invisible hand process (a). I now turn to the "invisible hand" passage in WN to show how it conforms to this hypothesis.

c. Promoting Unintended Ends in WN

In this section I argue that in WN the invisible hand is meant to illuminate how agents can produce regular outcome patterns that instantiate the theoretical link between (a) Smith's definition of a nation's wealth and (b) their own attempts at profit maximization, even if they are unaware of this theoretical link. Recognizing this will illuminate the significant differences between Smithian social explanations and invisible hand explanations.

In WN the "invisible hand" occurs in the midst of a withering attack on mercantilism and the merchants that profit from the policies promoted by it:

> But the annual revenue of every society is always precisely equal to the exchangeable value of the whole annual produce of its industry, or rather is precisely the same thing with that exchangeable value. As every individual, therefore, endeavours as much as he can both to employ his capital in the support of domestick industry, and so to direct that industry that its produce may be of the greatest value; every individual necessarily labours to render the annual revenue of the society as great as he can. He generally, indeed, neither intends to promote the publick interest, nor knows how much he is promoting it. By preferring the support of domestick to that of foreign industry, he intends only his own security; and by directing that industry in such a manner as its produce may be of the greatest value, he intends only his own gain, and he is in this, as in many other cases, led by an invisible hand to promote an end which was no part of his intention. Nor is it always the worse for the society that it was no part of it. By pursuing his own interest he frequently promotes that of the society more effectually than when he really intends to promote it. I have never known much good done by those who affected to trade for the publick good. It is an affectation, indeed, not very common among merchants, and very few words need be employed in dissuading them from it. What is the species of domestick industry which his capital can employ, and of which the produce is likely to be of the greatest value, every individual, it is evident, can, in his local situation, judge much better than any statesman or lawgiver can do for him. The statesman, who should attempt to direct private

people in what manner they ought to employ their capitals, would not only load himself with a most unnecessary attention, but assume an authority which could safely be trusted, not only to no single person, but to no council or senate whatever, and which would nowhere be so dangerous as in the hands of a man who had folly and presumption enough to fancy himself fit to exercise it. (WN 4.2.9, 455–6)

In polemical context Smith is arguing against mercantilist claims that a nation's "wealth consisted in gold and silver, and that those metals could be brought into a country which had no mines only by the balance of trade, or by exporting to a greater value than it imported" (WN 4.1.35, 450). These general mercantilist doctrines have been successfully marshaled by merchant/employer interests in favor of protectionist import tariffs—that is, "high duties, or by absolute prohibitions" (WN 4.2.1, 456) that "create monopoly of the home-market to the produce of domestick industry" (WN 4.2.11, 456). Thus, Smith is taking on intellectual doctrines that have supported *particular* producer interests against consumers, exporters, and nonprotected industries. In a letter to Smith, Burke describes how Wedgewood "pretends indeed that he is actuated, (and so he told me,) by nothing but a desire of the publick good" (May 1, 1775, Letter 145, Corr. 181).[2] But these protected producer interests have been able to appeal to mercantile *theory* to claim that protecting them is in the nation's interest because it is said to make the country wealthy. This is why the passage starts with Smith's alternative definition of national wealth, which is "the exchangeable value of the whole annual produce of its industry."

As the quoted "invisible hand" paragraph reveals, Smith also assumes that merchants aim to maximize profit. This is a property of being a merchant. Smith does not think everybody is (always) aiming to maximize profit; tor example, many landowners support laws that leave land "uncultivated" because these laws (progeniture, entail, etc.) maintain the "exclusive privilege of the nobility to the great offices and honours of their country" (WN 3.2.6–7, 385; of course these "offices and honours" can be profitable, too, but that's compatible with the point being made).

Moreover, in context Smith argues that "upon equal or nearly equal profits, every wholesale merchant naturally prefers the home-trade to the foreign trade of consumption, and the foreign trade of consumption to the carrying trade" (WN 4.2.6, 454). The reason for this universal ("every") preference is what we could call risk aversion. As Smith explains:

In the home-trade his capital is never so long out of his sight as it frequently is in the foreign trade of consumption. He can know better the character and situation of the persons whom he trusts, and if he

---

[2] In context, Wedgewood is opposing a patent by Champion, a friend of Burke's.

should happen to be deceived, he knows better the laws of the country from which he must seek redress. In the carrying trade, the capital of the merchant is, as it were, divided between two foreign countries, and no part of it is ever necessarily brought home, or placed under his own immediate view and command. (WN 4.2.6, 454. The "carrying trade" means shipping other people's goods to and from other countries—in Smith's time the Dutch were the main rivals for the British carrying trade.)

Now we can turn to a closer inspection of the "invisible hand" paragraph. In it Smith argues, first, that—*contra* the mercantilists, who are said to claim that a nation's wealth consists of its holdings of gold and silver—a nation's (economic) wealth consists in its ability to produce goods that can be sold: "the annual revenue of every society is always precisely equal to the exchangeable value of the whole annual produce of its industry, or rather is precisely the same thing with that exchangeable value." Therefore, at a given time a country aims to have the highest possible annual revenue given its capital. Now given this definition of wealth,[3] it follows trivially, as a conceptual truth, that anybody who increases the amount of stuff that can be sold (that is, that has exchange value) is also inevitably contributing to generating national economic wealth. (There are some non-trivial assumptions built into this claim, but that need not concern us here—below we will see that Smith also recognizes exceptions.) This is why Smith can simply assert that regardless of what the merchant says (and Smith suggests that we have little reason to believe there is much conviction when he is talking about trading in the national interest), the employer need not intend or know that he is promoting national wealth by intending to maximize his profits.

The reason why the merchant does not know he is contributing to national wealth by his profit-seeking activity is that he is laboring with a faulty ideology supplied by mercantilist theorists that are articulating his interests. Smith does not claim that the merchant can never know that his activities may contribute to national wealth; in fact, it follows from Smith's account that once the merchant is familiar with a correct (that is, *Smith's*) political economy, he can also intend to promote national wealth just in virtue of pursing maximal profit. This is not to deny that according to Smith "generally" there need not be such intent, just that sometimes there could be. In the "invisible hand" passage, Smith is not claiming that a "society" has no other "interests" than national wealth. Smith does say that by intending to maximize profit, merchants or employers "frequently" promote "the interests of" society more effectively than when they really intend to promote it." This explicitly and very carefully also allows that a merchant can promote other interests of society in other ways.

---

[3] It is very unusual that Smith insists on an equality rather than a proportionality in his technical economics. See Chapter 13 for details.

Before I turn to the status of the invisible hand, we should not ignore that the point of the passage is to insist that the government should not tell merchants how to pursue their economic affairs either directly (by edict) or indirectly (by tariffs and export bounties). Even the indirect means are, according to Smith, "evident violations of natural liberty, and therefore unjust" (WN 4.5.b.16, 531). It may be "evident," but in context Smith does not provide a moral argument (for more detail see Pack and Schliesser 2017).

Smith does have three other arguments for this "evident" claim. The first argument is epistemic: "every individual, it is evident, can, in his local situation, judge much better than any statesman or lawgiver can do for him." Given the extremely limited data available to eighteenth-century statesmen, Smith need not produce much more of an argument. I assume Smith also would have thought his claim evident even in circumstances where the government drowns in extremely fine-grained data because at bottom his claim is about the significance—to adapt (and slightly transform) a phrase introduced by Knud Haakonssen (1981: 79–82; see also Fiori 2001: 435)—of contextual judgment (see Smith's treatment at WN 4.2.11, 456). An outsider can rarely have the relevant skills appropriate to what I have been calling environmental rationality in most particular situations (here: "the species of domestick industry which his capital can employ, and of which the produce is likely to be of the greatest value"). As Smith puts it, individuals in "their local situations" must "generally be able to judge better … than the legislator can do" (WN 4.5.b.16, 531). Smith does not claim, however, that individuals are infallible judges of their own situation; they can "hurt" themselves, too (WN 4.5.b.16, 531).

The second argument is practical. The government would be taking on tasks that are not only unnecessary but also—Smith implies—burdensome. This means that the opportunity costs are going to be considerable for little or no gain.

The third argument is moral-political. Even if a government could overcome the epistemic barriers to directing individuals on how they should pursue their own economic interests, Smith claims that it still should not be given such "authority." It would be "dangerous," especially if the government is overconfident enough to pursue such interventions. Smith does not, in fact, explain what he has in mind, but he distrusts arbitrary (that is, non-rule-governed) government power and advocates that government should stay out of people's lives.

Just as he does in TMS, Smith deploys the phrase "invisible hand" in his own voice here. But what does the claim amount to? Here the unintended and unknown consequence that merchants bring about is fairly immediate and also, in principle, knowable to them once an aspect of the correct political economy becomes more widely known. It is in this respect very unlike the "very slow and gradual consequence of a certain propensity" (WN 1.2.1, 25) that I discussed in Section a of Chapter 2 or the "trinkets and baubles fitter to be the play-things of children" (WN 3.4.15, 421) passage I discussed in Section b above.

I elaborate on my view by contrasting it to Michel Foucault's analysis; he insists that Smith is committed to the claim that

> Everyone must be uncertain with regard to the collective outcome if this positive collective outcome is really to be expected. Being in the dark and the blindness of all the economic agents are absolutely necessary. The collective good must not be an objective ... Invisibility is not just a fact arising from the imperfect nature of human intelligence which prevents people from realizing that there is a hand behind them which arranges or connects everything that each individual does on their own account. Invisibility is absolutely indispensable. It is an invisibility which means that no economic agent should or can pursue the collective good. (Foucault 2008: 279–80)

Foucault conflates here two features in Smith. First, Smith's insistence that "never ... much good" is "done by those who affected to trade for the publick good" does not require that individuals do not know that if by legally pursuing profits for their own enterprise (in a competitive environment) they can indirectly promote the public interest. If that were right, then by Foucault's logic, Smith should have never published WN (in English). As we have seen, the reason why merchants do not know that they are contributing to national wealth by their profit-seeking activity is that they are laboring with a faulty ideology supplied by mercantilists in the service of merchants' interests. Regardless of what Smith may have thought about intervening in the course of history, he clearly did think that people could learn to understand their own situations in improved fashion.

Second, it also does not follow from Smith's account that the collective or "public" good can never be pursued. As George Stigler (1971) famously noted (and bemoaned), Smith's account of politics presupposes some public-spiritedness, at least when it comes to institutional design and rule-setting. Arguably, WN is a contribution to promoting such public-spiritedness in its readers against the (mercantile) "wretched spirit of monopoly" (WN 4.2.21, 461; 4.3.a.1, 474; 4.3.c.9–10, 493, etc.). As Smith put it in TMS:

> Nothing tends so much to promote public spirit as the study of politics, of the several systems of civil government, their advantages and disadvantages, of the constitution of our own country, its situation, and interest with regard to foreign nations, its commerce, its defence, the disadvantages it labours under, the dangers to which it may be exposed, how to remove the one, and how to guard against the other." (TMS 4.1.11, 186)

This is not to say that all genuinely "publick spirited purposes" are endorsed by Smith—sometimes these are undertaken by people with flawed business sense (WN 2.2.73, 313) or flawed economic theory (WN 5.1.e.40, 758).

Of course, Foucault is right that according to Smith no economic agent should by trading pursue the collective good. And Foucault is certainly right that according to Smith "it is impossible for the sovereign to have a point of view on the economic mechanism which totalizes every element and enables them to be combined artificially or voluntarily" (Foucault 2008: 280). As Smith puts it:

> [T]he sovereign is completely discharged from a duty, in the attempting to perform which he must always be exposed to innumerable delusions, and for the proper performance of which no human wisdom or knowledge could ever be sufficient; the duty of superintending the industry of private people and of directing it towards the employments most suitable to the interest of society. (WN, 4.9.51, 687; quoted by Foucault 2008: 281)

The claim that government cannot direct others in managing "the totality of the economic process" (Foucault 2008: 282) is, in fact, compatible with the sovereign being able to run a particular business at a profit (not that Smith recommends this generally): "The post-office, another institution for the same purpose, over and above defraying its own expence, affords in almost all countries a very considerable revenue to the sovereign" (WN 5.1.d.3, 724). Thus, first, Smith's fundamental argument against trading on behalf of the public good is, while certainly epistemic, ultimately moral as well. Second, his argument against the state's ability to superintend and direct individual economic agents is epistemic.

Even so, Foucault draws an interesting implication from Smith's account:

> Economics is an atheist discipline: economics is a discipline without God; economics is discipline without totality: economics is a discipline that begins to demonstrate not only the pointlessness, but also the impossibility of a sovereign point of view over the totality of the state that he has to govern. ... Liberalism acquired its modern shape precisely with the formation of this essential incompatibility between the non-totalizable multiplicity of economics subjects of interests and the totalizing unity of the juridical sovereign. (Foucault 2008: 282)

Of course, when he calls economics "an atheist discipline," Foucault does not mean that economics can prove the nonexistence of God (Foucault is certainly aware of the providential interpretation of the invisible hand [Foucault 2008: 278]). Rather, he means that at the core of Smith's science there is a commitment to a fundamental epistemic humility: the "totality" of economic activity is beyond our reach. But *this* authentic, Smithian claim is not made in the invisible hand passage; rather, it is made in Smith's concluding paragraphs of WN's Book 4, when he summarizes his fundamental criticism of mercantilism and physiocracy: "All systems either of preference or of restraint, therefore, being thus completely taken away, the obvious and simple system of natural liberty establishes itself of its own accord" (WN, 4.9.51, 687). The point of this instance of natural law doctrine[4] is neatly captured by Foucault: "the disqualification of the very possibility of an economic sovereign, amounts to a challenge to the police state ... it is the critique of this paradoxical idea of total economic freedom and absolute despotism which they physiocrats tried to maintain the theory of economic evidence" (Foucault 2008: 284, 286). If one follows this thought, one can say, then, that Ricardo (or Samuelson) made economics a "theist" (in Foucault's, not the ordinary, sense) discipline again despite Smith's best efforts otherwise.

In contrast to Foucault's analysis in WN, Smith clearly indicates that the invisible hand also applies to "many other cases," but this means it does not always do so. Smith is frustratingly vague about the character of those other cases, but one can say some things about the character of these nevertheless.

For example, we know that "the violence and injustice of the rulers of mankind" does not have positive unintended consequences. It has, after all, no "remedy" (WN 4.3.c.9, 493; recall my argument in Chapter 6 against the idea that Smith provides us with a theodicy). Smith never claims that in any given bad situation eventually good things will start to happen. Thus, if the "other cases" involve rulers, it must be in circumstances in which they, in pursuing their own perceived interests, either reduce their power for mischief or bring about the rule of law. Following Hume, Smith suggests that this happens when foreign luxury and a culture of conspicuous consumption are introduced in, say, feudal circumstances (WN 3.4.4, 412). But this case is also notably different from WN's invisible hand passage we are discussing here—the rulers who pursue their own interests are not, in fact, necessarily always adding to the national wealth (even if they have lots of other beneficial consequences). It would depend on the degree to which they were industrious or promoted industry (in adding to the exchange value of the country's annual produce) in order to pay for the foreign goods. If they were merely appropriating the fruits of other people's industry, then they are not, in fact, adding to the national wealth.

Thus, it appears as if in WN's "invisible hand" passage, the relevant "other cases" involve economic agents *qua* profit maximizers—that is, people who employ capital (this can be landowners, manufacturers, mine owners, and rulers *qua* farmers/landowners/owners of mines) and who—note the significance of "security" (WN 4.2.9, 455)!—have a reasonable expectation to keep the fruits of their labor (WN 4.5.b.43, 540). This is to say, given (a) Smith's definition of a nation's wealth, (b) profit maximizers, and—as Rosenberg emphasized in a classic 1960 article—(c) a certain institutional framework, then (d) the "invisible hand" will "frequently" lead to beneficial economic consequences to the nation.

---

[4] For Smith and natural law, see Haakonssen 1981 and Young 1997. For a nice introduction that treats Smith and Hayek as belonging to a continuous natural law tradition, see Angner 2007, especially Chapters 3 and 4. One can recognize natural law elements throughout Smith's writings without endorsing that he is a natural law philosopher.

By why only "frequently" and not always? In fact, Smith explicitly denies that all profit maximizers will produce beneficial economic consequences to the nation, and he names the species: they are in his terminology "projectors"—that is, economic agents who "promise" themselves "extraordinary profits." Smith claims that "more frequently, perhaps," this is not so (WN 1.10.b.43, 131–2; Levy 1987 nicely shows how Smith considers "projectors" as gamblers with other people's money). For some of the economic havoc that the "golden dreams" of "the most distinct vision of this great profit" (WN 2.2.69, 310) create, see WN 2.2.57–77, 304–17. Smith's hostility toward such projectors accounts for his defense of (modest) usury laws (WN 2.4.15, 357ff); that is, legal restrictions on interest. Bentham famously argued against Smith's argument (see Levy 1987 and Hollander 1999 for excellent treatments). Moreover, as noted above, Smith also denies that all economic agents are, in fact, profit maximizers. Giant landlords who have inherited their estates are also unlikely to be good at estate management (WN 3.2.7, 385; see Rashid 2009); slaveholding continues when "the law allows it," despite its lack of profitability, because of prideful humanity's "love" of domineering (WN, 4.7.b.62, 589).

What has been shown here? For Smith there are theoretical reasons to believe that if (a) through (c) hold, in fact, then it is trivially the case that capitalists can, by pursuing their own profit-seeking interests (reliably, but not necessarily), contribute to the nation's wealth without even knowing or intending the consequence. But there is no evidence in WN that when (a) through (c) are absent, we are still in the realm of "invisible hand" explanations. This is because in WN the backbone of Smith's invisible hand is the theoretical link between (a) and (b). Without these there is—to use Smith's phrase—"no connecting chain" (recall Astronomy, 3.2–3, EPS 49–50!) to link the phenomena.

In particular, there is no evidence that Smith's treatment of the division of labor that is a consequence of a "very slow and gradual consequence of a certain propensity" (WN 1.2.1, 25) is also an instance of an invisible hand explanation because there is no equivalent theory (to the relationship between (a) and (b)) that can link the propensities to the consequences. For (recall from Section a of Chapter 2), these are an instance of "historical explanation," and one significant feature of a historical explanation, as I understand it, is (recall) that the stable consequence would not have been in "view" (or predictable) to observers of human nature at an early time (and, so, not capable of being intended), but only visible retrospectively after the fact. In Sections c and d of Chapter 12, I round out my treatment of Smithian social explanation.

d. Comparing the Three Invisible Hands

I conclude that in TMS and WN Smith uses the "invisible hand" in consistent fashion to describe a very particular kind of mechanism. Any given iteration of such a mechanism is a relatively short-term process in which the agent produces unintended and to him unknown consequences. Of course, with relatively stable background conditions the invisible hand process can be repeated indefinitely. Crucially, the consequences are, in principle, knowable to the right kind of observer at the time either theoretically informed or by accumulated common sense.

We can say that Smithian invisible hand processes are, in fact, cases where the agent could have known better in an epistemic sense. However, the moral valence of the two cases in TMS and WN is not the same: the profit-maximizing businessman is being prudent and by acting prudently serves the greater good (given the larger institutional context) regardless of his intentions of doing so, while the unfeeling landlord is acting without propriety and misses his opportunity to serve the good (in manly fashion, etc.), although the end result may be for the best.

Moreover, Smithian invisible hand processes are not identical to Smithian social explanation. The latter are cases where the consequences are visible or knowable only after the fact. Generally, to complete the process they take place over much longer amounts of time than any given invisible hand process. Smithian social explanations can include invisible hand processes as sub-components (or mechanisms) but should not be conflated with these.

Thus, at first blush, conceptually there seems to be no connection at all between the invisible hand of Jupiter and Smith's invisible hand in TMS and WN. In TMS and WN Smith's invisible hand is not an error theory, but a truth hidden from agents that they could have known. Moreover, while Smith clearly signals that he finds the attribution of particular providence superstitious, he seems to allow the implication that the invisible hand in TMS and WN is at least somewhat in the service of larger processes that promote general providence. After all, in both TMS and WN the invisible hand promotes "the multiplication of the species." This conforms nicely to "the propagation of the species" as one of (two of) "the great ends" which the "great Director of nature intended to produce" (TMS 2.1.5.10, 77–8; this is compatible with their being more ends for us humans). So, it seems that Smith claims that when we uncover the sometimes hidden mechanisms of nature, we discern features of general providence (as Viner initially insisted; in recent times Evensky has argued this case).

Nevertheless, it is peculiar that Smith insists that multiplication is the great providential end while "to invent and improve all the sciences and arts, which ennoble and embellish human life" is merely a byproduct. Smith never claims that the worship or love of God or doing good deeds promotes the intended outcome of providence.

If there is a connection between the invisible hand of Jupiter and Smith's invisible hand, it can only be made visible by reflection on Smith's philosophy of science and his understanding of the nature of philosophy more generally. This is because we left a crucial question hanging in our treatment in Section a in discussing the displacement of "the lowest and most pusillanimous superstition" by philosophy; this is compatible with Smith's claiming *either* that with natural philosophy we move to civilized noble truths *or* that natural philosophy itself is a species of magnanimous superstition. Thus, before I turn to a closer analysis of the methods of WN, I offer a detailed account of what we might call Smith's "philosophy of science" or his "historical and social epistemology."

11

Philosophy of Science

In this chapter I articulate Smith's philosophy of science. In the first section I emphasize the significance of his social conception of science—science takes place, not always comfortably, within a larger society and is itself a social enterprise in which our emotions play a crucial role. Even so, throughout the chapter I also emphasize that Smith views science ultimately in terms of a reason-giving enterprise, akin to how he understands the role of the impartial spectator. In the second and third sections I explain Smith's attitude to theorizing and its relationship, if any, to Humean skepticism. I argue first that Smith distinguishes between considerations that go into theory acceptance and those that enter the possibility of criticism; I also argue that while Smith accepts fallibilism and is in many respects a proto-Kuhnian (embracing scientific revolutions and even instances of psychological incommensurability), his philosophy is not an embrace of Humean skepticism (or skeptical realism). I argue that his is a modest realism. In the final section I explore the implications of Smith's analysis of scientific systems as machines. I argue that while he shares with Hume the wish that science can be a kind of neutral instrument in establishing facts of the world, he may not have shared Hume's hope that science could ever be a completely neutral instrument in deciding questions about the factual existence of a deity.

a. Philosophy Within the Division of Labor

Recall that during the eighteenth century, "science," "philosophy," and "natural philosophy" tend to be used interchangeably; Smith is no exception. To characterize Smith's views I generally follow his practice unless I note my deviation explicitly. In this section I argue that according to Smith science takes place within a larger, sometimes hostile social context.

According to Smith, "Philosophy is the science of connecting principles of nature" (Astronomy 2.12, EPS 45). Philosophy is just one trade among many. In the first chapter of the first book of WN, Smith prominently includes "philosophers" as being part of the division of labor (WN 1.1.9, 21–2); shortly thereafter he derides their "vanity" to think otherwise (WN 1.2.4, 29). Thus, philosophy takes place within society; it is possible only after "law has established order and security, and subsistence ceases to be precarious, the curiosity of mankind is increased, and their fears diminished. The leisure which they then enjoy renders them more attentive to the appearance of nature" (Astronomy 3.3, EPS 50). Moreover, Smith's invocation of philosophy as one among many trades and his emphasis on the lack of difference between the "philosopher and common street porter" (WN 1.2.4, 28) signals at the start of WN that his theorizing also applies to the "trade and occupation" of "speculation" (WN 1.1.9, 21; on this theme, see Levy 1992b; Peart and Levy 2005).

According to Smith, the philosopher's trade is "not to do any thing, but to observe every thing; and, who, upon that account, are often capable of combining together the powers of the most distant and dissimilar objects" (WN 1.1.9, 21). In principle, philosophy has the most comprehensive perspective of nature in order to successfully intervene in nature. Thus, Smith understands philosophy not as primarily speculative, but as a theory-driven, action-enabling (combining the powers of distant objects) activity.[1] Sometimes Smith emphasizes the technological benefits of philosophy by way of "improvements in machinery" (WN 1.1.9, 21; Aspromourgos 2013: 269). But only "some" of the improvements are said to result from men of speculation; "many" are due to "the makers of the machines" (WN 1.1.9, 21). In TMS the tendency to emphasize the usefulness of the "abstruser sciences" is explained as a *post facto* rhetorical response to depreciation of those who have "no taste for such sublime discoveries" (Hume's treatment of Newton in "Of the Middle Station of Life" may be Smith's target). Elsewhere Smith writes, "the most precise knowledge of the relative situation of" very distant objects "could be of no other use than to satisfy the most unnecessary curiosity" (External Senses, 51, EPS 151). Of course, even the most abstruse sciences may have some use: "The utility of those sciences, either to the individual or to the public, is not very obvious, and to prove it requires a discussion which is not always very easily comprehended" (TMS 4.2.7, 189).

In fact, according to Smith, the origins of philosophy are not really well understood by the action-enabling activities: "Wonder . . . and not any expectation of advantage from its discoveries, is the first principle which prompts mankind to the study of philosophy . . . and they pursue this study for its own sake, as an original pleasure or good in itself, without regarding its tendency to procure them the means of other pleasures" (Astronomy 3.3, EPS 51). Thus, on Smith's account, any given philosopher might well understand philosophy as a purely theoretical enterprise with intrinsic worth, but to do so is in fact not to have the wider view that is characteristic of philosophy; one misses an essential feature: philosophy's capacity to facilitate harnessing natural powers (living and non-living). Such a philosopher is like the merchant who operates with a false (mercantile) theory about the

---

[1] To prefigure one of my later conclusions: note Smith's use of "powers." Whatever these turn out to be, they are real entities that can be manipulated by those in the know.

nature of natural wealth (discussed in Section c of Chapter 10). Therefore, from a contemporary perspective one can say that according to Smith theoretical reason is pursued as an intrinsic good that has come to have as a *foreseeable* byproduct technological improvements.

Such a blindness to the wider perspective on philosophy's nature among philosophers may itself be the consequence of stage-dependent economic prosperity. Smith agrees with Hume (cf. "The Rise and Progress of the Arts and Sciences") that "in the progress of society," philosophy becomes a specialist trade, itself "subdivided into a great number of different branches, each of which affords occupation to a peculiar tribe or class of philosophers" (WN 1.1.9, 21–2). In fact, it is only after the "progress of refinement" (that is, at a relatively late stage of civilization) that "philosophy and rhetoric came into fashion." Then the "better sort of people ... send their children to the schools of philosophers and rhetoricians, in order to be instructed in the fashionable sciences" (WN 5.1.f.43, 777). The division of labor that enables the growth of opulence creates conditions that stimulate interest in philosophy, which itself must be cultivated: "for a long time," "demand for it" was "small" (WN 5.1.f.43, 777). Once there is a larger demand for philosophy, this enables the division of labor within philosophy, which, in turn, leads to improvements in machinery that enhance productivity, the division of labor, and a virtuous cycle of opulence (see C. Smith 2006). All of this is conducive to mark philosophy off as a trade among many within society.

Once specialization has taken place among philosophers, one might wonder how is it possible "to observe every thing" and combine "together the powers of the most distant and dissimilar objects." As we have seen at the start of WN, the division of labor causes us to have very partial views of the whole (WN 1.1.2, 14; see Levy 1995). So how can philosophers be proper philosophers if they participate in the division of labor? This issue only becomes more pressing if one thinks that the content of somebody's philosophy tends to represent his or her partial, class-interest "progress of opulence" (WN 4.intro.2, 428; recall the discussion in Chapter 8).

Given Smith's account of philosophy, what claim can it make to comprehensiveness, impartiality, and truth? Because Smith's own ambitions as a systematic philosopher were announced in the last paragraph of the first edition of TMS (1759), and reaffirmed in the "Advertisement" to the last edition (1790), we also may formulate this as a problem about how Smith understands his own theoretical activity.

To put the issue in terms of the concepts being developed in this book: from the perspective of environmental rationality (that is, in a properly functioning person) there is a reciprocal relationship between the habituated mental anticipations and sound judgment (recall my discussion in Section c of Chapter 3), the relationship between environmental rationality and philosophy is not straightforward. This is because environmental rationality tends *not* to be trained up on the "most distant and dissimilar objects." According to Smith, philosophy starts in two species of wonder, and wonder is the unpleasant passion that opens up the possibility for adjusting existing environmental rationality (recall the treatment of the intellectual passions in Section e of Chapter 3). It turns out that the "great objects" in the heavens supply the first philosophical systems according to Smith (Astronomy 4.1, EPS 53), but one's ordinary environmental rationality is generally not cultivated observing the stars (even if one allows that within Ancient civilizations folk may have been more attentive to them for navigational and hunting needs).

Recall that the content of the first species of wonder is: <a painful uncertainty, lack of filling-location in the natural taxonomy (for the idea of the triggering object)>. This content produces a quite vehement physiologic and behavioral response. Unlike most of the natural sentiments, which are fitted toward highly specific triggering objects, the intellectual sentiments are observer-relative:

> The same orders of succession, which to one set of men seem quite according to the natural course of things, and such as require no intermediate events to join them, shall to another appear altogether incoherent and disjointed, unless some such events be supposed: and this for no other reason, but because such orders of succession are familiar to the one, and strange to the other. (Astronomy 2.11, EPS 44)

The expert eye and the untrained eye do not see the same "things," and consequently they have different occasions for wonder (Astronomy 2.2, EPS 38). Therefore, technical skill and theoretical reason involve a reshaping of what I have been calling "environmental rationality." But this can create circumstances in which what may seem sound judgment to the non-expert is discerned otherwise by the expert (and vice versa). The manifest and scientific image can come into conflict, after all (Sellars 1963).

Moreover, since Socrates' trial, if not Anaxagoras's banishment, philosophy's relationship to society is not as unproblematic as Smith seems to suggest here. It's not only the philosophers' "vanity" that causes them to think they are different from the ordinary bulk of mankind: even in classical Athens the activities of philosophers can lead to negative reactions. (This is the conceit behind the dialogue in Section XI of Hume's First *Enquiry*.) Smith knows this. He writes, for example, that "in Ancient times some philosophers" of the "Italian School" (that is, Pythagoreans) taught their doctrines to pupils only "under the seal of the most sacred secrecy, that they might avoid the fury of the people, and not incur the imputation of impiety" (Astronomy 4.4, 55–6). And, in WN he notes that the "schools" of the philosophers "were not supported by the publick. They were for a long time barely tolerated by it" (WN 5.1.f.43, 777). In fact, one may think that philosophers' emphasis on the usefulness of their activities is precisely the rhetorical response required to society's disapproval (TMS 4.2.7, 189; cf. WN 5.1.f.43, 778). Smith taught a regular class on rhetoric while he was a professor at

Glasgow; he is aware of its power (Ross 1995: 128ff; for important discussion, see Brown 1994 and Fleischacker 2004: 12–5).

Smith's comment on the Italian School echoes a claim by John Toland (offered in the context of his genealogy of the immortality of the soul):

> But in all sects there never wanted particular persons who really opposed the soul's immortality, though they might accommodate their ordinary language to the belief of the people: for most of the philosophers (as we read) had two sorts of doctrines, the one internal and the other external, or the one private and the other public; the latter to be indifferently communicated to all the world, and the former only very cautiously to their best friends, or to some few others capable of receiving it, and that would not make any ill use of the same. Pythagoras himself did not believe the transmigration which has made him so famous to posterity, for in the internal or secret doctrine he meant no more than the eternal revolution of forms in matters, those ceaseless vicissitudes and alternations, which turns everything into all things and all things into anything, as vegetables and animals become part of us, we become part of them, and both become parts of a thousand other things in the universe. (Toland, *Letters to Serena*, II. 56–7; I have modernized Toland's spelling)

In context, Toland bases his claim about Pythagoras on an interpretation of Timaeus Locrus. In his account of the "systems of nature," Smith remarks in passing, "The same notion, of the spontaneous origin of the world, was embraced, too, as the same author tells us, by the early Pythagoreans, a sect, which, in the antient world, was never regarded as irreligious" (Ancient Physics 9, EPS 113; in context, Smith is citing Aristotle's *Metaphysics*).

Therefore, regardless of whether Smith has read Toland (Smith is notoriously ungenerous in his citations [Rashid 1990]), he is aware of the existence of a Toland-like claim about the Pythagoreans, and a few lines down Smith also cites Toland's source, Timaeus Locrus. One might think from these lines that Smith thinks that Pythagorean esotericism is a modern invention (of, say, Toland), to be rejected by more careful readings. But as we have seen, in his own voice Smith affirms that in Ancient times some philosophers of the "Italian School" taught their doctrines to pupils only "under the seal of the most sacred secrecy, that they might avoid the fury of the people, and not incur the imputation of impiety" (Astronomy 4.4, 55–6; according to Smith, in addition to Pythagoras, the major figures in the school consist of "Empedocles, . . . Archytas, . . . Timaeus, and . . . Ocellus the Lucanian").

Smith, thus, explicitly accepts that at least some philosophers taught esoteric doctrines in order to avoid popular condemnation. Smith also contests it about others; see his very long footnote on Plato at EPS 122. My point here is not to insist that such readings about the Pythagorean school are right; rather, we cannot ignore that it seems to be a trope in the eighteenth century. Such tropes about esoteric teachings are not inventions of the eighteenth century, however: we find the attribution of an esoteric doctrine explicitly in Cicero's widely read dialogue *On the Nature of the Gods*; there one of the speakers says, "undoubtedly closer to truth is the claim made the fifth book of his 'Nature of the Gods' by Posidonius, whose friendship we all share: that Epicurus does not believe in any gods, and that the statements which he made affirming the immortal gods were made to avert popular odium" (Cicero, *De Natura Deorum* 1.123). Either way, Smith is aware that society can be hostile to philosophical doctrines; he knew of the troubles of his teacher, Hutcheson, and his friend, Hume, directed to them by religious fanatics. As is well known, Smith refused to publish Hume's Dialogues, but his obituary, a "very harmless Sheet of paper, which I happened to Write concerning the death of our late friend Mr Hume, brought upon me ten times more abuse than the very violent attack I had made upon the whole commercial system of Great Britain" (Letter 208, To Andreas Hold, October 1780, Corr. 251).

The point here is not to draw implications of Smith's interest in esotericism to make claims about his own mode of presentation. Rather, I introduce the material to argue that Smith is clearly aware that the potential conflict between the manifest and scientific image can be quite significant, and that he is familiar with the material that suggests that corrections to expectations built into environmental rationality in light of scientific developments need not be a smooth process. As I argue in the next section, for Smith science is embedded in society and it has itself a social dimension.

b. Social Epistemology and the Impartial Spectator

In this section I explore the details of Smith's social epistemology and the roles of the intellectual sentiments in it. I focus on the role of scientific legislators who initiate scientific revolutions and on how Smith conceptualizes their role in changing the norms of scientific inquiry. Along the way, I emphasize that according to Smith the aesthetic sentiments are not by themselves necessarily truth-apt even in a rigorous mathematical-scientific context.

For Smith, philosophy is originally aimed at calming the imagination: "Philosophy . . . endeavours to introduce order into this chaos of jarring and discordant appearances, to allay this tumult of the imagination" (Astronomy 2.12, EPS 45–6). In WN, when Smith discusses "natural and moral philosophy" (5.1.f.26, 767–70), he emphasizes, echoing Astronomy, how they both originate in wonder and curiosity (WN 5.1.f.24, 767), and that they appeal, at least in part, to the "beauty of a systematical arrangement" (5.1.f.25, 768; on the importance of beauty and aesthetic considerations in what we would call science and philosophy, see also TMS 1.1.4.3, 20, and Astronomy 4.13, EPS 62).

In Section e of Chapter 3 I treated Smith's account of the intellectual sentiments in relative isolation from the social context of inquiry, but this is not Smith's stance toward the life of the mind. Smith notes that theoretical "men are fond of paradoxes, and of appearing to understand what surpasses the comprehension of ordinary people" (WN 4.9.38, 678–9; see also Astronomy 4.33, EPS 75). It is "admiration" that generates applause for the "intellectual virtues" (TMS 1.1.4.3, 20; on "admiration," see also Astronomy Intro.5–7, EPS 34, and 4.5, EPS 56ff; WN 4.9.38, 678–9). Throughout his writings on science, Smith always calls attention to the significance of status seeking (that is, obtaining admiration). Given that philosophy is just one of the trades, his account of admiration fits nicely with the psychology of "professional" ambition in WN, which is articulated in terms of the desire to emulate and eagerness to gain public admiration (5.1.f.4, 759–60; 1.10.b.23–5, 123–4). To be clear, the admiration for one's intellectual virtues need not be derived from just anybody: "attracting the attention of scarce any body but the most studious and careful observer. They are the wise and the virtuous chiefly, a select, though, I am afraid, but a small party, who are the real and steady admirers of wisdom and virtue" (TMS 1.3.3.2, 62). Not all spectators, not even all the neutral ones, are studious.

Thus, while it is not utility or love of gain that prompts and sustains theoretical activity, love of (exploring seeming) paradox, the desire to extinguish wonder, love of admiration, and the appeal of beauty are far more important motivational pulls. Because some of these involve the *moral* sentiments (or derived passions), they involve reliable expectations about responses by others. Expected social passions are, in fact, governed by norms (recall Section e of Chapter 3); they are cultivated sentiments. Thus, perhaps inspired by Hume (Treatise 1.4.1.2), Smith's understanding of people engaged in inquiry involves the social nature of inquiry itself and (in addition) its relationship to a wider social world.

Philosophical or scientific inquiry is like all the other professions: "rivalry and emulation will render excellency . . . an object of ambition, and frequently occasion the very greatest exertions" (WN 5.1.f.4,759–60). All people, including philosophers, routinely desire and seek approval from others. Smith emphasizes that philosophers may be motivated by desire for the right kind of (sometimes posthumous) fame (TMS 3.2.8, 117; D'Alembert 1995: 93 also has no doubt about this).

If one is a member of a community with fairly exact and clear standards and one's actions accord with those values, the need for overt public approval diminishes because one feels a sense of self-approval and security in one's behavior; one knows, as Smith claims to be "probable" of Newton, that one is *praiseworthy* even in the absence of public praise—the mind is tranquil in its "independency" of public opinion (TMS 3.2.20, 124; cf. 3.3.30–3, 149–52). Smith believes that success in mathematics and natural philosophy admits "either of clear demonstration, or very satisfactory proof" (TMS 3.2.18, 123; 4.2.7, 189). Once mathematicians and natural philosophers have internalized the criteria and methods of "clear demonstration, or very satisfactory proof" valued by their disciplines, they need not worry about public opinion—because they have already adopted the perspective of the impartial spectator. Smith does not think that mathematicians or natural philosophers are by nature either prone to less uncertainty or better at internalizing norms than others; there are just relatively clear standards in these fields. Smith contrasts such fields (with "clear demonstration, or very satisfactory proof") with the "very noble and beautiful arts, in which the degree of excellence can be determined only by a certain nicety of taste, of which the decisions, however, appear always, in some measure, uncertain" (TMS 3.2.18, 123). To be sure, Smith does not deny here that there are standards in the arts.

Sometimes there are competing *technical* standards within the sciences: for example, Smith points out that the Copernican system was accepted by "astronomers only" but that the "learned in all other sciences, continued to regard it with the same contempt as the vulgar" (Astronomy 4.36, EPS 77). Smith thinks that "the coherence, which it bestowed upon the celestial appearances, the simplicity and uniformity which it introduced into the real directions and velocities of the Planets," attracted the astronomers to the Copernican system that "thus connected together so happily, the most disjointed of those objects that chiefly occupied their thoughts." Meanwhile, philosophers concerned with local terrestrial motion dreamed up objections against it (Astronomy 4.38, EPS 77–9). This delayed the adoption of the Copernican hypothesis. Thus, a focus on different domains of study can lead different groups of experts to embrace different standards of evidence and systems (Skinner 1996: 44).

Smith acknowledges that sometimes the better theory need not gain such acceptance among nonspecialists and the "vulgar" (Astronomy 4.35–8, EPS 76–8), who, for example, exhibit the "prejudice of mankind" and the "prejudice of sense, confirmed by education" against Copernicanism. Smith believes that the educated are not immune from the "prejudices" of the vulgar; when some such beliefs are "natural," they could even corrupt the thinking of Aristotle, the most "renowned philosopher" (Ancient Physics 10, EPS 116; cf. Hanley 2010, who uses these passages for an argument that Smith adopts the Humean framework of natural beliefs in the service of so-called skeptical realism [see Section c below]). Smith here is willing to suggest that from a certain theoretical standpoint, ordinary environmental rationality, which is constitutive of good judgment about ordinary affairs, is itself a prejudice in need of correction.

In particular, Smith does not ignore the situation in which natural philosophers, such as Descartes, Galileo, or Newton, attempt to change or legislate new criteria for a scientific community. He is mindful of the existence of those scientific legislators:

> It is the acute and delicate discernment of the man of taste, who distinguishes the minute, and scarce perceptible difference of beauty and deformity; it is the comprehensive accuracy of the experienced mathematician, who unravels, with ease, the most intricate and perplexed

proportions; *it is the great leader in science and taste, the man who directs and conducts our own sentiments*, the extent and superior justness of whose talents astonish us with wonder and surprise, who excites our admiration, and seems to deserve our applause: and upon this foundation is grounded the greater part of the praise which is bestowed upon what are called the intellectual virtues. (TMS 1.1.4.3, 20; emphasis added)

The "great leader in science" is no mere problem solver or theory constructer; he understands existing norms in a fundamental way. Smith also implies that "the leader ... who directs and conducts our own sentiments" sets standards for others to emulate. Some great scientists do not merely conform to existing values, but introduce new standards. He describes them as "splendid characters, the men who have performed the most illustrious actions, who have brought about the greatest revolutions, both in situations and opinions of mankind" (TMS 6.3.28, 250; he calls Hume the "most illustrious philosopher" at WN 5.i.g.3, 790).

So, when a natural philosopher contemplates and presents his results, this involves reference to the norms of one's intellectual community: the impartial spectator within anticipates how a scientist's (idealized) audience will judge a new theory, and provides self-approbation (TMS 3.2.3, 114) and tranquility (Astronomy 4.13, EPS 61), as well as sometimes an expectation about the reaction of ordinary people. Of course, when a natural philosopher proposes changes in the standards of an intellectual community, then such tranquility can be expected if and only if one imagines that the impartial spectator will eventually approve of one's improvements; sometimes one's imagination will project such approbation on to posterity (TMS 1.3.1.14, 48–9 and 6.3.5, 238–9).

According to Smith there are, in practice, two kinds of standards by which one judges one's efforts (recall also Section f of Chapter 5):

> The one is the idea of exact propriety and perfection, so far as we are each of us capable of comprehending that idea. The other is that degree of approximation to this idea which is commonly attained in the world, and which the greater part of our friends and companions, of our rivals and competitors, may have actually arrived at. We very seldom (I am disposed to think, we never) attempt to judge of ourselves without giving more or less attention to both these different standards ... In all the liberal and ingenious arts, in painting, in poetry, in music, in eloquence, in philosophy, the greatest artist feels always the real imperfection of his own best works, and is more sensible than any man how much they fall short of that ideal perfection of which he has some conception, which he imitates as well as he can, but which he despairs of ever equalling ... [Boileau said] no great man was ever completely satisfied with his own works. (TMS 6.3.23–6, 247–8; see also TMS 1.1.5.9, 26)

Hence, on Smith's account the great scientist is satisfied only when he (momentarily) compares his own work to that of his peers—hat is, when he directs his imitative attention toward the second standard (Chandler 2013). The first standard can always inspire critical reflection. In Section b of Chapter 3, I argued that according to Smith we innately start, in part, with "some conception"—not the whole concept—of the "idea of exact propriety and perfection" (cf. Hanley 2013: 233). If one does not find my argument persuasive there, one has to claim that Smith assumes that all individuals, or the subcultures they belong to, have access to some such immanent criticism. That's not an implausible assumption. (He may have thought the problem was solved in Hume's Treatise 1.2.4.24–5). Either way, "real imperfection" is present in all of man's works, so there will always be room for criticism (see also TMS 1.1.5.8, 25). This is the source of Smith's fallibilism.

In fact, the possibility of criticism is crucial to understanding Smith's stance toward theoretical reason. Smith calls attention to how natural philosophy is a discursive practice offering reasons to adopt a theory (External Senses 12, EPS 137; see also Wightman 1975: 61. For the general importance of persuasion in Smith's thought, see Fleischacker 2004, 92–4). This resembles how Smith treats the moral deliberation of our impartial spectator within when, say, we attempt to act with self-command and propriety. This is why he represents the impartial spectator as a "voice" of "reason" (TMS 3.3.4, 137). Smith identifies simplicity, coherence, distinctness, comprehensibility, lack of reasonable competitors, and predicting the phenomena among such reasons within natural philosophy (External Senses 18, EPS 140; Astronomy 4.15, EDPS 63–4); many of these are still a staple in any discussion of theoretical virtues. Thus, according to Smith, theory acceptance in natural philosophy is not driven merely by arbitrary appeals to the passions and sentiments. (For a similar conclusion, but with a different argument, see Skinner 1996: 41.) Natural philosophy is, in addition to all kinds of evidential practices, an ongoing conversation with appeals to the intellectual, cultivated judgments of the participants in light of sometimes conflicting epistemic virtues. (See Fleischacker 1999 for the important role of judgment in Smith.)

One of my favorite examples of Smith's commitment to such a critical stance is exhibited by a very subtle criticism of Isaac Newton in Astronomy: Smith remarks at length on the adoption of the Copernican system. While Smith is not blind to the efforts by Kepler and Galileo or Descartes and Gassendi, the crucial episode in his narrative is his treatment of the status of the post-Galilean contribution of the astronomer Cassini. When Smith first drafted Astronomy (probably in the 1740s), Cassini's son and grandson were, in fact, known for opposing Newton's view on the shape of the Earth advocated by Maupertuis in a celebrated dispute that Smith alludes to in Astronomy (4.73, EPS 101).

Smith explains that Cassini's observations, which establish that the four known satellites of Jupiter and the five known satellites of Saturn obey Kepler's equal area rule and Kepler's harmonic rule, were regarded by most astronomers and natural philosophers (he mentions Voltaire, Cardinal of Polignac, McLaurin [*sic*]) as decisive "demonstration" for the Copernican hypothesis. As Smith notes, even Newton seems to appeal to it as a source of "principal evidences for the truth of" the Copernican "hypothesis" (4.58, EPS 90–1). The appeal is to the preservation of the "analogy of nature"—that is, to the similarity between the orbits of the planets around the sun, and the moons of Jupiter and Saturn around these respective planets. This analogy does not hold in the Ptolemaic and Tychonic systems. So far so good.

As an important, clarificatory aside, this analogical use of Cassini's observations is an extension of the Galilean arguments from analogy that Philo admires so much in Hume's Dialogues. On Philo's views such arguments would provide more proofs for the fortifications supporting Copernican theory. Cleanthes and Philo have a heated exchange in which Philo explains how he understands the status of Copernicanism:

[Cleanthes:] And a caviller might raise all the same objections to the Copernican system, which you have urged against my reasonings. Have you other earths, might he say, which you have seen to move? Have . . .

Yes! cried Philo, interrupting him, we have other earths. Is not the moon another earth, which we see to turn round its centre? Is not Venus another earth, where we observe the same phenomenon? Are not the revolutions of the sun also a confirmation, from analogy, of the same theory? All the planets, are they not earths, which revolve about the sun? Are not the satellites moons, which move round Jupiter and Saturn, and along with these primary planets round the sun? These analogies and resemblances, with others which I have not mentioned, are the sole proofs of the Copernican system; and to you it belongs to consider, whether you have any analogies of the same kind to support your theory.

In reality, Cleanthes, continued he, the modern system of astronomy is now so much received by all enquirers, and has become so essential a part even of our earliest education, that we are not commonly very scrupulous in examining the reasons upon which it is founded. It is now become a matter of mere curiosity to study the first writers on that subject, who had the full force of prejudice to encounter, and were obliged to turn their arguments on every side in order to render them popular and convincing. But if we peruse Galileo's famous Dialogues concerning the system of the world, we shall find, that that great genius, one of the sublimest that ever existed, first bent all his endeavours to prove, that there was no foundation for the distinction commonly made between elementary and celestial substances. The schools, proceeding from the illusions of sense, had carried this distinction very far; and had established the latter substances to be impenetrable, incorruptible, unalterable, impassible; and had assigned all the opposite qualities to the former. But Galileo, beginning with the moon, proved its similarity in every particular to the earth; its convex figure, its natural darkness when not illuminated, its density, its distinction into solid and liquid, the variations of its phases, the mutual illumina- tions of the earth and moon, their mutual eclipses, the inequalities of the lunar surface, etc. After many instances of this kind, with regard to all the planets, men plainly saw that these bodies became proper objects of experience; and that the similarity of their nature enabled us to extend the same arguments and phenomena from one to the other." (Dialogues 2.26–27)

Philo and Cleanthes *agree* that the positive argument on behalf of Copernicanism is *strictly* analogical. These arguments go beyond *mere* analogy, because there are converging arguments for the claim that the Earth is one planet among others. The analogical evidence is, thus, in modern terminology robust; this is why these argu- ments provide "proofs." "Proof" is the highest epistemic category for matters of fact in Hume's system (see, especially, the footnote at the start of EHU 6; it falls a bit short of demonstrable certainty, but that is unattainable for factual matters). These are said to offer "confirmation" of Copernican theory. Philo is careful, however, not to claim that these provide a "certain proof" (the highest form of certainty in matters of fact; for this locution, see e.g., Dialogues 9.11).

Silvia Manzo (2009) has nicely shown that Hume almost certainly consulted Galileo's *Dialogues* in composing this passage.[2] Philo points out that if one wishes to understand theory acceptance one often finds the most detailed arguments in favor of a doctrine in the theory's early days because they have to overcome steady opposition if not downright skepticism. Philo is clearly charmed by Galileo, whom he calls "one of the sublimest" geniuses that ever existed.[3] No doubt Philo (and probably Hume) also finds Galileo's anti-clericalism and anti-authoritarianism appealing. Because Philo (and Cleanthes does not demur) also claims Galileo's analogical arguments are the "sole" proofs for Copernicanism, he also appears unaware of the fact that after Huygens and Newton, qualitatively different kinds

---

[2] There are some differences between Salviati and Philo, however. Where Salviati blames "Aristotle" for the distinction between "celestial and elementary … parts," Philo blames "the schools" for the distinction between "elementary and celestial … substances." Besides a subtle shift in culprits, note the reversal of order and the move from parts to substances. A more important difference is that Philo attributes the origin of the schools' mistake to "the illusions of sense" whereas Salviati attributes Aristotle's mistake to the "diversity of local motions." This difference is not a mere rhetorical or stylis- tic flourish, but a change in content. While Salviati and Philo are both offering an error-theory, Salviati explains that the error is due to the complex nature of the phenomena; Philo is making a skeptical point. For Salviati the moon and the Earth only agree "in some things," while for Philo they agree "in every particular."

[3] This fits with other evidence from Hume: if we ignore the contribution to public utility altogether, Galileo would merit highest esteem ("Of the Middle Station of Life," EMPL 550). It is a bit strange that Hume is so unwilling to acknowledge "virtue and usefulness to the public" of Galileo (whose work was

of evidence emerged for Copernicanism. In Dialogues, the engagement with Copernicanism is entirely pre-Newtonian in character.

It is unclear how to take Philo's arguments in Part 2 of Dialogues. The status of analogical argument comes under fire throughout the remainder of Dialogues, but without touching on Copernicanism. Philo returns to the status of Copernicanism in the last, twelfth part of the Dialogues in a passage that is notorious because it seems to reflect Philo's concession to the argument from design. He says:

> A purpose, an intention, a design, strikes every where the most care-less, the most stupid thinker; and no man can be so hardened in absurd systems, as at all times to reject it. That Nature does nothing in vain, is a maxim established in all the schools, merely from the contempla-tion of the works of Nature, without any religious purpose; and, from a firm conviction of its truth, an anatomist, who had observed a new organ or canal, would never be satisfied till he had also discovered its use and intention. One great foundation of the Copernican system is the maxim, That Nature acts by the simplest methods, and chooses the most proper means to any end; and astronomers often, without think-ing of it, lay this strong foundation of piety and religion. The same thing is observable in other parts of philosophy: and thus all the sciences almost lead us insensibly to acknowledge a first intelligent Author; and their authority is often so much the greater, as they do not directly pro-fess that intention. (Dialogues 12.2,)

If we leave aside here his commitment to a "first intelligent Author" (see Section d below), Philo seems to be endorsing simplicity as a feature of nature and of Copernicanism. No doubt this illuminates why explanatory reductionism is an attractive strategy (Hazony 2014). Thus, a fruitful way to read Philo in Dialogues is to see his acceptance of Copernicanism turn on analogical arguments that pro-vide explanatory reductionism (not to mention that Galileo has successfully criti-cized the rivals of Copernicanism). But it is by no means clear that Philo is also offering an endorsement of Copernicanism in Part 12. This is because the passage above is provided in the context of an error theory; the context explains why "all the sciences," including ones—Galenism!—rejected by Philo, "lead us insensibly to acknowledge a first intelligent author." This is compatible with the claim that Copernicanism is an obvious improvement over the Ptolemaic system without requiring an endorsement of it.

However, the treatment of Copernicanism and Galileo is echoed in History, and there can be no doubt that Hume is speaking in his own voice there. In the

---

intended to be applied to calculating proper trajectories of cannonballs and finding longitude at sea, not to mention the important work on strength of materials—it seems Hume did not read Galileo's *Two New Sciences*!) or Newton (who even served in the Mint).

Appendix to the section on King James I, Hume offers a summary of the life of Bacon in which Galileo and Copernicanism play a central role:

> The great glory of literature in this island, during the reign of James, was lord Bacon [...] [he] is justly the object of great admiration. If we consider him merely as an author and philosopher, the light in which we view him at present, though very estimable, he was yet inferior to his cotemporary Galileo, perhaps even to Kepler. Bacon pointed out at a distance the road to true philosophy: Galileo both pointed it out to others, and made himself considerable advances in it. The Englishman was ignorant of geometry: The Florentine revived that science, excelled in it, and was the first that applied it, together with experiment, to natural philosophy. The former rejected, with the most positive disdain, the system of Copernicus: The latter fortified it with new proofs, derived both from reason and the senses. [...] Galileo is a lively and agreeable, though somewhat a prolix writer. But Italy, not united in any single government, and perhaps satiated with that literary glory, which it has possessed both in ancient and modern times, has too much neglected the renown which it has acquired by giving birth to so great a man. That national spirit, which prevails among the English, and which forms their great happiness, is the cause why they bestow on all their eminent writers, and on Bacon among the rest, such praises and acclamations, as may often appear partial and excessive. (History, Volume 5: 153–4)

First, Galileo is introduced as a yardstick by which admiration of Bacon, who still has pride of place in the Introduction to Treatise, is devalued (see Schliesser 2014). The passage leaves no room for doubt that Bacon's opposition to Copernicanism and his ignorance of geometry are reasons for censure. Kepler, who is barely mentioned, and Galileo share advocacy of Copernicanism and possess ample geometric skills. Second, if we leave aside Galileo's writing style, Hume commends him for his methodology of "reason and the senses." In context, it is clear that Hume is pointing to Galileo's use of mathematics and its interplay with experiment/observation in natural philosophy. It is a significant passage because it is one of the very few places where Hume shows recognition of the important role of mathematics within natural philosophy (cf. de Pierris 2006: 320).

Third, Hume is explicit that Galileo "fortified" the "system of Copernicus" with "new proofs." Here Hume makes a distinction between the evidence for Copernicus as marshaled by Copernicus and the new arguments that Galileo supplied. In ways unremarked upon in Treatise or elsewhere, Hume seems aware that for Copernicus's explanatory reductionism to succeed, it required Galilean arguments of diverse kind. Thus, Hume's treatment of Copernicanism in his own voice does not simply echo Philo's argument in Dialogues. Besides Hume's willingness to distinguish between Copernicus and Galileo, there are two other differences. First, in his own voice Hume is silent on the analogical and aesthetic arguments that are said to support Copernicanism in Dialogues; the passage above is compatible with these, of course. Second, Hume's awareness of the interplay of mathematics and experiment/observation is the most sophisticated observation he makes about the practice of the new, post-Galilean natural philosophy.

Now we can return to Smith's argument in the astronomy on Cassini's observations; recall that Smith is careful not to endorse this argument of Voltaire, Maclaurin, and others: "Yet, an analogy of this kind, it would seem, far from a demonstration, could afford, at most, but the shadow of a probability" (Astronomy 4.58, EPS 91). Smith explicitly denies that Cassini's observations provide conclusive evidence for the Copernican theory; at best, they raise the probability of the thesis, and then in an extremely limited fashion. It follows by implication that if Cassini's observations were not decisive, then on Smith's view Galileo's earlier and less sophisticated analogical arguments were even less successful.

Smith is correct in thinking that Cassini's observations do not provide a principled explanation of why all the orbits in the planetary systems act like the planetary orbits in the solar system. This requires what Smith calls Newton's "physical account" (Astronomy 4.67, EPS 97)—that is, something more than an appeal to aesthetic and analogical considerations. Smith recognizes that the demonstrative part of Newton's exposition concerns the conditional, if/then, relationship between the nature of the force and the planetary orbits. But Smith stresses that Newton did not rest with this: "Having thus shown that gravity might be the connecting principle which joined together the movements of the Planets, he endeavoured next to prove that it really was so" (Astronomy 4.67, EPS 98). Smith goes on to describe how the moon-test, Newton's amazing (entirely unsuspected by contemporary astronomers) prediction that a mutual attraction between Jupiter and Saturn would be strong enough to perturb their orbits when near conjunction, Newton's treatment of the lunar orbit, Newton's account of the shape of the Earth, Newton's treatment of the comets, and many other observations "fully confirmed Sir Isaac's System" (Astronomy 4.72, EPS 101; for a modern treatment see Harper 2011). Smith lists a number of surprising, different, and independent kinds of evidence for accepting the Copernican hypothesis.

In his exposition of Newton's system, Smith explicitly returns to the status of Cassini's observations. Newton provides what is missing in the original discussion about Cassini's observations. Newton unified and reduced many apparently disconnected planetary phenomena to a "familiar principle of connection"—that is, universal gravity. As Smith sums up his discussion of Newton:

> Allow his principle, the universality of gravity, and that it decreases as the squares of the distance increase, and all the appearances, which he joins together by it, necessarily follow [. . .] It is every where the most precise and particular that can be imagined, and ascertains the time,

the place, the quantity, the duration of each individual phaenomenon,
to be exactly such, by observation, they have been determined to be.
(Astronomy 4.76, EPS 104)

According to Smith, Newton's theory is not merely a more accurate and beautiful device for predicting known and previously unknown phenomena, but
it is also a tool for use in engaging in further, and fundamentally qualitatively
improved, kinds of inquiry. Moreover, Newton provides a principled—we would
say dynamic—account of why the relative motions of bodies appear a certain
way, and this account is fully confirmed by the phenomena. Note that Smith side-
steps debates over the nature of gravity; like the historical Newton, Smith is a
causal realist about gravity without requiring an explanation for its mechanism
(Ducheyne 2011; Schliesser 2011).

Smith is unimpressed by the pre-Newtonian evidential status of analogical
and aesthetic arguments in favor of Copernicanism: "an analogy of this kind, it
would seem, far from a demonstration, could afford, at most, but the shadow of
a probability." While at a certain level of generality this mistrust of analogy has a
Humean flavor, Smith is far more dismissive of the pre-Newtonian "abstruse analogies" in favor of Copernicus, even if Cassini's observations "establish" Keplerian
motion "as a law of the system." These pre-Newtonian arguments are not proofs
but "shadows of probabilities." That is, Smith accepts in ways that Hume never
did that Newton provided a whole new kind of evidence (Schliesser 2009, 2010).
Newton could offer a physics in which all the major features of Copernicanism
could really be hoped to be explained.

Smith is aware that besides Galileo and Copernicus there were others, especially Descartes, who contributed to the acceptance of Copernican theory long
before there were solid Newton proofs:

> The Cartesian philosophy begins now to be almost universally rejected,
> while the Copernican system continues to be universally received.
> Yet, it is not easy to imagine, how much probability and coherence
> this admired system was long supposed to derive from that exploded
> hypothesis [. . .] when the world beheld that complete, and almost per-
> fect coherence, which the philosophy of Des Cartes bestowed upon the
> system of Copernicus, the imaginations of mankind could no longer
> refuse themselves the pleasure of going along with so harmonious an
> account of things. (Astronomy 4.65, EPS 97)

Thus, Smith emphasizes that the grounds of acceptance of a theory may be multiple and appear more solid than they really are.

It is such discrepancy between the conditions of acceptance and evidential
solidity that opens the door to a critical stance toward any accepted theory. This is
why it matters that Smith insists that "even McLaurin [sic], who was more capable

of judging; nay, Newton himself" (4.58, EPS 90–1) overemphasized the significance of Cassini's observations. (Maclaurin was the most prominent Scottish Newtonian in the second quarter of the eighteenth century.) Smith does not allow group consensus to close the door to ongoing critical reflection on the theory.

A subtle consequence of Smith's analysis is that he is aware that Newton's work shifted the norms of scientific success. He adopts the perspective of a post-Newtonian in judging the evaluative standards of earlier generations. (Recall his own critical attitude toward Plato on infanticide.) Newton is one of those scientific legislators (TMS 1.1.4.3, 20) who cause "revolutions." As Smith puts it near the start of his essay:

> [Philosophy] is the most sublime of all the agreeable arts, and its revolutions have been the greatest, the most frequent, and the most distinguished of all those that have happened in the literary world. Its history ... must ... be the most entertaining and the most instructive. Let us examine ... the different systems of nature, which, in these western parts of the world ... have successively been adopted by the learned and ingenious; and without regarding their absurdity or probability, their agreement with truth and reality, let us consider them only in that particular point of view which belongs to our subject; and content ourselves with inquiring how far each of them was fitted to soothe the imagination, and to render the theatre of nature more coherent, and therefore a more magnificent spectacle, than otherwise it would have appeared to be. According as they have failed or succeeded in this, they have constantly failed or succeeded in gaining reputation and renown to their authors; and this will be found to be the clew that is most capable of conducting us through all the labyrinths of philosophical history ... in general, [that] no system, how well soever in other respects supported, has ever been able to gain any general credit on the world, whose connecting principles were not such as were familiar to all mankind. (Astronomy 2.12, EPS 46)

It is then no surprise that in recent scholarly discussions Smith's astronomy has been linked regularly to Kuhn's philosophy of scientific revolutions. Although ever since Montaigne skeptics had speculated that the replacement of Ptolemy with the Copernican system could be replaced by some further new system, Smith's generation is among the first to see regular and successive revolutions in the history of astronomy and, perhaps, sciences and other forms of inquiry more broadly (Cohen 1985; Schliesser 2005). Smith also recognizes features of Kuhnian incommensurability. As he writes,

> As this doctrine of specific Essences seems naturally enough to have arisen from that ancient system of Physics ... and which is, by no

means devoid of probability, so many of the doctrines of that system,
which seem to us, who have been long accustomed to another, the most
incomprehensible. (Physics 10, EPS 128)

Strictly speaking, Smith is silent on incommensurability, which involves the inability to find a common measure between two competing theories. All he speaks
about is the lack of intelligibility when trying to understand a theory from a different intellectual epoch. But clearly (not unlike Kuhn) Smith thinks this lack of
intelligibility can be overcome by the historian's imagination. But as we have seen,
during his argument Smith is less descriptive and more evaluative than this statement (and the comparison with Kuhn) would have suggested.

Above I remarked (without fully explaining) that wonder opens up the possibility for adjusting the existing manifest image. As we have seen, throughout
his treatment of the sciences, Smith emphasizes how far removed from common
sense the contents of highly successful scientific theories can be: for example,
the Copernican hypothesis means that Earth and the planets are traveling with
"a rapidity that almost passes all human comprehension" (External Senses 12,
EPS 137). Smith's narrative in Astronomy exhibits that the norms of acceptance
of a theory in the astronomical community can evolve and diverge from those of
the wider public; coherence, predictive power, and so forth are factors, but in the
course of successive "revolutions" of systems, this list can be expanded.

Even before his discussion of Copernicus, Smith shows that technical criteria of theory acceptance can change and develop. For example, one innovation in
astronomy is the demand for a physical explanation of the phenomena. Smith's
recognition of this point is why he thematically links the origins of Copernicanism
with the demand for a consistent physical theory by Purbach and Regiomantus:

> When you have convinced the world, that an established system ought
> to be corrected, it is not very difficult to persuade them that it should
> be destroyed. Not long, therefore, after the death of Regiomontanus,
> Copernicus began to meditate a new system, which should connect
> together the celestial appearances, in a more simple as well as a more
> accurate manner, than that of Ptolemy. (Astronomy 4.27, EPS 71)

Simplicity, distinctness, coherence, comprehensibility or intelligibility, lack of
reasonable competitors, and predicting and accounting for the phenomena do not
exhaust the reasons for accepting a theory; in Astronomy Smith writes,

> For, though it is the end of Philosophy, to allay that wonder, which
> either the unusual or seemingly disjointed appearances of nature excite,
> yet she never triumphs so much, as when, in order to connect together
> a few, in themselves, perhaps, inconsiderable objects, she has, if I may
> so, created another constitution of things, more easily attended to, but

more new, more contrary to common opinion and expectation, than any of those appearances themselves. (Astronomy 4.33, EPS 75)

Now part of Smith's claim is that in offering an explanation scientists remove the possible disorder that threatens our environmental rationality and substitute for it a new "connection" among the objects that can facilitate the train of ideas in the imagination. Thus, it is a mark of a successful theory that it is unexpected, even surprising, and, in doing so, creates a new order. (See also the comments on Reamur's *History of Insects* in Edinburgh Review 9, EPS 249.) While Hume had castigated the greedy embrace by philosophers of theories that have "the air of a paradox" and who are thereby distancing themselves from the "unprejudiced notions of mankind" (Treatise 1.2.1.1), Smith does not criticize these "triumphs." Yet such a theory, almost "another constitution of things," will, once it becomes part of the rejigged scientific image of a group of experts, almost certainly create a feeling of wonder and surprise, which may induce reflections on its metaphysical or conceptual foundations and perhaps spur on the development of new theories. Smith's philosophy of science does not see science as a mere extension of common sense—there can be genuine discontinuities between the expert's view of the world and common life, although there is always a possibility of connecting these two into a provisionally stable, environmental rationality.

But it turns out that Smith also insists on limits. First, he mocks gently the kind of aesthetic escapism that the life of mind can generate:

Those philosophers transported themselves, in fancy, to the centres of these imaginary Circles, and took pleasure in surveying from thence, all those fantastical motions, arranged, according to harmony and order, which had been the end of all their researches to bestow upon them. Here, at last, they enjoyed that tranquillity [sic] and repose which they had pursued through all the mazes of this intricate hypothesis; and here they beheld this, the most beautiful and magnificent part of the great theatre of nature, so disposed and constructed, that they could attend, with ease and delight, to all the revolutions and changes that occurred in it. (Astronomy 4.13, EPS 62)

The aesthetic pleasure of the astronomers is achieved through the workings of the imagination; by seeing the world theoretically, or in "constructed" fashion, they can make the phenomena tractable and achieve tranquility of mind. But note that the aesthetic emotions are not necessarily truth-apt; sometimes the practice of astronomy is a kind of escapism that never connects with any reality behind appearances.

Second, according to Smith, satisfying evaluative criteria adopted by a present or future community of inquirers (cf. TMS 3.2.20–2, 124–5) can provide one with public reasons to reject the assumptions of everyday life. By contrast, when discussing the relative merits of moral theories, he claims that the expert may reject common sense, but that the cost (in persecution, disbelief, rejection, satire, etc.) may be high: "the author who should assign, as the cause of any natural senti-ment, some principle which neither had any connexion with it, nor resembled any other principle which had some such connexion, would appear absurd and ridic-ulous to the most injudicious and unexperienced reader" (TMS 7.2.4.14, 314–5). The context suggests that Smith can imagine that an account could be dreamed up by a judicious and experienced reader that would explain human behavior in terms that are unfamiliar to people. Yet, such an account would receive a hostile reception. While theories of natural philosophy successfully create "another con-stitution of things ... contrary to common opinion" (Astronomy 4.33, EPS 75), this should be avoided in the case of moral philosophy.

An account of moral life that is phrased in familiar terms can gain approval as long as it has some truth. This is why Smith often sounds like a so-called com-monsense philosopher when discussing moral philosophy (WN 5.f.26, 769; see Fleischacker 2004: 22). This is so even though Smith believes that common sense itself is quite rare; in fact, if common sense were more common, then more people would be able to prevent their vanity from being the foundation of various vices (TMS 3.2.4, 115). This suggests that Smith's public presentation of his own moral and political views will emphasize the ways in which his views cohere with com-mon sense or common life. Smith does not emphasize his own novelty.

While moral philosophy must make occasional concessions to the sensibility of common life, natural philosophy can triumph by opposing it. Of course, the con-flict between the vulgar and the astronomers over the Copernican hypothesis is, as the trial of Galileo demonstrates, not always without dangers. But apparently Smith does not think there needs to be a permanent tension between natural science and political (or religious) authority. I return to this issue once more in Section d.

c. Copernicus and Newton: Modest Scientific Realism

In this section I argue that Smith is not a Humean skeptic or a skeptical realist, but a modest scientific realist about the then-recent achievements of Newton.

Recall that Smith defines philosophy as "the science of connecting principles of nature" (Astronomy 2.12, EPS 45) that is directed at "combining together the powers of the most distant and dissimilar objects" (WN 1.1.9, 21). These claims exhibit a realist commitment that shows up in a variety of places in Smith's phi-losophy. For example, in External Senses, Smith describes planets—in Newtonian fashion—as "masses of motion" (12, EPS 137).

Even so, many have discerned a skeptical stance in Smith's psychologi-cal account of theory acceptance (Cremaschi 1989; Pack 1991: 114; Griswold 1999: Chapters 4, 8, and Epilogue; Rothschild 2001: 138–40, 229). In 2005, while writing about (and against) this skeptical interpretation, I acknowledged that "the examples of Smith's acceptance of invisible forces are compatible with a kind of 'skeptical realism' that has recently been attributed to Hume (Wright 1983)." A few years later Ryan Hanley wrote a brilliant paper defending such a skeptical realist interpretation of Smith, centering on Smith's embrace of Humean natural beliefs (Hanley 2010).

It is easy to see why people would have attributed a skeptical position to Smith. Recall the quoted the passage in which Smith writes, "Let us examine . . . the different systems of nature, which, in these western parts of the world . . . have successively been adopted by the learned and ingenious; and without regarding their absurdity or probability, their agreement with truth and reality." It is no surprise that the proto-Kuhnian rhetoric in Astronomy and the common association of Smith with Hume facilitate such an interpretation.

Moreover, Astronomy ends with the following reflexive evaluation on his description of Newton's system:

> And even we, while we have been endeavouring to represent all philosophical systems as mere inventions of the imagination, to connect together the otherwise disjointed and discordant phaenomena of nature, have insensibly been drawn in, to make use of language expressing the connecting principles of this one, as if they were the real chains which Nature makes use of to bind together her several operations. Can we wonder then, that it should have gained the general and complete approbation of mankind, and that it should now be considered, not as an attempt to connect in the imagination the phaenomena of the Heavens, but as the greatest discovery that ever was made by man, the discovery of an immense chain of the most important and sublime truths, all closely connected together, by one capital fact, of the reality of which we have daily experience. (4.76, 105)

According to many commentators, Smith's use of "as if" seems to lend support to such a skeptical interpretation.

Throughout this book (and echoing Fleischacker 2012), I have provided considerable evidence that we have to be very cautious about reading Humean commitments into Smith's philosophy. Moreover, in the previous section I provided considerable evidence of Smith's nonskeptical treatment of the nature of philosophy. Rather than recycling all of this here, I offer an alternative argument that reminds us of the distance between Smith and Hume, in the context of Hume's skepticism and Smith's nonskeptical position.

In the First *Enquiry*, Hume treats the unknown source of the nourishment of bread as an example of our "ignorance of natural powers"—that is, how "nature has kept us at a great distance from all her secrets" (EHU 4.16). In Astronomy, Smith carefully circumscribes the "us" implicit in Hume's bread example. Smith discusses the example only as an instance of the difference between the "bulk of mankind" and "philosophers." The former "seldom had the curiosity to inquire" about how bread is "converted into flesh and bones," while the latter have tried to find the connecting "chain" that can explain the "nourishment of the human body" (2.12, EPS 45). Smith treats the example not as a confirmation of a kind of skepticism about possible knowledge of nature, but rather as a research problem not unlike the attempts to "connect the gravity, elasticity, and even the cohesion of natural bodies, with some of their other qualities" (EHU 4.12).

Therefore, the response to the Humean example shows that for Smith there is some distinction between the "bulk of mankind" and "philosophers;" it manifests itself in a difference in curiosity. This difference is largely the effect of the division of labor, from "habit, custom and education" (WN 2.2.4, 28–9). For Smithian philosophers inquiry never need come to an end.

There is a related point to be made. Hume interprets Newton's achievements in general as supporting his "true philosophy"—as showing there are limits to inquiry that need to be respected. In History he writes, "While Newton seemed to draw off the veil from some of the mysteries of nature, he shewed at the same time the imperfections of the mechanical philosophy; and *thereby* restored her ultimate secrets to that obscurity, in which they ever did and ever will remain" (Book 6, 542; emphasis added). Hume treats Newton's refutation of the mechanical philosophy as decisive evidence for the claim that nature will remain unknowable in principle. But there are no equivalent statements in Smith (see also Montes 2004 and Berry 2006).

Ever since at least Montaigne's response to Copernicus, a pessimistic meta-induction over the history of science is a known skeptical argument. Given Smith's huge admiration of Swift (Hanley 2008), there is no doubt he is familiar with the treatment of the argument in *Gulliver's Travels*:

> [Aristotle's ghost] freely acknowledged his own mistakes in natural philosophy, because he proceeded in many things upon conjecture, as all men must do; and he found that Gassendi, who had made the doctrine of Epicurus as palatable as he could, and the vortices of Descartes, were equally exploded. He predicted the same fate to ATTRACTION, whereof the present learned are such zealous asserters. He said, that new systems of nature were but new fashions, which would vary in every age; even those who pretend to demonstrate them from mathematical principles would flourish but a short period of time, and be out of vogue when that was determined. (Chapter VIII of Voyage III; Smith owned Swift's *Works* (see Yanaihara 1966: 91))

I am unfamiliar with a place where Smith discusses such a pessimistic meta-induction argument head on. Now if Smith had agreed with the pessimistic meta-induction argument, it would have been easy for him to suggest so in Astronomy.

On balance, I would agree with those who argue that Smith is, in general, committed to a form of inference to the best explanation (Kim 2012).

There is a further argument to treat Smith as resistant to Humean-style skepticism. Recall from Section b in Chapter 3 that Smith is explicitly committed to what I have called "proto-passions" (his "anticipations" of nature). The contents of these passions always involve a feeling of desire (joy) or aversion (etc.) toward some anticipated triggering object. Thus, part of the structure of the world is built into our passions, thus facilitating the development of our ordinary environmental rationality.

In fact, as Glenney (2011) has emphasized, throughout External Senses Smith argues that our sensory modalities refer to a world outside of themselves—this is most prominently so in touch—and he does so in the service of (not entirely convincing) arguments against skepticism. According to Smith the solidity of an object makes us feel "as something altogether external to us, so we necessarily conceive it as something altogether independent of us" (External Senses 9, EPS 136). In context Smith is explaining why we "commonly" adopt a substance-oriented language and ontology. Either way, Smith's analysis suggests that some of the more extreme, external-world types of skepticism or phenomenalism are nonstarters given the kind of natures we have. As Smith puts it:

> solidity, the compressibility or incompressibility, of the resisting substance, the certainty of our distinct sense and feeling of its Externality, or of its entire independency upon the organ which perceives it, or by which we perceive it, cannot in the smallest degree be affected by any such system. (External Senses 18, EPS 140)

In context, Smith means by "system" a system of nature. In effect, he is claiming that because of our embodiment and the external-world orientation of many of our sense modalities and proto-passions, we simply cannot even be argued into believing external-world skepticism. Smith grants, however, that not all modalities are alike in this respect; for example, "the sensations of heat and cold do not necessarily suggest the presence of any external object, we soon learn from experience that they are commonly excited by some such object" (External Senses 21, EPS 141). If we had had different kinds of sense modalities—more akin to heat and cold detection—then certain forms of skepticism would have been more open to argument, according to Smith. But he dismisses this option: "It is probable, however, not only that no man, but that no animal was ever born without the Sense of Touching, which seems essential to, and inseparable from, the nature of animal life and existence. It is unnecessary, therefore, to throw away any reasoning, or to hazard any conjectures, about what might be the effects of what I look upon as altogether an impossible supposition" (External Senses 49, EPS 150). Whatever we may think of Smith's handling of the logically and metaphysically possible here, it is clear that he is committed to the Lockean claim that touch—and, thus, commitment to external-world reality—is an intrinsic feature of our nature (on Locke see Shockey 2007). The necessity involved is *felt*; that is sufficient in Humean context. In effect, the essay, Smith returns to Berkeley—Hume had adopted Berkeley's arguments to skeptical ends—in order to refute Hume (and Berkeley).

So, while in External Senses Smith acknowledges his ample debt to Berkeley, he thinks there are non-trivial differences in the status of the sensible qualities; according to Smith touching is very different from tasting, smelling, hearing, and heat/cold sensation (External Senses 36, EPS 145–6) and vision (External Senses 49, EPS 150; in context, the main point of Smith's analysis is to offer a profound and considered response to the so-called Molyneux question [Glenney 2011]).

But what about the "as if" passage noted at the start of this section? My non-skeptical reading emphasizes a different sentence in the same paragraph. This is because Smith is aware that when one is confronted by the explanatory robust, predictive, beautiful, and magnificent system (etc.), such as Newton's in his day, even "the most skeptical cannot avoid feeling" that its principles have a "degree of firmness and solidity" (Astronomy, 4.76, EPS 105). This is meeting Humean skeptics on their own ground, for Humeans have no access to an alternative perspective than one's (proper) feelings. Smith's "as if" is not a concession to the skeptic; rather, he is merely explaining why he has *abandoned* the method he had intended to pursue in his essay ("even we, while we have been endeavouring to represent all philosophical systems as mere inventions of the imagination") and using realist language. So, while one can always try to find grounds for criticizing accepted theories, one cannot always avoid treating these as capturing reality within the scientific image.

Smith's commitment to a modest scientific realism is, however, not the end of the matter. This is because Smith's genealogical essays on the history of philosophy and philosophizing also have an unexpected, further concern that is not skeptical itself, but connects to other Humean concerns with ways in which theorizing aids superstition.

d. Magnanimous Superstition

In this section I argue that in Astronomy Smith explores the complex relationship between the development of science and the development of religion. I argue that Smith's narrative does not convey the expectation that science is ever cleansed of all superstition.

In Astronomy, Smith claims that the systems of philosophers

> [in] many respects resemble machines. A machine is a little system, created to perform, as well as to connect together, in reality, those different movements and effects which the artist has occasion for. A system

is an imaginary machine invented to connect together in the fancy those different movements and effects which are already in reality performed. The machines that are first invented to perform any particular movement are always the most complex, and succeeding artists generally discover that, with fewer wheels, with fewer principles of motion, than had originally been employed, the same effects may be more easily produced. (Astronomy 4.19, EPS 66)

In fact, throughout his writings Smith distinguishes among three kinds of uses of "machines:" (i) imaginary machines—that is, especially, scientific theories; (ii) actual (designed) mechanical devices of the sort, say, found behind the scenes in the theater (i.e., the "machinery of the opera-house" [Astronomy 2.9, EPS 42]); and (iii) the Platonic and later also Epicurean doctrine of nature viewed as "complete machine" (Ancient Physics 9, EPS 119; see also the treatment of Descartes in Astronomy).

While technology is a foreseeable byproduct, systems that calm the wonder-induced discomfort of the imagination are the main primary products of the philosopher's labor (WN 1.1.9, 21–2 and 5.1.f.26–34, 769–73). The comparison between machines and the systems of philosophers pertains in Smith's use to their similar pattern of development—that is, that within a theoretical framework there is often a regular tradeoff between simplicity of principles and expansion of application. This relates to the development of an accepted theory. The replacement of one theory with the next, a "revolution," is motivated, among other things, by the fact that the new theory has simpler principles and a wider application (of predictions, etc.; Astronomy 4.18–19, EPS 65–7).

Smith makes clear that the development and evolution of all such systems have a fairly regular sequence: a system is constructed with the aid of the imagination to provide coherence to the appearances. As time passes, irregularities are discovered, and successive, gradual modifications are introduced into the system, leading toward more complexity; eventually, new requirements are put on the system or new phenomena are discovered that lead to conflicting accounts or dissatisfaction. This makes it likely that the system will be replaced by a new system, and so the process starts anew. Of course, this does not address the situation in which no satisfactory system has been created at all; Smith explicitly bemoans the lack of progress and "obscurity" in the "chemical philosophy" (Astronomy 2.12, 46).

There is some evidence that Smith viewed his own relationship to previous contributions to political economy as a closer approximation to the truth (see also Montes 2003). In WN, in the process of an extensive, critical discussion of the Physiocratic system, popular in France, he was led to remark on this system:

This system, however, with all its imperfections is, perhaps, the nearest approximation to the truth that has been yet published upon the subject of political oeconomy, and is upon that account well worth the consideration of every man who wishes to examine with attention the principles of that very important science. (WN 4.9.38, 678–9)

Smith greatly admires the Physiocrats; according to Dugald Stewart, Smith's first biographer, Smith would have dedicated WN to Quesnay, "the very ingenious and profound author of this [Physiocratic] system" (WN IV.ix.27, 672) if the French physician had lived. There is no doubt, however, that he thought he had advanced beyond the Physiocrats (4.9.50, 687); perhaps he even thought he had achieved the truth, and no mere approximation to truth, about political economy. WN is obviously written in a confident tone; sometimes Smith is willing to assert his views "with a degree of probability that approaches almost to certainty" (1.11.n.3, 257).

Let's return to the main argument. In Smith's hands the machine metaphor in the sense of a scientific system emphasizes four distinct but mutually resonating things:

(a) The constructed nature of philosophical systems—they are inventions that change over time, and this is, in fact, one of the major themes of Astronomy.
(b) The comparison among machines, systems, and languages is used to imply that their pattern of development is a gradual, even predictable, affair, at least until a revolution takes place (Languages, 223–4).
(c) Systems are effective ways to convey abundant information—they provide efficient explanatory accounts.
(d) The machine metaphor reminds us that systems are tools to engage in further research.

The idea that scientific theories can be compared to machines goes back at least to a fascinating passage in Cicero's On the Nature of the Gods:

But if all the parts of the universe have been so appointed that they could neither be better adapted for use nor be made more beautiful in appearance, we must investigate whether this is chance, or whether the condition of the world is such that it certainly could not cohere unless it were controlled by intelligence of divine providence. If, then, nature's attainments transcend those achieved by human design, and if human skill achieves nothing without the application of reason, we must grant that nature too is not devoid of reason. It can surely not be right to acknowledge as a work of art a statue or a painted picture, or to be convinced from distant observation of a ship's course that its progress is controlled by reason and human skill, or upon examination of the design of a sundial or a water-clock to appreciate that calculation of the time of day is made by skill and not by chance, yet none the less to consider that the universe is devoid of purpose and reason, thought it embraces those very skills, and the craftsmen who wield them, and all else beside?

Our friend Posidonius has recently fashioned a planetarium; each time it revolves, it makes the sun, moon, and planets reproduce the movements which they make over a day and a night in the heavens. Suppose someone carried this to Scythia or to Britain. Surely no one in those barbarous regions would doubt that that planetarium had been constructed by a rational process. Yet our opponents [the Epicureans] here profess uncertainty whether the universe, from which all things take their, has come into existence by chance or some necessity, or by divine reason and intelligence. Thus, they believe Archimedes more successful in his model of the heavenly revolutions than nature's production of these, even though nature's role is considerably more ingenious than such representations. (Cicero 1978: 78)[4]

There are many arguments from design; I dub the main one articulated in the quoted passage by Cicero's Stoic character, Quintius Lucilius Balbus, the "Posidonian argument." It deploys—in David Sedley's felicitous phrase—the "structural resemblance of state-of-the-art-planetary mechanism to the celestial globe" (Sedley 2007: 207). This is because it relies on the supposition that everybody (even barbarians) will grant that a sophisticated complex machine, which is a scientific representation of nature, must be the product of intelligent design, and then (once granted) it turns to suggest that the represented complex (beautiful, well-adapted, etc.) machine must itself also have an intelligent author.[5] (For a very careful analysis of the argument, see Hunter 2009.)

The most famous version of the Posidonian argument during the early modern period is probably to be found in Boyle, who frequently "compares the world as a whole with a clock" (I am indebted to Durland 2015). This argument does more than just defend the "corpuscular hypothesis." Here's one of Boyle's celebrated instances of the analogy:

'tis like a rare Clock, such as may be that at Strasbourg, where all things are so skilfully contriv'd, that the Engine being once set a Moving, all things proceed according to the Artificers first design, and the Motions of the little Statues, that at such hours perform these or those things, do not require, like those of Puppets, the peculiar interposing of the Artificer, or any Intelligent Agent imployed by him, but perform their functions upon particular occasions, by vertue of the General and Primitive Contrivance of the whole Engine. (Boyle 1996: 13)

---

[4] I have made some minor modifications.

[5] As Sedley notes, the represented world need not be itself a mechanism (207).

Boyle uses the world-clock analogy to drive home the idea that God's *general* providence works by general and original (this captures the sense of Boyle's "primitive" in
light of the "first design") causes.[6] Boyle's argument seems familiar to us, educated as
we are to see Darwinism, in part, as a response to Paley's watch (see Boyle 1991: xvi).

In the *Usefulness of Natural Philosophy*, Boyle adds two claims to his treatment
of the Strasbourg clock:[7] (i) "the various motions of the wheels and other parts
concur to exhibit the phenomena designed by the artificer in the engine" and (ii)
"might to a rude Indian seem to be more intelligent than Cunradus Dasypodius
himself" (Boyle 1991: 160; Conrad Dasypodius was the designer of the famous
Strasbourg clock). Here I ignore Boyle's shocking disregard of the intellectual
achievements of Indian civilization(s). The phenomena exhibited by the (second)
Strasbourg clock were primarily astronomical—that is, it was a gigantic, massive
planetarium in which heavenly motions and phenomena were faithfully represented.[8] Boyle's version of the Posidonian argument (astronomical clock, ignorant
foreigner) was familiar enough such that Locke would offer his own variant of it
(without mention of Boyle) at *Essay* 3.6.9 (see also 3.6.3).[9]

Hume alludes to a version of the argument in the First *Enquiry*, but without
connecting it to design arguments (First *Enquiry* 4.4). He also has a character,
Cleanthes, propose an argument very similar to the Posidonian argument in his

---

[6] To modern eyes it is tempting to read the "general" causes as laws of nature, but in this passage
Boyle could also be relying on the traditional idea that the clock has a real essence (the hidden-from-
sight "contrivance") from which effects follow in exception-less fashion (such a world would also be
amenable to description by laws of nature, of course).

[7] In his works Boyle uses the Strasbourg clock to offer many different kinds of arguments to design.
Many of these are logically distinct from the Posidonian argument.

[8] Check out this wonderful image: https://en.wikipedia.org/wiki/Strasbourg_astronomical_
clock#Second_clock

[9] In fact, as is well known, *Essay* 3.6.9 anticipates Newton's treatment of our lack of knowledge of
God's substance in *General Scholium*. Here is Newton:

> A blind man has no idea of colours, so have we no idea of the manner by which the all-wise
> God perceives and understands all things. He is utterly void of all body and bodily figure, and
> can therefore neither be seen, nor heard, not touched; nor ought he to be worshipped under
> the representation of any corporeal thing. We have ideas of his attributes, but what the real
> substance of anything is, we know not. In bodies we see only their figures and colours, we hear
> only the sounds, we touch only their outward surfaces, we smell only the smells, and taste the
> savours; but their inward substances are not to be known, either by our senses, or by any reflex
> act of our minds; much less then have we any idea of the substance of God.

In Locke we find pretty much the same claims, except that they are contextualized by the
Posidonian argument:

> Our faculties carry us no further towards the knowledge and distinction of substances, than
> a collection of those sensible ideas which we observe in them; which, however made with the
> greatest diligence and exactness we are capable of, yet is more remote from the true internal
> constitution from which those qualities flow, than, as I said, a countryman's idea is from the
> inward contrivance of that famous clock at Strasburg, whereof he only sees the outward figure

Dialogues (in which the world is itself treated as "one great machine, subdivided into an infinite number of lesser machines" (Dialogues 2.5; it is then discussed from various angles throughout Dialogues; cf. 2.14ff, 5.7, 7.3 and 7.8, 7.15, and 12.5). As many scholars have recognized, Dialogues is, of course, full of allusions to Cicero's *The Nature of the Gods*.

This is not the place to analyze the full afterlife of this argument and all the variety of possible interpretations of it (see Hunter 2009). In addition to the familiar design arguments there is also a kind of transcendental argument lurking in Cicero's passage. Clarke develops it in his *A Demonstration of the Being and Attributes of God* (1705), which is a response to Hobbes, Spinoza, and Toland (for details see Schliesser [2018]). We can reconstruct Clarke's argument—perhaps anachronistically—as follows:

(I) A necessary condition of the possibility of an (intended) successful scientific representation or concrete model of (a region of) nature is that (a region of) nature is orderly;

(II) (A region of) Nature's hidden order could not be the product of chance [as suggested by Epicureanism] or necessity [as suggested by Spinozism], but only by God;

(III) Science produces successful representations and successful concrete models of (a region of) nature.[10]

and motions [this is a reference back to *Essay* 3.6.3]. There is not so contemptible a plant or animal, that does not confound the most enlarged understanding . . . It is evident the internal constitution, whereon their properties depend, is unknown to us: for to go no further than the grossest and most obvious we can imagine amongst them, What is that texture of parts, that real essence, that makes lead and antimony fusible, wood and stones not? What makes lead and iron malleable, antimony and stones not? And yet how infinitely these come short of the fine contrivances and inconceivable real essences of plants or animals, every one knows. The workmanship of the all-wise and powerful God in the great fabric of the universe, and every part thereof, further exceeds the capacity and comprehension of the most inquisitive and intelligent man, than the best contrivance of the most ingenious man doth the conceptions of the most ignorant of rational creatures. Therefore we in vain pretend to range things into sorts, and dispose them into certain classes under names, by their real essences, that are so far from our discovery or comprehension. A blind man may as soon sort things by their colours, and he that has lost his smell as well distinguish a lily and a rose by their odours, as by those internal constitutions which he knows not.

As I discuss in Section d, both Hume and Smith discuss our lack of knowledge of the hidden, causal powers of ordinary stuff in terms of the nutritious features of bread. To the best of my knowledge, Newton mentions neither the Posidonian argument nor the Strasbourg version explicitly. A generation later, however, the Newtonians are associated with the Strasbourg clock in a popular work, *Sir Isaac Newton's Philosophy Explain'd For the Use of the Ladies* by Francesco Algarotti (translated in 1739); see Dialogue 1: http://www.newtonproject.sussex.ac.uk/view/texts/normalized/OTHE00106.

[10] Strictly speaking this premise is stronger than is required logically. All that's needed is the possibility of successful scientific representation. I thank Andrew Bailey for discussion.

(IV) ∴ There is a God (of order).

Some such argument would have been familiar to Smith because it was popular in the hands of Newtonian natural theologians of which Clarke, who appeals to this particular Cicero passage and the history of scientific success, was among the most prominent. One interesting feature of this transcendental argument is that science would not be a neutral means toward establishing a designing God (I dub this the "neutrality requirement"), but rather that science presupposes for its very possibility of success a commitment to such a designing God.

It seems that Smith's understanding of science commits him to (I). Moreover, he seems to accept (III) a history of scientific success culminating in Newton (Astronomy 4.76; EPS 104). However, in Section f of Chapter 5, I suggested that Smith rejects (II) because he claims in his own voice "Fortune, which governs the world" (TMS 2.3.1, 104). I suggested that Smith's embrace of the piacular points toward an acknowledgment of the Epicurean system, which was then commonly associated with either the rule of chance or Spinozist necessitarianism—both of which are compatible with the rule of Fortune as presented by Smith.

But TMS 2.3.1, 104, can be balanced by plenty of passages in which he seems to accept (IV) without any need for an argument. As I have noted throughout this book, Smith often talks about the "Author of nature." But it is worth noting that there are also passages that indicate reservations about such a claim. For example, Smith introduces Plato's cosmogony as follows:

> As soon as the Universe was regarded as a complete machine, as a coherent system, governed by general laws, and directed to general ends, viz. its own preservation and prosperity, and that of all the species that are in it; the resemblance which it evidently bore to those machines which are produced by human art, necessarily impressed those sages with a belief, that in the original formation of the world there must have been employed an art resembling the human art, but as much superior to it, as the world is superior to the machines which that art produces. The unity of the system, which, according to this ancient philosophy, is most perfect, suggested the idea of the unity of that principle, by whose art it was formed; and thus, as ignorance begot superstition, science gave birth to the first theism that arose among those nations, who were not enlightened by divine Revelation. (Ancient Physics 9, EPS 113)

Thus, it seems that on Smith's conception design is woven into our very conceptions of scientific representations. This does not mean, of course, he himself also understands the world as a giant machine. Smith explicitly cites Cicero as his source on the doctrines of Plato (EPS 114), and presumably he is relying on *On the Nature of the Gods*.

In the quoted passage there are undeniable echoes of Cicero's design argument; I have in mind not just the appeal to the analogy between manmade machines and the world machine, but also the claim that "the world is superior to the machines which that art produces." (Recall "nature's attainments transcend those achieved by human design.") Even so, the echoes are not decisive—neither Posidonius nor Archimedes is mentioned, and Smith need not have accepted the claim that the world is a machine. What follows does not require that Smith understands his own arguments in light of Cicero's design argument, but it is illuminating, I think, to see Smith's narrative in light of the transcendental interpretation of Cicero's argument and, especially, the nature of the neutrality requirement of science.

This is because Smith's main historical claim in the passage (quoted from EPS 113) is that theism is a natural, even immediate consequence of the scientific (or natural philosophic) mindset completely distinct from the introduction of Judaism or Christianity. This is a subtle correction to Hume's argument on the origin of cosmogony in the *Natural History of Religion*, where, in his treatment of Greek natural philosophy, Hume had claimed that "it was pretty late too before these be thought themselves of having recourse to a mind or supreme intelligence, as the first cause of all" (N 4.10). Thus, while Hume treats theism as a kind of alien infection of even Greek science, Smith treats it as natural consequence of the scientific mindset.[11]

I leave aside, momentarily, what this entails for *Smith's* views on the existence of God, for it follows from Smith's position that science cannot act as a neutral means toward establishing the existence of God. If we view science as a discovery machine (as Smith does), then science cannot be neutral on God's existence. This is because on Smith's view the existence of God is *presupposed* in scientific practice, if not conceptually (if he accepts something like the Posidonian argument) then at least psychologically (based on his historical analysis). So it is no surprise

---

[11] The differences between Hume and Smith are also evident in on their treatment of Thales (treated by Hume as the founder of natural philosophy in the Introduction to Treatise). Hume writes:

It will be easy to give a reason, why Thales, Anaximander, and those early philosophers, who really were atheists, might be very orthodox in the pagan creed; and why Anaxagoras and Socrates, though real theists, must naturally, in ancient times, be esteemed impious. The blind, unguided powers of nature, if they could produce men, might also produce such beings as Jupiter and Neptune, who being the most powerful, intelligent existences in the world, would be proper objects of worship. But where a supreme intelligence, the first cause of all, is admitted, these capricious beings, if they exist at all, must appear very subordinate and dependent, and consequently be excluded from the rank of deities. Plato (de leg. lib. x.) assigns this reason for the imputation thrown on Anaxagoras, namely his denying the divinity of the stars, planets, and other created objects. (N [ZZ].1)

Hume treats Thales and Anaximander as proto-Spinozists, yet not impious. By contrast, while Smith agrees that Thales was the founders of one of the first "philosophical sects" (Astronomy 3.6, EPS 52), following the authority of Aristotle, Smith treats the accounts by Plutarch and Apuleius of Thales' astronomical discoveries as historical fictions, and presents Thales' cosmology as an anthropocentric and "confused an account of things" (Astronomy 4.5. EPS 56; see also Astronomy 3.6, EPS 52). Empedocles is treated as the first philosopher with something approaching an orderly system.

that Newtonian natural religion discovers evidence of God everywhere it looks.[12] From *within* science one must accept God's existence either as an inductive inference to the best explanation (recall Kim 2012) or as a kind of indispensability argument.[13] Thus, it looks like he accepts (IV) after all.

If Smith accepted the authority of (Newton's) natural philosophy without qualification, that would be the end of the matter, but his position is more complex. Recall that Smith writes, "as ignorance begot superstition, science gave birth to the first theism" (Ancient Physics 9, EPS 113). It is very tempting to think that insofar as science is contrasted with ignorance, theism is contrasted with superstition. Yet, the larger paragraph from which the analogy is quoted is rhetorically more complex, for Smith writes:

> Their ignorance, and confusion of thought, necessarily gave birth to that pusillanimous superstition, which ascribes almost every unexpected event, to the arbitrary will of some designing, though invisible beings, who produced it for some private and particular purpose. The idea of an universal mind, of a God of all, who originally formed the whole, and who governs the whole by general laws, directed to the conservation and prosperity of the whole, without regard to that of any private individual, was a notion to which they were utterly strangers. (Ancient Physics 9, EPS 112)

Smith seems to distinguish between a variety of superstitions; one of the scales seems to go from pusillanimous superstition to magnanimous superstition. A very natural reading of the quoted passage is that the second (more Stoic) providential God is a kind of magnanimous superstition. This second species of superstition *is* the one associated with eighteenth-century, Newtonian natural religion (e.g., the writings of Samuel Clarke, Colin Maclaurin, or Smith's own teacher, Hutcheson). It seems, then, that for Smith even "heroic magnanimity" can occur in a superstitious system (reasonings of the Stoics "confound and perplex the understanding" [TMS 7.2.1.47, 293]) and superstitious men (see the description of Caesar at TMS 1.3.3.8, 65).

By contrast, Smith describes the dying Hume as magnanimous but (in reading Lucian) not superstitious (see Chapter 15 for details). But that implies that if Cicero's transcendental design argument is an instance of magnanimous superstition and Smith models his treatment of science on it, then Smith is treating science as a species of *magnanimous* superstition![14]

---

[12] This God is not anthropocentric because, as he explains in the *General Scholium*, Newton takes it to be obvious that beings in other solar systems will also admire the beauty of God's creation (see Smeenk and Schliesser 2013: 146).

[13] I thank Daniel Moerner for emphasizing the abductive nature of the argument.

[14] Smith never explicitly notes the possibility that the commitment to natural order (or design) presupposed by science is what a Kantian might call a "regulative principle." This would not help the Newtonians, who require it as an ontological principle, but it would help illuminate Smith's authorial stance in Astronomy.

Andrew Corsa has suggested a useful way of understanding the distinction between pusillanimous and magnanimous superstition. Magnanimous superstition is a consequence of taking the universe to be machine-like. Scientific theory involves imaginary machines. Irregular events come, as it were, "from the machine," even if a deity is responsible for the machine itself. By contrast, pusillanimous superstition does not involve machine metaphors, and irregular events are attributed directly to gods or spirits. The distinction, thus, marks a contrast between pre-technological and technological worldviews.

There is another passage that bears on the interpretation of Smith developed here. In Ancient Physics, Smith explicitly describes the origin of polytheism as instances of "vulgar superstition," and he concludes his description of polytheism with "the lowest and most pusillanimous superstition supplied the place of natural philosophy" (Astronomy 3.2, EPS 49–50; this long paragraph includes Smith's reference to "the invisible hand of Jupiter" discussed in Section a of Chapter 10). Smith then makes the transition to claim that:

> But when law has established order and security, and subsistence ceases to be precarious, the curiosity of mankind is increased, and their fears are diminished. The leisure which they then enjoy renders them more attentive to the appearances of nature, more observant of her smallest irregularities, and more desirous to know what is the chain which links them all together. That some such chain subsists betwixt all her seemingly disjointed phaenomena, they are necessarily led to conceive; and that magnanimity, and cheerfulness, which all generous natures acquire who are bred in civilized societies, where they have so few occasions to feel their weakness, and so many to be conscious of their strength and security, renders them less disposed to employ, for this connecting chain, those invisible beings whom the fear and ignorance of their rude forefathers had engendered. (Astronomy 3.3, EPS 50)

Smith then argues that the same social conditions (law, some prosperity, leisure, etc.) that make science possible also make magnanimity and cheerfulness possible. (See Smith's description of Hume in the "Letter to Strahan" discussed in Chapter 15.) The development of science itself is then understood as a gradual refining away (to use an eighteenth-century metaphor) of superstitious elements. But Smith leaves unclear if on his account we ought to expect science ever to be cleansed of all superstition. This parallels the conclusion we found at the bottom of Smith's treatment of the piacular in Section e(iii) in Chapter 5.

12

The Methodology of *Wealth of Nations*

This chapter aims to give an interpretation of Smith's main methods in WN. I do so by focusing on the crucial analytical distinction between natural and market prices. I argue that Smith postulates a "natural course" of events in order to stimulate research into institutions and other causes that cause actual events to deviate from it. Smith's employment of the fiction of a natural price should, thus, not be seen as an instance of general or partial equilibrium analysis, but, instead, as part of a theoretical framework that will enable observed deviations from expected regularities to improve his theory. For Smith, scientific theory is, among other functions, a research tool that allows for a potentially open-ended process of successive approximation. I argue that this accords with Smith's views on methodology as articulated in EPS. By way of illumination, Smith's explanation of the introduction of commerce in Europe is contrasted with that of Hume as presented in "Of Commerce."

In the most lengthy section (Section b), I look at Smith's distinction between natural and market prices. I focus on Smith's account of the causes of the deviations of market prices from natural prices. Smith is committed to two, mutually reinforcing, elements of one evidential strategy: (i) to use deviations from expected regularities to uncover the causes at work in political economy and (ii) to enable discovery of these causes to generate successive improvements in the theoretical idealization (or theoretical models) that was used to generate predictions. Echoing Montes (2004), I provide some evidence that Smith was aware of the method; I focus on a very insightful passage in Astronomy in which Smith takes Descartes to task for trying to explain away deviations from general rules instead of explaining them. Along the way, I discuss Smith's treatment of labor markets and his long "digression" on silver.

Joseph Schumpeter (1954) maintained that Smith was at most a grand synthesizer of economic ideas that were being discussed widely at the time; Rashid (1990) has developed this line of argument and demonstrated that Smith was rather ungenerous about his debts to others. However, a focus on the origin of the content of Smith's doctrines obscures the fascinating evidential strategies in Smith's work. Recall that Smith praises Galileo's use of "reason and experience" (Astronomy 4.44, EPS 83). Part of the aim of this chapter is to explain what Smith means by the interplay of "reason and experience."

In Section c I provide further, albeit much more schematic, evidence from WN for my reading of Smith. I focus on Book 3 of WN, where Smith postulates a "natural" development of societies from hunting, to pasturage, to agriculture, to commerce. I show that Smith's employment of a counterfactual four-stage theory is also designed to allow deviations from the natural course to provide a refined, realistic causal explanation of historical events. By way of illumination, I contrast Smith's explanation of the introduction of commerce in Europe with that of his friend and forerunner David Hume. I suggest, however, that Hume's essay "Of the Populousness of Ancient Nations" (1750–1) may have inspired Smith to develop his method.

In Section d, I show that my reading of the method of WN is in accord with Smith's methodologic views on science as revealed by Astronomy. I focus on some of Smith's views on the nature of scientific theories—or "machines." It turns out that for Smith, theories are tools for further research. This may seem an obvious use for a theory, but taking this idea seriously creates a shift in perspective; it makes one ask: How does this theory allow one to find and analyze data that can be turned into evidence? (Harper 2011). What kind of research can one do to improve the theory? I suggest that Smith is committed to something akin to a process of successive approximation.

a. Reflexivity

In this brief section, I argue that Smith is reflexive about his own enterprise even in WN. At the start of WN, he observes, "Those theories [of political economy] have a considerable influence, not only upon the opinions of men of learning, but upon the public conduct of princes and sovereign states" (Introduction and Plan of the Work, 8, 11). Smith signals a contrast between the opinions of "men of learning" and the public conduct of "princes." Theories not only attempt to explain and predict economic behavior, but through the actions of rulers also deliberately or unintentionally influence it. Thus, they run the risk, for example, of becoming self-fulfilling or self-refuting prophecies.

In addition, the passage also shows his awareness of the risk that scientific experts will become the (paid) spokespeople for the partial interest of the dominant class or rank of a particular society or stage of development (as Smith implies has happened with the authors defending mercantilism); they then peddle "wrong" systems. Despite his terseness, Smith's remark reveals methodologic self-awareness and sophistication.

WN is a very long treatise—about a thousand pages. Despite the remark just quoted, there are, nevertheless, very few methodologic comments in the book, especially when we compare it to other seventeenth- and eighteenth-century treatises that often contain important statements on method or rules of reasoning. Instead we find many elaborate descriptions and homely examples. Even though

Smith calls his book "a speculative work" (WN 5.3.68, 934), he clearly does not want to limit its appeal to "men of learning".

At one point he says the following about his readership: "this book may come into the hands of many people who are not men of business, and as the effects of this practice upon the banking trade are not perhaps generally understood even by men of business themselves, I shall endeavour to explain it as distinctly as I can" (WN 2.2.66, 309).[1] He clearly and evidently expects a diverse readership; this means that he understands himself as writing for a heterogeneous audience. It is no surprise, then, that his rhetoric has attracted considerable interest (see, especially, Brown 1994; Tribe 1999; Fleischacker 2004; Phillips 2006; Christie 1987 is sadly neglected). Sometimes Smith is even apologetic for being "obscure" and "extremely abstracted" (e.g., WN 1.4.43, 46). Either way, Smith leaves it to the reader to figure out his methods. In this chapter we are almost exclusively focused on a topic of interest only to a narrow segment of these "men of learning."

b. Natural and Market Prices

In this section, I explain the contrast that Smith draws between natural and market prices. I provide a rather detailed case study on behalf of my general methodologic theses. The detail is necessary not only because of the intricacy and subtlety of Smith's thought, but also because it is widely agreed that Smith's account of natural price is one of the key elements of the analytical or theoretical core of WN. Hence, this is a crucial test case of any account that is offered as an interpretation of substantive parts of the methodology or theory of WN.

At the start of Chapter 7 of Book 1, Smith writes,

> When the price of any commodity is neither more nor less than what is sufficient to pay the rent of the land, the wages of the labour, and the profits of the stock employed in raising, preparing, and bringing it to market, according to their natural rates, the commodity is then sold for what may be called its natural price. The commodity is then sold precisely for what it is worth, or for what it really costs the person who brings it to market; for though in common language what is called the prime cost of any commodity does not comprehend the profit of the person who is to sell it again, yet if he sells it at a price which does not allow him the ordinary rate of profit in his neighbourhood, he is evidently a loser by the trade; since by employing his stock in some other

---

[1] This is a striking exception to Smith's general presumption that economic agents understand their own interests; the complexity of financial services has always made it special (see his critical discussion of the engineered opacity of financial products, the so-called bills of exchange; WN 2.2.67–75, 309–15).

way he might have made that profit. His profit, besides, is his revenue, the proper fund of his subsistence ... Though the price, therefore,
which leaves him this profit is not always the lowest at which a dealer
may sometimes sell his goods, it is the lowest at which he is likely to
sell them for any considerable time; at least where there is perfect liberty, or where he may change his trade as often as he pleases. The actual
price at which any commodity is commonly sold is called its market
price. It may either be above, or below, or exactly the same with its natural price. (WN 1.7.4–7, 72–3)

There is a lot to unpack here. I focus on the purpose of the distinction between
natural and market prices, and how one would go about measuring the natural
price. First I explain a few background features of Smith's framework. For Smith,
the price of a commodity is a composite of rents, wages, and profits. This is, of
course, an oversimplification; strictly speaking, it is a composite of rents, wages,
profits, and the cost of raw materials and instruments used up, but the latter
resolves itself ("immediately or ultimately") into one of the three component
parts. Smith explicitly rejects the idea that there is a fourth part to the natural
rate (WN 1.6.11, 68). What is true for a single commodity is also true for the
"whole annual produce of a society, or what comes to the same thing, the whole
price of that annual produce."

Thus, these three components correspond to the three great classes in society: landowners, workers, and merchants (WN 1.6.17–9, 69–70 and 1.11.p.7,
265). Smith wrote in a time when the service part of the economy was not very
developed yet, although it is surprising he does not mention it in the early chapters of WN because he later devotes considerable space to banking, insurance,
education, clergy, and law (but see Rosenberg 1968; for comments on the relationship between "annual produce" and a modern conception of "national income,"
see O'Donnell [1990, 30ff]).

Smith assumes that in "every society or neighbourhood" there will be "an ordinary or average" rate of wages, profits, and rents. These average rates will be called
the natural rates (for wages and so on) "at the time and place in which they commonly prevail" (WN I.7.1–3, 72). If one knows these average rates, one can then
estimate the natural price. For simplicity's sake, assume that Smith's concept of
a "society or neighbourhood" is not problematic; in Chapter 6, I had argued that
a "society" just is some combination of laws and productive capacity shared by a
particular "neighborhood," or "different employments, and ... different laws and
policy" (WN 1.7.36, 80).

It is worth stressing that the price is only said to be "natural" in a situation
of what Smith calls "perfect liberty"—that is, when the labor and commodity
markets, especially, are competitive and free (WN 1.7.27, 78). Although capital
markets were also not free (as Smith explains, in many countries the exportation
of gold was forbidden and interest rates were regulated), Smith often seems to

assume, following Hume, that regulations against the movement of capital are much more ineffective than other economic statutes (WN 2.3.23, 340; on Smith's concept of capital, see Aspromourgos 2013: 270–5). The "natural price" is, then, the counterfactual, localized price of a good if there were not all kinds of obstacles preventing the free movement of capital, labor, and goods (Marshall came close to seeing this, but Andrews 2015 is correct to criticize him, although my position is at odds with Andrews's claim that it is the reproduction price). That is to say, it comes down to what the world would be like if there were no impediments to the mobility of resources. This situation did not exist in Smith's time (or ours); thus, the natural price can, at best, only be estimated.

One might think that there were natural prices for some goods in Smith's time, but even if there were free markets in a particular commodity, the factors of production would still be influenced by the obstacles in other markets. (For the systemic element in Smith's understanding see Skinner (1979, 1996), and my discussion below.)

The situation of perfect liberty is not a necessary condition for the price of a commodity to be or reach its natural price. Even if there were no complete mobility of resources in an economy, fluctuations in short-run market prices may, for whatever reason, make a commodity occasionally reach its natural price. Smith is clear that except when an economy operates in perfect liberty, this is unlikely to happen very often or last very long; "what is sufficient to pay the rent of the land, the wages of the labour, and the profits of the stock employed in raising, preparing and bringing it to market" is in most non-perfect-liberty conditions almost always going to be different from, and usually more than, what is said to be the natural price of a commodity (WN 1.7.30, 79).

But how does one go about estimating the natural price of a good? How does one discover what the average rates of rent, wages, and profit are? Moreover, how does one go about figuring out what they would be in nonexistent circumstances? To put it crudely, according to Smith, rent and wages rise with the increasing prosperity of society (for explicit statements on wages see WN 1.8.21–2, 86–7, and on rents see 1.11.p.1, 264). By contrast, Smith thinks that in rich societies the rate of profit would be low (WN 1.9.20, 113), while in poor societies it would be high, and "it is always highest in countries which are going fastest to ruin" (WN 1.11.p.10, 266). Smith claims that in prosperous countries—that is, those in which capital had already been accumulated—"mutual competition" among merchants, who have abundant sources of capital, would drive down profit rates (WN 1.9.2, 105), while poor and declining countries would scare off merchants, thus increasing potential profit for the adventurous few. For Smith high wages and high profits do not tend to go together. However, he did recognize an exception to this general rule in "the peculiar circumstances of new colonies," where profits, due to relative lack of stock, and wages, due to high growth, could both be high (WN 1.8.11, 109). One may be tempted to claim that Smith thought that the rate of growth determines the rate of profit, but he thought that the unusual circumstance of the

American colonies (abundant fertile land, unusually low prices for land, etc.) was an exception that proved the rule. Of course, the rate of growth can influence the rate of profit for Smith.

The high or low rates of land rent are the effect of high or low prices (WN 1.11.a.8, 162); rents shadow prices. For Smith the rates of rent are the result of haggling between landowners and farmers, influenced by their relative power to supply and demand. (Of course, Smith repeatedly points out that the legal structure influences the types of leases and land ownership. I am also ignoring the status of mine and house rents for the sake of brevity.) Wages, however, are not only set by the demand and supply of labor (and the effort, skill, security, public esteem, and probability of success involved; see WN 1.10.b.1–33, 116–28), but they are also influenced by guild policies, fixed wage scales, and various regulations that benefit the merchants and tradesmen at the expense of the workers, who were denied attempts to combine (recall the discussion of WN 1.10.c.61, 157–8 in Section e in Chapter 8).

For Smith, wages would be a cause of high or low prices (WN 1.11.a.8, 162)— that is, high wages, a sign of a growing economy, would lead to higher prices, unless, of course, productivity would grow at the same rate (WN 1.11.o.1, 260). Apparently, Smith does not think that it would be difficult to estimate the average rent. He may be confident about this because the information on rents was (for tax purposes) a matter of public record published in registries (WN 5.2.c.1–d.9, 828– 40, although WN 5.2.c.21, 834, shows awareness of incentives for fraud on part of lessor and lessee). Smith's relative optimism on this score may, as Jen Boobar first suggested to me, also be due to the fact that many rents were paid in corn, thus standardizing measurement (see Section c in Chapter 8). Smith admits, however, that "[I]t is not easy . . . to ascertain what are the average wages of a labourer even in a particular place, and at a particular time" (WM 1.9.3, 105; see also the important discussion at WN 1.8.34, 93–5). At best one can determine what the usual (a phrase Smith uses as well) wages are. This does not seem to worry him much. Generally, when Smith makes claims about wages, he keeps his sources of information obscure (with a few exceptions, such as historical documents at WN 1.8.34, 94–5, and personal conversation at 1.10.b.50, 134; see Fleischacker 2004: 36–44, for more detailed discussion).

Figuring out the average rate of profits is even more difficult. For competitive reasons, merchants have a strong incentive to hide their profits (WN 1.7.21, 77). Also, due to price changes and chance (sinking of ships, fires in storehouses, etc.) the rate of "profits of stock" for an individual merchant could fluctuate wildly,

> [N]ot only from year to year, but from day to day, and almost from hour to hour. To ascertain what is the average profit of all the different trades carried on in a great kingdom, must be much more difficult; and to judge of what it may have been formerly, or in remote periods of time, with any degree of precision, must be altogether impossible. (WN 1.9.3, 105)

There can be, thus, no doubt that Smith was acutely conscious of the limited accuracy of data available to him. (See also his remark on the "somewhat uncertain" information on claims about quality at 1.11.o.5, 261.) In fact, unless the taxman or the government had shown interest in the past, there would be little reason to expect any data on an industry (see, e.g., WN 4.5.a.33, 521).[2] Smith notes the near-total absence of reliable data and the fudging of the contemporary practitioners of "Political Arithmetick" (WN 4.5.b.30, 534–5, and Letter No. 249 to George Chalmers, November 10, 1758). ("Political Arithmetick" is roughly the eighteenth-century version of social science statistics; see Redman 1997: 142–51, for an introduction to the ideas of Petty, King, and Davenant, especially. See also her account of Smith's views on "Political Arithmetick" [Redman 1997: 230–3].)[3]

There is a potential confusion in Smith. When one subtracts wages and rent from the natural price of a commodity, "profit" seems to refer to the margin left over that accrues to the manufacturer or trader. This is an understanding of profit that in modern terms is described as the ratio of flow profits to flow costs, or profit margin. But sometimes, as in the quote from WN 1.9.3, 105, Smith seems to be referring to what moderns call the ratio of flow profits to capital stock, or return on investment. The modern conceptual apparatus assumes a distinction between flow and stock (see Mirowski 1988: 205ff). Smith probably assumed that profit margins and rate of profit on stock are connected. It appears he thought that an increase of stock would stimulate competition and increase wages, and drive down profits (WN 1.9.2, 105). He seems not to have envisioned the possibility that one could have a low margin on an individual commodity, yet still have a high rate of return on one's investment or high margins with low returns on investment. Nevertheless, in what follows, I accept Smith's argument at face value; I treat him as saying that profits on stock and profit margins are tightly related. There is another problem in Smith: when he writes about "the profit of stock" he sometimes means the rate of profit and not the total amount of profit. In general, the context makes it clear what he means.

Inspired, perhaps, by David Hume, who called interest the "barometer" of the state (Hume's "Of Interest," EMPL 303), and Turgot, who called it the "thermometer" (Turgot [1770] 1889, §LXXXIX), Smith proposes measuring interest rates to indirectly measure the average rate of profit. For Smith, the rate of profit influences the rate of interest: "wherever a great deal can be made by the use of money, a great deal will commonly be given for the use of it; and . . . wherever little can be made by it, less will commonly be given for it" (WN 1.9.4, 105). In the definition, but not elsewhere (WN 5.3, 907–47), Smith ignores the effects of government borrowing. Smith thought that in his own time interest rates were about

---

[2] This anticipates part of Piketty's argument for the role of taxation; the taxman's interest generates incentives for the collection of reliable data (Piketty 2014: 12; 570).

[3] Smith was distinctly reserved about the application of mathematical techniques in the human sciences; see Chapter 13.

half profit rates. It is only a rough indicator, however, because "The proportion which the usual market rate of interest ought to be to the ordinary rate of clear profit, necessarily varies as profit rises or falls." Smith thinks interest is made up of two components: "insurance" against loss of the capital and a compensation for opportunity costs, "sufficient recompence for the trouble of employing the stock" (WN 1.9.22, 114; cf. Turgot [1770] 1889, §LXXIII), where he insists that interest is a form of compensation for opportunities [of profit or revenue] forgone). Smith is not contradicting himself by claiming, on the one hand, that short-term interest rates are determined by the supply and demand of loanable funds, while, on the other hand, claiming that interest rates themselves can be analyzed into two different components.

In risky or very stable countries, either component may have a different weighting. Of course, various governments have attempted to fix the rate of interest, so Smith warns the reader to focus, on the whole, on market rates, although sometimes those are secret. In general, he thinks that in most countries there are "several very safe and easy methods of evading the law" (WN 1.9.9, 107; see also 2.4.16, 358). This would make figuring out the exact market rates of interest not a simple task. Nevertheless, Smith thinks that, especially in England, the fixed rates often "follow" the market rates of interest (WN 1.9.5, 106), so the problem should not be exaggerated.

Incidentally, at WN 2.4.17, 358, we learn that the rate of interest influences the price of land, so indirectly at least, interest rates will influence the size of the rent (WN 4.7.c58, 611). Moreover, if the natural price of a commodity is the result of adding up its constitutive components, then high rent will cause high prices, and so on. Here I can only give a glimpse of the interconnected relationships among all factors in Smith's economic system; see Skinner (1979, 1996) for more details.

Moreover, even if the movement of capital were free, the rate of profit is influenced by the existence of monopolies and market barriers that can artificially inflate or lower the rate. Thus, even if one used market interest rates to get at average profit rates, one is not measuring the natural rate of profit. (Marx complains about this; 1968, Part II: 229.) Finally, Smith notes about the natural rate of profit, rent, and wages that "in every society this rate varies according to their circumstances, according to their riches or poverty, their advancing, stationary, or declining condition" (WN 1.7.33, 80). This implies that the natural price of a commodity only changes when the circumstances of a society change (O'Donnell 1990: 90–6). No wonder Smith never attempts to calculate a natural price in the whole of WN! (For a critical evaluation, see O'Donnell 1990: 10ff, 85, 157, 214–8.)

Incidentally, part of Smith's argument against the colonial monopolies is that it raises the rate of profit in one sector and advances its interests at the expense of all other sectors by hurting their rate of profit and consumers generally (WN 4.7.c.60, 612). Some critics have been puzzled by an element of Smith's argument. Although he clearly shows that other sectors—and consumers in general—are hurt by the monopoly trade, it could be the case that the exorbitant profits from the colonial trade raise the general rate of profit. Smith has no trouble conceding this while still maintaining his polemic against monopolies. After all, he makes it clear in WN that high rates of profit are, in general, a bad thing. It is only readers who presuppose that Smith is a spokesperson for the profit-seeking class who will see a paradox here (e.g., at the height of the depression, Max Lerner in the preface to the 1937 edition of WN).[4]

To be clear: the factors that make up a "natural" price (i.e., wages, rent, and profit) exist only in certain economic arrangements or stages of economic development. Specifically, there is no rent in a hunting society (WN 5.i.b.2, 709), and many shepherd societies may not have stable property arrangements. Thus, the theory being described and defended in Books 1 and 2 of WN is applicable in only a limited domain (i.e., societies with property and ones that have at least some freemen [for if all the labor were performed by slaves there would be no wages] and merchants). By contrast, the natural course of things in Book 3 covers several more stages. (This is not to say that certain aspects of the theory as developed in Books 1 and 2 cannot be extended or adapted to cover other periods or levels of development.) The extent of this domain is constrained by features of, say, the legal structure of the society under analysis, as it is in this case of the theory of Book 1. But one can imagine that other human institutions (e.g., the existence of different modes of production or the establishment of new categories of income) will structure and constrain the contents of the possible generalizations.

Smith's theory in Books 1 and 2 is, thus, context-sensitive to the laws and institutions of a society. (See Hutchison 1978, 10; Hutchison points out on p. 7 that subsequent economists assumed a fairly stable social and political environment.) As Smith explains:

> [T]hough pecuniary wages and profit are very different in the different employments of labour and stock; yet a certain proportion seems commonly to take place between both the pecuniary wages in all the different employments of labour, and the pecuniary profits in all the different employments of stock. This proportion, it will appear hereafter, depends partly upon the nature of the different employments, and partly upon the different laws and policy of the society in which they are carried on. But though in many respects dependent upon the laws and policy, this proportion seems to be little affected by the riches or poverty of that society; by its advancing, stationary, or declining condition; but to remain the same or very nearly the same in all those different states. (WN 1.7.36, 80)

---

[4] After granting that Smith was "something of a revolutionary," he adds that "He was on the economic side, the philosopher of the capitalist revolution, as John Locke was its philosopher on the political side" (Lerner, Introduction, 1937: x).

Smith does not emphasize the context-sensitive nature of his work in WN, and he expects the learned reader to keep it in mind. He was too optimistic on this issue.

So what does Smith want to do with this notion of a natural price? Why would he risk the criticism of his close friend, Hume, who upon reading of WN claimed that "I cannot think, that the rents of Farms makes any part of the Price of the Produce, but that the price is determined altogether by the Quantity and the Demand?" (Hume's Letter No. 150 to Smith, April 1, 1776, 186, Corr. 186). Ricardo and his followers would echo this criticism. Smith agrees that this was indeed the case for short-run market prices (WN 1.7.8, 73; O'Donnell 1990: 89–90, claims that in Smith the market price is the short period, while the natural price is the long period [WN 1.7.4–7, 72–3]). In the next section I argue for the potential epistemic payoff of Smith's approach.

c. Deviations from Nature, "The Price of Free Competition"

In this section I argue that Smith's methodology creates an invitation not only to determine the nature of and the causal role that human institutions play in economic life, but also to improve on his theory, if necessary. The political, far-reaching significance of this is the possibility to make the world conform to theory: if the natural system of liberty is ever implemented, the calculations required to establish an exact natural price would also become more tractable.

Many commentators note the indebtedness of Smith to Petty and the Physiocrats, especially Cantillon and Turgot (for useful corrective, see Groenewegen 2009). Yet neither their *Le prix veritable* nor *Le prix mitoyen* conforms to Smith's understanding of natural price (see Turgot [1770] 1889, §XXXI and §XXXII). Turgot's notion of *Le Prix fondamental* (see his letter to Hume, March 25, 1767) comes very close because it includes the wages and profits (but not rent). However, Turgot views it as a minimum price below which the market price cannot fall; this is not true in Smith's theory. Perhaps inspired by Petty 1662, who uses "natural price" in a proto-labor theory of value (Persky 1990: 188), Hume also employs the phrase "natural price" in "Of Taxes" (EMPL 345), but does so in a casual fashion. If even Hume cannot see any use for a natural price, why would Smith introduce this abstract and hard-to-measure concept?

Let us grant on behalf of Smith that the natural price is a kind of useful fiction. Whatever the metaphysical status of this fiction—1.7.20, 77 (to be quoted below) makes it tempting to view it something more akin to a center of gravity in physics and less akin to, say, a unicorn—can we say more about it on conceptual grounds? For example, the (average) market price of labor can be below, at, or above the natural price. Smith thinks, however, that most market prices are (well) above the natural price. For example, if the market price of a good remained below the natural price, then workers "will withdraw a part of their labour" (WN 1.7.13, 75) or farmers and merchants would move into more profitable areas (e.g., 111.b.23, 168). Of course, if the market wage rate dropped below the subsistence rate, then the workers would starve and, thus, ultimately reduce the availability of labor (see Hill and Montag 2014 for the significance of this). As we have already seen with his interest in the economic causes of infanticide, Smith does not think this is merely a hypothetical situation (e.g., WN 1.8.26, 92; 1.8.40, 98; 5.2.k.7–8, 872–3; for a discussion of other causes of famine see WN 4.5.b.6–9, 526–8). A declining populace would shrink demand and this in turn (setting off a vicious cycle) would shrink the division of labor, and so forth. (For more on Smith's views on famine, see Rothschild 2001: 73–86.)

Smith assumes that, in general, market prices will be more frequently above natural prices: "the market price of any particular commodity, though it may continue long above, can seldom continue long below its natural price" (1.7.30, 79). Smith does not discuss examples where the market price of a good is below a natural price (so, in practice, he agrees with Turgot). For Smith, prices are nearly always seen falling to the natural rate (e.g., WN 1.11.g.21–2, 219–20); changes in technology and productivity or supply factors can alter the natural price (see O'Donnell 1990: 255, n. 26). Smith says in a famous passage:

> [B]ut though the market price of every particular commodity is in this manner continually gravitating, if one may say so, towards the natural price, yet sometimes particular accidents, sometimes natural causes, and sometimes particular regulations of police [i.e., public administration], may, in many commodities keep up the market price, for a long time together, a good deal above the natural price. (WN 1.7.20, 77)

This passage is central to debates about the degree to which Smith anticipated modern equilibrium theories (Hollander 1973 and O'Donnell 1990 offer conflicting accounts). That debate misses the reasons why Smith developed his conceptual apparatus and fails to grasp the logic of Smith's enterprise. While Smith uses imagery that is often suggestive of an equilibrium model, his only explicit mention of the word "equilibrium" is, as Leon Montes (2003) has emphasized, in the context of an attack on the Mercantilist system (WN 4.3.c.2, 489). It is by no means clear that he means to endorse an equilibrium conception of the economy there.[5]

Smith's use of gravitational metaphor may have been influenced by Turgot ([1770] 1889 §LXXXVIII and §LXXXIX; see Rothschild 2001: 76ff for useful comments on the contrast between Turgot and Smith on general equilibrium). Because of Smith's use of "gravitating," one could be tempted to hear an echo of

---

[5] I do not mean to deny that there are equilibrium-generating mechanisms with hydrostatic imagery in Smith thought, but Smith's views on population also suggest he would have been excited to learn of dynamic disequilibrium theories.

Newton's theory of universal gravity in this passage (cf. Redman 1997: 219), but the comparison is misleading if only because the natural price is not also gravitating toward the market price—that is, the gravitation is not mutual. For, in Newton "all attraction is (by Law III) mutual" (*Principia*, Book 3, Proposition 5, Theorem 5, Corollary 1). In fact, Smith's statement is closer to a description of Aristotelian gravity, in which matter gravitates toward its natural place (*Physics* 8.4, 255b13–17 [Bodnar 2016]; see also Section a and b in Chapter 13). Yet, Smith was aware that Newton's theory implied universal, mutual, simultaneous attraction (Astronomy 4.67–76, EPS 98–104). Smith explicitly writes about the "mutual attraction of the Planets" (Astronomy 4.67–68, EPS 99).

Rather, for Smith the natural price is the (counterfactual!) "price of free competition" (WN 1.7.27, 78; see also 1.7.6, 73; 1.7.30, 79; O'Donnell 1990: 58–61, 93–96) and, without it, the market price will almost always deviate from it. Of course, most of WN is a lament about the political interventions in such competition.

Smith informs his readers that there are three types of reasons for "deviations, whether occasional or permanent, of the market price of commodities from the natural price" (WN 1.7.32, 80):

(1) when, regardless of high prices, supply is limited due to natural causes (e.g., the vineyards of particular soils in France, 1.7.24, 78);
(2) the existence of legal monopolies that keep the market "under-stocked, by never supplying the effectual demand" (1.7.26, 78);
(3) various trade and labor regulations that lower "competition [in a trade] to a smaller number than might otherwise go into them" (1.7.28, 79).

Smith makes it clear that these circumstances can "endure for many centuries" (1.7.31, 79). For Smith, the difference between the latter two types of cause is just a matter of degree; trade and labor regulations are "a sort of enlarged monopolies" (1.7.28, 79). Of these three reasons, (2) and (3) are frequently the consequence of mercantilist policies.

Note that in the quote (WN 1.7.28, 79) about the third type of reason on why a market price may deviate from the natural price, Smith uses counterfactual language. The natural path is one that would happen if it were not for obstacles to competition. (See Maifreda 2012: 100ff for a fascinating genealogy of counterfactual conception of prices.) That is to say, the discussion of the natural prices is designed to promote the following question: What cause(s) or reasons prevent the market price from falling to the natural price? And, within Smith's explanatory scheme, the natural response is that, except for a few goods whose supply cannot be increased, human institutions, policies, laws, and so forth prevent market prices from falling to natural prices. The discrepancies between market prices and estimated natural prices are caused by human intervention. By contrast, subsequent Ricardian economics made determining the natural rates of wages, profit, and rent the object of analysis of economic theory (O'Donnell 1990: 55).

From the perspective of Smith's economics one can say that instead of having general, trans-stadial, validity, such theories must assume constant background conditions.

A large part of the take-home message of Smith's argument in Books 1 and 2 of WN is that the natural price is not only the most efficient but also the fairest price. In Smith's time most inefficiencies were also welfare-reducing (see Rothschild 2001, Chapter 4, for a discussion of passages that show how for Smith efficiency and fairness are often connected). It is easy to see part of Smith's argument: not only do existing regulations cause market prices to favor the well-connected (rent-seeking) few and to raise the price of all goods for all consumers, hence lowering their welfare, they also provide false signals; from the vantage point of "equity" (WN 1.8.36, 96) they distort investment decisions. (On the importance of justice in WN, see Brubaker 2002 and Werhane 1991: 82.) In fact, if Smith's system is "fully implemented" it would not allow steep inequalities to arise (see Boucoyannis 2013 for a very thorough and important version of this argument). Smith probably did not foresee the possibility that there could be a negative trade-off between efficiency and welfare.

In effect, Smith provides a detailed analytical argument for Montesquieu's claim that "it is competition that puts a just price on goods" (*The Spirit of the Laws*, Part 4, Book 20, Chapter 9; for mention of Montesquieu in WN, see 1.9.17, 112–3; 2.4.9, 353; 4.9.47, 684; and 5.1.f.40, 775; of course, Montesquieu was anticipated by a whole host of earlier writers in the Scholastic just price tradition, but Smith tends to ridicule the Scholastics). By avoiding "just price" terminology with its Scholastic connotations, Smith can ignore the intellectual baggage associated with it. (For Smith and the Scholastics see Young 1997 or Young and Gordon 1996). Michel Foucault captures the point nicely:

> [The natural price] will be profitable to the seller, but also to the buyer; to both buyer and seller. That is to say, the beneficial effects of competition will not be divided unequally between them and necessary to the advantage of one at the expense of the other. The legitimate game of natural competition that is to say, competition under conditions of freedom, can only lead to a dual profit. The fluctuation of the price around the value ... brings into play a mechanism of mutual enrichment: maximum profit for the seller, minimum expense for the buyer. (Foucault 2008: 53–4)

To be clear: according to Smith the profit to the seller could be higher under less competitive conditions, but as Foucault emphasizes according to Smith the profit that the seller gains under competitive conditions does not come at the expense of others. In fact, Foucault is quite generous here to Smith. Compared to the treatment in Book 2 of the *Inquiry* of Smith's great rival, James Steuart, Smith underdescribes the "fluctuation of the price around value;" in Smith we find little detailed description or conceptual analysis of the mechanisms of price formation (cf. Steuart 1966).

So, I agree with Deborah Redman when she claims that Smith "abstracts from the real world to determine a typical—what he terms natural—representation of the facts." But this abstraction, which Smith presents in an extremely gentle fashion to his readers, is only the first step. By specifying *in advance* what could be a cause for a deviation from the natural price, Smith allows the "men of learning" among his readers to quantify and exploit discrepancies from these idealizations to improve his theory. Here I mean by the term "idealization" a situation that would hold exactly in certain specifiable circumstances. Smith tells us to expect a gap between his theory (the natural price) and the facts (the market price); methodologically, it is an invitation not only to determine the nature of and causal role that human institutions play in economic life, but also to improve on his theory, if necessary.

Of course, *politically* it may be an invitation to help make the world conform to theory. If the natural system of liberty is ever implemented, the calculations required to establish an exact natural price would also become more tractable. Smith's political project, thus, makes a "science of Man" more possible. As we have already seen, Smith is extremely aware that such implementation may generate conflict and downside risks. This is why (recall Section a of Chapter 1) he promotes gradualism in the implementation of policies, even those in accord with his own system, on grounds of "humanity" and fear of "disorder" (WN 4.2.40, 469).

i. Newton's Fourth Rule of Reasoning

In this section I explore the link between Smith's methodology and a crucial feature of Newton's methodology (Montes 2003). I argue that Smith's thinking is in accord with a very important feature of Newton's methodology: empirical exceptions to general rules, even minor ones, should be investigated because they open up either the possibility of discovering interesting refinements to general rules or the possibility of formulating a more sophisticated new theory. As Newton writes:

> In experimental philosophy, propositions gathered from phenomena by induction should be considered either exactly or very nearly true notwithstanding any contrary hypotheses, until yet other phenomena make such propositions either more exact or liable to exceptions (*Principia*, Book III, Rule IV)

The fourth rule says that we should treat well-confirmed propositions as true (or nearly true) until there are deviations that promote new research, which, in turn, will lead us to refine our original propositions or reject them for new ones. That is, Newton accepts that physical inquiry may be open-ended. As he writes in the Preface to *Principia*, "the principles set down here will shed some light on either this mode of philosophizing or some truer one" (Newton 1999: 383; for discussion see G. E. Smith 2002, Harper 2011, and, especially, G. E. Smith 2014).

One can see in the fourth rule a principle of the fallibility of induction (Force 1987: 180–7; Redman 1997: 79–82, endorses Force's view). It does implicitly accept that the future may bring surprises and new evidence, and, thus, anticipates one of Hume's major insights. But it avoids Hume's more skeptical conclusions (for more on Hume and the fourth rule, see Schliesser 2004). Instead, the fourth rule is (1) a proposal of how to treat Newton's system—that is, as true until proven otherwise—and (2) an encouragement to find and exploit known deviations from the regularities he has established in order to make them "more exact." It is true that Newton recognizes in the last three words of the first sentence of the fourth rule that regularities can have exceptions. But, regardless of what Newton means by "phenomena" and "hypotheses," all he is saying in the fourth rule—and this is clearly stated in the second sentence—is that one must not be distracted by possible differing explanations for the found regularities until one has empirical reason to do so.

ii. Descartes and Kepler's Irregularities

I have no direct evidence that Smith found his method by reading Newton, but in this section I offer evidence that it is not unlikely. One might think that to pay attention to empirical exceptions is just obviously sound methodology, and not especially Newtonian. But this is a methodologic achievement of Newton. I have already shown that Smith was a very astute reader of Newton in Astronomy. Of course, Smith praises Newton's style of presentation in LRBL (see ii.132–4, LRBL 145–6), but here I am not concerned with Smith's views on different modes of presentation.

Nevertheless, as Smith's eighteenth-century editors of EPS recognized, in Astronomy, Smith's treatment of Newton is not exhaustive. One could reasonably doubt that Smith learned to think about the evidential import of deviations from regularities by reading Newton. I do not have conclusive evidence for this, but this does not mean there is no evidence at all that Smith was unaware of the point. In this section, I present Smith's criticism of Descartes' methodology. This shows that Smith was aware of the methodology that I ascribe to him, regardless of its source.

To show the significance for science—in Smith's philosophy of science—of discrepancies between scientific theories and data, it is useful to recall that in Astronomy there are for Smith two related species of wonder (Astronomy 2.5–9, EPS 40–2). "New and singular" events (Astronomy 2.3, EPS 39) or unusual relations (2.6, EPS 40) excite wonder in people's imagination and make the mind's customary procession between connecting principles falter; this causes "uncertainty and anxious curiosity" (2.4, EPS 40) and even "discomfort" and "tumult" in the "imagination" (2.12, EPS 45–6). The discomfort caused by the appearance(s) of exceptions to expected regularity, one's environmental rationality, first motivates inquiry (cf., by contrast, Berkeley: "exceptions from the general rules of Nature are proper to surprise and awe men into an acknowledgment of the Divine Being" [*A Treatise Concerning the Principles of Human Knowledge*, §63]). Smith provides a very similar account in WN (5.1.f.24–6, 767–770), although the emphasis on discomfort is absent, thus suggesting considerable continuity between the two works. It is noteworthy that in the WN account, Smith discusses both "natural" and "moral philosophy" (5.1.f.26, 767–8), clearly implying that his approach covers both areas. It is this that helps justify my appropriation of the material of Astronomy while interpreting WN. Of course, Smith does acknowledge historical differences (natural philosophy came first [WN 5.1.f.24, 768]) and believes that, in contrast to natural philosophy, where "absurd and ridiculous" systems can gain widespread credence, entirely false moral systems would never find any widespread acceptance (TMS 7.2.4.14, 313–4).

Here, I call special attention to a striking passage in Astronomy. Smith explains the downfall of the Cartesian system in terms of its inability and unwillingness to deal with the "detailed motions and all the minute irregularities" of the heavenly bodies. In Astronomy, Smith points out that Descartes' theory does not explain these deviations from general rules, but attempts to explain them away:

> So far, therefore, from accommodating his [Descartes'] system to all the minute irregularities, which Kepler has ascertained in the movements of the Planets; or from shewing, particularly, how these irregularities, and no other, should arise from it, he contented himself with observing, that perfect uniformity could not be expected in their motions, from the nature of the causes which produced them; that certain irregularities might take place in them, for a great number of successive revolutions, and afterwards give way to others of a different kind: a remark which, happily, relieved him from the necessity of applying his system to the observations of Kepler, and the other Astronomers. (Astronomy 4.66, EPS 97)

One may think that what Smith says here about Kepler is a bit strange because what Kepler had "ascertained" were mostly regularities—which regularities Descartes ignored (or rather, he denied that regularities could exist in this domain), contenting himself with irregularities instead. Kepler's regularities were irregularities from the dominant system(s) among astronomers when Kepler wrote; Kepler pointed to elliptical rather than circular orbits of planets. This is why in Section c of Chapter 3 I insisted that for Smith an "irregularity" is a deviation from either environmental rationality or theoretical reason trained up on systemic expectations.

The quoted passage shows that Smith is aware of the importance of pursuing empirical accuracy and exactitude in judging systems of nature even after general fit has been established. Elsewhere, he criticizes Descartes for claiming that it was not necessary "to suppose, that they [the orbits of the planets] described with geometrical accuracy, or even that they described always precisely the same figure. It rarely happens, that nature can be mathematically exact with regard to figure of the objects she produces" (4.64, EPS 95). Of course, the need to accommodate one's theory "to all the minute irregularities" is akin to what we would call careful curve-fitting, but what Smith has in mind is not merely curve-fitting. The passage from 4.66 (EPS 97), also shows he thinks that it is a legitimate requirement on a system that it should provide a systematic account of how discrepancies from regularities can arise within it. He means by this that a theory should both explain in advance what would count as evidence for or against it, and what type of deviations from regularities one could expect and explain with it. Smith implies about Cartesian-style theorizing that it does not have a feedback mechanism to allow empirical failures to improve one's theory.

Hence, it is not surprising that, in Astronomy, Smith calls attention to how deviations from Ptolemy's, Almamon's, and the Alphonsine tables inspired corrections to Ptolemy's system (4.26, EPS 70–1). Throughout Astronomy, Smith is getting at how the search for discrepancies from expected and clearly specified regularities can lead to refinement of existing or development of new theory (in addition to the passages about wonder, see also 4.7, EPS 58, and 4.60, EPS 91). This is very Newtonian (see G. E. Smith 2002 and 2014; for judicious remarks, see Wightman 1975: 62). A good theory may even lead not only to a qualitative change in the questions asked, but also to fundamentally different kinds of questions and criteria by which they are judged. (Recall Smith's treatment of Cassini in Section b of Chapter 11.)

It is useful to draw a contrast with Smith's celebrated contemporary, d'Alembert. We know that Smith read his *Preliminary Discourse to the Encyclopedia* (1751) (Edinburgh Review 6, EPS 246). D'Alembert also advocates that unusual events, or "monsters" (146), required special attention. They ought to be the topic of a special branch of natural history: "Errors or deviations of nature." But in the *Preliminary Discourse* d'Alembert overlooks the idea that they could be useful in refining the regularities found in nature. (In fact, the only use d'Alembert sees for "monsters" is "to pass from the prodigies of nature's deviations to the marvels of art" [146].) Thus, while d'Alembert emphasizes the importance of exactitude in science (95), he does not emphasize in his popular writings one of the most important benefits to be derived from it. If the empirical world cooperates, precision and exactitude allow one to get ever more rigorous about deviant data in order to marshal such data as potential evidence for better theories.

d. The Role of Institutions

In this section I explain the causal role of human institutions in WN. In particular, I explain how Smith's account can support counterfactual claims about these.

The theoretical fiction of a "natural price" not only calls attention to the distorting influences of human institutions but also points to an approach that can make evident the causes of the wealth of nations. Smith's science postulates the existence of the natural price and, more broadly, the natural course of economic development. Invoking the language of nature is obviously partly done for rhetorical purposes; to many eighteenth-century readers, deviations from nature will have seemed corrupt and flawed (Becker 1932). But discrepancies from the natural course of things also put the spotlight on the causes of wealth formation and retardation: human institutions (recall my discussion above of WN 1.7.24–31, 78–80). As Smith writes at the start of Book 3:

> That order of things which necessity imposes in general, though not in every particular country, is, in every particular country, promoted by the natural inclinations of man. If human institutions had never thwarted those natural inclinations, the towns could nowhere have increased beyond what the improvement and cultivation of the territory in which they were situated could support; till such time, at least, as the whole of that territory was completely cultivated and improved. (WN 3.1.3, 377; cf. 3.1.4, 378)

Smith uses counterfactual language to make his point. He presupposes what would have happened. Smith explains that it is the workings of institutions that prevent the natural course of things from taking place. Recall that for Smith human institutions include roads, bridges, canals, harbors, companies, schools, universities, religious orders/ministries, the monarchy, the armed forces, slavery, taxation policies, and legal arrangements (especially on land and inheritance of property).

It is tempting to graft Hume's distinction between the "natural" and "artificial" onto Smith's approach to institutions (Treatise 3.1.2.9). For Hume education (1.3.9.19), property, honor, custom, civil laws (2.1.10.1), justice (3.3.6.4), and, perhaps, all goal-directed human actions (3.1.2.9 and 3.2.6.6) are "artificial." If Smith thought of "artificial" institutions as deflecting the "natural" course of things, then his conception harks back to the traditional (pre-Cartesian) understanding of mechanics, which studied how human artifices change the course of nature (Pack and Schliesser 2017; cf. Sagar 2017).

Now, Smith had articulated the professed aim of Books 3 and 4 of WN at the end of Book 2:

> What circumstances in the policy of Europe have given the trades which are carried on in towns so great an advantage over that which is carried on in the country, that private persons frequently find it more for their advantage to employ their capitals in the most distant carrying trades of Asia and America, than in the improvement and cultivation of the

most fertile fields in their own neighbourhood, I shall endeavour to explain at full length in the two following books. (WN 2.5.37, 374–5)

Over the course of 300 pages, Smith explains why rather than being invested in nearby agriculture, capital generated by European (coastal) cities is invested in long-distance trading. This is the "unnatural and retrograde order" (WN 3.1.9, 380) to be accounted for. In Book 3, Smith lays out what he takes to be the natural, albeit not inevitable, course of civilizations, given the steady propensities of mankind, especially the propensity to barter, for example, in the service of "bettering one's condition" (see, e.g., WN 2.3.28, 341). It is a typical Smithian social explanation (see also the next section) that involves a normological generalization (in the quote from WN 3.1.3, 377, necessity only works its course "in general"). Smith is also adamant that "the manners and customs" that a government introduces can also cause an "unnatural and retrograde order" even long after the government has changed (WN 3.1.9, 380). In Book 4 he explores how mistaken and politically partial theories of political economy (that is, mercantilism and physiocracy) facilitated the "unnatural and retrograde order." Book 4 is, thus, an extended example of the negative effects of what Smith calls "wrong" theorizing.

Induced from the "natural inclinations of man" (WN 3.1.3, 377), Smith provides an idealized picture of how societies "naturally" develop. Stock must first be saved in a hunting or shepherding society before it can be directed to agriculture, then afterward to manufactures, and finally to foreign commerce (WN 3.1.8, 380). The rest of Book 3 is an exploration of why and how this natural path was not followed in Europe after the fall of the Roman Empire. In doing this, Smith is put in a position to provide a subtle picture of how wealth is created given certain fairly stable background conditions (e.g., location, climate, geography, etc.). Books 3 and 4 provide an account of legal frameworks and political arrangements that retard or encourage the "natural course" of things.

Once one pays attention one sees these themes already present in Books 1 and 2; also:

> China seems to have been long stationary, and had probably long ago acquired that full complement of riches which is consistent with the nature of its laws and institutions. But this complement may be much inferior to what, with other laws and institutions, the nature of its soil, climate, and situation might admit of. (WN 1.9.15, 111–2; WN 1.8.24, 89 and WN 4.9.40, 679–80; see Hanley 2014 on Smith's subtle engagement with China)

Note the counterfactual; China's stationary state is a consequence of its institutions. A different set of institutions would allow for the abolishment of famine and, perhaps, even open-ended growth.[6] Thus, instead of being merely a curious historical/sociological sideshow that illustrates Smith's wide range of interests, Book 3 is on my reading central to the science that Smith attempts to found. It is only a first stab at providing explanations of the comparative and historical performances of various European countries. In Book 5, he takes the lessons he has learned, including the law of unintended consequences, and applies them to his proposed design for many institutions. In a seminal article, Nathan Rosenberg argues that there was a systematic vision underlying Smith's policy recommendations: to provide "an exact, detailed specification of an optimal institutional structure" so that market forces could operate in a beneficent fashion (Rosenberg 1960: 570; see also Muller 1993 for elaboration).

e. Model, Cause, and Process; Smithian Social Explanation

Recall Smith's discussion at WN 1.7.20–32, 77–80, where after sketching an abstract "natural" model, he systematically laid out what causes could create "deviations, whether occasional or permanent, of the market price of commodities from the natural price" (WN 1.7.32, 80). Future researchers are in the position to do empirical work on measuring the extent of these causes. Down the road, this research can stimulate revision, if necessary, to the ideal model. A small-scale revision would be the discovery of causes other than institutions; this would be welcome, for it would not require wholesale change to the theoretical structure. It could be accommodated by merely adding the nature and extent, permanent or occasional, of this newly discovered cause to the list of possible deviations. One circumstance in which larger-scale revision would happen is if it turned out that Smith has ignored dominant causes that need to be accounted for, not merely as causes of deviation, but as elements of the "natural" model; one could imagine this to be the case if serious empirical flaws were found in his assumptions about human nature or if, say, the nature of exchange changed dramatically in technologically advanced societies.

But even if we ignore the most abstract level of Smith's theory, the methodologic structure of his theory (i.e., postulate a "natural" course and systematically stipulate causes that can make it deviate) is recapitulated on the component level (wages, rents, profits, etc.) of his natural price analysis (WN 1.8–11.d, 82–193). For example, after presenting a quick account of the origin of wage labor (1.8.1–10, 82–3), Smith provides a general model of the nature of property–wage relationships and how the circumstances of society impact the price of labor (1.8.11–57,

---

[6] During the decade after Smith's death, Malthus would take up this issue in a broadly Smithian framework, but here I remain agnostic about what Smith's position on population is.

83–103); as we have seen, WN 1.8 also contains some of Smith's most explicit language on the importance of improving the welfare of "Servants, labourers and workmen of different kinds, [which] make up the far greater part of every great political society" (WN 1.8.36, 96).

The crucial point is that the "money price of labor is necessarily regulated by two circumstances; the demand for labour, and the price of the necessaries and conveniences of life" (1.8.52, 103); the latter circumstance acts as a kind of constraint on the former. But shortly hereafter, Smith explains, while employing counterfactual language, that the model he had just provided is an idealized one; it only "would be the case in a society where things were left to follow their natural course, where there was perfect liberty, and where every man was perfectly free both to chuse what occupation he thought proper, and to change it as often as he thought proper" (WN 1.10.1, 116).

Now we can complete the explanation pattern we described in Section a of Chapter 2 and Sections b, c, and d of Chapter 10, where we identified the following four related aspects of Smith's social explanatory account:

(i) While propensities are themselves normological, their persistent triggering and expression can lead to nomological outcomes such that the outcome could not be otherwise—presumably as necessary that all humans are mortal.

(ii) (a) Stable consequences would not have been in "view" (or predictable) to observers of human nature at an early time (and so not capable of being intended). (b) To be a cause does not require temporal contiguity between the cause and the effect; the same cause(s) can do their work over enormous expanses of time.

(iii) Smith's account does require that after certain consequences become visible to observer-participants, they become self-reinforcing.

(iv) It supports counterfactual judgments—the process characterized by the Smithian social explanation describes not just what happened, but also how it differs from what would have happened without the process characterized by the Smithian social explanation.

So, in the long run and in the aggregate, normological propensities will produce initially unpredictable, albeit definite and determined outcomes. If one accepts that Smith accepts general final causes (Kleer 1995), then Smithian social explanation makes visible God's plan. By contrast, I read TMS 2.2.3.5, 87, as suggesting that the imputation of final causation is a kind of mistake that tempts philosophers regularly.

In addition, Smith recognizes two different kinds of causes that can produce deviations from the natural course of things: (1) those "arising from the Nature of the Employments themselves" (WN 1.10.b, 116–35) and, more important, (2) those "occasioned by the policy [i.e., administrative rules] of Europe,"

(WN 1.10.c, 135–59). Each kind of cause gets, in turn, subdivided into particular causes, all of which receive extensive treatment. Therefore, in addition to human propensities, which lead to a whole set of new propensities and ("natural") institutional outcomes, there are also second-order institutions or processes that can push the natural course of things from its expected path. Identifying the operation of such second-order courses is crucial to Smith's scientific enterprise.

To sum up briefly: on my reading, Smith offers (a) a "natural" model (based on certain assumptions of human nature, historical change, etc.) of what would be the case under ideal circumstances with (b) a list of factors (stipulated in advance) that will cause deviations from the idealization in order to (c) stimulate research on a part of his readers, both to (d) investigate the nature and extent of these causes, and if they do not turn out to be exhaustive, to what degree there are (e) new causes that need to be incorporated in the model, which, *in extremis*, (f) may be revised. Smith is starting, then, an open-ended process in which one moves from theory to facts and back (cf. G. E. Smith 2014). At the same time, Smith's detailed presentation of his idealizations provides a richly layered, systematic structure to help organize, interpret, and understand the phenomena under scrutiny. Smith helps the majority of his readers to make sense of the world they live in, while trying to prevent the political class (the "princes") from doing inadvertent harm to the societies they govern, and while offering a framework that will help the working poor without advocating dangerous revolutionary changes in society's structures. This, then, one assumes is what he would take to be an instance of a "right" sort of theorizing with little inductive risk.

f. Hume Versus Smith on the Introduction of Commerce

By way of illumination, I contrast Smith's method to Hume's treatment of the origins of commercial society in his essay "Of Commerce." (Here I emphasize the differences between Hume and Smith, but Smith's political economy is also heavily influenced by Hume; see Hayek 1967: 113; Rothschild 2001: 10; and the editor's introduction in Rotwein 1955.) There, Hume suggests we should "consult history" to explain the growth of foreign commerce. He claims it is an empirical fact that in Europe "foreign trade has preceded any refinement in home manufactures." He goes on to suggest that natural endowments such as "soil or climate" influence what commodity gets exchanged. For Hume, the actual historical record suggests that, in most nations, foreign commerce is prior to the expansion of local manufacturing ("Of Commerce," EMPL 263–4; recall that for Smith, in the natural course of events, foreign commerce comes *after* the development of local manufacturing). Hume is here a good empiricist, but he provides no explanatory strategy for thinking that this observation is not merely a contingent fact. Here he provides no theoretical structure for analyzing alternative historical paths.

In general, Hume thought, "it is the chief business of philosophers to regard the general course of things" and not worry too much about "exceptions" ("Of Commerce" 254–5). In Hume's theorizing, exceptions to general rules cannot provide further evidence in the development of theory; what they point to is the contingent nature of human history or the existence of many intervening causes that are not open to systematic investigation (see Schliesser 2004).

g. Hume's Natural Rate of Propagation and Smith's Digression on Silver

Nevertheless, I do not want to give the impression that Hume was a casual Empiricist in interpreting economic history. In particular, I argue that Hume lets his understanding of human nature constrain his interpretations of the historical record (Rotwein 1955). Thus, for example, before he introduces his discussion of the relationship between foreign commerce and local manufacture, he points out "Every thing in the world is purchased by labour; and our passions are the only causes of labour" ("Of Commerce," EMPL 261). In "Of Interest" Hume writes: "There is no craving or demand of the human mind more constant and insatiable than that for exercise and employment; and this seems the foundation of most of our passions and pursuits" (EMPL 300).

Moreover, not unlike Smith, Hume is quite serious about taking into account the institutional framework and "habits and manners" of a society when interpreting the historical record ("Of Interest," EMPL 298, and, especially, Ancient Nations, EMPL 381ff). It is worth looking at one of Hume's most sustained efforts at doing so.

In his essay on the population of ancient nations, Hume points out that, when facts are uncertain, it is appropriate to "intermingle the enquiry concerning the causes with that concerning facts" (EMPL 381). In this essay, Hume postulates a natural rate of propagation: slightly more than a doubling in every generation of the human species. (Strictly speaking, Hume does not call it a "natural rate," although a page later he says the rate "seems natural to expect.") Hume stipulates that "everything else being equal" (vegetation, climate, etc.), this rate can only be achieved under "wise, just, and mild government" with the "wisest institutions" (EMPL 382).[7] The natural rate is, thus, for Hume a counterfactual optimal rate. Hume infers what would be the case based on empirical observations of what is the case in, say, the American colonies and the quick rebound in population after plagues, as well as on facts about human nature (EMPL 381; presumably he is drawing on his Treatise, which had been based on "experiment and observation").

From a political perspective, Hume's point is important because population growth becomes a proxy for measuring good government. As the editor of EMPL,

---

[7] Hume did not pioneer *ceteris paribus* clauses (see Persky 1990: 188, especially on Petty).

David Miller, notes, this was a widely shared position in Hume's age. To be sure, Hume need not rely exclusively on population growth as a proxy for good government. In "That Politics may be reduced to a Science," Hume treats social unrest or criminality as evidence of defective institutions or bad leadership. So, in a good government, population grows without civil unrest or worse. (For Hume the lack of economic growth would produce famine and, thus, undermine population growth.) Hume applies this normative claim in his empirical research.

From a methodologic perspective, what's striking here is that Hume infers what would be the case in various places based on empirical observations of what is the case in, say, the American colonies (alas, Hume was not too bothered by the treatment of the natives) and the quick rebound in population after plagues as well as on facts about human nature. Hume uses this natural rate to reason from facts to causes as well as from causes to facts. So, for example, if there is reliable information that population is or was increasing in some locale, this is *prima facie* evidence for a mild government with a relatively sound economic policy, while he will infer the converse, too. Positing the natural rate, then, allows Hume to make inferences about the past and present.

Acceptance of the relationship between the nature of government and population also provides Hume with an important constraint on accepting the facts provided by various literary and political texts. Hume is, thus, self-consciously offering a principled evidential strategy to deal with a situation in which only limited data are available. (Alas, Hume does not allow historical facts to help him improve or refute the rule that he employs to interpret history with.)

Because Hume has little invested in laws as explanatory principles (I have argued that most of Hume's explanations are also what I call "normological"— that is, robust generalizations that allow exceptions [see Schliesser 2004]), his introduction of a *ceteris paribus* clause does not call for special comment from him. Hume is positing a (counterfactual) natural rate that rarely obtains in the real world. But even in the rare occasions when "wise, just, and mild government" and the "wisest institutions" obtain, it is possible for the (implied) local natural rate of population to vary. That's because Hume thinks the local natural rate is, in part, dependent on conditions of geography, climate, and so forth. Therefore, it is possible both to exceed the optimal rate locally (through artificial means) in the short run but not in the long run, as well as for the local natural rate to vary temporally and spatially—it's the *ceteris paribus* condition that helps specify the conditions for this variation.

Above, while discussing WN I.ix.3, 105 and I.xi.o.5, 261, I made a point of claiming that Smith was acutely conscious of the limited accuracy of data available to him. Of course, how to interpret the data may be just as problematic. Smith employs Hume's technique—of moving from causal theory to facts and vice versa while deploying something like a natural rate to constrain data—in at least one prominent place in WN (see also Hoover and Dowell 2001). In his very long "Digression concerning the Variations in the Value of Silver during the Course of the four last Centuries" at the end of the first book of WN (1.11.e, 195ff), Smith ingeniously employs his theory about the relationship among an increase in aggregate supply (the result of increase in agricultural output, in turn the effect of improved technology and cultivation), the price of corn (the eighteenth-century word for edible seeds), and the value of silver in order to attack mercantilism. The "Digression" tries to show that inflation (in the silver price of corn) is not an inevitable consequence of growing national wealth (WN 1.11.n.1, 255; 1.11.e.30, 207; Hueckel 2000: 323ff).

Smith assumes that an increase in supply caused by technological improvement will cause the value of items that always produce rent to decrease in proportion to the value of items that may or may not afford some rent: "materials of cloathing and lodging, the useful fossils and minerals of earth, the precious metals and the precious stones should gradually become dearer and dearer" (WN 1.11.d.1, 193; Smith recognizes that changes in supply and demand can alter this relationship; see also 1.11.i.3, 234). Assuming that corn is produced under conditions of constant resource costs "in every stage of improvement" (WN 1.11.e.28, 206), the silver price of corn should, with economic development, thus, decline. Unfortunately, for Smith, this only holds true "if particular accidents" (WN 1.11.d.1, 193), namely "the accidental discovery of more abundant mines," do not interfere (WN 1.11.n.1, 255). Thus, when under some circumstances rising nominal corn prices can reflect rising silver production, he must have another measure. Smith has resource to additional assumptions about the trend in the butcher's meat/corn price ratio as economies grow; a rising corn price of meat is, he believes, indicative of "progress of improvement" (WN 1.11.l.2, 237; 1.11.n.2–3, 256–7).

Based on these relationships, Smith can exhaustively state (WN 1.11.d.4–6, 194) all "possible combinations of events which happen in the progress of improvement" (1.11.d.7, 194—note the modality!) as they pertain to the relative prices of silver and corn. To be clear: Smith's analysis is focused on long-term prices. Short-term fluctuations indicate supply shocks, which are frequent in "turbulent and disorderly societies" (WN 1.11.e.23, 204; Smith has in mind feudalism here) or changes in weather patterns. Smith must also assume that improvements in the efficiency of producing corn are "counter-balanced" by other costs (such as the price of cattle and "the principal instruments of agriculture," WN 1.11.e.28, 206).

With this theoretical framework in place, and the availability of relatively reliable long-running data on the price of corn, Smith is able to impute the value of silver over a long period of time (O'Donnell 1990: 77–81). "With a degree of probability that approaches almost to certainty," Smith is in a position to infer from relative, "real" prices of different commodities (i.e., cattle, corn, vegetables, and manufacturers) the stage of improvement that an economy was in (WN 1.11.n.3, 257; for the nature of real price, see Section c in Chapter 8). This, in turn, allows him to make an empirical case for the causal claims against the mercantilists in the "conclusion" of his digression:

> As the wealth of Europe, indeed, has increased greatly since the discovery of the mines of America, so the value of gold and silver has gradually diminished. This diminution of their value, however, has not been owing to the increase of the real wealth of Europe, of the annual produce of its land and labour, but to the accidental discovery of more abundant mines than any that were known before. The increase of the quantity of gold and silver in Europe, and the increase of its manufactures and agriculture, are two events which, though they have happened nearly about the same time, yet have arisen from very different causes, and have scarce any natural connection with one another. The one has arisen from a mere accident, in which neither prudence nor policy either had or could have any share. The other from the fall of the feudal system, and from the establishment of a government which afforded to industry the only encouragement which it requires, some tolerable security that it shall enjoy the fruits of its own labour. (WN 1.11.n.1, 255–6)

Smith clearly thinks that his method has enabled him to distinguish apparent from real causes and to differentiate between natural connections and mere coincidences. This is why his conclusions are offered "with a degree of probability that approaches almost to certainty" (1.11.n.3, 257), while other opinions "scarce, perhaps, deserve the name of belief" (WN 1.11.h.11, 233). Smith offers what he takes to be compelling counterfactual arguments because he has an abstract theory about the natural course of events. (Compare this with Hume's much cruder argument in "Of Interest," which turns on an assumption about the proportionate nature of cause and effect [EMPL 296].) Smith's model is supplemented by crucial assumptions about the relative prices of goods and the "gradual" nature by which certain long-term causes are said to operate in the course of development (e.g., W.11.g.19, 218). The latter are constraints on his interpretation of the historical data.

In Ancient Nations, Hume has shown the way to this method to interpret the historical record. It is no coincidence that the constraint that is employed on interpreting historical data is of the same kind that, for Smith, enables the normatively desirable, real growth in wealth: a stable institutional framework that ensures a minimal protection for income earned from labor.

13

Smith and Anti-Mathematicism

I have no great faith in political arithmetick, and I mean not to
warrant the exactness of either of these computations.
—Adam Smith, *WN 4.5.b.30, 535*

The epigraph of this chapter tends to be interpreted as an expression of Smith's hostility toward "unreliable statistics" (Redman: 216 n. 22) and his rejection of Petty's mercantile or political orientation, which was tied up with British imperialist and colonial policies in Ireland. I agree with these claims. In this chapter, however, I argue that in addition, Smith in general is distinctly reserved about the application of mathematics to political economy and even other terrestrial sciences. In particular, I argue that Smith's strategy in these matters is an instance of what I call a "containment strategy." By this I mean that Smith restricts the *application* of mathematics to a fairly limited domain of inquiry. Smith was not alone in such a containment strategy: we find instances of it in Locke, Buffon (whom he admired), and Mandeville. Below I offer evidence from Buffon, Hume, and Mandeville for the existence of such strategies (on Locke, see Domski 2012). Their containment strategies are part of a wider trend of eighteenth-century "anti-mathematicism," by which I mean the expressed reservations about the authority and utility of the *application* of mathematical sciences.[1]

In treating Smith as instantiating such anti-mathematicism, I deviate from the recent tendency, including my own (Schliesser 2005 and 2006), of arguing that he meant to model WN on features of Newton's *Principia* (e.g., Redman 1997, Chapter 5; Montes 2003, 2004, 2006). To be clear: there is no doubt that Smith admired Newton: "The superior genius and sagacity of Sir Isaac Newton, therefore, made the most happy, and, we may now say, the greatest and most

---

[1] Eighteenth-century anti-mathematicism can be traced back to Spinoza's so-called Letter on the Infinite. In particular, the writings of Hume (especially Treatise 1.2.4.29 and 1.4.1.1–2) and Diderot offer examples of more comprehensive, rejectionist strategies in their anti-mathematicism. As I show, Smith's approach is more circumscribed. Even philosophers who were distinctly unsympathetic to Spinoza's project (e.g., the mature Berkeley) also engaged in anti-mathematicism. Spinoza was not the only seventeenth-century critic of the application of mathematics; see Peterman (2017) on Margaret Cavendish.

admirable improvement that was ever made in philosophy" (Astronomy 4.67, EPS 98). Moreover, the claim I am about to offer is compatible with the idea that (as I argued in Chapter 12) Smith adopted methodologic strategies that were made influential by Newton.

An early, respectful critic of Smith, Governor Pownall, seems to compare WN to *Principia*: WN is "a system, that might fix some first principles in the most important of sciences, the knowledge of the human community, and its operations. That might become principia to the knowledge of politick operations; as Mathematicks are to Mechanicks, Astronomy, and the other Sciences." Pownall goes on to attribute to Smith Newton's method of analysis and synthesis:

> you have, I find, by a truly philosophic and patient analysis, endeavoured to investigate analytically those principles, by which nature first moves and then conducts the operations of man in the individual, and in community: And then, next, by application of these principles to fact, experience, and the institutions of men, you have endeavoured to deduce synthetically, by the most precise and measured steps of demonstration, those important doctrines of practice, which your very scientifick and learned book offers to the consideration of the world of business. (A Letter from Governor Pownall to Adam Smith, Richmond, September 25, 1776; cf. Newton's *Opticks*, Query 31. The latter comment leads Redman 1997: 211 to connect Smith to *Opticks* rather than *Principia*.)

I do not contest Pownall's attribution of Newton's method of analysis and synthesis to Smith, although it is not the interpretation I advance. The method of analysis and synthesis as proposed by Newton (in Query 31 of the *Opticks* [see especially Ducheyne 2011]) is compatible with a non-mathematical approach, for what this method is really about is the discovery and composition of causes (see Demeter 2016 for how this was understood in the eighteenth century). Of course, in *Principia* these causes are abstract, mathematical quantities—that is, forces (Smeenk and Schliesser 2013)—but this is not required for the deployment of the method.

The Newtonian reading of Smith was also promoted by his greatest student, John Millar: "The Great Montesquieu pointed out the road. He was the Lord Bacon in this branch of philosophy. Dr. Smith is the Newton" (Millar 1803, Vol. 2: 429–30). While Millar is not an impartial observer, his reading of Smith seems to be invited by Smith in the conceptually and methodologically crucial Chapter 7 of Book 1 of WN, where Smith writes, "The natural price, therefore, is, as it were, the central price, to which the prices of all commodities are continually gravitating" (1.7.15, 75; recall also WN 1.7.20, 77). I return to Millar's claim in Section c of this chapter, but here I note that strictly speaking Smith's claim about the natural price is only a very imperfect Newtonian analogy. This is because in Newton, "all attraction is (by Law III) mutual" (*Principia*, Book 3, Proposition 5, Theorem 5, Corollary 1). In fact, as I noted above, Smith's statement is closer to a description of Aristotelian gravity.

In what follows, I motivate a reconsideration of Smith's views on the applicability of mathematics. In particular, I attribute to Smith a version of the containment strategy; I draw on passages in Buffon and Mandeville to illuminate this. I then offer a reinterpretation of Millar's testimony that, by drawing on some of Hume's account of proportionality, helps us better understand the way that number and quantity are treated in WN.

a. Smith's Newtonianism Reconsidered

In this section I argue that Smith probably accepts the containment strategy. I put the containment strategy in some historical context. I start my treatment by looking at a passage in one of Smith's posthumous essays (published in EPS) that has received little scholarly attention. It's the first paragraph of Ancient Physics, and at first sight its only significance is to function as a bridge between the developed argument of Astronomy and the more fragmentary claims of Ancient Physics and Ancient Logics. The paragraph reads as follows:

> From arranging and methodizing the System of the Heavens, Philosophy descended to the consideration of the inferior parts of Nature, of the Earth, and of the bodies which immediately surround it. If the objects, which were here presented to its view, were inferior in greatness or beauty, and therefore less apt to attract the attention of the mind, they were more apt, when they came to be attended to, to embarrass and perplex it, by the variety of their species, and by the intricacy and seeming irregularity of the laws or orders of their succession. The species of objects in the Heavens are few in number; the Sun, the Moon, the Planets, and the Fixed Stars, are all which those philosophers could distinguish. All the changes too, which are ever observed in these bodies, evidently arise from some difference in the velocity and direction of their several motions; but the variety of meteors in the air, of clouds, rainbows, thunder, lightning, winds, rain, hail, snow, is vastly greater; and the order of their succession seems to be still more irregular and unconstant. The species of fossils, minerals, plants, animals, which are found in the Waters, and near the surface of the Earth, are still more intricately diversified; and if we regard the different manners of their production, their mutual influence in altering, destroying, supporting one another, the orders of their succession seem to admit of an almost infinite variety. If the imagination, therefore, when it considered the appearances in the Heavens, was often perplexed, and driven out of

its natural career, it would be much more exposed to the same embarrassment, when it directed its attention to the objects which the Earth presented to it, and when it endeavoured to trace their progress and successive revolutions. (Ancient Physics 1, EPS 106)

Passages such as these are difficult to interpret because it is not easy to disentangle when Smith is merely summarizing other people's views or also subtly inserting his own perspective into the narrative. My reading assumes that here Smith is not making merely a historical point; this is not to deny that the hermeneutical situation is difficult given that the quoted passage is the opening paragraph to a treatment of Ancient physics, and elsewhere in this essay he writes in adopted voices of the people he is summarizing. As I have noted, there has been quite a bit of excellent scholarship on Smith's rhetoric (Brown 1994; Fleischacker 2004: 12ff; Phillips 2006), but the rhetoric of his essays is somewhat uncharted territory.

One important reason to think that in this paragraph Smith is speaking in his own voice is his claim that "The species of fossils, minerals, plants, animals, which are found in the Waters, and near the surface of the Earth, are still more intricately diversified." While Ancient writers such as Pliny noted the existence of fossils, the existence and meaning of fossils had become explosive material in the eighteenth century. In posthumously published work on earthquakes (1705), the secretary of the Royal Society, Robert Hooke, had used his work on fossils to argue that "There have been many other Species of Creatures in former Ages, of which we can find none at present; and that 'tis not unlikely also but that there may be divers new kinds now, which have not been from the beginning" (quoted in Gaukroger 2006: 503). By the time of Smith's death, the significance of a scientific study of fossils was well understood, especially by the two editors of the posthumous EPS. In 1785 Hutton gave a public lecture, "Concerning the System of the Earth, Its Duration, and Stability," at the University of Edinburgh. Due to the illness of Hutton, Smith's other eventual posthumous editor, Black, gave the lecture on Hutton's behalf. In the lecture Hutton used geological and fossil evidence to argue that the Earth was almost certainly older than the Biblical suggestion of 5,000 years (Dean 1992: 17ff). We do not know for sure if Smith attended the lecture, but it would have been amazing if he was unfamiliar with the contents.[2]

Clearly Hooke's "many other" is not the same as Smith's "infinite variety." But in his *Theory of the Earth* (1788), Hutton emphasizes the "infinite variety of mineral productions which we find in nature" (Hutton 1795, Chapter 2, Vol. 1, 90; according to Mizuta's catalogue of the library, Smith owned this book, but not the dissertation abstract of the 1785 lecture). Thus, Smith's phrasing may well be inspired by discussion with Hutton, whom he met weekly at the Oyster Club

---

[2] Dean makes clear how close Smith and Hutton were. I am indebted to Nicholas Phillipson for discussion on this point, too.

dinners (Phillipson 2010). Smith's interest in biology and botany is well attested. As Spencer Pack (2010: 105) has emphasized, there is evidence that Smith also took an interest in species extinction (WN 4.7.a.11, 560).

One cannot rule out that Hutton got the idea of an infinite variety from discussion with Smith, for it is generally assumed that Ancient Physics was written in the 1740s. One might suggest that Smith added the paragraph to Ancient Physics near the end of his life as a kind of bridge between Astronomy (a very mathematical science) and Ancient Physics (where no exactitude was forthcoming), but it may have been in the original manuscript.

In the quoted passage from Ancient Physics 1, Smith seems to be saying that (i) celestial phenomena are simple; (ii) phenomena in the atmosphere are a bit more complex; and (iii) terrestrial phenomena are infinitely complex. The simple, celestial phenomena are clearly capable of being subject of a science, but the terrestrial phenomena are, if they are subject to science at all, of a very different kind. Smith does not mention mathematics in the passage. Indeed, if there are literally an infinite variety of phenomena in a domain, then the application of mathematics to it may give false confidence in our ability to discern the genuine underlying connections. We may discern a robust, even causal pattern without doing justice to the complexity of the larger whole. Spinoza had made such an argument famous in his "Letter on the Infinite" and his "Letter on Worm in the Blood." (Schliesser 2016b). These letters had been attacked vehemently by Clarke and Maclaurin in works that Smith knew well (Schliesser 2012). Given the underdeveloped nature of the mathematics of infinity in the eighteenth century (Levy 1992a on Berkeley is very important), this kind of reasoning may explain Smith's lack of confidence in political arithmetic.

One might think that in the wake of Galileo, Descartes, Huygens, and Newton, no serious thinker would accept a division between terrestrial and celestial phenomena. But, in practice, epistemic differences between domains, especially over the application of mathematics, continued to be accepted by influential natural philosophers. I quote a prominent example, Buffon's Initial Discourse to his *Histoire Naturelle*:

> This union of mathematics and physics can be accomplished only for a very small number of subjects ... it is necessary that the phenomena we are concerned with explaining be susceptible to being considered in an abstract manner and that their nature be stripped of almost all physical qualities. For mathematics is inapplicable to the extent that subjects are not simple abstractions ... there are very few subjects in physics in which the abstract sciences can be applied so advantageously. And I scarcely see anything but astronomy and optics to which they might be of any great service. (Lyon 1976: 176)

I view this as a canonical statement of the so-called containment strategy. Buffon's rhetoric here ("abstract manner and that their nature be stripped of almost all physical qualities") deliberately echoes Newton, who had emphasized that "in philosophical disquisitions [i.e., natural philosophy] abstraction from our senses is required" (Scholium to the definitions, *Principia*, Newton 1999: 411; Domski 2012), but for a very different aim. In particular, Buffon claims that when we become unable to properly assign relevant causes—where such stripping of qualities (that is, abstraction) is impossible or causes us to "remove" too many qualities from a thing's essence—application of mathematics to nature is to be limited to astronomy and optics.[3]

We know that Smith was a careful, admiring, albeit not uncritical, reader of Buffon's writings on natural history, and he calls attention to Buffon's contributions to Diderot's *Encyclopedia* in his first publication. He treats Buffon's contributions as part of a larger system (which suggests familiarity with the unfolding *Histoire Naturelle*): "The system indeed of this Gentleman [Buffon], it may be thought, is almost entirely hypothetical; and with regard to the causes of generation such, that it is scarce possible to form any very determinate idea of it" (Edinburgh Review 8, EPS 248). Note, first, that Smith rejects here the hypothetical method associated with the Cartesian-Mechanical philosophy. Second, Smith emphasizes that there are parts of nature that cannot be known exactly ("determinate idea"). But despite some of his reservations, he treats Buffon's *Natural History* as a reliable empirical source on the extinction of the Cori (recall WN 4.7.a.11, 560).

Smith was also familiar with another prominent instance of anti-mathematicism. Mandeville had offered a very critical analysis of Hutcheson's application of mathematical techniques in the moral sciences:

> Mr. Hutcheson, who wrote the *Inquiry into the Original of our Ideas of Beauty and Virtue*, seems to be very expert at weighing and measuring the Quantities of Affection, Benevolence, &c. I wish that curious Metaphysician would give himself the Trouble, at his Leisure, to weigh two things separately: First, the real Love Men have for their Country, abstracted from Selfishness. Secondly, the Ambition they have, of being thought to act from that Love, tho' they feel none. I wish, I say, that this ingenious Gentleman would once weigh these two asunder; and afterwards, having taken in impartially all he could find of either, in this or any other Nation, shew us in his demonstrative way, what Proportion the Quantities bore to each other. (Mandeville, *The Fable of the Bees or Private Vices, Publick Benefits, sixth dialogue between Horatio and Cleomenes*; Mandeville 1988, Vol. 2: 345–6)

---

[3] Smith's account of abstraction is different than Buffon's more traditional analysis (recall Section b in Chapter 2).

Let's leave aside the question how fair Mandeville is to Hutcheson. Mandeville here resolutely puts on the table a number of serious problems for a quantitative science of human nature: how to measure directly or by proxy some of the hidden mental qualities that we are most interested in (theoretically or politically). Mandeville here calls attention to at least four distinct problems:

1. The way we reveal our motives may not track our genuine motives; we have a lot of incentives to disguise our real motives, after all.
2. Even allowing that outsiders or the persons concerned have access to motives, it is very difficult to disentangle different motives to action.
3. Even if we can disentangle motives to action, it is very difficult to weigh motives quantitatively.
4. Experts may not be unbiased spectators when they try to operationalize answers to these three problems.

Mandeville develops these four reservations about the application of mathematics to human sciences in the context of his critical treatment of attempts at mathematical medicine in more fine-grained and detailed matter in the third dialogue of the third edition (1730) of *A Treatise of the Hypochondriack and Hysterick Diseases*. While there is evidence that Hume may well have read Mandeville's *Treatise* (Wright 2009: 8–9), it is unclear if Smith did.[4] Either way, unlike Hutcheson, Smith (nor Hume) never seems to have been tempted to use quantitative methods to describe and track mental properties; in particular, he does not use price data for this.

A cautious critic may find the argument of this chapter rather speculative thus far. All I have shown is that Smith is almost certainly aware of the containment strategy and the existence of debates over the application of mathematics outside of mathematical physics. So far I have offered an ambiguous passage where he may seem to adopt the containment strategy, but that passage is not decisive given the lack of mention of mathematics if I wish to argue that Smith adopts the containment strategy. In addition, the argument as presented here can explain why Smith was not tempted by Hutcheson's application of mathematics to moral affairs and the absence from Smith of anything like Hutcheson's (proto-Utilitarian) commitment to the greatest happiness for the greatest number.[5]

---

[4] There is tantalizing evidence he may have. In Astronomy he writes, "In the same manner, a learned physician lately gave a system of moral philosophy upon the principles of his own art, in which wisdom and virtue were the healthful state of the soul" (II.12, EPS 47). The editors of EPS assume this is a reference to La Mettrie (47 n. 16), but it is just as likely to be Mandeville.

[5] I thank a perceptive referee for stimulating this thought. In Hutcheson the greatest happiness for the greatest number is not so much a decision rule as a means to argue for moral egalitarianism.

I argue that some of the best evidence about Smith's views on the limits of the application of mathematics comes from a careful analysis of his admiring writings about Newton. Consider the closing paragraph of Astronomy:

> [Newton's principles] not only connect together most perfectly *all the phaenomena of the Heavens*, which had been observed before his time, but those also which the persevering industry and more perfect instruments of later Astronomers have made known to us; have been either easily and immediately explained by the application of his principles, or have been explained in consequence of more laborious and accurate calculations from these principles, than had been instituted before. (Astronomy 4.76, EPS 105; emphasis added)

Here Smith tacitly limits Newton's achievement to the heavens. Neither here nor elsewhere in his essay does Smith mention how Newton accounted for the tides or the moon's attraction on the seas! In fact, in this passage and throughout the essay, Smith treats Newton the way Locke treats Newton—as offering a terrific *celestial* mechanics (Domski 2012).

Of course, arguments from omission do not settle anything, but there is another passage in which Smith discusses the crucial evidence produced by Maupertuis's voyage to Lapland that ended eighteenth-century debate over the status of Newton's system:

> The Earth had hitherto been regarded as perfectly globular, probably for the same reason which had made men imagine, that the orbits of the Planets must necessarily be perfectly circular. But *Sir Isaac Newton, from mechanical principles, concluded, that, as the parts of the Earth must be more agitated by her diurnal revolution at the Equator, than at the Poles, they must necessarily be somewhat elevated at the first, and flattened at the second.* The observation, that the oscillations of pendulums were slower at the Equator than at the Poles, seeming to demonstrate, that gravity was stronger at the Poles, and weaker at the Equator, proved, he thought, that the Equator was further from the centre than the Poles. All the measures, however, which had hitherto been made of the Earth, seemed to show the contrary, that it was drawn out towards the Poles, and flattened towards the Equator. Newton, however, preferred his mechanical computations to the former measures of Geographers and Astronomers; and in this he was confirmed by the observations of Astronomers on the figure of Jupiter, whose diameter at the Pole seems to be to his diameter at the Equator, as twelve to thirteen; a much greater inequality than could be supposed to take place betwixt the correspondent diameters of the Earth, but which was exactly proportioned to the superior bulk of Jupiter, and the superior rapidity

with which he performs his diurnal revolutions. The observations of
Astronomers at Lapland and Peru have fully confirmed Sir Isaac's system,
and have not only demonstrated, that the figure of the Earth is, in general,
such as he supposed it; but that the proportion of its axis to the diameter
of its Equator is almost precisely such as he had computed it. And of all the
proofs that have ever been adduced of the diurnal revolution of the Earth,
this perhaps is the most solid and satisfactory. (Astronomy 4.72, EPS 101;
emphasis added)

This is a long, complicated passage, and the speculative argument I am about to
offer is not simple. It had eluded me during the two decades I have been reflecting
on Astronomy.

Smith treats the Maupertuis expedition as settling two controversial, related
issues at once: (i) the Copernican hypothesis and (ii) the controversy over the
shape of the Earth, which pitted, in fact, three competing explanations: (a) one
offered by the Cassini family (the geographers), (b) one proposed by Huygens in
accord with his vortex theory of gravity, and (c) one proposed by Newton based
on universal gravitation. In Smith's hands Maupertuis shows that Copernicanism
is true and that Newton's account of the shape of the Earth "is, in general, such
as he supposed it."

In the passage, Smith is silent on the fact that Maupertuis's expedition also
settles another debate: (iii) the controversy between Newton and Huygens (and
the neo-Cartesians inspired by Huygens) over the status of universal gravity. In
Newton's theory the flattening at the poles has two sources. One is the rotation of
the Earth. Pendulum measurements at different latitudes as well as the measurements in Lapland and Peru fully confirm this. These thus prove Copernicanism
without a doubt. Second, universal gravity means that under the surface of
the Earth, gravity does not act inverse-square but $1/r$. This results in a different, inferred shape of the Earth in Newton's theory than the one inferred from
Huygens's theory. Newton and Huygens both recognized that this could let pendulum measurements on the shape of the Earth provide decisive empirical evidence in their dispute over the existence of universal gravity.

To avoid misunderstanding, note two things. First, Huygens accepted Newton's
inverse-square law for celestial gravity between planetary bodies. Second, Newton
and Huygens agree on the oblateness of the Earth (against the Cassinis); they
just have different values for the flattening at the poles (Schliesser and Smith,
forthcoming).

Maupertuis's evidence showed that Huygens' theory could not possibly be
true because all the measured systematic deviations from his theory were in the
wrong direction (Maglo 2003; Schliesser and Smith, forthcoming). The measurements in Lapland and Peru, thus, also showed decisively that universal gravity
really existed, leaving aside questions over its mechanism. Smith is entirely silent
on this point. To put all of this a bit technically: in all his writings, Smith treats

the Earth as a celestial body that can be fit into a widely successful astronomical scheme. Thus, Smith accepts the inverse law for celestial bodies (in accord with Huygens' position on Newton, in fact). But Smith never explicitly adopts the inverse law as explaining terrestrial phenomena, even though he clearly thinks that we have daily experience of gravity. As a consequence Smith implicitly confines Newtonian and mathematical science to the heavens without ever having to adopt the mathematical-Newtonian way in the human sciences.

Of course, skeptical readers may grant that it is surprising that Smith does not mention the tides or Newton's so-called Moon test; they may even grant that Smith indeed understood that he was qualifying Newton's achievement in the very passage that he is praising him. Even so, skeptics would argue, this does not settle that he accepts the containment strategy.

Fair enough, of course. But I can offer another detail in the passage quoted from Smith that makes sense on the reading I offer but is otherwise just plain strange. Smith writes that "the figure of the Earth is, in general, such as he supposed it." Smith's "in general" clearly limits the claim to precise accuracy of Newton's position. Yet, this stands in striking contrast to the claim of exactitude about the orbit and shape of Jupiter in the same paragraph. The only way to make sense of this purported contrast is that given the very different epistemic situations between Jupiter and Earth, Smith takes for granted that our evidential standards for Earth are going to be more exacting such that the very same kind of astronomical measurements will offer us claims with different epistemic value depending on the domain we apply them in. This may not convince the skeptics, but the cumulative argument offered here should shift the burden of evidence. On my reading these details make sense: Smith is adopting the containment strategy. No alternative reading of all these details has been offered yet.

In this section I have argued that there is a surprising amount of converging evidence that Smith accepts and deploys the containment strategy and—in accord with this—restricts Newton's achievements to the heavens. While my argument is by no means conclusive, of course, my approach can explain both the evidence of Smith's reservations about statistical reasoning and the absence in WN of mathematical modeling and theory-mediated measurement of the sort deployed by Newton in *Principia*. In the next section, I explain away some of the evidence that has prevented us from appreciating that Smith deployed the containment strategy.

b. The Road to True Philosophy

In this section I use Millar's claim that Smith is the "Newton" of his particular branch of philosophy as a jumping-off point to discuss Hume's views on the application of mathematics and then to compare these to Smith's. Millar's claim allows one to discern the moral motives common to the variety of eighteenth-century anti-mathematicism.

Recall the oft-quoted passage from John Millar: "The Great Montesquieu pointed out the road. He was the Lord Bacon in this branch of philosophy. Dr. Smith is the Newton." It is rarely commented that in Millar this appears in a footnote appended to a long passage from WN 5.i.g.25, 803. In that passage, Smith is basically extending the Humean point that "the clergy, like the great barons" are undone by an appetite for luxury goods such that over time they give up their ability to maintain retainers. It is a paradigmatic instance of Smithian social explanation. Throughout *An Historical View of the English Government*, Millar shows himself a careful reader of Hume's History, so it is unlikely he would have missed the Humean provenance of Smith's point. Moreover, the very phrasing of Millar's praise of Smith recalls two significant tropes in Hume—one from the Introduction to Hume's Treatise and the other from Hume's treatment of Bacon, Galileo, and Newton in his History. I discuss them in reverse historical order. First, consider the following two passages from History:

> If we consider [Bacon] merely as an author and philosopher, the light in which we view him at present, though very estimable, he was yet inferior to his contemporary Galileo, perhaps even to Kepler. Bacon pointed out at a distance the road to true philosophy: Galileo both pointed it out to others, and made himself considerable advances in it. (Vol. 5, 153)
>
> [T]here flourished during this period a Boyle and a Newton; men who trod, with cautious, and therefore the more secure steps, the only road, which leads to true philosophy. (Vol. 6, 542)

In fact, throughout Hume's History, he creates a narrative that starts during the "dark" ages, which are full of "ignorance and superstition" and are marked by a "false" philosophy and "false literature" (Livingston 1988, especially Chapters 2, 7, 8, and 9). From the dark ages onward, Hume artfully weaves an account of the rediscovery of the "road" to true philosophy in the margins of his more political and economic history (Schliesser 2014). Nowhere in his narrative does Hume claim that Newton completes the true philosophy.

The significance for Hume of these matters becomes clear if we turn to the official "Introduction" to his Treatise:

> 'Tis is no astonishing reflection to consider, that the application of experimental philosophy to moral subjects shou'd come after that to natural at the distance of above a whole century; since we find in fact, that there was about the same interval betwixt the origins of these sciences; and that reckoning from THALES to SOCRATES, the space of time is nearly equal to that betwixt my Lord Bacon and some late philosophers in England, who have begun to put the science of man on a new footing, and have engag'd the attention, and excited the curiosity

of the public ... Nor ought we to think, that this latter improvement in the science of man will do less honour to our native country than the former in natural philosophy, but ought rather to esteem it a greater glory, upon account of the greater importance of that science, as well as the necessity it lay under of such a reformation ... [W]e may hope to establish on them a science [of man], which will not be inferior in certainty, and will be much superior in utility to any other of human comprehension. (Treatise, Introduction, 7–8 and 10)

Within philosophy, Hume's project is explicitly aimed at creating a science of man that is more useful than and as certain as natural philosophy (Schliesser 2009; Hazony and Schliesser 2016). That is, Hume's project is fueled as much by epistemic as moral concerns. To put the matter concisely: Hume thinks that improving man's estate is more useful than the study of the heavens and the Newtonian natural religion and theology it supports.

Before I expand on my treatment of Hume and Smith and their alternative to mathematical exactitude, I conclude my discussion of Millar's footnote. Compared to Hume's distinctly English context (in the Introduction of the Treatise) for the improvements in the "science of man," Millar puts Smith in a more European framework (for a plausible explanation why Millar would do so, see Fleischacker 2004: 252). In effect, by putting Smith in the company of Montesquieu[6] and Newton, Millar effectively distances Smith from the association with Hume, but oddly enough he does so by using Humean tropes and in the context where Smith echoes Hume.

c. Anti-Mathematicism and Proportionality in Hume and Smith

Part of the critical side of Hume's project is, in fact, an attack on Newton's claim that the exactness of geometry makes mathematical physics an exact science. As Hume writes, "As the ultimate standard for these [geometric] figures is deriv'd from nothing but the senses and imagination, 'tis absurd to talk of any perfection beyond what these faculties can judge of" (Treatise 1.2.4.29). Anything we do with geometry is only roughly right:

[Geometric proofs] are not properly demonstrations, because built on ideas, which are not exact, and maxims, which are not precisely true. When geometry decides any thing concerning proportions of quantity, we ought not to look for the utmost precision and exactness. None of

---

[6] Despite the fact that it is regularly claimed that Montesquieu influenced Smith (e.g., Haakonssen 1981: 2), I am unaware of a comparative study, which would be very welcome.

its proofs extend so far. It takes the dimensions and proportions of figures justly; but roughly and with some liberty. (Treatise 1.2.4.17)

This has implications for the use of geometry in order to secure epistemic reliability. Hume concludes his discussion of geometry by writing that geometry "can never afford us any security" if our claim is, by its means, to have attained a certain understanding of nature. Thus, in Treatise, Hume's anti-mathematicism is broader than the containment strategy I have attributed to Smith. Note that it follows from Hume's approach in Treatise that the epistemic status of applications of mathematics is always going to be less than the science of man on which it is based. (See, especially, Treatise 1.4.1.1–2, which has been discussed by Meeker 2007; Hazony and Schliesser 2016.)

We are now in a position to understand how Hume thinks about the application of mathematics in political economy: even when we possess "proportions of quantity," we "ought not to look for the utmost precision and exactness." Recall (from Section c in Chapter 5) Hume's ninth rule of causal reasoning: "An effect always holds proportion with its cause" ("Of Interest," EMPL 297). If one assumes (or prescribes) that linear causal relationships are the only possible ones, this rule allows Hume to rule out competing claims that posit the existence of causal relationships that are not "proportional." Hume uses the rule as a constraint on theory. For example, in context (in "Of Interest") it plays a prominent role in Hume's political economy when he rejects mercantilism.

In Section c of Chapter 5 I pointed to the significance of the Humean foundations of proportional (moral) reasoning (see, e.g., Treatise 3.2.11.5,; 3.3.2.4). Hume's attraction to proportionality is easy to understand, for reasoning with proportions does not make exaggerated claims to exactitude. It also requires some (contextual) judgment. One cannot just follow a mechanical rule. This is why judgments of proportionality are central to Smith's moral psychology (again recall Section c of Chapter 5).

It should come, thus, as no surprise that we find proportional reasoning throughout WN (recall WN 1.7.36, 80 quoted above). Rather than multiplying (hundreds) of examples, let me just give a very prominent instance from Smith's "Introduction and Plan of the Work," where he is about to summarize "the second book:"

> Whatever be the actual state of the skill, dexterity, and judgment with which labour is applied in any nation, the abundance or scantiness of its annual supply must depend, during the continuance of that state, upon the proportion between the number of those who are annually employed in useful labour, and that of those who are not so employed. The number of useful and productive labourers, it will hereafter appear, is every where in proportion to the quantity of capital stock which is employed in setting them to work, and to the particular way in which it is so employed. The Second Book, therefore, treats . . . (WN Intro. 6, 11)

Thus, first, Smith is definitely interested in "quantity" and "number." But, second, rather than offering us equations or a mathematical model (cf. Samuelson 1977), he offers us proportions. Proportions are certainly part of a branch of (Ancient) mathematics, but deploying proportions is extremely useful when one has doubts about exactitude: a proportion can remain the same while the underlying empirical data vary. Reasoning with proportions is very useful when one is interested in robust patterns while not having epistemic access to all the micro-causes that generate and sustain them (as is characteristic of Smithian social explanation).

Thus, third, Smith's lack of faith in "political arithmetic" is, in fact, a recognition that in the face of human—perhaps infinite—variety, the science of the legislator should not make exaggerated claims to exactness. Given our recent bouts of expert overconfidence, Smith remains prescient: "The over-weening conceit which the greater part of men have of their own abilities, is an antient evil remarked by the philosophers and moralists of all ages" (WN 1.10.b.26, 124). As Mark Blaug put it: "for economic wisdom rather than theoretical elegance, Smith had no equal in the eighteenth and or even the nineteenth centuries" (Blaug 1996: 62).

One might object that in the passage above and throughout WN Smith appeals to "quantity" and "number," so let us reconsider (recall Section c of Chapter 8), for example, this influential passage:

> The real price of every thing, what every thing really costs to the man who wants to acquire it, is the toil and trouble of acquiring it. What every thing is really worth to the man who has acquired it, and who wants to dispose of it or exchange it for something else, is the toil and trouble which it can save to himself, and which it can impose upon other people. What is bought with money or with goods is purchased by labour, as much as what we acquire by the toil of our own body. That money or those goods indeed save us this toil. They contain the value of a certain quantity of labour which we exchange for what is supposed at the time to contain the value of an equal quantity. Labour was the first price, the original purchase-money that was paid for all things. It was not by gold or by silver, but by labour, that all the wealth of the world was originally purchased; and its value, to those who possess it, and who want to exchange it for some new productions, is precisely equal to the quantity of labour which it can enable them to purchase or command. (WN 1.5.2, 47–8)

Adopting the language of "precisely equal," Smith seems to imply to many, especially twentieth-century, readers that such magnitudes enter into an exact theoretical model that is capable of being reconstructed by a series of equations (e.g., Samuelson 1977). Given that "real price" and "quantity of labor" are measured, in part, by "money," this reading is extremely plausible. It would seem, then, that Smith ignores Mandeville's arguments about the difficulty of measuring or tracking mental quality (i.e., "toil and trouble"). Of course, such a model would have to be implicit to Smith's project because explicit equations are lacking in WN.

Yet, even explicit *computations* are extremely rare throughout WN. Strikingly enough, right at the start of book, just after introducing the first main idea—the division of labor—Smith writes, "Observe the accommodation of the most common artificer or day-labourer in a civilized and thriving country, and you will perceive that the number of people of whose industry a part, though but a small part, has been employed in procuring him this accommodation, *exceeds all computation*" (WN 1.1, 22; emphasis added). This passage sets up the famous *proportional* comparison between, on the one hand, "the European prince" and "the industrial and frugal peasant," and, on the other hand, the "African King" and the "ten thousand naked savages" (WN 1.1.11, 24). Rather than offering a ringing endorsement of quantitative methods in his science, Smith calls attention to our epistemic limitations right at the start of WN!

Recall from Section c of Chapter 8 that there is one exact measure in WN: "At the same time and place, therefore, money is the exact measure of the real exchangeable value of all commodities" (WN 1.5.19, 55). But the theoretical significance of this is undercut in the very next sentence: "It is so, however, at the same time and place only." No other measure is called "exact" in WN! By contrast, even though "labour be the real measure of the exchangeable value," it is not an exact measure. As Smith goes on to explain: "It is adjusted, however, not by any accurate measure, but by the higgling and bargaining of the market, according to that sort of rough equality which, though not exact, is sufficient for carrying on the business of common life" (WN 1.5.4, 49).

Smith makes another claim to precision in the passage leading up to his use of the "invisible hand" in WN. Recall (from Section c of Chapter 10), in his criticism of mercantilism, he writes that "the annual revenue of every society is always precisely equal to the exchangeable value of the whole annual produce of its industry, or rather is precisely the same thing with that exchangeable value" (WN 4.2.9, 455–6). Rather than measuring the annual revenue of a particular society, Smith treats it as a definition (which it is). And he uses this definition to correct the false mercantile theory (in which hoarding gold leads to wealth) that leads merchants to believe (falsely) that they are trading for the public good. Thus, Smith uses exactitude to make a politically significant conceptual claim, not to study data.

Finally, one may think that his claim "insurance, therefore, may be carried on successfully by a joint stock company," even "without any exclusive privilege" (that is, a monopoly or a restriction on competition), may be evidence to the contrary (WN 5.1.e.35, 756); after all, modern students of finance tend to think of insurance companies as using very precise probabilistic reasoning to handle risk proper (as opposed to Knightian uncertainty, which does not allow the assignation of probabilities; see Knight 1921). As it turns out, though, insurance fits my argument perfectly, because Smith's analysis of insurance is opposed to the modern one: "The value of the risk, either from fire, or from loss by sea, or by capture, though *it cannot, perhaps, be calculated very exactly,* admits, however, of such a gross estimation as renders it, in some degree, reducible to strict rule and method" (WN 5.1.e.35, 756; emphasis added). Thus, while he allows that insurance by a large company (or joint stock company) can be operated competitively on "strict rule and method" (and so avoid the principal-agent problems that Smith diagnoses as fatal to most large corporations in competitive environments), he does not think that the risk they insure against can be "calculated very exactly." But evidently he thinks that even with "gross estimation," profitable rule-following is possible in insurance.

I have argued that there is quite a bit of converging evidence that Smith accepts the containment strategy, and limits claims to mathematical exactness to the heavens. I have argued that in WN Smith primarily relies on proportional reasoning. Proportional reasoning is compatible with causal and counterfactual arguments of the sort we find in WN. But the moral is that even reasoning with quantities and number in Smithian political economy generally requires good judgment and cannot be reduced to mere mechanical rules. This fits nicely with Smith's moral philosophy (Fleischacker 1999), and it fits the spirit of Smith's criticism of the deleterious effects of too-technical metaphysics mentioned in the Introduction (TMS 3.3.14, 143; TMS 7.2.1.41, 291; WN 5.1.f.29, 770).

PART 3

PHILOSOPHERS

14

Religion

A chaste disciple of Epicurus.

—Lord Buchan

It is well known that Smith was extremely cautious about the public's response to theological unorthodoxy; he was not enthusiastic about appointing Hume to a position at Edinburgh, and he could not bring himself to publish Hume's Dialogues (Phillipson 2010). When we turn to analyze his own writings, we must not forget that he was not only a slow writer, but also a cautious writer when it came to theological affairs. As Gavin Kennedy has persuasively argued, this latter feature was well known among his friends, including William Robertson, who, in addition to being one of the outstanding historians of his generation, was also one of the leaders of the Moderate party in the Presbyterian General Assembly. In commenting on an ultimately suppressed preface in which James Hutton argued against Scriptural geology, Robertson advised Hutton to "consult our friend Mr. Smith" in order to render his work "a little more [orthodox] theological" (Kennedy 2013: 468; the letter can be consulted in Dean 1992: 23 with analysis). Kennedy nicely argues that Smith "was adept at using theological dressing when composing his arguments" (Kennedy 2013: 479).

Moreover, in Section a of Chapter 11, I argued that Smith affirms without condemnation that in classical times some philosophers of the "Italian School" taught their doctrines to pupils only "under the seal of the most sacred secrecy, that they might avoid the fury of the people, and not incur the imputation of impiety" (Astronomy 4.4, 55–6). So, given that on Smith's account the government must (recall) respect "the prejudices" of the people when it comes "to the happiness in a life to come" (WN 4.5.b.40, 539), there is no reason to expect Smith to be recklessly sincere in these matters.

Scholarly discussions of Smith's views on religion are bedeviled by two obsessively posed questions: (i) does the so-called invisible hand instantiate or rely on a providential order? and (ii) what are Smith's beliefs about the existence of God? I have addressed (i) in fine-grained detail in Chapter 10. In what follows I offer evidence that Smith may have been a deist, but given the tenor of the previous two paragraphs, it should be clear that I believe we cannot really know the answer to (ii). Let me offer one further argument to this effect. In his *Life of Adam Smith*, Rae reports that on their final meeting, while exiting the dining room and turning to his close friends Black and Hutton (the editors of EPS), Smith said:

> "I love your company, gentlemen, but I believe I must leave you to go to another world." These are the words as reported by Henry Mackenzie, who was present, in giving Samuel Rogers an account of Smith's death during a visit he paid to London in the course of the following year. But Hutton, in the account he gave Stewart of the incident, employs the slightly different form of expression, "I believe we must adjourn this meeting to some other place." (Rae 1895: 681)

Rae then comments: "Possibly both sentences were used by Smith, for both are needed for the complete expression of the parting consolation he obviously meant to convey—that death is not a final separation, but only an adjournment of the meeting" (681).[1] While Rae emphasizes the consoling intention, his approach seems to imply that Smith must have believed in something like heaven.

Yet, when we reflect on the theatricality of the reported event, another interpretation is equally plausible. As I recount in great detail in the next chapter, Smith was heavily involved in managing the public perception of Hume's final days. In particular, he was very eager to report that on his deathbed Hume was cheerfully reading Lucian's *Dialogues of the Dead*. It takes little imagination to see that while expressing utterly orthodox words, Smith is simultaneously capable of alluding to the title of Lucian's work and, thus, also his friend's example of facing death magnanimously. As I recount in more detail below, not unlike Smith's report of Hume, where Smith was absent at the actual moment of death, here, too, we receive witness of Smith approaching death without the testimony of the actual death scene.

In this chapter, I discuss two important aspects of Smith's philosophy of religion. In the first section I analyze Smith's analysis of the relationship between morality and theology. In the second, I treat Smith's political views on religion.

a. Biblical Revelation and Christian Theology

In this section I argue that, according to Smith, religion is constrained by the demands of morality. I also claim that Smith's treatment of revelation reveals that if he believed in a God, his views are more akin to Deism than Theism (in line with Evensky 2005: 23ff). He treats revelation as a significant sociologic phenomena, not a source of authoritative claims. I also claim that, according to Smith,

---

[1] MacKenzie was a successful novelist, who published *The Man of Feeling* (1771), perhaps the greatest novel about sympathy prior to Shelley's *Frankenstein* and Elliot's *Middlemarch*.

religion's main task is to ensure that people "fulfill all the obligations of morality" and to encourage them "to act from justice and beneficence."

Consider, first, the following passage:

> In the Decalogue we are commanded to honour our fathers and mothers. No mention is made of the love of our children. Nature had sufficiently prepared us for the performance of this latter duty. Men are seldom accused of affecting to be fonder of their children than they really are. They have sometimes been suspected of displaying their piety to their parents with too much ostentation. The ostentatious sorrow of widows has, for a like reason, been suspected of insincerity. (TMS 3.3.13, 142)

In this context, Smith treats the Ten Commandments sociologically, as an example of what "moralists" of all ages teach correctly. The Decalogue offers insight into which of our moral duties are innate (i.e., these do not need to be mentioned) and which duties require sanctions (i.e., the ones listed). The rules of revealed religion do not track the natural sentiments but help in their system of sanctions and rewards to cultivate some of our passions. Religion plays a role in stabilizing the derived sentiments. Given that here Smith treats revelation simultaneously as similar in kind to any other wise source of knowledge on human affairs as well as a reliable authority into how to engage with human nature, he understands Moses as a wise lawgiver (on this matter) but no more privileged than other "moralists." Smith's approach here has affinity with Chapter 3 of Spinoza's *Theological Political Treatise*. Insofar as Smith is committed to the existence of God, he is, thus, closer to Deism, which denies any special status to revelation, than to theism (in addition to Evensky, see Herzog 2013: 23).

If we are allowed to treat the whole list of Ten Commandments in such sociologic terms, then it appears that Smith thinks that the very idea of a monotheistic God is not natural (or innate) to us but requires social reinforcement mechanisms. This echoes, in fact, the first chapter of Hume's *Natural History of Religion*.

We find a similar (to TMS 3.3.13, 142) deflationary treatment of revelation in the midst of one of Smith's great set-pieces, the treatment of education of Book 5 of WN. At one point, he interrupts his narrative for what looks like a historical aside: "The antient Greek philosophy was divided into three great branches; physicks, or natural philosophy; ethicks, or moral philosophy; and logick. This general division seems perfectly agreeable to the nature of things" (WN 5.1.f.23, 766). What follows is a description of how, first, in account for natural phenomena, superstition turned into Greek natural philosophy (WN 5.1.f.24, 767–8); second, (a) how common "maxims" of living were, after the invention of writing, turned (b) by self-styled "wise men" into the great poetic works of, say, Theognis or Hesiod (WN 5.1.f.25, 768; see also LRBL 2.44, 104), and (c) with further development and—in light of the pattern of natural philosophy—"the maxims of common life were arranged in some methodical order, and connected together by a few common principles," into Greek moral philosophy (WN 5.1.f.25, 768–9); and third, the partisans "of each system of natural and moral philosophy naturally endeavoured to expose the weakness of the arguments adduced to support the systems which were opposite to their own. In examining those arguments, they were necessarily led to consider the difference between a probable and a demonstrative argument, between a fallacious and a conclusive one; and" so Logic came into being (5.1.f.26, 769–70).

In his treatment of the three-step origin of Greek moral philosophy (a–c above), Smith inserts as an example of the second step, (b) "wise sayings, like the Proverbs of Solomon," which are treated as on par with and no better than the cosmogonic poetry of the Greeks (i.e., Hesiod at WN 5.1.f.25, 768). Smith does not insert the Hebrew Bible into the origin of natural philosophy. Thus, Smith is flirting here again with a Spinozistic treatment of revelation in two senses: (i) the Bible is exclusively to be understood as a moral work and contains no worthy scientific teachings; (ii) it is capable of being historicized like any other human literary work. (Of course, Smith is not claiming this about the whole Bible.)

On (i) Smith stands far from the position of, say, Samuel Clarke's (1705) anti-Spinozistic (and anti-Hobbesian, anti-Toland, etc.) Boyle Lecture, *A Demonstration of the Being and Attributes of God*. In fact, after listing a large number of Newton's then recent discoveries, Clarke treats the history of scientific progress as an unfolding Biblical prophecy:

> We now see with how great reason the author of the Book of Ecclesiasticus after he had described the beauty of the Sun and Stars, and all then visible works of God in heaven and earth, concluded ch. 43, v 32 (as we after all the discoveries of later ages, may no doubt still truly say,) "There yet hid greater things than these, we have seen but a few of his Works." (A Demonstration XI, 232–3)

Newton's then recent discoveries are an important evidentiary signpost for understanding scientific progress as an open-ended unfolding and confirmation of confident Biblical prophecy. Even those who offer the most ardent of arguments that Smith is a "Christian" theist (Long 2009: 92) do not ascribe to Smith a position that goes beyond (i) and keep him far from Biblical literalist claims about science. In fact, in one of TMS's most pious-sounding passages ("the author of nature has made man the immediate judge of mankind, and has, in this respect, as in many others, created him after his own image"), Smith explicitly denies that any ongoing inquiry can reveal more about God's plan:

> If those infinite rewards and punishments which the Almighty has prepared for those who obey or transgress his will, were perceived as distinctly as we foresee the frivolous and temporary retaliations which we

may expect from one another, the weakness of human nature, astonished at the immensity of objects he so little fitted to its comprehension, could no longer attend to the little affairs of this world; and it is absolutely impossible that the business of society could have been carried on, if, in this respect, there had been a fuller revelation of the intentions of providence than that which has already been made. (TMS 128; withdrawn in TMS 6)

If we knew more of God's plan, we would (eventually) necessarily ("absolutely impossible") simply stop doing our moral duty. Smith here explicitly undercuts the argument—promoted in the General Scholium to Newton's *Principia* and countless latitudinarian Boyle lecturers and Newtonian popularizers—that scientific inquiry reveals to us more detail of God's plan. Our finite, human nature is—as it were—blinded by the perception of certain infinite objects.[2] In emphasizing this finitude, this scarcity of time, which is oriented "toward to the little affairs of this world," we find Smith embracing a form of leveling egalitarianism. As we have seen (recall Section a of Chapter 1), Smith treats homely proverbs and intellectual systems of thought as a means of coping with this finitude.

Moreover, if we reflect on the three great branches of learning that seem "perfectly agreeable to the nature of things" (WN 5.1.f.23, 766; note the Epicurean way this is phrased), Metaphysics and Theology are pointedly omitted originally. Initially, Smith includes treatment of "the gods" in the "superstitious phase" prior to natural philosophy (WN 5.1.f.24, 767), but he explicitly (and rather surprisingly) excludes the gods from the "philosophy phase:" "Superstition first attempted to satisfy this curiosity by referring all those wonderful appearances to the immediate agency of the gods. Philosophy afterwards endeavoured to account for them, from more familiar causes, or from such as mankind were better acquainted with, than the agency of the gods" (WN 5.1.f.24, 767). Thus, here (but not elsewhere), Smith treats the origins of Greek philosophy as a kind of naturalizing project.

What follows in WN is a story of the *corruption* of Greek philosophy by *Christianity* (in which Smith explains how a threefold division became a fivefold division due to the influence of Christianity):

[W]hatever was taught concerning the nature either of the human mind or of the Deity, made a part of the system of physicks. Those beings, in whatever their essence might be supposed to consist, were parts of the great system of the universe, and parts too productive of the most important effects. Whatever human reason could either conclude, or conjecture, concerning them, made, as it were, two chapters, though

[2] Yet elsewhere he adds—seemingly in passing—that "the universe may be conceived to be" as infinite (External Senses 11, EPS 137). Smith's relationship to the infinite deserves its own treatment.

no doubt two very important ones, of the science which pretended to give an account of the origin and revolutions of the great system of the universe. But in the [Medieval] universities of Europe, where philosophy was taught only as subservient to theology, it was natural to dwell longer upon these two chapters than upon any other of the science. They were gradually more and more extended, and were divided into many inferior chapters, till at last the doctrine of spirits, of which so little can be known, came to take up as much room in the system of philosophy as the doctrine of bodies, of which so much can be known. The proper subject of experiment and observation, a subject in which a careful attention is capable of making so many useful discoveries, was almost entirely neglected. The subject [metaphysics or pneumatics] in which, after a few very simple and almost obvious truths, the most careful attention can discover nothing but obscurity and uncertainty, and can consequently produce nothing but subtleties and sophisms, was greatly cultivated.

Wherein consisted the happiness and perfection of a man, considered not only as an individual, but as the member of a family, of a state, and of the great society of mankind, was the object which the ancient moral philosophy proposed to investigate. In that philosophy the duties of human life were treated of as subservient to the happiness and perfection of human life. But when moral, as well as natural philosophy, came to be taught only as subservient to theology, the duties of human life were treated of as chiefly subservient to the happiness of a life to come. In the antient philosophy the perfection of virtue was represented as necessarily productive, to the person who possessed it, of the most perfect happiness in this life. In the modern philosophy it was frequently represented as generally, or rather as almost always inconsistent with any degree of happiness in this life; and heaven was to be earned only by penance and mortification, by the austerities and abasement of a monk; not by the liberal, generous, and spirited conduct of a man. Casuistry and an ascetic morality made up, in most cases, the greater part of the moral philosophy of the schools. By far the most important of all the different branches of philosophy, became in this manner by far the most corrupted. (WN 5.1.f.28 and 30, 769–71)

Here Smith treats ancient accounts of the deity as "part of the great system of the universe" and not as in some sense beyond the universe. On Smith's account of ancient theology, which turns out not to have been absent from Greek philosophy after all, god is immanent in nature. This is an oddly Spinozistic reading of the Ancients (it is not a silly reading of Stoicism, of course, but this need not concern us here). The Gods play a role in cosmogony and cosmology, but (surprisingly enough, given the evidence available to him) not in the providential moral order. In Smith's hands theology is also restricted to the natural philosophy branch, and absent from Greek moral philosophy.

Moreover, echoing Spinoza, Smith treats theology's dominion over metaphysics and philosophy generally as an unmitigated intellectual disaster, leading philosophy into areas of "obscurity and uncertainty" (etc.). On balance, Smith thinks that (natural) philosophy should stick to the (Royal Society and Humean) method of "experiment and observation" in order to obtain knowledge of bodies—an eminently promising, even "useful" project. While the science of bodies need not be itself materialistic, in Smith's hands it is opposed to the science of spirits. Therefore, Smith does not only embrace experimental philosophy but also seems to embrace a surprisingly materialist version of it. Either way, Smith leaves extremely little room for a separate doctrine about immaterial souls as a matter of science.

Sadly, in this context we do not learn what the "simple and almost obvious truths" of metaphysics are that Smith thinks are available to all of us. But, pointedly, this excludes the Christian mysteries that even Protestants would have to embrace.

With that in mind, In the history of Ancient physics, Smith makes the following observation about the relationship between Aristotle and his scholastic interpreters:

> The revolutions of the Heavens, by their grandeur and constancy, excited his admiration, and seemed, upon that account, to be effects not unworthy a Divine Intelligence. Whereas the meanness of many things, the disorder and confusion of all things below, exciting no such agreeable emotion, seemed to have no marks of being directed by that Supreme Understanding. Yet, though this opinion saps the foundations of human worship, and must have the same effects upon society as Atheism itself, one may easily trace, in the Metaphysics upon which it is grounded, the origin of many of the notions, or rather of many of the expressions, in the scholastic theology, to which no notions can be annexed. (Ancient Physics 10, EPS 116)

Thus, according to Smith much of Christian theology got married to a conceptual framework that is not just inadequate, but unsuitable to it! On Smith's view human worship becomes senseless if God has no interest in our affairs. This is why Aristotle's doctrine about the unmoved mover "must have the same effects upon society as Atheism itself." Here Smith leaves unclear if these effects are pernicious (cf. Long 2009: 83). In WN Smith castigates Greek private and, especially, public morals (and compares these unfavorably to the classical Romans): "factions of the Greeks were almost always violent" (WN 5.1.f.40, 775–6). Romans' good morals are said to be a consequence, however, not of their religion but "probably more owing to the better constitution of their courts of justice" (WN 5.1.f.44, 779).

Let's return to WN 5.1.f.28 and 30, 769–71. In it, Christian theology is presented as an unmitigated disaster for the fate of moral philosophy, which is "most corrupted." Rather than focusing on the "happiness and perfection of human life," Christian duty orients us toward an afterlife and makes no contribution to happiness in this life. It's hard to shake the feeling that Smith thinks his own advocacy of commercial society is more conducive to moral philosophy and the moral way of life than Christian theology.[3]

Here Smith also rejects "the austerities and abasement of a monk" without qualification. As he puts it in TMS: "to compare . . . the futile mortifications of a monastery, to the ennobling hardships and hazards of war; to suppose that one day, or one hour, employed in the former should, in the eye of the great Judge of the world, have more merit than a whole life spent honourably in the latter, is surely contrary to all our moral sentiments" (TMS 3.2.35, 134; this echoes Hume's criticism of the monkish virtues Second *Enquiry*, EPM 9.3).

The passages I have just mentioned from TMS and WN are rarely discussed when treating Smith's views on revelation on theology. Speculation is, rather, centered on a long passage that Smith eventually removed from TMS. I quote before commenting on it:

> Man, when about to appear before a being of infinite perfection, can feel but little confidence in his own merit, or in the imperfect propriety of his own conduct. In the presence of his fellow-creatures, he may often [may even 2-5][4] justly elevate himself, and may often have reason to think highly of his own character and conduct, compared to the still greater imperfection of theirs. But the case is quite different when about to appear before his infinite Creator. To such a being, he can scarce imagine, that his littleness and weakness should ever seem to be [being, he fears, that his littleness and weakness can scarce ever appear] the proper object, either of esteem or of reward. But he can easily conceive, how the numberless violations of duty, of which he has been guilty, should render him the proper object of aversion and punishment; neither can he see any [and he thinks he can see no] reason why the divine indignation should not be let loose without any restraint, upon so vile an insect, as he is sensible [he imagines] that he himself must appear to be. If he would still hope for happiness, he is conscious [he suspects] that he cannot demand it from the justice, but that he must entreat it from the mercy of God. Repentance, sorrow, humiliation, contrition at the thought of his past conduct, are, [seem]

---

[3] Hanley 2009 explores Smith's doubts late in life about this.

[4] The words in brackets as well as the words in the last brackets of the passage were inserted in the second through fifth editions of TMS. The bracketed words in the remainder of the passage were added in the third through the fifth editions.

upon this account, the sentiments which become him, and seem to [and to] be the only means which he has left for appeasing that wrath which, he knows, he has justly provoked. He even distrusts the efficacy of all these, and naturally fears, lest the wisdom of God should not, like the weakness of man, be prevailed upon to spare the crime, by the most importunate lamentations of the criminal. Some other intercession, some other sacrifice, some other atonement, he imagines, [imagines] must be made for him, beyond what he himself is capable of making, before the purity of the divine justice can be reconciled to his manifold offences. The doctrines of revelation coincide, in every respect, with those original anticipations of nature; and, as they teach us how little we can depend upon the imperfection of our own virtue, so they show us, at the same time, that the most powerful intercession has been made, and that the most dreadful atonement has been paid for our manifold transgressions and iniquities. (TMS 91–2)

Let's assume for the sake of argument that Smith is entirely sincere in these lines. What is he, in fact, claiming here? No more than this: that when we are about to face our final judgment, we naturally believe that in the scales of divine justice we do not have enough weight to balance properly our "numberless violations of duty;" that we need some helping hand to atone for our sins. Revelation teaches us that Christ's death "paid for our manifold transgressions and iniquities." Smith is not claiming that (counterfactually) without revelation we would still believe that our sins are, in fact, atoned. Rather, without revelation we would naturally feel miserable about our chances of postmortem happiness. Of course, this realization makes us feel miserable in the present. As Smith puts it, even the "great Caesar," who may not have even believed in "infinite creator," felt "the avenging furies of shame and remorse."[5] His earthly misery is a product both of "his own memory and from that of other people, the remembrance of what he has done; that remembrance never fails to pursue him" (TMS 1.3.3.8, 65).

To put Smith's view in more deflationary economic terms, we naturally feel we lack purchasing power to bribe the great judge on our behalf. That is, we wish to treat him the way the inferior shepherds treat their clan-head, but we have run out of flock to share with him. (Recall WN 5.1.a.15, 697.) This prospect ruins our tranquility here on Earth. Luckily, Christian revelation teaches us that someone else has discharged our debt on our behalf, and this offers psychological comfort in the present. As Smith puts it in a slightly different context, "The consciousness that it is the object of such favourable regards, is the source of that inward tranquillity [sic] and self-satisfaction with which it is naturally attended, as the suspicion of the contrary gives occasion to the torments of vice" (TMS 3.1.7, 113).

---

[5] Smith seems to side here with Caesar's Republican critics.

One oddity about Smith's position expressed in the TMS 91–2 passage that he withdrew is that it coincides almost exactly with Spinoza's claim that

> for seeing we cannot by Natural Light, perceive that Simple Obedience is the way to Salvation, and God's special Grace and Favour hath by revelation only, and not by Reason, made it known unto us; the Scripture must certainly be a great help and consolation to all mankind; because tho' every Man may obey, yet in respect of the whole, there are very few, who by the dictates and conducts of Reason livery vertuously [sic], so that were it not for the Testimony of Scripture, me might doubt of most Men's Salvation. (TTP 15: 44–44; I have used here the 1737 translation, pp. 329–30)

However, it is compatible with Smith's position that if revelation had never occurred, and mankind had never been exposed to the idea of "infinite perfection," then Christ's atonement would not have been necessary for our tranquility of mind. This is because, as Smith puts it (in very Epicurean fashion): "the authority of religion is superior to every other authority. The fears which it suggests conquer all other fears" (WN 5.1.g.17, 797).

Admittedly, in the last paragraph I have gone, perhaps, beyond what is explicitly stated in Smith's text, but it is worth emphasizing that Smith's treatment of theological matters is framed nearly entirely by moral and political concerns. I am not the first to remark on this. For example, the co-editor of the Glasgow edition of TMS, D. D. Raphael, once noted correctly that in treating Smith's views on God and theology, for Smith a "theology is unacceptable if it fails to accord with 'all our moral sentiments' (TMS 3.2.33)" (Raphael 2007: 104). Yet Raphael does not pause to consider how, echoing Spinoza, Smith anticipates Kant in systematically subordinating theology to morality (Fleischacker 2004, Chapter 15):

> [R]eligion enforces the natural sense of duty. . . . And wherever the natural principles of religion are not corrupted by the factious and party zeal of some worthless cabal; wherever the first duty which it requires, is to fulfill all the obligations of morality; wherever men are not taught to regard frivolous observances, as more immediate duties of religion, than acts of justice and beneficence; and to imagine, that by sacrifices, and ceremonies, and vain supplications, they can bargain with the Deity for fraud, and perfidy, and violence, the world undoubtedly judges right in this respect. (TMS 3.5.13, 170)

Smith's point is very clear: religion's main task is (a) to ensure that people "fulfill all the obligations of morality" and (b) to encourage people "to act from justice and beneficence." This is undisguised Spinozism (cf. "the worship of God and obedience to him consist only in Justice and Loving-kindness, or in the love of one's neighbor" [TTP 14:28]). Smith is very careful not to spell out what the "natural principles" of a non-frivolous (or "true") religion are, although presumably they involve not treating God as an agent, who can be moved by incentives. That is, Smithian true religion does not include God in our political and moral economy. (It remains, of course, possible on this view that *we* are *in* God's economy.) Given that many religions do include lots of mechanisms by which adherents can try to gain God's favor, this suggests that such "natural principles" may be rarely instantiated in actual religions. (Smithian "natural principles" may be as rare as "natural sympathy" is [TMS 6.2.1.18, 224–5].)

Smith gives a further hint of what non-frivolous or true religion might be when he discusses Voltaire's play *Mahomet*: "False notions of religion are almost the only causes which can occasion any very gross perversion of our natural sentiments in this way; and that principle which gives the greatest authority to the rules of duty, is alone capable of distorting our ideas of them in any considerable degree" (TMS, 3.6.12, 176).

Now recall that Smith operates with a distinction between natural sentiments, which are more or less innate dispositions, and moral sentiments, which—based on our natural sentiments and propensities—are cultivated by the various institutions of society. Thus, Smith recognizes religion as a very powerful social force—in fact it is singled out here as the most significant source of the corruption of even our natural sentiments, so much so that it facilitates "horrid murder, that shocks all the principles of human nature" (TMS 3.6.12, 177; Minowitz 1993: 194). It is, in fact, the worst corruption of our passions that can occur, and, thus, politically dangerous and destabilizing (recall the discussion in Section a of Chapter 1 about religious faction in WN 5.1.g.8, 793; 5.1.g.15, 796; 5.1.g.29, 801; and 5.1.g.34–6, 808–9). Even our "disposition to admire, and almost to worship, the rich and the powerful, and to despise, or, at least, to neglect persons of poor and mean condition" corrupts only the moral sentiments, but not the natural sentiments (TMS 1.3.3.1, 61—Smith added this chapter to this sixth edition).

Moreover, it is unlikely that Smith thinks that true religion contains adherence to particular doctrines, because, as he writes in the same passage,

> concerning the particular commandments which that will may impose upon us, they differ widely from one another. In this, therefore, the greatest mutual forbearance and toleration is due; and though the defence of society requires that crimes should be punished, from whatever motives they proceed, yet a good man will always punish them with reluctance, when they evidently proceed from false notions of religious duty. (TMS 3.6.12, 176)

And here, again, we find Smith subtly introducing Spinozistic themes: he defends upholding obedience to the law as a supreme duty, while at the same time advocating doctrinal tolerance.

b. Anticlericalism and Freedom of Religion

In this section I explore the details of Smith's radical proposal to encourage both a very wide freedom of religion and the abandonment of an established religion. In doing so, I emphasize the anticlerical tenor of Smith's arguments. Having said that, Smith is not antireligious; large commercial society needs religion, and, in fact, he redeploys religious concepts to argue for freedom of thought.

While Smith hoped that education would lend genuine stability to government (WN 5.f.61, 788), he also recommended public "diversions" (e.g., "painting, poetry, musick, dancing" and "all sorts of dramatic representations and exhibitions") to "amuse" people's minds and make political and religious fanatics the objects of "ridicule" (WN 5.i.g.15, 796–7). In fact, although Smith is perfectly capable of treating the clergy in descriptive terms (e.g., TMS 5.25, 202–3), in his treatment of casuistry he reveals an anticlerical animus (e.g., TMS 7.4.18, 334; see also his treatment of monks and friars at TMS 3.2.34–5, 133–4; Minowitz 1993 develops this argument, perhaps to excess). He insists that "candour and moderation" are rarely found among existing leading clergy (WN 5.1.g.8, 793).

In WN Smith treats the clergy primarily as educators, who draw their salaries either from the state (or foundations) or from "the voluntary contributions of their hearers." The more secure the income of the clergy, the more likely they will be "men of learning and elegance" but likely "to lose the qualities, both good and bad, which [give] them authority and influence with the inferior ranks of people" (WN 5.1.g.1ff, 788ff). Smith quotes at considerable length from a Spinozistic argument by Hume, "the most illustrious philosopher and historian of the present age," to the effect that the "wise legislator" ought to "prevent" an "interested diligence of the clergy." Hume, therefore, advocates state-sponsored established religion in order to have a "salaried" and, therefore, reasonably contented and lazy clergy (WN 5.i.g.3–6, 790–1; see also Hume's "Of a Perfect Commonwealth").

Smith is adamantly opposed to established religion. He treats politically successful religions as lucky and intolerant partisans: "The sect which had the good fortune to be leagued with the conquering party, necessarily shared in the victory of its ally, by whose favour and protection it was soon enabled in some degree to silence and subdue all its adversaries. Their first demand was generally, that he should silence and subdue all their adversaries" (WN 5.i.g. 7, 792). Here Smith omits kind words for either the national churches of Scotland or England, which, after the Glorious Revolution of 1688, often appealed to providential plan in their public justification.

Instead Smith revives interest in the "plan of ecclesiastical government, or more properly of no ecclesiastical government, was what the sect called Independents, a sect no doubt of very wild enthusiasts, proposed to establish in England towards the end of the civil war" (WN 5.i.g.8, 793; for an excellent analysis, see Muller 1993, Chapter 12). Without an established religion, which would allow "every man to chuse his own priest and his own religion as he thought proper," and each religion treated equally under the law, Smith expected that "There would in this case, no doubt, have been a great multitude of religious sects. Almost every different congregation might probably have made a little sect by itself, or have entertained some peculiar tenets of its own" (WN 5.i.g.8, 793). Smith's hope in WN is that with near absolute freedom of religion (something neither Locke, Spinoza, nor Hume advocated), competition among religious sects will lead to a "pure and rational religion, free from every mixture of absurdity, imposture, or fanaticism, such as wise men have in all ages of the world wished to see established" (WN 5.i.g.8, 793).

Smith assumes that disestablishment will lead to an extreme proliferation "into two or three hundred, or perhaps into as many thousand small sects" (WN 5.i.g.8, 793). In context he does not offer a detailed explanation of why one would expect such a proliferation, but it seems clear that he thinks the division will be promoted by the entrepreneurial "zeal" of individual church leaders, who will promote themselves and different "particular" speculative "tenets" (WN 5.i.g.9, 793–4). Our earlier treatment of Smith's account of the establishment of "environmental rationality" (recall Section b of Chapter 3 and Section a of Chapter 10) can shed light on why he expects the proliferation of tenets absent state-sanctioned indoctrination. Religious, speculative tenets are not embedded and anchored in the kind of habits trained up, as it were, on the world's experienced order—they go beyond these (this is why I call them "speculative" here—see WN 5.1.f.26, 769).

Smith's arguments for such disestablishment are a mixture of prudential political considerations and sociologic ones. With extreme competition among lots of sects, Smith expects most of them to become relatively moderate in tone over time. In fact, he expects that

> The teachers of each little sect, finding themselves almost alone, would be obliged to respect those of almost every other sect, and the concessions which they would mutually find it both convenient and agreeable to make to one another, might in time probably reduce the doctrine of the greater part of them to that pure and rational religion. (WN 5.1.g.8, 793)

Smith does not really explain his grounds for optimism. It is by no means obvious why a free market in religious ideas would have to converge on religious tenets free from absurdity. (See Iannaccone 1991 for some empirical data on competitive religious "markets," but he leaves out doctrinal reasonableness.) Sadly, he also does not explain what the doctrinal contents of a "pure and rational" religion are, nor who the "wise" are.[6] It's also unclear why he thinks such a competition would

---

[6] For useful background, see Fraenkel 2012, but (sadly) he does not really take the story past Spinoza, so there are only passing mentions of the eighteenth century.

always lead to agreeable manners—he is certainly aware of the dangers of faction (TMS 6.2. 2. 12, 231; for discussion Brubaker 2006a; Peart and Levy 2009).

A related argument Smith offers is that he expects the competition of religions to maintain a "strict and austere system" of morality among the common people (WN 5.1.g.10, 794). Smith offers a functional argument for this outcome—it is economically expedient for the common people to have relatively strict mores and, therefore, relatively inexpensive taste:

> The vices of levity are always ruinous to the common people, and a single week's thoughtlessness and dissipation is often sufficient to undo a poor workman for ever, and to drive him through despair upon committing the most enormous crimes. The wiser and better sort of the common people, therefore, have always the utmost abhorrence and detestation of such excesses, which their experience tells them are so immediately fatal to people of their condition. (WN 5.1.g.10, 794)

One consequence of Smith's argument is that with rising prosperity and the lowering of the cost of living, a taste for (modest) luxury and less austere morals will be probable even among the poor.

A further argument that Smith offers is that as urbanization proceeds, people lack actual spectators on their conduct: "His conduct is observed and attended to by nobody, and he is therefore very likely to neglect it himself, and to abandon himself to every sort of low profligacy and vice." According to Smith, one "never emerges so effectually from this obscurity, his conduct never excites so much the attention of any respectable society, as by his becoming the member of a small religious sect" (WN 5.1.g.12, 795). Thus, religious sects become stand-ins for the impartial spectator within. Thus, "In little religious sects, accordingly, the morals of the common people have been almost always remarkably regular and orderly; generally much more so than in the established church" (WN 5.1.g.12, 796; for an excellent treatment of the positive role that religious virtues can play in commercial society, see Hanley 2009). But they do not do so perfectly: as Smith notes, "the morals of those little sects, indeed, have frequently been rather disagreeably rigorous and unsocial" (WN 5.1.g.12, 796).

In fact, it is in order to combat this potential "market failure in religion" that Smith suggests two state-sponsored remedies (as we have seen): first, the promotion of "the study of science and philosophy" among the common people, and, second, the "entire liberty" of people to promote "without scandal or indecency, to amuse and divert the people by painting, poetry, musick, dancing; by all sorts of dramatic representations and exhibitions, would easily dissipate, in the greater part of them, that melancholy and gloomy humour which is almost always the nurse of popular superstition and enthusiasm" (WN 5.1.g.14–5, 796).

Unlike his proposal for a parliamentary union between Great Britain and her American and Irish colonies, Smith does not treat his proposal for religious and cultural freedoms as unreachable given the political situation. There are no clear hints that he considers it utopian. Unlike his proposal for an Atlantic, parliamentary union, his disestablishment proposal was taken up with enthusiasm by the American Founders (Fleischacker 2002; McLean and Peterson 2010).

There are some peculiar aspects about Smith's proposal. First, it is remarkably non-factual; he makes no reference to the Dutch experiences with religious toleration. In fact, he only focuses on the likelihood of schism (WN 5.1.g.36, 808). His treatment is basically one extended thought experiment (or counterfactual supposition). The only empirical evidence he points to is a single sentence: his plan has already "been established in Pennsylvania, where, though the Quakers happen to be the most numerous, the law in reality favours no one sect more than another, and it is there said to have been productive of this philosophical good temper and moderation" (WN 5.1.g.8, 793). Smith provides no source or argument for the conclusion. It is tempting to think that he was echoing Benjamin Franklin, whom he knew personally (see Corr. 68, 73).

Smith's is also not an economic argument; he does not discuss or evaluate the argument popular in seventeenth-century Dutch Republican circles (e.g., Spinoza, the de la Court brothers, and echoed in Mandeville) that religious freedoms are supposed to be good for business by attracting skilled artisans and immigrants. He is also not tempted by the Spinozistic argument that cultural freedoms are good for technological development.

Another peculiarity is that in this chapter Smith cites Machiavelli approvingly and heaps praise on Hume; neither is exactly confidence-inspiring to Smith's religious readers. Are these the "wise" who would approve of the pure and rational religion that is the outcome of competitive religion? Smith never explains.

As I discuss at greater length in the next chapter, Smith was unwilling to get involved in the publication of Hume's Dialogues. Yet while he ends up disagreeing with Hume's proposal of state (financial and political) control over religion, the disagreement is primarily focused on means, not ends. Smith thinks his proposal leads to greater political stability for the state—in effect, the idea behind Smith's proposal is that the religious populace and their would-be leaders will be so distracted competing with each other and individually so small that they cannot effectively disturb the public peace or wield political power. Of course, that is all compatible with the further idea that keeping religion out of politics is in the interest of religion, too. Smith implies that political ambition corrupts religion (WN 5.1.g.7,792). Thus, in effect, Smith agrees with Spinoza that religions should focus primarily on morals and stay out of politics.

One final peculiarity about Smith's argument is that he does not connect it with one of his main concerns throughout WN: the freedom of movement and settlement that he promotes. The poor laws of England prevent the poor from leaving their parish (WN 1.10.c.44ff, 152ff): "To remove a man who has committed no misdemeanour from the parish where he chuses to reside, is an evident violation of natural liberty and justice" (WN 1.10.c.59, 157). Smith's disestablishment proposal effectively disconnects territory and religion from each other, yet he does not spell out this implication. It is hard to imagine he would not have noticed how the freedom of religion and freedom of movement would interact, especially because he discusses urbanization from the countryside (that is, movement between parishes) when he discusses the merits of his disestablishment proposal. Smith's proposal on religious disestablishment, thus, is remarkably disconnected from factual constraint. His discussion is, thus, very much in the spirit of Hume's way of proceeding in "Idea of a Perfect Commonwealth:" Hume had drawn the contours of the "most perfect in the kind, that we may be able to bring any real constitution or form of government as near it as possible" ("Idea of a Perfect Commonwealth" 2, EMPL 513–4).

I conclude with a general observation on Smith's strategy. Smith often appeals to religious-sounding language to argue for limitations on religion. Here is an example of this:

> Sentiments, designs, affections, though it is from these that according to cool reason human actions derive their whole merit or demerit, are placed by the great Judge of hearts beyond the limits of every human jurisdiction, and are reserved for the cognizance of his own unerring tribunal. That necessary rule of justice, therefore, that men in this life are liable to punishment for their actions only, not for their designs and intentions, is founded upon this salutary and useful irregularity in human sentiments concerning merit or demerit, which at first sight appears so absurd and unaccountable. (TMS 2.3.3.2, 105)

Here Smith expresses his doctrines in carefully constructed Theistic, and in context even Providentialist, language. (The larger context is Smith's treatment of moral luck; see Russell 1999, Garrett 2005, Flanders 2006, Hankins 2016, and my earlier Chapter 5 on the piacular.) In the quote, Smith relies on the fact that what may seem proper from the point of view of rationality is not always really the right thing to do in this world. This is, in fact, a fundamental Smithian commitment (recall the treatment of the piacular and TMS 1.3.3, 53 both in Chapter 5). In effect, here he appeals to God's design in order to insist that in this world there should be freedom of thought.

In this chapter I have shown that if we look at Smith's treatment of religion from a political perspective, his views are remarkably coherent and focused. While there is no doubt that, according to Smith, religions can play a positive role in socializing and monitoring the urban poor, most of his institutional reforms are designed to prevent the destabilization of public life by religious faction and Christian theology. In fact, on this point, Smith, the public thinker, departs from his gradualist and cautious political tendencies and advocates for disestablishment.

15

A Cheerful Philosophical Life

"I was lately reading the Dialogues of Lucian" [Smith reported Hume to have said on his deathbed] "in which he represents one Ghost as pleading for a short delay till he should marry a young daughter, another till he should finish a house he had begun, a third till he had provided a portion for two or three young Children, I began to think of what Excuse I could alledge [sic] to Charon in order to procure a short delay, and as I have now done everything that I ever intended to do, I acknowledge that for some time, no tolerable one occurred; at last I thought I might say, Good Charon, I have been endeavouring to open the eyes of people; have a little patience only till I have the pleasure of seeing the churches shut up, and the Clergy sent about their business; but Charon would reply, O you loitering rogue; that won't happen these two hundred; do you fancy I will give you a lease for so long a time? Get into the boat this instant."

—Adam Smith to Alexander Wedderburn

In this chapter I use Adam Smith's obituary of Hume, "Letter to Strahan" (published jointly with Hume's brief autobiography, "My Own Life" [hereafter Life]), to explore the rewards and purpose of doing philosophy in a commercial society according to Smith. I argue that he thinks that philosophers can enjoy the rewards of friendship in this life and immortality after their death if they are benefactors to humanity. I argue that, for Smith, friendship among equals is the most valuable goal.

a. The Commercial Philosopher

This section describes the circumstances of the publication of Hume's Life, and I call special attention to Smith's involvement with its publication while he simultaneously attempted to distance himself from Hume's Dialogues. Second, I offer a brief introduction to the significance of Hume's Life (see also Hanley 2002, Schliesser 2003, Corsa 2015).

Hume's Life ends on April 18, 1776, about four months before his death on August 25. He intended to have it published as the opening essay in the projected posthumous republication of all of his works. He also wanted to include works he had suppressed earlier in his career, including "Of Suicide," "Of the Immortality of the Soul," and, most famously, his Dialogues. Nearing death, Hume requested that Adam Smith arrange publication, but Smith declined. Even after Smith's initial demurral, Hume wanted Smith to ensure the piece's survival, leaving it to Smith's discretion when to publish it (Letters 156 and 157, Corr. 194–6). Although Smith agreed to take care of the Dialogues, and thought the book was "finely written," he confided to Strahan after Hume's death that he was willing to communicate the manuscript "only to a few people. When you read [the Dialogues] you will see my reasons." In particular, Smith was "resolved, for many reasons, to have no concern in the publication of those dialogues" (Letter 172, to Strahan, Corr. 211)

No part of the content of the Dialogues could have shocked anybody familiar with the details and implications of Hume's published philosophy. In a letter to Smith, Hume allows that he has become "sensible, that, both on account of the Nature of the Work, and of your Situation," that he understands that Smith would not rush into attaching him name to the piece (Letter 157, May 3, 1776, Corr. 196). At the time, Smith was not a university professor or a tutor anymore, but he may have worried that being caught up in religious-metaphysical controversy would distract from the reception of WN or a possible government appointment or preferment. After Hume's death, Smith was "still uneasy about the clamour which I foresee they will excite" (Letter 177A, unsent draft to Strahan, 216; see also Letter 177B, 217). The scholar David Raynor once plausibly suggested in private conversation that Hume's essay on the immortality of the soul (or the lack thereof) might have been the cause of Smith's recalcitrance, but I have been unable to find any evidence to back up Raynor's hunch. Smith's habitual prudence did not make this his finest hour.

Leaving aside Smith's own views about natural religion, Smith's stance is revealing for the light it sheds on his views about the existing limits to public enlightenment. He is willing to preserve—"if I should happen to die before they are published, I shall take care that my copy shall be as carefully preserved as if I was to live a hundred years" (Letter 166 to Hume, August 22, 1776, Corr. 206)— and circulate Hume's Dialogues to a hand-selected audience, but he is unwilling to see it in the public eye. We cannot know if he wishes to prevent this because he thinks ordinary people need (echoing Spinoza or Locke) a religion, if only to maintain social peace, and that the Dialogues would undermine this; or that he thinks we need to take the prejudices of ordinary people into account; or that he worries that religious fanatics would overreact. (These are compatible, of course.) Either way, my speculations fit with an important remark in WN:

The laws concerning corn may every where be compared to the laws concerning religion. The people feel themselves so much interested in what relates either to their subsistence in this life, or to their happiness in a life to come, that government must yield to their prejudices, and, in order to preserve the publick tranquillity [*sic*], establish that system which they approve of. It is upon this account, perhaps, that we so seldom find a reasonable system established with regard to either of those two capital objects. (WN 4.5.b. 40, 539)

Either way, evidently Smith thinks that the Dialogues are a "wrong" sort of philosophy, despite being worthy of study to the wise. (I return to this in the conclusion.)

Eventually, Hume decided to leave the Dialogues to his nephew to ensure that it would be published after his death (Letter 168, from Hume, 208). Despite Smith's qualms, publication of the Dialogues did not incite much public outcry. The same cannot be said for the reaction to Smith's brief comments on Hume's death in "Letter to Strahan:" "A single, and as, I thought a very harmless Sheet of paper, which I happened to Write concerning the death of our late friend Mr Hume," Smith wrote to a Danish friend, "brought upon me ten times more abuse than the very violent attack I had made upon the whole commercial system of Great Britain" (to Andreas Holt, October 26, 1780).

While Smith did not want to be associated with the publication of Hume's Dialogues, he took a great deal of interest in Hume's Life. On August 22, 1776, a few days before Hume's death, Smith wrote Hume requesting permission to

> add a few lines to your account, in my own name, of your behavior in this illness, if, contrary to my hopes, it should provide your last.... You have in a declining state of health, under an exhausting disease, for more than two years together, now looked at the approach, or what you believed to be the approach of Death with a steady cheerfulness such as very few men have been able to maintain for a few hours, tho' otherwise in the most perfect Health. (Letter 166, Corr. 206; I omit Smith's description of a conversation with Hume about Hume's imaginary dialogue with Charon, which I deal with below.)

In his last letter to Smith, Hume gave the requested permission (Letter 168, Corr. 208). Shortly after Hume's death, Smith circulated a draft of his addition to Hume's Life. He made some minor changes (see the exchange of Letters 171, 175, and 176 with John Home of Ninewells, 210 and 214–5) and sent Strahan a finished draft before the end of the year (Letter 178, to Strahan, November 9, 1776, 217–21). In a copy of an unsent draft letter to Strahan (Letter 177B, 216), Smith claims that he had not started writing his comments on Hume's life until a few weeks after Hume's death. It is, nevertheless, clear that he started thinking about writing it before Hume's death. Smith explicitly intended his short piece to be published jointly with Hume's autobiography and, more importantly, as a publication separate from Dialogues, although together with Hume's other works

(Letter 172, to Strahan, Corr. 211). In two (probably unsent) draft cover letters to Strahan, Smith talks of the "quiet" that his continuation of Hume's Life may cause in his own mind (Letters 177A and 177B, to Strahan, 216).

Smith's public discussion of Hume's private conduct may appear a bit surprising, because Smith is extremely guarded about keeping details of his own life from the public view, burning manuscripts on his deathbed. And when he writes Strahan to discourage him from publishing a collection of Hume's letters, he not only appeals to the contents of Hume's will but also claims that "Many things would be published not fit to see the light to the great mortification of all those who wish well to his memory" (Letter 181, 223–4). Some light is shed on Smith's course of action by the fact that Smith undoubtedly knew, for example, about James Boswell's visit to Hume on July 7, 1776. Although only one brief letter from Boswell to Smith is extant (Letter 122, 156), Boswell was well known to Smith, who was his college teacher at Glasgow in 1759–60. Boswell's diaries show that despite the antipathy between Johnson and Smith, Boswell met Smith in London on several occasions, even going out of his way to visit him. Boswell was convinced that Smith was an "infidel." Because Smith knew of Boswell's religiosity, Smith may have wanted to preempt a potentially unflattering account by Boswell of Hume's attitude toward death. This is not entirely groundless: on the day of Hume's burial, Boswell inspected the open grave and was seen following the corpse to the grave. In the final lines of Life, Hume boasts that "My friends never had occasion to vindicate any one circumstance of my character and conduct: not but that the zealots, we may well suppose, would have been glad to invent and propagate any story to my disadvantage, but they could never find any which they thought would wear the face of probability." Not only Smith, but also one of Hume's other friends, John Home the playwright (e.g., "Douglas"), wrote an account of Hume's dying days and both explicitly singled out his cheerful character. (See Schliesser 2003 for the documentation supporting this paragraph.)

Smith makes clear that he intends to portray Hume's behavior during his illness as an example of cheerfulness in the face of death. As he writes Hume:

> If you will give me leave I will add a few lines to your account of your own life; giving some account, in my own name, of your behaviour in this illness, if, contrary to my own hopes, it should prove your last. Some conversations we had lately together, particularly that concerning your want of an excuse to make to Charon, the excuse you at last thought of, and the very bad reception which Charon was likely to give it, would, I imagine, make no disagreeable part of the history. You have in a declining state of health, under an exhausting disease, for more than two years together, now looked at the approach, or what you at least believed to be the approach of Death with a steady cheerfulness such as very few men have been able to maintain for a few hours, tho' otherwise in the most perfect Health. (Letter 166 to Hume, August 22, 1776, Corr. 206)

I turn to the exchange about Charon below. But, first, Smith wants to present Hume as a model or exemplar of virtue. This echoes the epigraph from Lucan on the frontispiece of Book 3 of Hume's Treatise (*Durae semper virtutis amator, Quaere quid est virtus, et posce exemplar honesti*) as well as the preface to Spinoza's *Ethics IV* (*Per bonum itaque in sequentibus intelligam id quod certo scimus medium esse ut ad exemplar humanæ naturæ quod nobis proponimus, magis magisque accedamus*). There are, of course, many sources for such an idea. Smith had adopted the idea of a model of virtue in his own moral theory (recall Chapter 9):

> To deserve, to acquire, and to enjoy the respect and admiration of mankind, are the great objects of ambition and emulation. Two different roads are presented to us, equally leading to the attainment of this so much desired object; the one, by the study of wisdom and the practice of virtue; the other, by the acquisition of wealth and greatness. Two different characters are presented to our emulation ; the one, of proud ambition and ostentatious avidity; the other, of humble modesty and equitable justice. Two different models, two different pictures, are held out to us, according to which we may fashion our own character and behaviour; the one more gaudy and glittering in its colouring; the other more correct and more exquisitely beautiful in its outline: the one forcing itself upon the notice of every wandering eye; the other, attracting the attention of scarce any body but the most studious and careful observer. They are the wise and the virtuous chiefly, a select, though, I am afraid, but a small party, who are the real and steady admirers of wisdom and virtue. The great mob of mankind are the admirers and worshippers, and, what may seem more extraordinary, most frequently the disinterested admirers and worshippers, of wealth and greatness. (TMS 1.3.3.2, 62)

The two models desire (if one grants that a model can desire) the very same thing: "To deserve, to acquire, and to enjoy the respect and admiration of mankind, are the great objects of ambition and emulation." Here Smith does not deny that the "acquisitions of wealth and greatness" may meet this aim, but he does insist that the other model that engages in the ongoing "study of wisdom and the practice of virtue" is more correct and more beautiful to the discerning, cultivated eye. Smith echoes here Hume's EPM 7.16, which links the better sort of tranquility to "greatness of mind." (See also Corsa 2015; on the significance of such beauty Valihora 2001.)

Even so, in his "Letter to Strahan," Smith does not stress "humble modesty" but Hume's "steady cheerfulness." Hume does not write very often about cheerfulness, but the times he does so are very relevant to Smith's analysis of Hume's deathbed. Hume writes, "Prosperity is easily received as our due, and few questions are asked concerning its cause or author. It begets cheerfulness and activity and alacrity and a lively enjoyment of every social and sensual pleasure: And during this state of mind, men have little leisure or inclination to think of the unknown invisible regions" (N 3.4). Thus, prosperity-induced cheerfulness is the state of mind that keeps us from the religiously inspired terrors in the face of death.[1] Superficially this fits Hume's self-description in Life, where he describes his own prosperity and good cheer, but upon closer inspection this is not quite right: Hume calls attention to his good cheer despite the adversity he faces: "but being naturally of a cheerful" temper (Life 6; Hume is describing how the Treatise did not even "excite a murmur among the zealots.") Hume presents himself as naturally cheerful.

Thus, in Hume's analysis there are at least two kinds of cheerfulness: (i) prosperity-induced cheer and (ii) one belonging to one's natural temper. (Of course, one and the same person can experience both, and they can mutually reinforce each other.) In fact, Hume recognizes a third kind of cheerfulness: (iii) the one consequent on the practice of properly conceived (Humean) virtue. As Hume writes:

> But what philosophical truths can be more advantageous to society, than those here delivered, which represent virtue in all her genuine and most engaging charms, and make us approach her with ease, familiarity, and affection? The dismal dress falls off, with which many divines, and some philosophers have covered her; and nothing appears but gentleness, humanity, beneficence, affability; nay even, at proper intervals, play, frolic, and gaiety. She talks not of useless austerities and rigours, suffering and self-denial. She declares, that her sole purpose is, to make her votaries and all mankind, during every instant of their existence, if possible, cheerful and happy; nor does she ever willingly part with any pleasure but in hopes of ample compensation in some other period of their lives. (EPM 9.15; see also Treatise 2.2.11.2 and 2.3.5.4)

As we have seen, Hume associates the "dismall dress" of virtue with the "monkish virtues" of self-denial (EPM 9.3). Thus, Hume's cheerfulness is evidence not just of his (undeniable) prosperity and natural temper, but also that his philosophy and life are well integrated. In other words, in my terms, Hume presents himself as possessing philosophical integrity (recall Sections a of Chapter 1 and Section b of Chapter 9)—that is, a coherence between his stated moral theory and his own actions.

Smith also accepts close-enough versions of these three Humean species of cheerfulness (e.g., TMS 1.2.5.2, 42, where Humean temper is turned into a Smithian habit, and TMS 3.3.31, 149). But Smith also recognizes three additional

---

[1] In Spinoza's *Ethics* cheerfulness (*hilaritas*) is an active emotion connected to mind and body jointly (*Ethics* 3p11) and is always good (*Ethics* 4p42).

species of cheerfulness. The fourth is (iv) one consequent love (TMS 1.2.4.2, 39). A fifth kind of un-Humean cheerfulness is articulated here:

> Our happiness in this life is thus, upon many occasions, dependent upon the humble hope and expectation of a life to come: a hope and expectation deeply rooted in human nature; which can alone support its lofty ideas of its own dignity; can alone illumine the dreary prospect of its continually approaching mortality, and maintain its cheerfulness under all the heaviest calamities to which, from the disorders of this life, it may sometimes be exposed. That there is a world to come, where exact justice will be done to every man, where every man will be ranked with those who, in the moral and intellectual qualities, are really his equals … is a doctrine, in every respect so venerable, so comfortable to the weakness, so flattering to the grandeur of human nature, that the virtuous man who has the misfortune to doubt of it, cannot possibly avoid wishing most earnestly and anxiously to believe it. (TMS 3.2.33, 132)

Smith knows that Hume doubts it and has no desire to earnestly believe it. It is to Smith's credit that in his representation of the dying Hume he does not insinuate this aspect of his own views into his narrative.

Finally, there is (vi) cheerfulness consequent to great or heroic magnanimity (TMS 1.3.1.13–4, 47–9). Two examples Smith offers of this kind of cheerfulness are Cato's suicide "surrounded by his enemies" and Socrates on his deathbed in the *Phaedo*. The person asking for a model of virtue in Hume's epigraph to Part 3 of the Treatise is Cato. We can read Smith's obituary of Hume as offering an alternative to Socrates and Cato of an exemplar of virtue—one that does not require belief in the afterlife.[2] As Smith remarked eleven days before Hume's death in a letter to Alexander Wedderburn, "Poor David Hume is dying very fast, but with great chearfulness and good humour and with more real resignation to the necessary course of things, than any Whining Christian ever dyed with pretended resignation to the will of God" (Letter 163, 203). If this reading of the obituary is right, then Smith used the occasion of Hume's death to subtly supplement his own philosophical position.

Like Plato's absence from Socrates' death, Smith was not present for Hume's. Smith's account of Hume's final days accords well, despite some minor discrepancies, with the other available evidence; this includes not only Hume's and Smith's correspondence (and that of their friends) but also memoirs written by Boswell

---

[2] In Plutarch's rendition, before he commits suicide, Cato reads Plato's "On the Soul," known to us as the *Phaedo*, with its account of the immortality of the soul. In his *Letters*, Seneca suggests Cato required reading Plato in order to follow through on his intention (Letter 24). Here Seneca comes close to suggesting that, to put this in Smith's neo-Stoic conception, Plato's words were required for Cato's self-command.

and Home. In a separate letter to Strahan, Smith insists that his description of Hume's dying days is "very well authenticated" (Letter 172, 211). Even so, I treat "Letter to Strahan" less as a historical record, interesting as it is, and more as a literary effort to fix the public's "memory" of Hume as the model of a genuine philosopher in life and in the face of death.

Smith ends his "Letter to Strahan" with the following characterization: "Upon the whole, I have always considered him, both in his lifetime and since his death, as approaching nearly to the idea of a perfectly wise and virtuous man, as perhaps the nature of human frailty will permit" (Corr. 220). "Letter to Strahan" occasionally echoes Plato's description of Socrates' death in the *Phaedo*, where Socrates expounds his account of the immortality of the soul. This connection is especially significant given that Hume's essay on that topic was about to appear and provides guidance to interpreting Dialogues. And the details of Hume's death attracted widespread interest because he was thought to be an atheist by many who wanted to know how someone who does not believe in the afterlife faces death (Hobbes, Descartes, and Spinoza also attracted this kind of fascinated interest (see Van Bunge 2017)). This is illustrated by Boswell's account in which he maintains some ambiguity concerning the exact details of Hume's views on the existence and nature of God, but does report that Hume continued to deny an afterlife for his soul (Schliesser 2003).

One of the main implicit goals of Hume's Life appears to be his attempt to fix the cannon of his writings, especially because he knew it would be the first piece encountered in definitive editions of his works. While not providing much detail of the content of his works, in his Life Hume focuses on his material rewards for his literary output and related activities. Hume's Life serves as an example of how the values of commercial society, as defended in his own essays (especially "Of Commerce" and "Of Refinement in the Arts"), are fully compatible with and, in fact, enable a life of philosophy (Hanley 2002; Schliesser 2003). For Hume (sounding like Montesquieu), economic, social, and intellectual commerce reinforce each other: "The spirit of the age affects all the arts. . . . The more these refined arts advance, the more sociable men become . . . They flock into cities; love to receive and communicate knowledge . . . industry, knowledge, and humanity, are linked together by an indissoluble chain" ("Of Refinement in the Arts" 271). On the surface, at least, Hume's Life is a vindication of his social project: the various kinds of commerce and exchange, including those of the sentiments, the foundation of his ethical thought, have a politically and morally civilizing function. A philosopher can remain independent while thriving, despite adversity in the new cosmopolitan world of global trade in goods and ideas.

There is, however, a minor hint toward the end of Life that, for Hume, the best part of life is not exclusively focused on commerce of various kinds:

> I now reckon upon speedy dissolution . . . and what is more strange, have notwithstanding the great decline of my person, never suffered a moment's abatement of my spirits; insomuch, that were I to name the

period of my life, which I should most choose to pass over again, I might be tempted to point to this later period. I possess the same ardour as ever in study, and the same gaiety in company. I consider, besides, that a man of sixty-five, by dying cuts off only a few years of infirmities; and though I see many symptoms of my literary reputation's breaking out at last with additional luster, I knew that I could have but few years to enjoy it. It is difficult to be more detached from life than I am at present. (lx)

Despite his passion for literary fame, and his strong affirmation of commercial society and a life of worldly activity, Hume would, if forced to choose the part of life he could live again, pick the period in which he is most "detached" from life— that is, in which he spends his time studying and socializing. It is the time of his life in which Hume can write about his character as if he were a dead man (that is, in the past tense) "for that is the style I must now use in speaking of myself, which emboldens me the more to speak my sentiments" (xl). One ought not to dramatize Hume's choice; he is not rejecting the rewards of commercial life and worldly fame outright as unworthy of pursuit. The temptation of turning one's back on the world is itself only made possible by two important conditions: the achievement of worldly success (in the service of changing the world) in legal security, and a sense and awareness of the impending dissolution of his body. Commercial life, then, is not just compatible with the philosophical life, but, by enabling the conditions that allow for independence and the genuine possibility of being tempted by the detached view on life, also a means to it in Hume's account.

In "Letter to Strahan," Smith writes that "concerning [Hume's] philosophic opinions men will, no doubt judge variously, every one approving, or condemning them, according as they happen to coincide or disagree with his own" (xlviii). Smith seems to be admitting that there is no matter of fact that will settle one's views of Hume's philosophy. The same is not the case "concerning [Hume's] character and conduct," about which "there can scarce be a difference of opinion." Here Smith not only disassociates judgments of Hume's philosophical-theological views from his judgments of his character, but also seems to insist that it is judgments of character that ought to trump judgments of another person's philosophy (see my discussion of "true liberty" in Section c below).

Smith's move is, of course, only possible if the evidence of character is publicly available (in the way Hume's writings are); Hume was (like Rousseau and Voltaire) a public thinker and presented himself as such from the start of his career, when he tried "the taste of the public" (Treatise Ad.1), to the end, when he presented himself as trying to influence the public in his exchange with Charon (see the next section). And so judgments of Hume's character are public judgments.

Smith says:

His temper, indeed, seemed more happily balanced, if I may be allowed such an expression, than that perhaps of any other man I have ever

known. Even in the lowest state of his fortune, his great and necessary frugality never hindered him from exercising, upon proper occasions, acts both of charity and generosity. It was a frugality founded,
not upon avarice, but the love of independency. (xlviii)

The main point of this passage is Hume's balanced temper, but Smith also calls
attention to the fact that Hume was not always rich. Not surprisingly for the man
who encourages frugality (WN 2.3.28, 341; cf. TMS, 5.2.13, 209), Smith attributes
it to Hume, as Hume explicitly does in Life (xxxiv–xxxv; see also EPM 6.1.21 and
History 6.247). Smith defends Hume's frugality as a virtue not from a Christian
point of view, but because it is motivated by his laudable love of independence.
By stressing Hume's love of independence, Smith subtly shifts the emphasis away
from literary fame, Hume's self-described "ruling passion." But Smith also insists
that Hume was, at times, a generous and charitable person.

b. Hume's Exchange with Charon

In the letter to Hume in which Smith requests permission to add a few lines to his
Life, Smith is particularly eager to be allowed to report on a conversation about
an imaginary exchange between Hume and Charon (Letter 166, Corr. 206). Smith
describes this exchange first in the letter to Alexander Wedderburn, in the context of contrasting Hume to the "Whining Christians" (quoted above). The version presented in the "Letter to Strahan" is the most detailed:

[W]hen [Hume] was reading a few days before, Lucian's Dialogues of
the Dead, among all the excuses which are alleged to Charon [that is,
the ferryman who conveyed the dead to Hades] for not entering readily
into his boat, he could not find one that fitted him; he had no house to
finish, he had no daughter to provide for, he had no enemies upon whom
he wished to revenge himself. "I could not well imagine," said he, "what
excuse I could make to Charon in order to obtain a little delay. I have
done every thing of consequence which I ever meant to do, and I could
at no time expect to leave my relations and friends in a better situation
than that in which I am now likely to leave them; I, therefore, have all
reason to die contented." He then diverted himself with inventing several jocular excuses, which he supposed he might make to Charon, and
with imagining the very surly answers which it might suit the character of Charon to return to them. "Upon further consideration," said he,
"I thought I may say to him, Good Charon, I have been correcting my
works for a new edition. Allow me a little time, that I may see how the
Public receives the alterations." But Charon would answer, "When you
have seen the effect of these, you will be for making other alterations.

There will be no end of such excuses; so, honest friend, please step into the boat." But I might still urge, "Have a little patience, Good Charon, I have been endeavouring to open the eyes of the Public. If I live a few years longer, I may have the satisfaction of seeing the downfall of some of the prevailing systems of superstition." But Charon would then lose all temper and decency. "You loitering rogue, that will not happen these many hundred years. Do you fancy I will grant you a lease for so long a term? Get into the boat this instant, you lazy loitering rogue." (xlv–xlvi)

Smith includes the exchange to illustrate that Hume "approached dissolution" with "great cheerfulness" (xlvi). There is no mention of Hume's stance toward a Christian doctrine of the immortality of the soul. Hume is shown to have tranquility of mind and "magnanimity" without making "any parade" of it (xlvi); in Letter 166 to Hume, Smith refers to the "steady cheerfulness" of Hume (Corr. 206). For Smith, this kind of magnanimity is a great achievement because death "is the king of terrors" (TMS 6.3.6, 239). According to Smith, "War is the great school both for acquiring and exercising this species of magnanimity" (TMS 6.iii.6, 239). "No character is more admired," Smith wrote, "than that of the man who faces death with intrepidity, and maintains his tranquility and presence of mind" (6.3.17, 244). While Hume was no stranger to war, Smith's account is hard to believe. According to Boswell's report, Dr. Johnson, for example, has no doubt that Hume "lied" about facing death calmly. Johnson thinks Hume "had a vanity in being thought easy." (Boswell 1826: 138) Smith insists that Hume's vanity is not misplaced.

It is extremely important to Smith that Hume is portrayed as reading the ancient pagan satirist Lucian and not, say, the Bible or some pious work. Hume and Smith have a high opinion of Lucian. Lucian was "though licentious with regard to pleasure," in Hume's opinion, "yet, in other respects, a very moral writer" (EPM 6.1.21). It is clear from the context of these remarks that Hume thinks that Lucian is "a very moral writer" because of his public spirit. Elsewhere Hume praises Lucian for performing the "good office" of entirely opening the "eyes of mankind" by exposing the false prophet Alexander of Paphlagonia (EHU 10.2.23). For Hume, Lucian is a kindred spirit in combating systems of superstition—not the least because Lucian has no illusions about human nature.

Hume wants to live longer because, through his books, he has "been endeavouring to open the eyes of the Public." In his "Letter to Strahan," Smith shows that when in Hume's Life Hume writes that "almost all my life has been spent in literary pursuits and occupations," these pursuits are part of an Enlightenment project against superstition and ignorance in aid of the public. For Hume, "no qualities are more entitled to the general good-will and approbation of mankind, than beneficence and humanity, friendship and gratitude, natural affection and public spirit, or whatever proceeds from a tender sympathy with others, and a generous concern for our kind and species" (EPM 2.1.5). Hume's life of letters, devoted to public enlightenment in attacking religious systems of superstition, in the footsteps of Lucian, is a form of public service. Smith shows Hume attacking "wrong" systems of thought.

By reporting the imaginary exchange with Charon, Smith shows us Hume's benevolence and a generous concern for mankind. In the context of Hume's very human desire to live longer and with his imaginative abilities on display (he is creating a dialogue with a character from Lucian), the serious joke works because Hume's desire is shown to be an instance of public spirit. Hume's advocacy of public enlightenment against superstition and the values of commercial life, of which he benefited materially, have their source not only in Hume's pleasure, but also in his love of virtue or of humanity. For Hume, the presence of self-interest is no reason to reject the virtues displayed. Smith also does not insist on absolute purity of motives, as he believes Mandeville and Rousseau in different ways mistakenly attempt to do to recognize virtuous actions (TMS 7.2.4.12, 312, and Edinburgh Review 12, EPS 251). Hume's writings are a form of public generosity in the battle against superstitions.

The exchange with Charon makes clear, however, that Hume was aware that an attack on "the prevailing systems of superstition" is not guaranteed success. In Smith's narrative, Hume is presented as realizing that many centuries will pass before we can expect to see only "some" of the systems of superstition defeated; this suggests that at the end of his life, Hume was a pessimistic Enlightenment thinker. An implication of Smith's report is that the reception of Hume's works had taught him the limited impact of his words on most people's beliefs (cf. TMS 3.5.10, 168). Thus, while Hume's life and character show how a philosophical life can be lived with integrity in a commercial society, it also shows that most people will resist living a life without superstition. Yet, both Smith's "Letter to Strahan" (xliv–xlvii) and Hume's Life (xxxiii, xl) show the different positive effects on Hume's state of mind of reading other thinkers' works. Enlightenment can occur in a limited fashion.

It might be argued that I make too much of Smith's report of Hume's imaginary exchange with Charon; all this "jocular" conversation really is meant to show is that Hume faced death with "great cheerfulness" (xlvi). This is, in part, what marks Hume's magnanimity. (See also EPM 9.2) This is, as I asserted above, one of the main points of Smith's piece. Even so, it would be a mistake to focus exclusively on the relevance of Hume's unorthodox religious beliefs (e.g., his denial of the existence of an afterlife). This would be to underestimate the importance of the portrait of Hume reading Lucian's Dialogues of the Dead. This anecdote does not show that he merely "diverted himself." Smith shows that part of Hume's wisdom consists in his ability to entertain himself with "amusements" (xliv; see also Hume's "gaiety in company" [xl]) and serious topics (see Hume's "ardour ... in study" [xl])—sometimes these are the same, of course (for a nice example, see Hume's Letter 31, Corr. 33–6, occasioned by the reception of TMS). In Smith's portrayal, Hume follows Plato's suggestion for old men to combine play with high-minded seriousness (Laws 685AB; Menexenus 236C; also Laws 803BE). In his Life,

Hume calls his autobiography a "funeral oration" (xli). This mock-seriousness recalls Plato's *Menexenus*—another dialogue between the dead.

Smith agrees with Hume about fame: "The love of just fame, of true glory, even for its own sake, and independent of any advantage which he can derive from it, is not unworthy even of a wise man" (TMS 3.2.8, 117; see also 3.2.29, 127). But what if no fame is forthcoming? What are the genuine rewards, for the philosopher, of a commitment to opening up the eyes of the public, especially if this is a very futile enterprise? (So many centuries have passed since Lucian's time!) Moreover, although Hume's *Life* ultimately is a triumphant account of increasing material rewards and public recognition, there is no sense of inevitability. As Dugald Stewart, commenting on the fate of Smith's works, observes: "It is not often that a disinterested zeal for truth has so soon met with its just reward" ("Account of Smith," 4.29, EPS 323). In WN, Smith remarks that "Before the invention of the art of printing, a scholar and a beggar seem to have been terms very nearly synonymous" (WN 110.c.38, 149). Even after the invention of the printing press, Hume's experience was quite unusual: "The copy-money given me by the booksellers," Hume bragged, "much exceeded any thing formerly known in England" (xxxviii). Few men of letters could claim to be "independent" let alone "opulent" from their writing. Surely Hume's singular achievement does not warrant generalization; if anything, all it shows is that Hume is a winner of what Smith calls an imperfect "lottery" (WN 1.10.b.22, 123 and 1.10.c.37, 148).

What kind of rewards could motivate someone who desires independence in commercial society to choose the uncertain path of a career in letters? According to Smith's economic theorizing, people display both loss aversion and a tendency to overestimate their own luck and future payoffs when making decisions (e.g., WN 1.10.b.26, 124 ff; Ashraf et al. 2005). Smith denies philosophers a superior perspective on their own actions; aspiring philosophers may be just as deluded or overconfident as other people. In fact, according to Smith the scant rewards available to teachers and educators of mankind are, by making education affordable, "surely an advantage" to the "publick" at large (1.10.c.40, 151). It would be ironic if a philosopher's public service would derive from self-deception about available rewards (cf. TMS 4.1.9–10, 183–5).

When Smith turns to the question of what motivates somebody to become a philosopher, nowhere does he discuss monetary incentives or possible technological applications at all. As we have seen, he agrees with Plato that some people are gripped by the sensation of wonder when they confront the world of appearances (Astronomy 2.4, EPS 39–40; 2.12, EPS, 45–6; cf. Hume's Treatise 2.3.10.12). By trying to create a coherent picture of the world, they attempt to alleviate this painful sentiment of wonder (Astronomy 2.9, EPS 42–3; cf. WN). This desire for tranquility of mind originally motivates intellectual inquiry. Smith assures us that some philosophers, especially mathematicians with robust and attainable criteria of success, can attain it (recall TMS 3.2.20, 124). Nevertheless, this response is not very satisfying if one thinks that philosophers need some rewards to keep them going.

The last paragraph of Smith's "Letter to Strahan" begins as follows: "Thus died our most excellent, and never to be forgotten friend; concerning whose philosophical opinions men will, no doubt judge variously" (xlviii). Consider the phrase "never to be forgotten." He uses the locution also in a letter in remembrance of his old teacher, Francis Hutcheson (Letter 274, Corr. 309). As Smith writes in TMS: "Men of letters, though, after their death, they are frequently more talked of than the greatest princes or statesmen of their times, are generally, during their life, so obscure and insignificant that their adventures are seldom recorded by contemporary historians" (7.2.1.31, 285; cf. WN 1.10.c.39, 149–50).

In TMS, Smith draws a distinction between the qualities of generosity and humanity. For Smith, the virtue of humanity consists of "exquisite fellow-feeling," that is, perfect and refined sympathy, while the virtue of generosity consists of acts that include self-denial, self-command, sacrifice, and, often, public spirit.[3] For Smith, the generosity of public spirit often involves magnanimity (TMS 4.2.10–11, 190–2). Magnanimity is one of the most impressive virtues for Smith: "magnanimity amidst great distress appears always so divinely grateful" (TMS 1.3.13, 47); one of Smith's examples is Socrates' death scene, in which Smith imagines that Socrates can imagine posthumous approval for his disposition of "heroic magnanimity"! These are all instances of "proper and beneficent greatness of mind" (TMS 2.1.5.3, 74, which implies that some magnanimity may be malevolent).

Given Smith's repeated emphasis on Hume's gaiety and cheerfulness in the face of death, it is noteworthy that, in TMS, Smith calls special attention to Socrates' "triumphant gaiety" and the "gayest and most cheerful tranquility." Smith does not attribute Socrates' "noble and generous effort" to Socrates' belief in, say, the immortality of the soul; Smith insists, rather, that Socrates turns his eyes away "from what is either naturally terrible or disagreeable in his situation" (TMS 1.3.1.14, 48–9; Hume also calls Socrates "magnanimous," but for reasons different from Smith's, see EPM 7.17).

It is, therefore, important, that in his "Letter to Strahan," Smith attributes, besides generosity and cheerfulness, also "magnanimity" to Hume on several occasions (xlv–xlvi; see Corsa 2015). Smith believes that if the public knew the magnanimous man better, "they would esteem and love him." Smith argues that "there is an affinity . . . between the love of virtue and the love of true glory." The magnanimous man may despise existing public opinion, but "he has the highest value for those [views] which ought to be entertained of him" (TMS 7.2.4.10, 310–1). The reward, such as it is, for a philosopher does not generally come in this life, but in fame after death. As Dugald Stewart writes in his "Account of Smith:" "Philosophers (to use an expression of Lord Bacon's) are the 'servants of posterity'; and most of those who have devoted their talents to the best interests

---

[3] These qualities are gendered in Smith's hands: generosity is masculine and humanity is feminine. While on the whole Smith treats humanity as an authoritative moral virtue, it is worth noting that he tends to associate women with an excess of sympathy. This he treats as a minor blemish (Harkin 2013: 515–6).

of mankind, have been obliged, like Bacon, to 'bequeath their fame' to a race yet unborn, and to console themselves with the idea of sowing what another generation was to reap" (4.29, EPS 323).

There is ample evidence that Hume cared deeply about the opinions of his posthumous public concerning his character and ideas. Smith points out that until the very end Hume kept "correcting his own works for a new edition" (xliv), and Hume's jocular exchange with Charon implies that the reaction of the public influenced those "alterations" (xlvi). The fact that he composed his Life to be prefixed to the new edition suggests he wants the memory of who he was to be conjoined to the canonical part of what he produced. In reporting the exchange with Charon, Smith shows Hume's concern about the impact of his works on the public; Hume's detachment from life does not mean he does not care about his effect on the world. Even when being tempted by detachment, Hume would like to imagine that he is remembered as a public-spirited benefactor.

Smith's "Letter to Strahan" is, thus, an attempt to secure the appropriate basis for Hume's posthumous "memory"—one that is not based on the potential notoriety of the posthumous Dialogues and the accompanying essays on suicide and the immortality of the soul. Instead of focusing on Hume's "philosophical opinions," it shows how Hume "submitted [to the inevitability of death] with the utmost cheerfulness, and the most perfect complacency and resignation" (xliv). In Smith's account of Hume's death there is no talk of divine providence or the immortality of our souls, or about the consolation reflection on either can provide. Hume's apparent tranquility of mind and cheerfulness is a magnanimous act by a man who had achieved independence while being generous to the public.

c. Friendship, Sincerity, and Real Happiness

> Destroy love and friendship; what remains in the world worth accepting?
>
> —David Hume, "Of Polygamy and Divorces" (EMPL 185)

Smith believes that Hume approached "nearly to the idea of a perfectly wise and virtuous man, as perhaps the nature of human frailty will permit." So far, I have focused mostly on Hume's public generosity to explain why Smith thought that Hume was virtuous. One might argue that Hume's wisdom consists, for Smith, of his prudent way in expressing his public spirit. Certainly, this would fit Smith's generally cautious approach to public life. Nevertheless, this is not the view I defend here. Rather, Smith offers us an exemplary Hume. He, thus, answers the implied question in the epigraph drawn from Lucan on the frontispiece to Book 3 of Hume's Treatise by pointing to . . . Hume.[4]

---

[4] "*Durae semper virtutis amator, Quaere quid est virtus, et posce exemplar honesti.*—Lucan." See Russell 2008: 75–80 for a nice treatment of this passage in Hume.

Above I argue that, once Hume's material desires and need for public recognition were fulfilled, he could be tempted to prefer study and the "enjoyment . . . in the company of a few select companions," not the least of which was Adam Smith. "It was a friendship on both sides founded on the admiration of genius," Dugald Stewart remarked, "and the love of simplicity; and, which forms an interesting circumstance in the history of each of these eminent men, from the ambition which both have shewn to record it to posterity" ("Account of Smith" 1.13, 273; see Corsa 2015 on the relationship between simplicity and magnanimity). I focus on Smith's desire to make a public declaration of his friendship with Hume.

Once Hume resigned himself to death, "he continued to divert himself, as usual," Smith reported, "with correcting his own works for a new edition, with reading books of amusement, with the conversation of his friends; and, sometimes, in the evening, with a party at his favourite game of whist" (xliv). While I have been focusing on cheerfulness and magnanimity, friendship is the most important theme in the "Letter to Strahan." Smith starts by promising "some account of the behaviour of our late excellent friend, David Hume" (xliv; Hume's "friends" are invoked in the next paragraph, too). And (recall) the last paragraph begins as follows: "Thus died our most excellent, and never to be forgotten friend" (xlviii). Smith also mentions Hume's unnamed "most affectionate friends" (xlv), his "most intimate friends" (xlvi), and the frequent visits of Hume's friends to his deathbed (xlvi). Smith goes out of his way to quote selectively (he omits Hume's references to the Dialogues) from Hume's last letter to him; it starts with Hume calling Smith, "MY DEAREST FRIEND" (xlvii). "Letter to Strahan" is very short, but there are at least ten instances where Smith talks about Hume's friends and their friendship for Hume and Hume's friendship for them. Smith may be overdoing this talk of friendship; after all, in "Of Tragedy," Hume says, "Nothing endears so much a friend as sorrow for his death. The pleasure of his company has not so powerful an influence" (EMPL 222; cf. TMS 3.3.32, 151).

Smith's focus on friendship, however, connects with wider themes in Hume and Smith. They are adamant that commercial life, middle-class virtues, and friendship are compatible with each other and a life of philosophy. Hume brings these themes together in an essay he later withdrew, "Of the Middle Station of Life," in which he says that "These [men in the middle station] form most numerous Rank of men, that can be suppos'd susceptible of philosophy; and therefore, all Discourses of Morality ought principally to be address'd to them" (546), "the middle Station of Life, that is the most favourable to the acquiring of Wisdom and Ability as well as of Virtue," and "there is another Virtue, that seems principally to ly [sic] among Equals, and is, for that Reason, chiefly calculated for the middle Station of Life. This Virtue is FRIENDSHIP" (547). Hume says middle-class friends can be most confident of their mutual sincerity. This sincerity is not due to the absence of exchange; in fact, "commerce" and mutual "Obligations" secure genuine friendship (EMPL, 547; see also "Of Polygamy and Divorces," 189).

Smith endorses and explains this position by emphasizing even more than Hume the economic context:

> Colleagues in office, partners in trade, call one another brothers; and frequently feel towards one another as if they really were so. Their good agreement is an advantage to all; and, if they are tolerably reasonable people, they are naturally disposed to agree. We expect that they should do so; and their disagreement is a sort of a small scandal. (TMS 6.2.1.15, 223–4)

Commercial life brings people together as mutually advantageous friends. This is not an "unofficial side of Smith's picture" (Herzog 2013: 72) but is crucial to his broader defense of commerce. Because the benefits of such friendships are mutual, it can be sincere—*pace* Rousseau's famous line from the *Second Discourse*: "to be and to appear to be, became two things very different" (quoted by Smith in Edinburgh Review ¶4, EPS 252–3).

For Smith, friendship born of necessity is not merely compatible with prudence; it is crucial that "the prudent man . . . is always very capable of friendship" (TMS 6.1.9, 214). Prudence is the virtue most associated with middle-class values of hard work and industry (TMS 6.1.11, 215; the prudent man reappears in WN 1.4.2, 37; 1.5.21, 55, etc.). Friendship, not wealth, is the source of *true* happiness for Smith:

> there is a satisfaction in the consciousness of being beloved, which, to a person of delicacy and sensibility, is of more to importance to happiness, than all the advantage which he can expect to derive from it. What character is so detestable as that of one who takes pleasure to sow dissension among friends? (TMS 1.2.4.1, 39; see also 7.4.28, 337)

That wealth is not the source of true happiness is also mentioned in WN: "because happiness and misery, which reside altogether in the mind, must necessarily depend more upon the healthful or unhealthful, the mutilated or entire state of the mind, than upon that of the body" (WN 5.1.f.60, 787; recall from my discussion of TMS 4.1.9–10, 183–5, in Section a of Chapter 10 that Smith embraces an objective conception of well-being). If being prudent is a sufficient condition for being capable of friendship, and friendship is the major source of happiness, then real happiness is within reach of most people, given that Smith thought prudence was within reach of most people in commercial society:

> In the most glittering and exalted situation that our idle fancy can hold out to us, the pleasures from which we propose to derive our real happiness, are almost always the same with those which, in our actual, though humble stations, we have at all times at hand, and in our power.

> [W]hat the favourite of the king of Epirus said to his master, may
> be applied to men in all the ordinary situations of human life. When
> the King had recounted to him, in their proper order, all the conquests
> which he proposed to make, and had come to the last of them; And
> what does your Majesty propose to do then? said the Favourite.—I pro-
> pose then, said the King, to enjoy myself with my friends, and endeav-
> our to be good company over a bottle.—And what hinders your Majesty
> from doing so now? replied the Favourite. (TMS 3.3.31, 150)

Smith thinks that Hume was wise because he was able to keep his material gains
in perspective and continue to value the company of his true friends alongside his
public spirit.

So, according to Hume and Smith, sincere friendship is possible only when
there is an equitable exchange of needs and gifts. On the whole, Hume and Smith
associate this with the prudential middle class that commercial societies produce.
Nevertheless, this is not the only form of friendship recognized by Hume and
Smith; there is also philosophical friendship. Hume had signaled the significance
of this kind of friendship in the dedication to his *Four Dissertations* (which included
such crucial texts as "The Natural History of Religion" and "Of the Standard of
Taste"). Hume describes his political-theological ideal, "true liberty," as follows:

> Another instance of true liberty, of which antient times can alone afford
> us an example, is the liberty of thought, which engaged men of let-
> ters, however different in their abstract opinions, to maintain a mutual
> friendship and regard; and never to quarrel about principles, while
> they agreed in inclinations and manners. Science was often the sub-
> ject of disputation, never of animosity. Cicero, an academic, addressed
> his philosophical treatises, sometimes to Brutus, a stoic; sometimes to
> Atticus, an epicurean.

One feature of "true liberty," liberty of thought, has only existed in ancient times.
This feature allows one to keep disagreements over speculative matters (broadly
conceived; Hume includes "science" and [foundational] "principles" among
"abstract opinion") from spilling over into ferocious disputes. This echoes the
praise of Athens in the First *Enquiry* (EHU 11.2). Thus, Hume signals that he and
his intimates may be the first to have recovered this feature of true liberty. In his
obituary, Smith adopts this feature by insisting that friendship and speculative
disagreement are compatible (recall): "never to be forgotten friend; concerning
whose philosophical opinions men will, no doubt judge variously" (xlviii).

Here we do not need to explore all the aspects of Humean "true liberty" or
the ways the moderns go beyond the ancients in it. Part of the feature captured
in the dedication to Hume has to be in some sense a private (elitist) matter: it
is the ability to discuss speculative matters without animosity among (equal)

conversationalists. In Smith's obituary of Hume, Smith captured this as follows: "Mr. Hume's magnanimity and firmness were such, that his most affectionate friends knew, that they hazarded nothing in talking or writing to him as to a dying man, and that so far from being hurt by this frankness, he was rather pleased and flattered by it" ("Letter to Strahan," Corr. 219). Given that Hume's closest friends and even his critics almost certainly knew of Hume's lack of belief in the immortality of the soul, we can infer that they did not recycle fables about the afterlife with him (except as Lucian comedy).

Smith claims that in "civilized nations, the virtues ... are founded upon humanity" (TMS 5.2.8, 204), and he insists that sincerity itself is an achievement of commercial civilization: "A polished people being accustomed to give way, in some measure, to the movements of nature, become frank, open, and sincere." In contrast to Rousseau's picture, the further one is removed from "savagery" or "barbarism," the more possible sincerity becomes (TMS 5.2.11, 208; for the political significance of this, see Kapust & Schwartz 2016)). Finally, in commercial society the prudent man "is always sincere" (TMS 6.1.8, 214).

Nevertheless, Smith points out that the prudent man "is not always frank and open; and though he never tells any thing but the truth, he does not always think himself bound, when not properly called upon, to tell the whole truth" (TMS 6.1.8, 214). It is quite clear that while prudent friends may be sincere with each other, they would be foolish to tell each other the whole truth all the time. Excessive truth telling can cause hurt feelings and mutual irritation; it can be very bad for business, too. Even Hume says that only when he is detached from life and speaks in the past tense is he more "emboldened" to speak his "sentiments" (xl), but even then he does not promise to speak the whole truth. Complete frankness gets reserved for special occasions (cf. his letter to Oswald, November 1, 1750). But nowhere in TMS or WN does Smith tell us when this is the case.

Only in "Letter to Strahan" does Smith provide an example of someone speaking the whole truth. According to Smith, Hume's "magnanimity" enabled "frankness" between Hume and his friends. This frankness consists, at minimum, of Hume's friends being able to talk about Hume's death in his presence and with him; that is, they could speak the whole truth about Hume's situation. Smith claims that this frankness "pleased and flattered" Hume (xlv–xlvi).

In TMS Smith distinguishes between "inferior" and "superior prudence." Commercial society's emblematic prudential man exhibits prudence of the inferior kind. Superior prudence, however, when directed "to greater and nobler purposes than the care of health, the fortune, the rank, and reputation," involves the additional virtues of valor, extensive benevolence, sacred regard for justice, and proper self-command. This kind of superior prudence is reserved for generals, statesmen, legislators, and, when "carried to highest degree of perfection," philosophers. Superior prudence "supposes the utmost perfection of all the intellectual and moral virtues. It is the best head joined to the best heart. It is the most perfect wisdom combined with the most perfect virtue" (TMS 6.1.15, 216).

Because Smith calls special attention to Hume's magnanimity, it is clear that Hume is not serving as the model of the prudent man of the inferior kind. The portrayal of the "magnanimous" Hume in "Letter to Strahan" is not merely another example of Smith's defense of commercial society and typical prudent men in it. Smith thinks that if one possesses only inferior prudence, one is incapable of "performing the greatest and most magnanimous actions" (TMS 6.1.13, 216); these alone produce "real and solid glory." The motive is supplied by the "love of what is honourable and noble, of the grandeur, and dignity, and *superiority* of our own characters," (TMS 3.3.4, 137; emphasis added). For Smith to be properly magnanimous one must think oneself magnanimous.

Smith ends "Letter to Strahan" thus: "Upon the whole, I have always considered him, both in his lifetime and since his death, as approaching nearly to the idea of a perfectly wise and virtuous man, as perhaps the nature of human frailty will permit" (xlix). Hence, for Smith, Hume must be more than an exemplar of inferior prudence (recall also the treatment of the two standards at TMS 6.3.23–5, 247–8).

In a letter to Sir Gilbert Elliot, who had expressed concerns over Smith's account of the impartial spectator (Letter 40, Corr. 49), Smith says that his moral philosophy is designed to show that "real magnanimity and conscious virtue can support itself under the disapprobation of man-kind." That is, Smith's moral philosophy is designed to show how something akin to Hume's magnanimous life is possible. Thus, his "Letter to Strahan" is integral to his moral teaching.

Hume is one of the few people who possess the superior prudence that enables that rare combination of public spiritedness and magnanimity; for Smith, only someone like Hume can experience the kind of friendship in which the complete truth is said. In TMS, Smith speaks of the possibility and nature of such friendship in passionate terms:

> But of all attachments to an individual, that which is founded altogether upon the esteem and approbation of his good conduct and behaviour, confirmed by much experience and long acquaintance, is, by far, the most respectable. Such friendships, arising not from a constrained sympathy, not from a sympathy which has been assumed and rendered habitual for the sake of conveniency an accommodation; but from a natural sympathy, from an involuntary feeling that the persons to whom we attach ourselves are the natural and proper objects of esteem and approbation; can exist only among men of virtue. Men of virtue only can feel that entire confidence in the conduct and behaviour of one another, which can, at all times, assure them that they can never either offend or be offended by one another. . . . The attachment which is founded upon the love of virtue, as it is certainly, of all attachments, the most virtuous; so it is likewise the happiest, as well as the most permanent and secure. Such friendships need not be confined to

a single person, but may safely embrace all the wise and virtuous, with whom we have been long and intimately acquainted, and upon whose wisdom and virtue we can, upon that account, entirely depend. (TMS 6.2.1.18, 224–5; see also TMS 7.4.28, 337)

For Smith, echoing Aristotle, friendship between the wise and the virtuous is of an entirely different kind than that between men of inferior prudence, whose friendship is the product of necessity and habit. Friendship from natural sympathy, or what I earlier called "perfect sympathy," is the only certain reward for a philosopher in this life, if he is lucky to be in the vicinity of a fellow philosopher (in the broadest meaning of this word; it would include Hume's friendship with the playwright John Home).

Philosophical friendship is also founded on equality; it is based on mutual recognition of wisdom and virtue. This is quite rare because only the "most studious and careful observer" can discern the wise and virtuous; Smith has no doubt that there is only a "small party, who are the real and steady admirers of wisdom and virtue" (TMS 1.3.3.2, 62 and 6.2.1.20, 226; cf. Letter 31, from Hume, Corr. 33–6). Smith endorses, then, this feature of Hume's passionate elitism.

But while Smith provides examples or anecdotes for most claims he makes in TMS, he gives no example of sacred and venerable friendship among the wise and virtuous, let alone one that safely embraces all the wise and virtuous. Only in "Letter to Strahan" does he provide an example of genuine philosophical friendship—that is, between Hume and his closest intimates. But even in "Letter to Strahan," he says very little about the contents of their discussions. All of Smith's writings are marked by a restraint, or self-command, over his views on the highest, most ultimate matters. He says very little about the truths philosophers speak to each other. About this secrecy, Smith says:

> [a] certain reserve is necessary when we talk of our own friends, our own studies, our own professions. All these are objects which we cannot expect should interest our companions in the same degree in which they interest us. And it is for want of this reserve, that the one half of mankind make bad company to the other. A philosopher is company to a philosopher only; the member of a club, to his own little knot of companions. (TMS 1.2.2.6, 34; cf. TMS 6.3.31, 253)

PART 4

CONCLUSION

16

Conclusion

Adam Smith's historical significance is being rediscovered (e.g., Graeber 2014). For example, Smith frames the narrative of Jonathan Israel's third volume in his majestic reevaluation of the so-called radical Enlightenment: Smith's "definition" of "philosophy" as "'the science of the connecting principles of nature'" is introduced at the start of the volume (Israel 2013: 7). Israel's "epilogue" draws attention to Smith's remark (TMS 1.3.2.3, 53) "That kings are the servants of the people, to be obeyed, resisted, deposed or punished, as the public conveniency may require . . . is the doctrine of reason and philosophy; but it is not the doctrine of nature" (Israel 2013: 941). Israel reads this remark by Smith as Smith's criticism—a self-defeating criticism, in fact—of radical Enlightenment thinkers. Because Israel associates Smith's target (reason, public utility) with radical thought, he misses that Smith is, in fact, criticizing Locke's doctrine, which was the ideology of the Whig establishment of the right to revolution when there are great (abusive) "inconveniences" with continuing with established government (e.g., *Second Treatise*, §168).

At TMS (1.3.2.3, 53), Smith is not defending tradition but rather calling attention to the role (for good and for ill) of philosophy in providing justification for the status quo even when the actual doctrines it supplies have limited empirical adequacy (for the details, see Pack and Schliesser 2006). In larger context Smith is explaining how the corruption of our sentiments generates great social injustice and simultaneously a surprising element of stability to most established governments. Some social hierarchy, while founded on original injustices, turns out to be useful. This is not a defense of tradition "or veneration of rank" (Israel 2013: 237) but careful social analysis combined with considerable moral "indignation" (Israel 2013: 238)—no need to look at Smith's unpublished writings, it's right on the page, as discerned by Mary Wollstonecraft and Sophie de Grouchy, or so I argued throughout this book.

In Israel's narrative he wishes to disassociate the radical Enlightenment from the Terror that followed in the wake of its political success during 1789–92 (e.g., Israel 2013: 26ff). While Israel uses the radical/moderate split throughout his argument, he announces that until the storming of the Bastille, Enlightenment opinion "had remained broadly united," but that "during the summer of 1789 the heirs of the *philosophes* irrevocably split" (Israel 2013: 901). He then argues that the Assembly started to adopt the program of the radicals, and through it the rejection of all privilege (Israel 2013: 901ff), culminating in *The Declaration of the Rights of Man and Citizen*. A key move in his central argument is the rejection of the common idea of Rousseau's influence on sovereignty and the general will (914). By disconnecting Rousseau from the radicals, he can point to Rousseau's bad influence on the role of violence during the Terror (e.g., Israel 2013: 643, 814, 930ff, 946ff)—going so far as to claim that Rousseau was the "unique inspiration of what Robespierre insisted was the people's Revolution, that of 'virtue', not a revolution of philosophes" (Israel 2013: 948).

So, while Constant (2010) treats representative democracy as a product of the post-Napoleonic settlement and traces the Revolution back to Rousseau (and Mably), who unintentionally "furnished deadly pretexts for more than one kind of tyranny" (Constant 1819),[1] Israel only traces the bad developments and consequences of the French Revolution to Rousseau, and insists (against considerable evidence) that his radicals introduced modern representative democracy (Israel 2013: 815; see also De Dijn 2012).

Let's stipulate, for the sake of argument, that a moderate/radical distinction works as Israel intends, although the existence of a variety of anti-mathematicisms (see Chapter 13) cuts across his distinctions.[2] It is surprising that Israel never confronts what would be the key, moderate objection against the radicals: sudden changes are likely to lead—in the words of Smith—to destructive "disorder" (WN 4.2.40, 469; in context Smith is discussing the removal of trade barriers). Smith famously warns against the violent "madness of fanaticism" (TMS, 6.2.2.15, 232; see also 6.3.12, 242). Thus, even if the radicals did not intend the Terror, one could argue that by rapidly changing the laws and institutions of society, they paved the way for an unintentional and at the same time a foreseeable consequence of it. Given that Israel acknowledges Smith's "gradualism" (Israel 2013: 239), it is odd that he fails to discuss the objection that is central to Smith's public philosophy.

My point here is not that Smith foresaw the French Revolution, or that he accurately discerned the destructive consequences of Rousseau's rhetoric (although we have seen him worry about the latter), but rather to suggest that the reformist as opposed to the revolutionary position is not wholly without merit. Smith's philosophy is opposed to economic "shock therapy," "Big Bang liberalization," and other forms of sudden, revolutionary political and economic changes whether promoted by the so-called Left or Right. This is noteworthy because Smith's political gradualism is accompanied not by a philosophical or normative acceptance of the status quo (indeed, he attacks the mercantile-imperial system and many of its accompanying injustices relentlessly) but rather by various bold visions to

---

[1] http://oll.libertyfund.org/titles/2251#Constant_Liberty1521_28.

[2] I critically reviewed Israel in Schliesser 2015. but I wish to emphasize that Israel accurately discerned the racialized nature of Smith's proposed empire.

reimagine the future—not just, say, his famous "obvious and simple system of natural liberty" (WN 4.9.51, 687), which is by no means obvious, but also his bold plan to "complete" the "imperfect" British "constitution" for the ill-fated Atlantic empire (WN 4.7.c.77, 624). Smith's gradualism is not driven by what we would call a Burkean impulse to preserve, but rather to see normatively desirable consequences come to fruition over time.

As we have seen, Smith mixes moral ("humanity") and epistemic arguments for his gradualism. First, any legal status quo generates reasonable expectations and these ground claims to justice, even if these are merely derived rights. To violate these expectations is to incur justifiable resentment, even if the status quo exhibits injustices manifest to an impartial spectator. (Smith's argument mixes moral and political considerations on this point.) This is why, in addition to gradualism, Smith encourages ameliorative policies; the existence of reasonable expectations should never be an excuse to let injustices fester. We can recognize the merit of this, even if we fault some of Smith's decisions. Second, it is very likely that a sudden political change will have unforeseen consequences and, often, the downside risks are born by the politically least influential in society. Smith is clear that the downside risks include potential harms to innocent bystanders and, thereby, political "disorder."

Thus, I have argued that Smith understands his own gradualism as an instance of responsible ("right") public speech by the theorist—who theorizes in light of "equity" *about* the political from *within* the political order and extensive division of labor—in order to avoid the inductive risks associated with "wrong" theorizing. Throughout this monograph we have encountered at least two kinds of "wrong" theories: first, theories that are too partial to some powerful political interest (e.g., mercantilism and physiocracy) and, second, theories that encourage "crafty" politicians to meddle in people's lives and, thereby, generate too many opportunities for serious infringements on liberty (e.g., Mandeville and, presumably, James Steuart's political economy).

To be sure, I have not offered a defense of Smith to the effect that gradualism is always to be preferred over other forms of decisive action or inaction; I have merely attempted to sketch the contours of his position as a potentially attractive ideal to those would-be public philosophers who reject the futility of ideal theorizing and recoil from the dangerous, romantic decisionism of the self-described political realist. In so doing I have resisted, a few passing comments excepted, the temptation to apply the details of Smith's particular system to our times. This is because, on the view of Smith's meta-philosophy articulated in this book, philosophers of each generation anew need to develop in a systematic fashion particular normative and political ideals in light of our other systematic commitments that may guide policy in a humane fashion. But *how* to articulate and present those ideals as tools for social action in the service of humanity with integrity and with due attention to inductive risk can only be exhibited by way of critical reflection on proper models. This whole book has been one long argument for the idea that return to and study of such exemplars is a necessary, prefatory step in the renewal and re-articulation of the "old truths" of liberalism.

Finally, I have argued that Smith thinks there is also a dangerous form of theorizing (e.g., Hume's Dialogues) when it violates the public's "prejudices" (recall WN 4.5.b.40, 539). That is to say, while Smith does not seem to share Hume's skepticism(s) as such, I have argued that Smith is committed to the idea that superstition cannot be fully eliminated from our morality (e.g., the piacular) and even our science. Before we reject Smith in the name of truth, it is worth reminding ourselves that it remains an open, empirical question whether a humane, stable, and flourishing political order without prejudice and superstition is really possible for beings like us.

BIBLIOGRAPHY

Primary Sources

Adam Smith

Smith, Adam. "An Inquiry into the Nature and Causes of the Wealth of Nations." In *The Glasgow Edition of the Works and Correspondence of Adam Smith*, Vol. II, edited by R. H. Campbell, A. S. Skinner, and W. B. Todd. Indianapolis: Liberty Fund, 1981.

Smith, Adam. "Essays on Philosophical Subjects." In *The Glasgow Edition of the Works and Correspondence of Adam Smith*, Vol. III, edited by W. P. D. Wightman and J. C. Bryce. Indianapolis: Liberty Fund, 1982a.

Smith, Adam. "Lectures on Jurisprudence." In *The Glasgow Edition of the Works and Correspondence of Adam Smith*, Vol. V, edited by R. L. Meek, D. D. Raphael, and P. G. Stein. Indianapolis: Liberty Fund, 1982b.

Smith, Adam. "The Theory of Moral Sentiments." In *The Glasgow Edition of the Works and Correspondence of Adam Smith*, Vol. 1, edited by D. D. Raphael and A. L. Macfie. Indianapolis: Liberty Fund, 1984.

Smith, Adam. "Lectures on Rhetoric and Belles Lettres." In *The Glasgow Edition of the Works and Correspondence of Adam Smith*, Vol. IV, edited by J. C. Bryce. Indianapolis: Liberty Fund, 1985.

Smith, Smith. "Correspondence of Adam Smith." In *The Glasgow Edition of the Works and Correspondence of Adam Smith*, Vol. VI, edited by E. C. Mossner and I. S. Ross. Indianapolis: Liberty Fund, 1987.

David Hume

Hume, David. *The History of England from the Invasion of Julius Caesar to the Revolution in 1688* (foreword by William B. Todd), 6 vols. Indianapolis: Liberty Fund, 1983.

Hume, David. *Essays, Moral, Political, and Literary*, edited by Eugene F. Miller. Indianapolis: Liberty Fund, 1987.

http://www.davidhume.org/, edited by Amyas Merivale and Peter Millican, 2000–12.

Addison et al. *The Spectator*, Vol. 1, edited by Donald F. Bond. Oxford: Oxford University Press, 1987.

Berkeley, George. *The Querist containing several queries, proposed to the Public*. Glasgow: Robert & Andrew Foulis. 1751.

Berkeley, G. *Philosophical Works; Including the Works on Vision*, edited by M. Ayers. London: Dent, 1975.

Boswell, James. *The Life of Samuel Johnson, LL. D. By James Boswell, Esq*. Volume 3. Oxford: Talboys and Wheeler, 1826.

Boyle, Robert. *Selected Philosophical Papers of Robert Boyle*, edited by M. A. Stewart. Indianapolis: Hackett, 1991.

Boyle, Robert. *A Free Enquiry Into the Vulgarly Received Notion of Nature*, edited by Edward B. Davis and Michael Hunter. Cambridge: Cambridge University Press, 1996.

Chambers, Ephraim. *Cyclopædia, or, An universal dictionary of arts and sciences: containing the definitions of the terms, and accounts of the things signify'd thereby, in the several arts, both liberal and mechanical, and the several sciences, human and divine: the figures, kinds, properties, productions, preparations, and uses, of things natural and artificial: the rise, progress, and state of things ecclesiastical, civil, military, and commercial: with the several systems, sects, opinions, &c: among philosophers* . . . J. and J. Knapton [and 18 others]. London, 1728.

Cicero. *The Nature of the Gods*, translated by P. G. Walsh. Oxford: Oxford University Press, 1978.

Clarke, S. *A Demonstration of the Being and Attributes of God And Other Writings*, edited by E. Vailati. Cambridge: Cambridge University Press, 1998 [1705].

Constant, Benjamin. *The Liberty of Ancients Compared with that of Moderns* (Unknown, 1819). http://oll.libertyfund.org/titles/2251.

Constant, Benjamin. *De la liberté des anciens comparée à celle des modernes*. Fayard/Mille et une nuits, 2010.

d'Alembert, Jean le Rond. *Preliminary Discourse to the Encyclopedia of Diderot*, translated by Richard N. Schwab with the collaboration of Walter E. Rex. Chicago: University of Chicago Press, 1995, 3–140.

Darwin, C. *The Descent of Man*. London: Penguin, 2004 [1871].

De Grouchy, Sophie. *Letters on Sympathy*, translated by Sandrine Berges with a commentary and notes by Sandrines Berges and Eric Schliesser. Oxford: Oxford University Press, forthcoming.

Durkheim, Émile. *Les formes élémentaires de la vie religieuse*. Paris: F. Alcan, 1912

Edgeworth, Francis Ysidro. *Mathematical Psychics: An Essay on the Application of Mathematics to the Moral Sciences*. London: C. Kegan Paul, 1881.

Epictetus. *Discourses, Fragments, Handbook*, translated by Hard, Robin, and Christopher Gill. Oxford: Oxford University Press, 2014.

Hamiton, Alexander, et al. *Federalist Papers*. London: Penguin, 1987.

Hamilton, William. *Lectures on Metaphysics and Logic*, Vol. 2, edited by Rev. H. L. Mansell and J. Veitch. Edinburgh: William Blackwood and Sons, 1861.

Herschel, John F. W. *A Preliminary Discourse on the Study of Natural Philosophy*. London: Longman, Brown, 1830.

Hobbes, T. *Leviathan*, with selected variants from the Latin edition of 1668, edited by E. Curley. Indianapolis: Hackett, 1994.

Hutton, James. *Theory of the Earth*, in four parts, Vol. 1. London: Cadell, Junior and Davies, 1795 [1788].

Kail, Peter J. E. *Projection and Realism in Hume's Philosophy*. Oxford: Oxford University Press, 2007.

Kant, I. *What Does It Mean to Orient Oneself in Thinking?* Edited and translated by Allen W. Wood and George di Giovanni. Cambridge: Cambridge University Press, 2012 [1786].

Locke, John. *An Essay Concerning Human Understanding*, edited by Peter H. Nidditch. The Clarendon Edition of the Works of John Locke. Oxford: Oxford University Press, 1975.

Locke, John. *Some Thoughts Concerning Education*, edited by John W. Yolton and Jean S. Yolton. The Clarendon Edition of the Works of John Locke. Oxford: Oxford University Press, 1989.

Locke, John. *An Essay Concerning Toleration: And Other Writings on Law and Politics, 1667–1683*, edited by J. R. Milton and Philip Milton. The Clarendon Edition of the Works of John Locke. Oxford: Oxford University Press, 2006.

Malthus, Thomas Robert. *An Essay on the Principle of Population*, edited by D. Winch. Cambridge: Cambridge University Press, 1992.

Mandeville, Bernard. *The Fable of the Bees or Private Vices, Publick Benefits*, 2 vols., with a Commentary Critical, Historical, and Explanatory by F. B. Kaye. Indianapolis: Liberty Fund, 1988.

Marx, Karl. *Theories of Surplus-Value, Volume IV of Capital*, Part II. Translated and edited by S. Ryazanskaya. Moscow: Progress Publishers, 1968.

Mill, J. S. *On Liberty*, third ed. London: Longman, Green, Longman, Roberts & Green 1864.

Mill, John Stuart. *A System of Logic*, Vol. 1. London: John W. Parker, 1843.

Mill, John Stuart. *An Examination of Sir William Hamilton's Philosophy*. London: Longman, Green, Longman, Roberts & Green, 1865.

Millar, John. *An Historical View of the English Government: From the Settlement of the Saxons in Britain to the Revolution in 1688 in Four Volumes*, Vol. 2. London: J. Mawman, 1803.

Montesquieu, de Secondat, Charles, Baron. *Montesquieu: Spirit of the Laws*, edited by Anne M. Cohler, Basia Carolyn Miller, and Harold Samuel Stone. Cambridge Texts in the History of Political Thought. Cambridge: Cambridge University Press, 1989.

Newton, Isaac. *Opticks: Or a Treatise of the Reflections, Refractions, Inflections & Colours of Light*, based on the fourth edition, London, 1730. New York: Dover, 1952.

Newton, Isaac. *The Principia: Mathematical Principles of Natural Philosophy*, translated by I. B. Cohen and A. Whitman. Berkeley: University of California Press, 1999.

Nietzsche, Friedrich. *Zur Genealogie der Moral*. Leipzig: C. G. Neumann, 1887.

Paine, Thomas. *Common Sense with Agrarian Justice*. London: Penguin, 2004.

Rousseau, J. J. *Rousseau: The Discourses and Other Early Political Writings*, edited and translated by Victor Gourevitch. Cambridge: Cambridge University Press, 1997.

Shaftesbury. *Characteristics of Men, Manners, Opinions, Times*. Edited by Lawrence E. Klein. Cambridge: Cambridge University Press, 1999.

Smith, Adam. *The Theory of Moral Sentiments*, edited by R. Hanley. London: Penguin, 2010.

Spinoza. *Ethics*, translated by E. Curley. London: Penguin, 1904.

Spinoza, B. *The Collected Works of Spinoza*, translated by E. Curley. Princeton, NJ: Princeton University Press, 2016.

Starobinski, Jean. *Jean-Jacques Rousseau, Transparency and Obstruction*. Chicago: University of Chicago Press, 1988.

Steuart, J. *An Inquiry into the Principles of Political Oeconomy*, 2 vols., edited by A. Skinner. Chicago: The University of Chicago, 1966.

Stewart, Dugald. *Elements of the Philosophy of Mind*, Vol. 1. Edinburgh: A. Strahan & T. Cadell, 1792.

Toland, John. *Letters to Serena*. London: Bernard Lintot, 1704.

Turgot. *Reflections on the Formation and Distribution of Wealth*, translated by William J. Ashley. New York: Macmillan, [1770] 1889.

Vico, Giambattista. *The New Science of Giambattista Vico*, translated by Thomas Goddard Bergin and Max Harold Fisch. Ithaca, NY: Cornell University Press, 1984.

Voltaire. *The Philosophical Dictionary*, selected and translated by H. I. Woolf. New York: Knopf, 1924. Scanned by the Hanover College Department of History in 1995. Proofread and pages added by Jonathan Perry, March 2001. https://history.hanover.edu/texts/voltaire/volindex.html

Wollstonecraft, Mary. *A Vindication of the Rights of Woman*, edited by Sylvana Tomasseli. Cambridge: Cambridge University Press, 1995.

Secondary Sources

Anderson, Elizabeth. "Feminist Epistemology: An Interpretation and a Defense." *Hypatia* 10.3 (1995): 50–84.

Anderson, Elizabeth. "Thomas Paine's 'Agrarian Justice' and the Origins of Social Insurance." In *Ten Neglected Classics of Philosophy*, edited by E. Schliesser. Oxford: Oxford University Press (2016): 55–83.

Andrews, David. "Adam Smith's Natural Prices, the Gravitation Metaphor, and the Purposes of Nature." *Economic Thought* 3.1 (2014): 42–55.

Andrews, David. "Natural Price and the Long Run: Alfred Marshall's Misreading of Adam Smith." *Cambridge Journal of Economics* 39:1 (2015): 265–79.

Angner, Erik. *Hayek and Natural Law*. London: Routledge, 2007.

Arendt, Hannah. *Between Past and Future: Eight Exercises in Political Thought*, introduced by J. Kohn. London: Penguin, 2006.

Arrow, Kenneth J. "Methodological Individualism and Social Knowledge." *American Economic Review* 84.2 (1994): 1–9.

Ashraf, Nava, Colin F. Camerer, and George Loewenstein. "Adam Smith, Behavioral Economist." *Journal of Economic Perspectives* 19.3 (2005): 131–45.

Aspromourgos, Tony. "Adam Smith on Labour and Capital." In *The Oxford Handbook of Adam Smith*, edited by Christopher J. Berry, Maria Pia Paganelli, and Craig Smith. Oxford: Oxford University Press, 2013: 267–289.

Baker, K. M. "The Early History of the Term 'Social Science.'" *Annals of Science* 20 (1964): 211–26.

Baumstark, Moritz. "The End of Empire and the Death of Religion: A Reconsideration of Hume's Later Political Thought." In *Philosophy and Religion in Enlightenment Britain: New Case Studies*, edited by Ruth Savage. Oxford: Oxford University Press, 2012.

Baxter, Donald L. M. *Hume's Difficulty: Time and Identity in the Treatise.* London: Routledge, 2008.

Becker, Carl L. *The Heavenly City of the 18th-Century Philosophers.* New Haven, CT: Yale University Press, 1932.

Berges, Sandrine. "Is Motherhood Compatible with Political Participation? Sophie de Grouchy's Care-Based Republicanism." *Ethical Theory and Moral Practice* 18.1 (2015a): 47–60.

Berges, Sandrine. "Sophie de Grouchy on the Cost of Domination in the *Letters on Sympathy* and Two Anonymous Articles in *Le Républicain.*" *Monist* 98.1 (2015b): 102–12.

Berns, Laurence. "Aristotle and Adam Smith on Justice." *Review of Metaphysics* 48.1 (1994): 71–90.

Berry, Christopher J. "Adam Smith's Considerations on Language." *Journal of the History of Ideas* 35.1 (1974): 130–8.

Berry, Christopher J. "Smith and Science." In *The Cambridge Companion to Adam Smith*, edited by Knud Haakonssen. Cambridge: Cambridge University Press, 2006.

Berry, Christopher J. "An Outline of Life, Times, and Legacy." In *The Oxford Handbook of Adam Smith*, edited by Christopher J. Berry, Maria Pia Paganelli, and Craig Smith. Oxford: Oxford University Press, 2013: 77–102.

Biener, Z., and E. Schliesser. "The Certainty, Modality, and Grounding of Newton's Laws." In *The Monist: Special issue on "Laws of Nature"*, edited by Angela Breitenbach and Michela Massimi, 2017, in press.

Bittermann, Henry J. "Adam Smith's Empiricism and the Law of Nature: I." *Journal of Political Economy* 48.4 (1940): 487–520.

Blaug, Mark. "Welfare Indices in 'The Wealth of Nations.'" *Southern Economic Journal* 26.2 (1959): 150–3.

Blaug, Mark. "The Empirical Status of Human Capital Theory: A Slightly Jaundiced Survey." *Journal of Economic Literature* 14.3 (1976): 827–55.

Blaug. Mark. *Economic Theory in Retrospect*, fifth ed. Cambridge: Cambridge University Press, 1996.

Bodkin, Ronald G. "Women's Agency in Classical Economic Thought: Adam Smith, Harriet Taylor Mill, and JS Mill." *Feminist Economics* 5.1 (1999): 45–60.

Bodnar, Istvan. "Aristotle's Natural Philosophy." *Stanford Encyclopedia of Philosophy* (Winter 2016 Edition), edited by Edward N. Zalta. Forthcoming URL: http://plato.stanford.edu/archives/win2016/entries/aristotle-natphil/.

Boehm, M. "Hume's Foundational Project in the Treatise." *European Journal of Philosophy* 24 (2016): 55–77.

Boehm, Omri. *Kant's Critique of Spinoza.* Oxford: Oxford University Press, 2014.

Boucoyannis, Deborah. "The Equalizing Hand: Why Adam Smith Thought the Market Should Produce Wealth without Steep Inequality." *Perspectives on Politics* 11.04 (2013): 1051–70.

Boyd, Richard. "Adam Smith on Civility and Civil Society." In *The Oxford Handbook of Adam Smith*, edited by Christopher J. Berry, Maria Pia Paganelli, and Craig Smith. Oxford: Oxford University Press, 2013: 443–463.

Broad, C. D. "Review of PRIOR, A. N.—Logic and the Basis of Ethics." *Mind* 59 (1950): 392.

Brouwer, René. "Stoic Sympathy." In *Sympathy: A History*, edited by E. Schliesser. Oxford: Oxford University Press, 2015: 15–35.

Brown, Vivienne. *Adam Smith's Discourse: Canonicity, Commerce and Conscience.* London: Routledge, 1994.

Brown, Vivienne. "Agency and Discourse: Revisiting the Adam Smith Problem." In *The Elgar Companion to Adam Smith*, edited by Jeffrey T. Young. Cheltenham: Edward Elgar Publishing, 2009.

Brown, Vivienne, and Samuel Fleischacker, eds. *Essays on the Philosophy of Adam Smith: The Adam Smith Review*, Vol. 5. London: Routledge, 2010.

Brubaker, Lauren. *Adam Smith and the Limits of Enlightenment*. Dissertation defended at the University of Chicago, 2002.

Brubaker, Lauren. "Does the 'Wisdom of Nature' Need Help?" In *New Voices on Adam Smith*, edited by Leonidas Montes and Eric Schliesser. London: Routledge, 2006a.

Brubaker, Lauren. "Adam Smith on Natural Liberty and Moral Corruption: The Wisdom and Folly of Legislators?" In *Enlightening Revolutions: Essays in Honor of Ralph Lerner*, edited by S. Minkov. Lanham, MD: Lexington Books, 2006b.

Buchanan, James M., Robert D. Tollison, and Gordon Tullock. *Toward a Theory of the Rent-Seeking Society*. College Station, TX: Texas A & M University Press, 1980.

Campbell, Tom. *Adam Smith's Science of Morals*. London: Routledge, 1971.

Carrasco, María Alejandra. "Adam Smith's Reconstruction of Practical Reason." *Review of Metaphysics* 58.1 (2004): 81–116.

Catana, Leo. *The Historiographical Concept "System of Philosophy": Its Origin, Nature, Influence and Legitimacy*. Brill: Leiden and Boston, 2008.

Chandler, J. "Adam Smith as Critic." In *The Oxford Handbook of Adam Smith*, edited by Christopher J. Berry, Maria Pia Paganelli, and Craig Smith. Oxford: Oxford University Press, 2013: 126–142.

Christie, John R. R. "Adam Smith's 'Metaphysics of Language'." In *The Figural and the Literal: Problems of Language in the History of Science and Philosophy, 1630–1800*, edited by A. Benjamin et al. Manchester: Manchester University Press, 1987.

Clark, Andy. "Whatever Next? Predictive Brains, Situated Agents, and the Future of Cognitive Science." *Behavioral and Brain Sciences* 36.03 (2013): 181–204.

Cohen, I. Bernard. *Revolution in Science*. Cambridge, MA: Harvard University Press, 1985.

Cohon, Rachel. *Hume's Morality: Feeling and Fabrication*. Oxford: Oxford University Press, 2008.

Cohon, Rachel, and David Owen. "Hume on Representation, Reason and Motivation." *Manuscrito* 20 (1997): 47–76.

Corsa, Andrew J. "Modern Greatness of Soul in Hume and Smith." *Ergo, an Open Access Journal of Philosophy* 2 (2015).

Cremaschi, Sergio. "Adam Smith: Skeptical Newtonianism, Disenchanted Republicanism, and the Birth of Social Science." In *Knowledge and Politics: Case Studies in the Relationship Between Epistemology and Political Philosophy*, edited by Marcelo Dascal and Ora Gruengard. Boulder, CO: Westview Press (1989): 83–110.

Cropsey, Joseph. *Polity and Economy*. The Hague: Martinus Nijhoff, 1957.

Danesi, Marcel. *Vico, Metaphor, and the Origin of Language*. Bloomington, IN: Indiana University Press, 1993.

Darwall, Stephen. "Sympathetic Liberalism: Recent Work on Adam Smith." *Philosophy & Public Affairs* 28.2 (1999): 139–64.

Darwall, Stephen. "Equal Dignity in Adam Smith." *Adam Smith Review* 1 (2004): 129.

Darwall, Stephen L. *The Second-Person Standpoint: Morality, Respect, and Accountability*. Cambridge, MA: Harvard University Press, 2006.

Dean, Dennis R. *James Hutton and the History of Geology*. Ithaca, NY: Cornell University Press, 1992.

Debes, Remy. "Humanity, Sympathy and the Puzzle of Hume's Second Enquiry." *British Journal for the History of Philosophy* 15.1 (2007): 27–57.

De Dijn, Annelien. "The Politics of Enlightenment: From Peter Gay to Jonathan Israel." *Historical Journal* 55 (2012): 785–805.

Della Rocca, Michael. "Playing with Fire: Hume, Rationalism, and a Little Bit of Spinoza." In *The Oxford Handbook of Spinoza*, edited by M. Della Rocca. New York: Oxford University Press, 2014.

Della Rocca, Michael. "Interpreting Spinoza: The Real Is the Rational." *Journal of the History of Philosophy* 53:3 (2015): 523–35.

Demeter, Tamas. *David Hume and the Culture of Scottish Newtonianism: Methodology and Ideology in Enlightenment Inquiry*. Leiden: Brill, 2016.

Dennett, Daniel C. *Darwin's Dangerous Idea: Evolution and the Meaning of Life*. New York: Simon and Schuster, 1995.

Dent, Nicholas John Henry. *Rousseau: An Introduction to His Psychological, Social, and Political Theory*. Oxford: Blackwell, 1988.

De Pierris, Graciela. "Hume and Locke on Scientific Methodology." *Hume Studies* 32.2 (2006): 277–329.

Domski, Mary. "Locke's Qualified Embrace of Newton's *Principia*." In *Interpreting Newton: Critical Essays*, edited by Andrew Janiak and Eric Schliesser. Cambridge: Cambridge University Press, 2012.

Douglas, Heather. "Inductive Risk and Values in Science." *Philosophy of Science* 67.4 (2000): 559–79.

Ducheyne, Steffen. "The Main Business of Natural Philosophy." *Isaac Newton's Natural-Philosophical Methodology*, Vol. 29. Dordrecht: Springer, 2011.

Durland, Karann. *Analogies in Natural Philosophy, Natural Theology, and Hume's "Of a Particular Providence."* Presented at the International Hume Society meeting, Stockholm, 2015.

Ekelund, Robert Burton, and Robert D. Tollison. *Mercantilism as a Rent-Seeking Society: Economic Regulation in Historical Perspective*. College Station, TX: Texas A & M University Press, 1981.

Emilsson, Eyjólfur K. "Plotinus on Sympatheia." In *Sympathy: A History*. Oxford: Oxford University Press, 2015: 36–60.

Evensky, Jerry. *Adam Smith's Moral Philosophy: A Historical and Contemporary Perspective on Markets, Law, Ethics, and Culture*. Cambridge: Cambridge University Press, 2005.

Fiori, Stefano. "Visible and Invisible Order. The Theoretical Duality of Smith's Political Economy." *European Journal of the History of Economic Thought* 8.4 (2001): 429–48.

Firth, Roderick. "Ethical Absolutism and the Ideal Observer." *Philosophy and Phenomenological Research* 12.3 (1952): 317–45.

Fitzgibbons, Athol. *Adam Smith's System of Liberty, Wealth, and Virtue: The Moral and Political Foundations of the Wealth of Nations*. Oxford: Oxford University Press, 1995.

Flanders, Chad. "'This Irregularity of Sentiment': Adam Smith on Moral Luck." In *New Voices on Adam Smith*, edited by Leonidas Montes and Eric Schliesser. London: Routledge, 2006: 193–218.

Fleischacker, Samuel. *A Third Concept of Liberty: Judgment and Freedom in Kant and Adam Smith*. Princeton, NJ: Princeton University Press, 1999.

Fleischacker, Samuel. "Adam Smith's Reception Among the American founders, 1776–1790." *William and Mary Quarterly* 59.4 (2002): 897–924.

Fleischacker, Samuel. *On Adam Smith's" Wealth of Nations": A Philosophical Companion*. Princeton, NJ: Princeton University Press, 2004.

Fleischacker, Samuel. "Sympathy in Hume and Smith: a Contrast, Critique, and Reconstruction." In *Intersubjectivity and Objectivity in Adam Smith and Edmund Husserl*, edited by Christel Fricke and Dagfinn Føllesdal. Ontos: Verlag, 2012: 273–311.

Fleischacker, Samuel. "Adam Smith on Equality." In *The Oxford Handbook of Adam Smith*, edited by Christopher J. Berry, Maria Pia Paganelli, and Craig Smith. Oxford: Oxford University Press, 2013: 485–500.

Force, J. E. "Hume's Interest in Newton and Science." *Hume Studies* 13.2 (1987): 166–216.

Force, Pierre. *Self-interest before Adam Smith: A genealogy of economic science*. Cambridge: Cambridge University Press, 2003.

Forget, Evelyn L. "Cultivating Sympathy: Sophie Condorcet's 'Letters on Sympathy'." *Journal of the History of Economic Thought* 23.03 (2001): 319–37.

Forget, Evelyn L. "Evocations of Sympathy: Sympathetic Imagery in Eighteenth-Century Social Theory and Physiology." *History of Political Economy* 35.5 (2003): 282–308.

Forman-Barzilai, Fonna. "Smith on 'Connexion', Culture and Judgment." In *New Voices on Adam Smith*, edited by Leonidas Montes and Eric Schliesser. London: Routledge, 2006: 89–114.

Forman-Barzilai, Fonna. *Adam Smith and the Circles of Sympathy: Cosmopolitanism and Moral Theory*. Cambridge: Cambridge University Press, 2010.

Foucault, Michel. *The Birth of Biopolitics: Lectures at the Collège de France, 1978–1979*, translated by Graham Burchell. Houndmills: Palgrave MacMillan, 2008.

Fraenkel, Carlos. *Philosophical Religions from Plato to Spinoza: Reason, Religion, and Autonomy*. Cambridge: Cambridge University Press, 2012.

Frazer, Michael L. *The Enlightenment of Sympathy: Justice and the Moral Sentiments in the Eighteenth Century and Today*. Oxford: Oxford University Press, 2010.

Friedman, Michael. *Dynamics of Reason*. Stanford: Csli Publications, 2001.

Frierson, Patrick R. "Adam Smith and the Possibility of Sympathy with Nature." *Pacific Philosophical Quarterly* 87.4 (2006a): 442–80.

Frierson, Patrick. "Adam Smith and Environmental Virtue Ethics." In *New Voices on Adam Smith*, edited by Leonidas Montes and Eric Schliesser. London: Routledge, 2006b: 140–67.

Fry, Richard. "Skeptical Influences on Hume's View of Animal Reasoning." 2016 (unpublished).

Garrett, Aaron. "Hume's Revised Racism Revisited." *Hume Studies* 26.1 (2000): 171–8.

Garrett, Aaron. "Adam Smith on Moral Luck." In *Adam Smith Als Moralphilosoph*, edited by Christel Fricke and Hans-Peter Schütt. Berlin: Walter de Gruyter, 2005.

Garrett, Aaron. "Human Nature." In *The Cambridge History of Eighteenth-Century Philosophy*, edited by K. Haakonssen. Cambridge: Cambridge University Press, 2006: 160–233.

Garrett, Don. *Cognition and Commitment in Hume's Philosophy*. Oxford: Oxford University Press, 1997.

Gaukroger, Stephen. *The Emergence of a Scientific Culture: Science and the Shaping of Modernity, 1210–1685*. Oxford: Oxford University Press, 2006.

Gerschlager, Caroline. "Adam Smith and Feminist Perspectives on Exchange." In *Exchange and Deception: A Feminist Perspective*, edited by C. Gerschlager and M. Mokre. Dordrecht: Kluwer, 2002: 13–26.

Gellner, Ernest. *Nations and Nationalism*. London: Basil Blackwell Publisher, 1983.

Gill, Michael B. *The British Moralists on Human Nature and the Birth of Secular Ethics*. Cambridge: Cambridge University Press, 2006.

Gill, Michael B. "Humean Moral Pluralism." *History of Philosophy Quarterly* 28.1 (2011): 45–64.

Gill, Michael B. "Moral Pluralism in Smith and His Contemporaries." *Revue Internationale de Philosophie* 3 (2014a): 275–306.

Gill, Michael B. *Humean Moral Pluralism*. Oxford: Oxford University Press, 2014b.

Glenney, Brian. "Adam Smith and the Problem of the External World." *Journal of Scottish Philosophy* 9.2 (2011): 205–23.

Glenney, Brian. "Perception by Sympathy: Connecting Smith's 'External Senses' with his 'Sentiments'." *Adam Smith Review* 8 (2014): 241–255.

Goldstein, Jan E. *Console and classify: The French psychiatric profession in the nineteenth century*. Chicago: The University of Chicago Press, 2002.

Golemboski, David. "The impartiality of Smith's spectator: The problem of parochialism and the possibility of social critique." *European Journal of Political Theory* (2015): 1–20.

Graeber, David. *Deb: The First 5,000 Years*. Updated and expanded edition. New York: Melville House, 2014.

Griswold, Charles L. *Adam Smith and the Virtues of Enlightenment*. Cambridge: Cambridge University Press, 1999.

Griswold, Charles. L. "Imagination: Morals, Science and Arts." In *The Cambridge Companion to Adam Smith*, edited by K. Haakonssen. Cambridge: Cambridge University Press, 2006.

Groenewegen, Peter. "Adam Smith, the Physiocrats and Turgot." In *The Elgar Companion to Adam Smith*, edited by Jeffrey Young. Cheltenham: Edward Elgar, 2009.

Haakonssen, Knud. *The Science of a Legislator: The Natural Jurisprudence of David Hume and Adam Smith*. Cambridge: Cambridge University Press, 1981.

Hacking, Ian. *The Taming of Change*. Cambridge: Cambridge University Press, 1990.

Hanley, Ryan Patrick. "Hume's Last Lessons: The Civic Education of 'My Own Life'." *Review of Politics* 64.04 (2002): 659–85.

Hanley, Ryan Patrick. "Adam Smith, Aristotle and Virtue Ethics." In *New Voices on Adam Smith*, edited by Leonidas Montes and Eric Schliesser. London: Routledge, 2006.

Hanley, Ryan Patrick. "Style and Sentiment." *Adam Smith Review* 4 (2008): 88–105.

Hanley, Ryan Patrick. *Adam Smith and the Character of Virtue*. Cambridge: Cambridge University Press, 2009.

Hanley, Ryan P. "Scepticism and Naturalism in Adam Smith." *Adam Smith Review* 5 (2010): 198–212.

Hanley, Ryan Patrick. "David Hume and the 'Politics of Humanity'." *Political Theory* 39.2 (2011): 205–33.

Hanley, Ryan. "Political Economy and Individual Liberty." In *The Challenge of Rousseau*, edited by Eve Grace and Christopher Kelly. Cambridge: Cambridge University Press, 2012: 34–56.

Hanley, Ryan Patrick. "Adam Smith and Virtue." In *The Oxford Handbook of Adam Smith*, edited by Christopher J. Berry, Maria Pia Paganelli, and Craig Smith. Oxford: Oxford University Press, 2013: 219–240.

Hanley, Ryan Patrick. "The 'Wisdom of the State': Adam Smith on China and Tartary." *American Political Science Review* 108.02 (2014): 371–82.

Hanley, Ryan Patrick. "Fénelon's *Telemachus*." In *Ten Neglected Classics of Philosophy*, edited by E. Schliesser. Oxford: Oxford University Press, 2016: 26.

Hankins, Keith. "Adam Smith's Intriguing Solution to the Problem of Moral Luck." *Ethics* 126.3 (2016): 711–46.

Harkin, Maureen. "Natives and Nostalgia: The Problem of the 'North American Savage' in Adam Smith's Historiography." *Scottish Studies Review* 3.1 (2002): 21–32.

Harkin, Maureen. "Adam Smith's Missing History: Primitives, Progress, and Problems of Genre." *ELH* 72.2 (2005): 429–51.

Harkin, Maureen. "Adam Smith on Women." In *The Oxford Handbook of Adam Smith*, edited by Christopher J. Berry, Maria Pia Paganelli, and Craig Smith. Oxford: Oxford University Press, 2013: 501–521.

Harper, William L. *Isaac Newton's Scientific Method: Turning Data into Evidence About Gravity and Cosmology*. Oxford: Oxford University Press, 2011.

Harris. James A. *Hume: An Intellectual Biography*. Cambridge: Cambridge University Press, 2015.

Hayek, Friedrich August. "Dr. Bernard Mandeville." *Proceedings of the British Academy* 52 (1967). Reprinted as Chapter 16 in Hayek, Friedrich August (1978) *New Studies in Philosophy, Politics, Economics and the History of Ideas*, Routledge and Kegan Paul, London: 249–268.

Hayek, Friedrich August. *Constitution of Liberty: The Definitive Edition*, Vol. XVII, edited by R. Hamowy. Collected Works of F. A. Hayek. Chicago: The University of Chicago, 2011.

Hazony, Yoram. *The Philosophy of Hebrew Scripture*. Cambridge: Cambridge University Press, 2012.

Hazony, Yoram. "Newtonian Explanatory Reduction and Hume's System of the Sciences." In *Newton and Empiricism*, edited by Zvi Biener and Eric Schliesser. Oxford: Oxford University Press, 2014.

Hazony, Yoram, and Eric Schliesser. "Newton and Hume." In *The Oxford Handbook of David Hume*, edited by Paul Russell. Oxford: Oxford University Press, 2016.

Heath, Eugene. "Private Vices, Publick Benefits? The Contemporary Reception of Bernard Mandeville." *Hume Studies* 25.1/2 (1999): 225–40.

Heath, Eugene. "Adam Smith and Self-Interest." In *The Oxford Handbook of Adam Smith*, edited by Christopher J. Berry, Maria Pia Paganelli, and Craig Smith. Oxford: Oxford University Press, 2013: 241–265.

Herschell, John Frederick William. *A Preliminary Discourse on the Study of Natural Philosophy*. London: Longman. 1830.

Herzog, Lisa. *Inventing the Market: Smith, Hegel, and Political Theory*. Oxford: Oxford University Press, 2013.

Herzog, Lisa. "Adam Smith's Account of Justice Between Naturalness and Historicity." *Journal of the History of Philosophy* 52.4 (2014): 703–26.

Heydt, Colin. "'A Delicate and an Accurate Pencil': Adam Smith, Description, and Philosophy as Moral Education." *History of Philosophy Quarterly* 25.1 (2008): 57–73.

Hill, Mike, and Warren Montag. *The Other Adam Smith: Popular Contention, Commercial Society, and the Birth of Necro-Economics.* Palo Alto, CA: Stanford University Press, 2014.

Hollander, Samuel. *The Economics of Adam Smith*, Vol. 1. Toronto: University of Toronto Press, 1973.

Hollander, Samuel. "Jeremy Bentham and Adam Smith on the Usury Laws: A 'Smithian' Reply to Bentham and a New Problem." *Journal of the History of Economic Thought* 6.4 (1999): 523–51.

Holmes, Brooke. "Sympathy Between Hippocrates and Galen: The Case of Galen's Commentary on Epidemics II." In *Epidemics in Context: Hippocrates, Galen and Hunayn Between East and West*, edited by Peter E. Pormann. Berlin: De Gruyter, 2012.

Hont, Istvan. *Politics in Commercial Society.* Cambridge, MA: Harvard University Press, 2015.

Hont, Istvan, and Michael Ignatieff, editors. *Wealth and Virtue: The Shaping of Political Economy in the Scottish Enlightenment.* Cambridge: Cambridge University Press, 1983.

Hoover, Kevin D., and Michael E. Dowell. "Measuring Causes: Episodes in the Quantitative Assessment of the Value of Money." *History of Political Economy* 33.5 (2001): 137–61.

Hueckel, Glenn R. "On the 'Insurmountable Difficulties, Obscurity, and Embarrassment' of Smith's Fifth Chapter." *History of Political Economy* 32.2 (2000): 317–45.

Hueckel, Glenn. "In the Heat of Writing': Polemics and the 'Error of Smith' in the Matter of the Corn Bounty." In *The Elgar Companion to Adam Smith*, edited by Jeffrey Young. Cheltenham: Edward Elgar, 2009.

Humphries, Jane. "Childhood and child labour in the British industrial revolution1." *The Economic History Review* 66.2 (2013): 395–418.

Hunter, Graeme. "Cicero's Neglected Argument from Design." *British Journal for the History of Philosophy* 17.2 (2009): 235–45.

Hutchison, Terence Wilmot. *On Revolutions and Progress in Economic Knowledge.* Cambridge: Cambridge University Press, 1978.

Iannaccone, Laurence R. "The Consequences of Religious Market Structure: Adam Smith and the Economics of Religion." *Rationality and Society* 3.2 (1991): 156–77.

Israel, Jonathan. *Democratic Enlightenment: Philosophy, Revolution, and Human Rights, 1750–1790.* Oxford: Oxford University Press. 2013.

Kapust, Daniel J., and Michelle A. Schwarze. "The Rhetoric of Sincerity: Cicero and Smith on Propriety and Political Context." *American Political Science Review* 110.01 (2016): 100–111.

Kennedy, Gavin. "Adam Smith on Religion." In *The Oxford Handbook of Adam Smith*, edited by Christopher J. Berry, Maria Pia Paganelli, and Craig Smith. Oxford: Oxford University Press, 2013: 464–484.

Khalil, Elias L. "An Anatomy of Authority: Adam Smith as Political Theorist." *Cambridge Journal of Economics* 29.1 (2005): 57–71.

Kim, K. "Adam Smith's 'History of Astronomy' and View of Science." *Cambridge Journal of Economics* 36.4 (2012): 799–820.

Kleer, Richard A. "Final Causes in Adam Smith's Theory of Moral Sentiments." *Journal of the History of Philosophy* 33.2 (1995): 275–300.

Kleingeld, Pauline. "Kant's Second Thoughts on Race." *Philosophical Quarterly* 57.229 (2007): 573–92.

Knight, Frank H. *Risk, Uncertainty and Profit.* New York: Hart, Schaffner and Marx, 1921.

Kuhn, Thomas. *The Copernican Revolution; Planetary Astronomy in the Development of Western Thought.* Cambridge, MA: Harvard University Press, 1957.

Kuhn, Thomas. *The Structure of Scientific Revolutions*, second edition. Chicago: University of Chicago Press, 1970.

Kuiper, Edith. "Adam Smith and His Feminist Contemporaries." In *New Voices on Adam Smith*, edited by Leonidas Montes and Eric Schliesser. London: Routledge, 2006: 40–60.

Laing, B. M. "Hume and the Contemporary Theory of Instinct." *Monist* 36.4 (1926): 645–66.

Lawford-Smith, Holly. "Understanding political feasibility." *Journal of Political Philosophy* 21.3 (2013): 243–259.

Lerner, Max. "Introduction." In *Adam Smith, The Wealth of Nations.* New York: Random House (Modern Library edition), 1937.

Levy, David. "Adam Smith's Case for Usury Laws." *History of Political Economy* 19.3 (1987): 387–400.

Levy, David M. "Bishop Berkeley Exorcises the Infinite." *Hume Studies* 18.2 (1992a): 511–36.

Levy, David M. *The Economic Ideas of Ordinary People: From Preferences to Trade.* London: Taylor & Francis, 1992b.

Levy, David M. "The Partial Spectator in the *Wealth of Nations*: A Robust Utilitarianism." *European Journal of the History of Economic Thought* 2.2 (1995): 299–326.

Levy, David M. "Adam Smith's Rational Choice Linguistics." *Economic Inquiry* 35.3 (1997): 672–8.

Levy, David M. "Katallactic Rationality: Exploring the Links Between Co-operation and Language." *American Journal of Economics and Sociology* 58.4 (1999): 729–47.

Levy, David M., and Sandra J. Peart. "Analytical Egalitarianism, Anecdotal Evidence and Information Aggregation via Proverbial Wisdom." *Journal of Economic Methodology* 11.4 (2004): 411–35.

Levy, David M., and Sandra J. Peart. *Adam Smith & the Place of Faction* (October 13, 2007). Available at SSRN: http://ssrn.com/abstract=1022630 or http://dx.doi.org/10.2139/ssrn.1022630.

Levy, David M., and Sandra J. Peart. "Thinking About Analytical Egalitarianism." *American Journal of Economics and Sociology* 67.3 (2008a): 473–9.

Levy, David M., and Sandra Peart. *The Street Porter and the Philosopher: Conversations on Analytical Egalitarianism.* Ann Arbor: University of Michigan Press, 2008b.

Levy, David M., and Sandra J. Peart. "Adam Smith and the State: Language and Reform." In *The Oxford Handbook of Adam Smith*, edited by Christopher J. Berry, Maria Pia Paganelli, and Craig Smith. Oxford: Oxford University Press, 2013: 372–392.

Livingston, Donald W. *Philosophical Melancholy and Delirium: Hume's Pathology of Philosophy.* Chicago: University of Chicago Press, 1998.

Long, Brendan. "Adam Smith's Theism." In *The Elgar Companion to Adam Smith*, edited by Jeffrey Young. Cheltenham: Edwin Elgar, 2009.

Lomonaco, Jeffrey. "Adam Smith's 'Letter to the Authors of the *Edinburgh Review*'." *Journal of the History of Ideas* 63.4 (2002): 659–76.

Lyon, John. "The 'Initial Discourse' to Buffon's 'Histoire naturelle': The First Complete English Translation." *Journal of the History of Biology* 9.1 (1976): 133–81.

Macfie, A. L. *The Individual in Society.* London: George Allen & Unwin, 1967.

Macfie, Alec. "The Invisible Hand of Jupiter." *Journal of the History of Ideas* 32.4 (1971): 595–9.

MacLachlan, Alice. "Resentment and Moral Judgment in Smith and Butler." *Adam Smith Review* 5 (2010): 161–77.

Maglo, Koffi. "The Reception of Newton's Gravitational Theory by Huygens, Varignon, and Maupertuis: How Normal Science May Be Revolutionary." *Perspectives on Science* 11.2 (2003): 135–69.

Maifreda, Germano. *From Oikonomia to Political Economy*, translated by Loretta Valtz Mannucci. Farnham: Ashgate, 2012.

Manzo, Silvia. *David Hume and Copernicanism.* Hume Society, Halifax, August 2009.

McCloskey, Deirdre N. *The Bourgeois Virtues.* Chicago: University of Chicago Press, 2006.

McLean, Iain, and Scot M. Peterson. "Adam Smith at the Constitutional Convention." *Loyola Law Review* 56 (2010): 95.

Meek, Ronald L. "Smith, Turgot, and the "Four Stages" Theory." *History of Political Economy* 2.1 (1971): 9–27.

Meek, Ronald L. *Social Science and the Ignoble Savage.* Cambridge: Cambridge University Press, 1976.

Meeker, Kevin. "Hume on Knowledge, Certainty and Probability: Anticipating the Disintegration of the Analytic/Synthetic Divide?" *Pacific Philosophical Quarterly* 88.2 (2007): 226–42.

Minowitz, Peter. *Profits, Priests, and Princes: Adam Smith's Emancipation of Economics from Politics and Religion.* Palo Alto, CA: Stanford University Press, 1993.

Mirowski, Philip. *Against Mechanism: Protecting Economics from Science.* Lanham, MD: Rowman & Littlefield Publishers, 1988.

Montes, Leonidas. Smith and Newton: Some Methodological Issues Concerning General Economic Equilibrium Theory. *Cambridge journal of economics* 27.5 (2003): 723–47.

Montes, Leonidas. *Adam Smith in Context: A Critical Reassessment of Some Central Components of His Thought*. London: Palgrave Macmillan, 2004.

Montes, Leonidas. "On Adam Smith's Newtonianism and general economic equilibrium theory." *New Voices on Adam Smith*, edited by L. Montes & E. Schliesser. London: Routledge, 2006: 247–270.

Montes, Leonidas. "Newton's Real influence on Adam Smith and Its Context." *Cambridge Journal of Economics* 32.4 (2008): 555–76.

Montes, Leonidas. "Adam Smith on the Standing Army Versus Militia Issue: Wealth Over Virtue?" In *The Elgar Companion to Adam Smith*, edited by Jeffrey Young. Cheltenham: Edwin Elgar, 2009: 315–34.

Morrow, Glenn R. "The Significance of the Doctrine of Sympathy in Hume and Adam Smith." *Philosophical Review* 32.1 (1923): 60–78.

Muller, Jerry Z. *Adam Smith in His Time and Ours: Designing the Decent Society*. Princeton, NJ: Princeton University Press, 1993.

Muthu, Sankar. "Adam Smith's Critique of International Trading Companies Theorizing "Globalization" in the Age of Enlightenment." *Political Theory* 36.2 (2008): 185–212.

Nagel, Thomas. "Moral Luck." *Proceedings of the Aristotelian Society* 50 (1976): 115–51.

Nieli, Russell. "Spheres of Intimacy and the Adam Smith Problem." *Journal of the History of Ideas* 47.4 (1986): 611–24.

Norton, David Fate, and J. C. Stewart-Robertson. "Thomas Reid on Adam Smith's Theory of Morals." *Journal of the History of Ideas* 41.3 (1980): 381–98.

Nuzzo, Angelica. "The Standpoint of Morality in Adam Smith and Hegel." *Adam Smith Review* 5 (2010): 37–57.

O'Donnell, Rory. *Adam Smith's Theory of Value and Distribution: A Reappraisal*. London: Palgrave Macmillan, 1990.

Olsthoorn, Johan. "Two Ways of Theorizing Collective Ownership of the Earth." (unpublished).

Otten, Sarah. *'Real and Positive Hurt': An Examination of Justice in the Writings of Adam Smith*. Thesis submitted for the degree of Ph.D. at Trinity College Dublin, 2016.

Otteson, James R. *Adam Smith's Marketplace of Life*. Cambridge: Cambridge University Press, 2002a.

Otteson, James. "Adam Smith's First Market: The Development of Language." *History of Philosophy Quarterly* 19.1 (2002b): 65–86.

Owen, David. *Hume's Reason*. Oxford: Oxford University Press, 1999.

Pack, Spencer J. *Capitalism as a Moral System*. Cheltenham: Elgar, 1991.

Pack, Spencer J. "Adam Smith on the Virtues: A Partial Resolution of the Adam Smith Problem." *Journal for the History of Economic Thought* 19(Spring) (1997): 127–40.

Pack, Spencer J. *Aristotle, Adam Smith and Karl Marx: On Some Fundamental Issues in 21st-Century Political Economy*. Cheltenham: Edward Elgar Publishing, 2010.

Pack, Spencer J. "Adam Smith and Marx." In *The Oxford Handbook of Adam Smith*, edited by Christopher J. Berry, Maria Pia Paganelli, and Craig Smith. Oxford: Oxford University Press, 2013: 523–538.

Pack, Spencer J., and Eric Schliesser. "Smith's Humean Criticism of Hume's Account of the Origin of Justice." *Journal of the History of Philosophy* 44.1 (2006): 47–63.

Pack, S. J., and E. Schliesser. "Adam Smith, Natural Movement, and Physics." *Cambridge Journal of Economics*. 2017 (in press).

Paganelli, Maria Pia. "In Medio Stat Virtus: An Alternative View of Usury in Adam Smith's Thinking." *History of Political Economy* 35.1 (2003): 21–48.

Paganelli, Maria Pia. "The Adam Smith Problem in Reverse: Self-Interest in *The Wealth of Nations* and *The Theory of Moral Sentiments*." *History of Political Economy* 40.2 (2008): 365–82.

Paganelli, M. "Commercial Relations: From Adam Smith to Field Experiments." In *The Oxford Handbook of Adam Smith*, edited by Christopher I. Berry, Maria Pia Paganelli, and Craig Smith. Oxford: Oxford University Press, 2013: 333–351.

Peart, Sandra, and David M. Levy. *"The Vanity of the Philosopher": From Equality to Hierarchy in Post-Classical Economics.* Ann Arbor: University of Michigan Press, 2005.

Peart, Sandra J., and David M. Levy. "Adam Smith and the Place of Faction." In *The Elgar Companion to Adam Smith*, edited by Jeffrey Young. Cheltenham: Edward Elgar Publishing, 2009.

Peacock, A. T. "The Treatment of Public Finance." In *Essays on Adam Smith*. Oxford: Oxford University Press, 1975: 553–67.

Persky, J. "Ceteris Paribus." *Journal of Economic Perspectives* 4 (1990): 187–93.

Peterman, Alison. *The Inferior Spidermen: Cavendish on Pure and Applied Mathematics. Synthese*, 2017, in press.

Petty, William. *A Treatise of Taxes & Contributions, Shewing the Nature and Measures of Crown Lands, Assessments, Customs, Poll-Money, Lotteries, Benevolence, Penalties, Monopolies, Offices, Tythes, Raising of Coins, Harth-Money, Excize, etc.* London: Printed for N. Brooke, at the Angel in Cornhill, 1662.

Phillips, Mark Salber. "Adam Smith, Belletrist." In *The Cambridge Companion to Adam Smith*, edited by K. Haakonssen. Cambridge: Cambridge University Press, 2006.

Phillipson, Nicholas. *Adam Smith: An Enlightened Life.* London: Penguin, 2010.

Piketty, Thomas. *Capital in the Twenty-First Century.* Cambridge: Harvard University Press, 2014.

Pitts, Jennifer. *A Turn to Empire: The Rise of Imperial Liberalism in Britain and France.* Princeton, N.J.: Princeton University Press, 2009.

Prinz, Jesse. "Is Empathy Necessary for Morality." In *Empathy: Philosophical and Psychological Perspectives*, edited by Amy Coplan and Peter Goldie. Oxford: Oxford University Press, 2011: 211–29.

Prior, Arthur N. *Logic and the Basis of Ethics.* Oxford, Clarendon Press, 1949.

Rae, John. *Life of Adam Smith.* Auckland: The Floating Press, [1895] 2007.

Raphael, D. D. "Hume and Adam Smith on Justice and Utility." *Proceedings of the Aristotelian Society* 73.1 (1972): 87–104.

Raphael, David Daiches. *The Impartial Spectator: Adam Smith's Moral Philosophy.* Oxford: Oxford University Press, 2007.

Rashid, Salim. "The Irish School of Economic Development 1720–1750." *The Manchester School* 56.4 (1988): 345–69.

Rashid, Salim. "Berkeley's Querist and Its Influence." *Journal of the History of Economic Thought* 12(Spring) (1990), 38–60.

Rashid, Salim. *The Myth of Adam Smith.* Cheltenham: Edward Elgar Publishing, 1998.

Rashid, S. "Adam Smith and Economic Development." In *The Elgar Companion to Adam Smith*, edited by Jeffrey Young. Cheltenham: Edward Elgar, 2009: 211–28.

Rasmussen, Dennis C. "Does 'Bettering Our Condition' Really Make Us Better Off? Adam Smith on Progress and Happiness." *American Political Science Review* 100.03 (2006): 309–18.

Rasmussen, Dennis C. "Adam Smith and Rousseau: Enlightenment and Counter-Enlightenment." In *The Oxford Handbook of Adam Smith*, edited by Christopher J. Berry, Maria Pia Paganelli, and Craig Smith. Oxford: Oxford University Press, 2013: 54–76.

Rawls, John. *A Theory of Justice.* Cambridge, MA: Harvard University Press, 1971.

Redman, Deborah A. *The Rise of Political Economy as a Science Methodology and the Classical Economists.* Cambridge: MIT Press, 1997.

Risse, Mathias. *On Global Justice.* Princeton, NJ: Princeton University Press, 2012.

Rocknak, Stefanie. *Imagined Causes: Hume's Conception of Objects.* Dordrecht: Springer, 2012.

Rockoff, Hugh. "Adam Smith on Money, Banking, and the Price Level." In *The Oxford Handbook of Adam Smith*, edited by Christopher J. Berry, Maria Pia Paganelli, and Craig Smith. Oxford: Oxford University Press, 2013: 307–332.

Roelants, Nienke. *Lutheran Astronomers After the Fall (1540–1590): A Reappraisal of the Renaissance Dynamic of Science and Religion.* Dissertation Defended at Ghent University, 2013.

Rosen, Frederick. *Classical Utilitarianism from Hume to Mill.* London: Routledge, 2005.

Rosenberg, Nathan. "Some Institutional Aspects of the *Wealth of Nations*." *Journal of Political Economy* 68.6 (1960): 557–70.

Rosenberg, Nathan. "Mandeville and Laissez-Faire." *Journal of the History of Ideas* 24.2 (1963): 183–96.

Rosenberg, Nathan. "Adam Smith, Consumer Tastes, and Economic Growth." *Journal of Political Economy* 76.3 (1968), 361–74.

Ross, Ian Simpson. *The Life of Adam Smith*, first edition. Oxford: Clarendon Press, 1995.

Rothbard, Murray. *Economic Thought Before Adam Smith: An Austrian Perspective on the History of Economic Thought*, Vol. 1. Edward Elgar (1995), reprinted by Ludwig Von Mises Institute, Auburn, 2006.

Rothschild, Emma. "Adam Smith and Conservative Economics." *The Economic History Review* 45.1 (1992): 74–96.

Rothschild, Emma. "Adam Smith and the Invisible Hand." *American Economic Review* 84.2 (1994): 319–22.

Rothschild, Emma. *Economic Sentiments*. Cambridge, MA: Harvard University Press, 2001.

Rothschild, Emma, and Amartya Sen. "Adam Smith's Economics." In *The Cambridge Companion to Adam Smith*, edited by Knud Haakonssen. Cambridge: Cambridge University Press, 2006.

Rotwein, E., editor. *Writings on Economics*. Madison: University of Wisconsin Press, 1955.

Russell, Paul. "Smith on Moral Sentiment and Moral Luck." *History of Philosophy Quarterly* 16.1 (1999): 37–58.

Russell, Paul. *The Riddle of Hume's Treatise: Skepticism, Naturalism, and Irreligion*. Oxford: Oxford University Press, 2008.

Sabl, Andrew. *Hume's Politics: Coordination and Crisis in the* History of England. Princeton NJ: Princeton University Press, 2012.

Sagar, Sagar. "Beyond sympathy: Smith's rejection of Hume's moral theory," *British Journal for the History of Philosophy* (2017, forthcoming): http://dx.doi.org/10.1080/09608788.2016.1263598

Samuels, Warren J. *Erasing the Invisible Hand: Essays on an Elusive and Misused Concept in Economics*. Cambridge: Cambridge University Press, 2011.

Samuels, Warren J., and Steven G. Medema. "Freeing Smith from the 'Free Market': On the Misperception of Adam Smith on the Economic Role of Government." *History of Political Economy* 37.2 (2005): 219–26.

Samuelson, Paul A. "A Modern Theorist's Vindication of Adam Smith." *American Economic Review* 67.1 (1977): 42–9.

Schabas, Margaret. *The Natural Origins of Economics*. Chicago: University of Chicago Press Economics Books, 2006.

Schliesser, Eric. "'The Obituary of a Vain Philosopher': Adam Smith's Reflections on Hume's Life." *Hume Studies* 29.2 (2003): 327–62.

Schliesser, Eric. "Hume's Missing Shade of Blue Reconsidered from a Newtonian Perspective." *Journal of Scottish Philosophy* 2.2 (2004): 164–75.

Schliesser, Eric. "Some Principles of Adam Smith's Newtonian Methods in *The Wealth of Nations*." *Research in the History of Economic Thought and Methodology* 23.A (2005): 33–74.

Schliesser, Eric. "Adam Smith's Benevolent and Self-Interested Conception of Philosophy." In *New Voices on Adam Smith*, edited by Leonidas Montes and Eric Schliesser. London: Routledge, 2006.

Schliesser, Eric. "Hume's Newtonianism and Anti-Newtonianism," *The Stanford Encyclopedia of Philosophy* (Winter 2008 Edition), Edward N. Zalta (ed.), URL: https://plato.stanford.edu/archives/win2008/entries/hume-newton/.

Schliesser, Eric. "Hume's Attack on Newton's Philosophy." *Enlightenment & Dissent* 25 (2009): 167–203.

Schliesser, Eric. "Copernican Revolutions Revisited in Adam Smith by Way of David Hume." *Revista Empressa y Humanismo* 13.1 (2010): 213–48.

Schliesser, Eric. "Without God: Gravity as a Relational Quality of Matter in Newton's Treatise." In *Vanishing Matter and the Laws of Motion: Descartes and Beyond*, edited by D. Jalobeanu and P. Anstey. London: Routledge, 2011: 80–102.

Schliesser, Eric. "Newton and Spinoza: On Motion and Matter (and God, of Course)." *Southern Journal of Philosophy* 50.3 (2012): 436–58.

Schliesser, Eric. "Philosophic Prophecy." In *Philosophy and Its History: Aims and Methods in the Study of Early Modern Philosophy*, edited by Mogens Laerke, Justin E. H. Smith, and Eric Schliesser. Oxford: Oxford University Press, 2013.

Schliesser, Eric. *The Science of Man and the Invention of Usable Traditions. Conflicting Values of Inquiry.* Leiden: Brill, 2014: 306–36.

Schliesser, Eric. *Sympathy: A History.* Oxford: Oxford University Press, 2015.

Schliesser, Eric. "The Separation of Economics from Virtue: A Historical-Conceptual Introduction." In *Economics and the Virtues: Building a New Moral Foundation*, edited by M. White and J. Baker. Oxford: Oxford University Press, 2016a: 141–64.

Schliesser, Eric. "Spinoza and the Philosophy of Science: Mathematics, Motion, and Being." Oxford Handbooks Online. Oct. 30, 2016b. http://www.oxfordhandbooks.com/view/10.1093/oxfordhb/9780195335828.001.0001/oxfordhb-9780195335828-e-020.

Schliesser, Eric. "Sophie de Grouchy, Adam Smith, and the Politics of Sympathy." In *Feminism and the History of Philosophy*, edited by M. Lascano and E. O'Neill. Dordrecht: Springer (2017a, in press).

Schliesser, Eric. "Sophie de Grouchy, The Tradition(s) of Two Liberties, and the Missing Mother(s) of Liberalism." In *Women on Liberty*, edited by K. Detlefsen and J. Broad. Oxford: Oxford University Press (2017b, in press).

Schliesser, Eric. "Newton's Polemics with Spinozists in the General Scholium." In *Isaac Newton's General Scholium to the Principia: Science, Religion and Metaphysics*, edited by Steffen Ducheyne, Scott Mandelbrote, and Stephen D. Snobelen (forthcoming 2018).

Schliesser, Eric, and George E. Smith. "Huygens's 1688 Report to the Directors of the Dutch East India Company on the Measurement of Longitude at Sea and the Evidence it Offered Against Universal Gravity." *Archive for the History of Exact Sciences* (forthcoming).

Schumpeter, Joseph A. *History of Economic Analysis.* London: Routledge, 1954.

Schwarze, Michelle A., and John T. Scott. "Spontaneous Disorder in Adam Smith's Theory of Moral Sentiments: Resentment, Injustice, and the Appeal to Providence." *The Journal of Politics* 77.2 (2015): 463–476.

Sebastiani, S. *The Scottish Enlightenment: Race, Gender, and the Limits of Progress.* Basingstoke: Palgrave McMillan, 2013.

Sedley, David. *Creationism and Its Critics in Antiquity.* Berkeley: University of California Press, 2007.

Selby-Bigge, Lewis Amherst, ed. *British Moralists.* Vol. 2. Oxford: Claredon Press, 1897.

Seligman, Adam B. *The Idea of Civil Society.* Princeton, NJ: Princeton University Press, 1995.

Sellars, Wilfrid S. "Philosophy and the Scientific Image of Man." In *Frontiers of Science and Philosophy*, edited by Robert Colodny. Pittsburgh, PA: University of Pittsburgh Press (1962): 35–78.

Shin, Albert. *Adam Smith on the Nature and Authority of Conscience.* Diss. The University of California, Santa Barbara, 2014.

Shklar, Judith. "The Liberalism of Fear." In *Political Liberalism: Variations on a Theme*, edited by Shaun P. Young. Albany, NY: State University of New York Press, (1989): 149–66.

Shockey, R. Matthew. "Lockean Primary Quality Perception Reconstructed." *History of Philosophy Quarterly* 24.3 (2007): 221–35.

Sidgwick, Henry. *Outlines of the History of Ethics for English Readers.* London: Macmillan, 1892.

Simon, Fabrizio. "Adam Smith and the Law." In *The Oxford Handbook of Adam Smith*, edited by Christopher J. Berry, Maria Pia Paganelli, and Craig Smith. Oxford: Oxford University Press, 2013: 393–416.

Skinner, Andrew Stewart. *A System of Social Science: Papers Relating to Adam Smith*, second edition. Oxford: Oxford University Press, 1996 (first published 1979).

Skinner, Andrew Stewart. "The Mercantile System." In *The Elgar Companion to Adam Smith*, edited by Jeffrey Young. Cheltenham: Edward Elgar Publishing, 2009.

Smeenk, Christopher, and Eric Schliesser. "Newton's *Principia*." In *The Oxford Handbook of the History of Physics*, edited by Jed Z Buchwald and Robert Fox. Oxford: Oxford University Press, 2013: 109–65.

Smith, Craig. *Adam Smith's Political Philosophy: The Invisible Hand and Spontaneous Order.* London: Routledge, 2006.

Smith, Craig. "The Scottish Enlightenment, Unintended Consequences and the Science of Man." *Journal of Scottish Philosophy* 7.1 (2009): 9–28.

Smith, Craig. "Adam Smith and the New Right." In *The Oxford Handbook of Adam Smith*, edited by Christopher J. Berry, Maria Pia Paganelli, and Craig Smith. Oxford: Oxford University Press, 2013: 539–558.

Smith, G. E. "Newton's Methodology." In *The Cambridge Companion to Newton*, edited by I. Bernard Cohen and George E. Smith. Cambridge: Cambridge University Press, 2002: 138–173.

Smith, G. E. "Closing the Loop." In *Newton and Empiricism*, edited by Zvi Biener and Eric Schliesser. Oxford: Oxford University Press, 2014: 262–352.

Smith, Justin E. H. *Nature, Human Nature, and Human Difference: Race in Early Modern Philosophy.* Princeton, NJ: Princeton University Press, 2015.

Smith, Michael. *The Moral Problem.* Malden, MA: Blackwell, 1994.

Smith, Vernon L. "Constructivist and Ecological Rationality in Economics." *American Economic Review* 93.3 (2003): 465–508.

Spengler, Joseph J. "Adam Smith on Human Capital." *American Economic Review* 67.1 (1977): 32–6.

Stewart-Robertson, J. C., and David Fate Norton. "Thomas Reid on Adam Smith's Theory of Morals." *Journal of the History of Ideas* 45.2 (1984): 309–21.

Stigler, George J. "The Nature and Role of Originality in Scientific Progress." *Economica* 22.88 (1955): 293–302.

Stigler, George J. "Smith's Travels on the Ship of State." *History of Political Economy* 3.2 (1971): 265–77.

Taylor, Jacqueline. "Hume on the Importance of Humanity." *Revue Internationale de Philosophie* 1 (2013): 81–97.

Taylor, Jacqueline. "Hume on Pride and the Other Indirect Passions." In *The Oxford Handbook of Hume*, edited by James Harris. Oxford: Oxford University Press, 2016: 295.

Taylor, Jacqueline. "Mandeville and the Women" (forthcoming).

Tegos, Spiros. "Sympathie morale et tragédie sociale: Sophie de Grouchy lectrice d'Adam Smith." *Noesis* 21 (2013a). URL: http://noesis.revues.org/1865.

Tegos, Spiros. "Adam Smith: Theorist of Corruption." In *The Oxford Handbook of Adam Smith*, edited by Christopher J. Berry, Maria Pia Paganelli, and Craig Smith. Oxford: Oxford University Press, 2013b: 353–371.

Teixeira, Pedro N. "Dr. Smith and the Moderns." *Adam Smith Review* 3 (2007): 139.

Tribe, Keith. "Adam Smith: Critical Theorist?" *Journal of Economic Literature* 37.2 (1999): 609–32.

Valihora, Karen. "The Judgement of Judgement: Adam Smith's Theory of Moral Sentiments." *British Journal of Aesthetics* 41.2 (2001): 138–61.

Valihora, Karen. *Austen's Oughts: Judgment After Locke and Shaftesbury.* Newark: University of Delaware Press, 2010.

van Bunge, Wiep. "Spinoza's Life: 1677–1802." *Journal of the History of Ideas* 78.2 (2017): 211–231.

Van de Haar, Edwin. "Adam Smith on Empire and International Relations." In *The Oxford Handbook of Adam Smith*, edited by Christopher J. Berry, Maria Pia Paganelli, and Craig Smith. Oxford: Oxford University Press, 2013: 417–442.

Viner, Jacob. *The Role of Providence in the Social Order: An Essay in Intellectual History.* Princeton, NJ: Princeton University Press, 2015 [1972].

Vivenza, Gloria. "Adam Smith and Aristotle." In *The Elgar Companion to Adam Smith*, edited by Jeffrey Young. Cheltenham: Edward Elgar Publishing, 2009.

Waterman, Anthony M. C. "Economics as Theology: Adam Smith's Wealth of Nations." *Southern Economic Journal* 68.4. (2002): 907–21.

Weinstein, Jack Russell. *Adam Smith's Pluralism: Rationality, Education, and the Moral Sentiments.* New Haven, CT: Yale University Press, 2013.

Werhane, Patricia Hogue. *Adam Smith and His Legacy for Modern Capitalism.* Oxford: Oxford University Press, 1991.

Wight, Jonathan B. "Adam Smith and Greed." *Journal of Private Enterprise* 21.1 (2005): 46.

Wight, Jonathan B. "Adam Smith on Instincts, Affection, and Informal Learning: Proximate Mechanisms in Multilevel Selection." *Review of Social Economy* 67.1 (2009): 95–113.

Wightman, W. P. D. "Adam Smith and the History of Ideas." In *Essays on Adam Smith*. Oxford: Clarendon, 1975: 44–67

Williams, Bernard. "Moral Luck." *Proceedings of the Aristotelian Society*, Supplementary Volumes 50 (1976): 115–35.

Wimsatt, William C. "Developmental Constraints, Generative Entrenchment, and the Innate-Acquired Distinction." In *Integrating Scientific Disciplines*, edited by W. Bechtel. Dordrecht: Springer Netherlands (1986): 185–208.

Witztum, Amos, and Jeffrey T. Young. "Utilitarianism and the Role of Utility in Adam Smith." *European Journal of the History of Economic Thought* 20.4 (2013): 572–602.

Wokler, Robert. "Saint-Simon and the Passage from Political to Social Science." In *The Languages of Political Theory in Early-Modern Europe*, edited by Anthony Pagden. Cambridge: Cambridge University Press, 1987: 325–38.

Wright, John P. *The Sceptical Realism of David Hume*. Manchester: Manchester University Press, 1983.

Wright, John P. *Hume's 'A Treatise of Human Nature': An Introduction*. Cambridge: Cambridge University Press, 2009.

Yanaihara, Tadao. *A Full and Detailed Catalogue of Books Which Belonged to Adam Smith*. Tokyo: Iwanami Shoten, 1966 [1951].

Young, J. T. *Economics as a Moral Science*. Cheltenham: Edward Elgar Publishing, 1997.

Young, Jeffrey T., ed. *The Elgar Companion to Adam Smith*. Cheltenham: Edward Elgar Publishing, 2009.

Young, Jeffrey T., and Barry Gordon. "Distributive Justice as a Normative Criterion in Adam Smith's Political Economy." *History of Political Economy* 28.1 (1996): 1–25.

INDEX

Printed in the USA/Agawam, MA
January 30, 2018

668546.013